Rick Steves®

BEST OF

SPAIN

Contents

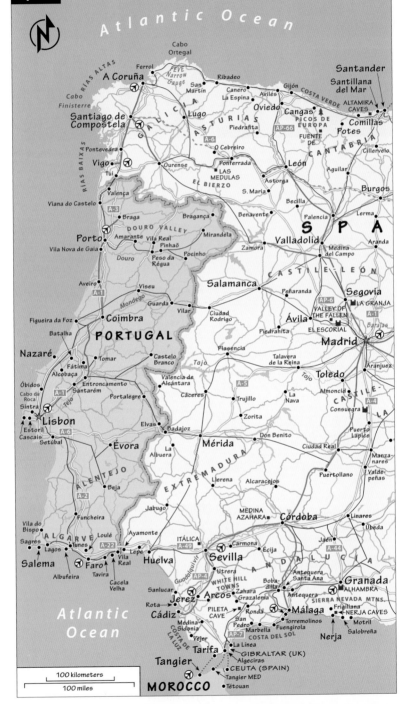

Spain

Atlantic Ocean

Cabo Ortegal

Cabo Finisterre

RIAS ALTAS

Ferrol
A Coruña
EFE Narrow Gauge
San Martín
Ribadeo
Canero
La Espina
Avilés
Gijón
COSTA VERDE
Santander
Santillana del Mar
ALTAMIRA CAVES
Comillas
Potes

Santiago de Compostela

GALICIA
Lugo
ASTURIAS
Oviedo
Cangas
PICOS DE EUROPA
FUENTE DÉ
CANTABRIA
Cillervelo

Piedrafita
AP-66

Pontevedra
RIAS BAIXAS
Vigo
Tui
O Cebreiro
Ponferrada
LAS MEDULAS
EL BIERZO
León
Astorga
S. Maria
Aguilar
Burgos

Ourense

Valença
A-3
Braga
Bragança
Mirandela
Zamora
Benavente
Becilla
Palencia
Lerma
Aranda

Viana do Castelo

DOURO VALLEY
Vila Real
Amarante
Pinhaõ
Valladolid
Medina del Campo
S P A

Porto
Vila Nova de Gaia
Douro
Peso da Régua
Pocinho
CASTILE-LEÓN

Aveiro
A-1
Viseu
Salamanca
Peñaranda
Segovia
LA GRANJA
AP-6
VALLEY OF THE FALLEN
A-1

Mondego
Guarda
Vilar
Ciudad Rodrigo
Ávila
EL ESCORIAL
Barajas

Figueira da Foz
Coimbra
Piedrahita
Madrid

Batalha
PORTUGAL
Plasencia
Talavera de la Reina
Toledo
Aranjuez

Nazaré
Tomar
Castelo Branco
Tajo
A-5
Tajo
Almoncid
CASTILE-

Fátima
Alcobaça
Entroncamento
Santarém
Valencia de Alcántara
Cáceres
Trujillo
La Nava
Consuegra
LA

Óbidos
A-1
Tejo
Portalegre
Zorita
Puerto Lapice

Cabo da Roca
Sintra
Elvas
Badajoz
Mérida
Don Benito
Ciudad Real
Manzanares

Estoril
Lisbon
A-6
Cascais
Setúbal
Évora
La Albuera
Llerena
Alcaracejos
Puertollano
Valde-peñas

ALENTEJO
A-2
Beja
EXTREMADURA
MEDINA AZAHARA
Córdoba
Linares
Úbeda

Jabugo
Funcheira

Vila do Bispo
Sagres
Lagos
Salema
ALGARVE
Loulé
Tunes
A-22
Albufeira
Faro
Tavira
Cacela Velha
Ayamonte
Lepe
Vila Real
ITÁLICA
A-49
Huelva
Guadalquivir
Carmona
Écija
Jaén
A-44
Sevilla
Utrera
WHITE HILL TOWNS
Bobadilla
Antequera
Santa Ana
Granada
ALHAMBRA

Sanlucar
Rota
Jerez
Arcos
Zahara
Grazalema
PILETA CAVE
Ronda
Antequera
SIERRA NEVADA MTNS.
Frigiliana
NERJA CAVES
Motril
Salobreña
Nerja

Cádiz
Medina Sidonia
San Pedro
AP-7
Marbella
Fuengirola
Torremolinos
Málaga
COSTA DEL SOL

COSTA DE LA LUZ
Vejer
Tarifa
La Línea
GIBRALTAR (UK)
Algeciras
CEUTA (SPAIN)

Tangier
Tangier MED
MOROCCO
Tétouan

Atlantic Ocean

100 kilometers

100 miles

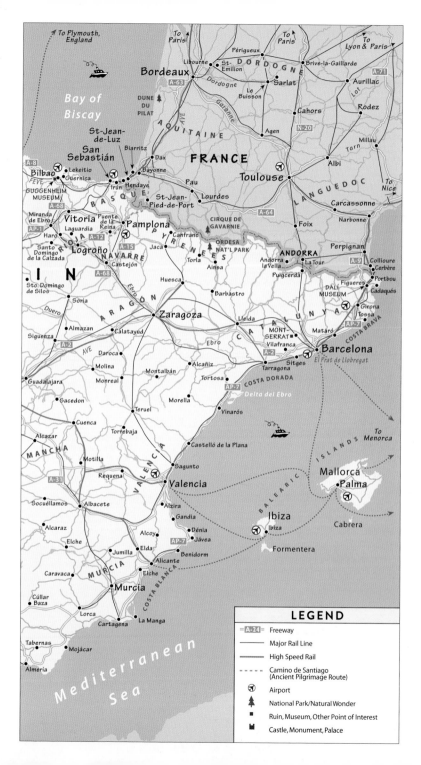

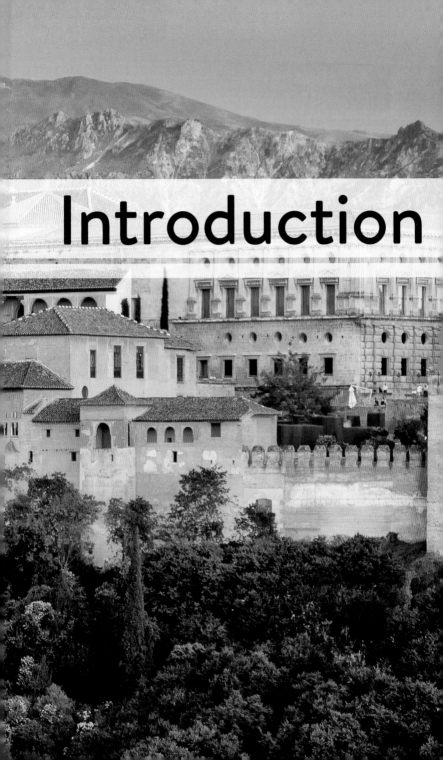

Introduction

Like a grandpa bouncing a baby on his knee, Spain is a mix of old and new, modern and traditional. Spain means massive cathedrals, world-class art, Moorish palaces, nonstop nightlife, whitewashed villages, and glorious sunshine. Spain has a richness of history and culture. From the stirring *sardana* dance in Barcelona to the sizzling rat-a-tat-tat of flamenco in Sevilla, this country creates its own beat amid the heat.

Spain's charm really lies in its people and their unique lifestyle. Even as the Spanish embrace modern times, their daily lives focus on friends and family, just as they always have. Many still follow the siesta schedule, shutting down work during the midday heat to enjoy the company of loved ones. In the cool of the evening, Spain comes back to life. Whole families stroll through the streets and greet their neighbors—a custom called the paseo. Spaniards are notorious night owls. The antidote for late nights? The next day's siesta.

You can see many European countries by just passing through, but Spain is a destination. Learn its history and accept the country on its own terms. Gain an appreciation for cured ham, dry sherry, and bull's-tail stew. When you go to Spain, go all the way.

THE BEST OF SPAIN

This book is all about Spain's top destinations, from its thriving cities to its authentic towns. The biggies on everyone's list are exuberant, trendy Barcelona and marvelous Madrid, the nation's capital. Buzzing with energy, Sevilla features flamenco and nightlife that doesn't quit. Granada has Spain's finest Moorish sight—the grand palace of the Alhambra. And no visit to Spain is complete without exploring its smaller towns, from historic Toledo to the sleepy whitewashed hill towns of Andalucía. In some cases, when there are interesting sights or towns near my top destinations, I cover these briefly (as "Near" sights), to help you enjoyably fill out a free day or a longer stay.

Beyond the major destinations, I also cover what I call the Best of the Rest—great destinations that don't quite make my top cut, but are worth seeing if you have more time or specific interests: the Basque Country, Santiago de Compostela, Córdoba, and the South Coast.

To help you link the top stops, I've included a two-week itinerary (see page 26), with tips to help you tailor it to your interests and available time.

THE BEST OF BARCELONA

Spain's second city and the proud capital of the Catalan people, Barcelona bubbles with life—from the tangled lanes of the Barri Gòtic to the elegant boulevards of the Eixample. A cradle of modern art, and home to Gaudí, Picasso, and Miró, the city itself is a dynamic work of art in progress, with everything—enthralling sights, man-made beaches, and a fun street scene—continually evolving. Join the parade of people and become part of the show.

❶ The **Ramblas**—Barcelona's long, tree-lined, pedestrian-friendly boulevard—spills gently down from the heart of the city to the harbor.

❷ The huge, unfinished church of Sagrada **Família,** with sequoia-sized columns and fantastical Neo-Gothic decor, feels both medieval and futuristic.

❸ Barcelonans crowd into lively bars to feast on **tapas**—small portions of olives, seafood, meatballs, and deep-fried tasties on a toothpick.

❹ In the shadow of the 700-year-old **cathedral** in the Barri Gòtic neighborhood, locals join hands in a communal circle to dance the sardana.

❺ Park Güell—with its colorful mosaics, wavy forms, and whimsical statues—is one of several fanciful sights by Antoni Gaudí, the master of Modernisme.

❻ The vibrant **Boqueria Market** along the Ramblas evokes deep passion among Spain's devout jamón-iphiles.

❼ In the shape of an animal's back with iridescent scales, Gaudí's **Casa Batlló** is a magical place.

❽ Near the busy downtown but a world away, the **beach at Barceloneta** is a balmy world of sand, surf, snack shacks, and slow sunsets.

❾ The numerous **street performers** express the spirit of this city—playful, nonconformist, spontaneous, and a bit theatrical.

THE BEST OF MADRID

Lively Madrid, both the nation's capital and its heart, is Spain on a grand scale, with stately squares and modern skyscrapers. The main square, Puerta del Sol, leads west to the lavish Royal Palace and east to the outstanding Prado art museum and Picasso's thought-provoking *Guernica*. With a compact core and a contemporary bar-hopping paseo, this sunny city is intimate, youthful, and welcoming.

❶ *Plaza Mayor—Madrid's historic center—is ringed by gloriously symmetrical buildings from the era of Spain's Golden Age.*

❷ *El Rastro, Europe's biggest flea market, is a field day for shoppers, browsers, people-watchers, and bar-hopping Madrileños.*

❸ *Spain's capital city offers a smorgasbord of culinary delicacies from across the country—including seafood from the Mediterranean coast.*

❹ *Escape the brutal Madrid sun in spacious Retiro Park, a leafy oasis a stone's throw from the Prado Museum.*

❺ *Spanish masterpieces (like Las Meninas) hang alongside Italian Renaissance works and more at the Prado, arguably Europe's greatest museum of paintings.*

❻ *A bear picks berries from a madroño tree—part of the city's coat of arms since medieval times, and now a statue in the city center.*

❼ *Puerta del Sol—the city's cultural heart and transportation hub—bustles with pedestrians, taxis, neon, demonstrations, and celebrations.*

THE BEST OF TOLEDO

The medieval skyline of Toledo, rising atop a hill lassoed by a river, captivated hometown boy El Greco as much as it does travelers today. Its winding streets are dotted with bakeries making sweet, colorful *mazapán,* and restaurants serving up savory roast suckling pig. Toledo's architecture reflects its Jewish, Moorish, and Christian roots, from the arches of a synagogue and the intricate designs of a mosque to the looming spires of a cathedral melding into medieval moonlight.

1 *The skyline of Toledo looks much the same today as when* **El Greco** *painted it four centuries ago, when he made the city his home.*

2 *Local cuisine specializes in game meats from the surrounding countryside—venison, partridge, and wild boar—with almond-sweet mazapán for dessert.*

3 *Perched strategically in the geographic center of Iberia along the Tajo River, Toledo grew to become the first capital of Spain.*

4 *To create Toledo's specialty, damascene, artisans inlay gold and silver wires into steel, making intricately patterned bowls, jewelry, and bull-fighting swords.*

5 *The vast cathedral has a collection of priceless paintings, including El Grecos, that would put any museum on the map.*

6 *The Sinagoga del Tránsito is richly decorated in Mudejar style.*

7 *Toledo's many souvenir shops sell locally hand-crafted knives, swords, maces, armor, and other nouveau antiques. I buy all my medieval weaponry here.*

THE BEST OF GRANADA

Set against a mountainous backdrop, Granada is crowned with the last vestige of Moorish rule in Iberia: the magnificent Alhambra—fortress, palace, and gardens. Beyond that unforgettable sight, Granada offers a historic cathedral and a truly Royal Chapel. Stroll the main square, Plaza Nueva, and two distinctive neighborhoods: the Alcaicería with its colorful market streets, and the hilly Albayzín, lined with funky teahouses and graced by the San Nicolás viewpoint where the day ends—and the night begins.

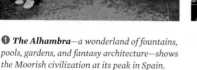

❶ The Alhambra—*a wonderland of fountains, pools, gardens, and fantasy architecture—shows the Moorish civilization at its peak in Spain.*

❷ *In* **flamenco,** *the women make graceful turns, the men do the machine-gun footwork, and castanets set the beat.*

❸ *Like an Arabian souk, Granada's* **Alcaicería** *marketplace is a maze of small shops selling leather purses, scarves, and trinkets.*

❹ *The Alhambra's* **intricate decoration** *is rooted in the Moors' reluctance to portray living crea-*

tures (that was God's work)—instead, they created art with calligraphy and stylized patterns.

❺ *Granada's* **terrace eateries** *come with world-class views.*

❻ *The tombs of the "Catholic Monarchs"—Ferdinand and Isabel—are the centerpiece of the* **Royal Chapel.**

❼ *Late-night visits to the* **Alhambra** *are romantic and less crowded.*

THE BEST OF ANDALUCÍA'S WHITE HILL TOWNS

The meandering "Route of the White Villages" wends through the hilly, wind-swept landscape of Andalucía, Spain's heartland. Of the many villages worth exploring, tiny Arcos de la Frontera and sturdy Ronda rise above the rest. Slow down and wander their lanes, enjoying the small architectural nuances, the quiet rhythm of life, and the sweeping territorial views.

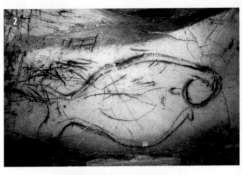

❶ Whitewashed villages with narrow lanes and timeless traditions, perched atop craggy bluffs—these are Spain's **pueblos blancos.**

❷ Inside the dank **Pileta Cave** you can see some of mankind's oldest creations—paintings of fish, horses, and goats by Paleolithic Michelangelos.

❸ In **Jerez de la Frontera,** you can watch balletic stallions prance and high-step to a classical music soundtrack.

❹ Many hill towns, such as Ronda, have **paradors**—historic luxury inns—where you can sleep with a view (or just settle for a drink on their veranda).

❺ Crowned by its cathedral, **Arcos de la Frontera** is not only quaint—it's also rustic, historic, and genuine.

❻ Ronda, the birthplace of **bullfighting,** has Spain's first bullring (which still operates), and the best museum on matadors and their craft.

❼ The festive city of Jerez de la Frontera is just a gateway to the White Hill Towns, but it's home to two Andalusian icons: fine horses and **dry sherry.**

THE BEST OF SEVILLA

Spain's most soulful city teems with people day and night. Its top sights are the cathedral and Royal Alcázar. Its top emotion is fervor, whether applied to Holy Week processions, bullfights, or riveting flamenco. Even the paseo goes on past midnight. Museums are plentiful and bars are hopping—but the main attraction is the nonstop city itself.

❶ *Elbowing your way through a crowded bar to order* **tapas** *and a small* caña *of beer is a classic Sevilla experience.*

❷ *Sevilla is home to some of Spain's most "Spanish" traditions, like* **flamenco dancing,** *which erupts spontaneously in late-night bars throughout the old town.*

❸ *Matadors relish showing off their technique, fancy outfits, and flair in Sevilla's popular* **bullfighting ring**.

❹ *The* **cathedral** *has the world's biggest church interior, and houses the world's largest altarpiece, a half-ton monstrance, and the tomb of Columbus.*

❺ *The* **Alcázar palace,** *with both Christian and Moorish elements, has lavish decor, quiet courtyards, and reminders of Columbus.*

❻ *Graceful statues of the Virgin Mary mourning her crucified son adorn many of* **Sevilla's churches**—*each one a different variation on sorrow.*

❼ *Andalusian pride is on display as Sevillans don their traditional outfits—dresses, mantillas, fans, brimmed hats—for the* **April Fair.**

❽ *Castle walls surround the* **Royal Alcázar,** *Sevilla's spectacular 10th-century palace.*

THE BEST OF THE REST

If you have the time and interest, splice any of the following destinations into your itinerary. In northeast Spain, the feisty Basque Country features the coastal resort of **San Sebastián,** the famous modern-art museum at **Bilbao,** and bull-running at **Pamplona.** In the far northwest, all roads lead to **Santiago de Compostela,** where pilgrims rejoice at the end of their long journey. **Córdoba** is home to Spain's (and Europe's) only mosque with a cathedral inside. The sunny South Coast boasts the beach town of **Nerja** and British-flavored **Gibraltar.**

❶ *Spain's often-overlooked progressive side is trumpeted boldly at the Guggenheim modern art museum in* **Bilbao.**

❷ *The* **Costa del Sol**—*home to sun, sand, and seafood—is heavily touristed, but there are still a few unspoiled beaches and quaint towns.*

❸ **Córdoba**'s *huge former mosque, with its forest of 800 red and blue columns, attests to the cultural vitality of the Moors' 700-year presence in Spain.*

❹ *For centuries, pilgrims have trekked across Europe to the Cathedral of* **Santiago de Compostela** *in Spain's northwest corner.*

❺ *Apes rule the* **Rock of Gibraltar.** *Hide your snacks or they'll grab them.*

❻ **Nerja** *is a relaxed Costa del Sol town, perfect for an evening paseo on its Balcony of Europe promenade.*

❼ *Locals throughout southern Spain get more excited about their many* **festivals** *than the tourists do.*

❽ *The Running of the Bulls in* **Pamplona** *is like surfing—you hope to catch a good wave and ride it.*

TRAVEL SMART

Approach Spain like a veteran traveler, even if it's your first trip. Design your itinerary, get a handle on your budget, make advance arrangements, and follow my travel strategies on the road. For my best advice on sightseeing, accommodations, restaurants, and transportation, see the Practicalities chapter.

Designing Your Itinerary

Decide when to go. Peak season—July through September—comes with crowds, heat, and higher prices, especially in the coastal areas. Air-conditioning is essential. Spring and fall (April, June, and Oct) offer the best combination of lighter crowds, good weather, and moderate prices. Off-season, November through March, prices drop, sights have shorter hours, and the weather is crisp.

Choose your top destinations. My itinerary (on page 26) gives you an idea of how much you can reasonably see in 14 days, but you can adapt it to fit your own interests and timeframe.

Art lovers are drawn to Madrid and Barcelona, which have the greatest collections of art and the most museums. Historians travel back in time to Granada's sprawling Moorish Alhambra, and to Toledo, with its concentrated mix of art and history within small-town walls. If you're fond of sleepy hill towns, get a good dose (or doze?) in Andalucía. Night owls have a hoot in Sevilla. Sun worshippers bask in Barcelona, San Sebastián (a Basque city that's fun for foodies, too), and little Nerja on the South Coast. Pilgrims head for Montserrat (near Barcelona) and Santiago de Compostela.

Draft a rough itinerary. Figure out how many destinations you can comfortably fit in the time you have. Don't overdo it—few travelers wish they'd hurried more. Allow enough days per stop: Figure on at least two days for major destinations (and at least three for Barcelona).

Staying in a home base—like Barcelona or Madrid—and making day trips can be more time-efficient than changing locations and hotels. Minimize one-night stands, especially consecutive ones; it can be worth taking a late-afternoon train ride or drive to get settled into a town for two nights.

Connect the dots. Link your desti-

nations into a logical route. Determine which cities you'll fly into and out of; begin your search for transatlantic flights at Kayak.com.

Decide if you'll travel by car or public transportation, or a combination. A car is helpful for exploring regions in-depth, such as Andalucía's hill towns (where public transit can be sparse and infrequent). But a car is useless in cities, and it's not necessary for connecting far-apart destinations (easier by train or even a short flight), unless you plan to make a lot of stops along the way.

Barcelona, perched at the far northeast corner of Spain, makes a good first or last stop for your trip. Given its fast AVE train connections with Madrid (three hours, simpler than flying), you could put off renting a car until after you see Barcelona, Madrid, and Toledo.

If relying on public transit, you'll probably use a mix of trains and buses. Trains are faster, but buses can reach a few places that trains can't.

Allot sufficient time for transportation in your itinerary. Whether you travel by train, bus, or car, it'll take a half-day to get between most destinations.

To determine approximate transportation times, study the driving chart (on page 428) or train schedules (at www.bahn.de or www.renfe.com). Spain's long distances can make it worth considering the option of flying for part of your trip; check Skyscanner.com for intra-European flights.

Plan your days. Fine tune your itinerary; write out a day-by-day plan of where you'll be and what you want to see. To help make the most of your time, I've suggested day plans for destinations. But check the opening hours of sights; avoid visiting a town on the one day a week that your must-see sight is closed. Also research whether any holidays or festivals will fall during your trip—these attract crowds and can close sights (for the latest, visit Spain's tourist website, www.spain.info).

Give yourself some slack. Nonstop sightseeing can turn a vacation into a blur. Every trip, and every traveler, needs downtime for doing laundry, picnic shopping, people-watching, and so on. Pace yourself. Assume you will return.

Ready, set... You've designed the perfect itinerary for the trip of a lifetime.

From cathedrals to back streets, Spain rewards eager learners.

THE BEST OF SPAIN IN 2 WEEKS

This unforgettable two-week trip will show you the very best that Spain has to offer. It's geared for public transportation (mainly trains and a few buses), but can be traveled by car. (Ideally, rent a car after you've visited Barcelona, Madrid, and Toledo, which are well connected by train.)

DAY	PLAN	SLEEP IN
	Arrive in Barcelona	Barcelona
1	Sightsee Barcelona	Barcelona
2	Barcelona	Barcelona
3	Barcelona	Barcelona
4	Travel to Madrid in the morning (3 hours by train)	Madrid
5	Sightsee Madrid	Madrid
6	More Madrid, then head to Toledo in the late afternoon (30 minutes by train, or 1 hour by bus)	Toledo
7	Sightsee Toledo	Toledo
8	Travel to Granada (6 hours by train or bus)	Granada
9	Sightsee Granada	Granada
10	More Granada, then travel to Ronda in the late afternoon (2.5 hours by train)	Ronda
11	Sightsee Ronda	Ronda
12	Travel to Arcos (2 hours by bus), sightsee Arcos	Arcos
13	Travel to Sevilla (2 hours by bus)	Sevilla
14	Sightsee Sevilla	Sevilla
	Linger in Sevilla, or fly out	

100 Kilometers

100 Miles

FRANCE

Santiago de Compostela

Bilbao
San Sebastián

ANDORRA

SPAIN

Pamplona

Montserrat

Salamanca

Segovia

Barcelona **4**

El Escorial

Madrid **2**

Toledo **2**

Córdoba

Mediterranean Sea

Sevilla **2**

Arcos ← **1** Grazalema

Granada **2**

Jerez

Nerja

Gibraltar (UK)

Ronda **2**

Atlantic Ocean

MOROCCO

ALGERIA

PORTUGAL

LEGEND

2 Number of Overnights

Trip Costs per Person

Run a reality check on your dream trip. You'll have major transportation costs in addition to daily expenses.

Flight: A round-trip flight from the US to Barcelona or Madrid costs about $1,000-2,000, depending on where you fly from and when.

Public Transportation: For a two-week trip, allow $300 for second-class trains ($450 for first class) and buses. Whether you get a rail pass in advance or buy train tickets as you go, you'll pay about the same—unless you take advantage of online discounts for advance ticket purchases. In some cases, a short flight can cost less than a long train ride.

Car Rental: Allow roughly $250 per week, not including tolls, gas, parking, and insurance. Rentals and leases (an economical way to go if you need a car for at least three weeks) are cheaper if arranged from the US.

Budget Tips: To cut your daily expenses, take advantage of the deals you'll find throughout Spain and mentioned in this book.

City transit passes (for multiple rides or all-day usage) decrease your cost per ride. Avid sightseers buy combo-tickets or passes that cover multiple museums. If a town doesn't offer deals, visit only the sights you most want to see. Seek out free sights and experiences (people-watching counts).

Book your rooms directly with the hotel via email or phone for the best rates. Some businesses—especially hotels and walking-tour companies—offer discounts to my readers. Some hotels offer discounts if you pay in cash and/or stay three or more nights (it pays to check online or ask). Rooms cost less outside of peak season (roughly November through March). And even seniors can stay in hostels (some have double rooms) for about $30 per person. Or check Airbnb-type sites for deals.

It's no hardship to eat cheap in Spain. You can get tasty, inexpensive meals at

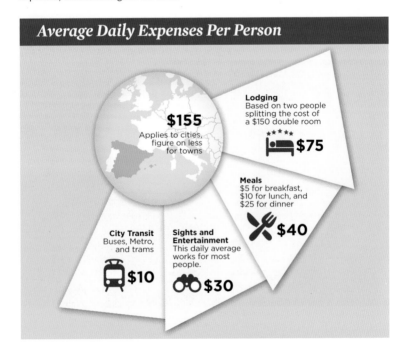

Average Daily Expenses Per Person

$155
Applies to cities, figure on less for towns

Lodging
Based on two people splitting the cost of a $150 double room
★★★★★ **$75**

Meals
$5 for breakfast, $10 for lunch, and $25 for dinner
$40

City Transit
Buses, Metro, and trams
$10

Sights and Entertainment
This daily average works for most people.
$30

tapas bars, sandwich shops, and other local chains. Cultivate the art of picnicking in atmospheric settings. When you splurge, choose an experience you'll always remember, such as a fun food-tasting tour or a dazzling flamenco show. Minimize souvenir shopping; focus instead on collecting wonderful memories.

Before You Go

You'll have a smoother trip if you tackle a few things ahead of time. For more info on these topics, see the Practicalities chapter (and www.ricksteves.com, which has helpful travel tips and talks).

Make sure your passport is valid. If it's due to expire within six months of your ticketed date of return, you need to renew it. Allow up to six weeks to renew or get a passport (www.travel.state.gov).

Arrange your transportation. Book your international flights. Figure out your main form of transportation in Spain. You can buy discounted train tickets online in advance, get a rail pass, rent a car, or book cheap European flights. (You can wing it once you're there, but it may cost more.) Drivers: Along with your license, consider bringing an International Driving Permit (sold at AAA offices in the US).

Book rooms well in advance, especially if your trip falls during peak season or any major holidays or festivals.

Reserve or buy tickets ahead for major sights. It's smart to reserve for Granada's Alhambra (up to three months in advance) to be assured of seeing its often sold-out Palacios Nazaríes. To beat the lines, reserve ahead for Madrid's Prado Museum. In Barcelona, reservations are required for the Palace of Catalan Music and recommended for the Picasso Museum, Sagrada Família, Casa Batlló, La Pedrera, Palau Güell, and Park Güell. Reservations are advised for the Dalí Theater-Museum in Figueres.

Hire guides in advance. Popular guides can get booked up; reserve by email as far ahead as possible.

Consider travel insurance. Compare the cost of the insurance to the cost of your potential loss. Check whether your existing insurance (health, homeowners, or renters) covers you and your possessions overseas.

Call your bank. Let them know you'll be using your debit and credit cards in Europe. Ask about transaction fees, and get the PIN number for your credit card. You won't need to bring euros for your trip; you can withdraw euros from cash machines in Europe.

Use your smartphone smartly. Sign up for an international service plan to reduce your costs, or rely on Wi-Fi in Europe instead. Download any apps you'll want on the road, such as maps, translation, transit schedules, and Rick Steves Audio Europe (see sidebar).

Pack light. You'll walk with your luggage more than you think. Bring a single carry-on bag and a daypack. Use the packing checklist in Practicalities as a guide.

Stick This Guidebook in Your Ear!

My free **Rick Steves Audio Europe app** makes it easy to download my audio tours of many of Europe's top attractions and listen to them offline on your travels.

For Spain, these include walking tours of Barcelona and Madrid, marked in this book with this symbol: ∩. The app also offers insightful travel interviews from my public radio show with experts from Spain and around the globe. It's all free! You can download the app via Apple's App Store, Google Play, or Amazon's Appstore. For more info, see RickSteves.com/audioeurope.

Travel Strategies on the Road

If you have a positive attitude, equip yourself with good information, and expect to travel smart, you will.

Read—and reread—this book. To have an "A" trip, be an "A" student. Note opening hours of sights, closed days, crowd-beating tips, and whether reservations are required or advisable. Check the latest at www.ricksteves.com/update.

Be your own tour guide. As you travel, get up-to-date info on sights, reserve tickets and tours, reconfirm hotels and travel arrangements, and check transit connections. Upon arrival in a new town, lay the groundwork for a smooth departure; confirm the train, bus, or road you'll take when you leave.

Give local tours a spin. Your appreciation of a city or region and its history can increase dramatically if you take a walking tour in any big city or even hire a private guide. If you want to learn more about any aspect of Spain, you're in the right place with experts happy to teach you.

Try alternatives to restaurants. Spanish restaurants are often closed when we're hungry. Compared to our standards, Spaniards eat late, having lunch—their biggest meal of the day—around 13:00 to 16:00, and dinner starting about 21:00. To cope, try picnics, sandwich shops, or tapas bars, where you can get a hearty snack or an assortment of tapas (appetizers that can add up to a tasty meal). In the bigger cities, consider taking a food tour; they're pricey but informative and delicious—filling you in while filling you up.

Outsmart thieves. Pickpockets abound in crowded places where tourists congregate. Treat commotions as smokescreens for theft. Keep your cash, cards, and passport secure in a money belt tucked under your clothes; carry only a day's spending money in your front pocket. Don't set valuable items down on counters or café tabletops, where they can be quickly stolen or easily forgotten.

Minimize potential loss. Keep expensive gear to a minimum. Bring photocopies or take photos of important documents (passport and cards) to aid in replacement if they're lost or stolen. Back up photos frequently.

Beat the summer heat. If you wilt easily, choose a hotel with air-conditioning, start your day early, take a midday siesta at your hotel, and resume your sightseeing later. Churches can offer a cool haven (but note that some enforce a modest dress code—no bare shoulders or shorts). Take frequent ice-cream breaks. Join in the paseo, when locals stroll in the cool of the evening.

Guard your time and energy. Taking a taxi can be a good value if it saves you a long wait for a cheap bus or an exhausting walk across town. To avoid long lines, follow my crowd-beating tips, such as making advance reservations or sightseeing early or late.

Be flexible. Even if you have a well-planned itinerary, expect changes, closures, sore feet, sweltering weather, and so on. Your Plan B could turn out to be even better. And if problems arise, keep things in perspective. You're on vacation in a beautiful country.

Attempt the language. Many Spaniards—especially those in the tourist trade and in big cities—speak English. But if you learn some Spanish, you'll get more smiles and make more friends. Practice the survival phrases near the end of this book and bring a phrase book.

Connect with the culture. Interacting with locals carbonates your experience. Enjoy the friendliness of the Spanish people. Ask questions—most locals are happy to point you in their idea of the right direction. Set up your own quest for the best main square, paella, paseo, or tapas bar. When an opportunity pops up, say *Sí.*

Spain...here you come!

Welcome to Rick Steves' Europe

Travel is intensified living—maximum thrills per minute and one of the last great sources of legal adventure. Travel is freedom. It's recess, and we need it.

I discovered a passion for European travel as a teen and have been sharing it ever since—through my tours, public television and radio shows, and travel guidebooks. Over the years, I've taught thousands of travelers how to best enjoy Europe's blockbuster sights—and experience "Back Door" discoveries that most tourists miss.

This book offers you a balanced mix of Spain's lively cities and cozy towns, from trendy Barcelona and upbeat Madrid to Andalucía's romantic hill towns. It's selective—rather than listing countless beach resorts, I recommend only my favorites (San Sebastián and Nerja). And it's in-depth: My self-guided museum tours and city walks provide insight into the country's vibrant history and today's living, breathing culture.

I advocate traveling simply and smartly. Take advantage of my money- and time-saving tips on sightseeing, transportation, and more. Try local, characteristic alternatives to expensive hotels and restaurants. In many ways, spending more money only builds a thicker wall between you and what you traveled so far to see.

We visit Spain to experience it—to become temporary locals. Thoughtful travel engages us with the world, as we learn to appreciate other cultures and new ways to measure quality of life.

Judging from the positive feedback I receive from readers, this book will help you enjoy a fun, affordable, and rewarding vacation—whether it's your first trip or your tenth.

¡Buen viaje! Happy travels!

Rick Steves

Barcelona

Barcelona may be Spain's second city, but it's undoubtedly the first city of the proud and distinct region of Catalunya. Catalan flags wave side by side with Spanish flags, and locals—while fluent in both languages—insist on speaking Catalan first. Joining hands to dance the patriotic *sardana* is a tradition that's going strong. This lively culture is on an unstoppable roll in Spain's most cosmopolitan corner.

The city itself is a work of art. Catalan architects, including Antoni Gaudí, Lluís Domènech i Montaner, and Josep Puig i Cadafalch, forged the Modernista style and remade the city's skyline into a curvy fantasy—culminating in Gaudí's over-the-top Sagrada Família, a church still under construction. Pablo Picasso lived here as a teenager, right as he was on the verge of reinventing painting; his legacy is today's Picasso Museum.

Barcelona bubbles with life—in the narrow alleys of the Barri Gòtic, along the pedestrian boulevard called the Ramblas, in the funky bohemian quarter of El Born, along the bustling beach promenade, and throughout the chic Eixample. The cafés are filled by day, and people crowd the streets at night, popping into tapas bars for a drink and a perfectly composed bite of seafood.

If you surrender to any city's charms, let it be Barcelona.

BARCELONA IN 3 DAYS

Day 1: In the cool of the morning, follow my Barri Gòtic Walk, exploring the winding lanes, unique boutiques, and historic cathedral.

Then take my Ramblas Ramble, strolling down the grand pedestrian boulevard—a festival of people-watching, street performers, and pickpockets. On the Ramblas, duck into La Boqueria Market for fresh produce and unforgettable taste treats. In the afternoon, head to the trendy El Born district to tour the Picasso Museum or Palace of Catalan Music, or both.

On any evening: Have a tapa-hopping dinner in El Born, the Barri Gòtic, or the Eixample. Take in some music (flamenco, guitar, concerts). Zip up to the hilltop of Montjuïc for the sunset, then down to the Magic Fountains (illuminated on weekends). Or stroll the long, inviting beach promenade.

Day 2: Tour the city's fanciful Modernista architecture. Marvel at the buildings on the Block of Discord and the street's masterpiece, Gaudí's La Pedrera. Tour Gaudí's soaring church, the Sagrada Família. Then head to his Park Güell, with its colorful mosaics, fountains, and stunning city views.

Day 3: Tour the museums on Montjuïc: The Catalan Art Museum displays top medieval sculptures, while Fundació Joan Miró features the hometown artist's whimsical work. The hilltop castle ramparts offer sweeping views. You could head back downtown (for museums, shopping, exploring) or take the slow, scenic cable-car from Montjuïc to the port—from here, it's easy to stroll the beach along Barceloneta, collect another sunset, and find your favorite *chiringuito* (beach bar).

Day Trips: Allot an extra day for a side trip: the holy site of Montserrat, with its dramatic mountain scenery, or Figueres, with its mind-bending Salvador Dalí museum.

Rick's Tip: *Don't miss out! To ensure you'll see Barcelona's top sights—the Picasso Museum, La Pedrera, Sagrada Família, Casa Batlló, and Park Güell—***book reserved-time tickets in advance.** *Casa Amatller and the Palace of Catalan Music require a guided tour, which also must be reserved in advance.*

ORIENTATION

Plaça de Catalunya, a large square at the center of Barcelona, divides the older and newer parts of town.

Below Plaça de Catalunya, the **Old City** (Ciutat Vella) is the compact core of Barcelona—ideal for strolling, shopping, and people-watching. It's a labyrinth of narrow streets once confined by medieval walls. The lively pedestrian drag called the **Ramblas** goes through the heart of the Old City from Plaça de Catalunya to the harbor. The Old City is divided into

thirds by the Ramblas and another major thoroughfare (running roughly parallel to the Ramblas), Via Laietana. Between the Ramblas and Via Laietana is the characteristic **Barri Gòtic** (BAH-ree GOH-teek, Gothic Quarter), with the cathedral as its navel. Locals call it "El Gòtic" for short. To the east of Via Laietana is the trendy **El Born** district (a.k.a. "La Ribera"), a shopping, dining, and nightlife mecca centered on the Picasso Museum and the Church of Santa Maria del Mar. To the west of the Ramblas is **El Raval** (rah-VAHL), enlivened by its university and modern-art museum. While rough-edged in places, it's the emerging lively, foodie zone.

The old harbor, **Port Vell,** gleams with landmark monuments and new developments. A pedestrian bridge links the Ramblas with the modern Maremagnum entertainment complex. On the peninsula across the quaint sailboat harbor is **Barceloneta,** a traditional fishing neighborhood with gritty charm and some good seafood restaurants. Beyond Barceloneta, a gorgeous man-made **beach** several miles long leads east to the commercial and convention district called the **Fòrum.**

Above the Old City, beyond the bustling hub of Plaça de Catalunya, is the elegant Eixample (eye-SHAM-plah) district, its grid plan softened by cutoff corners. Much of Barcelona's Modernista architecture is found here—especially along the swanky artery Passeig de Gràcia, in an area called **Quadrat d'Or** ("Golden Quarter"). To the east is the Sagrada Família; to the north is the **Gràcia** district and Antoni Gaudí's **Park Güell.**

The large hill overlooking the city to the southwest is **Montjuïc** (mohn-jew-EEK), home to some excellent museums (Catalan Art, Joan Miró).

Tourist Information

Barcelona's TI has several branches (central tel. 932-853-834, www.barcelonaturisme.cat). The primary TI is beneath the main square, **Plaça de Catalunya** (daily 8:30-

Greater Barcelona

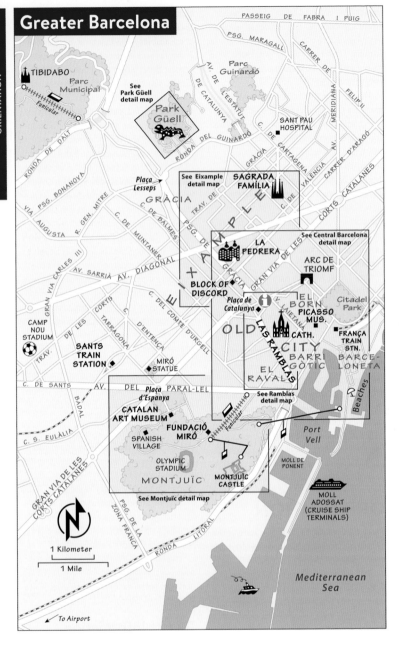

PASSEIG DE FABRA I PUIG

PSG. MARAGALL

CARRER DE

FELIP II

TIBIDABO

Parc Municipal

Funicular

RONDA DE DALT

PSG. BONANOVA

VIA AUGUSTA

R. GEN. MITRE

Parc Guinardó

AV. DE L'ESTATUT

DE CATALUNYA

See Park Güell detail map

Park Güell

RONDA DEL GUINARDÓ

C. DE CARTAGENA

SANT PAU HOSPITAL

AV. MERIDIANA

AV. D'ARAGÓ

CARRER D'ARAGÓ

Plaça Lesseps

GRACIA

C. DE BALMES

C. DE MUNTANER

TRAV. DE GRACIA

PSG. DE GRACIA

See Eixample detail map

SAGRADA FAMÍLIA

C. DE

CORTS CATALANES

VIA CARLES III

AV. SARRIA AV. DIAGONAL

C. DEL COMTE D'URGELL

C. D'ENTENÇA

EIXAMPLE

LA PEDRERA

GRAN VIA DE LES

GRACIA

BLOCK OF DISCORD

Plaça de Catalunya

See Central Barcelona detail map

ARC DE TRIOMF

EL BORN

PICASSO MUS.

Citadel Park

CAMP NOU STADIUM

DE LES CORTS

TARRAGONA

SANTS TRAIN STATION

MIRÓ STATUE

TRAV.

OLD CITY

LAS RAMBLAS

LA RIETANA

CATH.

BARRI GOTIC

EL RAVAL

FRANÇA TRAIN STN.

BARCE- LONETA

C. DE SANTS

AV.

BADAL

C. S. EULÀLIA

GRAN VIA DE LES CORTS CATALANES

DEL PARAL-LEL

Plaça d'Espanya

CATALAN ART MUSEUM

SPANISH VILLAGE

OLYMPIC STADIUM

MONTJUÏC

FUNDACIÓ MIRÓ

Funicular

MONTJUÏC CASTLE

See Montjuïc detail map

See Ramblas detail map

Beaches

Port Vell

MOLL DE PONENT

MOLL ADOSSAT (CRUISE SHIP TERMINALS)

PSG. DE LA ZONA FRANCA

RONDA LITORAL

Mediterranean Sea

N

1 Kilometer

1 Mile

To Airport

21:00, entrance just across from El Corte Inglés department store—look for red sign and take stairs down).

Other branches include a kiosk near the top of the **Ramblas** (#115), near the cathedral (inside City Hall at Ciutat 2), inside the base of the **Columbus Monument,** at the **airport** (terminals 1 and 2B), and at the **Sants train station.**

At any TI, pick up the monthly Visit *Barcelona* guidebook (with tips on sightseeing, shopping, events, and restaurants); *Time Out BCN Guide* (events, www.timeout.com/barcelona); *Barcelona Metropolitan* magazine (local topics and events, www.barcelona-metropolitan. com); and *Barcelona Prestige* (upscale dining and shopping, www.bcn-guide.com).

Modernisme Route: A handy map showing all 116 Modernista buildings is available online (www.barcelonabooks. com) or at the Institut Municipal del Paisatge Urbà, inside the Edificio Colón (Mon-Fri 9:00-14:00, closed Sat-Sun, Avinguda de les Drassanes 6, 21st floor, www.rutadelmodernisme.com). They also offer a sightseeing discount package (€12) with a great guidebook.

Regional Catalunya TI: The all-Catalunya TI, inside a former palace, can help with travel and sightseeing tips for the entire region (daily 10:00-21:00, Palau Moja, midway along the Ramblas at #118, Portaferrisa 1, tel. 933-162-740, www. palaumoja.com).

Sightseeing Passes: The Articket BCN pass covers admission to six art museums including the Picasso Museum, Catalan Art Museum, and Fundació Joan Miró (€30, valid 12 months; sold online or at museums and TIs, www.articketbcn.org). If you visit three or more covered museums, this ticket can save you money and time in line—and you can visit the Picasso Museum without a reservation.

Helpful Hints

Closed Days: Many sights are closed on Monday, including the Picasso Museum,

Catalan Art Museum, Palau Güell, Barcelona History Museum, Fundació Joan Miró, and Frederic Marès Museum. On Sunday, the food markets are closed, and some sights close early—check hours when planning your day.

Theft and Scam Alert: You're more likely to be pickpocketed in Barcelona—especially on the Ramblas and at the Sagrada Família—than about anywhere else in Europe. Leave valuables in your hotel and wear a money belt. Count your change carefully. Some areas of the Barri Gòtic and El Raval feel seedy and can be unsafe after dark.

Laundry: LavaXpres is near recommended Plaça de Catalunya and Ramblas hotels (self-service, English instructions, daily 8:00-22:00, Passatge d'Elisabets 3, www.lavaxpres.com).

Tours

WALKING TOURS

The **TI** at Plaça de Sant Jaume offers great guided walks through the **Barri Gòtic** (€16, daily at 9:30, 2 hours, groups limited to 35, buy online in advance—especially in summer, otherwise buy ticket 15 minutes early at the TI desk—not from the guide, tel. 932-853-832, www.barcelonaturisme.cat). The TI at Plaça de Sant Jaume also offers walks for **gourmets** (€22, Mon-Fri at 10:30, 2 hours) and fans of **Modernisme** (€16, April-Oct Wed and Fri at 18:00, off-season at 15:30, 2 hours).

The TI at Plaça de Catalunya offers a **Picasso** walk, through the streets of his youth and finishing in the Picasso Museum (€22, includes museum entry, runs Tue-Sat at 15:00, 2 hours including museum visit). It's always smart to reserve in advance and double-check departure times with the TI.

Discover Walks offers good walking tours in under two hours for €19-22. These include **Gaudí** (daily at 10:30, meet in front of KFC at Avinguda de Gaudí 2) and the **Ramblas and Barri Gòtic** (Tue,

BARCELONA AT A GLANCE

▲▲▲**Picasso Museum** Extensive collection offering insight into the brilliant Spanish artist's early years. **Hours:** Mon 10:00-17:00, Tue-Sun 9:00-20:30, Thu until 21:30, shorter hours and closed Mon in off-season. See page 64.

▲▲▲**Sagrada Família** Gaudí's remarkable, unfinished church—a masterpiece in progress. **Hours:** Daily 9:00-20:00, March and Oct until 19:00, Nov-Feb until 18:00. See page 76.

▲▲**Ramblas** Barcelona's colorful, gritty, tourist-filled pedestrian thoroughfare. See page 43.

▲▲**Palace of Catalan Music** Best Modernista interior in Barcelona. **Hours:** One-hour English tours daily 10:00-15:00, plus frequent concerts. See page 70.

▲▲**La Pedrera** (Casa Milà) Barcelona's quintessential Modernista building and Gaudí creation. **Hours:** Daily 9:00-20:00, Nov-Feb until 18:30. See page 73.

▲▲**Park Güell** Colorful Gaudí-designed park overlooking the city. **Hours:** Daily 8:00-21:30, Sept-Oct and April until 20:30, shorter hours in winter. See page 83.

▲▲**Catalan Art Museum** World-class showcase of this region's art. **Hours:** Tue-Sat 10:00-20:00 (Oct-April until 18:00), Sun 10:00-15:00, closed Mon year-round. See page 86.

▲**La Boqueria Market** Colorful but touristy produce market, just off the Ramblas. **Hours:** Mon-Sat 8:00-20:00, best mornings after 9:00, closed Sun, many stalls shut down early on Mon. See page 48.

▲**Palau Güell** Exquisitely curvy Gaudí interior and fantasy rooftop. **Hours:** Tue-Sun 10:00-20:00, Nov-March until 17:30, closed Mon year-round. See page 60.

▲**Maritime Museum** A sailor's delight, housed in a medieval shipyard. **Hours:** Daily 10:00-20:00. See page 60.

▲**Barcelona Cathedral** Colossal Gothic cathedral ringed by distinctive chapels. **Hours:** Generally open to visitors Mon-Fri 8:30-19:30, Sat-Sun until 20:00. See page 61.

▲**Gaudí Exhibition Center** Fine exhibit about the man who made Barcelona what it is today. **Hours:** Daily 10:00-20:00, Nov-Feb until 18:00. See page 64.

▲**Frederic Marès Museum** Quirky museum highlighted by Marès' collection of bric-a-brac from 19th-century Barcelona. **Hours:** Tue-Sat 10:00-19:00, Sun until 20:00, closed Mon. See page 64.

▲**Barcelona History Museum** One-stop trip through town history, from Roman times to today. **Hours:** Tue-Sat 10:00-19:00, Sun until 20:00, closed Mon. See page 64.

▲**Santa Caterina Market** Fine market hall built on the site of an old monastery and updated with a wavy Gaudí-inspired roof. **Hours:** Mon-Sat 7:30-15:30, open until 20:30 on Tue and Thu-Fri, closed Sun. See page 70.

▲**Church of Santa Maria del Mar** Catalan Gothic church. **Hours:** Generally open to visitors Mon-Sat 9:00-20:30, Sun from 10:00. See page 70.

▲**Casa Batlló** Gaudí-designed home topped with fanciful dragon-inspired roof. **Hours:** Daily 9:00-21:00. See page 70.

▲**Fundació Joan Miró** World's best collection of works by Catalan modern artist Joan Miró. **Hours:** Tue-Sat 10:00-20:00 (Thu until 21:00), Sun 10:00-15:00, shorter hours in winter, closed Mon year-round. See page 86.

▲**CaixaForum** Modernista cultural center featuring good temporary art exhibits. **Hours:** Daily 10:00-20:00. See page 91.

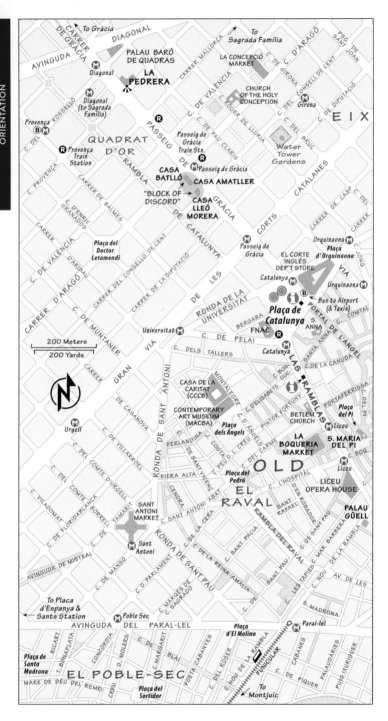

To Gràcia

DIAGONAL

CARRER DE GRACIA

AVINGUDA

To
Sagrada Família

C. DE GIRONA

C. D'ARAGÓ

PSG. DE
SANT JOAN

PALAU BARÓ
DE QUADRAS

Ⓜ Diagonal

LA
PEDRERA

CARRER MALLORCA

LA CONCEPCIÓ
MARKET

C. DEL CONSELL DE CENT

C. DE DIPUTACIÓ

Ⓜ Diagonal
(to Sagrada
Família)

C. DE VALÈNCIA

CHURCH
OF THE HOLY
CONCEPTION

EIX

Provença
Ⓑ Ⓜ

C. DEL ROSSELLÓ

C. DE ROGER DE LLÚRIA

Girona Ⓜ

Ⓡ Provença
Train
Station

QUADRAT
D'OR

PASSEIG
DE
RAMBLA

Ⓡ

Passeig de
Gràcia
Train Stn.

C. DE PAU CLARIS

C. DEL BRUC

Water
Tower
Gardens

CATALANES

C. DE PROVENÇA

Ⓜ Passeig de Gràcia

CARRER DE BALMES

CASA
BATLLÓ

GRÀCIA

CASA AMATLLER

CARRER DE CASP

C. DE

"BLOCK OF →
DISCORD"

CASA
LLEÓ
MORERA

DE

CARRER

C. D'ENRIC
GRANADOS

CORTS

CARRER

C. DE VALÈNCIA

D'ARIBAU

Plaça del
Doctor
Letamendi

CATALUNYA

LA

Passeig de
Gràcia

Ⓜ

Urquinaona Ⓜ

Plaça
d'Urquinaona

VIA

CARRER D'ARAGÓ

C. DE MUNTANER

C. DEL CONSELLO DE CENT

CARRER DE LA DIPUTACIÓ

DE

LES

EL CORTE
INGLÉS
DEP'T STORE

Catalunya Ⓜ

Urquinaona Ⓜ

200 Meters

RONDA DE LA
UNIVERSITAT

Bergara

Ⓘ Ⓑ

Bus to Airport
(& Taxis)

COMTAL

PORTAL DE L'ANGEL

200 Yards

Universitat Ⓜ

Plaça de
Catalunya

C. DE PELAI

FNAC Ⓡ

ANNA

SANTA ANNA C.

Catalunya Ⓜ

C. DELS TALLERS

CARRER

GRAN

DE CASANOVA

DE SANT ANTONI

MONTALEGRE

C.DE LA CANUDA

Ⓘ

LAS RAMBLAS

C. BON
SUCC

C.DE LA CANUDA

Urgell Ⓜ

CASA DE LA
CARITAT
(CCCB)

CONTEMPORARY
ART MUSEUM
(MACBA)

Plaça
dels Àngels

FERLANDINA

C. D'ELISABETS

PINTOR FORTUNY

PORTAFERRISSA

Plaça
del Pi

BETLEM
CHURCH

Ⓜ Liceu

S. MARIA
DEL PI

C. DE VILLARROEL

C. DEL COMTE D'URGELL

DE SANT VICENÇ

J. COSTA

P. L. CREU

C. D'EN XUCLÀ

DEL CARME

LA
BOQUERIA
MARKET

Ⓜ Liceu

C. DEL COMTE BORRELL

RIERA ALTA

PEU DE

Plaça del
Pedró

OLD

L'HOSPITAL

LICEU
OPERA HOUSE

C. DE FLORIDABLANCA

CENDRA

EL
RAVAL

SANT
RAFAEL

D'EN ROBADOR

PALAU
GÜELL

C. VILADOMAT

SANT
ANTONI
MARKET

C. DE TAMARIT

C. SANT ANTONI ABAT

RONDA DE SANT PAU

RAMBLA DEL RAVAL

DE SANT PAU

C. MÀR. BARBERA

DE LA RAMBLA

Ⓜ Sant
Antoni

C. DE MANSO

RONDA DE LA REINA AMALIA

SANT PACIÀ

SANT PAU

C. LES TÀPIES

AV. DE LES

AVINGUDA DE MISTRAL

C. DE PARLAMENT

C. DE LA CERA

C. NOU DE LA RAMBLA

To Plaça
d'Espanya &
Sants Station

C. MARQÈS DE
C. SAGRADO

DE

S. MADRONA

Ⓜ Poble Sec

AVINGUDA

DEL

PARAL-LEL

Plaça
d'El Molino

Ⓜ Paral-lel

Plaça de
Santa
Madrona

C. RICART

C. BONAPLATA

C. D. MOLERS

C. DE

C.MARGARIT

BLAI

POETA CABANYES

C. DEL ROSER

C. NOU DE LA RAMBLA

FUNICULAR

CABANES

C. DE PIQUER

PALAUDÀRIES

PUIG XURIGUER

MARE DE DÉU DEL REMEI

EL POBLE-SEC

CONCORDIA

CREU

Plaça del
Sortidor

To
Montjuïc

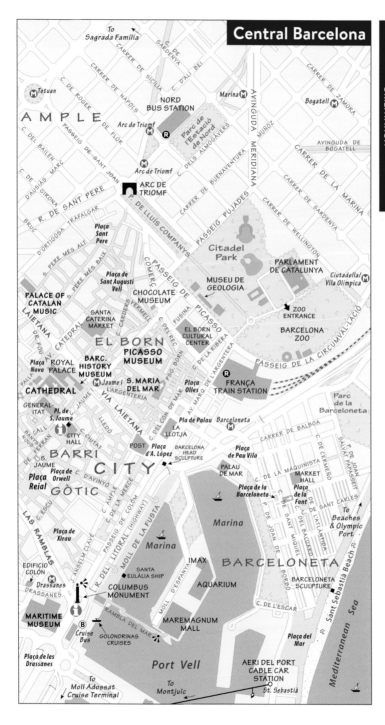

Central Barcelona

To Sagrada Família

C. DE SARDENYA
CARRER DE SICÍLIA
CARRER DE NÁPOLS
C. D'ALÍ BEI

Tetuan
C. DE ROGER DE FLOR

NORD
BUS STATION

Marina
AVINGUDA MERIDIANA
Bogatell
CARRER DE ZAMORA

AMPLE

Arc de Triomf

Parc de
l'Estació
de Nord

AVINGUDA DE
BOGATELL

CARRER DE LA MARINA

PASSEIG DE SANT JOAN

C. DEL BAILÉN
C. DE GIRONA
D'AUSIÀS MARC

Arc de Triomf

C. DELS ALMOGÀVERS

CARRER DE BUENAVENTURA MUÑOZ

CARRER DE SARDENYA

ARC DE
TRIOMF

R. DE SANT PERE

P. DE LLUÍS COMPANYS

CARRER DE WELLINGTON

BRUC
D'ORTIGOSA
TRAFALGAR

Plaça
Sant
Pere

S. PERE MÉS ALT

PASSEIG PUJADES

PASSEIG DE PICASSO

Plaça de
Sant Augustí
Vell

COMERÇ

Citadel
Park

PARLAMENT
DE CATALUNYA

Ciutadella/
Vila Olímpica

S. PERE MÉS BAIX

CHOCOLATE
MUSEUM

MUSEU DE
GEOLOGIA

PALACE OF
CATALAN
MUSIC

SANTA
CATERINA
MARKET

C. DEL REC
C. CARDERS

FUSINA

EL BORN
CULTURAL
CENTER

ZOO
ENTRANCE

LAIETANA
DR. POU

V. CATEDRAL

EL BORN

PICASSO
MUSEUM

BARCELONA
ZOO

PASSEIG DE LA CIRCUMVAL·LACIÓ

Plaça
Nova

ROYAL
PALACE

BARC.
HISTORY
MUSEUM

PG. BORN
C. DE LA RIBERA

CATHEDRAL

Jaume I

S. MARIA
DEL MAR

AV. MARQ. DE L'ARGENTERA

GENERAL-
ITAT

L'ARGENTERIA

Plaça
Olles

FRANÇA
TRAIN STATION

Parc
de la
Barceloneta

Pl. de
S. Jaume

VIA LAIETANA

C. DELGON DE MAR

Pla de Palau

Barceloneta

CARRER DE BALBOA

CALL
BANYS
NOUS

C. JAUME

C. CIUTAT

LLEDÓ

LA
LLOTJA

FERRAN

CITY
HALL

BARRI

POST

Plaça
d'A. López

BARCELONA
HEAD
SCULPTURE

Plaça
de Pau Vila

PALAU
DE MAR

C. DE LA MAQUINISTA

MARKET
HALL

P. DE JOAN DE BORBÓ
SALVAT PAPASSEIT

C. ESCU

S.
JAUME

Plaça de
Orwell

CITY
GÒTIC

C. D'AVINYÓ

PALAU
DE MAR

Plaça de la
Barceloneta

Plaça
de la
Font

C. DE SANT CARLES

To
Beaches
& Olympic
Port

Plaça
Reial

C. AMPLE

C. DE LA MERCÈ

P. DEL LITORAL (HIGHWAY)

Marina

P. DE JOAN DE BORBÓ

C. DEL BALUARD
C. DE SANT MIGUEL
C. DE L'ATLÀNTIDA

LAS RAMBLAS

Plaça de
Xirau

R. DEL LITORAL (HIGHWAY)

ANSELM CLAVÉ

PASSEIG DE COLÓM

MOLL DE LA FUSTA

Marina

IMAX

BARCELONETA

Sant Sebastià Beach

EDIFICIO
COLÓN

Drassanes

SANTA
EULÀLIA SHIP

AQUARIUM

BARCELONETA
SCULPTURE

DRASSANES

COLUMBUS
MONUMENT

C. DE L'ESCAR

MARITIME
MUSEUM

RAMBLA DEL MAR

MOLL D'ESPANYA

MAREMAGNUM
MALL

Mediterranean Sea

Cruise
Bus

GOLONDRINAS
CRUISES

Plaça del
Mar

Plaça de les
Drassanes

Port Vell

AERI DEL PORT
CABLE CAR
STATION

To
Moll Adossat
Cruise Terminal

To
Montjuïc

St. Sebastià

"You're Not in Spain, You're in Catalunya!"

The region of Catalunya, with Barcelona as its capital, has its own language, history, culture, and proud, independent spirit (you might see the popular nationalistic refrain above on T-shirts or stickers around town). Historically, Catalunya ("Cataluña" in Spanish, "Catalonia" in English) has often been at odds with the central Spanish government in Madrid.

The Catalan language and culture were discouraged or even outlawed at various times in the past, as Catalunya often chose the wrong side in wars and rebellions against the kings in Madrid. In the Spanish Civil War (1936-1939), Catalunya was one of the last pockets of democratic resistance against the military coup of fascist dictator Francisco Franco, who punished the region with four decades of repression.

After the end of the Franco era in the mid-1970s, the Catalan language made a huge comeback. Schools are now required by law to conduct classes in Catalan; most children learn Catalan first and Spanish second. While all Barcelonans still speak Spanish, nearly all understand Catalan, three-quarters speak Catalan, and half can write it.

Here are some helpful Catalan words and phrases:

Hello	*Hola* (OH-lah)
Please	*Si us plau* (see oos plow)
Thank you	*Gràcies* (GRAH-see-es)
Goodbye	*Adéu* (ah-DAY-oo)
Long live Catalunya!	*¡Visca Catalunya!* (BEE-skah kah-tah-LOON-yah)
avenue	*avinguda* (ah-veen-GOO-dah)
boulevard	*passeig* (PAH-sehj)
exit	*sortida* (sor-TEE-dah)
square	*plaça* (PLAH-sah)
street	*carrer* (kah-REHR)

Thu, and Sat at 15:00, meet in front of Liceu Opera House on the Ramblas, tel. 931-816-810, www.discoverwalks.com).

A dozen or so companies offer "free" walks that rely on—and expect—tips to stay in business. Try **Runner Bean Tours'** 2.5-hour, English-only walks, one on the Old City and the other covering Gaudí (both depart from Plaça Reial daily at 11:00, also at 16:30 March-Sept and 15:00 Oct-Dec, mobile 636-108-776, www.runnerbeantours.com).

LOCAL GUIDES

For a private guide or group tour, try **Barcelona Guide Bureau** (check website for prices; Via Laietana 50, tel. 932-682-422, www.barcelonaguidebureau.com); **José Soler** (€250/half-day per group, mobile 615-059-326, www.pepitotours.com, info@pepitotours.com); or **Live Barcelona** (from €195/3 hours, tel. 936-327-259, mobile 609-205-844, www.livebarcelona.com, info@livebarcelona.com).

GUIDED BUS TOURS

The **Barcelona Guide Bureau** offers various tours that include most sight admissions; their Montserrat tour is convenient if you don't want to deal with public transportation. Book tickets at a TI or online, or just show up at their departure point on Plaça de Catalunya in front of the Deutsche Bank (€35-74; tel. 933-152-261, www.barcelonaguidebureau.com). **Catalunya Bus Turístic** also runs excursions to nearby destinations, including **Salvador Dalí sights** in Figueres and Girona (€49-79, trips run April-Oct, depart from Plaça de Catalunya in front of El Corte Inglés, live trilingual commentary in Catalan, Spanish, and English; €5 extra for a more in-depth English audioguide; book at TIs, by phone, or online—10 percent web discount; tel. 932-853-832, www.catalunyabusturistic.com).

HOP-ON, HOP-OFF BUSES

The handy hop-on, hop-off **Bus Turístic,** which departs from Plaça de Catalunya, offers three multistop circuits in double-decker buses with headphone commentary. The two-hour blue route covers north Barcelona (most Gaudí sights, departs from El Corte Inglés). The two-hour red route covers south Barcelona (Barri Gòtic and Montjuïc, departs from the west—Ramblas—side of the square). The 40-minute green route covers the beaches and modern Fòrum complex from April-October (1 day-€30, 2 days-€40, buy on bus, at TI, or online, offers small discounts on major sights, daily 9:00-20:00 in summer, off-season until 19:00, buses run every 10-25 minutes, www.barcelonabusturistic.cat).

BARCELONA WALKS

These two self-guided walks take you through the old town—down the main boulevard ("Ramblas Ramble") and through the cathedral neighborhood

("Barri Gòtic Walk"). 🎧 My free Barcelona City Walk audio tour covers the Ramblas (in part) and the Barri Gòtic neighborhood.

Ramblas Ramble

For more than a century, this walk down Barcelona's main boulevard has been a magnet for visitors. Raft the river of Barcelonan life, passing a grand opera house, elegant cafés, flower stands, artists, street mimes, con men, and prostitutes. This one-hour stroll goes from Plaça de Catalunya gently downhill to the waterfront, with an easy return by Metro. The word "Ramblas" is plural; the street is actually a succession of five separately named segments. But street signs and addresses treat it as a single long street—"La Rambla," singular.

● Self-Guided Walk

• *Start your ramble on Plaça de Catalunya, at the top of the Ramblas.*

❶ Plaça de Catalunya

Dotted with fountains, statues, and pigeons, and ringed by grand buildings, this plaza is Barcelona's center. Plaça de Catalunya is the hub for the Metro, bus, airport shuttle, and Bus Turístic. Of the region's 7.4 million Catalans, more than half live in greater Barcelona. Plaça de Catalunya is their Times Square.

Geographically, the 12-acre square links the narrow streets of old Barcelona with the broad boulevards of the newer city (the Eixample). Four great thoroughfares radiate from here: The Ramblas is the popular tourist promenade. Passeig de Gràcia has fashionable shops and cafés (and noisy traffic). Rambla de Catalunya is equally fashionable but cozier and more pedestrian-friendly. Avinguda del Portal de l'Angel (shopper-friendly and traffic-free) leads to the Barri Gòtic.

At the Ramblas end of the square, the odd, inverted-staircase **monument** represents the shape of Catalunya. An

Plaça de Catalunya

inscription honors one of its former presidents, Francesc Macià i Llussà, who declared independence for the breakaway region in 1931. (It didn't quite stick.) Sculptor Josep Maria Subirachs, whose work you'll see at the Sagrada Família, designed it. These days, Catalans gather on the square by the tens of thousands to demonstrate passionately about whether Catalunya should be independent from Spain.

The giant El Corte Inglés department store towering above the square (on the northeast side) has just about anything you might need.

• *Cross the street, head down about 30 yards, and pause to take in the scene.*

❷ Head of the Ramblas

The street called the Ramblas slopes gently downhill from here to the harbor. It's dotted with trees and ironwork lampposts, lined with fanciful buildings, paved with colorful mosaics, and trod upon by thousands of people both day and night.

Start with the ornate, black and gold lamppost on your right. The base is a water tap called the **Fountain of Canaletes,** which has been a local favorite for more than a century. When Barcelona tore down its medieval wall and created this elegant promenade, this fountain was one of its early attractions. Legend says that a drink from the fountain ensures that you'll come back to Barcelona one day.

As you survey the Ramblas action, get your bearings for our upcoming stroll. You'll see the following features here and all along the way:

The **wavy tile work** of the pavers underfoot represent the stream that once flowed here. *Rambla* means "stream" in Arabic, and this used to be a drainage ditch along one of the medieval walls enclosing the Barri Gòtic (to the left). Look up to see the city's characteristic shallow **balconies.** The **plane trees** lining the boulevard are known for their toughness in urban settings. These deciduous trees let in maximum sun in the winter and provide maximum shade in the summer.

Nearby, notice the **chairs** fixed to the

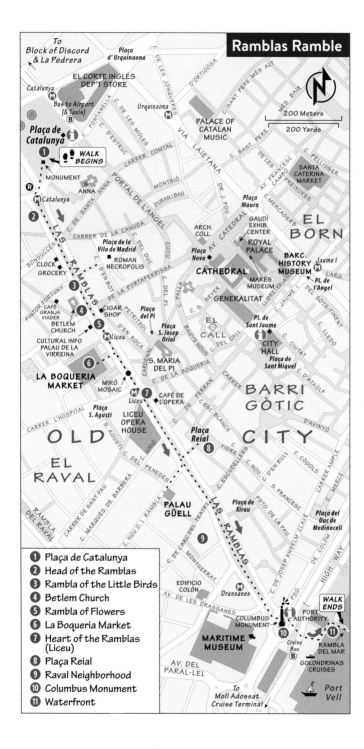

Ramblas Ramble

To Block of Discord & La Pedrera

Plaça d'Urquinaona

EL CORTE INGLÉS DEP'T STORE

Catalunya

Bus to Airport (& Taxis)

Urquinaona

Plaça de Catalunya

WALK BEGINS

MONUMENT

S. ANNA

Catalunya

200 Meters
200 Yards

D'ORTIGOSA

C. DE LES JONQUERES

C. FONTANELLA

C. D'ESTRUC

CARRER COMTAL

C. DE LES MOLES

PORTAL DE L'ANGEL

C. DE SANTA ANNA

MONTSIÓ

DURAN I BAS

DR. J. POU

PALACE OF CATALAN MUSIC

SANT PERE MÉS ALT

MES BAIX

VIA LAIETANA

C. SANT PERE

DE LES

AV. FRANCESC CAMBÓ

C. FELLISSER

SANTA CATERINA MARKET

Plaça Maura

C. MERCADERS

EL BORN

BONSUCCÉS

LAS RAMBLAS

CLOCK

GROCERY

PINTOR FORTUNY

CAFÉ GRANJA VIADER

BETLEM CHURCH

CULTURAL INFO PALAU DE LA VIRREINA

Plaça de la Vila de Madrid

ROMAN NECROPOLIS

CARRER DE LA CANUDA

C. DEL DUC

CUCU

C. DE LA PORTAFERRISSA

C. D'EN BOT

CIGAR SHOP

D'EN ROCA

Liceu

Plaça del Pi

Plaça S. Josep Oriol

C. PALLA

C. DEL PI

BANYS NOUS

S. MARIA DEL PI

ARCH. COLL.

Plaça Nova

AV. CATEDRAL

CATHEDRAL

MARÈS MUSEUM

GENERALITAT

C. S. BEYER

GAUDÍ EXHIB. CENTER

ROYAL PALACE

BARC. HISTORY MUSEUM

Jaume I

Pl. de l'Àngel

C. JAUME I

C. LLIBRETERIA

EL CALL

C. DEL CALL

Pl. de Sant Jaume

CITY HALL

Plaça de Sant Miquel

C. CIUTAT

L'ARG.

C. SOTS-TINENT

C. LLEDÓ

C. D'ATAÚLF

LA BOQUERIA MARKET

MIRÓ MOSAIC

Liceu

CAFÉ DE L'OPERA

Plaça S. Agustí

OLD EL RAVAL

CARRER L'HOSPITAL

C. ST. AGUSTÍ

LICEU OPERA HOUSE

C. DE LA BOQUERIA

C. DE FERRAN

C. DE L'UNIÓ

CESC BLANCS

Plaça Reial

C. VIDRERIA

BARRI GÒTIC

CITY

D'AVINYÓ

C. NOU D'EN RULL

C. CÒDOLS

C. ESCUDELLERS

PALAU GÜELL

C. NOU D. L. RAMBLA

C. DE PENEDÉS

C. DEL C. UNIÓ

CARRER DE SANT PAU

RAMBLA DEL RAVAL

C. MARQUES DE BARBERÀ

C. DE L'ARC DEL TEATRE

C. DE MONTSERRAT

Plaça de Xirau

LAS RAMBLAS

PSTG. DE LA PAU

S. FRANCESC

CARRER AMPLE

C. MERCE

Plaça del Duc de Medinaceli

EDIFICIO COLÓN

Drassanes

AV. DE LES DRASSANES

COLUMBUS MONUMENT

MARITIME MUSEUM

AV. DEL PARAL·LEL

To Moll Adossat Cruise Terminal

C. DE JOSEP ANSELM CLAVÉ

DE COLOM

P.S.G.

Cruise Bus

HIGH·WAY

PORT AUTHORITY

WALK ENDS

RAMBLA DEL MAR

GOLONDRINAS CRUISES

Port Vell

① Plaça de Catalunya
② Head of the Ramblas
③ Rambla of the Little Birds
④ Betlem Church
⑤ Rambla of Flowers
⑥ La Boqueria Market
⑦ Heart of the Ramblas (Liceu)
⑧ Plaça Reial
⑨ Raval Neighborhood
⑩ Columbus Monument
⑪ Waterfront

Leafy and broad, the Ramblas is a tourist magnet.

sidewalk at jaunty angles. It used to be that you'd pay to rent a chair here to watch the parade of passersby. Enjoy these chairs while you can—you'll find virtually no public benches or other seating farther down the Ramblas, only cafés that serve beer and sangria in just one (expensive) size: *gigante*.

Along this walk are **booths** that sell lottery tickets in support of ONCE, Spain's organization for the blind. You'll see **soccer souvenirs,** especially the scarlet and blue of FC Barcelona—known as Barça.
• *Continue strolling.*

Walk 100 yards farther to #115, with an entrance flanked by two columns and a fine facade struggling to be noticed above the Ramblas ruckus. This marks the venerable **Royal Academy of Science and Arts building** (now home to a performing-arts theater). The building is emblematic of the city's striking architecture from the late 1900s—an industrial boom time that brought lots of construction. Look up: The clock high on the facade marks official Barcelona time—synchronize. The **Carrefour** supermarket next door has cheap groceries (at #113).

• *Remember that each of the Ramblas segments has its own name. You're now standing at what was the…*

❸ *Rambla of the Little Birds (RIP)*

A generation ago, kids brought their parents here to buy birds, turtles, and hamsters. Today, none of the pet kiosks survive—there's not a bird in sight.
• *At #122 (the big, modern Citadines Hotel on the left), take a 100-yard detour through a modern passageway marked with the hotel's name to a restored…*

Roman Necropolis: Look down and imagine a 2,000-year-old road lined with tombs. Outside the walls of Roman cities, tombs typically lined the roads leading into town. Emperor Augustus spent time in modern-day Spain conquering new land, so the Romans incorporated Hispania into the empire's infrastructure. This road, Via Augusta, led into the Roman port of Barcino (today's highway to France still follows the route laid out by this Roman thoroughfare).

Canaletes fountain

Rambla of Flowers

• Return to the Ramblas and continue down 100 yards or so to the next cross street, Carrer de la Portaferrissa (on the left), to see the **decorative tile** over a fountain still in use by locals. The scene shows the original city wall with the gate that once stood here. Now cross the boulevard to the front of the big church.

❹ Betlem Church

This imposing church is dedicated to Bethlehem, and for centuries locals have flocked here at Christmastime to see nativity scenes. Its diamond-shaped stonework is 17th-century Baroque: Check out the sloping roofline, ball-topped pinnacles, corkscrew columns, and scrolls above the entrance.

This Baroque style is unusual in Barcelona because during the Baroque and Renaissance eras (1500-1800), Barcelona was broke: New World discoveries shifted lucrative trade to the Atlantic, and the Spanish crown kept unruly Catalunya on a short leash.

For a sweet treat, head around to the narrow lane on the far side of the church (Carrer d'en Xucla) to the recommended Café Granja Viader.

• Continue down the boulevard, through the stretch called the...

❺ Rambla of Flowers

This colorful block is lined with flower stands. Besides admiring the blossoms on display, gardeners will covet the seeds sold here for varieties of radishes, greens, peppers, and beans seldom seen in the US—including the iconic green Padrón pepper (if you buy seeds, you're obligated to declare them at US customs when returning home). At #99 (on the right), the **cultural center** in Palau de la Virreina sells tickets to dance and musical concerts (easier to buy here than at the main TI).

On the left, at #100, **Tabacs Gimeno** has been selling cigars since the 1920s. Step inside and appreciate the dying art of cigar boxes and hand-crafted pipes.

• A little farther on, across the street (opposite the Erotic Museum) is the arcaded entrance to Barcelona's great covered market, La Boqueria.

❻ La Boqueria Market

Since as far back as 1200, Barcelonans have brought their animal parts to this market, worth ▲. While tourists are drawn to the area around the main entry, locals know that the stalls up front pay the highest rent—and therefore inflate their prices and cater to out-of-towners. Skip the tempting but more expensive juices sold here and head to a booth farther in or along the sides (market open Mon-Sat 8:00-20:00, best mornings after 9:00, closed Sun, many stalls shut down early on Mon).

Stop in at the **Pinotxo Bar**—it's just inside the market, under the sign—and snap a photo of animated Juan giving a thumbs-up for your camera. The market and adjacent lanes are busy with tempting little eateries.

Stands show off seasonal fruits and vegetables The focus here is on Spanish specialties like olives and saffron. Full legs of *jamón* (ham) abound. Top quality *ibérico* (Iberian type) and *bellota* (acorn eaters) can cost €300 or more per hock. You'll see many types of the Catalan *botifarra* sausage. The fishmonger stalls could double as a marine biology lab. Fish is sold whole, not filleted—local shoppers like to look their dinner in the eye to be sure it's fresh.
• *After you've scoped out the market, head back to the street and continue down the Ramblas.*

You're skirting the old Barri Gòtic neighborhood. Glance left through a modern cutaway arch for a glimpse of the medieval church tower of **Santa Maria del Pi,** a popular venue for guitar concerts. This marks the Plaça del Pi and a great shopping street, Carrer Petritxol, which runs parallel to the Ramblas.

On the right side of the Ramblas (at #83), find the highly regarded **Escribà bakery,** with its appealing Modernista facade: Look for the *Antigua Casa Figueras* sign arching over the doorway, mosaics of twining plants, a stained-glass peacock, and undulating woodwork.

• *After another block, you reach the Liceu Metro station, marking the...*

❼ Heart of the Ramblas

At the Liceu Metro station's elevators, the Ramblas widens a bit into a small, lively square (Plaça de la Boqueria). Liceu marks the midpoint of the Ramblas between Plaça de Catalunya and the waterfront.

Underfoot, find the much trod-upon **Joan Miró mosaic** in red, white, yellow, and blue. The mosaic's black arrow represents an anchor, a reminder of the city's attachment to the ocean and a welcome to visitors arriving by sea. Miró's simple, colorful designs are found all over the city, from murals to mobiles to the La Caixa bank logo. The best place to see his work is in the Fundació Joan Miró at Montjuïc.

The surrounding buildings have playful ornamentation typical of the city. The **Chinese dragon** holding a lantern (at #82) decorates a former umbrella shop (notice the fun umbrellas perched high up). The dragon is an important symbol of Catalan pride for its connection to the local patron saint, St. George (Jordi).

A few steps down (on the right) is the **Liceu Opera House** (Gran Teatre del Liceu), which hosts world-class opera, dance, and theater (box office left of main entrance, open Mon-Fri 9:30-20:00). Opposite the opera house is **Café de l'Opera** (#74), an elegant stop for an expensive beverage. This bustling café, with Modernista decor and a historic atmosphere, boasts that it's been open since 1929, even during the Spanish Civil War.
• *We've seen the best stretch of the Ramblas; to cut this walk short, you could catch the Metro back to Plaça de Catalunya. Otherwise, let's continue to the port. The wide, straight street that crosses the Ramblas in another 30 feet (Carrer de Ferran) leads to Plaça de Sant Jaume, the governmental center.*

Head down the Ramblas another 50 yards (to #46), and turn left down an arcaded lane (Carrer de Colom) to the square called...

A *Chinese dragon ornament*

B *Joan Miró's mosaic*

C *Plaça Reial*

D *La Boqueria Market*

E *Columbus Monument*

F *Palau Güell*

❽ Plaça Reial

Dotted with palm trees, surrounded by an arcade, and ringed by yellow buildings with white Neoclassical trim, this elegant square has a colonial ambience. It comes complete with old-fashioned taverns (cervecerías), modern bars with patio seating, and a Sunday coin-and-stamp market. Completing the picture are Gaudí's first public works (the two colorful helmeted lampposts). The square is a lively hangout by day or by night.
• Head back out to the Ramblas.

Across the boulevard, a half-block detour down Carrer Nou de la Rambla brings you to **Palau Güell,** designed by Antoni Gaudí (on the left, at #3). Even from the outside, you get a sense of this innovative apartment, the first of Gaudí's Modernista buildings. As this is early Gaudí (built 1886-1890), it's darker and more Neo-Gothic than his more famous later work. The two parabolic-arch doorways and elaborate wrought-iron work signal his emerging nonlinear style. Completely restored in 2011, Palau Güell offers an informative look at a Gaudí interior (see page 83).
• Return to the Ramblas and keep heading down.

❾ Raval Neighborhood

The neighborhood on the right side of this stretch of the Ramblas is El Raval. In the last century, this was a rough neighborhood, home to sailors, prostitutes, and poor immigrants. Today, its new **Museum of Contemporary Art** and the massive **Sant Antoni market hall** are gentrifying the area, and it's becoming a bohemian-chic magnet for the young and trendy and the foodie crowd.

The skyscraper to the right of the Ramblas is the Edificio Colón. When built in 1970, the 28-story structure was Barcelona's first high-rise. Near the skyscraper is the Maritime Museum, housed in what were the city's giant medieval shipyards.
• Near the bottom of the Ramblas, take note of the Drassanes Metro stop, which can take you back to Plaça de Catalunya when you're ready. Up ahead is the...

❿ Columbus Monument

The 200-foot column honors Christopher Columbus, who came to Barcelona in 1493 after journeying to America. It was erected for the 1888 Universal Exposition, an international fair that helped vault a surging Barcelona onto the world stage.

A tiny elevator ascends to the top of the column, lifting visitors to a covered observation area for fine panoramas over the city (entrance/ticket desk is in the TI, inside the base of the monument; elevator-€6, daily 8:30-19:30, when crowded line may close up to an hour early).
• Scoot across the busy traffic circle and continue straight ahead to the water's edge. Turn left, walk 50 yards, and find a pedestrian bridge that juts out over the harbor for a good place from which to check out the...

⓫ Waterfront

For more than 2,000 years, this harbor with its bustling sea trade has been the reason Barcelona is on the world map. The wooden pedestrian **bridge** you're standing on is a modern extension of the Ramblas, called La Rambla de Mar ("Rambla of the Sea"). The bridge can swing out to allow boat traffic into the marina.

As you face Columbus, take in the sights. At the foot of the Ramblas are the docks with the golondrinas harbor-cruise boats (€7.70, daily about 11:30-19:00, more in summer, fewer in winter, tel. 934-423-106, www.lasgolondrinas.com). To the left of Columbus is the big Maritime Museum. Farther left, in the distance, is the majestic, 570-foot bluff of parklike **Montjuïc,** with a number of sights and museums reachable by cable car (as you can see). To the right of the Columbus statue, the frilly yellow building is the fanciful Modernista-style port-authority building. Stretching to the right of that is a delightful promenade along the seawall of Barcelona's Old Port (Port Vell); it's worth a stroll. Along the promenade is a permanently moored historic schooner,

Modernista port authority building and the Old Port

the **Santa Eulàlia** (part of the Maritime Museum). Finally, over your right shoulder is Maremagnum, a modern shopping mall and entertainment complex with an IMAX cinema, a huge aquarium, restaurants, and piles of people. Late at night, it's a rollicking youth hangout.

Barri Gòtic Walk

Barcelona's Barri Gòtic (Gothic Quarter) is a bustling world of shops, bars, and nightlife packed into narrow, winding lanes and undiscovered courtyards. This is Barcelona's birthplace—where the ancient Romans built a city, where medieval Christians built their cathedral, where Jews gathered together, and where Barcelonans lived within a ring of protective walls until the 1850s, when the city expanded.

Treat this 1.5-hour self-guided walk from Plaça de Catalunya to Plaça del Rei as a historical scavenger hunt. You'll focus on the earliest chunk of Roman Barcelona, right around the cathedral, and explore some legacy sights from the city's medieval era.

◑ Self-Guided Walk

• Start on Barcelona's grand main square, **Plaça de Catalunya.** From the northeast corner (between the giant El Corte Inglés department store and the Banco de España), head down the broad pedestrian boulevard called...

❶ Avinguda del Portal de l'Angel

For much of Barcelona's history, this was a major city gate. A medieval wall enclosed the city, and the entrance here—the "Gate of the Angel"—gave the street

Architectural details

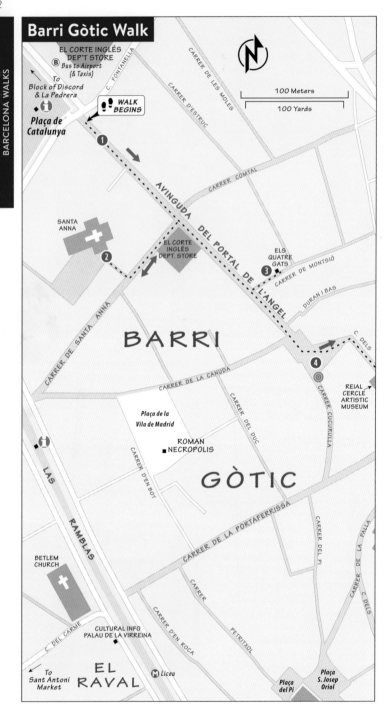

Barri Gòtic Walk

EL CORTE INGLÉS DEP'T STORE
B Bus to Airport (& Taxis)

To
Block of Discord
& La Pedrera

Plaça de
Catalunya

WALK
BEGINS

1

C. FONTANELLA

CARRER DE LES MOLES

CARRER D'ESTRUC

CARRER DE LES MOLES

CARRER COMTAL

SANTA
ANNA

AVINGUDA DEL PORTAL DE L'ANGEL

EL CORTE
INGLÉS
DEPT. STORE

2

ELS
QUATRE
GATS

3

CARRER DE MONTSIÓ

DURAN I BAS

BARRI

CARRER DE SANTA ANNA

C. DELS

4

CARRER DE LA CANUDA

REIAL
CERCLE
ARTISTIC
MUSEUM

Plaça de la
Vila de Madrid

CARRER DEL DUC

CARRER CUCURULLA

ROMAN
NECROPOLIS

GÒTIC

CARRER D'EN BOT

CARRER DE LA PORTAFERRISSA

CARRER DEL PI

CARRER DE LA PALLA

LAS

RAMBLAS

BETLEM
CHURCH

CARRER

DELS

CARRER D'EN ROCA

PETRITXOL

C. DEL CARME

CULTURAL INFO
PALAU DE LA VIRREINA

To
Sant Antoni
Market

EL
RAVAL

M Liceu

Plaça
del Pi

Plaça
S. Josep
Oriol

100 Meters

100 Yards

N

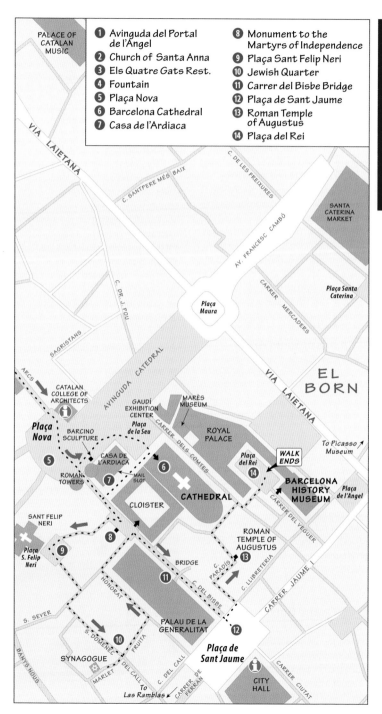

1 Avinguda del Portal de l'Àngel
2 Church of Santa Anna
3 Els Quatre Gats Rest.
4 Fountain
5 Plaça Nova
6 Barcelona Cathedral
7 Casa de l'Ardiaca
8 Monument to the Martyrs of Independence
9 Plaça Sant Felip Neri
10 Jewish Quarter
11 Carrer del Bisbe Bridge
12 Plaça de Sant Jaume
13 Roman Temple of Augustus
14 Plaça del Rei

PALACE OF CATALAN MUSIC

VIA LAIETANA

C. SANTPERE MÉS BAIX

C. DE LES FREIXURES

SANTA CATERINA MARKET

AV. FRANCESC CAMBÓ

C. DR. J. POU

CARRER MERCADERS

Plaça Santa Caterina

Plaça Maura

SAGRISTANS

VIA LAIETANA

EL BORN

ARCS

CATALAN COLLEGE OF ARCHITECTS

AVINGUDA CATEDRAL

GAUDÍ EXHIBITION CENTER

MARÈS MUSEUM

Plaça Nova

BARCINO SCULPTURE

Plaça de la Seu

CARRER DELS COMTES

ROYAL PALACE

To Picasso Museum

5

CASA DE L'ARDIACA

6

Plaça del Rei

WALK ENDS

14

ROMAN TOWERS

7

MAIL SLOT

CATHEDRAL

BARCELONA HISTORY MUSEUM

Plaça de l'Àngel

SANT FELIP NERI

CLOISTER

CARRER DEL VEGUER

Plaça S. Felip Neri

9

8

ROMAN TEMPLE OF AUGUSTUS

S. SEVER

HONORAT

BRIDGE

11

C. PARADÍS

13

C. LLIBRETERIA

CARRER JAUME I

C. DEL BISBE

S. DOMÈNEC

10

PALAU DE LA GENERALITAT

12

BANYS NOUS

SYNAGOGUE

MARLET

DEL CALL

FRUITA

C. DEL CALL

CARRER DE FERRAN

Plaça de Sant Jaume

CARRER CIUTAT

CITY HALL

To Las Ramblas

its name. An angel statue atop the gate purportedly kept Barcelonans safe from plagues and bid voyagers safe journey as they left the security of the city.

Although today this street has been globalized and sanitized, a handful of businesses with local roots survive. On the right at the first corner (at #25), a green sign and particularly appetizing display window mark **Planelles Donat**—long appreciated for its ice cream, sweet *turró* (or *turrón,* almond-and-honey candy), refreshing *orxata* (or *horchata,* almond-flavored drink), and *granissat* (or *granizado,* ice slush).

• *A block farther down, pause at Carrer de Santa Anna to admire the Art Nouveau awning at another* **El Corte Inglés** *department store. From here, take a half-block detour to the right on Carrer de Santa Anna. At #32 go through a large entryway to the pleasant, flower-fragrant courtyard of the...*

❷ Church of Santa Anna

This austere Catalan Gothic church—a 12th-century gem—was part of a convent and still has its marker cross standing outside. To the left of the cross, approach the gate, where you can peek inside the fine cloister—an arcaded walkway around a leafy courtyard. Climb the modern stairs across from the church for views of the bell tower. Inside the church you'll find a bare Romanesque interior, topped with an octagonal wooden roof. At the back of the nave, you'll find the cloister (€2, usually Mon-Sat 11:00-19:00, until 14:00 in Aug).

• *Backtrack to Avinguda del Portal de l'Angel. At Carrer de Montsió (on the left), just past the H&M store, side-trip a half-block to...*

❸ Els Quatre Gats

This restaurant (at #3) is a historic monument, tourist attraction, nightspot, and recommended eatery. It's famous for being the circa-1900 bohemian-artist hangout where Picasso nursed drinks with friends and had his first one-man show.

The building itself, by prominent architect Josep Puig i Cadafalch, represents Neo-Gothic Modernisme. Even if you don't eat or drink here, you can take a quick look around (ask "*Solo mirar, por favor?*").

• *Return to and continue down Avinguda del Portal de l'Angel. You'll soon reach a fork in the road and a building with a...*

❹ Fountain

The blue and yellow tilework, a circa-1918 addition to this even older fountain, depicts ladies with big jugs of water. In the 17th century this was the last watering stop for horses before leaving town. As recently as 1940, about 10 percent of Barcelonans still got their water from fountains like this.

• *You may feel the pull of wonderful little shops down the street to the right. But take the left fork, down Carrer dels Arcs. Just past the corner, you'll pass the* **Reial Cercle Artístic Museum,** *a private collection of Dalí's work (€10, daily 10:00-22:00). Continue and enter the large square called...*

❺ Plaça Nova

Two bold Roman towers flank a street leading off the square. These once guarded the entrance gate of the ancient Roman city of Barcino. The big stones that make up the base of the (reconstructed) towers are actually Roman. Near the base of the left tower, modern bronze letters spell out "BARCINO." The city's name may have come from Barca, one of Hannibal's generals, who is said to

Fountain with tilework

Picasso frieze on the Catalan College building

have passed through during Hannibal's roundabout invasion of Italy. At Barcino's peak, the Roman wall (see the section stretching to the left of the towers) was 25 feet high and a mile around, with 74 towers. It enclosed a population of 4,000.

One of the towers has a bit of reconstructed **Roman aqueduct** (notice the streambed on top). In ancient times, bridges of stone carried fresh water from the distant hillsides into the walled city.

Opposite the towers is the modern **Catalan College of Architects** building (Col·legi d'Arquitectes de Barcelona, TI inside), which is, ironically for a city with so much great architecture, quite ugly. The frieze was designed by Picasso (1962) in his distinctive simplified style. With just a few squiggly stick-figures, Picasso captured traditional Catalan activities. If you check out all three sides of the building, you'll see scenes suggesting music, bullfighting, sea trade, and the *sardana* dance. The branch-waving kings Picasso drew are the giant puppets (*gigantes*) paraded through the streets during local festivals. Picasso spent his formative years (1895-1904, age 14-23)

here in the old town. He drank with fellow bohemians at Els Quatre Gats (which we just passed) and frequented brothels a few blocks from here on Carrer d'Avinyó ("Avignon")—which inspired his influential Cubist painting *Les Demoiselles d'Avignon*.

• *Immediately to the left as you face the Picasso frieze,* **Carrer de la Palla** *is an inviting shopping street. But let's head left through Plaça Nova to take in the mighty...*

❻ Barcelona Cathedral

The facade is a virtual catalog of Gothic motifs. There's the pointed arch over the entrance and the stained-glass windows with elaborate stone tracery. Statues of robed saints stand in niches, and winged angels teeter on the octagonal bell towers. And the whole thing is topped with three tall steeples. These pointy spires are meant to give the impression of a church flickering with spiritual fires. This was the Gothic style called Flamboyant—meaning "flame-like." The area in front of the cathedral is where Barcelonans dance the *sardana* on weekends (see page 63).

The cathedral's interior—with its vast space, peaceful cloister, and many ornate chapels—is worth a visit (see Barcelona Cathedral listing later). If you interrupt this tour to visit the cathedral now, you'll exit the cloister a block down Carrer del Bisbe. From there you can circle back to the right, following the wall of the cathedral to visit stop #7—or skip #7 and step directly into stop #8.

As you stand in the square facing the cathedral, look far to your left to see the multicolored, wavy canopy marking the roofline of the **Santa Caterina Market.** The busy street between here and the market—called Via Laietana—is the boundary between the Barri Gòtic and the funkier, edgier **El Born** neighborhood.

• *For now, return to the Roman towers and pass between them to head up Carrer del Bisbe. Take an immediate left, up the ramp to the entrance of...*

Barcelona Cathedral

❼ Casa de l'Ardiaca

It's free to enter this mansion, which was once the archdeacon's residence and now functions as the city archives. The elaborately carved doorway is Renaissance. To the right of the doorway is a carved mail slot by 19th-century Modernista architect Lluís Domènech i Montaner. Enter a small courtyard with a fountain, then step inside the lobby of the city archives, (often featuring free exhibits). At the left end of the lobby, go through the archway and look down into the stairwell for a peek at impressive Roman stonework. Back in the courtyard, climb to the balcony for views of the cathedral steeple, gargoyles, and the small Romanesque chapel on the right—the only surviving 13th-century bit of the cathedral.

• *Return to Carrer del Bisbe and turn left. After a few steps, you reach a small square with a bronze statue ensemble.*

❽ Monument to the Martyrs of Independence

Five Barcelona patriots—including two priests—calmly receive their last rites before being garroted (strangled) for resisting Napoleon's occupation of Spain in the early 19th century. They'd been outraged by French atrocities in Madrid (depicted in Goya's famous *Third of May* painting in Madrid's Prado Museum). According to the plaque marking their mortal remains, these martyrs to independence gave their lives in 1809 *"por Dios, por la Patria, y por el Rey"*—for God, country, and king.

• *Exit the square down tiny Carrer de Montjuïc del Bisbe (to the right as you face the martyrs). This leads to the cute...*

❾ Plaça Sant Felip Neri

This shaded square serves as the playground of an elementary school and is often bursting with energetic kids speaking Catalan (just a couple of generations ago, this would have been illegal). The Church of Sant Felip Neri, which Gaudí attended, is still pocked with bomb damage from the Spanish Civil War. As a stronghold of democratic, anti-Franco forces, Barcelona saw a lot of fighting. A plaque on the wall (left of church door) honors the 42 killed—mostly children—in that 1938 aerial bombardment.

The buildings here were paid for by the guilds that powered the local economy. The shoemakers guild (to the right of the arch where you entered the square) is decorated above the windows with reliefs depicting boots.

• *Exit the square past the fun **Sabater Hermanos** artisanal soap shop, and head down Carrer de Sant Felip Neri. At the T-intersection, turn right onto Carrer de Sant Sever, then immediately left on Carrer de Sant Domènec del Call (look for the blue El Call sign). You've entered the...*

❿ Jewish Quarter (El Call)

In Catalan, a Jewish quarter goes by the name El Call—literally "narrow passage," for the tight lanes where medieval Jews were forced to live, under the watchful eye of the nearby cathedral. (At its peak, some 4,000 Jews were crammed into just a few alleys in this neighborhood.)

Walk down Carrer de Sant Domènec del Call, and pass through the charming little square (a gap in the dense tangle of medieval buildings cleared by another civil war bomb), where you will find a rust-colored sign displaying a map of the Jewish Quarter. Take the next lane to the right (Carrer de Marlet). On the right is the (literally) low-profile, four-foot-high entrance to what was likely Barcelona's **main synagogue** during the Middle Ages (Antigua Sinagoga Mayor, €2.50, Mon-Fri 10:30-18:30, Sat-Sun until 15:00, shorter hours off-season). The sparse interior includes access to two small subterranean rooms with Roman walls topped by a medieval Catalan vault. Look through the glass floor to see dyeing vats used for a later shop on this site run by former

Ⓐ *Roman towers on Plaça Nova*

Ⓑ *Carrer del Bisbe Bridge*

Ⓒ *Church of Sant Felip Neri*

Ⓓ *Monument to the Martyrs of Independence*

Ⓔ *Architectural detail, Casa de l'Ardiaca*

Jews who had been forcibly converted to Christianity.

• *From the synagogue, start back the way you came but then continue straight ahead, onto Carrer de la Fruita. At the T-intersection, turn left, then right, to find your way back to the Martyrs statue. From here, we'll turn right down Carrer del Bisbe to the...*

⑪ Carrer del Bisbe Bridge

This structure connects the Catalan government building (on the right) with what was the Catalan president's ceremonial residence (on the left). Though the bridge appears to be centuries old, it was constructed in the 1920s by Catalan architect Joan Rubió (a follower of Gaudí), who also did the carved ornamentation on the buildings.

• *Continue along Carrer del Bisbe to...*

⑫ Plaça de Sant Jaume

This stately central square of the Barri Gòtic takes its name from the Church of St. James (in Catalan: Jaume, JOW-mah) that once stood here. Set at the intersection of ancient Barcino's main thoroughfares, this square was once a Roman forum. In that sense, it's been the seat of city government for 2,000 years.

For more than six centuries, the **Palau de la Generalitat** (on the uphill side of the square) has housed the offices of the autonomous government of Catalunya. It always flies the Catalan flag next to the obligatory Spanish one. Above the building's doorway is Catalunya's patron saint—St. George (Jordi), slaying the dragon. From these balconies, the nation's leaders (and soccer heroes) greet the people on momentous days. The square is often the site of festivals or demonstrations.

Facing the Generalitat across the square is the **Barcelona City Hall** (Casa de la Ciutat).

Look left and right down the main streets branching off the square; they're lined with ironwork streetlamps and bal-conies draped with plants. Carrer de Ferran, which leads to the Ramblas, is classic Barcelona.

• *Facing the Generalitat, exit the square going up the second street to the right of the building, on tiny Carrer del Paradís. Follow this street as it turns right. When it swings left, pause at #10, the entrance to the...*

⑬ Roman Temple of Augustus (Temple Roma d'August)

You're standing at the summit of Mont Tàber, the Barri Gòtic's highest spot. A plaque on the wall by the entrance reads: "Mont Tàber, 16.9 meters" (elevation 55 feet). At your feet, a millstone inlaid in the pavement also marks a momentous spot. It was here that the ancient Romans founded the town of Barcino around 12 BC. They built a *castrum* (fort) on the hilltop, protecting the harbor, and this temple to honor their emperor, Augustus.

Go inside for a peek at the last vestiges of the imposing Roman temple (free, Tue-Sat 10:00-19:00, Sun until 20:00, Mon

Roman Temple of Augustus

until 14:00). All that's left are four columns and some fragments of the transept and its plinth (good English info on-site). The huge columns, dating from the late first century BC, are as old as Barcelona itself. They were part of the ancient town's biggest structure, dedicated to Augustus, who was worshipped as a god. These Corinthian columns (with deep fluting and topped with leafy capitals) were the back corner of a 120-foot-long temple that extended from here to Barcino's forum...Plaça de Sant Jaume, which you just visited.

• *Continue down Carrer del Paradís one block. When you bump into the back end of the cathedral, take a right, going down Carrer de la Pietat/Baixada de Santa Clara until you emerge into a square called...*

⑭ *Plaça del Rei*

The buildings enclosing this square exemplify Barcelona's medieval past. The central section (topped by a five-story addition) was the core of the **Royal Palace** (Palau Reial Major). A vast hall on its ground floor once served as the throne room and reception room. From the 13th to the 15th century, the Royal Palace housed Barcelona's counts as well as the resident kings of Aragon. In 1493, a triumphant Christopher Columbus, accompanied by six New World natives and several pure-gold statues, was welcomed home by King Ferdinand and Queen Isabel, who honored him with the title "Admiral of the Oceans."

To the right is the palace's church, the 14th-century **Chapel of Saint Agatha,** which sits atop the foundations of a Roman wall. To the left is the **Viceroy's Palace,** built in the 1500s for the right-hand man of the Spanish monarch, who was now located in far-off Castile.

SIGHTS

Near the Ramblas

▲PALAU GÜELL

This early building by Antoni Gaudí (completed in 1890) shows the architect taking his first tentative steps toward what would become his trademark curvy style. Dark and masculine, with castle-like rooms, Palau Güell (pronounced "gway") was custom built to house the Güell clan and gives an insight into Gaudí's artistic genius. The rooftop has his signature colorful tile mosaic chimneys and offers a panorama of the city. While some people will find this redundant if also visiting La Pedrera, others will appreciate this exquisite building for its delightfully loopy rooftop and far fewer crowds.

Cost and Hours: €12 timed-entry ticket includes good audioguide—buy in advance online, free first Sun of the month; open Tue-Sun 10:00-20:00, Nov-March until 17:30, closed Mon year-round; last entry one hour before closing, rooftop closes when raining; a half-block off the Ramblas at Carrer Nou de la Rambla 3, Metro: Liceu or Drassanes, tel. 934-725-775, www.palauguell.cat.

▲MARITIME MUSEUM (MUSEU MARÍTIM)

Barcelona's medieval shipyard, the best preserved in the entire Mediterranean, is home to an excellent museum near the bottom of the Ramblas. The museum's permanent collection covers the salty history of ships and navigation from the 13th to the 18th century (restoration projects on their permanent collection will eventually reveal pieces from the 18th to the 20th century). Even if you choose not to pay for a full visit, the building is worth a look; interesting free exhibits are in the lobby (inside the main entrance facing the water), where you can get a glimpse of the building's interior.

Cost and Hours: €10, free Sun from 15:00 and for kids 16 and under, ticket includes audioguide and visit to *Santa Eulàlia* boat; open daily 10:00-20:00, nice café with seating inside or out on the museum courtyard (free to enter), Avinguda de les Drassanes, Metro: Drassanes, tel. 933-429-920, www.mmb.cat.

Nearby: Your museum ticket includes entrance to the ***Santa Eulàlia,*** an early-20th-century schooner docked a short walk from the Columbus Monument (otherwise €3, Tue-Sun 10:00-20:30, Nov-March until 17:30, closed Mon year-round). On Saturday mornings, you can sail around the harbor on the schooner for three hours—reserve well in advance (Sat 10:00-13:00, €12 for adults, €6 for kids 6-14, tel. 933-429-920, reserves.mmaritim@diba.cat).

Barri Gòtic
▲BARCELONA CATHEDRAL (CATEDRAL DE BARCELONA)

The city's 14th-century, Gothic-style cathedral (with a Neo-Gothic facade) has played a significant role in Barcelona's history—but as far as grand cathedrals go, this one is relatively unexciting. Still, it's worth a visit to see its richly decorated chapels, finely carved choir, tomb of Santa Eulàlia, and restful cloister with gurgling fountains and resident geese.

Cost: Free to enter Mon-Sat before 12:30, Sun before 13:45, and daily after 17:45, but during those times you must pay €3 each to visit the choir or the terrace (the museum is closed during these hours, and church access may be limited during services). The church is open to tourists for several hours each afternoon (Mon-Sat 12:30-17:30, Sun 14:00-17:15), but you must pay €7 (covers admission to choir, terrace, and museum).

Hours: Cathedral generally open to visitors Mon-Fri 8:30-19:30, Sat-Sun until 20:00. The cathedral's three minor sights are open Mon-Sat (with different hours) and closed Sun: choir—9:00-19:00, terrace—9:00-18:00, museum—12:30-17:15. Both the choir and terrace may close ear-

lier on slow days.

Information: Tel. 933-151-554, www.catedralbcn.org.

Dress Code: The dress code is strictly enforced; don't wear tank tops, shorts, or skirts above the knee.

Getting In: The main, front door is open most of the time. While it can be crowded, the line generally moves fast. You can also enter directly into the cloister (through the door facing the *Martyrs* statue on the small square along Carrer del Bisbe) or through the side door (facing the Frederic Marès Museum along Carrer dels Comtes).

Visiting the Cathedral: This has been Barcelona's holiest spot for 2,000 years. The Romans built their Temple of Jupiter here. In AD 343, the pagan temple was replaced with a Christian cathedral. That building was supplanted by a Romanesque-style church (11th century). The current Gothic structure was started in 1298 and finished in 1450, during the medieval glory days of the Catalan nation. The facade was humble, so in the 19th century the proud local bourgeoisie (enjoying a second Golden Age) redid it in a more ornate, Neo-Gothic style. Construction was capped in 1913 with the central spire, 230 feet tall.

The nave is ringed with 28 **chapels.** Besides creating worship spaces, the walls defining these chapels serve as interior buttresses supporting the roof (which is why the exterior walls are smooth, without the normal Gothic buttresses outside). Barcelona honors many of the homegrown saints found in these chapels with public holidays. In the middle of the nave, the 15th-century choir (coro) features ornately carved stalls. During the standing parts of the Mass, the chairs were folded up, but VIPs still had those little wooden ledges to lean on. Each was creatively carved and—since you couldn't sit on sacred things—the artists were free to enjoy some secular and naughty fun here.

Look behind the **high altar** (beneath

Nave of Barcelona Cathedral

the crucifix) to find the bishop's chair (cathedra). As a cathedral, this church is the bishop's seat—hence its Catalan nickname of *La Seu.* To the left of the altar is the organ and the elevator up to the terrace. To the right of the altar, the wall is decorated with Catalunya's yellow-and-red coat of arms. Steps beneath the altar lead to the **crypt,** featuring the marble-and-alabaster sarcophagus (1327-1339) containing the remains of Santa Eulàlia. The cathedral is dedicated to this saint. Thirteen-year-old Eulàlia, daughter of a prominent Barcelona family, was martyred by the Romans for her faith in AD 304. Murky legends say she was subjected to 13 tortures.

The **elevator** in the left transept takes you up to the rooftop **terrace,** made of sturdy scaffolding pieces, for an expansive city view.

Exit through the right transept to enter the **cloister. Its arcaded walkway surrounds a lush** circa-1450 courtyard. Ahhhh. It's a tropical atmosphere of palm, orange, and magnolia trees; a fish pond; trickling fountains; and squawking geese. During the Corpus Christi festival in June, kids come here to watch a hollow egg

dance atop the fountain's spray. As you wander the cloister (clockwise), check out the coats of arms as well as the tombs in the pavement. These were for rich merchants who paid good money to be buried as close to the altar as possible. A few pavement stones here and there have the symbols of their trades: scissors, shoes, bakers, and so on. The resident **geese** have been here for at least 500 years. There are always 13, in memory of Eulàlia's 13 years and 13 torments.

The little **museum** (at the far end of the cloister; entry possible only during paid visiting hours) has the six-foot-tall 14th-century Great Monstrance, a ceremonial display case for the communion wafer that's paraded through the streets during the Corpus Christi festival. The next room, the Sala Capitular, has several altarpieces, including a pietà (*Desplà,* 1490) by Bartolomé Bermejo.

▲SARDANA DANCES

If you're in town on a weekend, you can see the *sardana,* a patriotic dance in which Barcelonans link hands and dance in a circle (Sun at 11:15, many Sat at 18:00, no

Circle Dances in Squares and Castles in the Air

From group circle dancing to human towers, Catalans have some interesting and unique traditions. A memorable Barcelona experience is watching (or participating in) the patriotic *sardana* dances. Locals of all ages seem to spontaneously appear. For some it's a highly symbolic, politically charged action representing Catalan unity—but for most it's just a fun chance to kick up their heels. All are welcome, even tourists cursed with two left feet. The dances are held in the square in front of the cathedral on Sundays at 11:15 (and many Saturdays at 18:00).

Participants gather in circles after putting their things in the center—symbolic of community and sharing (and the ever-present risk of theft). Holding hands, dancers raise their arms—slow-motion, *Zorba the Greek*-style—as they hop and sway gracefully to the music. The band (*cobla*) consists of a long flute, tenor and soprano oboes, strange-looking brass instruments, and a tiny bongo-like drum (*tamborí*). The rest of Spain mocks this lazy circle dance, but considering what it takes for a culture to survive within another culture's country, it is a stirring display of local pride and patriotism. During the 36 years of Franco dictatorship, the *sardana* was forbidden.

Another Catalan tradition is the **castell,** a tower erected solely of people. *Castells* pop up on special occasions, such as the Festa Major de Gràcia in mid-August and La Mercè festival in late September. Towers can be up to 10 humans high. Imagine balancing 50 or 60 feet in the air, with nothing but a pile of flesh and bone between you and the ground. The base is formed by burly supports called *baixos;* above them are the *manilles* ("handles"), which help haul up the people to the top. The *castell* is capped with a human steeple—usually a child—who extends four fingers into the air, representing the four red stripes of the Catalan flag. A scrum of spotters (called *pinyas*) cluster around the base in case anyone falls. *Castelleres* are judged both on how quickly they erect their human towers and how fast they can take them down. Besides during festivals, you can usually see *castells* in front of the cathedral on spring and summer Saturdays at 19:30 (as part of the Festa Catalana). If you've never seen this, it's worth searching for the spectacle on YouTube.

One thing that these two traditions have in common is their communal nature. Perhaps it's no coincidence, as Catalunya is known for its community spirit, team building, and socialistic bent.

dances in Aug, event lasts 1-2 hours, in the square in front of the cathedral; for details, see the sidebar).

▲GAUDÍ EXHIBITION CENTER

This center fills the stony complex of ancient and medieval buildings immediately to the left of the cathedral with a beautifully lit, thoughtful, and well-described exhibit. With plenty of historic artifacts, it provides the best introduction to Antoni Gaudí—the man and the architect. You'll spend about an hour following the included audioguide through six rooms on three floors.

Cost and Hours: €15; daily 10:00-20:00, Nov-Feb until 18:00, last entry one hour before closing; Pla de la Seu 7, Metro: Jaume I, tel. 932-687-582, www.gaudiexhibitioncenter.com. While a combo-ticket sold here includes entrance to the great Modernista sights, it's impractical considering the necessity of booking those sights in advance.

▲FREDERIC MARÈS MUSEUM (MUSEU FREDERIC MARÈS)

This delightful museum, adjacent to the cathedral, features the eclectic collection of Frederic Marès (1893-1991), a local sculptor and packrat. The museum sprawls through several old Barri Gòtic buildings around a peaceful courtyard. It offers a fascinating look at ancient Roman statues from this region and is an exquisite warehouse of Romanesque and Gothic Christian art from Catalunya.

Cost and Hours: €4.20, free first Sun of the month and all other Sun from 15:00; open Tue-Sat 10:00-19:00, Sun until 20:00, closed Mon; essential audioguide-€1, Plaça de Sant Iu 5, Metro: Jaume I, tel. 932-563-500, www.museumares.bcn.cat.

▲BARCELONA HISTORY MUSEUM (MUSEU D'HISTÒRIA DE BARCELONA)

This museum primarily contains objects from archaeological digs around Barcelona. But the real highlight is an underground labyrinth of excavated Roman ruins.

Cost and Hours: €7; includes audioguide and other MUHBA branches; free all day first Sun of month and other Sun from 15:00—but no audioguide during free times; open Tue-Sat 10:00-19:00, Sun until 20:00, closed Mon; Plaça del Rei, enter on Carrer del Veguer, Metro: Jaume I, tel. 932-562-122.

El Born

▲▲▲PICASSO MUSEUM (MUSEU PICASSO)

Pablo Picasso may have made his career in Paris, but the years he spent in Barcelona—from age 14 through 23—were among the most formative of his life. Here, young Pablo mastered the realistic painting style of his artistic forebears—and first felt the freedom that allowed him to leave that all behind and give in to his creative, experimental urges. When he left Barcelona, Picasso headed for Paris...and revolutionized art forever.

The pieces in this excellent museum capture that priceless moment just before this bold young thinker changed the world. While you won't find Picasso's famous later Cubist works here, you will enjoy a representative sweep of his early years, as well as works from his twilight years. It's the top collection of Picassos here in his native country and the best anywhere of his early years.

Cost and Hours: €12 for timed-entry ticket, free Thu from 18:00 and all day first Sun of month, must reserve ahead for free hours; open Mon 10:00-17:00, Tue-Sun 9:00-20:30, Thu until 21:30, shorter hours and closed Mon in off-season; audioguide-€5, Carrer de Montcada 15, tel. 932-563-000, www.museupicasso.bcn.cat.

Rick's Tip: *The* **Picasso Museum** *often sells out and there's nearly always a long line. Buy a* **timed-entry ticket** *in advance to avoid disappointment.*

Ticketing Tips: The ticketing part of the website can be temperamental—keep

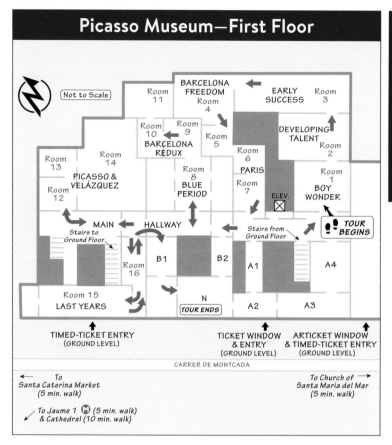

Picasso Museum—First Floor

Not to Scale

Room 11
BARCELONA FREEDOM
Room 4
EARLY SUCCESS
Room 3

Room 10
Room 9
DEVELOPING TALENT
Room 2

BARCELONA REDUX
Room 5
Room 6
PARIS
Room 1
BOY WONDER

Room 13
Room 14
PICASSO & VELÁZQUEZ
Room 8
BLUE PERIOD
Room 7
ELEV.

Room 12

MAIN
HALLWAY
Stairs to Ground Floor
Stairs from Ground Floor
TOUR BEGINS

B1
B2
A1
A4

Room 16
N
TOUR ENDS
A2
A3

Room 15
LAST YEARS

TIMED-TICKET ENTRY (GROUND LEVEL)
TICKET WINDOW & ENTRY (GROUND LEVEL)
ARTICKET WINDOW & TIMED-TICKET ENTRY (GROUND LEVEL)

CARRER DE MONTCADA

← To Santa Caterina Market (5 min. walk)
To Church of → Santa Maria del Mar (5 min. walk)

To Jaume 1 Ⓜ (5 min. walk) & Cathedral (10 min. walk)

trying. An **Articket BCN** (see page 37) allows you to enter the galleries whenever you wish (you must first obtain an admission ticket from the on-site Articket window—where you can also buy an Articket).

Day-of tickets (when available) are sold online (must purchase at least 2 hours before your visit). The museum's busiest times are mornings before 13:00, all day Tue, and during the free entry times.

Getting There: It's on Carrer de Montcada; the general ticket office is in the courtyard at #19, and the Articket BCN booth is at #23. From the Jaume I Metro stop, it's a quick five-minute walk. It's a 10-minute walk from the cathedral and many parts of the Barri Gòtic.

Services: The ground floor has a required bag check, a bookshop, and WC.

◑ SELF-GUIDED TOUR

The Picasso Museum's collection of nearly 300 paintings is presented more or less chronologically. With good text panels in every room providing context, it's easy to follow the evolution of Picasso's work. Don't be surprised if a painting described here is not on view; paintings are rotated in and out. But the themes and chronology remain constant.

BOY WONDER (ROOM 1)

Pablo's earliest art is realistic and earnest. His work quickly advanced from childish pencil drawings (from about 1890),

Pablo Picasso (1881-1973)

Pablo Picasso was the most famous and, for me, the greatest artist of the 20th century. He became the master of many styles (Cubism, Surrealism, Expressionism) and many media (painting, sculpture, prints, ceramics, assemblages). Still, anything he touched looked unmistakably like "a Picasso."

Born in Málaga, Spain, Picasso was the son of an art teacher. At a young age, he quickly advanced beyond his teachers. Picasso's teenage works are stunningly realistic and capture the inner complexities of the people he painted. As a youth in Barcelona, he fell in with a bohemian crowd that mixed wine, women, and art.

In 1900, at age 19, Picasso started making trips to Paris and moved there four years later. When his best friend, Spanish artist Carlos Casagemas, committed suicide, Picasso plunged into a **Blue Period** (1901-1904)—the dominant color in these paintings matches their melancholy mood and subject matter (emaciated beggars, hard-eyed pimps).

In 1904, Picasso got a steady girlfriend (Fernande Olivier) and suddenly saw the world through rose-colored glasses—the **Rose Period.** He played with the "building blocks" of line and color to find new ways to reconstruct the real world on canvas.

At his studio in Montmartre, Picasso and his neighbor Georges Braque worked together, in poverty so dire they often didn't know where their next bottle of wine was coming from. And then, at age 25, Picasso reinvented painting. Fascinated by the primitive power of African tribal masks, he sketched human faces with simple outlines and almond eyes. He sketched nudes from every angle, then experimented with showing several views on the same canvas. A hundred paintings and nine months later, Picasso gave birth to a monstrous canvas of five nude, fragmented prostitutes with mask-like faces—*Les Demoiselles d'Avignon* (1907).

This bold new style was called **Cubism.** With Cubism, Picasso shattered the Old World and put it back together in a new way. The subjects are somewhat recognizable (with the help of the titles), but they're built with geometric shards (let's call them "cubes")—like viewing the world through a kaleidoscope of brown and gray.

In 1918, Picasso traveled to Rome and entered a **Classical Period** (1920s) of more realistic, full-bodied women and children, inspired by the three-dimensional sturdiness of ancient statues. While he flirted with abstraction, through-

through a series of technically skilled **art-school works** (copies of plaster feet and arms), to oil paintings of impressive technique. His **portraits** demonstrate surprising psychological insight.

DEVELOPING TALENT (ROOM 2)

Pablo moved to Barcelona at age 14. During a summer trip to Málaga in 1896, he experimented with a series of fresh, Impressionistic-style landscapes (relatively rare in Spain at the time). As a 15-year-old, Pablo dutifully entered art-school competitions. His first big work, *First Communion,* tackled a prescribed religious subject, but Picasso made it an excuse to paint his family. His sister Lola was the model for the communicant, and the man beside her has the face of Picasso's father.

out his life Picasso always kept a grip on "reality." His favorite subject was people. The anatomy might be jumbled, but it's all there.

Though he lived in France and Italy, Picasso remained a Spaniard at heart, incorporating Spanish motifs into his work. Unrepentantly macho, he loved bullfights, seeing them as a metaphor for the timeless human interaction between the genders. To Picasso, the horse symbolizes the feminine, and the bull, the masculine. Spanish imagery—bulls, screaming horses, a Madonna—appears in Picasso's most famous work, *Guernica* (1937). The monumental canvas of a bombed village summed up the pain of Spain's brutal civil war (1936-1939) and foreshadowed the onslaught of World War II.

At war's end, Picasso left Paris behind, finding fun in the **south of France.** Sun! Color! Water! Freedom! Senior citizen Pablo Picasso was reborn, enjoying worldwide fame and the love of a beautiful young painter, Françoise Gilot. Bursting with creativity, Picasso cranked out a painting a day. His Riviera works set the tone for the rest of his life: sunny, lighthearted, and childlike; filled with motifs of the sea, Greek myths, and animals. His simple drawing of a dove holding an olive branch became an international symbol of peace.

Picasso made collages, built "statues" out of wood, wire, ceramics, papier-mâché, or whatever, and even turned everyday household objects into statues (like his famous bull's head made of a bicycle seat with handlebar horns). **Multimedia** works like these have become so standard today that we forget how revolutionary they once were. His last works have the playfulness of someone much younger. As it is often said of Picasso, "When he was a child, he painted like a man. When he was old, he painted like a child."

Find the portrait of his aunt Tía Pepa, painted in Málaga in 1896 (this and other family portraits are frequently rotated). Notice how ably Picasso captured the toughness of his aunt.

EARLY SUCCESS (ROOM 3)

In the large, classically painted *Science and Charity* (1897), Picasso used realistic means to represent subjects of social concern—a technique typical of the social realism movement of the late 19th century. The doctor (modeled on Pablo's father) represents science. The nun represents charity and religion. From the hopeless face and lifeless hand of the sick woman, it seems that Picasso believes nothing will save her from death.

Picasso traveled to Madrid to study. At

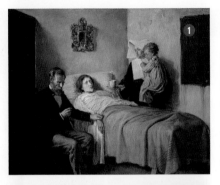

❶ *Picasso*, Science and Charity

❷ *Picasso*, Las Meninas

❸ *Picasso's menu design for Els Quatre Gats*

the Prado Museum, he learned by copying earlier Spanish masters, especially Diego Velázquez. An example of Picasso's impressive mimicry is sometimes displayed in this room—a nearly perfect copy of a **portrait of Philip IV** by Velázquez.

BARCELONA FREEDOM (ROOM 4)

In 1900 Picasso returned to Barcelona, where Art Nouveau was all the rage. He fell in with an avant-garde crowd, who congregated daily at Els Quatre Gats ("The Four Cats," a popular restaurant to this day). Picasso even created the **menu cover** for this favorite hangout. He painted **portraits** of his new friends (including Jaume Sabartés, who later became Picasso's personal assistant and donated the foundational works of this museum). Still a teenager, Pablo exhibited his first one-man show at Els Quatre Gats in 1900.

PARIS (ROOMS 6-7)

In 1900 Picasso made his first trip to Paris, and began sampling the contemporary art styles around him: He painted **cancan dancers** like Toulouse-Lautrec, **still lifes** like Paul Cézanne, brightly colored **Fauvist** works like Henri Matisse, and Impressionist **landscapes** like Claude Monet. In *The Waiting (Margot),* the subject— with her bold outline and strong gaze— pops out from the vivid, mosaic-like background.

BLUE PERIOD (ROOM 8)

Picasso traveled to Paris several times before settling there permanently in 1904. The suicide of his best friend Carlos Casagemas, his own poverty, and the influence of new ideas linking color and mood led Picasso to abandon jewel-bright color for his Blue Period (1901-1904). Now the artist was painting not what he saw, but what he felt. Painting misfits and street people, Picasso revealed the beauty in ugliness.

During a visit to Barcelona, Picasso painted a nighttime view over the **rooftops** of the city. His palette is still blue, but here we see proto-Cubism...five years before the first real Cubist painting.

ROSE PERIOD

Picasso finally lifted out of his funk after meeting a new lady, Fernande Olivier (a bronze bust of her from 1906 may be on view). He moved out of the blue and into the happier Rose Period (1904-1907), dominated by soft pink and reddish tones. (Other than the rarely displayed **Portrait of Bernadetta Bianco,** the museum is weak on Rose Period works.)

CUBISM

Pablo's role in the invention of the groundbreaking Cubist style (with his friend Georges Braque) is well known—at least I hope so, since this museum has no true Cubist paintings. The technique of "building" a subject with "cubes" of paint simmered in Picasso's artistic stew for years. The idea was to simultaneously see several 3-D facets of the subject.

BARCELONA REDUX (ROOMS 9-10)

Picasso spent six months back in Barcelona in 1917 (yet another girlfriend, a Russian ballet dancer, had a gig in town). The paintings in these rooms demonstrate the artist's irrepressible versatility: He had already developed Cubism, but continued to play with other styles. In **Woman with Mantilla,** we see a little Post-Impressionistic Pointillism in a portrait that is as elegant as a classical statue. Nearby, **Gored Horse** has all the anguish and power of his iconic *Guernica* (painted years later).

Remember that this museum has very little from the most famous and prolific "middle" part of Picasso's career—basically, from his adoption of Cubism to his sunset years on the French Riviera. (To fill in the gaps in his middle career, see the sidebar.)

PICASSO AND VELÁZQUEZ (ROOMS 12-14)

As a mature artist, Picasso turned to the great Old Masters for inspiration, and set about making a series of work related to what many consider the greatest paint-

ing by anyone, ever: Diego Velázquez's *Las Meninas.* The 17th-century original (in Madrid's Prado Museum) depicted the young maids of honor (or *meninas*) of the Spanish royal court. Pablo painted more than **40 interpretations** of the masterwork. Picasso deconstructed Velázquez and then injected light, color, and perspective as he improvised on the earlier masterpiece. In Picasso's big, black and white canvas, he more or less re-created Velázquez's painting in its entirety. But here, the king and queen (reflected in the mirror in the back of the room) are hardly seen, while the painter—the great Velázquez—towers above everyone. In other paintings in the series, Picasso focused on details—one maid of honor or a pair of them, or he zeroed in on just their faces.

LAST YEARS (ROOM 15)

Picasso spent the last 36 years of his life living simply in the south of France. With simple black outlines and Crayola colors, Picasso painted sun-splashed nature, peaceful doves, and the joys of the beach. He enjoyed life with his second (and much younger) wife, Jacqueline Roque.

His last works have the playfulness of someone much younger. As is often said of Picasso, in his youth he was taught to see the world like an adult, and in his golden years he enjoyed seeing and portraying the world with the freedom of a child.

Nearby (in Rooms B1, N, and B2), you'll see how in his later years Picasso became a master of other media besides painting. With his **ceramics,** he made bowls and vases in fun animal shapes, decorated with simple motifs.

Picasso died in 1973 with brush in hand. Sadly, since he vowed never to set foot in fascist, Franco-ruled Spain—the artist never returned to his homeland...and never saw this museum. But to the end, Picasso continued exploring and loving life through his art.

▲▲PALACE OF CATALAN MUSIC (PALAU DE LA MÚSICA CATALANA)

This concert hall, built in just three years, features an unexceptional exterior but boasts my favorite Modernista interior in town (by Lluís Domènech i Montaner). Its inviting arches lead you into the 2,138-seat hall, which is accessible only with a tour (or by attending a concert). A kaleidoscopic skylight features a choir singing around the sun, while playful carvings and mosaics celebrate music and Catalan culture. If you're interested in Modernisme, taking this tour is one of the best experiences in town—and helps balance the hard-to-avoid focus on Gaudí as "Mr. Modernisme."

Cost and Hours: €20, daily one-hour tours in English run every hour 10:00-15:00, tour times may change based on performance schedule, about six blocks northeast of cathedral, Carrer Palau de la Música 4, Metro: Urquinaona, tel. 932-957-200, www.palaumusica.cat.

Advance Reservations Required: You must buy tickets in advance to get a spot on an English guided tour (tickets available up to four months in advance—purchase yours at least two days before, though they're sometimes available the same day or the day before—especially Oct-March). You can buy tickets in person at the concert hall box office or at its Modernista ticket window to the left of the main concert hall entrance (box office open Mon-Sat 9:30-21:00, Sun 10:00-15:00, 10-minute walk from the cathedral or Picasso Museum). You can also purchase tickets over the phone (no extra charge, tel. 902-475-485) or on the concert hall website (€1 fee).

Concerts: An excellent way to see the hall is by attending a concert (300 per year, €20-150 tickets, see website for details and to buy tickets, box office tel. 902-442-882).

Rick's Tip: *Concerts advertised as "Palace of Catalan Music" are performed in two separate concert halls. To see the Modernista main concert hall,* **be sure the show is in Sala de Concerts**—*not the new Petit Palau hall.*

Palace of Catalan Music

Modernisme and the Renaixença

Modernisme is Barcelona's unique contribution to the Europe-wide Art Nouveau movement. Meaning "a taste for what is modern"—such as streetcars, electric lights, and big-wheeled bicycles—this free-flowing organic style lasted from 1888 to 1906.

Broadly speaking, there were two kinds of Modernisme (otherwise known as Catalan Art Nouveau). Early Modernisme has a Neo-Gothic flavor, clearly inspired by medieval castles and towers—logically, since architects wanted to recall the days when Barcelona was at its peak. From that starting point, Antoni Gaudí branched off on his own, adding the color and curves we most associate with the look of Barcelona's Modernisme.

Casa Amatller, with stepped roofline, and Casa Batlló, to the right

The aim was to create buildings that were both practical and decorative. To that end, Modernista architects experimented with new construction techniques. Their most important material was concrete, which they could mold to curve and ripple like a wave, and enliven with brightly colored glass and tile. Their structures were fully modern, but the decoration was a clip-art collage of natural images, exotic Moorish or Chinese themes, and fanciful Gothic crosses and knights to celebrate Catalunya's medieval glory days.

It's ironic to think that Modernisme was a response against the regimentation of the Industrial Age—and that all those organic shapes were only made possible thanks to Eiffel Tower-like iron frames. As you wander through the Eixample looking at all those fanciful facades and colorful, leafy, blooming shapes in doorways, entrances, and ceilings, remember that many of these homes were built at the same time as the first skyscrapers in Chicago and New York City.

Underpinning Modernisme was the Catalan cultural revival movement, called the Renaixença. Across Europe, it was a time of national resurgence. It was the dawn of the modern age, and downtrodden peoples—from the Basques to the Irish to the Hungarians to the Finns—were throwing off the cultural domination of other nations and celebrating what made their own culture unique. Here in Catalunya, the Renaixença encouraged everyday people to get excited about all things Catalan—from their language, patriotic dances, and inspirational art to their surprising style of architecture.

▲SANTA CATERINA MARKET (MERCAT DE SANTA CATERINA)

This eye-catching market hall's colorful, swooping roof covers a delightful shopping zone that caters more to locals than tourists. Come for the outlandish architecture, but stay for the food and the chance to picnic shop without the tourist logjam of La Boqueria. Besides fresh produce, it has many inviting eateries.

Cost and Hours: Free, Mon-Sat 7:30-15:30, until 20:30 on Tue and Thu-Fri, closed Sun, Avinguda de Francesc Cambó 16, www.mercatsantacaterina.cat.

▲CHURCH OF SANTA MARIA DEL MAR (BASÍLICA DE SANTA MARIA DEL MAR)

This "Cathedral of the Sea" was built entirely with local funds and labor, in the heart of the wealthy merchant El Born quarter. Proudly independent, the church features a purely Catalan Gothic interior that was forcibly uncluttered of its Baroque decor by civil war belligerents. On the big front doors, notice the figures of workers who donated their time and sweat to build the church. The stone they used was quarried at Montjuïc and had to be carried across town on the backs of porters called *bastaixos*.

Cost and Hours: Entry is free Mon-Sat 9:00-13:00 & 17:00-20:30, Sun 10:00-14:00 & 17:00-20:30. Entry is €5 (when the interior is illuminated and you have access to the choir and the crypt) Mon-Sat 13:00-17:00, Sun from 14:00. They offer €8 guided rooftop tours more or less on the hour during paid entry times (45 minutes, check for English tours and sign up at the door); Plaça Santa Maria, Metro: Jaume I, tel. 933-102-390, www.santamariadelmar-barcelona.org.

The Eixample
Block of Discord

At the center of this neighborhood is the Block of Discord, where three colorful Modernista facades compete for your attention: Casa Batlló, Casa Amatller, and Casa Lleó Morera (all on Passeig de Grà-cia—near the Metro stop of the same name—between Carrer del Consell de Cent and Carrer d'Aragó). All were built by well-known Modernista architects at the end of the 19th century. Because the mansions look as though they are trying to outdo each other in creative twists, locals nicknamed the noisy block the "Block of Discord." Of the three houses, two are open to visitors—Casa Batlló and the less-crowded Casa Amatller.

For a tour of the Eixample, download my free 🎧 Eixample Walk audio tour.

▲CASA BATLLÓ

While the highlight of this Gaudí-designed residence is the roof, the interior is also interesting—and much more over-the-top than La Pedrera's. The house features a funky mushroom-shaped fireplace nook on the main floor, a blue-and-white-ceramic-slathered atrium, and an attic with parabolic arches. There's barely a straight line in the house. You can also get a close-up look at the dragon-inspired

Church of Santa Maria del Mar

rooftop. The ticket includes a good (if long-winded) videoguide that shows the rooms as they may have been.

Cost and Hours: €24.50 timed-entry ticket includes videoguide—purchase in advance online; daily 9:00-21:00, check website for evening wine and music visits, Passeig de Gràcia 43, tel. 932-160-306, www.casabatllo.cat.

CASA MUSEU AMATLLER

The middle residence of the Block of Discord, Casa Amatller was designed by Josep Puig I Cadafalch in the late 19th century for the Amatller chocolate-making family. Only viewable via a group tour, it features mostly original furniture, placed just as the owners had it when they lived there. Admire the home's Neo-Catalan Gothic facade, with tiles and *esgrafiado* decoration.

Rick's Tip: *If you don't want to pay for a ticket, you can step inside* **Casa Amatller's foyer (free during opening hours)** *to see the Modernist stained-glass door and ceiling, and an elaborate staircase.*

Cost and Hours: €24 for one-hour English tour at 11:00, €19 for 40-minute videoguided group tour—generally on the hour and at :30 past the hour, admission includes treat from café; open daily 10:30-18:30, advance tickets available online, Passeig de Gràcia 41, tel. 934-617-460, www.amatller.org.

CASA LLEÓ MORERA

This house was designed by Lluís Domènech i Montaner and finished in 1906. The architect demolished and rebuilt the facade, embellishing it with galleries and balconies. To create the sculptural ornamentation, he hired the city's best craftsmen. Look for the recurring references to mulberries in the decoration—an allusion to the family name, Morera (mulberry). The interior is closed to visitors.

▲▲LA PEDRERA (CASA MILÀ)

One of Gaudí's trademark works, this house—built between 1906 and 1912—is an icon of Modernisme. The wealthy industrialist Pere Milà i Camps commissioned it, and while some still call it *Casa*

La Pedrera rooftop

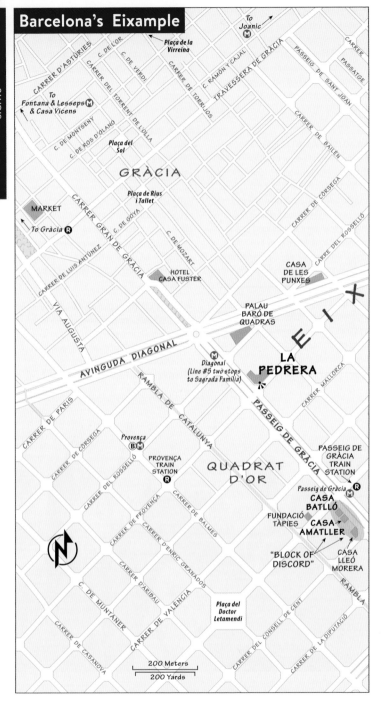

Barcelona's Eixample

To Joanic

Plaça de la Virreina

CARRER D'ASTÚRIES
C. DE L'OR
C. DE VERDI
CARRER DEL TORRENT DE L'OLLA
CARRER DE TORRIJOS
C. RAMÓN Y CAJAL
TRAVESSERA DE GRÀCIA
PASSEIG DE SANT JOAN
CARRER
PASSATGE

To Fontana & Lesseps & Casa Vicens

C. DE MONTSENY
C. DE ROS D'OLANO
CARRER DE BAILÉN

Plaça del Sol

GRÀCIA

Plaça de Rius i Tallet

CARRER DE CÓRSEGA

MARKET

CARRER GRAN DE GRÀCIA
C. DE GOYA
C. DE MOZART
CARRER DEL ROSSELLÓ

To Gràcia Ⓡ

CARRER DE LUIS ANTÚNEZ

HOTEL CASA FUSTER

CASA DE LES PUNXES

VIA AUGUSTA

PALAU BARÓ DE QUADRAS

EIX

AVINGUDA DIAGONAL

Diagonal (Line #5 two stops to Sagrada Família)

LA PEDRERA

RAMBLA DE CATALUNYA

CARRER MALLORCA

PASSEIG DE GRÀCIA

CARRER DE PARIS

CARRER DE CÓRSEGA

Provença
Ⓑ Ⓜ

PROVENÇA TRAIN STATION
Ⓡ

CARRER DEL ROSSELLÓ

QUADRAT D'OR

PASSEIG DE GRÀCIA TRAIN STATION

Passeig de Gràcia Ⓡ Ⓜ

CASA BATLLÓ

FUNDACIÓ TÀPIES

CASA AMATLLER

CARRER DE PROVENÇA

CARRER DE BALMES

CARRER D'ENRIC GRANADOS

"BLOCK OF DISCORD"

CASA LLEÓ MORERA

C. DE ARIBAU

RAMBLA

C. DE MUNTANER

CARRER DE VALÈNCIA

Plaça del Doctor Letamendi

CARRER DEL CONSELL DE CENT

CARRER DE LA DIPUTACIÓ

CARRER DE CASANOVA

200 Meters

200 Yards

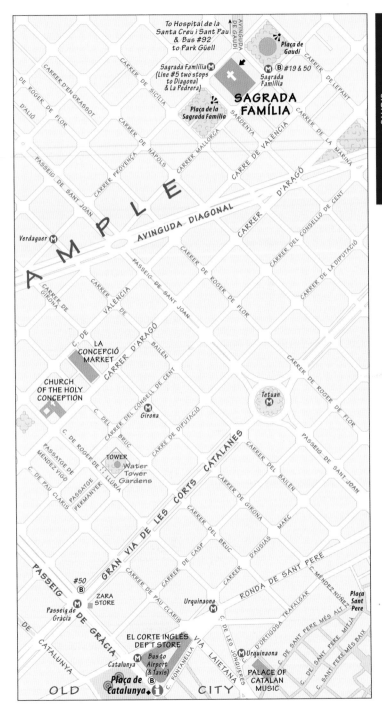

To Hospital de la
Santa Creu i Sant Pau
& Bus #92
to Park Güell

AVINGUDA
DE GAUDÍ

Plaça de
Gaudí

CARRER DE LEPANT

Sagrada Família Ⓜ
(Line #5 two stops
to Diagonal
& La Pedrera)

Ⓜ Ⓑ #19 & 50
Sagrada
Família

CARRER DE SICÍLIA

Plaça de la
Sagrada Família

CARRER DE NÁPOLS

SAGRADA
FAMÍLIA

SARDENYA

CARRER DE VALÈNCIA

CARRER DE LA MARINA

CARRER MALLORCA

DE ROGER DE FLOR

CARRER D'EN GRASSOT

CARRER DE NÁPOLS

CARRER PROVENÇA

CARRER PROVENÇA

CARRER MALLORCA

D'ALIÓ

PASSEIG DE SANT JOAN

A M P L E

AVINGUDA DIAGONAL

CARRER

D'ARAGÓ

CARRER DEL CONSELLO DE CENT

Verdaguer Ⓜ

CARRER DE GIRONA

CARRER DE VALÈNCIA

DE

PASSEIG DE SANT JOAN

CARRER DE ROGER DE FLOR

CARRER DE LA DIPUTACIÓ

C. DE

LA
CONCEPCIÓ
MARKET

BAILEN

CARRER D'ARAGÓ

CARRER

CHURCH
OF THE HOLY
CONCEPTION

C. DEL BRUC

CARRER DEL CONSELL DE CENT

Tetuan
Ⓜ

CARRER DE ROGER DE FLOR

Girona
Ⓜ

CARRER DE DIPUTACIÓ

PASSATGE DE
MENDEZ VIGO

C. DE ROGER DE LLÚRIA

CARRER DEL BRUC

PASSEIG DE SANT JOAN

C. DE PAU CLARIS

PASSATGE
PERMANYER

TOWER
Water
Tower
Gardens

GRAN VIA DE LES CORTS CATALANES

CARRER DEL BAILEN

CARRER DE GIRONA

MARC

CARRER DEL BRUC

CARRER DE CASP

D'AUSIAS

RONDA DE SANT PERE

Plaça
Sant
Pere

PASSEIG

#50
Ⓑ

DE GRÀCIA

ZARA
STORE

CARRER DE PAU CLARIS

Urquinaona
Ⓜ

TRAFALGAR

C. MÉNDEZ NÚÑEZ

Passeig de
Gràcia Ⓜ

C. D'ORTIGOSA

C. DE SANT PERE MÉS ALT

DE

CATALUNYA

EL CORTE INGLÉS
DEP'T STORE

VIA LAIETANA

C. DE LES JONQUERES

Urquinaona
Ⓜ

C. DE SANT PERE MÉS MITJÀ

C. DE SANT PERE MÉS BAIX

Bus to
Airport
(& Taxis)

Catalunya Ⓜ

C. FONTANELLA

PALACE OF
CATALAN
MUSIC

Plaça de
Catalunya ◆ Ⓑ Ⓒ

OLD

CITY

Milà, most call it *La Pedrera* (The Quarry) because of its jagged, rocky facade. While it's fun to ogle from the outside, it's also worth going inside, as it's arguably the purest Gaudí interior in Barcelona—executed at the height of his abilities (unlike his earlier Palau Güell)—and contains original furnishings. While Casa Batlló has a Gaudí facade and rooftop, these were appended to an existing building; La Pedrera, on the other hand, was built from the ground up according to Gaudí's plans. Your ticket includes entry to the interior (with the furnished apartment) and to the delightful rooftop, with its forest of tiled chimneys.

Cost and Hours: €22 timed-entry ticket includes good audioguide—purchase online in advance; open daily 9:00-20:30, Nov-Feb until 18:30; at the corner of Passeig de Gràcia and Provença (visitor entrance at Provença 261), Metro: Diagonal, info tel. 902-400-973, www.lapedrera.com.

Rick's Tip: *To enter* **La Pedrera without a wait,** *buy a €29 premium ticket, which allows you to arrive whenever you wish (no assigned entry time) and skip all lines, including those for audioguides and the elevator to the apartment and roof (sometimes a 30-minute wait).*

Nighttime Visits: After-hour visits dubbed "La Pedrera Night Experience" include a guided tour of the building (but not the apartment), along with a rooftop light show and glass of *cava* (€34; usually daily from 21:00). Another nighttime ticket (€59) includes the rooftop light show, plus dinner and a glass of *cava* at the on-site café. Options change frequently, so check online for the latest.

Concerts: On summer weekends, an evening rooftop concert series, "Summer Nights at La Pedrera," features live jazz and the chance to see the rooftop illuminated (€35, June-mid-Sept Fri-Sat at 20:15, book advance tickets online or by phone, tel. 902-101-212, www.lapedrera.com).

Visiting the House: A visit covers three sections—the rooftop, the attic, and the apartment. Enter and head up the elevator to the jaw-dropping **rooftop** to enjoy Gaudí's works and the views (note that the roof may close when it rains).

Follow the signs to go down to the **attic,** which houses a sprawling multimedia exhibit tracing the history of the architect's career, with models, photos, and videos of his work. It's all displayed under distinctive parabola-shaped arches.

Continue the visit by going downstairs to the typical bourgeois **apartment,** decorated as it might have been when the building was first occupied by middle-class urbanites (a 7-minute video explains Barcelona society at the time). Notice Gaudí's clever use of the atrium to maximize daylight in all the apartments.

Back at the **ground level** of La Pedrera, poke into the dreamily painted original entrance courtyard.

▲▲▲SAGRADA FAMÍLIA (HOLY FAMILY CHURCH)

Gaudí's grand masterpiece sits unfinished in a residential Eixample neighborhood 1.5 miles north of Plaça de Catalunya. An icon of the city, the Sagrada Família boasts bold, wildly creative, unmistakably organic architecture and decor inside and out—from its melting Glory Facade to its skull-like Passion Facade to its rainforest-esque interior.

Cost: Buy timed-entry tickets online in advance; basic ticket-€17 (church only, available only from 17:00), guided tour ticket-€26 (church and live guide), audio tour ticket-€25 (church and audioguide), church and tower ticket-€32 (church, audioguide, and tower elevator).

Hours: Daily 9:00-20:00, March and Oct until 19:00, Nov-Feb until 18:00, Metro: Sagrada Família, tel. 932-073-031, www.sagradafamilia.org.

Rick's Tip: *Buying a timed-entry ticket in advance for the* **Sagrada Família** *will save you time, money, and possibly the frustration of not getting in at all.*

Sagrada Família

Getting In: With ticket in hand (or on your phone), go through security and enter at the Nativity Facade side.

Tours: The 50-minute English tours run year-round; choose a tour time when you buy your ticket. Or rent the good 1.5-hour audioguide (€8 if purchased separately on-site, credit cards only, at desk to the right as you enter). There are often scalpers outside the gate selling admission with tours for those who don't have tickets.

Tower Elevators: Elevators on opposite sides of the church take you partway up the towers—one on the Passion Facade, and one on the Nativity Facade. The elevators go up only—to get down, you'll use a tightly wound, narrow staircase.

To ride an elevator, you must buy a Top Views combo-ticket. You'll choose the tower you want to visit and reserve an entry time (your entrance to the church will be assigned automatically, usually 15 minutes before your tower time). Towers can close when windy or rainy (if that happens, the tower portion of your ticket will be refunded).

The **Passion Facade elevator** takes you up a touch higher, and the stairs to come down are slightly wider than those descending from the **Nativity Facade elevator.** The facades are not joined, so it isn't possible to cross from one facade to the other, but you can cross a dizzying bridge between towers on the same facade.

BACKGROUND

Gaudí labored on Sagrada Família for 43 years, from 1883 until his death in 1926. Nearly a century on, people continue to toil to bring Gaudí's designs to life. After paying the admission price (becoming a partner in this building project), you will actually feel good. If there's any building on earth I'd like to see, it's the Basílica de la Sagrada Família...finished.

⊙ SELF-GUIDED TOUR

• *Before entering the church, start on the far side of the pond in the park that faces the Nativity Facade (east side, where the entry lines for individuals are located). From there, you're back far enough to take in the entire towering facade.*

❶ VIEW OF THE EXTERIOR FROM BEYOND THE POND

Stand and imagine how grand this church will be when completed. The eight 330-foot spires topped with crosses are just a fraction of this mega-church. When finished, it will have 18 spires. Four will stand at each of the three entrances. Rising above those will be four taller towers, dedicated to the four Evangelists. A tower dedicated to Mary (expected to be completed soon) rises still higher—400 feet. And in the very center of the complex will stand the grand 560-foot Jesus tower, topped with a cross that will shine like a spiritual lighthouse, visible even from out at sea.

The Nativity Facade—where tourists enter today—is only a side entrance to the church. The grand main entry will be around to the left. To accommodate the church's planned entrance esplanade, a nine-story apartment building will have to be torn down. (This is an ongoing controversy as authorities negotiate with landowners.)

The three facades—Nativity, Passion, and Glory—will chronicle Christ's life from birth to death to resurrection. Inside and out, a goal of the church is to bring the lessons of the Bible to the world. Despite his boldly modern architectural vision, Gaudí was fundamentally traditional and deeply religious. He designed the Sagrada Família to be a bastion of solid Christian values in the midst of what was a humble workers' colony in a fast-changing city. When Gaudí died, the only section that had been completed was the Nativity Facade (with its themes of birth and new life). Notice the dove-covered Tree of Life on top, with playful little creatures carved into nooks and crannies throughout, and a white pelican at the bottom. Because it was believed that this noble bird would feed its young with its own blood, the pelican was a common symbol in the Middle Ages for the self-sacrifice of Jesus.

The Nativity Facade's four spires are dedicated to apostles, and they repeatedly bear the word "sanctus," or holy. Their colorful ceramic caps symbolize the miters (formal hats) of bishops. The shorter spires (to the left) symbolize the Eucharist (communion), alternating between a chalice with grapes and a communion host with wheat.

The rest of the church, while inspired by Gaudí's long-range vision, has been designed and executed by others. This artistic freedom was amplified in 1936, when civil war shelling burned many of Gaudí's blueprints. Supporters of the ongoing work insist that Gaudí, who enjoyed saying, "My client [God] is not in a hurry," knew he wouldn't live to complete the church and recognized that later architects and artists would rely on their own muses for inspiration.

• Now move up to the viewing plaza in front of the Nativity Facade. Check out the small **bronze model** of how the church might look when completed. Then stand as far back as you can to take it all in.

❷ NATIVITY FACADE

This is the only part of the church essentially finished in Gaudí's lifetime (although the architect had intended for this facade to be painted). The four spires decorated with his naturalistic sculpture mark this facade as unmistakably part of his original design. Mixing Gothic-era symbolism, images from nature, and Modernista asymmetry, the Nativity Facade is the best example of Gaudí's original vision, and it established the template for future architects. Cleverly, this attractive facade was built and finished first to bring in financial support for the project.

The theme of the facade, which faces the rising sun, is Christ's birth. A statue above the doorway shows Mary, Joseph, and Baby Jesus in the manger, while a curious cow and donkey peek in. It's the Holy Family—or "Sagrada Família" (literally "sacred family")—to whom this church is dedicated. Flanking the doorway are the three Magi and adoring shepherds.

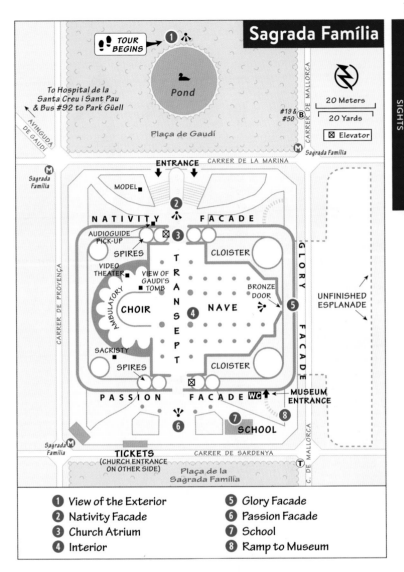

Sagrada Família

TOUR BEGINS

To Hospital de la Santa Creu i Sant Pau & Bus #92 to Park Güell

AVINGUDA DE GAUDÍ

Pond

Plaça de Gaudí

#19 & #50

CARRER DE MALLORCA

20 Meters

20 Yards

⊠ Elevator

Ⓜ Sagrada Família

ENTRANCE CARRER DE LA MARINA

Ⓜ Sagrada Família

MODEL■

NATIVITY ⚐ **FACADE**

AUDIOGUIDE PICK-UP ⊠

SPIRES

CLOISTER

VIDEO THEATER■

VIEW OF GAUDÍ'S TOMB■

CARRER DE PROVENÇA

AMBULATORY

CHOIR

T R A N S E P T

NAVE

BRONZE DOOR

G L O R Y

F A C A D E

UNFINISHED ESPLANADE

SACRISTY

SPIRES

CLOISTER

⊠

PASSION ⚐ **FACADE** WC ↑ **MUSEUM ENTRANCE**

SCHOOL

Ⓜ Sagrada Família

TICKETS (CHURCH ENTRANCE ON OTHER SIDE)

CARRER DE SARDENYA

Plaça de la Sagrada Família

C. DE MALLORCA

Ⓣ

❶ View of the Exterior
❷ Nativity Facade
❸ Church Atrium
❹ Interior
❺ Glory Facade
❻ Passion Facade
❼ School
❽ Ramp to Museum

Other statues at this height show Jesus as a young carpenter (right), the Holy Family fleeing to Egypt (left), and angels playing musical instruments. Much higher up, in the arched niche, Jesus crowns Mary triumphantly.

The doors in the middle of the facade (covered with small colorful bugs and leaves) were designed by head sculptor Etsuro Sotoo. Born in Japan, Sotoo visited Barcelona for the first time in 1978 and fell in love with the project. He worked hard to become a part of it and even converted to Catholicism.

• Now join the line and enter the ❸ church atrium (within your allotted window of time). If you purchased a tower ticket, a guard will direct you to your elevator. If you

Sagrada Família nave

amazing space. The morning light shines in through blues, greens, and other cool colors, whereas the evening light glows through reds, oranges, and warm tones. Gaudí envisioned an awe-inspiring symphony of colored light to encourage a contemplative mood.

At the center of the church stand four main columns, each marked with an Evangelist's symbol and name in Catalan: angel (Mateu), lion (Marc), bull (Luc), and eagle (Joan). These columns support a ceiling vault that's 200 feet high—and eventually will also support the central steeple (the Jesus tower with the shining cross).

The Holy Family is looking down from on high: Jesus is above the altar, Mary is in the left transept, and Joseph in the right transept.

Behind the high altar, peer down to see a surprisingly traditional space—the 19th-century Neo-Gothic building that Gaudí was originally hired to finish (talk about mission creep!). Today this is a **crypt** holding the tomb of Gaudí himself. A few steps away are two small theaters in adjacent side chapels. One shows a short **video** about the architect and his work.

• *Walk through the forest of massive columns to the opposite end of the church. The view from here is best for appreciating the majesty of the building's interior. (A big mirror is placed here to make admiring the ceiling easier.) Suspended high above the nave, the U-shaped **choir** can seat a thousand singers, who will eventually be backed by four organs. Doors here will one day open to the...*

Nativity Facade detail

purchased an audioguide (or would like to rent one now), go to that desk (on the right). Continue to the center of the church, near the altar, to survey the magnificent...

❹ INTERIOR

Typical of even the most traditional Catalan and Spanish churches, the floor plan is in the shape of a Latin cross, 300 feet long and 200 feet wide. Ultimately, the church will accommodate 8,000 worshippers. The crisscross arches of the ceiling (the vaults) show off Gaudí's distinctive engineering. The church's roof and flooring were only completed in 2010—just in time for Pope Benedict XVI to arrive and consecrate the church.

Part of Gaudí's religious vision was a love for nature. He said, "Nothing is invented; it's written in nature." Like the trunks of trees, these **columns** (56 in all) blossom with life, complete with branches, leaves, and knot-like capitals. The columns vary in color and material—brown clay, gray granite, dark gray basalt.

Light filtering through the stained-glass **windows** has the dappled effect of a rainforest canopy. Notice how splashes of color breathe even more life into this

❺ GLORY FACADE

While you can't go out what will one day be the main entrance, you can study a life-size image of the **bronze door** intended for this spot, emblazoned with the Lord's Prayer in Catalan and surrounded by "Give us this day our daily bread" in 50 languages. If you were able to exit through the actual door, you'd be face-to-face with drab, doomed apartment blocks. In the 1950s, the mayor of Barcelona, figuring this day would never really come, sold the land destined for the church project. Now the city must buy back these buildings in order to complete Gaudí's vision of a grand esplanade leading to this main entry. Four towers will rise. The facade's sculpture will represent how the soul passes through death, faces the Last Judgment, avoids the pitfalls of hell, and finds its way to eternal glory with God.

• *Head back up the nave, and exit through the left transept. To the left, notice the second* **elevator** *up to the towers. Before exiting, look down at the fine porphyry floor with scenes of Jesus' entry into Jerusalem. To the right, stroll through the* **sacristy,** *where you will find benches, candelabras, and sacristy furniture designed by Gaudí. Now head outside and down the ramp. Step away to take in the...*

❻ PASSION FACADE

Judge for yourself how well Gaudí's original vision has been carried out by later artists. The Passion Facade's four spires were designed by Gaudí and completed (quite faithfully) in 1976. But the lower

Sagrada Família Passion facade

part was only inspired by Gaudí's designs. The sculptures intended for this facade were interpreted freely and sternly (also controversially) by Josep Maria Subirachs (1927-2014), who completed the work in 2005.

Subirachs tells the story of Christ's torture and execution. The various scenes—Last Supper, betrayal, whipping, and so on—zigzag up from bottom to top, culminating in Christ's crucifixion over the doorway. The style is severe and unadorned, quite different from Gaudí's signature naturalism. But the bone-like archways are closely based on Gaudí's original designs. And Gaudí had made it clear that this facade should be grim and terrifying.

• *Now head into the small building outside the Passion Facade. This is the...*

❼ SCHOOL

Gaudí erected this school for the children of the workers building the church. Today, it displays a replica classroom and old photos of school activities during Gaudí's time.

• *Back outside, head down the ramp, where you'll find WCs and the entrance to the...*

❽ MUSEUM

Housed in what will someday function as the church crypt, the museum takes you through the past, present, and future of Sagrada Família's development.

Upon entering, you'll see **photos** (including one of the master himself) and a **timeline** illustrating how construction work has progressed from Gaudí's day to now. Before turning into the main hall, find **three different visions** for this church.

As you wander, notice how the **plaster models,** used for the church's construction, don't always match the finished product—these are ideas, not blueprints. The Passion Facade model shows Gaudí's original vision, with which Subirachs tinkered freely (see "Passion Facade," earlier). The models also make clear the influence of nature. The columns seem light, with branches springing forth and capitals that look like palm trees.

Exploring further, you'll find a small theater showing a worthwhile 11-minute movie; the Neo-Gothic 19th-century crypt where Gaudí is buried—look (steeply) down at his tomb; the actual workshop where artists employ the latest technology (such as 3-D printing) to test ideas; and an intriguing "Hanging Model" for Gaudí's unfinished Church of Colònia Güell (in a suburb of Barcelona).

Beyond the Eixample
▲▲PARK GÜELL

Designed as an upscale housing development for early-20th-century urbanites, this park is home to some of Barcelona's most famous symbols, including a dragon guarding a whimsical staircase and a wavy bench bordering a panoramic view terrace supported by a forest of columns. Gaudí used vivid tile fragments to decorate much of his work, creating a playful, pleasing effect.

Much of the park is free, but the part visitors want to see, the **Monumental Zone**—with all the iconic Gaudí features—has an admission fee and timed-entry ticket. Also in the park is the **Gaudí House Museum,** where Gaudí lived for a time—but it's not worth the entry fee for most travelers. Even without its Gaudí connection, Park Güell is simply a fine place to enjoy a break from a busy city, where green space is relatively rare.

Cost: €10 for timed-entry Monumental Zone ticket (buy online), includes shuttle to park from Alfons X Metro station (see below). It's smart to get a prepaid ticket online—while you can buy a ticket at the park, you'll likely have to wait hours to get in.

Hours: Daily 8:00-21:30, Sept-Oct and April until 20:30, shorter hours in winter.

Information: Tel. 934-091-831, www.parkguell.cat.

Getting There: Park Güell is about 2.5 miles from Plaça de Catalunya. A **taxi** from downtown to the front entrance is about €15. Otherwise, take the **Metro**

Park Güell stairway

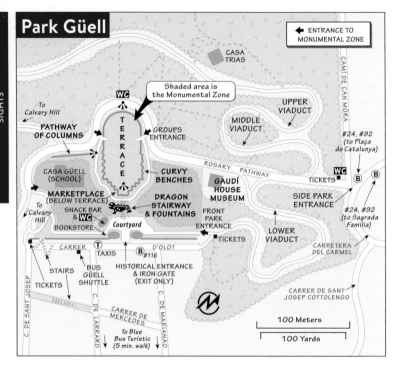

Park Güell

ENTRANCE TO MONUMENTAL ZONE

CASA TRIAS

Shaded area is the Monumental Zone

WC

To Calvary Hill

PATHWAY OF COLUMNS

TERRACE

GROUPS ENTRANCE

UPPER VIADUCT

MIDDLE VIADUCT

CAMÍ DE CAN MÓRA

#24, #92 (to Plaça de Catalunya)

CASA GÜELL (SCHOOL)

CURVY BENCHES

ROSARY PATHWAY

WC

TICKETS

B B

MARKETPLACE (BELOW TERRACE)

GAUDÍ HOUSE MUSEUM

SIDE PARK ENTRANCE

To Calvary Hill

SNACK BAR & WC

DRAGON STAIRWAY & FOUNTAINS

FRONT PARK ENTRANCE

#24, #92 (to Sagrada Família)

BOOKSTORE

Courtyard

TICKETS

LOWER VIADUCT

CARRETERA DEL CARMEL

CARRER

D'OLOT

T TAXIS

B #116

STAIRS

BUS GÜELL SHUTTLE

HISTORICAL ENTRANCE & IRON GATE (EXIT ONLY)

CARRER DE SANT JOSEP COTTOLENGO

TICKETS

C. DE SANT JOSEP

C. DE LARRARD

CARRER DE MERCEDES

C. DE MARIANAO

To Blue Bus Turístic (5 min. walk)

100 Meters

100 Yards

L4 (yellow) line to the Alfons X stop and ride the **Bus Güell shuttle** to the park (allow 15 minutes transit time on shuttle bus). Or, from Plaça de Catalunya, hop on either the blue **Bus Turístic** (stops about four blocks downhill from front entrance, on Travessera de Dalt) or **public bus #24**, which drops you at a side entrance.

Getting In: The Monumental Zone has several entrances; the most practical way in for tourists is on Carrer d'Olot (front entrance) or on Carretera del Carmel (side entrance). At either, you'll find a ticket office, WCs, and plenty of park staff to help orient you. Hang on to your ticket; you'll need to show it when you exit.

Overview: Gaudí intended this 30-acre garden to be a high-end community, with 60 upscale residences. Funded by his frequent benefactor Eusebi Güell, he began work on the project in 1900; however, the project stalled

in 1914, with the outbreak of World War I, and it never resumed. Only two houses were built, neither designed by Gaudí (one is now the Gaudí House Museum). Be thankful that the housing development faltered—as a park, this place is a delight. It offers a novel peek into Gaudí's eccentric genius in a setting that's wonderfully in keeping with the naturalism that pervades his work.

Visiting the Park: Enjoy Gaudí's **historical front entrance** (now exit only) with its palm-frond **gate** and gas lamps on either side, made of wrought iron. Gaudí's dad was a blacksmith, and he always enjoyed this medium.

Two Hansel-and-Gretel gingerbread lodges flank this former entrance, signaling to visitors that the park is a magical space. One building houses a bookshop; the other is home to the skippable **La Casa del Guarda,** a branch of the Barcelona History Museum.

Twin staircases curve upward, separated by three fountains stacked between them. The first, at the base of the steps, is rocky and leafy, typical of Gaudí's naturalism. Next is a red and gold Catalan shield, with the head of a serpent poking out. The third fountain is an icon of the park—and of Barcelona: a smiling dragon, slathered in colorful tile. The two grottos flanking the stairs were functional: One was a garage for Eusebi Güell's newfangled automobiles; the other was a cart shelter.

At the top of the dragon stairs, the **marketplace** (Hypostyle Room) was designed to house a produce market for the neighborhood's inhabitants. Eighty-six Doric columns—each lined at the base with white ceramic shards—populate the marketplace and add to its vitality. (Their main job, though, is to hold up the view terrace above.) Shards of white ceramic also cover the multiple domes of the ceiling. The four giant mosaic decorations overhead represent the four seasons.

As you continue up the left-hand staircase, look left, down the playful **Pathway of Columns.** Gaudí drew his inspiration from nature, and this arcade is like a surfer's perfect tube. Both structural and aesthetic, it is one of many clever double-decker **viaducts** that Gaudí designed for the grounds: vehicles up top, pedestrians in the portico down below.

The big pink house flanking the stairs is where Eusebi Güell lived. Now a school, this house predates the park project and was not designed by Gaudí.

At the top of the stairway, the **terrace** (Nature Square) boasts one of Barcelona's best views. (Find the Sagrada Família in the distance.) Functioning as both a seat and a balustrade, the 360-foot-long bench is designed to fit your body just so. As you wander, consider that, as a high-end housing development, Gaudí's project flopped (back then, high-society ladies didn't want to live so far from the cultural action). But a century later, as a park, it's a magnificent success.

Montjuïc

I've listed these sights by altitude, from the hill-topping castle down to the 1929 World Expo Fairgrounds at the base of Montjuïc ("Mount of the Jews"). If you're visiting them all, ride to the top by bus, funicular, or taxi, then visit them in this order so that most of your walking is downhill.

Getting to Montjuïc: You have several choices. The simplest is to take a **taxi** directly to your destination (about €12 from downtown).

Buses also take you up to Montjuïc. From Plaça de Catalunya bus #55 goes as far as Montjuïc's cable-car station/funicular. If you want to get higher (to the castle), ride the Metro or bus #50 from Plaça de Catalunya to Plaça d'Espanya, then make the easy transfer to bus #150 to ride all the way up the hill. Alternatively, the red Bus Turístic will get you to the Montjuïc sights.

Another option is by **funicular** (covered by Metro ticket, runs every 10 minutes 9:00-22:00). To reach it, take the Metro to the Paral-lel stop, then follow signs for *Parc Montjuïc* and the (mainly underground) funicular icon—you can enter the funicular without using another ticket. (If the funicular is closed, you'll find a shuttle bus.) From the top of the funicular, turn left and walk gently downhill for the Fundació Joan Miró and Catalan Art Museum.

For a scenic (if slow) approach to Montjuïc, you can ride the fun circa-1929 Aeri del Port **cable car** *(telefèric)* from the tip of the Barceloneta peninsula (across the harbor, near the beach) to the Miramar viewpoint park in Montjuïc. The cable car is expensive, loads excruciatingly slowly, and goes between two relatively remote parts of town, so it's only worthwhile for its sweeping views over town or to head back down to Barceloneta at the end of the day, as lines are shorter if you board in Montjuïc (€11 one-way, €16.50 round-trip, 3/hour, daily 11:00-17:30, June-Sept until 20:00, closed in high wind, tel. 934-414-820, www. telefericodebarcelona.com).

If you're only visiting the Catalan Art

Fundació Joan Miró

Museum and/or CaixaForum, you can take the Metro to Plaça d'Espanya and **walk** up (primarily riding handy escalators).

Getting Around Montjuïc: Up top, it's easy and fun to walk between the sights—especially downhill. You can also connect the sights using the red Bus Turístic or one of the public buses: Bus #150 does a loop around the hilltop and is the only bus that goes to the castle; on the way up, it stops at or passes near the CaixaForum, Catalan Art Museum, Fundació Joan Miró, the lower castle cable-car station/top of the funicular, and finally, the castle. On the downhill run, it loops by Avinguda Miramar, the cable-car station for Barceloneta. Bus #55 connects only the funicular/cable-car stations, Fundació Joan Miró, and the Catalan Art Museum.

▲FUNDACIÓ JOAN MIRÓ

This museum has the best collection anywhere of works by Catalan artist Joan Miró (ZHOO-ahn mee-ROH, 1893-1983). The museum displays an overview of Miró's oeuvre (as well as generally excellent temporary exhibits of 20th- and 21st-century artists).

Cost and Hours: €12, 2-for-1 tickets Thu from 18:00; open Tue-Sat 10:00-20:00 (Thu until 21:00), Sun 10:00-15:00, shorter hours in winter, closed Mon year-round; great videoguide-€5; 200 yards from top of funicular, Parc de Montjuïc, tel. 934-439-470, www.fundaciomiro-bcn.org.

▲▲CATALAN ART MUSEUM (MUSEU NACIONAL D'ART DE CATALUNYA)

This wonderful museum showcases Catalan art from the 10th century through the mid-20th century. Often called "the Prado of Romanesque art" (and "MNAC" for short), it holds Europe's best collection of Romanesque frescoes and offers a good sweep of modern Catalan art—fitting, given Catalunya's astonishing contribution to the Modern. It's all housed in the grand Palau Nacional (National Palace), an emblematic building from the 1929 World Expo, with magnificent views over Barcelona, especially from the building's rooftop terrace.

Cost and Hours: €12, free Sat from

Catalan Art Museum

15:00 and first Sun of month; open Tue-Sat 10:00-20:00 (Oct-April until 18:00), Sun 10:00-15:00, closed Mon year-round; worthwhile videoguide-€4; above Magic Fountains near Plaça d'Espanya—take escalators up; tel. 936-220-376, www.museunacional.cat.

Rooftop Terrace: You can visit the rooftop with your museum ticket; rooftop access is €2 without a ticket. To reach the terrace from the main entrance, walk past the bathrooms on the left and show your ticket to get on the elevator. You'll ride up nearly to the viewpoint, and from there hike up a couple of flights of stairs to the terrace. To take an elevator the whole way, go to the far end of the museum, through the huge dome room, to the far-right corner.

Visiting the Museum: As you enter, pick up a map. The left wing is Romanesque, and the right wing is Gothic, Renaissance, and Baroque. Upstairs is more Baroque, plus modern art, photography, coins, and more.

The MNAC's world-class collection of **Romanesque** (Romànic) art came mostly from a handful of Catalan village churches. In **Room 1,** you're greeted by a fresco of Mary painted in a re-created apse of one of the churches. **Room 2** has lively and colorful murals. In **Room 4,** one apse features saints in halos (Peter with his keys alongside Mary with a flaming chalice) and the countess who paid for the painting (lower right). The other apse has winged angels (seraphim) who appear to the prophets Isaiah (lower left) and Ezekiel (right), alongside Ezekiel's vision of the four-wheeled flaming chariot.

Rooms 5-7 focus on one of the most popular images in the medieval world: Christ in Majesty (a.k.a. the Pantocrator, or Ruler of All). Jesus is depicted inside an almond-shaped halo, seated on a throne, with one hand raised in blessing, the other holding an open Bible. He's surrounded by either seraphim or the four symbols of the Evangelists. Christ is always easy to identify—he's the only one with a cross in his halo. Room 7 puts all the Romanesque elements together for a great in situ experience—a replica church, with Christ in Majesty in the apse and other Romanesque themes.

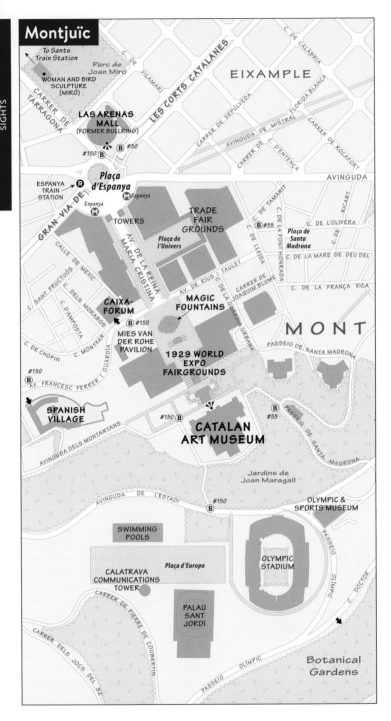

Montjuïc

To Sants
Train Station

Parc de
Joan Miró

WOMAN AND BIRD
SCULPTURE
(MIRÓ)

EIXAMPLE

C. DE CALABRIA

C. DE VILAMARI

LES CORTS CATALANES

CARRER DE SEPULVEDA

AVINGUDA DE MISTRAL

CARRER DE FLORIDA BLANCA

CARRER DE ROCAFORT

CARRER DE

C. D'ENTENÇA

LAS ARENAS
MALL
(FORMER BULLRING)

CARRER DE
TARRAGONA

#150 Ⓑ Ⓑ #50

Plaça
d'Espanya

ESPANYA
TRAIN
STATION Ⓡ

Ⓜ Espanya

Espanya Ⓜ

AVINGUDA

GRAN VIA DE

TOWERS

TRADE
FAIR
GROUNDS

C. DE TAMARIT

Ⓑ #55

Plaça de
Santa
Madrona

C. DE L'OLIVERA

C. DE LA
RICART

AV. DE LA REINA MARIA CRISTINA

Plaça de
l'Univers

C. DE LA FONT HONRADA

C. DE LLEIDA

C. DE LA MARE DE DÉU DEL

CALLE DE MEXIC

C. SANT FRUCTUOS

C. DELS MORABOS

C. D'AMPOSTA

CAIXA-
FORUM

Ⓑ #150

AV. DE RIUS I TAULET

C. DE LA GUARDIA URBANA

CARRER DE
JOAQUIM BLUME

C. DE LA FRANÇA XICA

MAGIC
FOUNTAINS

MONT

C. DE CHOPIN

C. MONTFAR

AV. DE LA GUARDIA

MIES VAN
DER ROHE
PAVILION

1929 WORLD
EXPO
FAIRGROUNDS

PASSEIG DE SANTA MADRONA

#150
Ⓑ
AV. FRANCESC FERRER I GUARDIA

SPANISH
VILLAGE

#150 Ⓑ

CATALAN
ART MUSEUM

Ⓑ
#55

PASSEIG DE SANTA MADRONA

AVINGUDA DELS MONTANYANS

Jardins de
Joan Maragall

AVINGUDA DE L'ESTADI

#150
Ⓑ

OLYMPIC &
SPORTS MUSEUM

SWIMMING
POOLS

Plaça d'Europa

OLYMPIC
STADIUM

PASSEIG OLIMPIC

CALATRAVA
COMMUNICATIONS
TOWER

C. DOCTOR.

CARRER DE PIERRE DE COUBERTIN

PALAU
SANT
JORDI

CARRER DELS JOCS DEL 92

PASSEIG OLIMPIC

Botanical
Gardens

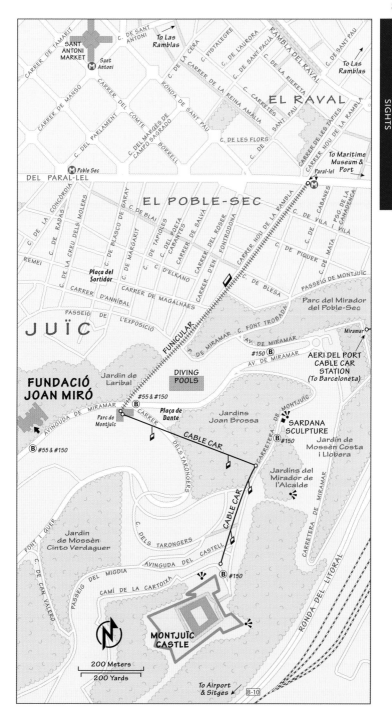

Browse through **Rooms 8-16,** seeing leafy column capitals, wooden crucifixes, and statues of Mary and the saints, until you spill back out into the main hall.

• *Cross the hall to the rooms of...*

Gothic Art: Picking up where Romanesque left off (c. 1300), fresco murals give way to vivid 14th-century wood-panel paintings of Bible stories. Make your way to **Room 26** (straight in, then to the left) and find the collection's highlight: a half-dozen paintings by the Catalan master Jaume Huguet (1412-1492), particularly his Consagració de San Agustín (Consecration of Saint Augustine).

These paintings (impressive enough on their own) were once part of a huge altarpiece—an estimated 40 feet tall and 30 feet wide—with some 20 paintings, done for a church in El Born. Huguet labored on the project for more than 20 years. The theme was the life of St. Augustine. It started with the painting of young Augustine (in black robe and red cap) dropping his pagan books to the floor as he realizes the truth and converts to Christianity. In other scenes Augustine wears his golden robes and bishop's hat as he's shown preaching at a pulpit, or disputing a heretic (in green who tumbles to the ground before the power of Augie's words), or kneeling to wash the feet of a pilgrim (who turns out to be Christ in disguise), or greeting a boy (who turns out to be a vision of young Jesus).

Huguet's masterpiece was the *Consecration* scene, where Augustine becomes bishop and is crowned with the hat. The details are incredible: the bright colors and gold leaf, the sober expressive faces, the brocaded robe with pictures of saints, and the early attempt at 3-D created by the floor tiles. Notice that this isn't simply a "painting"—it has a raised surface, like a cameo. It's a sheet of wood topped with molded stucco, then covered with paints and gold leaf. Nearby is Huguet's *Last Supper,* which was also part of the Augustine altarpiece.

• *The Gothic collection leads into...*

Renaissance and Baroque: Browse several rooms, watching as Renaissance artists make altarpieces more balanced and serene, with distant realistic backgrounds. You'll see Spain's Golden Age (Zurbarán, heavy religious scenes, and Spanish royals with their endearing underbites) and examples of Romanticism (dewy-eyed Catalan landscapes). Room 32 has El Greco's *Christ Carrying the Cross* and José de Ribera's saints with wrinkled foreheads. In addition, you'll find minor works by major—if not necessarily Catalan—masters like Velázquez, Goya, Tintoretto, Rubens, and Titian.

Rest of the Museum: The Gothic/Renaissance/Baroque exit spills out by the room of the huge **dome,** which has a cafeteria. From here, you can ride the glass elevator upstairs to the **modern art** section, where a big chronological clockwise circle from Room 1 covers Symbolism, Modernisme, fin de siècle fun, Art Deco, and more.

1929 World Expo Fairgrounds and Nearby

Nearly everything you see here dates from the 1929 World Expo (the exceptions are CaixaForum and Las Arenas mall). The expo's theme was to demonstrate how electricity was about more than lightbulbs: Electricity powered the funicular, the glorious expo fountains, the many pavilion displays, and even the flame atop the fountain marking the center of Plaça d'Espanya.

Getting There: The fairgrounds sprawl at the base of Montjuïc, from the Catalan Art Museum's doorstep to Plaça d'Espanya. It's easiest to see these sights on your way down from Montjuïc. Otherwise, ride the Metro to Espanya, then use the series of stairs and escalators to climb up through the heart of the fairgrounds (eventually reaching the Catalan Art Museum).

▲MAGIC FOUNTAINS
(FONT MÀGICA)
Music, colored lights, and huge amounts of water make an artistic and coordinated splash in the evening near Plaça d'Espanya.

Cost and Hours: Free, 20-minute shows start every half-hour; June-Sept Wed-Sun 21:30-22:30, April-May and Oct Thu-Sat 21:00-22:00, winter Thu-Sat 20:00-21:00 (no shows Jan-Feb); from the Espanya Metro stop, walk toward the towering National Palace.

▲CAIXAFORUM
The CaixaForum Social and Cultural Center is housed in one of Barcelona's most important Art Nouveau buildings. In 1911, Josep Puig i Cadafalch (a top architect often overshadowed by Gaudí) designed the Casaramona textile factory, using Modernista design in an industrial rather than a residential context. It functioned as a factory for less than a decade, then later served a long stint as a police station under Franco. Beautifully refurbished in 2002, the facility reopened as a great center for bringing culture and art to the people of Barcelona.

Cost and Hours: Free entrance to building, exhibits-€4, daily 10:00-20:00, Avinguda de Francesc Ferrer i Guàrdia 6, tel. 934-768-600, www.caixaforum.es/barcelona.

Visiting the Center: From the lobby, signs point to Sala 2, 3, 4, and 5; each typically hosts an outstanding temporary exhibition. Ride the escalator to the first floor, which features a modest but interesting exhibit about the history and renovation of the building, including a model and photos. Then head into the appealing red-brick courtyard to access the exhibition halls. The sight features some English descriptions. Take the stairs or elevator up to the Modernista Terrace (Planta 2, or look for signs to Aula 1). This terrace, boasting a wavy floor and bristling with fanciful brick towers, offers views over the complex and to Montjuïc.

LAS ARENAS (BULLRING MALL)
The grand Neo-Moorish Modernista plaça de toros functioned as an arena for bullfights from around 1900 to 1977, and then reopened in 2011 as a mall. The **rooftop terrace,** with stupendous views of Plaça d'Espanya and Montjuïc, is ringed with eateries (reachable by external glass elevator for €1 or from inside escalators/elevators for free). Besides getting a bird's-eye perspective of the fairgrounds, you can gaze down at Parc de Joan Miró, which includes the giant sculpture **Woman and Bird** (Dona i Ocell). Miró's sense of humor is evident—if the sculpture seems phallic, keep in mind that the Catalan word for "bird" is also slang for "penis."

Cost and Hours: Free, daily 10:00-22:00, outside elevator and restaurants open until 24:00, Gran Via de les Corts Catalanes 373, Metro: Espanya, exit following Sortida Tarragona signs, www.arenasdebarcelona.com.

The Beaches and Nearby
▲BARCELONA'S BEACHES
Barcelona has created a summer tourist trade by building a huge stretch of beaches east of the town center. From Barceloneta, an uninterrupted band of sand tumbles three miles northeast to the Fòrum.

The overall scene is great for sunbathing and for an evening paseo before dinner. It's like a resort island—complete with lounge chairs, volleyball, showers,

Nova Icària beach

WCs, bike paths, and inviting beach bars called *chiringuitos*. Each beach segment has its own vibe: Sant Sebastià (closest, popular with older beachgoers and families), Barceloneta (with many seafood restaurants), Nova Icària (pleasant family beach), and Mar Bella (attracts a younger crowd, clothing-optional).

Getting There: The Barceloneta Metro stop leaves you a long walk from the sand. To get to the beaches without a hike, take the bus. From the Ramblas, bus #59 will get you as far as Barceloneta Park; bus #D20 leaves from the Columbus Monument and follows a similar route. Bus #V15 runs from Plaça de Catalunya to the tip of Barceloneta (near the W Hotel).

Rick's Tip: Biking *is a joy in Citadel Park and along the beachfront. To rent a bike near the beach, try* **Barcelona Rent-A-Bike** *(€6/2 hours, €15/day, shorter hours in winter, Passeig de Joan de Borbó 35, www. barcelonarentabike.com).*

CITADEL PARK
(PARC DE LA CIUTADELLA)
In 1888, Barcelona's biggest, greenest park—originally the site of a much-hated military citadel—was transformed for a Universal Exhibition (world's fair). The stately Triumphal Arch at the top of the park, celebrating the removal of the citadel, was built as the main entrance. Inside you'll find wide pathways, plenty of trees and grass, a zoo, a museum of geology, and a castle-like former restaurant for the fair (closed to the public).

Enjoy the ornamental fountain that the young Antoni Gaudí helped design, and consider a jaunt in a rental rowboat on the lake in the center of the park. Check out the tropical Umbracle greenhouse and the Hivernacle winter garden, which has a pleasant café-bar (Mon-Sat 10:00-14:00 & 17:00-20:30, Sun 10:30-14:00, shorter hours off-season).

Cost and Hours: Park-free, daily 10:00 until dusk, north of França train station, Metro: Arc de Triomf, Barceloneta, or Ciutadella/Vila Olímpica.

EXPERIENCES

Shopping
The streets of the Barri Gòtic and El Born are bursting with characteristic hole-in-the-wall shops and delightful neighborhood boutiques, while the Eixample is the upscale "uptown" shopping district. The area around Avinguda del Portal de l'Angel (at the northern edge of the Barri Gòtic) has a number of department and chain stores.

Souvenir Items: In this artistic city, consider picking up prints, books, and posters. Museum gift shops (Picasso Museum and La Pedrera) offer a bonanza of classy souvenirs. Home decor shops sell Euro-housewares unavailable back home. Decorative tile and pottery (popularized by Moderist architects) can be a good keepsake. Foodies might bring back olive oil, wine, spices (such as saffron or sea salts), or *torró* (Catalan nougat). An *espardenya* (or *alpargata* in Spanish) is a soft-canvas, rope-soled shoe (known in the US as an espadrille). For a souvenir of Catalunyan culture, consider a Catalan flag, a dragon of St. Jordi, or a jersey or scarf from the wildly popular Barça soccer team.

Shopping Spots

BARRI GÒTIC
The wide Carrer de la Portaferrissa, between the cathedral and the Ramblas, is lined with mostly international clothing stores (H&M, Mango, etc.). For little local shops, plunge into some lanes just to the south. **Carrer de la Palla** is ideal for antiques. On **Carrer dels Banys Nous,** the sprawling **Oliver** shop sells home decor, women's clothing, and accessories. Directly across the lane, **Artesania Catalunya** is a large market-space run by the

Open-air market in the Barri Gòtic

city, featuring handmade items from Catalan artisans.

Plaça del Pi has worthwhile shops plus local food and crafts markets on many days. On **Carrer de Petritxol,** lined with art galleries and fancy jewelry shops, stop into **Granja La Pallaresa** for *churros con chocolate;* or try **Vicens,** a fancy sweets shop specializing in *torró.* **Carrer Ample** feels local but with little bursts of trendy energy (watch candy being made the old-fashioned way at **Papabubble**). Skinny **Carrer de Bonsuccés,** on the other side of the Ramblas, has fine boutiques.

EL BORN
This area is bohemian-chic, with funky shops, Santa Caterina Market, and unique boutiques. Look for interesting shops in the area around **Carrer del Rec** (boutiques), on **Carrer de l'Esparteria** (off Carrer del Rec), and the streets **between Carrer dels Banys Vells and Carrer de l'Argenteria** (artisan workshops and handmade clothing, accessories, and bags).

THE EIXAMPLE
This ritzy "uptown" district is home to some of the city's top-end shops. In general, you'll find a lot of big international names along **Passeig de Gràcia,** the main boulevard that runs from Plaça de Catalunya to the Gaudí sights—an area fittingly called the "Golden Quarter" (Quadrat d'Or). The "upper end" of Passeig de Gràcia has the fancier shops (Gucci, Luis Vuitton, and so on) while the southern part of the street is relatively "low-end" (Zara, Mango, H&M). One block to the west, **Rambla de Catalunya** holds more local (but still expensive) options: fashion, home decor, jewelry, perfume, and so on. The streets that connect Rambla de Catalunya to Passeig da Gràcia are also home to some fine shops, including some fun kitchen stores.

DEPARTMENT STORES
Plaça de Catalunya has a gigantic **El Corte Inglés** (with a supermarket in the basement and ninth-floor view cafeteria,

Mon-Sat 9:30-21:00, until 22:00 in summer, closed Sun). Across the square is **FNAC**—a French department store that sells electronics, music, books, and tickets for major concerts and events (Mon-Sat 10:00-22:00, closed Sun).

NIGHTLIFE

Barcelona is extremely lively after hours. People head out for dinner at 22:00, then bar-hop or simply wander the streets until well after midnight. Some days it seems that more people are out and about at 2:00 in the morning (party time) than at 2:00 in the afternoon (lunch time). The most "local" thing you can do here after sunset is to explore neighborhood watering holes and find your favorite place to enjoy a glass of wine.

PERFORMING ARTS

Barcelona always has a vast array of cultural events. Pick up the TI's free monthly *Time Out BCN Guide* and Visit *Barcelona* (both in English). **Palau de la Virreina,** an arts-and-culture information office, is also helpful (daily 10:00-20:30, Ramblas 99—see the "Ramblas Ramble" map, earlier, tel. 933-161-000, www.lavirreina.bcn.cat).

Tickets are available through venue websites, through TicketMaster or Telen-Trada, or through the box offices in the main El Corte Inglés department store or the giant FNAC electronics store (both on Plaça de Catalunya, extra booking fee), or at the ticket desk in Palau de la Virreina.

The **Palace of Catalan Music** offers everything from symphonic to Catalan folk songs to chamber music to flamenco (€20-150 tickets, purchase online or in person, box office open Mon-Sat 9:30-21:00, Sun 10:00-15:00, Carrer Palau de la Música 4, Metro: Urquinaona, box office tel. 902-442-882).

The **Liceu Opera House** (Gran Teatre del Liceu), right in the heart of the Ramblas, is a pre-Modernista, sumptuous venue for opera, dance, children's theater, and concerts (tickets from €10, buy tickets online up to 1.5 hours before show or in person, Ramblas 51, box office just around the corner at Carrer Sant Pau 1, Metro: Liceu, box office tel. 934-859-913, www.liceubarcelona.cat).

Some of Barcelona's top sights host good-quality concerts. On summer weekends, a classy option is the **"Summer Nights at La Pedrera"** concerts (see page 76). Also try the **Fundació Joan Miró** and **CaixaForum.**

Two famously Spanish types of music—flamenco and Spanish guitar—have little to do with Barcelona or Catalunya, but are performed to keep visitors happy. For **flamenco,** head to **Palau Dalmases** for high-quality performances (€25 includes a drink, daily at 19:30, additional shows Fri-Sun at 21:30, also hosts opera and jazz, Carrer de Montcada 20, tel. 933-100-673, www.palaudalmases.com). **Tarantos** is easy and inexpensive (€15; nightly at 19:30, 20:30, 21:30, and 22:30; Plaça Reial 17, tel. 933-191-789, go to www.masimas.com and click on "Tarantos").

Another option is the pricey (and relatively high-quality) **Tablao Cordobés** (€45 includes a drink, €80 includes mediocre buffet dinner and better seats, 3 performances/day, Ramblas 35, tel. 933-175-711, www.tablaocordobes.com).

For Spanish guitar, try **Church of Santa Maria del Pi** (€23 at the door, €4 less if you buy at least 3 hours ahead or online—look for ticket sellers in front of church and scattered around town, nightly at 21:00, Plaça del Pi 7; at Carrer de Ferran 28; tel. 647-514-513, www.maestrosdela-guitarra.com). The same company also does occasional concerts in the **Palace of Catalan Music** (€39-45). Similar guitar concerts are performed at the **Church of Santa Anna** (tel. 662-698-547, www.spanishguitarbarcelona.es).

After-Hours Hangout Neighborhoods

El Born: Passeig del Born, a broad parklike strip stretching from the Church of Santa

Maria del Mar up to the old market hall, is lined with inviting bars and nightspots. Wander the side streets for more options. **Miramelindo** is a favorite for mojitos (Passeig del Born 15). **La Vinya del Senyor** is a fine place for a glass of high-quality wine on the square in front of the Church of Santa Maria del Mar.

Plaça Reial and Nearby: This elegant-feeling square bustles with popular bars and restaurants offering pleasant outdoor tables at inflated prices—perfect for nursing a drink. Try the **Bar Club Ocaña,** at #13 (open nightly, reserve a table online at www.ocana.cat).

Carrer de la Mercè: This Barri Gòtic street near the harbor is lined with salty sailors' pubs and more youthful bars. The next street up, **Carrer Ample,** has a similar scene.

Barceloneta: This broad beach is dotted with *chiringuitos*—shacks selling drinks and snacks, creating a fun, lively scene on a balmy summer evening.

Montjuïc: Take in breathtaking views and the Magic Fountains show.

EATING

Barcelona, the capital of Catalan cuisine, offers a tremendous variety of colorful places to eat, ranging from workaday eateries to homey Catalan bistros *(cans)*, crowded tapas bars, and avant-garde restaurants.

Basque-style tapas places are popular and user-friendly. Just grab what looks good, order a drink, and save your toothpicks (they'll count them up at the end to tally your bill). I've listed several of these bars (including Taverna Basca Irati and Sagardi Euskal Taberna), but there are many others. Look for *basca* or *euskal* (both mean "Basque").

Budget Meals: Sandwich shops serve made-to-order bocadillos. Choose between bright (mass-produced) chains such as **Bocatta** and **Pans & Company,** or colorful hole-in-the-wall spots. **Mucci's**

Pizza has good, fresh pizza slices and empanadas (just off the Ramblas, at Bonsuccés 10 and Tallers 75). **Wok to Walk** has takeaway noodle and rice dishes (branches near Plaça de Sant Jaume and Liceu Metro station). **Buenas Migas** serves quiche, salads, and pastas (locations at Baixada de Santa Clara 2, Plaça de la Sagrada Família 17, and Plaça del Bonsuccés 6). Kebab places are another standby for quick and tasty meals. For a fast, affordable lunch with a view, the ninth-floor cafeteria at **El Corte Inglés department store** on Plaça de Catalunya can't be beat. Picnickers can buy groceries at the basement supermarket in El Corte Inglés, or at **La Boqueria Market** on the Ramblas.

Near the Ramblas

Do not eat or drink at the tourist traps on the Ramblas. Within a few steps, you'll find handy lunch places, an inviting market hall, and some good vegetarian options.

Lunching Simply yet Memorably near the Ramblas

Although these places are enjoyable for a lunch break from sightseeing, many are also open for dinner.

$$ Taverna Basca Irati serves 40 kinds of hot and cold Basque *pintxos* for €2 each. These are small open-faced sandwiches—a baguette slice topped with something tasty. Muscle in through the hungry crowd, get an empty plate from the waiter, and then help yourself. Every few minutes, waiters circulate with platters of new, still-warm munchies. Grab one as they pass by...it's addictive (you'll be charged by the number of toothpicks left on your plate). For drink options, look for the printed menu on the wall in the back. Wash down your food with Rioja (full-bodied red wine), Txakolí (sprightly Basque white wine), or *sidra* (apple wine). Open daily (11:00-24:00, a block off the Ramblas, behind arcade at Carrer del

Tapas can be a fun snack or add up to a light meal.

Cardenal Casanyes 17, Metro: Liceu, tel. 933-023-084).

$$ Restaurant Elisabets is a rough little neighborhood eatery popular for its €12 "home-cooked" three-course lunch special; even cheaper *menú rapid* options are available (13:00-16:00 only). Apparently, locals put up with the service for the tasty food (cash only, Mon-Sat 7:30-23:00, closed Sun and Aug, 2 blocks west of Ramblas on far corner of Plaça del Bonsuccés at Carrer d'Elisabets 2, Metro: Catalunya, tel. 933-175-826).

$$ Café Granja Viader is a quaint time capsule, family-run since 1870. They boast about being the first dairy business to bottle and distribute milk in Spain. This feminine-feeling place—specializing in baked and dairy treats, toasted sandwiches, and light meals—is ideal for a traditional breakfast. Or indulge your sweet tooth: Try a glass of *orxata* (or *horchata*—*chufa*-nut milk, summer only), *llet mallorquina* (Majorca-style milk with cinnamon, lemon, and sugar), *crema catalana* (crème brûlée, their specialty), or

suis ("Swiss"—hot chocolate with a snow-cap of whipped cream). *Mel i mató* is fresh cheese with honey...very Catalan (Mon-Sat 9:00-13:00 & 17:00-21:00, closed Sun, a block off the Ramblas behind Betlem Church at Xuclà 4, Metro: Liceu, tel. 933-183-486).

$$ Restaurante Nuria is a big, venerable standby that's been overlooking all the Ramblas action since 1926. It's a low-stress, hardworking place with a menu designed to please tourists: pizza, burgers, paellas, and salads (daily 24/7, Rambla de Canaletes 133, tel. 933-023-847). They have a fancier place upstairs.

$$ Biocenter, a Catalan soup-and-salad restaurant busy with local vegetarians, takes its cooking very seriously and feels a bit more like a real restaurant than most (weekday lunch specials include soup or salad and plate of the day, Mon-Sat 13:00-23:00, Sun until 16:00, two blocks off the Ramblas at Carrer del Pintor Fortuny 25, Metro: Liceu, tel. 933-014-583).

La Boqueria Market: If you're in La Boqueria and ready for lunch, a snack, or

Catalan Cuisine

Like its culture and language, Catalan food is a fusion of styles and influences. Cod, hake, tuna, squid, and anchovies appear on many menus, and you'll see Catalan favorites such as *fideuà,* a thin, flavor-infused noodle served with seafood—a kind of Catalan paella—and *arròs negre,* black rice cooked in squid ink. *Pa amb tomàquet* is the classic Catalan way to eat your bread—toasted white bread with olive oil, tomato, and a pinch of salt. It's often served with tapas and used to make sandwiches. As everywhere in Spain, Catalan cooks love garlic and olive oil—many dishes are soaked in both.

Catalan cuisine can be heavy for Americans more accustomed to salads, fruits, and grains. A few perfectly good vegetarian and lighter options exist, but you'll have to seek them out. The secret to getting your veggies at restaurants is to order two courses, because the first course generally has a green option. Resist the cheese-and-ham appetizers and instead choose first-course menu items such as creamed vegetable soup, *parrillada de verduras* (sautéed vegetables), or *ensalada mixta*. (Spaniards rarely eat only a salad, so salads tend to be small and simple—just iceberg lettuce, tomatoes, and maybe olives and tuna.)

While the famous cured *jamón* (ham) is not as typically Catalan as it is Spanish, you'll still find lots of it in Catalunya. Another popular Spanish dish is the empanada—a pastry turnover filled with seasoned meat and vegetables. The cheapest meal is a simple *bocadillo de jamón* (ham sandwich on a baguette), sold virtually everywhere.

a drink, there are several high-energy bars that would love to take your money. The Pinotxo Bar (just to the right as you enter) has a waiter beloved for his smile and his double thumbs up.

Barri Gòtic

$$$ Café de l'Academia is a delightful place on a pretty square tucked away in the heart of the Barri Gòtic—but patronized mainly by the neighbors. They serve refined cuisine with Catalan roots, using what's fresh from the market. The candlelit, air-conditioned interior is rustic yet elegant, with soft jazz, flowers, and modern art. And if you want to eat outdoors on a convivial, mellow square...this is the place. Reservations are a must, though if you show up without one, try asking to sit at the bar (lunch specials, open Mon-Fri 13:00-15:30 & 20:00-23:00, closed Sat-Sun, near the City Hall square, off Carrer de Jaume

I up Carrer de la Dagueria at Carrer dels Lledó 1, Metro: Jaume I, tel. 933-198-253).

$$$ La Vinateria del Call, buried deep in the Jewish Quarter, is one of the oldest wine bars in town. It offers a romantic restaurant-style meal of tapas with fine local wines. Eating at the small bar by the entrance is discouraged, so I'd settle in at a candlelit table. They have more than 100 well-priced wines, including a decent selection of Catalan wines at €2.50 a glass. Three or four plates of their classic tapas will fill two people (daily 19:30-24:00; with back to church, leave Plaça de Sant Felip Neri and walk two short blocks to Sant Domènec del Call 9; Metro: Jaume I, tel. 933-026-092).

$$$ Els Quatre Gats ("The Four Cats") was once the haunt of the Modernista greats—including a teenaged Picasso, and architect Josep Puig i Cadafalch, who designed the building. You

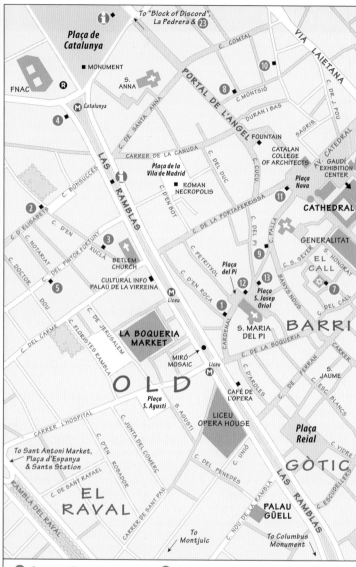

Plaça de Catalunya

MONUMENT

FNAC

Catalunya

S. ANNA

To "Block of Discord", La Pedrera & ㉓

C. COMTAL

PORTAL DE L'ANGEL

VIA LAIETANA

C. DR. J. POU

C. MONTSIÓ

DURAN I BAS

SAGRIS

C. DE SANTA ANNA

CARRER DE LA CANUDA

C. DEL DUC

FOUNTAIN

CATALAN COLLEGE OF ARCHITECTS

CATEDRAL

GAUDÍ EXHIBITION CENTER

Plaça de la Vila de Madrid

ROMAN NECROPOLIS

C. CUCU

Plaça Nova

C. BONSUCCÉS

LAS RAMBLAS

C. D'EN BOT

C. DE LA PORTAFERRISSA

C. PALLA

CATHEDRAL

C. D' ELISABETS

C. D'EN

C. NOTARIAT

C. DEL PINTOR FORTUNY

XUCLA

BETLEM CHURCH

CULTURAL INFO PALAU DE LA VIRREINA

C. DOCTOR

C. D'EN ROCA

C. DEL PI

C. PETRITXOL

Plaça del Pi

C. S. SEVER

GENERALITAT

EL CALL

S. HONORAT

BANYS NOUS

Plaça S. Josep Oriol

C. DEL CALL

DOU

LA BOQUERIA MARKET

C. DEL CARME

C. FLORISTES

RAMBLA

C. DE JERUSALEM

Liceu

MIRÓ MOSAIC

Liceu

S. MARIA DEL PI

C. DE LA BOQUERIA

BARRI

CARDENAL

CARRER

S. JAUME

C. D'AROLES

C. DE FERRAN

C. ESC. BLANCS

OLD

Plaça S. Agustí

CAFÉ DE L'OPERA

S. AGUSTI

LICEU OPERA HOUSE

Plaça Reial

CARRER L'HOSPITAL

C. JUNTA DEL COMERÇ

C. D'EN ROBADOR

C. VIDRE

To Sant Antoni Market, Plaça d'Espanya & Sants Station

C. DE SANT RAFAEL

EL RAVAL

RAMBLA DEL RAVAL

CARRER DE SANT PAU

C. DEL PENEDÈS

C. UNIÓ

GÒTIC

C. NOU DE LA RAMBLA

PALAU GÜELL

LAS RAMBLAS

C. ESCUDELLERS

To Montjuïc

To Columbus Monument

① Taverna Basca Irati
② Restaurant Elisabets
③ Café Granja Viader
④ Restaurante Nuria
⑤ Biocenter
⑥ Café de l'Academia
⑦ La Vinateria del Call
⑧ Els Quatre Gats
⑨ Xaloc

⑩ Onofre Vinos y Viandas
⑪ Bilbao Berria Pintxos & Tapas
⑫ Bar del Pi
⑬ El Drac de Sant Jordi
⑭ Carrer de la Mercè Tapas Bars
⑮ Sagardi Euskal Taberna
⑯ Vegetalia Vegetarian Restaurant
⑰ El Senyor Parellada

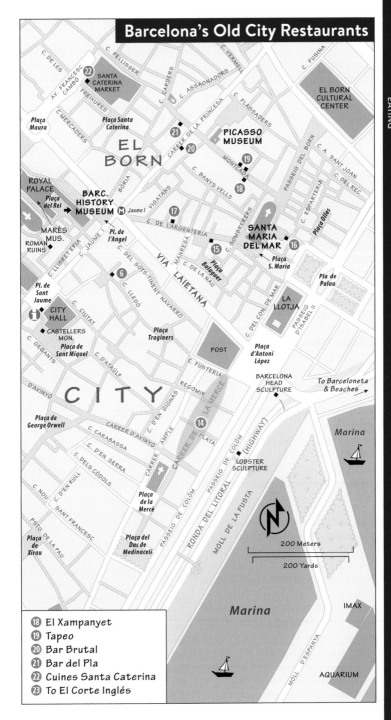

Barcelona's Old City Restaurants

EL BORN CULTURAL CENTER

SANTA CATERINA MARKET

22

Plaça Maura

Plaça Santa Caterina

EL BORN

21

20

PICASSO MUSEUM

19

18

ROYAL PALACE

Plaça del Rei

BARC. HISTORY MUSEUM

Jaume I

SANTA MARIA DEL MAR

16

Plaça S. Maria

MARÈS MUS.

ROMAN RUINS

Pl. de l'Angel

17

15

Plaça Balaguer

Pla de Palau

Pl. de Sant Jaume

6

VIA LAIETANA

LA LLOTJA

CITY HALL

CASTELLERS MON.

Plaça de Sant Miquel

Plaça Traginers

POST

Plaça d'Antoni López

C I T Y

BARCELONA HEAD SCULPTURE

To Barceloneta & Beaches

Marina

Plaça de George Orwell

14

LOBSTER SCULPTURE

Plaça de la Mercè

Marina

Plaça del Duc de Medinaceli

200 Meters

200 Yards

IMAX

Plaça de Xirau

AQUARIUM

- 18 El Xampanyet
- 19 Tapeo
- 20 Bar Brutal
- 21 Bar del Pla
- 22 Cuines Santa Caterina
- 23 To El Corte Inglés

can snack or drink at the bar, or go into the back for a sit-down meal after 19:00. While touristy (less so later), the food and service are good, and the prices aren't as high as you might guess (weekday lunch specials, daily 9:00-24:00, just steps off Avinguda del Portal de l'Angel at Carrer de Montsió 3, Metro: Catalunya, tel. 933-024-140).

$$$ **Xaloc** is a good place in the old center for nicely presented gourmet tapas. It has a woody, modern, relaxed, and spacious dining room with a fun energy, attentive service, and reasonable prices. The walls are covered with *ibérico* hamhocks and wine bottles. They focus on home-style Catalan classics—and though the food here doesn't impress locals, tourists find the place comfortable. A bowl of gazpacho, plate of ham, *pa amb tomàquet* (comes free), and nice glass of wine make a fine light meal (daily, 13:00-17:00 & 19:00-23:00, a block toward the cathedral from Plaça de Sant Josep Oriol at Carrer de la Palla 13, Metro: Catalunya, tel. 933-011-990).

$$$ **Onofre Vinos y Viandas,** owned and run by Marisol and Ángel, is a tiny wine bar (20 wines by the glass) with a few simple tables behind walls of wine bottles. Foodie but without pretense, it has few tourists and a fun, creative, accessible menu—be adventurous and try the brandy foie shavings. For a gastronomic treat highlighting house favorites and seasonal specials, you can trust your hosts and order the €40-per-person "Marisol Extravaganza" (daily 10:00-16:30 & 19:30-24:00, near the Palace of Catalan Music, Carrer de les Magdalenes 19, tel. 933-176-937).

$$ **Bilbao Berria Pintxos and Tapas** is a hardworking tapas bar, like its Basque sisters around town. It faces the cathedral, with tables outside on the square (15 percent surcharge to sit there), and sells little open-faced sandwiches and fun bites for €2 per toothpick. Grab a plate and pick what you want, buffet-style (Plaça Nova 3, tel. 933-170-124).

On Plaça de Sant Josep Oriol: To enjoy the most inviting square in the Gothic Quarter with a meal, consider these simple eateries, both with a few tables on the square: $$ **Bar del Pi** is a hardworking bar serving salads, sandwiches, and tapas (daily 9:00-23:00). $ **El Drac de Sant Jordi** has a fun budget formula—€10 for any four tapas, a drink, and a tiny dessert (daily 12:00-22:00).

Tapas on Carrer de la Mercè

This area lets you experience a rare, unvarnished bit of old Barcelona with great tascas—colorful local tapas bars. The neighborhood's dark, the regulars are rough-edged, and you'll get a glimpse of a crusty Barcelona from before the affluence hit. Try $ **Bar Celta** (marked la pulpería, at #9); $ **La Plata** (#28); and $ **Cerveceria Vendimia,** at the north end of Carrer de la Mercè (#46).

El Born

El Born sparkles with eclectic and trendy as well as subdued and classy little restaurants hidden in the small lanes surrounding the Church of Santa Maria del Mar. Consider starting off your evening with a glass of fine wine at one of the *enotecas* on the square facing the church (such as La Vinya del Senyor). Many restaurants and shops in this area are, like the Picasso Museum, closed on Mondays. For all of these eateries, use Metro: Jaume I.

$$ **Sagardi Euskal Taberna** offers an array of Basque goodies—tempting *pintxos* and *montaditos* (small open-faced sandwiches) at €2 each—along its huge bar. Ask for a plate and just take whatever looks good. You can sit on the square with your plunder for about 20 percent extra. Wash it down with Txakolí, a Basque white wine poured from the spout of a huge wooden barrel into a glass as you watch. Study the two price lists—bar and terrace—posted at the bar (daily 12:00-24:00, Carrer de l'Argenteria 62, tel. 933-199-993).

$$ Vegetalia Vegetarian Restaurant, facing the Monument of Catalan Independence and the Church of Santa Maria del Mar, is a basic vegetarian diner with a cheery, healthy-feeling interior (good three-course lunch special, daily from 11:00, tel. 930-177-256).

$$$ El Senyor Parellada, filling a former cloister, is an elegant restaurant with a smart, tourist-friendly waitstaff. It serves a fun menu of Mediterranean and Catalan cuisine with a modern twist, all in a classy chandeliers-and-white-tablecloths setting (daily 13:00-15:45 & 20:30-23:30, Carrer de l'Argenteria 37, 100 yards from Jaume I Metro stop, tel. 933-105-094).

$$ El Xampanyet ("The Little Champagne Bar"), a colorful family-run bar with a fun-loving staff (Juan Carlos, his mom, and the man who may be his father). It specializes in tapas and anchovies—and their cheap homemade *cava* (Spanish champagne) goes straight to your head. Don't be put off by the seafood from a tin: Catalans like it this way. A *sortido de fumats* (assorted plate of small fish) with *pa amb tomàquet* makes for a fun meal. This place is filled with tourists during the sightseeing day, but it's jam-packed with locals after dark. The scene is great, but—especially during busy times—it's tough without Spanish skills. When I asked about the price, Juan Carlos said, "Who cares? The ATM is just across the street" (same price at bar or table, Tue-Sun 12:00-15:30 & 19:00-23:00, closed Sun evening and Mon, a half-block beyond the Picasso Museum at Carrer de Montcada 22, tel. 933-197-003).

$$ Tapeo is a mod, classy alternative to the funky Xampanyet across the street. It serves high-end tapas at a long, sit-down bar and tiny tables with stools. This small space fills quickly so go early to get a seat (Tue-Sun 12:00-16:00 & 19:00-24:00, closed Mon, Carrer de Montcada 29, tel. 933-101-607).

$$$ Bar Brutal is a creative, fun-loving, and edgy bohemian-chic place with a young, local following. It serves a mix of Spanish and Italian dishes with an emphasis on wines—especially natural wines, with plenty available by the glass (Mon-Sat 13:00-24:00, closed Sun, Carrer de Princesa 14, tel. 932-954-797).

$$$ Bar del Pla is a favorite near the Picasso Museum. This classic diner/bar—overlooking a tiny crossroads next to Barcelona's oldest church—serves traditional Catalan dishes, *raciones,* and tapas. Their *croquetas,* mushrooms with wasabi, and crispy oxtail with foie gras are highlights. They also have a local IPA on tap. Prices are the same at the bar or at a table; eating at the bar puts you in the middle of a great scene (Mon-Sat 12:00-23:00, closed Sun, reservations smart; leaving the Picasso Museum, head right two blocks past Carrer de la Princesa to Carrer de Montcada 2; tel. 932-683-003, www.bardelpla.cat).

At Santa Caterina Market

$$ Cuines Santa Caterina, bright and modern, has shared tables under the open rafters of a modern market hall. There's also a handy tapas bar and fine self-service outdoor seating on the square. Their menu—with vegetarian, international, and Mediterranean dishes, all made from market-fresh and seasonal ingredients—cross-references everything on an innovative grid (outside tables OK for both restaurant and tapas bar, daily 12:30-16:00 & 19:30-23:00, Avinguda de Francesc Cambó 16, tel. 932-689-918, no reservations).

Eixample

The people-packed boulevards of the Eixample are lined with appetizing eateries featuring breezy outdoor seating. Choose between a real restaurant or an upscale tapas bar (for the best variety, walk down Rambla de Catalunya).

Restaurants

$$ La Rita is a fresh and dressy little restaurant serving Catalan and Medi-

Restaurants & Hotels in Barcelona's Eixample

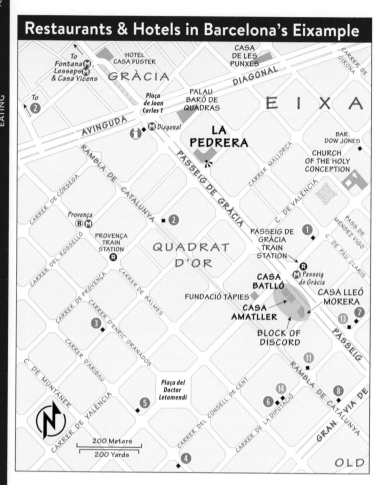

terranean cuisine near the Block of Discord. Their €11 lunch and €16 dinner *menú* specials are a great value. Arrive early...or wait (daily 13:00-15:45 & 20:00-23:00, near corner of Carrer de Pau Claris and Carrer d'Aragó at d'Aragó 279, a block from Metro: Passeig de Gràcia, tel. 934-872-376).

$$ La Bodegueta is an atmospheric below-street-level bodega serving hearty wines, homemade vermouth, *anchoas* (anchovies), tapas, and *flautas*—sandwiches made with flute-thin baguettes. On a nice day, it's great to eat outside, sitting in the median of the boulevard

under shady trees. Its three-course lunch special with wine is a deal (Mon-Fri only, 13:00-16:00). A long block from Gaudí's La Pedrera, this makes a fine sightseeing break (Mon-Sat 7:00-24:00, Sun from 18:00, at intersection with Carrer de Provença, Rambla de Catalunya 100, Metro: Provença, tel. 932-154-894). La Bodegueta has another location nearby—similar style and format but more comfortable and spacious (Carrer de Balmes 213).

$$$ Restaurante la Palmera serves a mix of Catalan, Mediterranean, and French cuisine in an elegant room with bottle-lined walls. This untouristy place

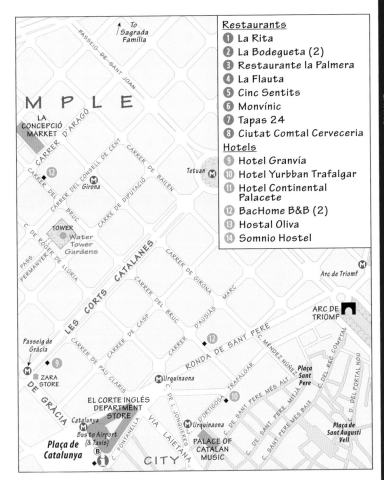

Restaurants
1. La Rita
2. La Bodegueta (2)
3. Restaurante la Palmera
4. La Flauta
5. Cinc Sentits
6. Monvínic
7. Tapas 24
8. Ciutat Comtal Cerveceria

Hotels
9. Hotel Granvía
10. Hotel Yurbban Trafalgar
11. Hotel Continental Palacete
12. BacHome B&B (2)
13. Hostal Oliva
14. Somnio Hostel

offers great food, service, and value—for me, a very special meal in Barcelona. They have three zones: the classic main room, a more forgettable adjacent room, and a few outdoor tables. I like the classic room. Reservations are smart (creative €24 six-plate *degustation* lunch—also available at dinner Sun and Tue-Thu, open Mon-Sat 13:00-15:45 & 19:45-23:30, closed Sun, Carrer d'Enric Granados 57, at the corner with Carrer Mallorca, Metro: Provença, tel. 934-532-338, www.lapalmera.cat).

$$ La Flauta fills two floors with enthusiastic eaters (I prefer the ground floor). It's fresh and modern, with a fun,

no-stress menu featuring small plates, creative *flauta* sandwiches, and a three-course lunch deal. Consider the list of *tapas del día*. Good wines by the glass are listed on the blackboard, and solo diners get great service at the bar (Mon-Sat 7:00-24:00, closed Sun, upbeat and helpful staff, no reservations, just off Carrer de la Diputació at Carrer d'Aribau 23, Metro: Universitat, tel. 933-237-038).

$$$$ Cinc Sentits ("Five Senses"), with only about 30 seats, is my gourmet recommendation for those who want to dress up and spend more money. At this chic, minimalist, slightly snooty place, all the attention goes to the fine service and beautifully presented dishes. The €55 *formula* lunch *menú* and the *quatre plats* (€90) and *sis plats* (€120) dinner menús are unforgettable extravaganzas. Each comes with a wine-pairing option (€65-70). Expect *menús* only—no à la carte. It's run by Catalans who lived in Canada (so there's no language barrier) and serve avant-garde cuisine inspired by Catalan traditions and ingredients. Reservations are essential (Tue-Sat 13:30-15:00 & 20:30-22:00, closed Sun-Mon, near Carrer d'Aragó at Carrer d'Aribau 58, between Metros: Universitat and Provença, tel. 933-239-490, www.cincsentits.com, maître d' Eric).

$$$$ Monvínic ("World of Wine")—a sleek, trendy wine bar that's evangelical about local wine culture—has an open kitchen, a passion for fine food, and little pretense. Considered one of the top wine bar/restaurants in town, their renowned chef creates Catalan and Mediterranean dishes for enjoying with the wine. Diners can use an iPad to read descriptions of the 50 open bottles. The faces of farmers—the unsung heroes of the food industry—are projected on the wall. Staff don't turn the tables and hope you'll spend the evening, so reserve in advance. For a more casual visit, they have a tapas bar (no reservations) in front where you'll also be empowered by an iPad and wine (Tue-Fri 13:00-23:00, Mon and Sat from 19:00, closed Sun, starters designed to share, creative tapas, lunch specials, Diputació 249, Metro: Passeig de Gràcia, tel. 932-726-187, www.monvinic.com).

Tapas Bars

Many trendy and touristic tapas bars in the Eixample offer a cheery welcome and slam out the appetizers. These two are particularly handy to Plaça de Catalunya and the Passeig de Gràcia artery (closest Metro stops: Catalunya and Passeig de Gràcia).

$$$ Tapas 24 makes eating fun. This local favorite, with a few street tables, fills a spot a few steps below street level with happy energy, funky decor, and good yet pricey tapas. Along with daily specials and fine breakfasts, the menu has all the typical standbys and quirky inventions. The *tapas del día* list is particularly good. The owner, Carles Abellan, is one of Barcelona's hot chefs; although his famous fare is pricey, you can enjoy it without going broke. Prices are the same whether you dine at the bar, a table, or outside. Come early or wait; no reservations are taken (daily 9:00-24:00, just off Passeig de Gràcia at Carrer de la Diputació 269, tel. 934-880-977).

$$ Ciutat Comtal Cerveceria is an Eixample favorite, full of tourists, with an elegant bar and tables plus good seating out on the Rambla de Catalunya for all that people-watching action. It's packed after 21:00, when you'll likely need to put your name on a list and wait. While it has no restaurant-type menu, the varied list of tapas and *montaditos* is easy, fun, high-quality, and includes daily specials (daily 8:00-24:00, facing the intersection of Gran Via de les Corts Catalanes and Rambla de Catalunya at Rambla de Catalunya 18, tel. 933-181-997).

SLEEPING

Despite being Spain's most expensive city, Barcelona has reasonably priced rooms. Cheap places are more crowded in summer; fancier business-class hotels fill up in winter and may offer discounts on weekends and in summer. When considering relative hotel values, in summer and on weekends you can often get modern comfort in centrally located business-class hotels for about the same price (€130) as you'll pay for ramshackle charm.

Near Plaça de Catalunya

These modern hotels are on big streets within two blocks of Barcelona's exuberant central square, where the Old City meets the Eixample. As business-class hotels, they have hard-to-pin-down prices that fluctuate with demand. In summer and on weekends, supply often far exceeds the demand, and many of these places cut prices. Some of my recommended hotels are on Carrer Pelai, a busy street; for these, request a quieter room in back.

$$$$ Hotel Catalonia Plaça Catalunya has four stars, an elegant old entryway with a modern reception area, splashy public spaces, slick marble and hardwood floors, 150 comfortable rooms, and a garden courtyard with a pool a world away from the big-city noise. It's a bit pricey for the room quality—you're paying for the posh lobby (air-con, elevator, a half-block off Plaça de Catalunya at Carrer de Bergara 11, Metro: Catalunya, tel. 933-015-151, www.hoteles-catalonia.com, catalunya@hoteles-catalonia.es).

$$$$ Hotel Midmost is an oasis a little west of Plaça de Catalunya. It has 56 rooms with luxurious, four-star style; a seaside-lounge-inspired rooftop terrace; and a mini pool to relax (family rooms, air-con, elevator, Carrer de Pelai 14, Metro: Universitat, tel. 935-051-100, www.hotel midmost.com, info@hotelmidmost.com).

$$$ Hotel Ginebra is a modern version of the old-school *pensión*, with 18 rooms in a classic, well-located building at the corner of Plaça de Catalunya (RS%—use code "HGinebra-RickSteves" and print voucher, family rooms, breakfast extra, laundry, air-con, elevator, Rambla de Catalunya 1, Metro: Catalunya, tel. 932-502-017, www.hotelginebra.com.es, info@barcelonahotelginebra.com, Brits Alfred and Ivon).

$$$ Hotel Reding Croma, on a quiet street a 10-minute walk west of the Ramblas and the Plaça de Catalunya action, is a slick and sleek place renting 44 basic but mod rooms on color-themed floors (RS%, air-con, elevator, Carrer de Gravina 5, Metro: Universitat, tel. 934-121-097, www.hotelreding.com, recepcion@hotelreding.com).

$$$ Hotel Lleó (YAH-oh) is well-run, with 92 big, bright, and comfortable rooms; a great breakfast room; and a generous lounge (air-con, elevator, small rooftop pool, Carrer de Pelai 22, midway between Metros: Universitat and Catalunya, tel. 933-181-312, www.hotel-lleo.com, info@hotel-lleo.com).

$$ Hotel Atlantis is solid, with 50 big, nondescript, slightly dated rooms and fair prices for the location (includes breakfast, air-con, elevator, Carrer de Pelai 20, midway between Metros: Universitat and Catalunya, tel. 933-189-012, http://hotelatlantis-atbcn.com, inf@hotelatlantis-bcn.com).

$$ Hotel Denit is a small, stylish, 36-room hotel on a pedestrian street two blocks off Plaça de Catalunya. It's chic, minimalist, and fun: Guidebook tips decorate the halls, and the rooms are sized like T-shirts, from small to extra-large (includes breakfast, air-con, elevator, Carrer d'Estruc 24, Metro: Catalunya, tel. 935-454-000, www.denit.com, info@denit.com).

On or near the Ramblas

These places are generally family-run, with ad-lib furnishings, more character, and lower prices.

$$$ Hotel Continental Barcelona, in a building overlooking the top of the Ramblas, offers classic, tiny view-balcony opportunities if you don't mind the noise. Its 40 rooms are quite comfortable and the staff is friendly. Choose between your own little Ramblas-view balcony (where you can eat your breakfast) or a quieter back room. J. M.'s (José María's) free breakfast and all-day snack-and-drink bar are a plus (RS%, air-con, elevator, quiet terrace, Ramblas 138, Metro: Catalunya, tel. 933-012-570, www.hotelcontinental.com, barcelona@hotelcontinental.com).

$$ Hostal Grau is a homey, family-run, and extremely eco-conscious hotel with custom recycled furniture and organic bedding. It has 25 crisp, impeccable, and cheery rooms a few blocks off the Ramblas in the colorful university district. Double-glazed windows keep it quiet (some rooms with balconies, family

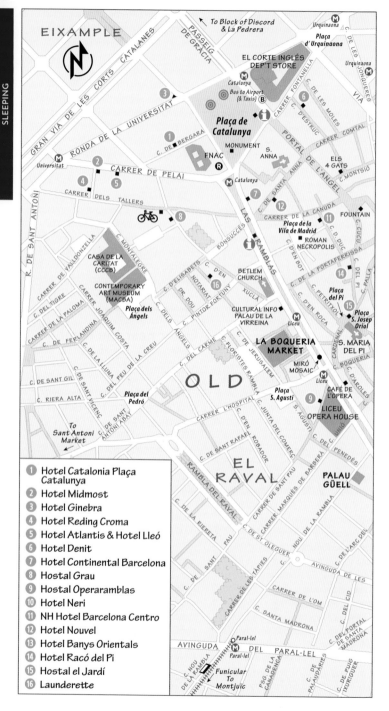

① Hotel Catalonia Plaça Catalunya
② Hotel Midmost
③ Hotel Ginebra
④ Hotel Reding Croma
⑤ Hotel Atlantis & Hotel Lleó
⑥ Hotel Denit
⑦ Hotel Continental Barcelona
⑧ Hostal Grau
⑨ Hostal Operaramblas
⑩ Hotel Neri
⑪ NH Hotel Barcelona Centro
⑫ Hotel Nouvel
⑬ Hotel Banys Orientals
⑭ Hotel Racó del Pi
⑮ Hostal el Jardí
⑯ Launderette

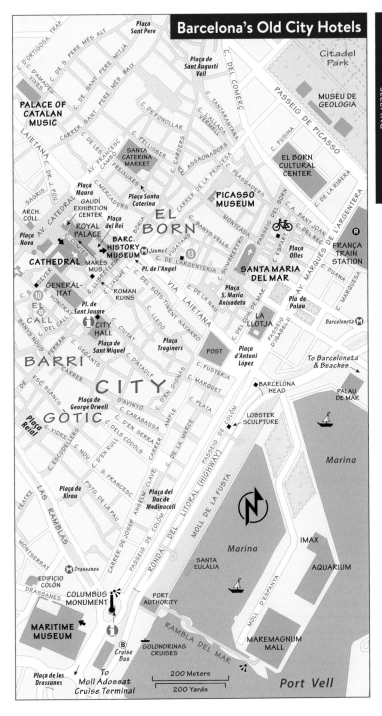

Barcelona's Old City Hotels

Citadel Park

MUSEU DE GEOLOGIA

PASSEIG DE PICASSO

Plaça Sant Pere

Plaça de Sant Augustí Vell

C. DEL COMERÇ

C. D'ORTIGOSA TRAF.
C. D'AMADEU VIVES
C. DE S. PERE MÉS ALT
C. DE SANT PERE MÉS BAIX
C. DE SANT PERE MÉS ALT
C. DE SANT PERE MÉS BAIX

PALACE OF CATALAN MUSIC

C. TANTARANTANA
C. L'ALLADA VERMELL
C. DE FONOLLAR

C. FUSINA

EL BORN CULTURAL CENTER

C. PELLISSER
AV. FRANCESC CAMBÓ
C. DE LES FREIXURES
CARDERS
C. ASSAONADORS
C. DE LA PRINCESA
C. FLASSADERS

SANTA CATERINA MARKET

C. DE LA RIBERA

Plaça Maura
GAUDÍ EXHIBITION CENTER
ARCH. COLL.
C. MERCADERS
Plaça Santa Caterina
EL BORN
PICASSO MUSEUM
MONTCADA

PASSEIG DEL BORN
C. A. SANT JOAN
C. DEL REC
C. ESPARTERIA
MARQUES DE L'ARGENTERA

Plaça del Rei
ROYAL PALACE
BORIA
C. BANYS VELLS
Plaça Olles
FRANÇA TRAIN STATION

Plaça Nova
AV. CATEDRAL
BARC. HISTORY MUSEUM
MARES MUS
Jaume I
C. VIGATANS
C. L'ARGENTERIA
13
SANTA MARIA DEL MAR
C. SOMBRERERS
C. DUANA
C. MARQUESA

CATHEDRAL
C. SEVER
C. COMTES
C. LLIBRETERIA
Pl. de l'Angel
Plaça S. Maria Anisadeta
Pla de Palau
Barceloneta

GENERAL-ITAT
C. S. HONORAT
ROMAN RUINS
C. DEL SOTS-TINENT NAVARRO
LA LLOTJA
PASSEIG D'ISABEL II
To Barceloneta & Beaches

EL CALL
BANYS NOUS
C. DEL CALL
Pl. de Sant Jaume
CITY HALL
C. CIUTAT
C. LLEDÓ
VIA LAIETANA
C. DE LA NAU
PALAU DE MAR

BARRI
C. FERRAN
C. GEGANTS
Plaça de Sant Miquel
C. DATAULF
Plaça Traginers
POST
Plaça d'Antoni López

CITY
CARRER
D'AVINYÓ
C. D'EN GIGNAS
C. FUSTERIA
BARCELONA HEAD

GÒTIC
DE ESC. BLANCS
Plaça de George Orwell
C. CARABASSA
C. D'EN SERRA
C. MARQUET
C. PLATA
LOBSTER SCULPTURE

Plaça Reial
C. VIDRES
C. ESCUDELLERS
C. NOU
C. D'EN RULL
C. DELS CÒDOLS
AMPLE
C. DE LA MERCÈ
PASSEIG DE COLOM
Marina

LAS RAMBLAS
Plaça de Xirau
PSTG. DE LA PAU
S. FRANCESC
Plaça del Duc de Medinaceli
CARRER DE JOSEP ANSELM CLAVÉ
PASSEIG DE COLOM
RONDA DEL LITORAL (HIGHWAY)
MOLL DE LA FUSTA
N
Marina
IMAX
AQUARIUM

MONTSERRAT
Drassanes
SANTA EULÀLIA
MOLL D'ESPANYA

EDIFICIO COLÓN
DRASSANES
COLUMBUS MONUMENT
PORT AUTHORITY
MAREMAGNUM MALL

MARITIME MUSEUM
Plaça de les Drassanes
B Cruise Bus
GOLONDRINAS CRUISES
RAMBLA DEL MAR
Port Vell

To Moll Adossat Cruise Terminal

200 Meters
200 Yards

rooms, strict cancellation policy, air-con, elevator, 200 yards up Carrer dels Tallers from the Ramblas at Ramelleres 27, Metro: Catalunya, tel. 933-018-135, www.hostalgrau.com, bookgreen@hostalgrau.com, Monica).

$$ Hostal Operaramblas, with 68 simple rooms 20 yards off the Ramblas, is clean, modern, and a great value. The street can feel a bit seedy at night, but it's safe, and the hotel is very secure (RS%—use code "operaramblas," air-con in summer, elevator, Carrer de Sant Pau 20, Metro: Liceu, tel. 933-188-201, www.operaramblas.com, info@operaramblas.com).

Old City

These accommodations are buried in Barcelona's Old City, mostly in the Barri Gòtic.

$$$$ Hotel Neri is posh, pretentious, and sophisticated, with 22 rooms spliced into the ancient stones of the Barri Gòtic, overlooking an overlooked square (Plaça Sant Felip Neri) a block from the cathedral. It has pricey modern art on the bedroom walls, dressed-up people in its gourmet restaurant, and high-class service (air-con, elevator, rooftop tanning deck, Carrer de Sant Sever 5, Metro: Liceu or Jaume I, tel. 933-040-655, www.hotelneri.com, info@hotelneri.com).

$$$ NH Hotel Barcelona Centro, with 156 rooms and tasteful chain-hotel predictability, is professional yet friendly, buried in the Barri Gòtic just three blocks off the Ramblas (air-con, elevator, Carrer del Duc 15, Metro: Catalunya or Liceu, tel. 932-703-410, www.nh-hotels.com, nhbarcelonacentro@nh-hotels.com).

$$$ Hotel Nouvel, in an elegant, Victorian-style building on a handy pedestrian street, is less business-oriented and offers more character than the others listed here. It boasts royal lounges and 78 comfy rooms (air-con, elevator, Carrer de Santa Anna 20, Metro: Catalunya, tel. 933-018-274, www.hotelnouvel.com, info@hotelnouvel.com).

$$$ Hotel Banys Orientals, a modern, boutique-type place, has a people-to-people ethic and refreshingly straight prices. Its 43 restful rooms are located in the El Born district on a pedestrianized street between the cathedral and Church of Santa Maria del Mar (air-con, elevator, Carrer de l'Argenteria 37, 50 yards from Metro: Jaume I, tel. 932-688-460, www.hotelbanysorientals.com, reservas@hotelbanysorientals.com).

$$$ Hotel Racó del Pi, part of the H10 hotel chain, is a quality, professional place with generous public spaces and 37 modern, bright, quiet rooms. It's located on a wonderful pedestrian street immersed in the Barri Gòtic (air-con, around the corner from Plaça del Pi at Carrer del Pi 7, three-minute walk from Metro: Liceu, tel. 933-426-190, www.h10hotels.com, h10.raco.delpi@h10hotels.com).

$ Hostal el Jardí offers 40 clean, remodeled rooms on a breezy square. Many of the tight, plain, comfy rooms come with petite balconies (for an extra charge) and enjoy an almost Parisian feel. It's a good deal only if you value the quaint-square-with-Barri-Gòtic ambience—you're definitely paying for the location. Book well in advance, as this family-run place has an avid following (air-con, elevator, some stairs, halfway between Ramblas and cathedral at Plaça Sant Josep Oriol 1, Metro: Liceu, tel. 933-015-900, www.eljardi-barcelona.com, reservations@eljardi-barcelona.com).

Eixample

For an uptown, boulevard-like neighborhood, sleep in the Eixample, a 10-minute walk from the Ramblas action. Most of these places use the Passeig de Gràcia or Catalunya Metro stops. Because these stations are so huge—especially Passeig de Gràcia, which sprawls underground for a few blocks—study the maps posted in the station to establish which exit you want before surfacing.

$$$$ Hotel Granvía, filling a palatial, brightly renovated 1870s mansion, offers a large, peaceful sun patio, several comfortable common areas, and 58 spacious, modern, business-style rooms (RS%—free breakfast with this book, family rooms, air-con, elevator, Gran Via de les Corts Catalanes 642, Metro: Passeig de Gràcia, tel. 933-181-900, www.hotelgranvia.com, hgranvia@nnhotels.com).

$$$$ Hotel Yurbban Trafalgar is a small, classy boutique hotel with 56 rooms and a masculine-minimalist decor. Their rooftop bar, tiny pool, and views alone are worth the price of your stay (air-con, free self-service laundry, gym, near the Palace of Catalan Music at Carrer de Trafalgar 30, a long block from Metro: Urquinaona, tel. 932-680-727, www.yurbban.com, trafalgar@yurbban.com).

$$$ Hotel Continental Palacete, with 22 small rooms, fills a 100-year-old chandeliered mansion. With flowery wallpaper and ornately gilded stucco, it's gaudy in the city of Gaudí, but it's also friendly, quiet, and well-located. Guests have unlimited access to the outdoor terrace and the "cruise-inspired" fruit, veggie, and drink buffet (RS%, includes breakfast, air-con, two blocks northwest of Plaça de Catalunya at corner of Rambla de Catalunya and Carrer de la Diputació, Rambla de Catalunya 30, Metro: Passeig de Gràcia, tel. 934-457-657, www.hotelcontinental.com, palacete@hotelcontinental.com).

$$ BacHome B&B has two bright and comfortable locations in traditional Eixample buildings on Carrer Bruc. BacHome Terrace (at #14) has 10 rooms and a pleasant outdoor terrace. BacHome Gallery (#96) has seven rooms and common areas with big windows looking out onto the city (includes breakfast, air-con, elevator, Metro: Urquinaona, tel. 620-657-810, www.bachomebarcelona.com, reservations@bachomebarcelona.com).

$$ Hostal Oliva, family-run with care, is a spartan, old-school place with 15 basic, bright, high-ceilinged rooms. It's on the fourth floor of a classic old Eixample building—with a beautiful mahogany elevator—in a perfect location, just a couple of blocks above Plaça de Catalunya (corner of Passeig de Gràcia and Carrer de la Diputació, Passeig de Gràcia 32, Metro: Passeig de Gràcia, tel. 934-880-162, www.hostaloliva.com, info@hostaloliva.com).

Hostels

¢ Somnio Hostel, a smaller place, has nine simple rooms (RS%, cheaper rooms with shared bath, private rooms available, air-con, Carrer de la Diputació 251, second floor, Metro: Passeig de Gràcia, tel. 932-725-308, www.somniohostels.com, info@somniohostels.com). They have a second location that's five blocks farther out.

TRANSPORTATION

Getting Around Barcelona

Barcelona's Metro and bus system is run by **TMB**—Transports Metropolitans de Barcelona (tel. 902-075-027, www.tmb.cat). Ask for TMB's excellent Metro/bus map at the TI, larger stations, or the TMB information counter in the Sants train station.

By Metro

The city's Metro, among Europe's best, connects just about every place you'll visit. A **single-ride ticket** (bitllet senzill) costs €2.20. The **T10 Card**—€10.20 for 10 rides—is a great deal (cutting the per-ride cost by more than half). The card is shareable, even by companions (insert the card in the machine per passenger). The back of your T10 card will show how many trips were taken, with the time and date of each ride. One "ride" covers you for 1.25 hours of unlimited use on all Metro and local bus lines, as well as local rides on the Renfe and Rodalies de Catalunya train lines (including the ride to the train station) and the suburban FGC trains. Transfers made within your 1.25-hour limit are not counted as a new ride, but you still must revalidate your T10 Card whenever you transfer.

Multiday **"Hola BCN!" travel cards** are also available (€15/2 days, €22/3 days,

€28.50/4 days, €35/5 days).

Buy tickets from ticket machines in the Metro station. They're easy—just press "English" to start. They'll give you the whole array of tickets you can buy, from individual to T10. Most machines accept coins, bills, and credit/debit cards.

Whatever type of ticket you use, insert it in the turnstile, retrieve it, and walk through. To exit, you don't need to insert it into the turnstile, but keep it until you have exited in case an inspector asks to see it.

Barcelona has several color-coded Metro lines. Most useful for tourists is the **L3 (green)** line. Handy city-center stops on this line include (in order):

Sants Estació: Main train station

Espanya: Plaça d'Espanya, with access to the lower part of Montjuïc and trains to Montserrat

Paral-lel: Funicular to the top of Montjuïc

Drassanes: Bottom of the Ramblas, near Maritime Museum and Maremagnum mall

Liceu: Middle of the Ramblas, near the heart of the Barri Gòtic and cathedral

Plaça de Catalunya: Top of the Ramblas and main square with TI, airport bus, and lots of transportation connections

Passeig de Gràcia: Classy Eixample street at the Block of Discord; also connection to L2 (purple) line to Sagrada Família and L4 (yellow) line (described below)

Diagonal: Gaudí's La Pedrera

The **L4 (yellow)** line, which crosses the L3 (green) line at Passeig de Gràcia, has a few helpful stops, including **Jaume I** (between the Barri Gòtic/cathedral and El Born/Picasso Museum) and **Barceloneta** (at the south end of El Born, near the harbor action).

By Bus

Given the excellent Metro service, it's unlikely you'll spend much time on **local buses** (also €2.20, covered by T10 Card, insert ticket in machine behind driver). However, buses are useful for reaching Park Güell, connecting the sights on Montjuïc, and getting to the beach. (Note that #24 bus route to Park Güell may change; check locally.) For information on **hop-on, hop-off bus tours,** see page 43.

By Taxi

Barcelona is one of Europe's best taxi towns. Taxis are plentiful and honest, and cab rates are reasonable (€2.10 drop charge, about €1/kilometer, figure €10 from Ramblas to Sants station; slightly more expensive "Tarif 2" rates are in effect weekdays 20:00-8:00 as well as holidays, "Tarif 3" rates apply on weekend evenings 20:00-6:00, surcharges for large suitcases, Sants train station, airport or cruise port, other fees posted in window).

Arriving and Departing
By Plane

Most flights use Barcelona's **El Prat de Llobregat Airport;** a few budget flights use a smaller airstrip farther away, called **Girona–Costa Brava Airport.** Information on both airports can be found on the official Spanish airport website: www.aena-aeropuertos.es.

EL PRAT DE LLOBREGAT AIRPORT

Barcelona's primary airport is eight miles southwest of town (code: BCN, info tel. 913-211-000). It has two large terminals, linked by shuttle buses. Terminal 1 serves Air France, Air Europa, American, British Airways, Delta, Iberia, Lufthansa, United, Vueling, and others. EasyJet, Ryanair, and minor airlines use the older Terminal 2, which is divided into sections A, B, and C.

Terminal 1 and the bigger sections of Terminal 2 (A and B) each have a post office, a pharmacy, a left-luggage office, plenty of good cafeterias in the gate areas, and ATMs.

Getting Downtown: To reach central Barcelona cheaply and quickly, take the bus or train (about 30 minutes on either).

The **Aerobus** (#A1 and #A2, corresponding with Terminals 1 and 2) picks up immediately outside the arrivals lobby of both terminals and makes several stops downtown, including at Plaça de Catalunya, near many of my recommended hotels (returning from downtown, buses leave from in front of El Corte Inglés). Either way it's very easy: Buses depart about every five minutes (30-40 minutes, runs from 5:30 to 24:00, buy €6 ticket from driver, tel. 902-100-104, www.aerobusbcn.com).

The **Renfe train** (on the "R2 Nord" Rodalies line) leaves from Terminal 2 and involves more walking. Head up the escalators and down the long orange-roofed skybridge to reach the station (2/hour at about :08 and :38 past the hour, 20 minutes to Sants station, 25 minutes to Passeig de Gràcia station—near Plaça de Catalunya; €4.10 or covered by T10 Card—described on page 109—which you can purchase from machines at the airport train station). If you are arriving or departing from Terminal 1, you will have to use the airport shuttle bus to connect with the train station, so allow extra time (10 buses/hour, 7-minute ride between terminals).

By **Metro,** take the L9 Sud (orange) line from either Terminal 1 or 2, to Zona Universitária, then transfer to the L3 (green) line and ride to a downtown stop (Passeig de Gràcia, Plaça de Catalunya, or Liceu). To reach the airport from downtown via Metro, take line L3 to Zona Universitária, and transfer to line L9 in the direction of Aeroport T1 (runs about every 10 minutes 5:00 until late; 20-30 minute ride; use €4.60 *Billet Aeroport* or any "Hola BCN!" travel card—the T10 and single-ride Metro tickets do not work for this ride).

A **taxi** between the airport and downtown costs about €32 (including €3 airport supplement).

GIRONA-COSTA BRAVA AIRPORT
Some budget airlines use this airport, located 60 miles north of Barcelona near Girona (code: GRO, tel. 972-186-600, www.aena-aeropuertos.es). If you're arriving on a Ryanair flight, you can take a bus (#604), run by Ryanair and operated by Sagalés, to the Barcelona Nord bus station (departs airport about 20-25 minutes after each arriving flight, 1.25 hours, €16, tel. 902-361-550, www.sagales.com). You can also take a Sagalés bus (#602, about every 10 minutes, 1.5 hours, €2.75) or a taxi (€25) to the town of Girona, then catch a train to Barcelona (at least hourly, 1.5 hours, €15-20). A taxi between the Girona airport and Barcelona costs at least €130.

Rick's Tip: *Remember,* **Barcelona makes a good first or last stop for your trip.** *With the speedy AVE train, Barcelona is only three hours away from Madrid—easier than flying. If you want to rent a car, start your trip in Barcelona, take the train or fly to Madrid, and see Madrid and Toledo, all before picking up a car—cleverly saving on several days of rental fees.*

By Train
Virtually all trains end up at Barcelona's **Sants train station,** west of the Old City. AVE trains from Madrid go only to Sants station. But many other trains also pass through other stations en route, such as **França station** (between the El Born and Barceloneta neighborhoods), or the downtown **Passeig de Gràcia** or **Plaça de Catalunya** stations (which are also Metro stops—and very close to most of my recommended hotels). Figure out which stations your train stops at (ask the conductor), and get off at the one most convenient to your hotel.

SANTS TRAIN STATION
Barcelona's big white main train station offers many services. In the large lobby area, you'll find a TI, ATMs, handy shops and eateries, pay WCs, car-rental kiosks, and, in the side concourse, a classy, quiet Sala Club lounge for travelers with first-class reservations. Sants is the only Barcelona station with luggage storage (€6/

Barcelona's Public Transportation

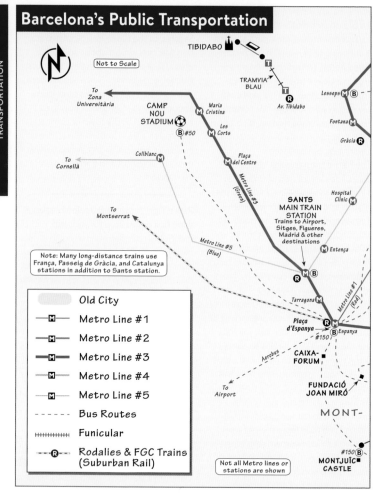

up to 2 hours, €10/day, daily 5:30-23:00, follow signs to *consigna*; go toward track 14, then exit the main building toward the parking lot and go down to level -1).

In the vast main hall is a very long wall of ticket windows. Figure out which one you need before you wait in line (all are labeled in English). Generally, windows 1-7 (on the left) are for local commuter and *media distancia* trains, such as to Sitges; windows 8-21 handle advance tickets for long-distance (*larga distancia*) trains beyond Catalunya; windows 22-26

give information—go here first if you're not sure which window you want; and windows 27-31 sell tickets for long-distance trains leaving today. These window assignments can shift in off-season. The information booths by windows 1 and 21 can help you find the right line and can provide some train schedules.

Scattered nearby are train-ticket vending machines. The red-and-gray machines sell tickets for local and *media distancia* trains within Catalunya. The purple machines are for national Renfe

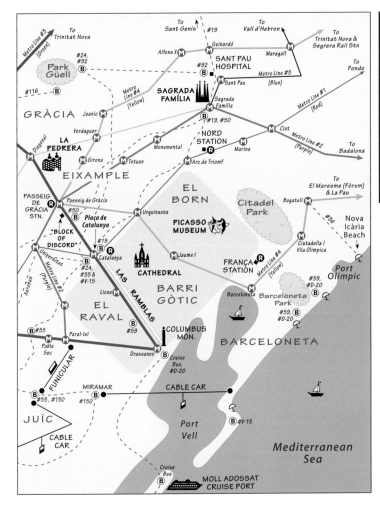

trains; these machines can also print out prereserved tickets if you have a confirmation code. And the orange machines sell local *Rodalies* train tickets. There are usually attendants around the machines to help you.

Getting Downtown: To reach the center of Barcelona, take a train or the Metro. To ride the subway, follow signs for the Metro (red M), and hop on the L3 (green) or L5 (blue) line, both of which link to useful points in town. Purchase tickets for the Metro at touch-screen machines near the tracks (where you can also buy the cost-saving T10 Card, explained earlier).

To zip downtown even faster (just five minutes), you can take any Rodalies de Catalunya suburban train from track 8 (R1, R3, or R4) to Plaça de Catalunya (departs at least every 10 minutes). Your long-distance Renfe train ticket comes with a complimentary ride on Rodalies, as long as you use it within three hours before or after your travels. Look for a code on your ticket labeled *Combinat Rodalies* or *Combinado Cercanías*. Go to the orange commuter ticket machines, touch *Combinat Rodalies,* type in your code, and the machine will print your ticket. There is usually an attendant around to help you.

TRAIN CONNECTIONS

Unless otherwise noted, all of the trains listed below depart from Sants station; however, remember that some trains also stop at other stations more convenient to the downtown tourist zone: França station, Passeig de Gràcia, or Plaça de Catalunya. Figure out if your train stops at these stations (and board there) to save yourself the trip to Sants.

If departing from the downtown Passeig de Gràcia station, where three Metro lines converge with the rail line, you might find the underground tunnels confusing. You can't access the Renfe station directly from some of the entrances. Use the northern entrances to this station (rather than the southern "Consell de Cent" entrance, which is closest to Plaça de Catalunya). Train info: Tel. 912-320-320, www.renfe.com.

From Barcelona by Train to Madrid: The AVE train to Madrid is faster than flying (when you consider that you're zipping from downtown to downtown). The train departs at least hourly. The non-stop train is a little more expensive but faster (€130, 2.5 hours) than the train that makes a few stops (€110, 3 hours). Regular reserved AVE tickets can be prepurchased (often with a discount) at the Renfe website and printed from an email or at the station. You can also download a ticket

QR code on a smartphone. If you have a rail pass, most trains require paid reservations; see the "Transportation" section of the Practicalities chapter.

From Barcelona by Train to: Montserrat (departs from Plaça d'Espanya—*not* from Sants, 1-2/hour, 1 hour, €22 round-trip, includes cable car or rack train to monastery), **Figueres** (hourly, 1 hour via AVE or Alvia to Figueres-Vilafant; hourly, 2 hours via local trains to Figueres station), **Sevilla** (2/day direct, more with transfer in Madrid, 5.5 hours), **Granada** (2/day, 8 hours via AVE and connecting bus, transfer in Antequera), **Córdoba** (4/day direct, 5 hours, many more with transfer in Madrid), **Salamanca** (6/day, 7 hours, change in Madrid from Atocha station to Chamartín station via Metro or *cercanías* train; also 1/day with a change in Valladolid, 8.5 hours), **San Sebastián** (2/day direct, 6 hours).

By Bus

Most buses depart from the Nord bus station at Metro: Arc de Triomf, but confirm when researching schedules (www.barcelonanord.com). Destinations served by Alsa buses (www.alsa.es) include **Madrid** and **Madrid's Barajas Airport** (nearly hourly, 8 hours), and Salamanca (2/day, 12 hours). Reservations are smart for long-distance destinations, especially during the busy summer season.

One bus departs daily for the **Montserrat** monastery, leaving from Carrer de Viriat near Sants station (1.5 hours).

NEAR BARCELONA

Two fine sights are day-trip temptations from Barcelona. Pilgrims with hiking boots head 1.5 hours into the mountains for the most sacred spot in Catalunya: **Montserrat.** Fans of Surrealism can enjoy a stop at the Dalí Theater-Museum in **Figueres** (one to two hours from Barcelona).

Montserrat

With its unique rock formations, mountaintop Benedictine monastery, and spiritual connection with the Catalan people, Montserrat has been Catalunya's most important pilgrimage site for a thousand years. In a quick day trip, you can view the mountain from its base, ride a funicular up to the top of the world, tour the basilica, touch a Black Virgin's orb, and hike down to a sacred cave.

Getting There

Barcelona is connected to the valley below Montserrat by a convenient train; from there, a cable car or rack railway

(your choice) takes you up to the mountaintop. Driving or taking the bus round out your options.

By Train Plus Cable Car or Rack Railway: Trains leave from Barcelona's Plaça d'Espanya Montserrat. Take the Metro to Espanya, then follow signs for Montserrat (showing a graphic of a train and the *FGC* symbol—for Ferrocarrils de la Generalitat de Catalunya) to the FGC station. Once there, find the track for train line R5 (direction: Manresa, 1-2/hour—usually at :36 and/or :56; hang onto your train ticket; you'll need it to exit the FGC station when you return to Plaça d'Espanya).

You'll ride about an hour on the train. For the cable car, get out at the Montserrat-Aeri station; for the rack railway, continue another few minutes to the next station—Monistrol de Montserrat (or simply "Monistrol de M.").

Tickets: The various available combo-tickets all begin with the train from Barcelona and include either the cable car or rack

Montserrat

railway—specify one or the other when you buy the ticket (same price for either).

The basic option is to buy a **train ticket** to Montserrat (€22 round-trip, includes cable car or rack railway to monastery, www.fgc.es). Two **combo-tickets** offered by the train company cover transportation and various admissions (€35 Trans Montserrat and €54 Tot Montserrat).

You can get advice about your ticket choice and return schedules at the Montserrat Cremallera (rack railway) or cable-car information booths at Plaça d'Espanya station (daily 8:00-14:00). Then purchase any of these options from the ticket machines. If you buy your ticket online (www.montserratvisita.com), you must take your purchase voucher to the Cremallera rack-railway information booth during open hours (daily 8:00-14:00) to receive an actual ticket.

Rick's Tip: *Should you choose* **the cable car or rack train?** *For scenery and fun, pick the little German-built cable car. Make your way to the cable car quickly when you reach Montserrat-Aeri station, or you may have to wait to go up.*

Cable Car: Departing the train at Montserrat-Aeri, follow signs to the cable-car station (covered by your train or combo-ticket; 4/hour, 5-minute trip, daily 10:00-19:00, www.aeridemontserrat.com). On the way back down, give yourself enough time to catch a Barcelona-bound train (these leave at :05 and :45 past the hour Mon-Fri, only at :45 Sat-Sun).

Rack Railway: From the Monistrol de Montserrat station, catch the Cremallera rack railway up to the monastery (covered by your train or combo-ticket, hourly, 20-minute trip, www.cremallerademontserrat.com). On the return trip, this train departs the monastery at :15 past the hour, allowing you to catch the Barcelona-bound train leaving Monistrol de Montserrat at :45 past the hour. The last convenient connection leaves

the monastery at 19:15 (Sat-Sun at 20:15). Confirm the schedule when you arrive, as specific times can change year to year.

By Car: Drivers can find pay parking at the sight, but it may be easier to park your car down below and ride the cable car or rack railway up; there is plenty of free parking at the Monistrol-Vila rack-railway station (cable car-€7 one-way, €11 round-trip; rack railway-€6.90 one-way, €11.50 round-trip).

By Bus: One bus per day connects downtown Barcelona directly to the monastery (departs from Carrer de Viriat near Barcelona's Sants station daily at 9:15, return trip at 18:00 June-Sept, at 17:00 Oct-May, €5 each way, 1.5 hours, operated by Autocares Julià, www.autocaresjulia.es).

Orientation

However you make your way up to the Montserrat monastery, it's easy to get oriented once you arrive at the top. Everything is within a few minutes' walk of your entry point. All of the transit options—including the rack railway and cable car—converge at one big station. Above that are the funicular stations: one up to the ridge top, the other down to the Sacred Cave trail. Across the street is the TI, and above that is the main square.

Rick's Tip: To beat the crowds, arrive early or late, *as tour groups mob the place midday. Crowds are less likely on weekdays and worst on Sundays.*

Tourist Information: The helpful TI is right across from the rack-railway station (daily, tel. 938-777-701, www.montserratvisita.com). A good audioguide, available only at the TI, describes the general site and basilica.

Sights

▲▲BASILICA

Although there's been a church here since the 11th century, the present structure was built in the 1850s, and the facade only

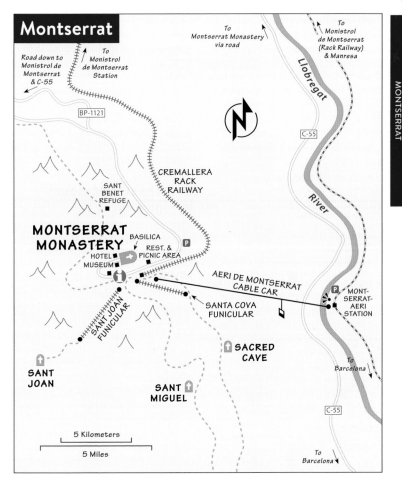

Montserrat

Road down to Monistrol de Montserrat & C-55

To Monistrol de Montserrat Station

To Montserrat Monastery via road

To Monistrol de Montserrat (Rack Railway) & Manresa

Llobregat

River

C-55

BP-1121

N

CREMALLERA RACK RAILWAY

SANT BENET REFUGE

MONTSERRAT MONASTERY

BASILICA

REST. & PICNIC AREA

HOTEL MUSEUM

P

AERI DE MONTSERRAT CABLE CAR

MONT-SERRAT-AERI STATION

P

SANT JOAN FUNICULAR

SANTA COVA FUNICULAR

SACRED CAVE

SANT JOAN

SANT MIGUEL

To Barcelona

C-55

5 Kilometers

5 Miles

To Barcelona

---

dates from 1968. The decor is Neo-Romanesque, so popular with the Romantic artists of the late 19th century. The basilica itself is ringed with interesting chapels, but the focus is on the Black Virgin (La Moreneta) sitting high above the main altar (keep an eye on the time if you want to see the statue—viewing hours are below).

Cost and Hours: Free; La Moreneta viewable Mon-Sat 8:00-10:30 & 12:00-18:30, Sun 19:30-20:15; church itself has longer hours and daily services; www.abadiamontserrat.net.

Visiting the Basilica: Montserrat's top attraction, the small wood statue of the

Black Virgin, was discovered in the Sacred Cave in the 12th century. Legend says she was carved by St. Luke, brought to Spain by St. Peter, hidden away in the cave during the Moorish invasions, and miraculously discovered by shepherd children.

To see the statue, join the line of pilgrims (along the right side of the church). Though Mary is behind a protective glass case, the royal orb she cradles in her hands is exposed. Pilgrims touch Mary's orb with one hand and hold their other hand up to show that they accept Jesus.

Immediately after La Moreneta, to the right, is the delightful Neo-Romanesque prayer **chapel,** where worshippers can sit behind the Virgin and pray. You'll exit by walking along the **Ave Maria Path** (along the outside of the church), with thousands of colorful votive candles. Before you leave the inner courtyard, pop in to the humble little room with the many votive offerings left as part of a prayer request or as thanks for divine intercession.

Rick's Tip: *If you're here late in the afternoon,* **check the funicular schedule** *before heading up to Sant Joan Chapel or down to the Sacred Cave to make sure you'll get back in time. You wouldn't want to miss the final ride down the mountain to* **catch the train to Barcelona.**

▲SANT JOAN FUNICULAR AND HIKES
This funicular climbs 820 feet above the monastery in five minutes. At the top, you are at the starting point of a 20-minute walk that takes you to the Sant Joan Chapel (follow sign for *Ermita de St. Joan*). Other hikes also begin at the trailhead by the funicular (get details from TI before you ascend). The most popular is a 45-minute, mostly downhill loop back to the monastery (go left from the funicular station; the trail—marked *Monestir de Montserrat*—will first go up to a rocky crest before heading downhill).

Cost and Hours: Funicular—€8.45 one-way, €13 round-trip, covered by Trans Montserrat and Tot Montserrat combo-tickets, goes every 20 minutes.

SACRED CAVE (SANTA COVA)
The Moreneta was originally discovered in the Sacred Cave, a 40-minute hike down from the monastery. The path (c. 1900), designed by Modernista architects including Gaudí and Josep Puig i Cadafalch, is lined with Modernista statues corresponding to the Mysteries of the Rosary. A three-minute funicular ride cuts 20 minutes off the hike.

Cost and Hours: Funicular—€3.40 one-way, €5.20 round-trip, €16.50 combo round-trip for both Sant Joan and Santa Cova, covered by Trans Montserrat and Tot Montserrat combo-tickets, goes every 20 minutes, more often with demand.

Eating

Montserrat is designed to feed hordes of pilgrims and tourists: You'll find cafeterias, restaurants, bars, and a grocery store with simple sandwiches. But the best option is to **pack a picnic** from Barcelona, especially if you plan to hike.

Dalí Theater-Museum in Figueres

The town of Figueres (feeg-YEHR-ehs), an hour from Barcelona by fast train, is of sightseeing interest mainly for its ▲▲▲ Salvador Dalí Theater-Museum. Ever the entertainer and promoter, Dalí personally conceptualized, designed, decorated, and painted it to showcase his life's work. The museum fills a former theater and contains the artist's mausoleum (his tomb is in the crypt below center stage). It's also a kind of mausoleum to Dalí's creative spirit.

Getting There

Figueres has two train stations on opposite sides of town: **Figueres-Vilafant** (served by about hourly high-speed train from Barcelona's Sants station) and **Figueres** (slower regional train departs from Barcelona's Sants station or from the Renfe station at Metro: Passeig de Gràcia; hourly).

From Figueres-Vilafant station, take the **bus** marked *Estació AVE-Figueres* (€1.70, buy ticket from driver), and get off at the Rambla stop—ask the driver for the museum. **Taxis** charge €10 to and from the station. From Figueres station, simply follow *Museu Dalí* signs (and the crowds) for the 15-minute walk to the museum.

Orientation

Cost: €14; purchase a timed-entry ticket online in advance. Your ticket includes the nearby Museu Empordà (two floors of Catalan paintings).

Dalí Theater-Museum

Hours: July-Sept daily 9:00-20:00; April-June same hours but closed Mon, Oct-March Tue-Sun 9:30-18:00—except from 10:30 Nov-Feb, closed Mon; last entry 45 minutes before closing, tel. 972-677-500, www.salvador-dali.org.

Rick's Tip: *It's important to* **reserve ahead online** *for the Salvador Dalí Theater-Museum, which can be a mob scene, especially when bad weather drives beach crowds here. You can make a reservation as little as two hours in advance.*

Visiting the Museum: Dalí worked here over many years and personally designed the core of the museum (Rooms 1 through 18). Even the building's exterior—painted pink, studded with golden loaves of bread, and topped with monumental eggs and a geodesic dome—exudes the artist's outrageous public persona. There's no logical order for a visit (that would be un-Surrealistic). I've written this loose commentary to attach some meaning to your visit.

Courtyard (Ground Floor): Step into the courtyard (with its audience of golden statues) and face the stage (visible through the window wall). You know how you can never get a cab when it's raining? Pop a coin into Dalí's personal 1941 Cadillac and it rains inside the car. Look above, atop the tire tower: That's the boat Dalí enjoyed with his soul mate, Gala—his emotional life preserver, who kept him from going overboard.

Stage/Cupola (Ground Floor): Now cross through the courtyard and go up to the stage. On the left, squint at the big digital Abraham Lincoln, and president #16 comes into focus. Approach the painting to find that Abe's facial cheeks are Gala's butt cheeks—or use the coin-operated telescope (at the far end) or your phone's camera to focus on his face.

Treasures Room (Ground Floor): Under Lincoln, a door leads to Room 4, with the best collection of original Dalí oil paintings in the museum. (Many artworks displayed elsewhere in the building are prints.) You'll see Cubist visions of Dalí's hometown and dreamy portraits of Gala.

Downstairs Crypt (Lower Level): Make your way downstairs, below the

Salvador Dalí (1904-1989)

Born in Figueres to a well-off family, Dalí showed talent early. After a breakthrough art exhibit in Barcelona in 1925, Dalí moved to Paris. He hobnobbed with fellow Spaniards Pablo Picasso and Joan Miró, along with a group of artists exploring Sigmund Freud's theory that we all have a hidden part of our mind, the unconscious "id," which surfaces when we dream. Dalí became the best-known spokesman for this group of Surrealists, channeling his id to create photorealistic dream images (melting watches, burning giraffes) set in bizarre dreamscapes.

His life changed forever in 1929, when he met an older, married Russian woman named Gala who would become his wife, muse, model, manager, and emotional compass. Dalí's popularity spread to the US, where he (and Gala) weathered the WWII years.

In the prime of his career, Dalí's work became less Surrealist and more classical, influenced by past masters of painted realism (Velázquez, Raphael, Ingres) and by his own study of history, science, and religion. He produced paintings of historical events (e.g., Columbus discovering America, the Last Supper) that were collages of realistic scenes floating in surrealistic landscapes, peppered with cryptic symbols.

Dalí—an extremely capable technician—mastered many media, including film. *An Andalusian Dog* (*Un Chien Andalou*, 1929, with Luis Buñuel) was a cutting-edge montage of disturbing, eyeball-slicing images. He designed Alfred Hitchcock's big-eye backdrop for the dream sequence of *Spellbound* (1945). He made jewels for the rich and clothes for Coco Chanel, wrote a novel and an autobiography, and pioneered what would come to be called "installations." He also helped develop "performance art" by showing up at an opening in a diver's suit or by playing the role he projected to the media—a super-confident, waxed-mustached artistic genius.

stage, and pay respect at the artist's crypt, within dimly lit rooms filled with golden sculptures.

Mae West Room (First Floor): Back upstairs and to the right (as you face the stage), head into the famous Mae West Room (Room 11), a tribute to the sultry seductress. Dalí loved her attitude. Climb to the vantage point where the sofa lips, fireplace nostrils, painting eyes, and drapery hair come together to make the face of Mae West.

Smoking Lounge (First Floor): Circle around to Room 15, with purple walls, labeled "Palace of the Wind" (just above the entrance). Formerly the theater's smoking lounge, it displays portraits of Gala and Dalí (with a big eye, big ear, and a dark side) bookending a Roman candle of creativity. The fascinating ceiling painting shows the feet of Gala and Dalí as they bridge the earth and the heavens.

Nearby: As you leave the theater through the turnstile gate, hook right around the corner to pop into the adjacent, not-to-be-missed Dalí's Jewels exhibit (*Dalí-Joies,* covered by your theater ticket). It shows sketches and paintings of jewelry Dalí designed, and the actual pieces jewelers made from those surreal visions.

BEST OF THE REST

BASQUE COUNTRY

Stretching about 100 miles—from Bilbao, Spain, north to Bayonne, France—the ancient, free-spirited land of the Basques is famous for its beaches, culinary scene, and scintillating modern architecture. It's also simply beautiful.

San Sebastián, with its sparkling, picturesque beach framed by looming green mountains, has a charming old town with gourmet *pintxos* (tapas) spilling out of every bar. On-the-rise **Bilbao** is worth a look for its landmark Guggenheim Museum and its atmospheric old town. The thriving town of **Pamplona** hosts the world-famous Running of the Bulls.

One day is enough for a quick sample of the Basque Country, but two or three days lets you breathe deep and hold it in. If you want to slow down and focus on Spain, spend one day relaxing in San Sebastián and the second side-tripping to Bilbao. For a third day, add Pamplona.

The Basque Country is connected by good roads and public transportation. Buses generally run faster and more frequently than trains. Drivers can choose between speedy toll roads or the free, scenic back roads with lots of twists and turns.

San Sebastián

Shimmering above the breathtaking Concha Bay, elegant and prosperous San Sebastián ("Donostia" in Euskara, the Basque language) has a favored location with golden beaches, capped by twin peaks at either end and a cute little island offshore. With a romantic setting, a soaring statue of Christ gazing over the city, and a late-night lively old town, San Sebastián has a mini Rio de Janeiro aura. It's also one of Spain's culinary capitals.

Day Plan

Stroll the two-mile-long beach promenade with the locals, and explore the old town and port. Enjoy the delightful aquarium, Monte Urgull, or the Museum of San Telmo, focusing on Basque culture. A key ingredient of any visit to San Sebastián is enjoying *pintxos* in the old-town bars.

Orientation

San Sebastián can be divided into three areas: Playa de la Concha (best beaches), the shopping district (Centro), and the grid-planned old town (Parte Vieja). A busy drag called Alameda del Boulevard (or just "Boulevard") stands where the city wall once ran, and separates the Centro from the old town. It's all bookended by Monte Urgull on the east end of the bay, and Monte Igueldo to the west.

Tourist Information: San Sebastián's TIs are located at Alameda del Boulevard 8 and next to the Renfe train station (both open daily, tel. 943-481-166, www.sansebastianturismo.com).

Local Guides: For cultural or food tours, consider Agustin Ciriza (€160/group for city tours, www.gorilla-trip.com) or Gabriella Ranelli (€295/half-day, www.tenedortours.com).

Getting There

San Sebastián has two train stations: Renfe (long-distance destinations within Spain) and Amara EuskoTren (Basque destinations). The Renfe station is just across the river from the Centro shopping district. To get to the old town, you can walk 10-15 minutes, catch bus #9 to the Boulevard stop (€1.75, pay driver onboard), or take a taxi (€6.20). Most **buses** arrive at the underground bus station located next to the Renfe station.

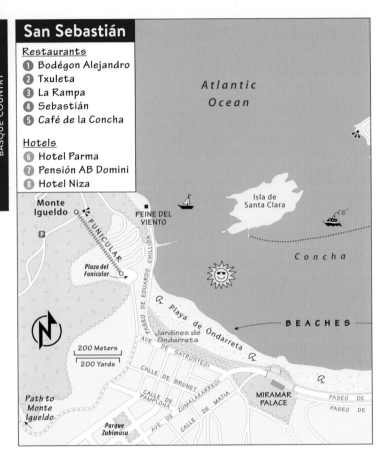

San Sebastián

Restaurants
1. Bodégon Alejandro
2. Txuleta
3. La Rampa
4. Sebastián
5. Café de la Concha

Hotels
6. Hotel Parma
7. Pensión AB Domini
8. Hotel Niza

Atlantic Ocean

Isla de Santa Clara

PEINE DEL VIENTO

Monte Igueldo

FUNICULAR

Plaza del Funicular

Concha

PASEO DE EDUARDO CHILLIDA

Playa de Ondarreta

Jardínes de Ondarreta

BEACHES

AVE. DE SATRUSTEGI

200 Meters
200 Yards

CALLE DE BRUNET

CALLE DE PAMPLONA

CALLE DE ZUMALAKARREGI

AVE. DE ZUMALAKARREGI

CALLE DE MATIA

MIRAMAR PALACE

PASEO DE
PASEO DE

Path to Monte Igueldo

Parque Zubimusu

The EuskoTren station is directly south of Centro, about 15 minutes on foot from the old town (or catch bus #21, #26, or #28).

An easy regional bus (#E21) connects the **San Sebastián airport** to Plaza de Gipuzkoa in town (about hourly, 35 minutes, www.ekialdebus.net). A taxi into town costs about €38.

Drivers should take the Amara freeway exit, follow *Centro Ciudad* signs into the city center, and park in a pay lot (many are well-signed—the Kursaal underground lot is the most central).

Sights

▲▲OLD TOWN (PARTE VIEJA)

Huddled in the shadow of its once-protective Monte Urgull, the old town is where San Sebastián was born about 1,000 years ago. The grid plan of streets hides heavy Baroque and Gothic churches, surprise plazas, and fun little shops, including venerable pastry stores, rugged produce markets, Basque-independence souvenir shops, and seafood-to-go delis. The highlight of the old town is its array of incredibly lively tapas bars.

The main square, Plaza de la Constitución, is where bullfights used to be held. Notice the seat numbering on the balco-

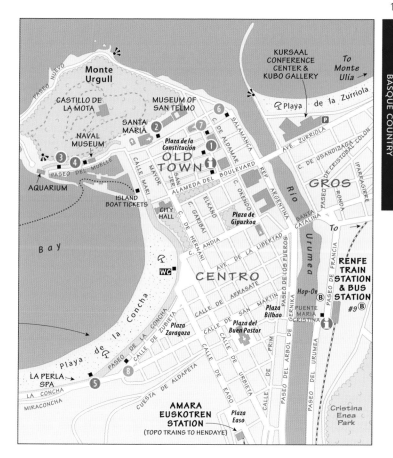

nies: The city retained rights to the balconies, which it could sell as box seats.

▲▲MUSEUM OF SAN TELMO (SAN TELMO MUSEOA)

This fascinating place is the largest museum of Basque culture in Spain and well worth a visit. Exhibits of archaeological and ethnographic artifacts demonstrate the traditional folkways of Basque life and vividly tell the history of the region. Its art collection features a few old-school gems (El Greco, Rubens, Tintoretto), while 19th- and 20th-century paintings by Basque artists offer an interesting glimpse into their spirit.

Cost and Hours: €6, free on Tue, open Tue-Sun 10:00-20:00, closed Mon,

Plaza Zuloaga 1, tel. 943-481-580, www.santelmomuseoa.eus.

▲BRETXA PUBLIC MARKET (MERCADO DE LA BRETXA)

Wandering through the public market is a fun way to get in touch with San Sebastián and Basque culture. Although the sandstone market building has been converted into a modern shopping complex, the farmers' produce market thrives here (lined up outside along the side of the mall), as does the fish and meat market (underground—to get there, find the big glass cube in the square, where an escalator takes you down).

Hours: Mon-Sat 8:00-21:00, closed Sun, Bretxa Plaza.

Who Are the Basques?

So just who are the Basques? Even for Basques, that's a difficult question. Widespread Spanish and French immigration has made it difficult to know who actually has Basque ethnic roots. And so today, anyone who speaks the Basque language, Euskara, is considered a Basque. With its seemingly impossible-to-pronounce words filled with k's, tx's, and z's (restrooms are *komunak: gizonak* for men and *emakumeak* for women), Euskara makes speaking Spanish suddenly seem easy. Kept alive as a symbol of Basque cultural identity, Euskara typically is learned proudly as a second or third language.

Basque sailors were some of the first and finest in Europe, as they built ever-better boats to venture farther into the Atlantic in search of whales and cod. By the mid-15th century, they were venturing a thousand miles from home into the far northern Atlantic Ocean. Despite lack of physical evidence, many historians surmise that the Basques must have sailed to Newfoundland before Christopher Columbus landed in the Caribbean.

When the Spanish era of exploration began, Basques played a key role as sailors and shipbuilders. Columbus' *Santa María* was likely Basque built, and his crew included many Basques. History books teach that Ferdinand Magellan was the first to circumnavigate the globe, with the footnote that he was killed partway around. Who took over the helm for the rest of the journey, completing the circle? It was his Basque captain, Juan Sebastián de Elcano. And a pair of well-traveled Catholic priests, known for their far-reaching missionary trips that led to founding the Jesuit order, were also Basques: St. Ignatius of Loyola and St. Francis Xavier.

Rick's Tip: *Small* **boats cruise from the old town's port to the island** *in the bay (Isla de Santa Clara), where you can* **hike the trails**—*pack a picnic before setting sail (€4 round-trip, www.motorasdelaisla.com).*

▲▲AQUARIUM

San Sebastián's aquarium is surprisingly good. Upstairs are displays on whaling, shipbuilding, legal versus illegal pirating, fishing, and local oceanography. Downstairs, a mesmerizing 45-foot-long tunnel is filled with more than 30 local species of sea life, flopping and flying over you in a tank holding nearly 400,000 gallons of water.

Cost and Hours: €13, €6.50 for kids under 13; daily 10:00-21:00, closes earlier in off-season, last entry one hour before closing; audioguide-€2, at the end of Paseo del Muelle, tel. 943-440-099, www.aquariumss.com.

▲MONTE URGULL

This hill and park area watches over the old town. The once-mighty castle (Castillo de la Mota) atop the hill deterred most attackers, allowing the city to prosper in the Middle Ages. The free **Casa de la Historia** museum within the castle covers San Sebastián history; it has access to the statue of Christ's view over the city. But the best views from the hill are from the **Battery of Santiago** ramparts (to Christ's far right). Bring a picnic or stop by the free-spirited **Café El Polvorín** for good sangria and picturesque vistas. Near sea level, a walkway allows you to stroll the mountain's entire perimeter (from Hotel Parma to the aquarium).

▲▲LA CONCHA BEACH AND PROMENADE

The shell-shaped Playa de la Concha, the pride of San Sebastián, has one of

San Sebastián's beach and Monte Urgull

Europe's loveliest stretches of sand. Lined with a two-mile-long promenade, it allows even backpackers to feel aristocratic. There are free showers, and *cabinas* provide lockers, showers, and shade for a fee.

$$ Café de la Concha serves reasonably priced, mediocre food, but you can't beat the location of its terrace overlooking the beach.

Eating

Pintxo Bar-Hopping: Basque tapas bars distinguish themselves by laying out big platters of help-yourself goodies. This user-friendly system lets you point to—or simply take—what looks good. If you can't get the bartender's attention to serve you a particular *pintxo,* don't be shy—watch other people; if they are serving themselves, grab what you want and munch away. You pay when you leave; just keep a mental note of the tapas you've eaten.

San Sebastián's old town provides the ideal backdrop for tapas-hopping. Calle Fermín Calbetón has the best concentration of bars; the streets San Jerónimo and 31 de Agosto are also good. Most places are open from around noon to 15:00, close for the afternoon, then reopen in the evening.

Restaurants in the Old Town: For places serving modern Basque cuisine, try **$$$ Bodégon Alejandro** (closed Sun night and Mon, Calle Fermín Calbetón 4) or **$$ Txuleta** (closed Mon evening and Tue, Plaza de la Trinidad 2). For seafood along the port, there's the upscale **$$$$ La Rampa** (closed Wed, Paseo del Muelle 26) or the more traditional **$$$ Sebastián** (closed Tue, Paseo del Muelle 14).

Sleeping

To sleep near the old town, try the well-located **$$$$ Hotel Parma** (RS%, www.hotelparma.com) or the delightful **$$$ Pensión AB Domini** (San Juan 8, www.abpensiones.es). **$$$$ Hotel Niza** is right on the beach (Zubieta 56, www.hotelniza.com).

Bilbao

In recent years, Bilbao (bil-BOW, rhymes with "cow") has seen a transformation like no other Spanish city. Entire sectors of the industrial city have been cleared away to allow construction of a new convention center, shops, apartment buildings, and the stunning Guggenheim Museum.

Day Plan

For most visitors, the Guggenheim is the main draw (and many could spend the entire day there). But with a little more time, it's worth hopping on a tram to explore the atmospheric old town or taking a walk along the Nervión River promenade.

Rick's Tip: *Don't bother coming to Bilbao on* Monday, *when the* Guggenheim Museum is closed *(except July-Aug).*

Orientation

The city hugs the Nervión River as it curves through town. The Guggenheim is more or less centrally located near the top of that curve; the bus station is to the west; the old town (Casco Viejo) and train stations are to the east.

Tourist Information: Bilbao's main TI is next to the Renfe station at Plaza Circular (daily, tel. 944-795-760); there's another near the main entrance of the Guggenheim (daily, Alameda Mazarredo 66, www.bilbaoturismo.net).

Local Guide: Knowledgeable Bilbao guide Iratxe Muñoz offers tours of the city and Guggenheim (contact for rates, iratxe.m@apite.eu).

Getting There

Bilbao's **Renfe station** (serving most of Spain—Madrid: 2/day, 5 hours; Barcelona: 2/day, 7 hours; Salamanca: 3/day, 6 hours) is on the river in central Bilbao (tram stops: Abando, Arriaga).

Euskotren trains from San Sebastián arrive at the **Zazpikaleak/Casco Viejo station** (hourly, scenic 2.5-hour trip, but bus is faster) in the old town near Plaza Nueva (tram stop: Arriaga). Buses stop at the **Termibús station** (San Sebastián: 2/hour, 1.5 hours; Pamplona: 6/day, 2 hours), about a mile southwest of the Guggenheim (tram stop: San Mamés).

From Bilbao's compact **airport,** the handy, green Bizkaibus #3247 takes you directly to the city center (€1.45); a taxi into town costs about €25. **Drivers** should head to the big underground parking garage near the Guggenheim (take the exit marked *Centro* and follow signs to Guggenheim).

Getting Around: Most travelers—whether arriving by train, bus, or car—will want to go straight to the Guggenheim. Thanks to a perfectly planned **tram system** (EuskoTren Tranbia), this couldn't be easier. From any point of entry, simply buy a €1.50 single-ride ticket at a user-friendly green machine (€4.40 for an all-day pass, www.euskotren.es).

Sights

▲▲▲GUGGENHEIM BILBAO

Even if you're not turned on by contemporary art, the Guggenheim building itself—designed by Frank Gehry—is a must-see experience. Its 20 galleries, on three floors, are full of surprises, and it's well worth the entry fee just to appreciate the museum's structural design, which is a masterpiece in itself.

Cost and Hours: €13, includes audioguide; Tue-Sun 10:00-20:00, closed Mon except in July-Aug; café, tram stop: Guggenheim, Avenida Abandoibarra 2, tel. 944-359-080, www.guggenheim-bilbao.es.

Tours: A free and excellent audioguide is included with a regular entry ticket. The museum offers two free guided tours in English: a 30-minute tour of the art on exhibit (Mon-Fri at 17:00, Sat-Sun at 12:30), and a 60-minute tour about the building (Mon-Fri at 12:30, Sat-Sun at 17:00). Show up at least 30 minutes early to put your name on the list at the information desk.

Guggenheim Bilbao

Visiting the Museum: Guarding the main entrance is artist Jeff Koons' 42-foot-tall **West Highland Terrier.** Its 60,000 plants and flowers, which blossom in concert, grow through steel mesh. Although the sculpture was originally intended to be temporary, the people of Bilbao fell in love with *Puppy*—so they bought it.

Enter the **atrium.** This acts as the heart of the building, pumping visitors from various rooms on three levels out and back. The architect invites you to caress the sensual curves of the walls. There are virtually no straight lines (except the floor). Notice the sheets of glass that make up the staircase and elevator shafts—overlapping each other like a fish's scales.

From the atrium, step out onto the riverside **terrace.** The "water garden" lets the river symbolically lap at the base of the building. The terrace is home to some unusual sculptures, including a 30-foot-tall bronze and steel **spider** (by French-American artist Louise Bourgeois).

Step back inside. Gehry designed the vast **ground floor** mainly to house often huge modern-art installations. While most of the collection comes and goes, Richard Serra's enormous *Matter of Time* sculpture in the largest gallery (#104) is permanent. Who would want to move those massive metal coils?

You can't fully enjoy the museum's architecture without taking a stroll up and down each side of the river along the handsome promenade and over the two modern **pedestrian bridges.** The building's skin—shiny and metallic, with a scale-like texture—is made of thin titanium, carefully created to give just the desired color and reflective quality.

FUNICULAR DE ARTXANDA

Opened in 1915, this funicular still provides *bilbainos* with a green escape. The three-minute ride offers sweeping views of the city on the way to the top of Mount Artxanda, where there's a park,

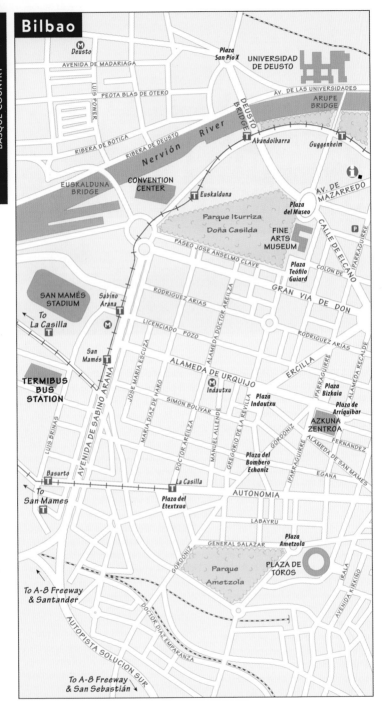

Bilbao

Deusto

AVENIDA DE MADARIAGA

PEOTA BLAS DE OTERO

LUIS POWER

Plaza San Pío X

UNIVERSIDAD DE DEUSTO

AV. DE LAS UNIVERSIDADES

ARUPE BRIDGE

DEUSTO BRIDGE

RIBERA DE BOTICA

RIBERA DE DEUSTO

Nervión River

Abándoibarra

Guggenheim

EUSKALDUNA BRIDGE

CONVENTION CENTER

Euskalduna

Parque Iturriza Doña Casilda

Plaza del Museo

AV. DE MAZARREDO

FINE ARTS MUSEUM

CALLE DE ELCANO

PASEO JOSE ANSELMO CLAVE

Plaza Teófilo Guiard

PARRAGUIRRE

SAN MAMÉS STADIUM

Sabino Arana

RODRIGUEZ ARIAS

GRAN VIA DE DON

COLON DE

To La Casilla

LICENCIADO POZO

ALAMEDA DOCTOR AREILZA

RODRIGUEZ ARIAS

San Mamés

JOSE MARIA ESCUZA

ALAMEDA DE URQUIJO

ERCILLA

ALAMEDA RECALDE

TERMIBUS BUS STATION

AVENIDA DE SABINO ARANA

MARIA DIAZ DE HARO

SIMÓN BOLIVAR

Indautxu

MANUEL ALLENDE

Plaza Indautxu

PARRAGUIRRE

Plaza Bizkaia

Plaza de Arriquibar

AZKUNA ZENTROA

DOCTOR AREILZA

GREGORIO DE LA REVILLA

GORDONIZ

IPARRAGUIRRE

ALAMEDA DE SAN MAMES

FERNANDEZ

LUIS BRIÑAS

Basurto

Plaza del Bombero Echaniz

EGANA

To San Mames

La Casilla

AUTONOMIA

Plaza del Etextxua

LABAYRU

GORDONIZ

GENERAL SALAZAR

Plaza Ametzola

To A-8 Freeway & Santander

Parque Ametzola

PLAZA DE TOROS

IRALA

AVENIDA KIRKINO

DOCTOR DIAZ EMPARANZA

AUTOPISTA SOLUCION SUR

To A-8 Freeway & San Sebastián

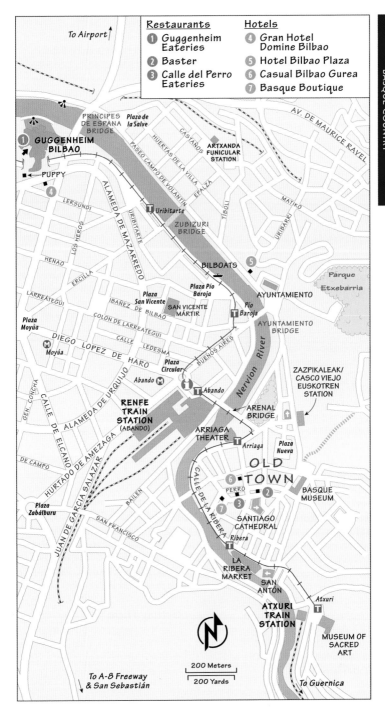

Restaurants
1 Guggenheim Eateries
2 Baster
3 Calle del Perro Eateries

Hotels
4 Gran Hotel Domine Bilbao
5 Hotel Bilbao Plaza
6 Casual Bilbao Gurea
7 Basque Boutique

To Airport

PRINCIPES DE ESPAÑA BRIDGE
Plaza de la Salve

1 GUGGENHEIM BILBAO

PUPPY

4

CASTAÑOS

HUERTAS DE LA VILLA

EPALZA

ARTXANDA FUNICULAR STATION

AV. DE MAURICE RAVEL

PASEO CAMPO DE VOLANTIN

ALAMEDA DE MAZARREDO

URIBITARTE

LERSUNDI

LOS HEROS

HENAO

ERCILLA

LARREATEGUI

Plaza Moyúa

DIEGO LOPEZ DE HARO

Moyúa

GEN. CONCHA

CALLE DE ELCANO

ALAMEDA DE URQUIJO

DE CAMPO

JUAN DE GARCIA SALAZAR

HURTADO DE AMEZAGA

BAILEN

SAN FRANCISCO

Plaza Zabálburu

IBAÑEZ DE BILBAO

COLÓN DE LARREATEGUI

CALLE LEDESMA

Plaza San Vicente

SAN VICENTE MÁRTIR

Uribitarte

ZUBIZURI BRIDGE

BILBOATS

Plaza Pío Baroja

Pío Baroja

AYUNTAMIENTO

MATIKO

URIBARRI

TIBOLI

Parque Etxebarria

5

AYUNTAMIENTO BRIDGE

Nervion River

BUENOS AIRES

Plaza Circular

Abando

Abando

RENFE TRAIN STATION (ABANDO)

ARENAL BRIDGE

ARRIAGA THEATER

Arriaga

Plaza Nueva

ZAZPIKALEAK/ CASCO VIEJO EUSKOTREN STATION

OLD TOWN

6 PERRO
7 3 2

SANTIAGO CATHEDRAL

Ribera

LA RIBERA MARKET

SAN ANTÓN

ATXURI TRAIN STATION

Atxuri

BASQUE MUSEUM

MUSEUM OF SACRED ART

Calle de la Ribera

To A-8 Freeway & San Sebastián

N

200 Meters
200 Yards

To Guernica

restaurants, and a sports complex. Bring a picnic on a sunny afternoon.

Cost and Hours: €3.25 round-trip, leaves every 15 minutes, daily 7:15-22:00, until 23:00 in summer; Plaza del Funicular.

OLD TOWN

Bilbao's old town, with tall, narrow lanes lined with thriving shops and tapas bars, is worth a stroll. Wind up to Old Bilbao's centerpiece, the **Santiago Cathedral,** a 14th-century Gothic church with a tranquil interior that has been scrubbed clean inside and out (€5 combo-ticket includes audioguide, daily July-Aug 10:00-21:00, Sept-June until 19:00, Plaza Santiago 1).

On a quick visit, the only old-town museum worth considering is the **Basque Museum** (Euskal Museoa), showing lovingly assembled artifacts of Basque heritage in a 16th-century convent (€3, Mon and Wed-Fri 10:00-19:00, Sat 10:00-13:30 & 16:00-19:00, Sun 10:00-14:00, closed Tue, Miguel de Unamuno Plaza 4, www. euskal-museoa.org/es).

Picknickers like the **Ribera Market** (Mercado de la Ribera). Stroll the stalls for the freshest fish, shop for produce, and admire a series of Art Deco stained-glass panels on the top floor. There's a stylish *cervecería* and a few *pintxo* bars on the ground floor (closed Sun).

Eating

Near the Guggenheim Museum, the easiest choice is the good **$$$ bar** in the museum itself or the adjacent, more chic **$$$ Bistro** (reservations smart, www. bistroguggenheimbilbao.com). In the Old Town you'll find plenty of options on the lanes near the cathedral. I like the hip little bar **$$ Baster** (just behind the cathedral, closed Mon), but it's worth checking out the offerings on Calle del Perro, including **$$ Xukela Bar,** for tasty tapas, and three sit-down restaurants virtually next door to each other: **Egiluz, Río-Oja,** and **Rotterdam.**

Sleeping

Near the Guggenheim Museum, **$$$$ Gran Hotel Domine Bilbao** is the place for well-heeled modern-art fans (Alameda Mazarredo 61, www. hoteldominebilbao.com). In the old town, try the bright and modern **$$ Hotel Bilbao Plaza** (Paseo Campo Volantín 1, www.hotelbilbaoplaza.com), the well-priced **$$ Casual Bilbao Gurea** (Calle Bidebarrieta 14, www.casualgurea.com,) or the classy **$$ Basque Boutique** (Calle de la Torre 2, www.basqueboutique.es).

Pamplona

Proud Pamplona is best known as the host of one of Spain's (and Europe's) most famous festivals: the Running of the Bulls (held in conjunction with the Fiesta de San Fermín, July 6-14). But there's more to this town than bulls—and, in fact, visiting at other times is preferable to the crowds and 24/7 party atmosphere that seize Pamplona during the festival.

Day Plan

Take my "Pamplona Walk" to trace the path of the Running of the Bulls, then visit the bullring exhibit.

Orientation

Most everything of interest is in the tight, twisting lanes of the old town, centered on the main square, Plaza del Castillo.

Tourist Information: Pamplona's TI is located next to City Hall (daily, closed Mon off-season and during Fiesta de San Fermín, Calle San Saturnino 2, tel. 948-420-700, www.turismodepamplona.es).

Local Guide: Francisco Glaría is top-notch (€140/half-day, www.novotur.com).

Getting There

Note that Pamplona's **bus station** is closer to the old town (about 10 minutes on foot) than the train station, and that some connections are faster by bus (San Sebastián: 10/day, 1 hour; Bilbao: 6/day, 2 hours; Madrid: 8/day—most with transfer, 6 hours).

The **Renfe station** is farther from the center, across the river to the northwest (San Sebastián: 3/day, 2 hours; Madrid: 6/day direct, 3.5 hours). It's easiest to hop on public bus #9 (€1.35, every 15 minutes) to the big Plaza Príncipe de Viana traffic circle, south of the old town.

Drivers will find handy **parking** right at Plaza del Castillo and Plaza de Toros, where the bullring is. From Pamplona's **airport,** a taxi to the city center costs around €12.

Rick's Tip: *Visit the last weekend in September for* **a fiesta with no bull:** *San Fermín Txikito is practically tourist-free, featuring concerts, brass bands, food competitions, and parades of giant mannequins.*

◯ *Pamplona Walk*

Even if you're not in town for the famous San Fermín festival, you can still get a good flavor of the town by following in the foot- and hoof-steps of its participants. This self-guided walk takes you through the town center along the same route of the famous Running of the Bulls.

• *Begin by the river, at the...*

Bull Corral: During the San Fermín festival, the bulls are released from here at 8:00 each morning. They first run up Cuesta de Santo Domingo; signs labeled *El Encierro* mark their route. Follow them.

• *A few blocks ahead on the right is the...*

Museum of Navarre (Museo de Navarra): This museum, worth ▲, has four floors of artifacts and paintings celebrating the art of this region, from prehistoric to modern (€2, free Sat afternoons and all day Sun, open Tue-Sat 9:30-14:00 & 17:00-19:00, Sun 11:00-14:00, closed Mon, Santo Domingo 47, www.museodenavarra.navarra.es). Check out the **adjoining church** (on the left as you exit,

show museum ticket), with its impressive golden Baroque-Rococo altarpiece depicting the Annunciation.

• *Continue along Cuesta de Santo Domingo. Embedded in the wall on your right, look for the small shrine containing an image of San Fermín. Farther up on your left is the food market of Santo Domingo, and ahead in the square is...*

City Hall (Ayuntamiento): The festival of San Fermín begins and ends on the balcony of this building (with the flags). Look in the direction you just came (the route of the bulls), and find the line of metal squares in the pavement—used to secure barricades for the run. The inner space is for journalists and emergency medical care; spectators line up along the outer barrier.

• *Follow the route of the bulls two blocks down Calle de Mercaderes to the intersection with Calle de la Estafeta. Turn right onto...*

Calle de la Estafeta: At this turn, the bulls—who are now going downhill—begin to lose their balance, often sliding into the barricade. Once the bulls regain their footing, they charge up the middle of La Estafeta. Notice how narrow the street is: No room for barricades...no escape for the daredevils trying to outrun the bulls.

Partway down the first block on the right, look for the hole-in-the-wall **Pastas Caseras Beatriz** shop (at #22)—most locals just call it "Beatriz"—makers of the best chocolate treats in Pamplona.

• *La Estafeta eventually leads you right to Pamplona's...*

Bullring (Plaza de Toros): Here's where the bulls meet their fate, but it's used for bullfights only nine days each summer (during the festival).

Look for the big bust of **Ernest Hemingway,** celebrated by Pamplona as if he were a native son. Hemingway came here for the first time during the 1923 Running of the Bulls. Inspired by the spectacle and the gore, he later wrote about the event in his classic *The Sun Also Rises.* He said

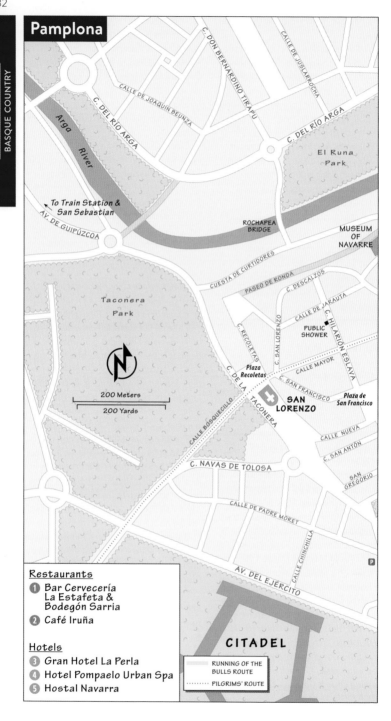

Pamplona

CALLE DE JUSLARROCHA

C. DON BERNARDINO TRAPU

CALLE DE JOAQUÍN BEUNZA

C. DEL RÍO ARGA

C. DEL RÍO ARGA

Arga River

El Runa Park

To Train Station & San Sebastian

AV. DE GUIPÚZCOA

ROCHAPEA BRIDGE

MUSEUM OF NAVARRE

CUESTA DE CURTIDORES

PASEO DE RONDA

C. DESCALZOS

CALLE DE JARAUTA

Taconera Park

C. RECOLETAS

C. SAN LORENZO

C. HILARIÓN ESLAVA

PUBLIC SHOWER

CALLE MAYOR

Plaza Recoletas

C. DE LA TACONERA

C. SAN FRANCISCO

SAN LORENZO

Plaza de San Francisco

200 Meters

200 Yards

CALLE BOSQUECILLO

CALLE NUEVA

C. SAN ANTÓN

C. NAVAS DE TOLOSA

SAN GREGORIO

CALLE DE PADRE MORET

CALLE CHINCHILLA

AV. DEL EJÉRCITO

CITADEL

Restaurants

1 Bar Cervecería
   La Estafeta &
   Bodegón Sarria
2 Café Iruña

Hotels

3 Gran Hotel La Perla
4 Hotel Pompaelo Urban Spa
5 Hostal Navarra

RUNNING OF THE BULLS ROUTE

PILGRIMS' ROUTE

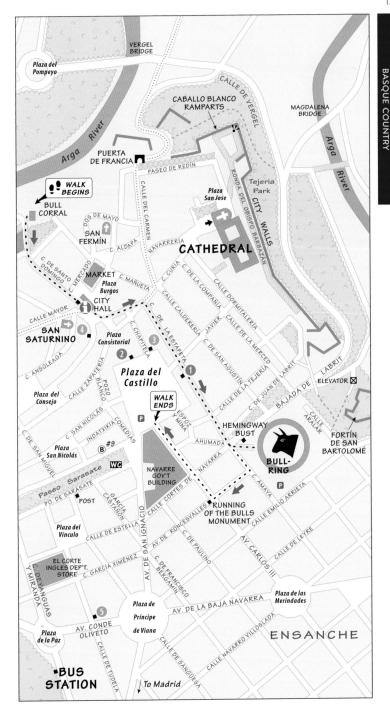

Pamplona's Running of the Bulls

Running of the Bulls monument

that he enjoyed seeing two wild animals running together: one on two legs, and the other on four.

If you've always wanted to **tour a bullring,** this is your chance. The city recently opened an exhibit (worth ▲) that gives a behind-the-scenes look at this iconic space (€6, audioguide included, April-Oct Tue-Sat 10:30-19:30, Sun until 14:30, closed Mon; Feb-March weekends only 10:30-14:30, closed Nov-Jan; tel. 948-225-389, www.feriadeltoro.com).

• *Walk 20 yards while keeping the bullring on your left, then cross the busy street and walk a block into the pedestrian zone (on Avenida de Roncesvalles) to the life-size...*

Running of the Bulls Monument (Monumento al Encierro): This statue shows 6 bulls, 2 steer, and 10 runners in action. Find the self-portrait of the sculptor (bald, lying down, and about to be gored). The statue has quickly become a local favorite.

• *Facing the monument, turn right and walk two blocks up the street to the main square...*

Plaza del Castillo: While not as grand as Spain's top squares, Pamplona's has something particularly cozy and livable about it. Several Hemingway sights surround this square. The recommended Gran Hotel La Perla, in the corner, was his

favorite place to stay. It recently underwent a head-to-toe five-star renovation, but Hemingway's room was kept exactly as he liked it. He also was known to frequent Bar Txoko at the corner opposite La Perla (as well as pretty much every other bar in town) and the venerable Café Iruña, which has a separate "Hemingway Corner" room, with a life-size statue of "Papa" to pose with.

Eating

The best concentration of trendy tapas bars is on and near Calle de la Estafeta; my favorites here are **$$ Bar Cervecería La Estafeta** (at #54) and **$$ Bodegón Sarria** (at #52). On Plaza del Castillo (#44), **$$$ Café Iruña** clings to its connection to Hemingway; while the food is mediocre, the ambience is great.

Sleeping

$$$$ Gran Hotel La Perla is the town's undisputed top splurge (Plaza del Castillo 1, www.granhotellaperla.com). **$$ Hotel Pompaelo Urban Spa** has 30 modern rooms located just next to the City Hall (Plaza Consistorial 3, www.hotelpompaelo.com). **$ Hostal Navarra** is the best value in Pamplona (RS%, Calle Tudela 9, www.hostalnavarra.com).

BEST OF THE REST

Santiago de Compostela

Santiago de Compostela has long had a powerful and mysterious draw on travelers: More than a thousand years' worth of Christian pilgrims have trod the desolate Camino de Santiago trail across the north of Spain with this glorious cathedral as their destination. If you decide to visit, you—like a millennium's worth of pilgrims before you—will find it's worth the trek.

Day Plan

The city has one real sight: the cathedral, with its fine museum and the surrounding squares. The rest of your visit is for munching seafood, pilgrim-watching, and browsing the stony streets. The highlight of a visit just may be hanging out on the cathedral square at about 10:00 to welcome pilgrims completing their long journey.

Orientation

The tourist's Santiago is small: You can walk across the historical center in about 20 minutes. There you'll find the city's centerpiece—the awe-inspiring cathedral—as well as several other churches, a maze of pretty squares, a smattering of small muse-

ums, and a bustling restaurant scene.

Tourist Information: The **TI** is at Rúa do Vilar 63 (daily, tel. 981-555-129, www.santiagoturismo.com).

Local Guides: The going rate is about €100 for 3.5 hours. **Patricia Furelos** (patriciafurelos@yahoo.es) and **Manuel Ruzo** (manuel@artnaturagalicia.com) are equally good.

Getting There

Santiago's biggest downside is its location: Except by air, it's a very long trip from any other notable stop in Spain (by train from Madrid: 6/day, 5.5 hours; from San Sebastián: 2/day, 10.5 hours).

The **train station** is on the southern edge of the modern Céntrico district, a 10-minute walk from the historical center. A taxi will cost about €8.

From the **bus station,** northeast of the cathedral, it's about a 15-minute, mostly downhill walk to the center. Either hop on bus #5 and take it to the market or Praza de Galicia, or grab a taxi to the center (about €8).

A bus connects the **airport** to the bus station, train station, and then to Praza de Galicia at the south end of the historical center (€3, 45 minutes, www.empresa-freire.com). A taxi into town costs €21.

There are only two **freeway** off-ramps to the city. The north exit (#67) is best for the airport and the old center. The parking lot (aparcadoiro) closest to the cathedral is 400 yards up Avenida de Xoán XXIII.

Rick's Tip: There are **beautiful views** back toward the cathedral from the city's pretty Alameda Park. From the cathedral, follow Rúa do Franco to the end, enter the park and continue up Paseo de Santa Susana to the viewpoint (mirador).

Sights

▲▲SANTIAGO CATHEDRAL (CATEDRAL DE SANTIAGO)

Santiago's cathedral isn't the biggest in Spain, nor is it the most impressive. Yet it's certainly the most mystical, exerting a spiritual magnetism that attracts people from all walks of life and from all corners of the globe. Put yourself in the well-worn shoes of the millions of pilgrims who have trekked many miles to this powerful place.

Cost and Hours: Free, daily 7:00-21:00, www.catedraldesantiago.es. Ask about guided tours at the ticket counter. Large backpacks aren't allowed in the church.

◑ SELF-GUIDED TOUR

• *Begin facing the cathedral's main facade, in the big square called...*

Praza do Obradoiro: Find the pavement stone with the scallop shell right in the middle of this square. For more than a thousand years, this spot has been where millions of tired pilgrims have taken a deep breath and thought to themselves: "I made it!" To maximize your chance of seeing pilgrims, be here at about 10:00—the last stop on the

Camino de Santiago is two miles away, and pilgrims try to get to the cathedral in time for the 12:00 Mass.

• *Bear in mind that the cathedral will be under restoration until 2021, but take a look at the...*

Cathedral Facade: Twelve hundred years ago, a monk followed a field of stars (probably the Milky Way) to the little Galician village of San Fiz de Solovio and discovered what appeared to be the long-lost tomb of St. James. On July 25, 813, the local bishop declared that St. James' remains had been found. They set to building a church here and named the place Santiago (St. James) de Compostela (*campo de estrellas,* or "field of stars," for the celestial bodies that guided the monk).

Originally a simple chapel, the cathedral you see today has gradually been added to over the last 12 centuries. Atop the middle steeple is St. James (dressed like the pilgrim he was). Beneath him is his tomb, marked by a star. On either side of the tomb are Theodorus and Athanasius, James' disciples who brought his body to Santiago. On the side pillars are, to the left, James' father, Zebedee; and to the right, his mother, Salomé.

Santiago Cathedral

The History of the Camino

The Camino de Santiago—the "Way of St. James"—is Europe's ultimate pilgrimage route. Since the Middle Ages, pilgrims have trod hundreds of miles across northern Spain to pay homage to the remains of St. James in his namesake city, Santiago de Compostela (Santiago is Spanish for St. James).

The first person to undertake the Camino de Santiago was Santiago himself. After the death of Christ, the apostles scattered to the corners of the earth to spread the Word of God. Supposedly, St. James went on a missionary trip from the Holy Land all the way to the northwest corner of Spain.

According to legend, St. James' remains were discovered in 813 in the town that would soon bear his name. This put Santiago de Compostela on the map. In 951 the bishop of Le Puy in France walked to Santiago de Compostela to pay homage to the relics. As other pilgrims followed his example, the Camino de Santiago informally emerged. Then, in the 12th century, Pope Callistus II decreed that any person who walked to Santiago in a Holy Year, confessed his or her sins, and took communion at the cathedral would be forgiven. This opportunity made the Camino de Santiago one of the most important pilgrimages in the world.

By 1130 the trek was so popular that it prompted French monk Aimery Picaud to pen a chronicle of his journey, including tips on where to eat, where to stay, the best way to get from place to place, and how to pack light and use a money belt. This *Codex Calixtinus* (Latin for "Camino Through the Back Door") was the world's first guidebook—the great-great-granddaddy of the one you're holding right now.

By the age of Columbus, the Renaissance, and the Reformation, interest in the Camino dropped way off. For the next centuries, and as recently as a few decades ago, only a few hardy souls still followed the route.

Many years later, in the late 1960s, a handful of parish priests along the Camino began working to recover the route, establishing associations of "friends of the Camino" that would eventually agree on a path and mark it. The plan worked: In 1987 the European Union designated the Camino as Europe's first Cultural Itinerary. The route has enjoyed a huge renaissance of interest, with more than 200,000 pilgrims each year trekking to Santiago.

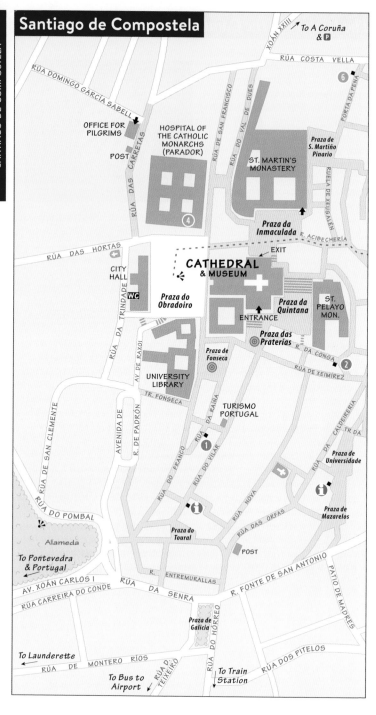

Santiago de Compostela

To A Coruña & 🅿

RÚA COSTA VELLA

6

PORTA DA PEN.

RÚA DOMINGO GARCÍA SABELL

XOÁN XXIII

OFFICE FOR PILGRIMS

POST

RÚA DAS CARRETAS

HOSPITAL OF THE CATHOLIC MONARCHS (PARADOR)

RÚA DE SAN FRANCISCO

RÚA DO VAL DE DUES

ST. MARTIN'S MONASTERY

Praza de S. Martiño Pinario

RUELA DE XEUSALEN

Praza da Inmaculada

R. ACIBECHERÍA

4

RÚA DAS HORTAS

RÚA DA TRINDADE

CITY HALL

WC

EXIT

CATHEDRAL & MUSEUM

Praza do Obradoiro

ENTRANCE

Praza da Quintana

ST. PELAYO MON.

R. DA CONGA

AV. DE RAXOL

Praza das Praterías

2

Praza de Fonseca

RÚA DE XEIMÍREZ

UNIVERSITY LIBRARY

TR. FONSECA

TURISMO PORTUGAL

RÚA DE SAN CLEMENTE

AVENIDA DE

R. DE PADRÓN

RÚA DO FRANCO

RÚA DO VILAR

RÚA DA RAINA

1

ℹ

RÚA DA CALDEIRERÍA

TR. DA

Praza de Universidade

ℹ

RÚA NOVA

RÚA DAS ÓRFAS

Praza de Mazarelos

RÚA DO POMBAL

Alameda

To Pontevedra & Portugal

Praza do Toural

POST

AV. XOÁN CARLOS I

RÚA CARREIRA DO CONDE

R. ENTREMURALLAS

RÚA DA SENRA

R. FONTE DE SAN ANTONIO

PÁTIO DE MADRES

To Launderette

RÚA DE MONTERO RÍOS

RÚA D. TEIXEIRO

Praza de Galicia

RÚA DO HÓRREO

To Bus to Airport

To Train Station

RÚA DOS PITELOS

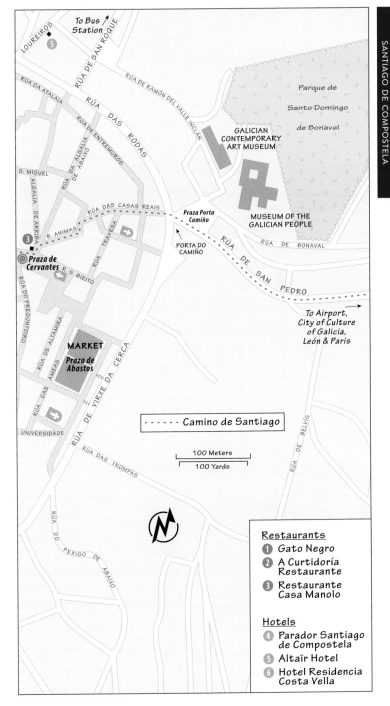

To Bus Station

LOUREIROS 5

RÚA DE SAN ROQUE

RÚA DA ATALAIA

RÚA DE RAMÓN DEL VALLE INCLÁN

RÚA DAS RODAS

RÚA DE ENTREMUROS

RÚA DA ALGALIA DE ABAIXO

S. MIGUEL

ALGALIA DE ARRIBA

3

RÚA DAS CASAS REAIS

R. ANIMAS

RÚA TRAVESA

Praza Porta Camiño

PORTA DO CAMIÑO

GALICIAN CONTEMPORARY ART MUSEUM

Parque de Santo Domingo de Bonaval

MUSEUM OF THE GALICIAN PEOPLE

RÚA DE BONAVAL

RÚA DE SAN PEDRO

Praza de Cervantes

R. S. BIEITO

RÚA DO PREGUNTOIRO

RÚA DE ALTAMIRA

RÚA DAS AMEAS

MARKET
Praza de Abastos

RÚA DE VIRXE DA CERCA

UNIVERSIDADE

RÚA DAS TROMPAS

RÚA DO PEXIGO DE ABAIXO

RÚA DE BELVÍS

To Airport, City of Culture of Galicia, León & Paris

- - - - - Camino de Santiago

100 Meters
100 Yards

Restaurants
1 Gato Negro
2 A Curtidoría Restaurante
3 Restaurante Casa Manolo

Hotels
4 Parador Santiago de Compostela
5 Altaïr Hotel
6 Hotel Residencia Costa Vella

• *Enter the cathedral and make your way to the rear of the nave to find the display about the...*

Portico of Glory: This portico (which may be hidden under scaffolding while being restored to all its glory) used to be the main facade of the cathedral, sculpted in about 1180. Pretend you're a medieval pilgrim, and you've just walked 500 miles to reach this cathedral. You're here to request the help of St. James in recovering from an illness or to give thanks for a success.

You can't read, but you can tell from the carved images that this magnificent door represents the Glory of God. Old Testament prophets on the left announce Christ's coming. New Testament apostles on the right spread his message. Jesus reigns directly above, approachable to the humble Christian pilgrim via St. James with his staff.

Below St. James is a column with the Tree of Jesse—showing the genealogy of Jesus, with Mary near the top and, above her, the Holy Trinity: Father, Son, and a dove representing the Holy Spirit.

As a pilgrim, you would place your hand into the well-worn finger holes on the column (see five grooves at about chest level) and bow your head, giving thanks to St. James for having granted you safe passage.

• *Now turn around to continue up the nave until you reach the...*

High Altar: The big gold altar has three representations of St. James in one place: Up top, on a white horse, is James the *Matamoros*—Moor-Slayer; below that (just under the canopy) is pilgrim James; and below that is a stone Apostle James—pointing down to his tomb.

• *Following the pilgrims' route, go down the ambulatory on the left side of the altar and walk down the little stairway on your right to the...*

Tomb of St. James: There he is, in the little silver chest, marked by a star—

Santiago. Pilgrims kneel in front of the tomb and make their request or say their thanks.

• *Continue through the little passage and up the stairs. At the very back of the church (behind the altar) is the greenish...*

Holy Door: This special door is open only during Holy Years, when pilgrims use it to access the tomb and statue of the apostle. The door, sculpted by a local artist for the 2004 Holy Year, shows six scenes from the life of St. James. At the bottom, the little snail is the symbol of the pilgrim...slow and steady, with everything on its back.

• *There's one more pilgrim ritual to complete.*

Hug St. James: Opposite the Holy Door, find a little door—perhaps with a line of pilgrims (closed 13:30-16:00 and after 20:00). Climb the stairs under the huge babies, and find a stone statue of St. James—gilded and caked with precious gems. Embrace him from behind and enjoy a saint's-eye view of the cathedral.

▲▲CATHEDRAL MUSEUM (MUSEO CATEDRAL DE CATEDRAL)

The cathedral's museum shows off some interesting pieces from the fine treasury collection and artifacts from the cathedral's history. Your admission ticket includes a look inside Gelmírez Palace and its exhibit about current restoration efforts.

Cost and Hours: €6, daily 9:00-20:00, Nov-March from 10:00, last entry one hour before closing, tel. 881-557-945, ticket office at entrance to the right of the main stairs into cathedral, www.catedral desantiago.es.

▲▲MARKET (MERCADO DE ABASTOS)

This wonderful market, housed in Old World stone buildings, offers a good opportunity to do some serious people-watching (Mon-Sat 8:00-14:00, closed Sun). It's busiest and best on Saturday, when villagers from the countryside come to sell things. Keep an eye out for

Tiny percebes *are a local specialty.*

the specialties you'll want to try later—octopus, shrimp, crabs, lobsters, and expensive-as-gold *percebes* (barnacles).

Local gooseneck barnacles, called *percebes*, are a delicacy. Two beers and a small 100-gram plate to split with your travel partner make for a wonderful snack. Just twist, rip, and bite: It's a bit like munching the necks off butter clams. I ask for toasted bread on the side.

For the freshest *percebes* at half the price—and twice the experience—buy them at the market, then let **Mariscomanía** boil them for you right there in their market café. They'll boil up any seafood (or meat) you buy in the market (it takes just a few minutes), charging €5 per person for table service (Tue-Sat 9:00-15:00, closed Sun-Mon, aisle 5 in the market, tel. 981-560-982).

Eating

With the coast just 20 miles away, the city is swimming in fresh seafood. Rúa do Franco is lined with eateries, including the no-frills seafood tapas bar, **$$ O Gato Negro** (closed Mon and Sun evening, near Rúa do Franco on side street Rúa da Raiña). **$$$ A Curtidoría Restaurante** offers good paella and fish plates (Rúa da Conga 2). The popular **$ Restaurante Casa Manolo** serves a generous €10 fixed-price meal (daily for lunch and dinner but Sun lunch only, at the bottom of Praza de Cervantes).

Sleeping

The trickiest dates to book here are Easter Sunday weekend and the days around the Feast of St. James (July 25—reserve your rooms well ahead).

$$$$ Parador Santiago de Compostela has the best address in Santiago—and prices to match (Praza do Obradoiro 1, www.paradores-spain.com). **$$ Altaïr Hotel** is surprisingly affordable (breakfast included for Rick Steves readers, Rúa dos Loureiros 12, www.altairhotel.net). Lovely **$ Hotel Residencia Costa Vella** overlooks a peaceful garden (Rúa Porta da Pena 17, www.costavella.com).

Madrid

Today's Madrid is upbeat and vibrant. You'll feel it. Look around—just about everyone has a twinkle in their eyes. Like its population, the city is relatively young. In medieval times, it was just another village, wedged between the powerful kingdoms of Castile and Aragon. When newlyweds Ferdinand and Isabel united those kingdoms in 1469, Madrid—at the center of Spain—became the focal point of a budding nation. By 1561, Spain ruled the world's most powerful empire, and Madrid was transformed into a European capital. By 1900, Madrid had 575,000 people.

Today, the hub of Spain—with more than 3 million people—is working hard to make itself more livable with urban improvements such as pedestrianized streets, parks, and commuter lines. Fortunately, the historic core is intact and easy to navigate.

So, dive headlong into the grandeur and intimate charm of Madrid. Feel the vibe in the main square, Puerta del Sol—the pulsing heart of Spain itself. The lavish Royal Palace, with its gilded rooms and frescoed ceilings, rivals Versailles. The Prado has Europe's top collection of paintings, and nearby hangs Picasso's chilling masterpiece, *Guernica*. Retiro Park invites you to take a shady siesta. Be sure to save some energy for after dark, when Madrileños pack the streets for an evening paseo and *tapeo* (tapas crawl) that can continue past midnight. Lively Madrid has enough street-singing, bar-hopping, and people-watching for everyone.

MADRID IN 2 DAYS

Day 1: Get your bearings with my self-guided city walk, which loops from Puerta del Sol to the Royal Palace and back—with a tour through the Royal Palace in the middle. Linger in Madrid's grand public spaces, such as Puerta del Sol and Plaza Mayor. Your afternoon is free for other sights, shopping, or exploring.

On any evening: Have a progressive tapas dinner at a series of characteristic bars. Join the evening paseo; my favorite time is right before sunset, when beautifully lit people fill the city. Take in a flamenco or zarzuela performance.

Day 2: Take a brisk, 20-minute good-morning-Madrid walk along Calle de las Huertas to the Prado, where you'll enjoy some of Europe's best art (reserve in advance). Enjoy an afternoon siesta—or rent a rowboat—in nearby Retiro Park. Then tackle modern art at the Reina Sofía museum, which displays Picasso's *Guernica* (closed Tue).

Day Trips: Toledo works as a day trip, but is worth two days and nights if you have the time and interest. Allow a half-day if you want to see El Escorial (Inquisition palace). Figure on one day to visit small-town Segovia (ancient Roman aqueduct), and if you add the university town of Salamanca, you'll have a pleasant two-day side-trip.

ORIENTATION

Madrid's historic core is compact and manageable. Frame it off on your map: The square called Puerta del Sol marks the center of Madrid. Everything described here is within about a 20-minute stroll or a €7 taxi ride of this central square. To the west is the Royal Palace. To the east are the great art museums: Prado, Reina Sofía, and Thyssen-Bornemisza. North of Puerta del Sol is Gran Vía, a broad east-west boulevard bubbling with elegant shops and cinemas. Between Gran Vía and Puerta del Sol is a lively pedestrian shopping zone. And southwest of Puerta del Sol is Plaza Mayor, the center of a 17th-century, slow-down-and-smell-the-cobbles district.

Handy for exploring, a wonderful chain of pedestrian streets crosses the city east to west, from the Prado to Plaza Mayor (along Calle de las Huertas) and from Puerta del Sol to the Royal Palace (on Calle del Arenal). Stretching north from Gran Vía, Calle de Fuencarral is a trendy shopping-and-strolling pedestrian street.

Tourist Information

Madrid's city-run TIs share a website (www.esmadrid.com), a central phone number (tel. 914-544-410), and hours (daily 9:30-20:30 or later). The best and most central city TI is on **Plaza Mayor.**

Additional branches are scattered all over the city, often in freestanding kiosks. Look for them near the **Prado** (facing the Neptune fountain), in front of the **Reina Sofía** art museum (across the street from the Atocha train station, in the median of the busy road), along Gran Vía at **Plaza de Callao,** at **Plaza de Colón** (in the underground passage accessed from Paseo de la Castellana and Calle de Goya), inside **Palacio de Cibeles** (up the stairs, and to the right), and at the **airport** (Terminals 2 and 4).

Regional Turismo Madrid TIs (privately run and therefore profit-motivated) share a website (www.turismomadrid.es), a phone number (tel. 902-100-007), and hours (Mon-Sat 8:00-20:00, Sun 9:00-14:00). The main branch is just east of Puerta del Sol at **Calle de Alcalá 31;** branches are also inside the **Sol Metro station** (inside the underground corridor; this branch open daily 8:00-20:00), at **Chamartín train station** (near track 20), at **Atocha train station** (AVE arrivals side; this branch open Sun until 20:00), and at the **airport** (Terminals 1 and 4). The regional TIs hand out a handy **public transportation map,** marked with bus routes.

Sightseeing Pass: If you want to visit the Prado, Thyssen-Bornemisza, and Centro de Arte Reina Sofía art museums during daytime hours, you can skip ticket lines and save a few euros by buying the **Paseo del Arte combo-ticket,** though keep in mind that the Prado and Reina Sofía are free in the evenings, and the Thyssen-Bornemisza permanent collection is free on Mondays (€30, sold at each museum, good for a year).

Helpful Hints

Theft and Safety: Be wary of **pickpockets** —anywhere, anytime, but especially in crowded areas such as Puerta del Sol (the central square), the busy street between Puerta del Sol and the Prado (Carrera de San Jerónimo), El Rastro (the flea market), Gran Vía (the paseo zone: Plaza del

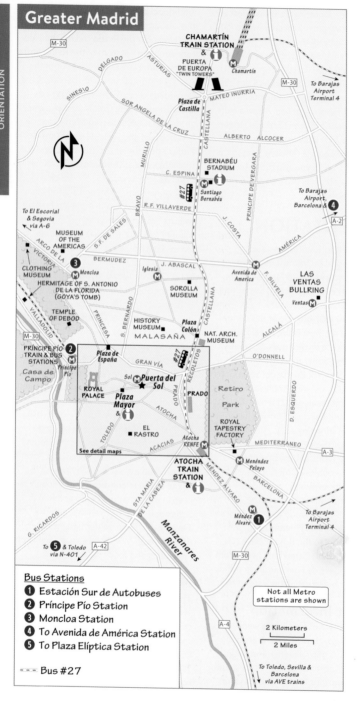

Greater Madrid

M-30

CHAMARTÍN
TRAIN STATION
&
PUERTA
DE EUROPA
"TWIN TOWERS"
M Chamartín

DELGADO
ASTURIAS
SINESIO
M-30
To Barajas
Airport
Terminal 4

SOR ANGELA DE LA CRUZ
MATEO INURRIA
Plaza de
Castilla

MURILLO
CASTELLANA
ALBERTO ALCOCER

C. ESPINA
BERNABÉU
STADIUM
#27
Santiago
Bernabéu
PRÍNCIPE DE VERGARA

To Barajas
Airport,
Barcelona & 4
A-2

R.F. VILLAVERDE
BRAVO
J. COSTA

To El Escorial
& Segovia
via A-6

ARCO DE LA
VICTORIA
MUSEUM
OF THE
AMERICAS
3
CLOTHING
MUSEUM
M Moncloa
HERMITAGE OF S. ANTONIO
DE LA FLORIDA
(GOYA'S TOMB)
TEMPLE
OF DEBOD
VALLADOLID
M-30

S.F. DE SALES
BERMUDEZ
S. BERNARDO
PRINCESA
Iglesia
M
J. ABASCAL
SOROLLA
MUSEUM
CASTELLANA
AMÉRICA
F SILVELA
M Avenida de
América
LAS
VENTAS
BULLRING
M Ventas

HISTORY
MUSEUM
MALASAÑA
Plaza
Colón
NAT. ARCH.
MUSEUM
ALCALÁ
O'DONNELL

PRÍNCIPE PÍO
TRAIN & BUS
STATIONS
Casa de
Campo
2
M Príncipe
Pío
Plaza de
España
GRAN VÍA
#27
RECOLETOS

ROYAL
PALACE
Plaza
Mayor
&
EL
RASTRO
M Sol
Puerta del
Sol
TOLEDO
ATOCHA
ACACIAS
PRADO
PRADO
Retiro
Park
ROYAL
TAPESTRY
FACTORY
D. ESQUERDO
MEDITERRANEO
A-3

See detail maps

Atocha
RENFE
M
ATOCHA
TRAIN
STATION
&

STA. MARIA
DE LA CABEZA
MENDEZ ALVARO
M Menéndez
Pelayo
BARCELONA

G. RICARDOS
To 5 & Toledo
via N-401
A-42
Manzanares
River
M-30
A-4
M Méndez
Alvaro 1
To Barajas
Airport
Terminal 4

Not all Metro
stations are shown

Bus Stations
1 Estación Sur de Autobuses
2 Príncipe Pío Station
3 Moncloa Station
4 To Avenida de América Station
5 To Plaza Elíptica Station

2 Kilometers
2 Miles

--- Bus #27

To Toledo, Sevilla &
Barcelona
via AVE trains

Callao to Plaza de España), anywhere on the Metro, bus #27, and at the airport. Someone wearing a heavy jacket in summer is likely a pickpocket. Teenagers (and younger) may dress like Americans and work the areas near big sights. Assume any fight or commotion is a distraction. Wear your money belt.

Call the **SATE line** in an **emergency** (24-hour tel. 902-102-112) for help with anything from canceling stolen credit cards to reporting a crime to the police (central police station, daily 9:00-24:00, near Plaza de Santo Domingo at Calle Leganitos 19). They will even act as an interpreter.

Prostitutes over 18 can solicit legally. They line Calle de la Montera, leading from Puerta del Sol to Plaza Red de San Luis. And don't stray north of Gran Vía around Calle de la Luna and Plaza Santa María Soledad.

Laundry: Try **Colada Express** at Calle Campomanes 9 (self-service daily 9:00-22:00, free Wi-Fi, tel. 657-876-464) or **Lavandería** at Calle León 6 (self-service—Mon-Sat 9:00-22:00, Sun 12:00-15:00; full-service—Mon-Sat 9:00-14:00 & 15:00-20:00, tel. 914-299-545).

Tours

WALKING TOURS
Across Madrid, run by art history professor Almudena Cros, offers specialized tours, including one on the Spanish Civil War that draws on her family's history (generally €70/person, 8 people max, book well in advance, mobile 652-576-423, www.acrossmadrid.com, info@acrossmadrid.com). **Stephen Drake-Jones** has led walks of historic old Madrid for decades and loves to teach history (€95 for 3.5-hour tour with three stops for drinks and tapas; daily at 11:00, 8 people max, www.wellsoc.org, mobile 609-143-203, chairman@wellsoc.org).

LOCAL GUIDES
Frederico and Cristina and their team lead city walks and family tours of Madrid and tours to nearby towns (prices per

group: €160/2 hours, €200/4 hours; mobile 649-936-222, www.spainfred.com, info@spainfred.com). **Letango Tours** offers private tours, packages, and stays all over Spain with a focus on families and groups (€275/group, 5 people max, kids free, 3-plus hours, www.letango.com, tours@letango.com). **Madridivine** guide David Gillison shares his love for his adopted city through food and walking tours (€200/group, 6 people max, 3-hour tour, food and drinks extra, www.madridivine.com, info@madridivine.com).

HOP-ON, HOP-OFF BUS
Madrid City Tour makes two different hop-on, hop-off circuits through the city: historic and modern. The two routes intersect at the south side of Puerta del Sol and in front of Starbucks across from the Prado. Your ticket covers both loops (€21/1 day, €25/2 days, buy ticket from driver; daily March-Oct 9:30-22:00, Nov-Feb 10:00-18:00; recorded narration, 16-21 stops, 1.5 hours, departs every 15 minutes, www.madridcitytour.es).

HISTORIC CORE WALK

Madrid's historic center is pedestrian-friendly and filled with spacious squares, a trendy market, bulls' heads in a bar, and a cookie-dispensing convent. Allow about two hours for this self-guided, mile-long walk that loops from Madrid's central square, Puerta del Sol, to the Royal Palace and back to the square (Metro: Sol).

🎧 Download my free Madrid audio tour, which complements this walk.

➲ Self-Guided Walk
• *Start in the middle of the square, by the equestrian statue of King Charles III, and survey the scene.*

❶ *Puerta del Sol*
The bustling Puerta del Sol, rated ▲▲, is Madrid's center. Over the years, the

MADRID AT A GLANCE

▲▲▲**Royal Palace** Spain's sumptuous, lavishly furnished national palace. **Hours:** Daily 10:00-20:00, Oct-March until 18:00. See page 161.

▲▲▲**Prado Museum** One of the world's great museums, loaded with masterpieces by Diego Velázquez, Francisco de Goya, El Greco, Hieronymus Bosch, Albrecht Dürer, and more. **Hours:** Mon-Sat 10:00-20:00, Sun until 19:00. See page 172.

▲▲▲**Centro de Arte Reina Sofía** Modern-art museum featuring Picasso's epic masterpiece *Guernica.* **Hours:** Mon and Wed-Sat 10:00-21:00, Sun until 19:00, closed Tue. See page 186.

▲▲▲**Paseo** Evening stroll among the Madrileños. **Hours:** Sundown until the wee hours. See page 192.

▲▲**Puerta del Sol** Madrid's lively central square. See page 147.

▲▲**Thyssen-Bornemisza Museum** A great complement to the Prado, with lesser-known yet still impressive works and an especially good Impressionist collection. **Hours:** Mon 12:00-16:00, Tue-Sun 10:00-19:00. See page 184.

▲▲**National Archaeological Museum** Traces the history of Iberia through artifacts. **Hours:** Tue-Sat 9:30-20:00, Sun until 15:00, closed Mon. See page 190.

▲▲**Flamenco** Captivating music and dance performances, at various venues throughout the city. **Hours:** Shows nightly, but some places closed on Sun. See page 192.

▲▲**Plaza Mayor** Historic cobbled square. See page 154.

▲▲**Retiro Park** Festive green escape from the city, with rental rowboats and great people-watching. **Hours:** Closes at dusk. See page 190.

▲**Bullfighting** Spain's controversial pastime. **Hours:** Most Sundays and holidays March-mid-Oct, plus almost daily early May-early June. See page 194.

▲**Royal Botanical Garden** A relaxing museum of plants, with specimens from around the world. **Hours:** Daily May-Aug 10:00-21:00, April and Sept until 20:00, shorter hours off-season. See page 190.

▲**El Rastro** Europe's biggest flea market, filled with bargains and pickpockets. **Hours:** Sun 9:00-15:00, best before 11:00. See page 191.

▲**Zarzuela** Madrid's delightful light opera. **Hours:** Evenings. See page 193.

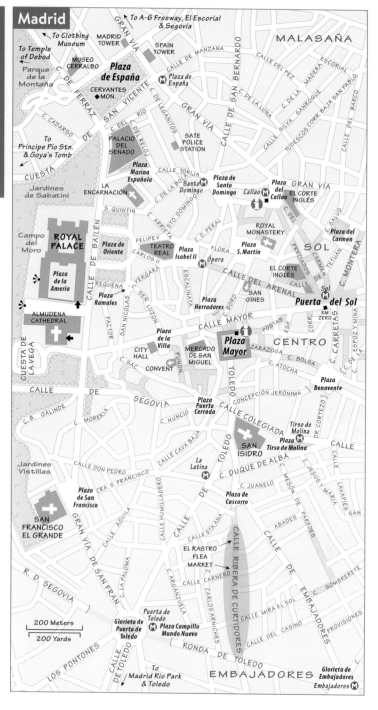

Madrid

To A-6 Freeway, El Escorial & Segovia

MALASAÑA

To Clothing Museum

To Temple of Debod

MADRID TOWER

SPAIN TOWER

MUSEO CERRALBO

Parque de la Montaña

CALLE DE MANZANA

CALLE DEL PEZ

ESCORIAL

CALLE DE SAN BERNARDO

C. DE LA MADERA

CALLE SILVA

SANROQUE

C. DE LA LUNA

CALLE DE LA

TUDESCOS CORR. BAJA SAN PABLO

CALLE DEL BARCO

Plaza de España

CERVANTES MON.

Plaza de España

GRAN VÍA

C. DE FERRAZ

SAN VICENTE

C. DEL RÍO

C. DE LEGANITOS

GRAN VÍA

C. DE LA

SATE POLICE STATION

C. CADARSO

To Príncipe Pío Stn. & Goya's Tomb

PALACIO DEL SENADO

Plaza Marina Española

CALLE TORIJA

CALLE DE LA BOLA

Plaza de Santo Domingo

GRAN VÍA

Plaza del Callao

EL CORTE INGLÉS

CUESTA

LA ENCARNACIÓN

C. DE PELIGRO

Santo Domingo

Callao

Jardines de Sabatini

S. QUINTIN

C. DE ARRIETA

STO. DOMINGO

Plaza del Carmen

Campo del Moro

ROYAL PALACE

FELIPE V

TEATRO REAL

CARLOS II

VERGARA

C. P. PERAL

ROYAL MONASTERY

Plaza S. Martín

EL CORTE INGLÉS

SOL

PRECIADOS

CARMEN

C. DE TETUÁN

C. MONTERA

Plaza de Oriente

Plaza Isabel II

FLORA

Ópera

Plaza de la Amería

Plaza Ramales

CALLE DE BAILÉN

REQUENA

C. SER LUZON

ESCALINATA

SAN NICOLAS

C. BORDO

Plaza Herradores

CALLE DEL ARENAL

SAN GINES

CALLE

Puerta del Sol

Sol

KM ZERO

ALMUDENA CATHEDRAL

FACTOR

Plaza de la Villa

CALLE MAYOR

POSTAS

ESP.

CORR.

C. CARRETAS

C. DE ESPOZ Y MINA

CUESTA DE LA VEGA

CITY HALL

C. SAC.

CONVENT

MERCADO DE SAN MIGUEL

PUÑON

Plaza Mayor

ZARAZOGA

C. BOLSA

CENTRO

CALLE

DE

SEGOVIA

C. NUNCIO

Plaza Puerta Cerrada

C. ATOCHA

Plaza Benavente

C. B. GALINDE

C. MORERIA

CALLE COLEGIADA

CONCEPCIÓN JERÓNIMA

DR. CORTEZO

Tirso de Molina

CALLE

Jardines Vistillas

CALLE DON PEDRO

CRA. S. FRANCISCO

CALLE CAVA BAJA

SAN ISIDRO

La Latina

C. DUQUE DE ALBA

Plaza Tirso de Molina

C. JESÚS Y MARÍA

LAVAPIÉS

SAN

Plaza de San Francisco

GRAN VÍA DE SAN FRAN

CALLE AGUILA

CALLE HUMILLADERO

C. JUANELO

Plaza de Cascorro

C. STA. ANA

ABADES

MESON DE PAREDES

SAN FRANCISCO EL GRANDE

LA PALOMA

EL RASTRO FLEA MARKET

CALLE CARNERO

C. ARGANZUELA

CARLOS ARNICHES

CALLE RIBERA DE CURTIDORES

CALLE MIRA EL SOL

CALLE DEL CASINO

C. SOMBRERETE

CALLE

DE

EMBAJADORES

PROVISIONES

C.

R. D. SEGOVIA

LOS PONTONES

CALLE DE TOLEDO

Puerta de Toledo

Glorieta de Puerta de Toledo

Plaza Campillo Mundo Nuevo

RONDA

DE

TOLEDO

To Madrid Rio Park & Toledo

EMBAJADORES

Glorieta de Embajadores

Embajadores

200 Meters
200 Yards

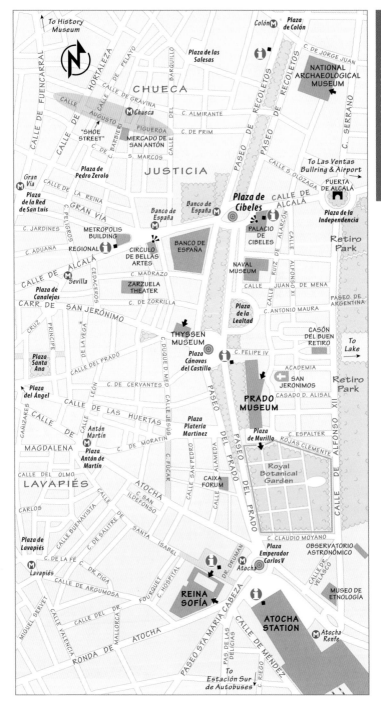

To History Museum

Colón Ⓜ Plaza de Colón

C. DE JORGE JUAN

Plaza de las Salesas

NATIONAL ARCHAEOLOGICAL MUSEUM

CHUECA

CALLE DE FUENCARRAL
HORTALEZA
CALLE DE PELAYO
BARQUILLO
CALLE DE GRAVINA
C. ALMIRANTE
CALLE AUGUSTO
Ⓜ Chueca
C. DE PRIM
FIGUEROA
"SHOE STREET"
C. DE BARBIERI
MERCADO DE SAN ANTÓN
S. MARCOS

JUSTICIA

PASEO DE RECOLETOS
PASEO DE RECOLETOS
C. SERRANO

To Las Ventas Bullring & Airport

Plaza de Pedro Zerolo

Gran Vía Ⓜ
CALLE DE LA REINA
Plaza de la Red de San Luis
GRAN VÍA
C. PELIGROS

Banco de España
Plaza de Cibeles
CALLE DE ALCALÁ

PUERTA DE ALCALÁ

Plaza de la Independencia

C. JARDINES
C. ADUANA
METROPOLIS BUILDING
REGIONAL
CÍRCULO DE BELLAS ARTES
Banco de España
BANCO DE ESPAÑA
PALACIO DE CIBELES
C. DE ALARCÓN

Retiro Park

CALLE DE ALCALÁ
CEDACEROS
Ⓜ Sevilla
C. MADRAZO
ZARZUELA THEATER
C. DE ZORRILLA
NAVAL MUSEUM
CALLE RUIZ
ALFONSO XI
JUAN DE MENA
PASEO DE ARGENTINA

Plaza de Canalejas
CARR. DE SAN JERÓNIMO
Plaza de la Lealtad
C. ANTONIO MAURA

CRUZ
PRÍNCIPE
CALLE DE LA VEGA
C. DUQUE D. MED
THYSSEN MUSEUM
Plaza Cánovas del Castillo
C. FELIPE IV
CASÓN DEL BUEN RETIRO
To Lake

Plaza Santa Ana
CALLE DEL PRADO
LEÓN
C. DE CERVANTES
ACADEMIA
SAN JERÓNIMOS
Retiro Park

Plaza del Ángel
CAÑIZARES
CALLE DE LAS HUERTAS
CALLE JESÚS
PRADO MUSEUM
CASADO D. ALISAL
XII

CALLE DE
Antón Martín Ⓜ
C. DE MORATÍN
Plaza Platería Martínez
Plaza de Murillo
C. ESPALTER
ROJAS CLEMENTE

MAGDALENA
Plaza Antón de Martín
C. SAN PEDRO
C. FÚCAR
Royal Botanical Garden
CALLE DE ALFONSO

CALLE DEL OLMO
LAVAPIÉS
ATOCHA
C. SAN ILDEFONSO
CAIXA FORUM

CARLOS
CALLE BUENAVISTA
C. DE SALITRE
SANTA ISABEL

Plaza de Lavapiés
C. DE LA FÉ
C. DR. PIGA
C. DE DRUMAN
Plaza Emperador Carlos V
OBSERVATORIO ASTRONÓMICO

Ⓜ Lavapiés
CALLE DE ARGUMOSA
FOURQUET
C. HOSPITAL
Ⓜ Atocha
C. CLAUDIO MOYANO
CALLE DR. VELASCO
MUSEO DE ETNOLOGÍA

MIGUEL SERVET
CALLE VALENCIA
CALLE DEL DR. MALLORCA
REINA SOFÍA
CALLE SANTA MARÍA CABEZA
CALLE DE MÉNDEZ
ATOCHA STATION
Ⓜ Atocha Renfe

RONDA DE ATOCHA
PASEO STA MARÍA CABEZA
PAS. DE LAS DELICIAS
C. RIEGO

To Estación Sur de Autobuses

square has undergone a facelift to become a mostly pedestrianized and wide-open gathering place. It's a magnet for strolling locals, sightseers, pickpockets, revelers, and cartoon characters who pose for photos for a fee. It's also a popular site for political demonstrations and national celebrations, and it's a transportation hub for the Metro and *cercanías* (suburban trains).

The equestrian statue in the middle of the square honors **King Charles III** (1716-1788). His enlightened urban policies earned him the affectionate nickname "the best mayor of Madrid." He decorated city squares with beautiful fountains, got those meddlesome Jesuits out of city government, established the public-school system, mandated underground sewers, opened his private Retiro Park to the public, built the Prado, made the Royal Palace the wonder of Europe, and generally cleaned up Madrid.

Head to the slightly uphill end of the square and find the **statue of a bear** pawing a tree—locals love it. This image has been a symbol of Madrid since medieval times. Bears used to live in the royal hunting grounds outside the city. And the *madroño* trees produce a berry that makes the traditional *madroño* liqueur.

Charles III faces a red-and-white building with a bell tower. This was Madrid's first post office, which Charles III founded in the 1760s. Today it's the **county governor's office,** home to the "president" who governs greater Madrid. The building is notorious for having once been dictator Francisco Franco's police headquarters. A tragic number of those detained and interrogated by the Franco police tried to "escape" by jumping out its windows to their deaths.

Crowds fill the square on New Year's Eve as the rest of Spain watches the Times Square-style action on TV. The bell atop the governor's office chimes 12 times, while Madrileños eat one grape for each ring to bring good luck through each of the next 12 months.

• *Cross the square and street to the governor's office.*

Puerta del Sol

Look down at the sidewalk directly in front of the entrance to the governor's office. The plaque marks **"kilometer zero,"** the symbolic center of Spain, from which the country's six main highways radiate (as the plaque shows). Standing on the zero marker with your back to the governor's office, get oriented visually, using an imaginary clock: Directly ahead, at 12 o'clock, is the famous *Tío Pepe* **sign.** This big neon billboard—25 feet high and 80 feet across—pictures a jaunty Andalusian *caballero* with a sombrero and guitar. He's been advertising a local sherry wine since the 1930s.

Beyond the sign is a thriving **pedestrian commercial zone,** anchored by the huge department store, El Corte Inglés. At two o'clock starts the seedier Calle de la Montera, a street with shady characters and prostitutes that leads to the trendy, pedestrianized Calle de Fuencarral. At three o'clock is the biggest Apple store in Europe; the Prado is about a mile farther to your right. Back over at 10 o'clock is the pedestrianized street called Calle del Arenal...where we'll finish this walk.

Now turn around. On the walls flanking the entrance to the governor's office are **two white marble plaques.** These commemorate two important dates, when Madrileños came together in times of dire need. The plaque on the right marks an event from 1808. An angry crowd gathered here to rise up against an invasion by France. Suddenly, French soldiers stormed the square and began massacring the Spaniards. The event galvanized the country, which eventually drove out the French. The painter Francisco de Goya, whose studio was not far from here, captured the event in his famous painting, *The Third of May,* which is in the Prado Museum.

The plaque to the left of the entry remembers a more recent tragedy, on March 11, 2004. That's when brave Spanish citizens helped fellow citizens in the wake of horrific terrorist bombings in the city. We have our 9/11—Spain has its 3/11.

On the corner of Puerta del Sol and Calle Mayor (downhill end of Puerta del Sol) is the busy, recommended *confitería* **La Mallorquina,** *"fundada en 1.894."* Go inside for a tempting peek at racks with goodies hot out of the oven. The crowded takeaway section is in front; the stand-up counter is in back. Enjoy observing the churning energy of Madrileños popping in for a fast coffee and a sweet treat. The shop is famous for its *Napolitana* pastry (like a squashed, custard-filled croissant). Or sample Madrid's answer to doughnuts, *rosquillas* (*tontas* means "silly"—plain, and *listas* means "all dressed up and ready to go"—with icing). Buy something...there's no special system, just order and pay. The café upstairs is more genteel, with nice views of the square.

Before leaving the shop, find the tile above the entrance door with the 18th-century view of Puerta del Sol. This was before the square was widened, when a church stood at its top end. Compare this with today's view out the door. Puerta del Sol ("Gate of the Sun") is named for a long-gone gate with the rising sun carved onto it, which once stood at the eastern edge of the old city. From here, we begin our walk through the historic town that dates back to medieval times.

• *Head west on busy Calle Mayor, just past McDonald's. Go a few steps up the side-street on the left, then angle right on the pedestrian-only street called...*

❷ *Calle de Postas*

The street sign shows the post coach heading for that famous first post office. Medieval street signs posted on the lower corners of buildings included pictures so the illiterate (and monolingual tourists) could "read" them. Fifty yards up the street on the left, at Calle San Cristóbal, is Pans & Company, a popular Catalan sandwich chain offering healthy choices. While Spaniards tend to consider American fast food unhealthy—culturally and

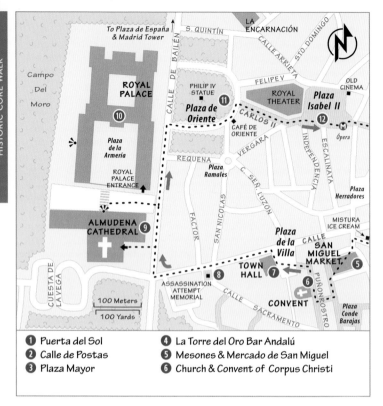

Campo
Del
Moro

ROYAL PALACE

Plaza de la Armería

ROYAL PALACE ENTRANCE

ALMUDENA CATHEDRAL

CUESTA DE LA VEGA

100 Meters
100 Yards

To Plaza de España & Madrid Tower

CALLE DE BAILÉN

S. QUINTÍN

LA ENCARNACIÓN

CALLE ARRIETA

STO. DOMINGO

FELIPE V

PHILIP IV STATUE

Plaza de Oriente

CARLOS II

CAFÉ DE ORIENTE

REQUENA

VERGARA

C. SEN. LUZON

Plaza Ramales

FACTOR

SAN NICOLAS

ROYAL THEATER

Plaza Isabel II

Ópera

INDEPENDENCIA

ESCALINATA

Plaza Herradores

MISTURA ICE CREAM

Plaza de la Villa

CALLE

SAN MIGUEL MARKET

PUÑONROSTRO

TOWN HALL

CONVENT

ASSASSINATION ATTEMPT MEMORIAL

CALLE SACRAMENTO

Plaza Conde Barajas

1 Puerta del Sol
2 Calle de Postas
3 Plaza Mayor

4 La Torre del Oro Bar Andalú
5 Mesones & Mercado de San Miguel
6 Church & Convent of Corpus Christi

physically—they love it. McDonald's and Burger King are thriving in Spain.

• *Continue up Calle de Postas, and take a slight right on Calle de la Sal through the arcade, where you emerge into...*

3 *Plaza Mayor*

This vast, cobbled square (worth ▲▲) dates back to Madrid's glory days, the 1600s, when this—not Puerta del Sol—was Madrid's main square *(plaza mayor)*. The **equestrian statue** (wearing a ruffled collar) honors Philip III, who made this square the centerpiece of the budding capital in 1619. The square is 140 yards long and 100 yards wide, enclosed by four-story buildings with symmetrical windows, balconies, slate roofs, and steepled towers. Each side of the square is uniform, as if a grand palace were turned

inside-out. This distinct "look," pioneered by architect Juan de Herrera (who finished El Escorial), is found all over Madrid.

This site served as the city's 17th-century open-air theater. Upon this stage, much Spanish history has been played out. The square's lampposts have reliefs

Plaza Mayor

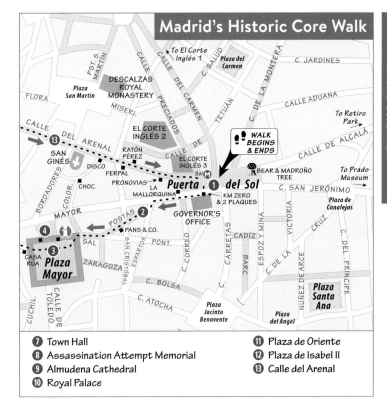

Madrid's Historic Core Walk

7 Town Hall
8 Assassination Attempt Memorial
9 Almudena Cathedral
10 Royal Palace
11 Plaza de Oriente
12 Plaza de Isabel II
13 Calle del Arenal

on the benches below illustrating major episodes: bullfights, dancers and masked revelers at Carnevale, royal pageantry, a horrendous fire in 1790, and events of the gruesome **Inquisition**. During the Inquisition, many were tried here—suspected heretics, Protestants, Jews, tour guides without a local license, and Muslims whose "conversion" to Christianity was dubious. The guilty were paraded around the square before their executions, wearing placards listing their many sins (bleachers were built for bigger audiences, while the wealthy rented balconies). The heretics were burned, and later, criminals were slowly strangled as they held a crucifix, hearing the reassuring words of a priest as the life was squeezed out of them.

The square's buildings are mainly private apartments. Want one? Costs run from €400,000 for a tiny attic studio to €2 million and up for a 2,500-square-foot flat. The square is painted a democratic shade of burgundy—the result of a city-wide poll. Since the end of decades of dictatorship in 1975, Spain has had a passion for voting. Three colors were painted as samples on the walls of this square, and the city voted for its favorite.

The building to Philip's left, on the north side beneath the twin towers, was once home to the baker's guild and now houses the **TI,** which is wonderfully air-conditioned.

A stamp-and-coin market bustles at Plaza Mayor on Sundays (10:00-14:00). Day or night, Plaza Mayor is a colorful place to enjoy an affordable cup of coffee or overpriced food. Throughout Spain, lesser *plazas mayores* provide peaceful pools in the whitewater river of Spanish life.

• Head to #26, under the arcade just to the left of the twin towers. This is a bar called…

❹ La Torre del Oro Bar Andalú

For some fascinating (if gruesome) bull-fighting lore, step inside. Order a drink at the bar and sightsee while you sip. Warning: First check the price list posted outside the door to understand the price tiers: "barra" indicates the price at the bar; "terraza" is the price at an outdoor table. A caña (small draft beer), Coke, or agua mineral should cost about €3. Your drink may come with a small, free tapa, per the old Spanish tradition. But to avoid being charged by surprise, clarify, "Gratis?" (Free?)

The interior is a temple to bullfighting, festooned with gory decor. Notice the breathtaking action captured in the many photographs. Look under the stuffed head of Barbero the bull (center, facing the bar). At eye level you'll see a puntilla, the knife used to put poor Barbero out of his misery at the arena. Just to the left of Barbero is a photo of longtime dictator Franco with the famous bullfighter Man-uel Benítez Pérez—better known as El Cordobés, the Elvis of bullfighters and a working-class hero. At the top of the stairs going down to the WC, find the photo of El Cordobés and Robert Kennedy—look-ing like brothers. Three feet to the left of them (and elsewhere in the bar) is a shot of Che Guevara enjoying a bullfight. At the end of the bar, in a glass case, is the "suit of lights" the great El Cordobés wore in an ill-fated 1967 fight, in which the bull gored him. El Cordobés survived; the bull didn't. In the same case, notice the photo of a matador (not El Cordobés) horrify-ingly hooked by a bull's horn.

Leaving the bull bar, consider taking a break at one of the tables on Madrid's grandest square. Cafetería Margerit (nearby) occupies Plaza Mayor's sunniest corner and is a good place to enjoy a cof-fee with the view. The scene is easily worth the extra euro you'll pay for the drink.

• Leave Plaza Mayor on Calle de Ciudad Rodrigo (at the northwest corner of the square), passing a series of solid turn-of-the-20th-century storefronts and sandwich joints, such as Casa Rúa (to the left), famous for cheap bocadillos de calamares—fried squid rings on a small baguette. Mistura Ice Cream (across the lane at Ciudad Rodrigo 6) serves fine coffee and quality ice cream. Emerging from the arcade, turn left and head downhill toward the iron-covered market hall. Before entering the market, look down a street to the left called Cava de San Miguel.

❺ Mesones and Mercado de San Miguel

Lining Cava de San Miguel is a series of traditional dive bars called mesones. If you like singing, sangria, and sloppy people, come back after 22:00 to visit one. These cave-like bars, stretching far back from the street, get packed with Madrileños out on dates who—emboldened by sangria and the setting—are prone to breaking out in song. It's a lowbrow, electric-keyboard, karaoke-type ambience, best on Friday and Saturday nights.

For a much more refined setting, wan-der through the Mercado de San Miguel (daily 10:00-24:00). This historic iron-and-glass structure from 1916 stands on the site of an even earlier marketplace. Renovated in the 21st century, the city's oldest surviving market hall now hosts

Mercado de San Miguel

some 30 high-end vendors of fresh produce, gourmet foods, wines by the glass, tapas, and full meals. Locals and tourists alike pause here for the food, natural-light ambience, and social scene.

• *Exit the market at the far end and turn left, heading downhill on Calle del Conde de Miranda. At the first corner, turn right and cross the small plaza to the brick church in the far corner.*

❻ Church and Convent of Corpus Christi

The proud coats of arms over the main entry announce the rich family that built this Hieronymite church and convent in 1607. In 17th-century Spain, the most prestigious thing a noble family could do was build and maintain a convent. To harvest all the goodwill created in your community, you'd want your family's insignia right there for all to see. (You can see the donating couple, like a 17th-century Bill and Melinda Gates, kneeling before the communion wafer in the central panel over the entrance.) Inside is a cool and quiet oasis with a Last Supper altarpiece.

Now for a unique shopping experience. A dozen steps to the right of the church entrance is its convent—the big brown door on the left at Calle del Codo 3 (Mon-Sat 9:30-13:00 & 16:30-18:30, closed Sun). The sign reads *Venta de Dulces* (Sweets for Sale). Buzz the *monjas* button, then wait patiently for the sister to respond over the intercom. Say *"dulces"* (DOOL-thays), and she'll let you in. When the lock buzzes, push open the door, turn on the lights, walk straight in and to the left, then follow the sign to the *torno*—the lazy Susan that lets the sisters sell their baked goods without being seen. Scan the menu, announce your choice to the sequestered sister (she may say some options are not available), place your money on the *torno*, and your goodies (and change) will appear. *Galletas* (shortbread cookies) are the least expensive (a *medio-kilo* costs about €10). Or try the *pastas de almendra* (almond cookies).

• *Continue uphill on Calle del Codo, where, in centuries past, those in need of bits of armor shopped. Bend sharply left with the street and head toward Plaza de la Villa. Before entering the square, notice an **old door** to the left of the **Real Sociedad Económica** sign, made of wood lined with metal. This is considered the oldest door in*

Church and Convent of Corpus Christi

Town Hall

town on Madrid's oldest building—inhabited since 1480. It's set in a Mudejar keyhole arch. Look up to see a tower, once used as a prison. Now continue into the square called Plaza de la Villa, dominated by Madrid's...

❼ Town Hall

The impressive structure features Madrid's distinctive architectural style—symmetrical square towers, topped with steeples and a slate roof...Castilian Baroque. Over the doorway, the three coats of arms sport many symbols of Madrid's rulers: Habsburg crowns on each, castles of Castile (in center shield), and the city symbol—the berry-eating bear (shield on left). This square was the ruling center of medieval Madrid in the centuries before it became an important capital.

Imagine how Philip II took this city by surprise in 1561 when he decided to move the capital of Europe's largest empire (even bigger than ancient Rome) from Toledo to humble Madrid. Located in the geographical center of the country, it united the two great kingdoms of Philip's great-grandparents, Ferdinand and Isabel. Philip II went on a building spree, and his son Philip III continued it. And this building reflects the hasty development. It's glorious, yes—but like much of Madrid, it's built with inexpensive brick rather than costly granite.

The statue in the little garden is of Philip II's admiral, Don Alvaro de Bazán, who defeated the Turkish Ottomans at the battle of Lepanto in 1571. This was Spain's last great victory. Mere months after Bazán's death in 1588, his "invincible" Spanish Armada was destroyed by England...and Spain's empire began its slow fade.

• From here, walk along busy, bus-lined Calle Mayor, which leads downhill (along the right side of the Town Hall) toward the Royal Palace. A few blocks down Calle Mayor is a small plaza in front of a church, where you'll find the...

❽ Assassination Attempt Memorial

This statue memorializes a 1906 assassination attempt. The target was Spain's King Alfonso XIII and his bride, Victoria Eugenie, as they paraded by on their wedding day. While the crowd was throwing flowers, an anarchist (as terrorists used to be called) threw a bouquet lashed to a bomb from a balcony at #84 (across the street). He missed the royal newlyweds, but killed 28 people. The king and queen went on to live to a ripe old age, producing many great-grandchildren, including the current king, Felipe VI.

• Continue down Calle Mayor one more block to a busy street, Calle de Bailén. Take in the big, domed...

❾ Almudena Cathedral

Madrid's massive, gray-and-white cathedral (Catedral de Nuestra Señora de la Almudena, 110 yards long and 80 yards high) opened in 1993, 100 years after workers started building it. (This is the side entrance for tourists, €1 donation requested). That year, Pope John Paul II consecrated Almudena, ending Madrid's 300-year stretch of requests for a cathedral of its own.

If you go in, you'll see colorful paintings, a striking 15th-century Gothic altarpiece, and a glittering 5,000-pipe organ in the rear of the nave. The church's historic highlight is directly behind the altar: a 13th-century coffin of painted leather on wood. Now empty, it once held Madrid's patron saint, Isidro. The story goes that Isidro was a humble farmer but exceptionally devout. One day, angels agreed to plow his fields so he could devote himself to praying. When Isidro died, he was buried in this simple coffin. Forty years later, the coffin was opened, and his body was still perfectly preserved. This miracle convinced the pope to canonize Isidro. He is now the patron saint of farmers, and of the city of Madrid.

• Leave the church from the transept where you entered, go out to the street, and turn left. Hike around the church to its rarely used front door. Climb the cathedral's front steps and face the imposing...

❿ Royal Palace

Since the ninth century, this spot has been Madrid's center of power: from Moorish castle to Christian fortress to Renaissance palace to the current structure, built in the 18th century. With its expansive courtyard surrounded by imposing Baroque architecture, it represents the wealth of Spain before its decline. Its 2,800 rooms, totaling nearly 1.5 million square feet, make it Europe's largest palace.

• You could visit the palace now, using my self-guided tour (see page 162). Or, to follow the rest of this walk back to Puerta del Sol, continue one long block north up Calle de Bailén to where the street opens into...

⓫ Plaza de Oriente

As its name suggests, this square faces east. The grand yet people-friendly plaza is typical of today's Europe, where energetic governments are converting car-congested wastelands into inviting public spaces. Where's the traffic? Under your feet. The Madrid mayor who spearheaded the project earned the nickname "The Mole" for all the digging he did.

Notice the quiet. You're surrounded by more than three million people, yet you can hear the birds, bells, and fountain. The park is decorated with statues of Visigothic kings who ruled from the fifth to eighth century. Romans allowed them to administer their province of Hispania on the condition that they'd provide food and weapons to the empire. The Visigoths inherited real power after Rome fell, but lost it to invading Moors in 711. The fine bronze equestrian statue of Philip IV faces the 1,700-seat **Royal Theater** (Teatro Real), built in the mid-1800s and rebuilt in 1997. It hosts traditional opera, ballets, concerts, and that unique Spanish form of light opera called zarzuela.

• Walk along the Royal Theater, on the right side, to the...

⓬ Plaza de Isabel II

This square is marked by a statue of Isabel II, who ruled Spain in the 19th century. Although she's immortalized here, the conservative Isabel had a rocky reign. A revolution in 1868 forced her to abdicate and live out her life in exile. Today, Isabel's statue stands before her most lasting legacy—the Royal Theater she built.

Facing the theater is an **old cinema** (now closed). This grand old movie palace from the 1920s is another example of Spain's persistent conservatism. As the rest of the world embraced Hollywood movies and their liberal mores, Spain approached it cautiously. During Franco's rule, foreign movies were allowed only if they were dubbed into Spanish, so his

Almudena Cathedral

Plaza de Oriente

censors could edit out sexual innuendo or liberal political references. Strangely, that tradition of dubbing continues even in today's more liberal Spain.

• From here, follow Calle del Arenal, walking gradually uphill. You're heading straight to Puerta del Sol.

⓭ Calle del Arenal

As depicted on the tiled street signs, this was the "street of sand"—where sand was stockpiled during construction. Each cross street is named for a medieval craft that, historically, was plied along that lane (for example, "Calle de Bordadores" means "Street of the Embroiderers"). Wander slowly uphill. As you stroll, imagine this street as a traffic inferno—which it was until the city pedestrianized it a decade ago. Notice also how orderly the side streets are. Where a mess of cars once lodged chaotically on the sidewalks, bollards (bolardos) now keep vehicles off the walkways.

Continue 200 yards up Calle del Arenal to the brick **St. Ginés Church** (on the right), which means temptation to most locals. From the uphill corner of the church, look to the end of the lane where—like a high-calorie red-light

zone—a neon sign spells out Chocolatería San Ginés...every local's favorite place for hot chocolate and churros (always open). The charming bookshop clinging like a barnacle to the wall of the church has been selling books on this spot since 1650.

Next door is the **Joy Eslava disco,** a former theater famous for operettas in the Gilbert and Sullivan days and now a popular club. In Spain, you can do it all when you're 18 (buy tobacco, drink, drive, serve in the military). This place is an alcohol-free disco for the younger kids until midnight, when it becomes a thriving adult space, with the theater floor and balconies all teeming with clubbers. Their slogan: "Go big or go home."

Farther up on the right (at #7) is **Ferpal,** an old-school deli with an inviting bar and easy takeout options. Wallpapered with ham hocks, it's famous for selling the finest Spanish cheeses, hams, and other tasty treats. Spanish saffron is half what you'd pay for it back in the US. While they sell quality sandwiches, cheap and ready-made, it's fun to buy some bread and—after a little tasting—choose a ham or cheese for a memorable picnic or snack. If you're lucky, you may get to taste a tiny

Calle del Arenal

bit of Spain's best ham *(Ibérico de vellota)*. Close your eyes and let the taste fly you to a land of very happy acorn-fed pigs.

Across the street, in a little mall (at #8), are a couple of sights celebrating the beloved **"Ratón Pérez"**—Perez the Mouse—who first appeared in a children's book in the late 1800s and serves as Spain's tooth fairy. Find the six-inch-tall bronze statue in the lobby, and then head upstairs to the fanciful Casita Museo de Ratón Pérez (€3, daily, Spanish only), with a fun window display.

Just uphill (at #6, on the left) is an official retailer of **Real Madrid** football (soccer) paraphernalia. Many European football fans come to Madrid simply to see its 80,000-seat Bernabéu Stadium. Madrid is absolutely crazy about football. They have two teams: the rich and successful Real Madrid, and the working-class underdog, Atlético. It's like the Yankees vs. the Mets.

Across the street at #5 is **Pronovias,** a famous Spanish wedding-dress shop that attracts brides-to-be from across Europe. These days, the current generation of Spaniards often just shack up without getting married. Those who do get married are more practical—preferring a down payment on a condo to a fancy wedding with a costly dress.

• *You're just a few steps from where you started this walk, at Puerta del Sol. Back in the square, you're met by a statue popularly known as* **La Mariblanca.** *At least 400 years old, it represents a kind of Spanish Venus. Today, La Mariblanca stands tall amid all the modernity, as she blesses the people of this great city.*

Rick's Tip: *For a walk down* **Spain's version of Fifth Avenue,** *stroll the* **Gran Vía,** *starting near Plaza de Cibeles and ending at Plaza de España. You'll enjoy early 20th-century architecture while strolling along with workaday Madrileños.*

SIGHTS

▲▲▲ROYAL PALACE

Spain's Royal Palace (Palacio Real) is Europe's third-greatest palace, after Versailles and Vienna's Schönbrunn. It has arguably the most sumptuous original interior, packed with tourists and royal antiques.

The palace is the product of many kings over several centuries. Philip II (1527-1598) made a wooden fortress on this site his governing center when he established Madrid as Spain's capital. When that palace burned down, the current structure was built by King Philip V (1683-1746). Philip V wanted to make it his own private Versailles, to match his French upbringing: He was born in Versailles—the grandson of Louis XIV—and ordered his tapas in French. His son, Charles III (whose statue graces Puerta del Sol), added interior decor in the Italian style, since he'd spent his formative years in Italy. These civilized Bourbon kings were trying to raise Spain to the cultural level of the rest of Europe. They hired foreign artists to oversee construction and established local Spanish porcelain and tapestry factories to copy works done in Paris or Brussels. Over the years, the palace was expanded and enriched, as each Spanish king tried to outdo his predecessor.

Today's palace is ridiculously supersized—with 2,800 rooms, tons of luxurious tapestries, a king's ransom of chandeliers, frescoes by Tiepolo, priceless porcelain, and bronze decor covered in gold leaf. The royal family actually lives in a mansion a few miles away, but this place still functions as the ceremonial palace, used for formal state receptions, royal weddings, and tourists' daydreams.

Cost and Hours: €10, €11 with special exhibits; open daily 10:00-20:00, Oct-March until 18:00, last entry one hour before closing; from Puerta del Sol, walk 15 minutes down pedestrianized Calle del

Royal Palace

Arenal (Metro: Ópera); palace can close for royal functions—confirm in advance.

Information: Tel. 914-548-800, www. patrimonionacional.es.

Crowd-Beating Tips: The palace is free for EU citizens—and most crowded—Monday-Thursday 18:00-20:00 in summer and 16:00-18:00 in winter. On any day, arrive early or go late to minimize lines and crowds.

Visitor Information: Short English descriptions posted in each room complement what I describe in my tour. The museum guidebook demonstrates a passion for meaningless data.

Tours: The €3 **audioguide** is good. Or download in advance the helpful **app,** "Royal Palace of Madrid" ($2). You can also join a €4 **guided tour.** Check the time of the next English-language tour and decide as you buy your ticket; the tours are dry, depart sporadically, and aren't worth a long wait.

Length of This Tour: Allow an hour and a half.

Services: Free lockers, a WC, and a gift shop are just past the ticket booth. Upstairs you'll find a more serious bookstore with good books on Spanish history.

Eating: Though the palace has a refreshing air-conditioned **$ cafeteria** upstairs in the ticket building (with salad bar), I prefer to walk a few minutes and find a place near the Royal Theater or on Calle del Arenal. The recommended **$$$ Café de Oriente,** boasting good lunch specials and fin-de-siècle elegance, is pricey but memorable, in a delightful park setting opposite the palace off Plaza de Oriente.

⊖ SELF-GUIDED TOUR

You'll follow a simple one-way circuit on a single floor covering more than 20 rooms.

• *Buy your ticket, proceed outside, stand in the middle of the vast open-air courtyard, and face the palace entrance.*

❶ Palace Exterior: The palace sports the French-Italian Baroque architecture so popular in the 18th century—heavy columns, classical-looking statues, a balustrade roofline, and false-front entrance. The entire building is made

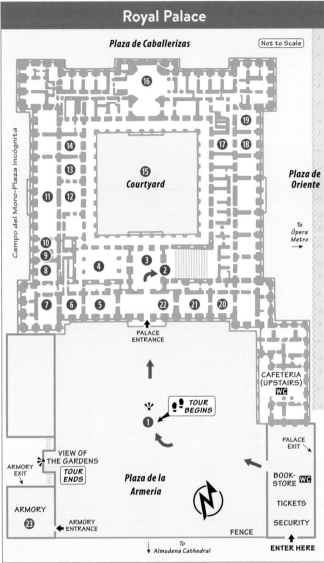

Royal Palace

Plaza de Caballerizas

Not to Scale

Campo del Moro-Plaza Incógnita

⑯

⑲

⑭

⑬

⑰ ⑱

⑮
Courtyard

⑪ ⑫

Plaza de
Oriente

⑩
⑨
⑧

To
Ópera
Metro
→

④ ❸ ❷

❼ ❻ ❺ ㉒ ㉑ ⑳

PALACE
ENTRANCE

↑

↓
TOUR
BEGINS

❶

CAFETERIA
(UPSTAIRS)
WC

PALACE
EXIT
↘

VIEW OF
THE GARDENS

ARMORY
EXIT
→

TOUR
ENDS

Plaza de la
Armería

N

BOOK-
STORE   WC

TICKETS

ARMORY

㉓

ARMORY
ENTRANCE
←

SECURITY

FENCE

To
↓ Almudena Cathedral

ENTER HERE
↑

❶ Palace Exterior	❽ Charles III Salon	⑯ Royal Chapel
❷ Palace Lobby (Ground Floor) & Grand Stairs	❾ Porcelain Room	⑰ Queen's Boudoir
	⑩ Yellow Room	⑱ Stradivarius Room
❸ Hall of Halberdiers	⑪ Gala Dining Room	⑲ Crown Room
❹ Hall of Columns	⑫ Cinema Room	⑳ Official Antechamber
❺ Drawing Room	⑬ Silver Room	㉑ Official Waiting Room
❻ Antechamber	⑭ Crockery & Crystal Rooms	㉒ Throne Room
❼ Gasparini Room	⑮ Courtyard	㉓ Armory

Spain's Royal Families: From Habsburg to Bourbon

Spain as we know it was born when four long-established medieval kingdoms were joined by the 1469 marriage of Ferdinand, ruler of Aragon and Navarre, and Isabel, ruler of Castile and León. The so-called "Catholic Monarchs" (Reyes Católicos) wasted no time in driving the Islamic Moors out of Spain (the Reconquista). By 1492, Isabel and Ferdinand had conquered a fifth kingdom, Granada, establishing more or less the same borders that Spain has today.

This was an age when "foreign policy" was conducted, in part, by marrying royal children into other royal families. Among the dynastic marriages of their children, Isabel and Ferdinand arranged for their third child, Juana "the Mad," to marry the crown prince of Austria, Philip "the Fair." This was a huge coup for the Spanish royal family. A member of the Habsburg dynasty, Philip was heir to the Holy Roman Empire, which then encompassed much of today's Austria, Czech Republic, Slovakia, Hungary, Transylvania, the Low Countries, southern Italy, and more. When Juana's brothers died, making her ruler of the kingdoms of Spain, it paved the way for her son, Charles, to inherit the kingdoms of his four grandparents—creating a vast realm and making him the most powerful man in Europe. He ruled as Charles I (king of Spain, from 1516) and Charles V (Holy Roman Emperor, from 1519).

He was followed by Philip II, Philip III, Philip IV, and finally Charles II. Over this period, Spain rested on its Golden Age laurels, eventually squandering much of its wealth and losing some of its holdings. Arguably the most inbred of an already very inbred dynasty (his parents were uncle and niece), Charles II was weak, sickly, and unable to have children, ending the 200-year Habsburg dynasty in Spain with his death in 1700.

Charles II willed the Spanish crown to the Bourbons of France, and his grand-nephew Philip of Anjou, whose granddaddy was the "Sun King" Louis XIV of

of gray-and-white local stone (very little wood) to prevent the kind of fire that leveled the previous castle. Imagine the place in its heyday, with a courtyard full of soldiers on parade, or a lantern-lit scene of horse carriages arriving for a ball.
• Enter the palace. You'll find an info desk, cloakrooms, and the meeting point for guided tours.

❷ Palace Lobby and Grand Stairs: In the old days, horse-drawn carriages would drop you off inside this covered arcade. Today, stretch limos do the same thing for gala events. When you reach the foot of the Grand Stairs, you'll see a statue of a toga-clad Charles III—the man most responsible for the lavish rooms you're about to see.

Gazing up the imposing staircase, you can see that Spain's kings wanted to make a big first impression. Whenever high-end dignitaries arrive, fancy carpets are rolled down the stairs (notice the little metal bar-holding hooks). Begin your ascent, up steps that are intentionally shallow, making your climb slow and regal. At the first landing, the burgundy coat of arms represents the current king, Felipe VI. He's part of a long tradition of kings stretching back to Ferdinand and Isabel. Overhead, the white-and-blue ceiling fresco opens up to a heavenly host of graceful female

France, took the throne. But the rest of Europe feared allowing the already powerful Louis XIV to add Spain (and its vast New World holdings) to his empire. Austria, the Germanic States, Holland, England, and Catalunya backed a different choice (Archduke Charles of Austria). So began the War of Spanish Succession (1700-1714), involving all of Europe. The French eventually prevailed, and with the signing of the Treaty of Utrecht (1713), Philip gave up any claim to the French throne. This let him keep the Spanish crown but ensured that his heirs—the future Spanish Bourbon dynasty—couldn't become too powerful by merging with the French Bourbons.

In 1714, the French-speaking Philip became the first king of the Bourbon dynasty in Spain (with the name Philip V). He breathed new life into the monarchy, which had grown ineffectual and corrupt under the Habsburgs. After the old wooden Habsburg royal palace burned on Christmas Eve of 1734, Philip (who was born at Versailles) built a new and spectacular late-Baroque-style palace as a bold symbol of his new dynasty. This is the palace that wows visitors to Madrid today. Construction was finished in 1764, and Philip V's son Charles III was the palace's first occupant (you'll see his decorations if you visit the palace's interior).

The Bourbon palace remained the home of Spain's kings from 1764 until 1931, when democratic elections led to the Second Spanish Republic and forced King Alfonso XIII into exile. After Francisco Franco took power in 1939, he sidelined the royals by making himself ruler-for-life. But later he handpicked as his successor Alfonso XIII's grandson, the Bourbon Prince Juan Carlos, whom Franco believed would continue his hardline policies. When Franco died in 1975, Juan Carlos surprised everyone by turning power over to Spain's parliament. Today Spain is a constitutional monarchy with a figurehead Bourbon king, Felipe VI, son of Juan Carlos I (who abdicated in 2014).

Virtues perched on a mountain of clouds, bestowing their favors on the Spanish monarchy.

Continue up to the top of the stairs. Before entering the first room, look to the right of the door to find a white marble bust of Felipe VI's great-great-g-g-g-great-grandfather Philip V, who began the Bourbon dynasty in Spain in 1700 and had this palace built.

• Now enter the first of the rooms.

❸ Hall of Halberdiers (Royal Guard): Immediately you get a sense of the palace's opulence, brought to you by the man portrayed over the fireplace: Charles III. Charles also appears overhead in the ceiling fresco as the legendary hero Aeneas, standing in the clouds of heaven. Charles hired the great Venetian painter Giambattista Tiepolo to do this room and others (see the "Tiepolo's Frescoes" sidebar, later). The fresco's theme, of Vulcan forging Aeneas's armor, relates to the room's function as the palace guards' lounge.

Notice the two fake doors painted on the wall to give the room a more regal symmetry. The old clocks are among hundreds amassed by Spain's royal family. And throughout the palace, pay attention to the carpets. Some are from the 18th century and others are new, but all were produced by the same Madrid royal tapestry factory and woven by hand.

The giant **portrait** depicts Spain's royal family: King Felipe (right), his dad and mom Juan Carlos I and Sofía (center), and his two sisters (left). It was Juan Carlos who resumed the monarchy in the 1970s after Francisco Franco's dictatorial regime. Unfortunately, J. C. showed poor judgment in flaunting his wealth during Spain's recent economic crisis, and was pressured to hand over the crown to his son, Felipe.
• Proceed into the...

❹ **Hall of Columns:** In Charles III's day, this sparkling, chandeliered venue was the grand ballroom and dining room. The tapestries (like most in the palace) are 17th-century Belgian, from designs by Raphael. Appropriately, the ceiling fresco (by Jaquinto, following Tiepolo's style) depicts a radiant young Apollo driving the chariot of the sun, while Bacchus enjoys wine, women, and song with a convivial gang. The message: A good king drives the chariot of state as smartly as Apollo, so his people can enjoy life to the fullest.

Today this space is used for intimate concerts as well as important ceremonies. This is where Spain formally joined the European Union in 1985, where Spaniards honored their national soccer team after their 2010 World Cup victory, and where Juan Carlos I signed his abdication in 2014.
• The next several rooms were the living quarters of King Charles III (r. 1759-1788). First comes his ❺ drawing room (with red-and-gold walls), where the king would enjoy the company of a similarly great ruler—the Roman emperor Trajan—depicted "triumphing" on the ceiling. The heroics of Trajan, born in Spain, naturally made the king feel good. Next, enter the blue-walled...

❻ **Antechamber:** This was Charles III's dining room. The gilded decor you see here and throughout the palace is bronze with gold leaf. The furnishings reflect the tastes of various kings and queens who've inhabited this palace. The four paintings are of Charles III's son and successor, King Charles IV (looking a bit like a dim-witted George Washington), and his wife, María Luisa (who wore the pants in the palace). They're by Francisco de Goya, who also made copies of these portraits (now in the Prado) to meet the demand for his work. Velázquez's famous painting, *Las Meninas* (also in the Prado), originally hung in this room.

The 12-foot-tall clock—in porcelain, bronze, and mahogany—sits on a music box. Reminding us of how time flies, it depicts Cronus, the god of time, both as a child and as an old man. The palace's clocks are wound—and reset—once a week to keep them accurate.

❼ **Gasparini Room:** (Gasp!) The entire room is designed, top to bottom, as a single gold-green-rose ensemble: from the frescoed ceiling to the painted stucco figures, silk-embroidered walls, chandelier, furniture, and multicolored marble floor. Each marble was quarried in, and represents, a different region of Spain. Birds overhead spread their wings, vines sprout, and fruit bulges from the surface. With curlicues everywhere (including their reflection in the mirrors), the room dazzles the eye and mind. It's a triumph of the Rococo style, with exotic motifs such as the Chinese people sculpted into the corners of the ceiling. (These figures, like many in the palace, were formed from stucco, or wet plaster.) The fabric gracing the walls was recently restored. Sixty people spent three years replacing the rotten silk fabric and then embroidering the original silver, silk, and gold threads back on.

Note the table with the Roman temple, birds, and flowers in the design. This was a typical souvenir from any aristocrat's trip to Rome in the mid-1800s. The chandelier, the biggest in the palace, is mesmerizing, especially with its glittering canopy of crystal reflecting in the wall mirrors. This was the king's dressing room. For a divine monarch, dressing was a public affair. The court bigwigs would assemble here as the

A *Grand Stairs*

B *Armory*

C *Gasparini Room*

D *Gala Dining Hall*

E *Porcelain Room*

F *Stradivarius Room*

G *Throne Room*

king, standing on a platform—notice the height of the mirrors—would pull on his leotards and adjust his wig.

• *In the next small room, the silk wallpaper is from modern times—note the intertwined "J. C. S." of former monarchs Juan Carlos I and Sofía. Pass through the silk room to reach...*

❽ Charles III Salon: This was Charles III's grand bedroom, where he died in 1788. His grandson, Ferdinand VII, redid the room to honor the great man. The room's color scheme recalls the blue robes of the religious order of monks Charles founded here. A portrait of Charles on the wall shows him also in blue. The ceiling fresco shows Charles (kneeling, in armor) establishing his order, with its various (female) Virtues. Along the bottom edge (near the harp player), find the baby in his mother's arms—that would be Ferdy himself, the long-sought male heir, preparing to continue Charles' dynasty.

The chandelier is shaped like a fleur-de-lis (the symbol of the Bourbon family) and capped with a Spanish crown. As you exit, notice the thick walls between rooms. These hid service corridors for servants, who scurried about mostly unseen.

❾ Porcelain Room: This tiny but lavish room is paneled with green-white-gold porcelain garlands, vases, vines, babies, and mythological figures. The entire ensemble was disassembled for safety during the civil war. (Find the little screws in the greenery that hides the seams between panels.) Notice the clock in the center with Atlas supporting the world on his shoulders.

❿ Yellow Room: This was a study for Charles III. The chandelier was designed to look like a temple with a fountain inside. Its cut crystal shows all the colors of the rainbow. Stand under it, look up, and sway slowly to see the colors glitter. This brilliantly lit room gives a glimpse of what the entire palace would look like whenever it was lit up for an occasion.

• *And if it were a special occasion, the next room is where everyone would gather and be dazzled.*

⓫ Gala Dining Room: This, perhaps the grandest room in the palace, is the main party room. The parquet floor was the preferred dancing surface when balls were held in this fabulous room. Note the golden vases from China and fine tapestries. The ceiling fresco depicts Christopher Columbus kneeling before Ferdinand and Isabel, presenting exotic souvenirs and his new, native friends.

Imagine this hall in action when a foreign dignitary dines here. Up to 12 times a year, the king entertains as many as 144 guests at this bowling lane-size table. If needed, the table can be extended the entire length of the room. The king and queen preside from the center. Find their chairs (slightly higher than the rest, and pulled out from the table a bit). The tables are set with fine crystal and cutlery. And the whole place glitters as the 15 chandeliers (and their 900 bulbs) are fired up.

• *Pass through the next room, originally where the royal string ensemble played for parties next door, but now known as the* **⓬ Cinema Room** *because the royal family once enjoyed Sunday afternoon movies here. From here, move into the...*

⓭ Silver Room: Some of this 19th-century silver tableware—knives and forks, bowls, salt and pepper shakers, and the big punch bowl—is used in the Gala Dining Room on special occasions. If you look carefully, you can see quirky royal accessories, including a baby's silver rattle and fancy candle snuffers.

⓮ Crockery and Crystal Rooms: The oldest and rarest pieces belonged to the man who built this palace—Philip V. His china actually came from China, before that country was opened to the West. Soon, other European royal families were opening their own porcelain works (such as France's Sèvres or Germany's Meissen) to produce high-quality knockoffs (and cutesy Hummel-like figurines). The porcelain technique itself was kept a royal secret. As you leave, check out

Isabel II's excellent 19th-century crystal ware.

• *Exit to the hallway and notice the interior courtyard you've been circling one room at a time.*

⑮ Courtyard: The royal family lived on this spacious middle floor, staff lived upstairs, and the kitchens, garage, and storerooms were on the ground level. The courtyard took on a new use in the 21st century, when King Felipe VI had his royal wedding reception in this courtyard, which was decorated like a palace room. Felipe married journalist Letizia Ortiz, a commoner (for love), and the two make a point to be approachable with their subjects—they're very popular.

• *Between statues of two of the giants of Spanish royal history (Isabel and Ferdinand), you'll enter the...*

⑯ Royal Chapel: This huge domed chapel is best known for royal funerals. The royal coffin lies in state here before making the sad trip to El Escorial to join the rest of Spain's past royalty. The glass coffin contains the entire body of St. Felix, given to the Spanish king by the pope in the 19th century. Note the glassed-in "crying room" to the left for royal babies. The royals rarely worship here (they prefer the adjacent cathedral), but the thrones are here just in case.

• *Continue around the courtyard, through the green* **⑰ Queen's Boudoir***—where royal ladies hung out—and into the...*

⑱ Stradivarius Room: Of all the instruments made by renowned violin maker Antonius Stradivarius (1644-1737), only 300 survive. This is the world's best collection and the only matching quartet set: two violins, a viola, and a cello. Charles III fiddled around with these. Today, a single Stradivarius could sell for $15 million.

• *The next room (on the left) is the...*

⑲ Crown Room: In the middle of the room is the scepter of the last Spanish king of the Habsburg family, Charles II, from

the 17th century. Alongside is the stunning crown of Charles III, from the succeeding (and current) dynasty, the Bourbons. There's the 2014 proclamation from when Juan Carlos abdicated, and another from when Felipe VI accepted. Notice which writing implement each man chose to sign with: Juan Carlos' traditional classic pen and Felipe VI's modern one. The fine inlaid marble table was used when King Juan Carlos signed the treaty finalizing Spain's entry into the European Union in 1985.

• *Walk back through the Stradivarius Room and into the courtyard hallway, passing the skippable Stucco Room. Cross over the top of the Grand Stairs, then continue your visit in the blue-wallpapered...*

⑳ Official Antechamber: Here, amid royal portraits, ambassadors would wait for their big moment when they met the king in the (upcoming) Throne Room. Tiepolo's ceiling fresco, of Jason returning with the Golden Fleece, would remind them of the exclusive company the Spanish monarch kept, as a Knight of the Golden Fleece.

• *After waiting here, ambassadors were called into the next room, the red-wallpapered...*

㉑ Official Waiting Room: Here dignitaries would have to wait a bit longer—awed by the rich tapestries, paintings, and Tiepolo's reverent ceiling fresco of the Spanish monarchy. Even today, officials are received in this room by royalty for an official photo op to remember their big moment.

• *And now we've reached the grand finale, the...*

㉒ Throne Room: This room, where the Spanish monarchs preside, is one of the palace's most glorious. The throne stands under a gilded canopy, on a raised platform, guarded by four lions (symbols of power found throughout the palace). The coat of arms above the throne shows the complexity of the Spanish empire across Europe—which, in the early 18th century, included Naples, Sicily, parts of

Tiepolo ceiling fresco in the Throne Room

the Netherlands, and more. Though the room was decorated under Charles III (late 18th century), the throne dates from 2014. Traditionally, a new throne is built for each king or queen, with a gilded portrait on the back. Felipe VI decided to keep things simple—his throne has only a crown.

Today, this room is where the king's guests salute him before they move on to state dinners. He receives them relatively informally...standing at floor level, rather than seated up on the throne.

The room holds many of the oldest and most precious things in the palace: silver-and-crystal chandeliers (from Venice's Murano Island), elaborate lions, and black bronze statues from the fortress that stood here before the 1734 fire. The 12 mirrors, impressively large in their day, each represent a different month.

The ceiling fresco (1764) is the last great work by Tiepolo, who died in Madrid in 1770. His massive painting (88 feet by 32 feet) celebrates the vast Spanish empire—upon which the sun also never set. The Greek gods look down from the clouds, overseeing Spain's empire, whose

Tiepolo's Frescoes

In 1762, King Charles III invited Europe's most celebrated palace painter, Giambattista Tiepolo (1696-1770), to decorate three rooms in the newly built palace. Sixty-six-year-old Tiepolo made the trip from Italy with his two well-known sons as assistants. They spent four years atop scaffolding decorating in the fresco technique, troweling plaster on the ceiling and quickly painting it before it dried.

Tiepolo's translucent ceilings seem to open up to a cloud-filled heaven, where Spanish royals cavort with Greek gods and pudgy cherubs. Tiepolo used every trick to "fool the eye" (trompe l'oeil), creating dizzying skyscapes of figures tumbling at every angle. He mixes 2-D painting with 3-D stucco figures that spill over the picture frame. His colorful, curvaceous ceilings blend seamlessly with the flamboyant furniture of the room below. Tiepolo's Royal Palace frescoes are often cited as the final flowering of Baroque and Rococo art.

territories are represented by the people and exotic animals ringing the edges of the ceiling. Follow the rainbow to the macho red-caped conquistador who motions toward the big bale of booty and the people he's conquered—feather-wearing Native Americans.

Admire Tiepolo's skill: At the far end of the room, he makes a pillar seem to shoot straight up into the sky. The pillar's pedestal has an inscription celebrating Tiepolo's boss, Charles III ("Carole Magna"). Notice how the painting spills over the gilded wood frame, where 3-D statues recline alongside 2-D painted figures. All of the throne room's decorations—the fresco, gold garlands, mythological statues, wall medallions—unite in a multimedia extravaganza dedicated to the glory of Spain.

• *Your tour of the palace is done. But, if you want one more interesting collection, you'll find it back outside. Exit down the same grand stairway you climbed at the start. Cross the big courtyard, heading to the far-right corner to the...*

🚩 **Royal Armory:** Here you'll find weapons and armor belonging to many great Spanish historical figures. While some of it was for battle, kings also wore armor for royal hunts, sporting events (such as jousting tournaments), and official ceremonies. Much of this armor dates from Habsburg times, before this palace was even built. Circle the big room clockwise.

In the three glass cases on the left, you'll see the oldest pieces in the collection. In the central case (case III) are the shield, sword, belt, and dagger of Boabdil, the last Moorish king, who surrendered Granada in 1492. In case IV, the armor and swords belonged to Boabdil's conqueror, King Ferdinand.

The center of the room is filled with knights in armor on horseback. Many of the pieces belonged to the two great kings who ruled Spain at its 16th-century peak, Charles V (a.k.a. the Holy Roman Emperor) and his son, Philip II.

The long wall on the left displays a full array of Charles V's personal armor. At the far end, the mannequin of Charles on horseback wears the same armor and assumes the same pose as in Titian's famous painting of him (in the Prado).

The opposite wall showcases the armor and weapons of Philip II, the king who impoverished Spain with his wars against the Protestants, beginning the country's downward slide. Philip anticipated that debt collectors would ransack his estate after his death and specifically protected his impressive collection of armor by founding this armory.

Downstairs is more armor, mostly from the 17th century. The pint-size armor you may see wasn't for children to fight in.

Rather, it's training armor for noble youngsters, who as adults would be expected to ride, fight, and play gracefully in these clunky getups. Before you leave, notice the life-saving breastplates dimpled with bullet dents (to right of exit door).

• *Climb the steps from the armory exit to the viewpoint.*

View of the Gardens: Looking down from this high bluff, it's clear why rulers have built on this strategically located spot since the ninth century. The vast palace backyard, once the king's hunting ground, is now a city park, dotted with fountains.

• *Whew. After all those rooms, frescoes, chandeliers, knickknacks, kings, and history, consider a final stop in the palace's upstairs café for a well-deserved rest.*

Madrid's Museum Neighborhood

Three great museums, all within a 10-minute walk of one another, cluster in east Madrid. The Prado is Europe's top collection of paintings. The Thyssen-Bornemisza sweeps through European art from old masters to moderns. And the Centro de Arte Reina Sofía has a choice

Prado Museum

selection of modern art, starring Picasso's famous Guernica.

If visiting all three museums, you can skip ticket lines and save a few euros by buying the **Paseo del Arte combo-ticket** (€30, sold at the museums).

Rick's Tip: *To really save money,* **visit when the sights are free:** *every evening for the Prado, every evening but Tuesday (when it's closed) for the Reina Sofía, and Mondays for the Thyssen-Bornemisza's permanent collection.*

▲▲▲PRADO MUSEUM (MUSEO NACIONAL DEL PRADO)

With more than 3,000 canvases, including entire rooms of masterpieces by superstar painters, the Prado (PRAH-doh) is my vote for the greatest collection anywhere of paintings by the European masters. The museum is the place to enjoy the holy trinity of Spanish painters—El Greco, Velázquez, and Goya—including Velázquez's *Las Meninas,* considered by many to be the world's finest painting, period. You'll also find paintings by Italian and Flemish masters, including Hieronymus Bosch's fantastical *Garden of Earthly Delights* altarpiece.

Cost: €15, additional (obligatory) fee for occasional temporary exhibits, free Mon-Sat 18:00-20:00 and Sun 17:00-19:00, temporary exhibits discounted during free hours, under age 18 always free.

Hours: Mon-Sat 10:00-20:00, Sun until 19:00.

Information: Tel. 913-302-800, www.museodelprado.es.

Crowd-Beating Tips: The only place to buy tickets on-site is the ground level of the Goya Entrance, where ticket-buying lines can be long. To save time, buy your ticket ahead for an extra fee of €0.50 per ticket (www.museodelprado.es, can buy same-day tickets if available—if the ticket line's long, check on your phone). Those with a Paseo del Arte combo-ticket

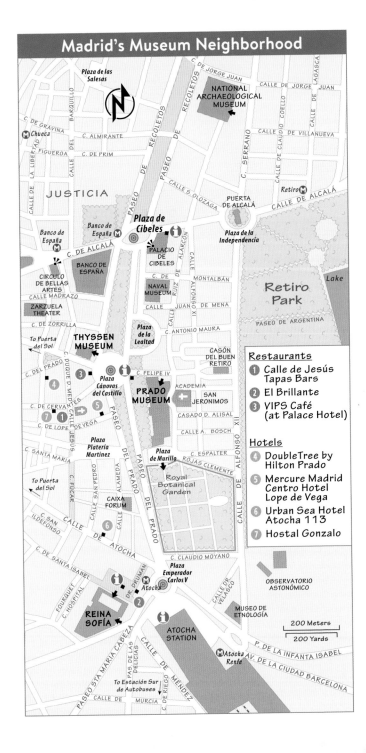

Madrid's Museum Neighborhood

Restaurants
1. Calle de Jesús Tapas Bars
2. El Brillante
3. VIPS Café (at Palace Hotel)

Hotels
4. DoubleTree by Hilton Prado
5. Mercure Madrid Centro Hotel Lope de Vega
6. Urban Sea Hotel Atocha 113
7. Hostal Gonzalo

(described earlier) can go straight to any entrance. To save time, buy it online or at the less-crowded Thyssen-Bornemisza or Reina Sofía museums. The Prado is generally less crowded at lunchtime (13:00-16:00), when there are fewer groups, and on weekdays. It's busiest on free evenings and weekends.

Getting There: It's at the Paseo del Prado. The nearest **Metro** stops are Banco de España (line 2) and Atocha (line 1), each a five-minute walk from the museum. It's a 15-minute **walk** from Puerta del Sol.

Getting In: The **Jerónimos Entrance,** where our tour begins, is the main entry (but no ticket sales). It's tucked around behind the north end of the building (to the left, as you face the Prado from the main road). The nearby **Goya Entrance,** also at the north end, has the ticket office and a museum entrance just above. The **Murillo Entrance** (south/right end, as you face the building) is mostly for student groups, but if you have a ticket, they may let you slip in. All entrances have airport-type security.

Tours: The audioguide is a helpful supplement to my self-guided tour, allowing you to wander and dial up commentary on 250 masterpieces as you come across them (€4-6 depending on if there's a temporary exhibit). Skip the Prado's Second Canvas smartphone app.

Length of This Tour: Allow at least two hours.

Services: The Jerónimos Entrance has an information desk, bag check, audioguides, bookshop, WCs, and café. Larger bags must be checked.

Eating: The museum's self-service **$ cafeteria/restaurant** is just inside the Jerónimos Entrance (Mon-Sat 10:00-19:30, Sun until 18:30, hot dishes served only 12:30-16:00). Across the street from the Goya Entrance, you'll find **$$ VIPS,** a popular chain restaurant, handy for a cheap and filling salad or sandwich, with outdoor tables facing the Neptune fountain (daily 9:00-24:00, across the boulevard from north end of Prado at Plaza de Canova del Castillo, under Palace Hotel).

Next door is Spain's first Starbucks, opened in 2001. A strip of wonderful **$$ tapas bars** is just a few blocks west of the museum, lining Calle de Jésús (see page 195). If you want to take a break outside the Prado for lunch, you can reenter the museum on the same ticket as long as you get it stamped at a desk marked "*Educación,*" near the Jerónimos Entrance.

⊘ SELF-GUIDED TOUR

The vast Prado Museum sprawls over four floors. This tour is designed to hit the highlights with a minimum of walking and in a (roughly) chronological way. We'll see altarpieces of early religious art, the rise of realism in the Renaissance, the royal art of Spain's Golden Age, and the slow decline of Spain—bringing us right up to the cusp of the modern world. Paintings are moved around frequently, and rooms may be renumbered—if you can't find a particular work, ask a guard.

• *Enter at the Jerónimos Entrance, pick up a museum map, and locate where you are: Level 0, at the Jerónimos Entrance. Our first stop should be nearby, in Room 56A. To get there, find the corridor (near the security checkpoint) to the* **Edificio Villanueva.** *Head down the corridor about 30 yards and turn right into Room 55, then immediately right again (into 55A), then left into Room 56A. Let's kick off this tour of artistic delights with a large three-panel painting of* The Garden of Earthly Delights.

❶ HIERONYMUS BOSCH

In his cryptic triptych *The Garden of Earthly Delights* (El Jardín de las Delicias, c. 1505), the early Flemish painter Bosch (c. 1450-1516) paints a wonderland of eye-pleasing details. The message is that the pleasures of life are fleeting, and we'd better avoid them or we'll wind up in hell.

This altarpiece has a central scene and two hinged outer panels. All of the images work together to teach a religious message. Imagine the altarpiece closed (showing the back side). The world is gray and bare, before God's creation. Now open it up, bring on the people, and splash into this colorful *Garden of Earthly Delights*.

The left panel is Paradise, showing naked Adam and Eve before original sin. Everything is in its place, with animals behaving virtuously. Innocent Adam and Eve get married, with God himself performing the ceremony.

The central panel is a riot of naked men and women on a perpetual spring break—eating, dancing, kissing, cavorting with strange animals, and contorting themselves into a *Kama Sutra* of sensual positions. Men on horseback ride round and round, searching for but never reaching the elusive Fountain of Youth. Humankind frolics in earth's "Garden," oblivious to where they came from (left) and where they may end up...

Now, go to hell (right panel). It's a burning Dante's *Inferno*-inspired wasteland where genetic-mutant demons torture sinners. Everyone gets their just desserts, like the glutton who is eaten and re-eaten eternally, the musician strung up on his own harp, and the gamblers with

their table forever overturned. In the center, hell is literally frozen over. A creature with a broken eggshell body hosting a tavern, tree-trunk legs, and a hat featuring a bagpipe (symbolic of hedonism) stares out—it's the face of Bosch himself.

If you want more Bosch, check out the nearby table featuring his **Seven Deadly Sins** (*Los Pecados Capitales,* late 15th century). Each of the four corners has a theme: death, judgment, paradise, and hell. The fascinating wheel, with Christ in the center, names the sins in Latin (lust, envy, gluttony, and so on), and illustrates each with a vivid scene that works as a slice of 15th-century Dutch life.

Nearby, another Bosch triptych, **The Hay Wain** (*El Carro de Heno,* c. 1516), has still more vivid imagery about the consequences of sin and the transience of earthly life.

• *Let's move on to the source of European painting as we know it: the Italian Renaissance. Backtrack through Rooms 55A and 55 to reach the corridor. At the corridor, turn right and go past the elevators (remember them—we'll use the elevators later). About 30 yards along, turn right into Room 49—a large, long, sage-green hall labeled XLIX. You've reached...*

Bosch, The Garden of Earthly Delights

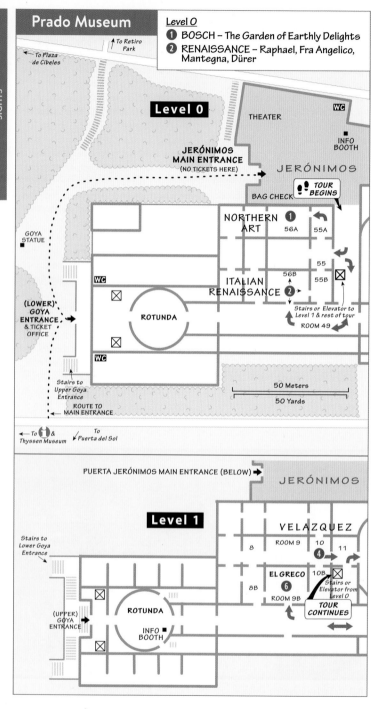

Prado Museum

Level 0

❶ BOSCH – The Garden of Earthly Delights
❷ RENAISSANCE – Raphael, Fra Angelico, Mantegna, Dürer

↑ To Retiro Park
← To Plaza de Cibeles

Level 0

THEATER

WC

INFO BOOTH

JERÓNIMOS MAIN ENTRANCE
(NO TICKETS HERE)

JERÓNIMOS

👣 TOUR BEGINS

BAG CHECK

NORTHERN ART ❶
56A 55A

GOYA STATUE

WC

(LOWER) GOYA ENTRANCE & TICKET OFFICE

ITALIAN RENAISSANCE ❷
56B 55B
55

ROTUNDA

Stairs or Elevator to Level 1 & rest of tour

ROOM 49

WC

Stairs to Upper Goya Entrance

ROUTE TO MAIN ENTRANCE

50 Meters
50 Yards

← To ⓘ & Thyssen Museum
↙ To Puerta del Sol

PUERTA JERÓNIMOS MAIN ENTRANCE (BELOW) ➡

JERÓNIMOS

Level 1

VELAZQUEZ

Stairs to Lower Goya Entrance

8   ROOM 9   10   11

❹

EL GRECO ❻
8B   ROOM 9B   10B
Stairs or Elevator from Level 0

(UPPER) GOYA ENTRANCE

ROTUNDA

INFO BOOTH

TOUR CONTINUES

Level 1

❸ VELÁZQUEZ – Las Meninas

❹ More Velázquez

❺ TITIAN – Court Paintings

❻ EL GRECO – Various Works

❼ RUBENS – The Three Graces

❽ GOYA – The Family of Charles IV; Nude Maja & Clothed Maja

❾ GOYA – Tapestry Cartoons (upstairs on Level 2)

Level 0

❿ GOYA – Dark Paintings

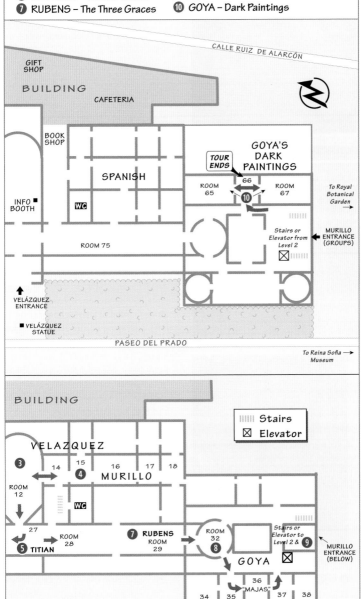

❷ THE RENAISSANCE

During its Golden Age (the 1500s), Spain may have been Europe's richest country, but Italy was still the most cultured. Spain's kings loved how Italian Renaissance artists captured a three-dimensional world on a two-dimensional canvas, bringing Bible scenes to life and celebrating real people and their emotions.

• *Start midway down Room 49, on the right-hand wall, with a guy in red painted by Raphael.*

Raphael (1483-1520) was the undisputed master of realism. When he painted *Portrait of a Cardinal* (*El Cardenal,* c. 1510-11), he showed the sly Vatican functionary with a day's growth of beard and an air of superiority, locking eyes with the viewer. The cardinal's slightly turned torso is as big as a statue. Nearby are several versions of *Holy Family* and other paintings by Raphael.

• *Now climb the four stairs in the middle of the room, up to Room 56B.*

Fra Angelico's *The Annunciation* (*La Anunciación,* c. 1426) is half medieval piety, half Renaissance realism. In the crude Garden of Eden scene (on the left), a scrawny, sinful First Couple hovers unrealistically above the foliage, awaiting eviction. The angel's Annunciation to Mary (right side) is more Renaissance, both with its upbeat message (that Jesus will be born to redeem sinners like Adam and Eve) and in the budding photorealism, set beneath 3-D arches. (Still, aren't the receding bars of the porch's ceiling a bit off? Painting three dimensions wasn't that easy.)

Also in Room 56B, the tiny *Dormition of the Virgin* (*El Tránsito de la Virgen*), by **Andrea Mantegna** (c. 1431-1506), shows his mastery of Renaissance perspective. The apostles crowd into the room to mourn the last moments of the Virgin Mary's life. The receding floor tiles and open window in the back create the subconscious effect of Mary's soul finding its way out into the serene distance.

Ⓐ *Raphael,* Portrait of a Cardinal

Ⓑ *Fra Angelico,* The Annunciation

Ⓒ *Mantegna,* Dormition of the Virgin

• *To see how the Renaissance spread to northern lands, step into the adjoining Room 55B (to the left, as you face the main hall).*

Albrecht Dürer's *Self-Portrait (Autorretrato),* from 1498, is possibly the first time an artist depicted himself. The artist, age 26, is German, but he's all dolled up in a fancy Italian hat and permed hair. He'd recently returned from Italy and wanted to impress his countrymen with his sophistication. Dürer (1471-1528) wasn't simply vain. He'd grown accustomed, as an artist in Renaissance Italy, to being treated like a prince. Note Dürer's signature, the pyramid-shaped "A. D." (D inside the A), on the windowsill.

Nearby are Dürer's 1507 panel paintings of *Adam* and *Eve*—the first full-size nudes in Northern European art. Like Greek statues, they pose in their separate niches, with three-dimensional, anatomically correct bodies. This was a bold humanist proclamation that the body is good, man is good, and the things of the world are good.

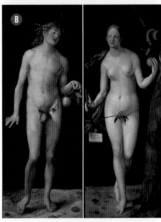

• *Renaissance art soon spread to Europe's richest country—Spain. Backtrack down the four steps into Room 49, and make a U-turn to the left, to reach those elevators we saw earlier. Take the elevator up to level 1, and turn left into Room 11. A painting here (by Velázquez) of a radiant Greek god surprising a gang of startled workmen introduces us to the main feature of Spanish art—unflinching realism.*

Let's begin next door, in the large, lozenge-shaped Room 12.

❸ VELÁZQUEZ, *LAS MENINAS*

Diego Velázquez (vel-LAHTH-keth, 1599-1660) was the photojournalist of court painters, capturing the Spanish king and his court in formal portraits that take on aspects of a candid snapshot. Room 12 is filled with the portraits Velázquez was called on to produce. Kings and princes prance like Roman emperors. Get up close and notice that his remarkably detailed costumes are nothing but a few

Ⓐ *Dürer,* Self-Portrait
Ⓑ *Dürer,* Adam and Eve
Ⓒ *Velázquez,* Las Meninas

messy splotches of paint—the proto-Impressionism Velázquez helped pioneer.

The room's centerpiece, and perhaps the most important painting in the museum, is Velázquez's **Maids of Honor** (**Las Meninas,** c. 1656). It's a peek at nannies caring for Princess Margarita and, at the same time, a behind-the-scenes look at Velázquez at work. One hot summer day in 1656, Velázquez (at left, with paintbrush and Dalí moustache) stands at his easel and stares out at the people he's painting—the king and queen. They would have been standing about where we are, and we see only their reflection in the mirror at the back of the room. Their daughter (blonde hair, in center) watches her parents being painted, joined by her servants (meninas), dwarves, and the family dog. At that very moment, a man happens to pass by the doorway at back and pauses to look in. Why is he there? Probably just to give the painting more depth.

This frozen moment is lit by the window on the right, splitting the room into bright and shaded planes that recede into the distance. The main characters look right at us, making us part of the scene, seemingly able to walk around, behind, and among the characters.

If you stand in the center of the room, the 3-D effect is most striking. This is art come to life.

• Facing this painting, leave to the left, pass through Room 11, and enter Room 10.

❹ MORE VELÁZQUEZ

Velázquez enjoyed capturing light— and capturing the moment. **The Feast of Bacchus** (Los Borrachos, c. 1628-29) is a group selfie in a blue-collar bar. A couple of peasants mug for a photo-op with a Greek god—Bacchus, the god of wine. This was an early work, before Velázquez got his court-painter gig, and shows off his admiration for "real" people. Hardworking farmers enjoying the fruit of their labor deserved portraits, too. Notice the almost-sacramental presence of the ultrarealistic bowl of wine in the center, as Bacchus, with the honest gut, crowns a fellow hedonist.

• Backtrack through the big gallery with Las Meninas, and continue straight ahead into Room 14.

Velázquez's boss, King Philip IV, had an affair, got caught, and repented by commissioning **The Crucified Christ** (Cristo Crucificado, c. 1632). Christ hangs his head, humbly accepting his punishment. Philip would have been left to stare at the slowly dripping blood, contemplating how long Christ had to suffer to atone for Philip's sins. This is an interesting death scene. There's no anguish, no tension, no torture. Light seems to emanate from Jesus as if nothing else matters. The crown of thorns and the cloth wrapped around his waist are particularly vivid. Above it all, a sign reads in three languages: "Jesus of Nazareth, King of the Jews."

• Continue on through Room 15 (with Velázquez's insightful portraits of the royal court **dwarves**) and into Rooms 16 and 17.

Take a moment to appreciate these paintings by one of Velázquez's admirers: Bartolomé Murillo. **Murillo** (1618-

Murillo, The Immaculate Conception of Los Venerables

1682) soaked up Velazquez's unflinching photorealism, but added a spoonful of sugar. In his most famous works—called *The Immaculate Conception*—Murillo put a human face on the abstract Catholic doctrine that Mary was conceived and born free of original sin. His "immaculate" virgins float in a cloud of Ivory Soap cleanliness, radiating youth and wholesome goodness. Mary wears her usual colors—white for purity and blue for divinity. Murillo's sweet and escapist work must have been very comforting to the wretched people of his hometown of Sevilla, which was ravaged by plague in 1647-1652.

• *Backtrack to the* Meninas *room (12) and turn left. You'll exit into the museum's looooong grand gallery (Rooms 25-29) and come face-to-face with a large canvas of a knight on horseback.*

❺ TITIAN'S COURT PAINTINGS

Spain's Golden Age kings Charles V and Philip II both hired Europe's premier painter—Titian the Venetian (c. 1485-1576)—to paint their portraits.

Titian, The Emperor Charles V at Mühlberg

In ***The Emperor Charles V at Mühlberg*** (*Carlos V en la Batalla de Mühlberg*, 1548), the king rears on his horse, points his lance at a jaunty angle, and rides out to crush an army of Lutherans. Having inherited kingdoms and baronies through his family connections, the Holy Roman Emperor Charles V (who was also King Charles I of Spain) was the world's most powerful man in the 1500s. (You can see the suit of armor depicted in the painting in the Royal Palace.)

In contrast (just to the right), Charles I's son, ***Philip II*** (*Felipe II*, c. 1550-1551), looks pale, suspicious, and lonely—a scholarly and complex figure. He moved Spain's capital from Toledo to Madrid and built the austere, monastic palace at El Escorial. These are the faces of the Counter-Reformation, as Spain took the lead in battling Protestants. Both father and son had one thing in common: underbites, a product of royal inbreeding (which Titian painted...delicately).

• *Philip II amassed a surprisingly large collection of Titian's Renaissance playmates, which you could seek out elsewhere on this floor. But let's turn to a quite different painter that Philip hired—El Greco.*

Facing Charles and Philip, turn right, walk about 30 yards, and turn right at the first door, into Room 9B.

❻ EL GRECO

El Greco (1541-1614) was born in Greece (his name is Spanish for "The Greek"), trained in Venice, then settled in Toledo—60 miles from Madrid. His paintings are like Byzantine icons drenched in Venetian color and fused in the fires of Spanish mysticism. The El Greco paintings displayed here rotate, but they all glow with his unique style.

In ***Christ Carrying the Cross*** (*Cristo Abrazado a la Cruz*, c. 1602), Jesus accepts his fate, trudging toward death with blood running down his neck. He hugs the cross and directs his gaze along the crossbar. His upturned eyes (sparkling with a streak of white paint) lock onto his next stop—heaven.

Ⓐ *El Greco*, Christ Carrying the Cross

Ⓑ *El Greco*, The Nobleman with His Hand on His Chest

Ⓒ *Rubens*, The Three Graces

Ⓓ *Goya*, The Family of Charles IV

Ⓔ *Goya*, Nude Maja

Ⓕ *Goya*, Third of May, 1808

The Adoration of the Shepherds (*La Adoración de los Pastores,* c. 1614—likely next door in room 10B), originally painted for El Greco's own burial chapel in Toledo, has the artist's typical two-tiered composition—heaven above, earth below. The long, skinny shepherds are stretched unnaturally in between, flickering like flames toward heaven.

El Greco's portraits of Spanish nobles and saints (such as **The Nobleman with His Hand on His Chest,** *El Caballero de la Mano al Pecho,* c. 1580) focus on their aristocratic expressions. A man's hand with his fingers splayed out, but with the middle fingers touching, was El Greco's trademark way of expressing elegance (or was it the 16th-century symbol for "Live long and prosper"?). Several paintings have El Greco's signature written in faint Greek letters—"Doménikos Theotokópoulos," El Greco's real name.

• *While El Greco was painting austere Christian saints, other European artists were painting in a dramatic new style—Baroque.*

Return to the main gallery, turn left, pass by Charles and Philip again, and proceed to the gallery's far end (technically Rooms 28 and 29) for the large, colorful, fleshy canvases by...

❼ RUBENS

A native of Flanders, Peter Paul Rubens (1577-1640) painted Baroque-style art meant to play on the emotions, titillate the senses, and carry you away. His paintings surge with Baroque energy and ripple with waves of figures. Surveying his big, boisterous canvases, you'll notice his trademarks: sex, violence, action, emotion, bright colors, and ample bodies, with the wind machine set on full. Gods are melodramatic, and nymphs flee half-human predators. Rubens painted the most beautiful women of his day—well-fed, no tan lines, squirt-gun breasts, and very sexy.

Rubens' **The Three Graces** (*Las Tres Gracias,* c. 1630-1635) celebrates cellulite. The ample, glowing bodies intertwine as the women exchange meaningful glances.

The Grace at the left is Rubens' young second wife, Hélène Fourment, who shows up regularly in his paintings.

• *Rubens, El Greco, Titian, and Velázquez had all made their living working for Europe's royalty. But that world was changing, and revolution was in the air. No painter illustrates the changing times more than our final artist—Goya.*

From Rubens, continue to the end of the long main gallery and enter the round Room 32, where you'll see royal portraits by Goya.

❽ GOYA—COURT PAINTER

Follow the complex Francisco de Goya (1746-1828) through the stages of his life—from dutiful court painter, to political rebel and scandal maker, to the disillusioned genius of his "black paintings."

In the group portrait **The Family of Charles IV** (*La Familia de Carlos IV,* 1800), the royals are all decked out in their Sunday best. Goya himself stands at his easel to the far left, painting the court (a tribute to Velázquez in *Las Meninas*) and revealing the shallowness beneath the fancy trappings. Charles, with his ridiculous hairpiece and goofy smile, was a vacuous, henpecked husband. His toothless yet domineering queen upstages him, arrogantly stretching her swanlike neck.

• *Exit to the right across a small hallway and turn left to find Room 36, where you'll find Goya's most scandalous work.*

Rumors flew that Goya was fooling around with the vivacious Duchess of Alba, who may have been the model for two similar paintings, **Nude Maja** (*La Maja Desnuda,* c. 1800) and **Clothed Maja** (*La Maja Vestida,* c. 1808). A *maja* was a trendy, working-class girl. Whether she's a duchess or a *maja,* Goya painted a naked lady—an actual person rather than some mythic Venus. According to a believable legend, the two paintings were displayed in a double frame, with the Clothed Maja sliding over the front to hide the Nude Maja from inquisitive minds.

• *Just off the next room, you'll find an elevator and a staircase (farther down the hall). You could use one of them to head up to level 2, to Rooms 85-87 and 90-94, to see Goya's* ❾ *tapestry cartoons—displays of his designs for tapestries (known as "cartoons") for nobles' palaces.*

Otherwise, take the elevator or stairs down to level 0, then go up and down the stairs (across the Murillo Entrance) to Room 66. Entering, start to the left, in Room 65, with powerful military scenes.

❿ GOYA—DARK PAINTINGS

Despite working for Spain's monarchs, Goya became a political liberal and a champion of the Revolution in France. But that idealism was soon crushed when the supposed hero of the Revolution, Napoleon, morphed into a tyrant and invaded Spain. Goya, who lived on Madrid's Puerta del Sol, captured the chaotic events that unfolded there.

In *The Second of May, 1808* (*El 2 de Mayo de 1808*, 1814), Madrid's citizens rise

Goya, Saturn

up to protest the occupation in Puerta del Sol, and the French send in their dreaded Egyptian mercenaries. They plow through the dense tangle of Madrileños, who have nowhere to run. The next day, *The Third of May, 1808* (*El 3 de Mayo de 1808*, 1814), the French rounded up ringleaders and executed them. The colorless firing squad—a faceless machine of death—mows them down, and they fall in bloody, tangled heaps. Goya throws a harsh prison-yard floodlight on the main victim, who spreads his arms Christ-like to ask, "Why?"

• *Finish the tour with Goya's final, late-in-life paintings. Turn about-face to the "black paintings" in Room 67.*

Depressed and deaf from syphilis, Goya retired to his small home and smeared its walls with his **"black paintings"**—dark in color and in mood. During this period in his life, Goya would paint his nightmares... literally. The style is considered Romantic—emphasizing emotion over beauty—but it foreshadows 20th-century Surrealism with its bizarre imagery, expressionistic and thick brushstrokes, and cynical outlook.

Stepping into Room 67, you are surrounded by art from Goya's dark period. These paintings are the actual murals from the walls of his house, transferred onto canvas. In *Saturn* (*Saturno*, c. 1820-1823), the king of the Roman gods—fearful that his progeny would overthrow him—eats one of his offspring. Saturn, also known as Cronus (Time), may symbolize how time devours us all.

• *There's a lot more to the Prado, but there's also a lot more to Madrid. The choice is yours.*

▲▲THYSSEN-BORNEMISZA MUSEUM (MUSEO DEL ARTE THYSSEN-BORNEMISZA)

Locals call this stunning museum simply the Thyssen (TEE-sun). It displays the impressive collection that Baron Thyssen (a wealthy German married to a former Miss Spain) sold to Spain for $350 million. The museum offers a unique chance

Thyssen-Bornemisza Museum

to enjoy the sweep of all of art history—including a good sampling of the "isms" of the 20th century—in one collection. It's basically minor works by major artists and major works by minor artists. (Major works by major artists are in the Prado.) But art lovers appreciate how the good baron's art complements the Prado's collection by filling in where the Prado is weak—such as Impressionism, which is the Thyssen's forte.

Cost and Hours: €12, includes temporary exhibits, timed ticket required for temporary exhibits, free for kids under age 18, free on Mon; permanent collection open Mon 12:00-16:00, Tue-Sun 10:00-19:00; temporary exhibits stay open Sat until 21:00; audioguide-€5 for permanent collection, €4 for temporary exhibits, €7 for both; Second Canvas Thyssen is a decent, free app that explains major works; located kitty-corner from the Prado at Paseo del Prado 8 in Palacio de Villahermosa (Metro: Banco de España); tel. 917-911-370, www.museothyssen.org.

Services: The museum has free baggage storage (bags must fit through a small x-ray machine), a cafeteria and restaurant, free Wi-Fi, and a shop/bookstore.

Visiting the Museum: After purchasing your ticket, continue down the wide main hall past larger-than-life paintings of former monarchs Juan Carlos I and Sofía, and then paintings of the baron (who died in 2002) and his art-collecting baroness, Carmen. At the info desk, pick up a museum map. Each of the three floors is divided into two areas: the permanent collection (numbered rooms) and additions from baroness Carmen since the 1980s (lettered rooms). The permanent collection has the heavyweight artists (Rubens, Rembrandt, Manet, Monet, Picasso, Braque, Bacon), although Carmen's wing is also intriguing. Ascend to the top floor and work your way down, taking a delightful walk through art history. Visit the rooms on each floor in numerical order, from Primitive Italian (Room 1) to Surrealism and Pop Art (Rooms 45-48).

Rick's Tip: *If you're tired and want to* **get from the Thyssen to the Reina Sofía,** *hail a cab at the gate to zip straight there, or take bus #27 from the square with the Neptune fountain.*

▲▲▲CENTRO DE ARTE REINA SOFÍA

Home to Picasso's *Guernica,* the Reina Sofía is one of Europe's most enjoyable modern-art museums. Its exceptional collection of 20th-century art is housed in what was Madrid's first public hospital. The focus is on 20th-century Spanish artists—Picasso, Dalí, Miró, and Gris—but you'll also find works by Kandinsky, Braque, Magritte, and other giants of modern art. Many works are displayed alongside continuously running films that place the art into social context. Those with an appetite for modern and contemporary art can spend several delightful hours in this museum.

Cost and Hours: €10 (includes most temporary exhibits), free if you're under 18 or over 65; open Mon and Wed-Sat 10:00-21:00, Sun until 19:00 (fourth floor not accessible Sun after 15:00), closed Tue. The museum is free—and often crowded—Mon and Wed-Sat 19:00-21:00 and Sun 13:30-19:00 (must pick up a ticket to enter).

Information: Tel. 917-741-000, www.museoreinasofia.es.

Centro de Arte Reina Sofía

Getting There: It's a block from the Atocha Metro stop, on Plaza Sánchez Bustillo (at Calle de Santa Isabel 52). In the Metro station, follow signs for the Reina Sofía exit. Emerging from the Metro, walk straight ahead a half-block and turn right on Calle de Santa Isabel. You'll see the tall, exterior glass elevators that flank the museum's main entrance.

A second entrance in the newer section of the building sometimes has shorter lines, especially during the museum's free hours. To get there, face the glass elevators and walk left around the old building to the large gates of the red-and-black Nouvel Building.

Tours: The hardworking audioguide is €5.50.

Services: Bag storage is free. The *librería* just outside the Nouvel wing has a larger selection of Picasso and Surrealist reproductions than the main gift shop at the entrance.

Eating: The museum's **$$ café** (a long block around the left from the main entrance) is a standout for its tasty cuisine. The square immediately in front of the museum is ringed by fine places for a simple meal or drink. My favorite is **$$ El Brillante,** a classic dive offering pricey tapas and baguette sandwiches (long hours daily, two entrances—one on Plaza Sánchez Bustillo, the other at Plaza del Emperador Carlos V 8, tel. 915-286-966). A 10-minute walk north is my favorite strip of **tapas bars,** on Calle de Jesús (for details, see page 195).

❍ SELF-GUIDED TOUR

The permanent collection is divided into three groups: art from 1900 to 1945 (second floor, including *Guernica*), art from 1945 to 1968 (fourth floor), and art from 1962 to 1982 (adjoining Nouvel wing). Temporary exhibits are scattered throughout. While the collection is roughly chronological, it's displayed thematically, with each room clearly labeled with its theme.

For a good first visit, pick up a free map and ride the fancy glass elevator to level 2 and tour that floor counterclockwise (Modernism, Cubism, Picasso's *Guernica*, Surrealism), then see post-WWII art on level 4, and finally descend to the Nouvel wing for the finale.

• *On level 2, begin in Room 201—located between the two elevators—which introduces you to the dawn of the 20th century.*

MODERNISM (ROOM 201)

The 20th century—accelerated by technology and shattered by war—would produce the exciting and turbulent modern art showcased in this museum. The collection kicks off with engravings by the 19th-century artist Goya, often considered the first "modern" painter. He used art to express his inner feelings and address social injustice, and his dynamic style anticipated the formless chaos of Modern Art.

You may also see early works by young Pablo Picasso—a precocious teenager who skipped his art classes to sketch works by Goya, Velázquez, and El Greco in the Prado. In 1900, 19-year-old Pablo moved to the world's art capital, Paris, where the Modern Art revolution was about to begin.

• *We'll tour this floor counterclockwise (in reverse order to how the rooms are numbered). Start in Room 210.*

CUBISM (ROOMS 210, 208, 207)

In Paris, Picasso and his roommate Georges Braque invented a new way of portraying the world on a canvas—Cubism. They shattered the world into a million pieces, then reassembled the shards and "cubes" onto a canvas. It was a way of showing a three-dimensional object on a two-dimensional surface. (Imagine walking around a statue to take in all the angles, and then attempting to put it on a 2-D plane.)

Room 210 makes it clear that Cubism was very much a Spaniard-driven movement. Picasso was soon joined in Paris by Madrid's own Juan Gris. Gris adored

Picasso (the feeling wasn't mutual) and added his own spin on the Cubist style. Gris used curvier lines, brighter colors, and more recognizable images, composing his paintings as if he was pasting paper cutouts on the canvas to make a collage.

Proceed through the rest of the Cubism exhibit (Rooms 208 and 207), tracing the development of this cornerstone of Modernism. You'll see how various artists took up this same idea but expressed it in different ways.

• *Continuing counterclockwise, you enter Room 206 ("Guernica and the 1930s"). Make your way through this wing and find the big room with a movie screen-sized canvas. You've reached what is likely the reason for your visit...*

PICASSO'S *GUERNICA* (ROOM 206)

Perhaps the single most impressive piece of art in Spain is Pablo Picasso's *Guernica* (1937). The monumental canvas—one of Europe's must-see sights—is not only a piece of art but a piece of history, capturing the horror of modern war in a modern style.

While it's become a timeless classic representing all war, it was born in response to a specific conflict—the Spanish Civil War (1936-1939), which pitted the democratically elected Second Republican government against the fascist general Francisco Franco. Franco won and ended up ruling Spain with an iron fist for the next 36 years. At the time Franco cemented his power, *Guernica* was touring internationally as part of a fundraiser for the Republican cause. With Spain's political situation deteriorating and World War II looming, Picasso in 1939 named New York's Museum of Modern Art as the depository for the work. It was only after Franco's death, in 1975, that *Guernica* ended its decades of exile. In 1981 the painting finally arrived in Spain (where it had never before been), and it now stands as Spain's national piece of art.

Guernica—The Bombing: On April 26, 1937, Guernica—a Basque market town in northern Spain and an important Republican center—was the target of the world's first saturation-bombing raid on civilians. Franco gave permission to his fascist confederate Adolf Hitler to use the town as a guinea pig to try out Germany's new air force. The raid leveled the town, causing destruction that was unheard of at the time (though by 1944, it would be commonplace).

News of the bombing reached Picasso in Paris, where coincidentally he was just beginning work on a painting commission awarded by the Republican government. Picasso scrapped his earlier plans and immediately set to work sketching scenes of the destruction as he imagined it. In a matter of weeks, he put these bomb-shattered shards together into a large mural (286 square feet). For the first time, the world could see the destructive force of the rising fascist movement—a prelude to World War II.

Guernica—The Painting: The bombs are falling, shattering the quiet village. A woman howls up at the sky (far right), horses scream (center), and a man falls from a horse and dies, while a wounded woman drags herself through the streets. She tries to escape, but her leg is too thick, dragging her down, like trying to run from something in a nightmare. On the left, a bull—a symbol of Spain—ponders it all, watching over a mother and her dead baby...a modern pietà. A woman in the center sticks her head out to see what's happening. The whole scene is lit from above by the stark light of a bare bulb. Picasso's painting threw a light on the brutality of Hitler and Franco, and suddenly the whole world was watching.

Picasso's abstract, Cubist style reinforces the message. It's as if he'd picked up the shattered shards and pasted them onto a canvas. The black-and-white tones are as gritty as the black-and-white newspaper photos that reported the bombing. The drab colors create a depressing, almost nauseating mood.

Picasso chose images with universal symbolism, making the work a commentary on all wars. Picasso said that the central horse, with the spear in its back, symbolizes humanity succumbing to brute force. The fallen rider's arm is severed and his sword is broken, more symbols of defeat. The bull, normally a proud symbol of strength and independence, is impotent and frightened. Between the bull and the horse, the faint dove of peace can do nothing but cry.

The bombing of Guernica—like the entire civil war—was an exercise in brutality. As one side captured a town, it might systematically round up every man, old and young—including priests—line them up, and shoot them in revenge for atrocities by the other side.

Thousands of people attended the Paris exhibition, and *Guernica* caused an

Picasso, Guernica

immediate sensation. They could see the horror of modern war technology, the vain struggle of the Spanish Republicans, and the cold indifference of the fascist war machine. Picasso vowed never to return to Spain while Franco ruled (the dictator outlived him).

With each passing year, the canvas seemed more and more prophetic—honoring not just the hundreds or thousands who died in Guernica, but also the estimated 500,000 victims of Spain's bitter civil war and the 55 million worldwide who perished in World War II. Picasso put a human face on what we now call "collateral damage."

• *After seeing* **Guernica,** *view the additional exhibits here and in adjoining rooms that put the painting in its social context, then continue counterclockwise to Room 205.*

SURREALISM AND SALVADOR DALÍ (ROOM 205)

Another Spaniard in Paris—Salvador Dalí (1904-1989)—helped found another groundbreaking Modern Art style, Surrealism. Dalí arrived in Jazz Age Paris in

Dalí, The Invisible Man

the 1920s, in the wake of World War I. He hung out with his idols, fellow Spaniards Picasso, Gris, and Joan Miró, as well as an international set.

Disillusioned by the irrationality of the war, they rebelled against traditional mores and the shackles of the rational mind. Influenced by Freud's theories about the power of the subconscious, they let their emotions and primal urges speak freely on the canvas. They painted imagery from their dreams (mindscapes, rather than landscapes). They captured the realm beyond the world we see—it was "sur-real."

You'll see Dalí's distinct, melting-object style. Dalí places familiar items in a stark landscape, creating an eerie effect. Figures morph into misplaced faces and body parts. Background and foreground play mind games—is it an animal (seen one way) or a man's face? A waterfall or a pair of legs? It's a wide shot...no, it's a close-up. Look long at paintings like Dalí's *The Endless Enigma* (1938) and *The Invisible Man* (1929-1932); they take different viewers to different places.

Face of the Great Masturbator (1929) is psychologically exhausting, depicting in its Surrealism a lonely, highly sexual genius in love with his muse, Gala (while she was still married to a French poet). This is the first famous Surrealist painting.

During this productive period, Dalí collaborated with Luis Buñuel on the classic Surrealist film *Un Chien Andalou* (***The Andalusian Dog,*** 1928, in the adjoining room). Buñuel and Dalí were members of the Generation of '27, a group of nonconformist Spanish bohemians whose creative interests had a huge influence on art and literature in their era.

• *Head up to level 4, where the permanent collection continues. Start in Room 401 and circle this floor counterclockwise.*

POST-WWII ART (1945-1968)

The organizing theme in this part of the museum is "Art in a Divided World"—a world upset by war, divided by the Iron

Curtain, and under the constant threat of nuclear war. The collection starts in the troubled wake of World War II, with canvases that are often distorted, harsh-colored, and violent-looking. With Europe in ruins, the center of the art world was moving from Paris to New York City. You'll see the distorted yet recognizable figures of Picasso give way to purely abstract art. The final rooms (423-429) bring in the 1960s, with its Pop Art—everyday pop-culture objects displayed as art.

• End your visit in the **Nouvel wing,** *where you'll see art from the 1960s to the 1980s. The easiest "connection" between the main building and Nouvel wing is to descend to level 2, make your way to Room 206.01, enter the Nouvel wing, descend the stairs to level 1, and start your visit in Room 104.01. But regardless of where you start, the Nouvel wing is made for browsing.*

Near the Prado
▲▲RETIRO PARK (PARQUE DEL BUEN RETIRO)
Once the private domain of royalty, this majestic park has been a favorite of Madrid's commoners since Charles III decided to share it with his subjects in the late 18th century. Siesta in this 300-acre green-and-breezy escape from the city. At midday on Saturday and Sunday, the area around the lake becomes a street carnival, with jugglers, puppeteers, and lots of local color. These peaceful gardens offer great picnicking and people-watching (closes at dusk). From the Retiro Metro stop, walk to the big lake (El Estanque), where you can rent a rowboat. Past the lake, a grand boulevard of statues leads to the Prado.

▲ROYAL BOTANICAL GARDEN (REAL JARDÍN BOTÁNICO)
After your Prado visit, you can take a lush and fragrant break in this sculpted park. Wander among trees from around the world, originally gathered by—who else?—the enlightened King Charles III. This garden was established when the Prado's building housed the natural science museum. A flier in English explains that this is actually more than a park—it's a museum of plants.

Cost and Hours: €4, daily May-Aug 10:00-21:00, April and Sept until 20:00, shorter hours off-season, entrance opposite the Prado's Murillo/south entry, Plaza de Murillo 2, tel. 914-203-017.

▲▲NATIONAL ARCHAEOLOGICAL MUSEUM (MUSEO ARQUEOLÓGICO NACIONAL/MAN)
This museum takes you on a chronological walk through the story of Iberia. With a well-curated, rich collection of artifacts and tasteful multimedia displays (well-described in English), the museum shows off the wonders of each age: Celtic pre-Roman, Roman, a fine and rare Visigothic section, Moorish, Romanesque, and beyond. A highlight is the Lady of Elche (Room 13), a prehistoric Iberian female bust and a symbol of Spanish archaeology.

Retiro Park

National Archaeological Museum

You may also find underwhelming replica artwork from northern Spain's Altamira Caves (big on bison), giving you a faded peek at the skill of the cave artists who created the originals 14,000 years ago.

Cost and Hours: €3, free on Sat after 14:00 and all day Sun; open Tue-Sat 9:30-20:00, Sun until 15:00, closed Mon; multimedia guide—€2; 20-minute walk north of the Prado at Calle Serrano 13, Metro: Serrano or Colón, tel. 915-777-912, www.man.es.

EXPERIENCES

Shopping

Madrileños have a passion for shopping. It's a social event, often incorporated into the afternoon paseo, which eventually turns into drinks and dinner. Most shoppers focus on the colorful pedestrian area between and around Gran Vía and Puerta del Sol. Here you'll find H&M and Zara clothing, Imaginarium toys, FNAC books and music, and a handful of small local shops. The fanciest big-name shops (Gucci, Prada, and the like) tempt strollers along Calle Serrano, northwest of Retiro Park. For trendier chains and local fashion, head to pedestrian Calle Fuencarral, Calle Augusto Figueroa, and the streets surrounding Plaza de Chueca (north of Gran Vía, Metro: Chueca).

EL CORTE INGLÉS DEPARTMENT STORE

The giant El Corte Inglés, with several buildings strung between Puerta del Sol and Plaza del Callou, is a handy place to pick up just about anything you need. **Building 3,** full of sports equipment, books, and home furnishings, is closest to Puerta del Sol. **Building 2,** a block up from Puerta del Sol on Calle Preciados, has a handy info desk, travel agency/box office for local events, souvenirs, toiletries, a post office, men's and women's fashions, and a vast basement supermarket with edible souvenirs. Farther north on Calle

del Carmen toward Plaza del Callao is **Building 1,** with electronics, another travel agency/box office, and the "Gourmet Experience"—a floor filled with fun eateries and a rooftop terrace for diners.

All El Corte Inglés department stores are open daily (Mon-Sat 10:00-22:00, Sun 11:00-21:00, tel. 913-798-000, www.elcorteingles.es).

▲EL RASTRO FLEA MARKET

Europe's biggest flea market is a field day for shoppers, people-watchers, and pickpockets (Sun only, 9:00-15:00). It's best before 11:00, though bargain shoppers like to go around 14:00, when vendors are more willing to strike end-of-day deals. Thousands of stalls titillate more than a million browsers with mostly new junk. Locals have lamented the tackiness of El Rastro lately—on the main drag, you'll find cheap underwear and bootleg CDs, but no real treasures.

Rick's Tip: El Rastro offers a fascinating chance to see gangs of young **thieves** *overwhelming and ripping off naive tourists while plainclothes police circulate and do their best.* **Don't even bring a wallet.** *The pickpocket action is brutal.*

For an interesting market day (Sun only), start at Plaza Mayor, where Europe's biggest stamp and coin market thrives. Watch old-timers paging lovingly through each other's albums, looking

El Rastro flea market

for win-win trades. When you're done, head south or take the Metro to Tirso de Molina. Walk downhill, wandering off on side streets to browse antiques, old furniture, and garage sale-style sellers who often simply throw everything out on a sheet. On Plaza del Campillo del Mundo Nuevo, kids and adults leaf through each other's albums of soccer cards and negotiate over trades.

A typical Madrileño's Sunday could involve a meander through the Rastro streets with several stops for *cañas* (small beers) at the gritty bars along the way.

Madrid offers intimate flamenco venues.

Nightlife

Those into clubbing may have to wait until after midnight for the most popular places to even open, much less start hopping. Spain has a reputation for partying very late and not stopping until offices open in the morning. (Spaniards, who are often awake into the wee hours of the morning, have a special word for this time of day: *la madrugada*.) If you're out early in the morning, it's hard to tell who is finishing their day and who's just starting it. Even if you're not a party animal after midnight, make a point to be out with the happy masses, luxuriating in the cool evening air between 22:00 and midnight. The scene is absolutely unforgettable.

▲▲▲ PASEO

Just walking the streets of Madrid seems to be the way Madrileños spend their evenings. Even past midnight on a hot summer night, entire families with little kids are strolling, enjoying tiny beers and tapas in a series of bars, licking ice cream, and greeting their neighbors. Good areas to wander include from Puerta del Sol to Plaza Mayor and down Calle del Arenal until you hit Plaza de Isabel II; the pedestrianized Calle de las Huertas from Plaza Mayor to the Prado; along Gran Vía from about Plaza de Callao to Plaza de España; and, to window shop with the young and trendy, up Calle de Fuencarral (keep going until you hit traffic).

▲▲ FLAMENCO

Although Sevilla is the capital of flamenco, Madrid has a few easy and affordable options. And on summer evenings, Madrid puts on live flamenco events in the Royal Palace gardens (ask TI for details). Among the listings below, Casa Patas is grumpy, while Carboneras is friendlier—but Casa Patas has better-quality artists and a riveting seriousness. Regardless of what your hotel receptionist may tell you, flamenco places other than the ones I recommend are filled with tourists and pushy waiters.

Taberna Casa Patas attracts big-name flamenco artists. You'll quickly understand why this intimate venue (30 tables, 120 seats) is named "House of Feet." Since it is for locals as well as tour groups, the flamenco is contemporary and may be jazzier than your notion—it depends on who's performing (€38 includes cover and first drink, Mon-Thu at 22:30, Fri-Sat at 20:00 and 22:30, closed Sun, about 1.5 hours, reservations smart, no flash cameras, Cañizares 10, tel. 913-690-496, www.casapatas. com). Its restaurant is a logical spot for dinner before the show (€30 dinners, Mon-Thu from 20:00, Fri-Sat from 18:30).

Las Carboneras, more downscale, is an easygoing, folksy little place a few steps from Plaza Mayor with a nightly hour-long flamenco show (€36 includes entry and a drink, €71 gets you a table up front with dinner and unlimited cheap drinks if you reserve ahead, manager Enrique promises a €5/person discount if you book directly and show this book, daily at 20:30, also Mon-Thu at 22:30 and Fri-Sat at 23:00, reservations recommended, Plaza del Conde de Miranda 1, tel. 915-428-677, www.tablaolascarboneras.com).

Las Tablas Flamenco offers a less-expensive nightly show respecting the traditional art of flamenco. You'll sit in a plain room with a mix of tourists and cool, young Madrileños in a nondescript office block just over the freeway from Plaza de España (€29 with drink, reasonable drink prices, shows daily at 20:00 and usually also at 22:00, 1.25 hours, corner of Calle de Ferraz and Cuesta de San Vicente at Plaza de España 9, tel. 915-420-520, www.lastablasmadrid.com).

▲ ZARZUELA

For a delightful look at Spanish light opera that even English speakers can enjoy, try zarzuela. Guitar-strumming Napoleons in red capes; buxom women with masks, fans, and castanets; Spanish-speaking pharaohs; melodramatic spotlights; and aficionados clapping and singing along from the cheap seats, where the acoustics are best—this is zarzuela...the people's opera. Originating in Madrid, zarzuela is known for its satiric humor and surprisingly good music. Performances occur evenings at Teatro de la Zarzuela, which alternates between zarzuela, ballet, and opera throughout the year. The TI's monthly guide has a special zarzuela section.

Getting Tickets: Prices range from €18-50, less for restricted-view seats, 50 percent off for those over 65, Teatro de la Zarzuela box office open Mon-Fri 12:00-20:00 and Sat-Sun 14:30-18:00 for advance tickets or until showtime for same-day tickets, near the Prado at Jovellanos 4, Metro: Sevilla or Banco de España, tel. 915-245-400, http://teatrodelazarzuela.mcu.es. To purchase tickets online, go to www.entradasinaem.es and select "*Espacios*" ("Spaces") to find Teatro de la Zarzuela; you'll receive an email with your tickets, which you need to print before you arrive at the theater.

ROOFTOP BARS

Madrid has several great rooftop bars, offering slightly overpriced drinks with views over the sprawling city center. At most of these, you'll pay €5 for a beer or wine, and €8-10 for a cocktail. Here are a few good options: To be right in the heart of the action, **Taberna Puertalsol** sits atop the El Corte Inglés department store (Building 3) right on Puerta del Sol; just head into the store and ride the elevator to Floor 5 (daily 12:30-late, Puerta del Sol 10). The classic **Circulo de Bellas Artes** skyscraper at Calle de Alcalá 42 is capped with the **Azotea** cocktail bar, offering reasonably priced drinks overlooking the start of Gran Vía (€4 to ride the elevator). Near the Plaza de España end of Gran Vía, the **Dear Madrid** hotel has a rooftop bar—called **Nice to Meet You**—on its 14th floor (Gran Vía 80).

Circulo de Bellas Artes rooftop bar

▲ BULLFIGHTING

Madrid's Plaza de Toros hosts Spain's top bullfights on most Sundays and holidays from March through mid-October, and nearly every day during the San Isidro festival (early May–early June—often sold out long in advance). Fights start between 17:00 and 19:00 (early in spring and fall, late in summer). The bullring is at the Ventas Metro stop (a 25-minute Metro ride from Puerta del Sol, tel. 913-562-200, www.las-ventas.com).

Getting Tickets: Prices range from €5 to €150. There are no bad seats at Plaza de Toros; paying more gets you in the shade and/or closer to the gore. (The action often intentionally occurs in the shade to reward the expensive-ticket holders.) To be close to the bullfighters, choose areas 8, 9, or 10; for shade: 1, 2, 9, or 10; for shade/sun: 3 or 8; for the sun and cheapest seats: 4, 5, 6, or 7. Note these key words: *corrida*—a real fight with professionals; *novillada*—rookie matadors, younger bulls, and cheaper tickets.

Getting tickets through your hotel or a booking office is convenient, but they add 20 percent or more and don't sell the cheapest seats. Two booking offices sell tickets online and in person. The easiest place is **Bullfight Tickets Madrid** at Plaza del Carmen 1 (Mon-Sat 9:00-13:00 & 16:30-19:00, Sun 9:30-14:00, tel. 915-319-131, www.bullfightticketsmadrid.com; run by José and his English-speaking son, also José, will deliver to your hotel). Another option is Toros La Central at Calle Victoria 3 (Mon-Fri 10:00-14:30 & 16:30-20:00, Sat-Sun 10:00-13:00, tel. 915-211-213, www.toroslacentral.es).

To save money, you can stand in the ticket line at the bullring. Except for important bullfights—or during the San Isidro festival—there are generally plenty of seats available.

For a dose of the experience, you can buy a cheap ticket and just see a couple of bullfights. Each takes about 20 minutes, and the event consists of six bulls over two hours.

EATING

In Spain, only Barcelona and the Basque Country rival Madrid for taste-bud thrills.

Fine Dining

$$$$ Restaurante Casa Paco feels simple, even basic, but it's a Madrid tradition. It's a worthwhile splurge if you want to dine out well and carnivorously (Tue-Sat

Madrid hosts Spain's top bullfights.

13:00-16:00 & 20:00-24:00, Sun 13:00-16:00, closed Mon, Plaza de la Puerta Cerrada 11, tel. 913-663-166, www.casa-paco1933.es).

$$$$ Sobrino del Botín is a hit with many Americans because "Hemingway ate here." It's grotesquely touristy, pricey, and the last place "Papa" would go now... but still, people love it and go for the roast suckling pig, their specialty (daily 13:00-16:00 & 20:00-24:00, a block downhill from Plaza Mayor at Cuchilleros 17, tel. 913-664-217, www.botin.es).

$$$$ Casa Lucio is a favorite splurge for traditional specialties among power-dressing Madrileños. This is a good restaurant for a special night out and a full-blown meal, but you pay extra for this place's fame (daily 13:00-16:00 & 20:30-24:00, closed Aug, Calle Cava Baja 35; reserve several days in advance—and don't even bother on weekends; tel. 913-653-252, www.casalucio.es).

$$$ El Caldero ("The Pot") is a romantic spot and a good place for paella and other rice dishes. A classy, in-the-know crowd appreciates its subdued elegance and crisp service (Tue-Sat 13:30-16:30 & 20:30-24:00, Sun-Mon 13:30-16:30, Calle de las Huertas 15, tel. 914-295-044).

$$$$ La Bola Taberna, touristy but friendly, cozy, and tastefully elegant, specializes in *cocido Madrileño*—Madrid stew. The stew, made of various meats, carrots, and garbanzo beans in earthen jugs, is a winter dish, prepared here for the tourists all year. Reservations are smart (cash only, daily lunch seatings at 13:30 and 15:30, dinner 20:30-23:00, closed Sun in July-Aug, midway between Royal Palace and Gran Vía at Calle Bola 5, tel. 915-476-930, http://labola.es).

Tapas-Hopping from Bar to Bar

For maximum fun, people, and atmosphere, go mobile for dinner: Do the *tapeo*, a local tradition of going from one bar to the next, munching, drinking, and socializing. The real action begins late (around 21:00). While the energy is fun and local later in the evening, you may find it easier to get service and a spot by dining earlier—which is still late by American standards.

There are tapas bars almost everywhere, but two areas in the city center are particularly rewarding for a bar-crawl meal: **Calle de Jesús** (near the Prado) is the easiest, with several wonderful and

Choosing tapas

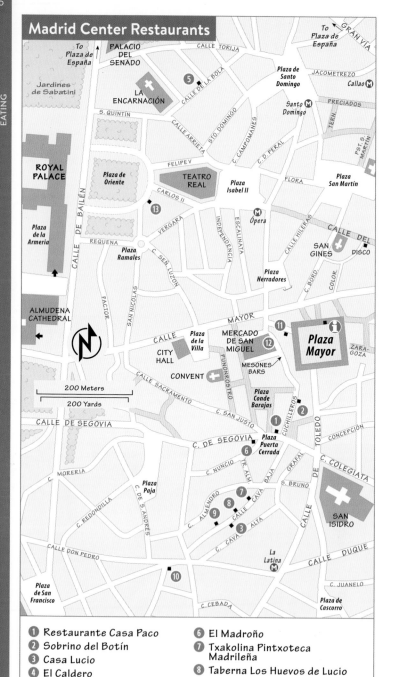

Madrid Center Restaurants

1. Restaurante Casa Paco
2. Sobrino del Botín
3. Casa Lucio
4. El Caldero
5. La Bola Taberna
6. El Madroño
7. Txakolina Pintxoteca Madrileña
8. Taberna Los Huevos de Lucio
9. Taberna Tempranillo

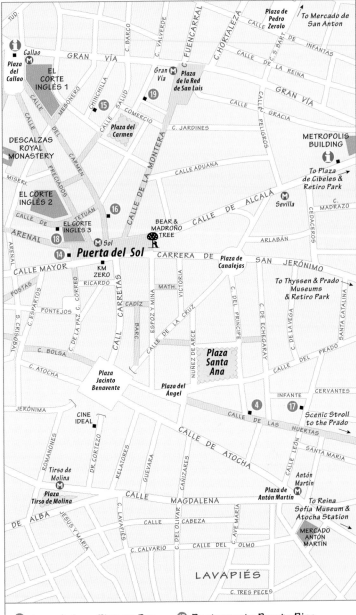

⑩ Juana la Loca Pintxos Bar
⑪ Casa Rúa
⑫ Mercado de San Miguel
⑬ Café de Oriente
⑭ La Mallorquina

⑮ Restaurante Puerto Rico
⑯ Restaurante-Cafeteria Europa
⑰ Casa Gonzalez
⑱ Casa Labra Taberna Restaurante
⑲ Artemisia

diverse places in a two-block row, while trendy **Calle Cava Baja** has fancier offerings and feels most energetic.

The Great Tapas Row on Calle de Jesús

For locations, see the map on page 173.

$$ Cervecería Cervantes serves hearty *raciones*, specializes in octopus, and has both a fine bar and good restaurant seating (intersection of Plaza de Jesús and Calle de Cervantes, tel. 914-296-093).

$$ Taberna de la Daniela Medinaceli, part of a local chain, is popular for its specialty *cocido madrileño*—a rich chickpea-based soup. It has a lovely dining area if you want to settle in for a while (Plaza de Jesús 7, tel. 913-896-238).

$$ La Dolores, with a rustic little dining area, has been a hit since 1908 and is still extremely popular. Its canapés (little sandwiches) are listed on the wall (Plaza de Jesús 4, tel. 914-292-243).

$$ Cervezas La Fabrica packs in seafood lovers at the bar; a quieter back room is available for those preferring a table. Prices are the same in both spots. They serve a nice *cava* (Spanish sparkling wine), which goes well with seafood (Calle de Jesús 2, tel. 913-690-671).

$$ Cervecería Los Gatos is a kaleidoscope of Spanish culture, with chandeliers swinging above wine barrels in the intense bar area and characteristic tables in the more peaceful zone behind (Calle de Jesús 2, tel. 914-293-067).

$$$ Taberna Maceira is a Galician place with a wonderfully woody and rustic energy. A sit-down restaurant (not a bar), it specializes in octopus, cod, *pimientos de Padrón* (green peppers), and *caldo gallego* (white bean soup)—all classic Galician specialties of northwest Spain (Mon-Sat 13:00-16:00 & 20:30-24:00, closed Sun, Calle de Jesús 7, tel. 914-291-584).

Tapas on Calle Cava Baja

$$$ El Madroño ("The Berry Tree," a symbol of Madrid), more of a cowboy

Breakfast in Madrid

Many hotels don't include (or even offer) breakfast, so you may be out on the streets first thing looking for a place to eat. My typical breakfast, found at any corner bar: *café con leche, tortilla española* (a slice of potato omelet), and *zumo de naranja natural* (fresh-squeezed orange juice). Nontouristy cafés offer a hot drink and a pastry, with perhaps a potato omelet and sandwiches (toasted cheese, ham, or both). Touristy places will have a *desayuno* menu with various ham-and-eggs deals. Try *churros* at least once; if you're not in the mood for heavy chocolate, go local and dip your *churros* in a *café con leche*. Get advice from your hotel staff for their favorite breakfast place. If all else fails, a Starbucks is often nearby.

bar, serves all the clichés. Inside, study the coats of arms of Madrid through the centuries as you try a *vermut* (vermouth) on tap. Or ask for a small glass (*chupito*) of the *licor de madroño*. Indoor seating is bright and colorful; the sidewalk tables come with good people-watching (daily 8:00-24:00, a block off the top of Calle Cava Baja at Plaza de la Puerta Cerrada 7, tel. 913-645-629).

$$ Txakolina Pintxoteca Madrileña is a thriving bar serving elaborately composed, Basque-style *pinchos* (fancy open-faced sandwiches—*pintxo* in Basque) to a young crowd (Calle Cava Baja 26, tel. 913-664-877).

$$ Taberna Los Huevos de Lucio is a jam-packed bar serving good tapas, salads, *huevos estrellados* (fried eggs over fried potatoes), and wine. If you'd like to make it a sit-down meal, head to the tables in the back (avoid the basement, Calle Cava Baja 30, tel. 913-662-984).

$$ Taberna Tempranillo, ideal for hungry wine lovers, offers fancy tapas and fine wine by the glass (see listing on the board or ask for their English menu). While there are a few tables, the bar is just right for hanging out (closed Aug, Calle Cava Baja 38, tel. 913-641-532).

$$ Juana la Loca Pintxos Bar ("Crazy Juana") overlooks a lonely square at the top end of Calle Cava Baja (on the left). It feels more sophisticated and civilized, with elegant *raciones*, refined-yet-tight seating, gorgeously presented dishes from a foodie menu, and reasonable prices considering the quality. Their classic is the runny *tortilla de patatas*, with piles of decadently caramelized onions (Plaza Puerta de Moros 4, tel. 913-665-500).

Eating Reasonably
On or near Plaza Mayor
Calamari Sandwiches: Plaza Mayor is famous for its *bocadillos de calamares.* For a tasty squid-ring sandwich, line up at **$ Casa Rúa** at Plaza Mayor's north-west corner, a few steps up Calle Ciudad Rodrigo (daily 11:00-23:00).

$$ Mercado de San Miguel: This early-20th-century market sparkles after a recent renovation and bustles with a trendy food circus of eateries (daily 10:00-24:00).

Facing the Royal Palace: $$$ Café de Oriente is recommended mostly for its location next to the National Theater and overlooking Plaza de Oriente. It's a venerable and elegant (and expensive) opera-type café with fine tables on the square (Plaza de Oriente 2, tel. 915-413-974, www.cafedeoriente.es, more interesting menu after 20:00).

Near Puerta del Sol and Plaza Mayor
$$ La Mallorquina ("The Girl from Mallorca"), on the downhill end of Puerta del Sol, is a venerable pastry shop serving the masses at the bar (cheap *Napolitana* pastries and *rosquillas*—doughnuts) and takeout on the ground floor. But upstairs is a refined little 19th-century café—popular for generations. It offers an accessible menu and a relative oasis of quiet (daily 9:00-21:00, closed mid-July-Aug).

$$ Restaurante Puerto Rico, a simple, no-nonsense place, serves good meals for great prices to smart Madrileños in a long, congested hall (daily 13:00-24:00, Chinchilla 2, between Puerta del Sol and Gran Vía, tel. 915-219-834).

$$$ Restaurante-Cafeteria Europa is a fun, high-energy scene with a mile-long bar, old-school waiters, local cuisine, and a fine €12 fixed-price lunch special available inside (daily 7:00-24:00, next to Hotel Europa, 50 yards off Puerta del Sol at Calle del Carmen 4, tel. 915-212-900).

$$$ Casa Gonzalez, a revered gourmet cheese-and-wine shop with a circa-1930s interior. Away from the tourist scene, it offers a genteel opportunity to enjoy a plate of first-class cheese and a fine glass of wine with friendly service and a fun setting (40 wines by the glass, Mon-Sat 9:30-24:00, Sun 11:30-17:00, Calle de León 12, tel. 914-295-618, Francisco and Luciano).

$ Casa Labra Taberna Restaurante is famous as the birthplace of the Spanish Socialist Party in 1879...and as a spot for great cod. Their tasty little *tajada de bacalao* dishes put them on the map. It's a wonderful scene with three distinct sections: the inexpensive stand-up **bar** (line up for cod and croquettes, power up to the bar for drinks); a peaceful little **sit-down area** in back (still cheap); and a fancy, more expensive **restaurant** (daily 11:00-15:30 & 18:00-23:00, a block off Puerta del Sol at Calle Tetuán 12, tel. 915-310-081).

Vegetarian: $$ Artemisia is a hit with vegetarians and vegans who like good, healthy food without the typical hippie ambience that comes with most veggie places (weekday lunch specials, open daily 13:30-16:00 & 20:30-23:30, north of Puerta del Sol at Tres Cruces 4, a few steps off Plaza del Carmen, tel. 915-218-721).

SLEEPING

Madrid has plenty of centrally located budget hotels and *pensiones*. Most of the accommodations I've listed are within a few minutes' walk of Puerta del Sol.

Most of the year you should be able to find a sleepable double for €70, a good double for €100, and a modern, air-conditioned double with all the comforts for €150. Anticipate full hotels only in May (the San Isidro festival, celebrating Madrid's patron saint with bullfights and zarzuelas—especially around his feast day on May 15), around Easter, during LGBT Pride Week at the end of June, and in September (when conventions can clog the city). During the hot months of July and August, prices can be soft—ask for a discount.

With all of Madrid's street noise, I'd request the highest floor possible. Cheaper places have very thin walls and doors, so you might get noise from within and without (pack earplugs). Breakfast is generally not offered—when it is, it's often expensive (about €15).

Midrange and Fancier Places
Near Puerta del Sol and Gran Vía

These hotels are located in and around the pedestrian zone north and west of Puerta del Sol. Use Metro: Sol unless noted otherwise.

$$$$ Hotel Liabeny feels like a grand Old World hotel, with a marble-and-wood lobby, an eager-to-please concierge, and 213 plush, spacious, business-class rooms offering all the comforts (air-con, elevator, sauna, gym, off Plaza del Carmen at Salud 3, tel. 915-319-000, www.liabeny.es, reservas@hotelliabeny.com).

$$$$ Hotel Ópera, with 79 classy rooms, is located just off Plaza Isabel II, a four-block walk from Puerta del Sol toward the Royal Palace (RS%, includes breakfast, air-con, elevator, sauna and gym, ask for a higher floor—there are

nine—to avoid street noise, Cuesta de Santo Domingo 2, Metro: Ópera, tel. 915-412-800, www.hotelopera.com, reservas@hotelopera.com). Hotel Ópera's cafetería is deservedly popular. Consider their "singing dinners"—great operetta music with a delightful dinner—offered nightly (around €60, reservations smart, call 915-426-382 or reserve at hotel).

$$$ Hotel Intur Palacio San Martín is perfectly tucked away from the hustle of the center next to the Descalzas Royal Monastery. It has a beautiful atrium lounge with a vertical garden and 94 comfortable rooms combining modern flair with respect for tradition (air-con, elevator, Plaza San Martín 5, tel. 917-015-000, www.hotel-inturpalaciosanmartin.com, sanmartin@intur.com).

$$$ Hotel H10 Villa de la Reina, filling a former bank building right along the pulsing Gran Vía, has an elegant, early 20th-century drawing-room lobby and 74 rooms (air-con, elevator, Gran Vía 22, tel. 915-239-101, www.h10hotels.com, H10.villa.delareina@H10hotels.com).

$$$ Hotel Preciados, a four-star business hotel, has 100 welcoming, modern rooms as well as elegant lounges. It's well-located and reasonably priced for the luxury it provides (free mini-bar, air-con, elevator, pay parking, just off Plaza de Santo Domingo at Calle Preciados 37, Metro: Callao, tel. 914-544-400, www.preciadoshotel.com, preciadoshotel@preciadoshotel.com).

$$$ Hotel Francisco I is on a lively pedestrian street midway between the Royal Theater and Puerta del Sol. It has a mod lobby and 93 rooms (air-con, elevator, Calle del Arenal 15, tel. 915-480-204, www.hotelfrancisco.com, info@hotelfrancisco.com).

$$ Hotel Europa, with sleek marble, red carpet runners along the halls, happy Muzak charm, and an attentive staff, is a solid value. It rents 100 squeaky-clean rooms, many with balconies overlooking the pedestrian zone or an inner courtyard.

The hotel has an honest ethos and offers a straight price (family rooms, air-con, elevator, Calle del Carmen 4, tel. 915-212-900, www.hoteleuropa.eu, info@hoteleuropa.eu, run by Antonio and Fernando Garaban and their helpful and jovial staff, Javi, Jim, and Tomás). The recommended **$$ Restaurante-Cafeteria Europa** is a lively and convivial scene—fun for breakfast.

$$ Hotel Moderno, renting 90 rooms, has a quiet, professional, and friendly atmosphere; a comfy first-floor lounge; and a convenient location close to Puerta del Sol (air-con, elevator, Calle del Arenal 2, tel. 915-310-900, www.hotel-moderno.com, info@hotel-moderno.com).

Near Plaza Mayor
$$$ Petit Palace Posada del Peine feels like part of a big, modern chain (which it is), but fills its well-located old building with fresh, efficient character. Behind the ornate Old World facade is a comfortable business-class hotel with 67 rooms (air-con, elevator, Calle Postas 17, tel. 915-238-151, www.petitpalace.com, posadadelpeine@petitpalace.com).

$$ Hotel Plaza Mayor, with 41 solidly outfitted rooms, is tastefully decorated and beautifully situated a block off Plaza Mayor. It occupies an enticing middle ground between pricey business-class hotels and the basic *hostales* (breakfast included for Rick Steves readers who book by email, air-con, elevator, Calle de Atocha 2, tel. 913-600-606, www.h-plaza-mayor.com, info@h-plazamayor.com).

Near the Prado
For locations, see the map on page 173.

$$$$ DoubleTree by Hilton Prado has the predictable class of an American chain, but feels more like a European boutique hotel—with 61 rooms, an attentive staff, and a handy location tucked down a quieter side street near the Prado (air-con, elevator, Calle San Agustín 3, tel. 913-600-820, www.doubletree3.hilton.com).

$$$ Mercure Madrid Centro Hotel Lope de Vega offers good business-class hotel value near the Prado. It is a "cultural-themed" hotel inspired by 17th-century writer Lope de Vega. With 59 rooms, it feels cozy and friendly for a formal hotel (family rooms, air-con, elevator, very limited pay parking—reserve ahead, Calle Lope de Vega 49, tel. 913-600-011, www.accor.com, H9618@accor.com).

Cheap Sleeps
Near Plaza del Carmen
These three are in the same building at Calle de la Salud 13, north of Puerta del Sol. It overlooks Plaza del Carmen—a little square with a sleepy, almost Parisian ambience.

$ Hostal Acapulco, a cheery oasis, rents 16 bright rooms with a professional, hotelesque feel. The neighborhood is quiet enough that it's smart to request a room with a balcony (family room, air-con, elevator, fourth floor, reasonable laundry service, overnight luggage storage, parking—reserve ahead, tel. 915-311-945, www.hostalacapulco.com, hostal_acapulco@yahoo.es, Ana, Marco, and Javier).

$ Hostal Triana, also a good deal, is bigger—with 40 rooms—and offers a little charm for a little less money (most rooms have air-con, others have fans; elevator and some stairs, first floor, tel. 915-326-812, www.hostaltriana.com, triana@hostaltriana.com, Victor González).

¢ Pensión Arcos is tiny, granny-run, and old-fashioned—it's been in the Hernández family since 1936. You can reserve by phone (in Spanish), and you must pay in cash—but its five rooms are clean, extra quiet, and served by an elevator. You also have access to a tiny roof terrace and a nice little lounge. For cheap beds in a great locale, assuming you can communicate, thisplace is unbeatable (cheaper rooms with shared bath, air-con, closed Aug, fifth floor, tel. 915-324-994, Anuncia and Sabino).

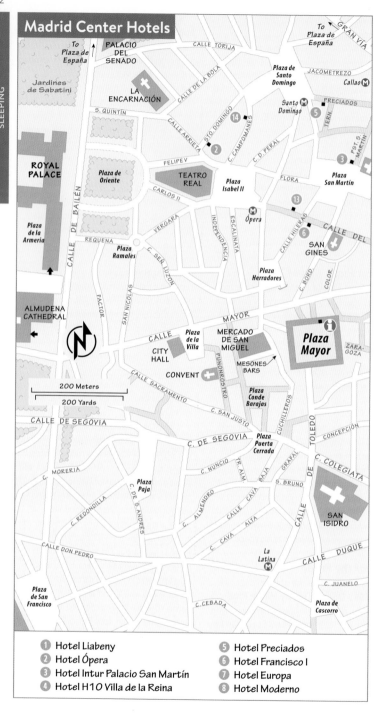

Madrid Center Hotels

To
Plaza de
España

GRAN VÍA

To
Plaza de
España

CALLE TORIJA

PALACIO
DEL
SENADO

Plaza de
Santo
Domingo

JACOMETREZO

Callao **M**

Jardines
de Sabatini

LA
ENCARNACIÓN

CALLE DE LA BOLA

Santo
Domingo **M**

PRECIADOS

5

TERN

S. QUINTÍN

CALLE ARRIETA

STO. DOMINGO

14

C. CAMPOMANES

PST. S.
MARTÍN

2

C. D. PERAL

3

ROYAL
PALACE

CALLE DE BAILÉN

Plaza de
Oriente

FELIPE V

TEATRO
REAL

Plaza
Isabel II

FLORA

Plaza
San Martín

CARLOS II

13

Plaza
de la
Armería

REQUENA

VERGARA

INDEPENDENCIA

ESCALINATA

M
Ópera

CALLE HILERAS

6

CALLE DEL

Plaza
Ramales

C. SEN LUZÓN

SAN
GINES

FACTOR

SAN NICOLAS

Plaza
Herradores

C. BORD

COLOR.

ALMUDENA
CATHEDRAL

N

MAYOR

CALLE

Plaza
de la
Villa

MERCADO
DE SAN
MIGUEL

Plaza
Mayor

i

ZARA-
GOZA

CITY
HALL

PUÑONROSTRO

MESONES
BARS

CONVENT

CALLE SACRAMENTO

C. SAN JUSTO

Plaza
Conde
Barajas

CUCHILLEROS

200 Meters

200 Yards

CALLE DE SEGOVIA

C. DE SEGOVIA

Plaza
Puerta
Cerrada

CALLE DE TOLEDO

CONCEPCIÓN

C. DE COLEGIATA

C. NUNCIO

FR. ALM.

C. MORERÍA

C. DE S. ANDRÉS

Plaza
Paja

C. ALMENDRO

CALLE CAYA BAJA

S. BRUNO

GRAFAL

CALLE DE

SAN
ISIDRO

C. REDONDILLA

CALLE DON PEDRO

C. CAVA ALTA

La
Latina **M**

CALLE DUQUE

C. JUANELO

Plaza
de San
Francisco

C. CEBADA

Plaza de
Cascorro

1 Hotel Liabeny

2 Hotel Ópera

3 Hotel Intur Palacio San Martín

4 Hotel H10 Villa de la Reina

5 Hotel Preciados

6 Hotel Francisco I

7 Hotel Europa

8 Hotel Moderno

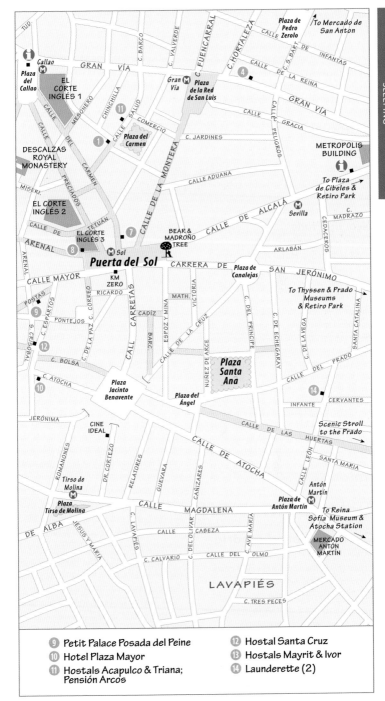

9 Petit Palace Posada del Peine
10 Hotel Plaza Mayor
11 Hostals Acapulco & Triana;
Pensión Arcos
12 Hostal Santa Cruz
13 Hostals Mayrit & Ivor
14 Launderette (2)

Near Plaza Mayor

$ Hostal Santa Cruz, simple and well-located, has 16 rooms at a good price (air-con, elevator, Plaza de Santa Cruz 6, second floor, tel. 915-222-441, www.hostalsantacruz.com, info@hostalsantacruz.com).

$ Hostal Mayrit and Hostal Ivor rent 28 rooms with thoughtful touches on pedestrianized Calle del Arenal. This is a very handy location, so prices are at the higher end of the range (air-con, elevator, near Metro: Ópera at Calle del Arenal 24, reception on third floor, tel. 915-480-403, www.hostalivor.com, reservas@hostalivor.com).

Near the Prado

For locations, see the map on page 173.

$$ Urban Sea Hotel Atocha 113 is a basic but contemporary option with 36 minimalist, well-worn rooms between the Prado and the Reina Sofía, near the Atocha train station (small rooftop terrace, self-service snacks, Calle de Atocha 113, tel. 913-692-895, www.blueseahotels.com, recepcionatocha@blueseahotels.es).

$ Hostal Gonzalo has 15 basic but comfortable rooms on the third floor. Well-run by friendly and helpful Javier and Antonio, it's popular with European budget travelers (air-con, elevator, Cervantes 34, third floor, Metro: Antón Martín—but not handy to Metro, tel. 914-292-714, www.hostalgonzalo.com, hostal@hostalgonzalo.com).

TRANSPORTATION

Getting Around Madrid

Madrid's **Metro** is simple, speedy, and cheap (www.metromadrid.es). It costs €1.50 for a **single ride** within zone A, which covers most of the city, but not trains out to the airport. A **10-ride ticket** is €12.20 and valid on the Metro and buses; it can be shared by several travelers with the same destination (two people taking five rides should get one).

To buy either a single ride or 10-ride ticket, you'll first have to buy a rechargeable red **Multi Card** (tarjeta) for €2.50 (nonrefundable—consider it a souvenir). So, the first time you buy a Metro ticket, it'll cost €4 and be issued on the card; thereafter, you can reload the card with additional rides (viajes) for €1.50 each. Ticket machines ask you to punch in your destination from the alphabetized list (follow the simple prompts) to load up the correct fare. You can also buy or reload Multi Cards at newspaper stands and Estanco tobacco shops.

Study your Metro map. Lines are color-or-coded and numbered; use end-of-the-line station names to choose your direction of travel. When entering the Metro system, touch your Multi Card against the yellow pad to open the turnstile (no need to touch it again to exit). Once in the Metro station, signs direct you to the train line and direction (e.g., Linea 1, *Valdecarros*). To transfer, follow signs in the station leading to connecting lines. Once you reach your final stop, look for the green *salida* signs pointing to the exits. Use the helpful neighborhood maps to choose the right *salida* and save yourself lots of walking.

By Bus: City buses, though not as easy as the Metro, can be useful. You can use a **Multi Card** loaded with a 10-ride ticket (see details earlier). But for **single rides,** you'll buy a ticket on the bus, paying the driver in cash (€1.50; bus maps at TI or info booth on Puerta del Sol, maps usually posted at bus stops, buses run 6:00-24:00, much less frequent *Buho* buses run all night). The EMT Madrid app finds the closest stops and lines and gives accurate wait times (there's a version in English). Bus info: www.emtmadrid.es.

By Taxi or Uber: Madrid's taxis are reasonably priced and easy to hail. A green light on the roof and/or the word *Libre* on the windshield indicates that a taxi is available. After the drop charge (about €3), the per-kilometer rate depends on the time: *Tarifa 1* (€1.05/kilometer) is

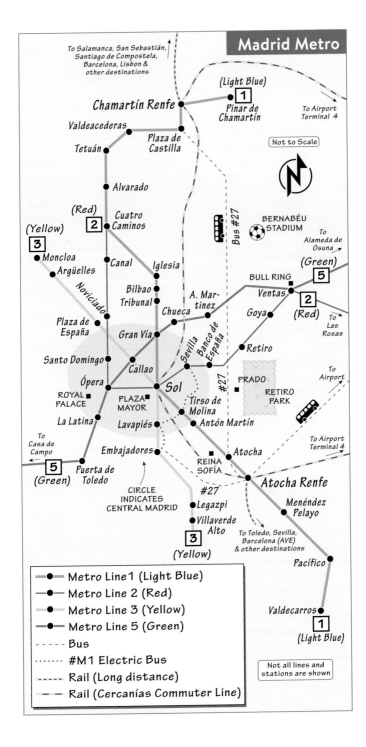

Madrid Metro

To Salamanca, San Sebastián, Santiago de Compostela, Barcelona, Lisbon & other destinations

(Light Blue)
1

Chamartín Renfe
Pinar de Chamartín

To Airport Terminal 4

Valdeacederas
Plaza de Castilla

Tetuán

Not to Scale

Alvarado

BERNABÉU STADIUM

Bus #27

To Alameda de Osuna

(Red)
2
Cuatro Caminos

(Yellow)
3

Moncloa
Argüelles

Canal
Iglesia

(Green)
5

BULL RING

Noviciado

Bilbao
Tribunal

A. Martinez

Ventas

2
(Red)

Goya

To Las Rosas

Chueca

Plaza de España

Gran Vía

Sevilla
Banco de España

Retiro

Santo Domingo

Callao

Ópera

Sol

To Airport

ROYAL PALACE

PLAZA MAYOR

#27

PRADO

RETIRO PARK

La Latina

Lavapiés

Tirso de Molina

Antón Martín

To Casa de Campo

Embajadores

REINA SOFÍA

Atocha

To Airport Terminal 4

5
(Green)

Puerta de Toledo

CIRCLE INDICATES CENTRAL MADRID

#27

Atocha Renfe

Menéndez Pelayo

Legazpi

Villaverde Alto

3
(Yellow)

To Toledo, Sevilla, Barcelona (AVE) & other destinations

Pacífico

Valdecarros

1
(Light Blue)

Not all lines and stations are shown

Legend:

●━━● Metro Line 1 (Light Blue)
●━━● Metro Line 2 (Red)
●━━● Metro Line 3 (Yellow)
●━━● Metro Line 5 (Green)
- - - - Bus
·········· #M1 Electric Bus
- · - · - Rail (Long distance)
—··— Rail (Cercanías Commuter Line)

charged Mon-Fri 6:00-21:00; *Tarifa 2* (€1.20/kilometer) is valid after 21:00 and on Saturdays, Sundays, and holidays. If your cabbie uses anything other than *Tarifa 1* on weekdays (shown as an isolated "1" on the meter), you're being cheated.

Legitimate extra charges include the €3 supplement for leaving any train or bus station, €20 per hour for waiting, and €5 if you call to have the taxi come to you. Make sure the meter is turned on as soon as you get into the cab so the driver can't tack anything onto the official rate. If the driver starts adding up "extras," look for the sticker detailing all legitimate surcharges (should be on the passenger window).

Uber works in Madrid pretty much like it does at home. An Uber ride can be slightly cheaper than a taxi outside of peak times.

Arriving and Departing
By Plane

ADOLFO SUÁREZ BARAJAS AIRPORT

Ten miles east of downtown, Madrid's modern airport has four terminals. Terminals 1, 2, and 3 are connected by long indoor walkways (about a 10-minute walk apart); the newer Terminal 4 is farther away, and also has a separate satellite terminal called T4S. Be clear on which terminal your flight uses before heading to the airport. To transfer between Terminals 1-3 and Terminal 4, you can take a 10-minute shuttle bus (free, leaves every 10 minutes from departures level), or ride the Metro (stops at Terminals 2 and 4). Make sure to allow enough time if you need to travel between terminals (and then for the long walk within Terminal 4 to the gates). For more information about navigating this massive airport, go to www.aena-aeropuertos.es (airport code: MAD).

Services: At the Terminal 1 arrivals area, you'll find the helpful Turismo Madrid TI (Mon-Sat 8:00-20:00, Sun 9:00-14:00, tel. 913-058-656), **ATMs,** a **flight info office** (freestanding info counter in airport lobby, open daily 24 hours, tel. 902-353-570), a **post office** window, a **pharmacy, eateries,** and **car rental** agencies. Upstairs at the check-in level, Terminal 1 has an El Corte Inglés travel agency. The super-modern Terminal 4 offers essentially the same services, as well as a **Renfe office** (where you can get train info and buy long-distance train tickets, long hours daily, tel. 902-320-320). You'll find **baggage storage** (*consigna*) in Terminals 1, 2, and 4.

Handy Domestic Flights: Consider flying between Madrid and other cities in Spain. Domestic airline Vueling (www.vueling.com) is popular for its discounts (e.g., Madrid-Barcelona flight as cheap as €30 if booked in advance).

GETTING BETWEEN THE AIRPORT AND DOWNTOWN

By Public Bus: The yellow **Exprés Aeropuerto** runs between all terminals of the airport and downtown, making three stops: O'Donnell, Plaza de Cibeles, and Atocha train station (€5, pay driver in cash, departs from arrivals level every 15-20 minutes, ride takes about 40 minutes, runs 24 hours a day). Once at Atocha, you can take a taxi or the Metro to your hotel. The bus back to the airport leaves Atocha from near the taxi stand on the *cercanías* side. From 23:30 to 6:00, the bus only goes to Plaza de Cibeles.

Bus #200 (from all terminals) is less handy than the express bus because it leaves you farther from downtown (at the Metro stop at Avenida de América, northeast of the historical center). This bus departs from the arrivals level about every 10 minutes and takes about 20 minutes to reach Avenida de América (runs 6:00-24:00, buy €1.50 ticket from driver, or get a Multi Card with 10 shareable rides—see "Getting Around Madrid," earlier).

By *Cercanías* Train: From Terminal 4, passengers can ride a *cercanías* train to either of Madrid's stations (€2.60, 2/ hour, 25 minutes to Atocha, 12 minutes to Chamartín). Those returning to Madrid's airport by AVE train from elsewhere in Spain can transfer for free to the *cercanías* at Atocha: Scan your AVE ticket at the *cercanías* ticket machine to receive a ticket for the airport train. Be sure to board a train labeled T-4. For terminals 1, 2, or 3, the bus is a more convenient choice.

By Metro: Considering the ease of riding the Exprés Aeropuerto bus in from the airport, I wouldn't recommend taking the Metro. The subway involves two transfers to reach the city; it's not difficult, but usually involves climbing some stairs (for Metro tips, see "Getting Around Madrid," earlier).

By Minibus Shuttle: The AeroCity shuttle bus provides door-to-door transport in a seven-seat minibus with up to three hotel stops en route. It's promoted by hotels, but if you want door-to-door service, simply taking a taxi generally offers a better value (www.aerocity.com).

By Taxi: With cheap and easy alternatives available, there's not much reason to take a taxi unless you have lots of luggage or just want to go straight to your hotel. If you do take a taxi between the airport and downtown, the flat rate is €30. There is no charge for luggage. **Uber** also serves the airport, and the fare is usually about the same. Plan on getting stalled in traffic.

By Train

Madrid's two train stations, Chamartín and Atocha, are both on Metro and *cercanías* (suburban train) lines with easy access to downtown Madrid. Chamartín handles most international trains and the AVE (AH-vay) train to and from Segovia. Atocha generally covers southern Spain, as well as the AVE trains to and from Barcelona, Córdoba, Sevilla, and Toledo. Many train tickets include a *cercanías* connection to or from the train station.

Buying Train Tickets: Train station ticket counters can have long lines, especially during high season or holidays. Consider buying tickets online or at a travel agency. There's an El Corte Inglés travel agency at Atocha station (Mon-Fri 8:00-22:00, Sat 10:00-14:00, closed Sun, small fee, on ground floor of AVE side at the far end); you'll also find travel agencies at the El Corte Inglés department store (Building 2) on Calle Preciados, a block from Puerta del Sol (Mon-Sat 10:00-22:00, Sun 11:00-21:00) and at the airport. Train info: Tel. 912-320-320, www.renfe.com.

Traveling Between Chamartín and Atocha Stations: You can take the Metro (line 1, 30-40 minutes, €1.50), but the *cercanías* trains are faster (6/hour, 13 minutes, Atocha-Chamartín lines C1, C3, C4, C7, C8, and C10 each connect the two stations, lines C3 and C4 also stop at Puerta del Sol, €1.70). If you have a rail pass or regular train ticket to Madrid, you can get a free transfer. Go to the *cercanías* touch-screen ticket machine and choose *combinado cercanías,* then either scan the bar code on your train ticket or punch in a code (labeled *combinado cercanías*), and choose your destination. These trains depart from Atocha's track 6 and generally Chamartín's track 1, 3, 8, or 9—check the *salidas inmediatas* board to be sure).

CHAMARTÍN STATION

The TI is near track 20. The impressively large information, tickets, and customer-service office is at track 11. You can relax in the Sala VIP Club if you have a first-class rail pass and first-class seat or sleeper reservations (between tracks 13 and 14, cooler of free drinks). Baggage storage *(consigna)* is across the street, opposite track 17. The station's Metro stop is also called Chamartín (not "Pinar de Chamartín").

ATOCHA STATION

The station is split in two: the AVE side (mostly long-distance trains) and the *cercanías* side (mostly local trains to the suburbs—called *cercanías*—and the Metro for connecting into downtown). These two parts are connected by a corridor of shops and eateries. Each side has separate schedules and customer-service offices. To get to Atocha, use the "Atocha Renfe" Metro stop (not "Atocha").

Ticket Offices: The *cercanías* side has two offices—a small one for local trains and a big one for major trains (such as AVE). The AVE side has a pleasant, airy office that sells tickets for AVE and other long-distance trains. In the ticket hall, there are three types of sales points: *venta anticipada* (tickets in advance), *salida inmediata* (immediate departures—only tickets for certain designated trains, leaving soon, can be purchased here), and *salidas hoy* (departures today, but only for certain destinations—for example, Toledo). When you enter the ticket office, grab a number from a machine. If the line at one office is long, check the other offices. The machines (in the ticket office and scattered around the station) usually don't work with American credit cards.

AVE Side: Located in the cavernous old brick station building, the AVE area boasts a lush, tropical garden filling its grand hall. It's used by AVE trains and other fast trains (Grandes Líneas). In the AVE side, you'll find a customer service and information office (under the escalators), a spacious ticket office (facing the garden, on the right side), a long-hours pharmacy (just past the ticket office), a handful of cafés and restaurants, and a pay WC. Baggage storage (*consigna*) is at the far end of the garden. Be clear on which level to catch your train: Some departures leave from the lower level (marked as *planta baja* on departure boards); others leave from the "first floor" (marked as *plta. primera,* ride up the escalators or elevators).

Cercanías Side: This is where you'll find the local *cercanías* trains, *regionales* trains, some eastbound faster trains, and the "Atocha Renfe" Metro stop. The *Atención al Cliente* office in the *cercanías* section has information only on trains to destina-tions near Madrid. Most AVE trains will pull in on this side—clearly marked signs lead you to a direct route to the *cercanías* train that goes to the airport, or to the Metro, taxi stand, or back to the AVE side.

Terrorism Memorial: The terrorist bombings of March 11, 2004, took place in Atocha and on local lines going into and out of the station. Security is understandably tight here. A moving memorial is in the *cercanías* part of the station (on the upper level, above the Atocha Renfe Metro stop). Walk inside and under the cylinder to read the thousands of condolence messages in many languages. The 36-foot-tall cylindrical glass memorial towers are visible from outside on the street.

AVE TRAINS

Spain's bullet train opens up good itinerary options. You can get from Madrid's Atocha station to **Barcelona** nonstop in 2.5 hours (at nearly 200 mph), with trains running almost hourly. The AVE train is faster and easier than flying, but not necessarily cheaper. Second-class tickets are about €110-130 one-way; first-class tickets are €180. Advance purchase and online discounts are available through the national rail company (Renfe), but sell out quickly. Save by not traveling on holidays. Your ticket includes one commuter-train transfer in Madrid or Barcelona.

The AVE is also handy for visiting **Sevilla** (and, on the way, **Córdoba**). Consider this exciting, exhausting day trip: 7:00-depart Madrid, 8:45-12:40-in Córdoba, 13:30-20:45-in Sevilla, 23:15-back in Madrid.

Other AVE destinations include **Toledo, Segovia, Valencia, Alicante,** and **Malaga.** Prices vary with times, class, and date of purchase—they're usually cheapest up to two months ahead. Eurail Pass holders pay a seat reservation fee (for example, Madrid to Sevilla is €13 second class, and Madrid to Toledo is €4; must purchase at Renfe ticket windows—not available at ticket machines). Reserve each AVE segment ahead.

TRAIN CONNECTIONS

Below I've listed both non-AVE and (where available) AVE trains.

From Madrid by Train to: Toledo (AVE or cheaper Avant: nearly hourly, 30 minutes, from Atocha), **El Escorial** (*cercanías*, 2/hour, from Atocha and Chamartín, but bus is better), **Segovia** (AVE, Alvia, Avant: 8-10/day, 30 minutes plus 20-minute shuttle bus into Segovia center, from Chamartín, take train going toward Valladolid), **Salamanca** (4/day on speedy Alvia, 1.5 hours; or 7/day on much slower regional Media Distancia train, 3 hours; both from Chamartín), **Santiago de Compostela** (6/day, 5-5.5 hours, longer trips transfer in Ourense), **Barcelona** (AVE: at least hourly, 2.5-3 hours from Atocha), **San Sebastián** (6/day, 5-8 hours, from Chamartín), **Bilbao** (2-4/day, 5-7 hours, some transfer in Zaragoza, from Chamartín), **Pamplona** (6/day direct, 3.5 hours, more with transfer in Zaragoza, from Atocha), **Granada** (2/day on Altaria, 4.5 hours; also 2/day with transfer to AVE in Málaga, 4 hours), **Sevilla** (AVE: hourly, 2.5 hours, departures from 16:00-19:00 can sell out far in advance, from Atocha), **Córdoba** (AVE: almost hourly, 2 hours; Altaria trains: 4/day, 2 hours; all from Atocha), **Málaga** (AVE: 12/day, 2.5-4 hours, from Atocha).

By Bus

Madrid has several major bus stations with good Metro connections. Several routes also serve Barajas Airport's Terminal 4. Multiple bus companies operate from these stations, including Alsa (www.alsa.es) and Avanza (www.avanzabus.com). If you take a taxi from any bus station, you'll be charged a legitimate €3 supplement (not levied for trips to the station).

Plaza Elíptica Station: Served by Alsa. Buses to Toledo leave from here (2/hour, 1-1.5 hours, *directo* faster than *ruta*, Metro: Plaza Elíptica).

Estación Sur de Autobuses (South Station): Served by Alsa, Socibus, and Avanza. From here, buses go to **Salamanca** (hourly express, 2.5-3 hours, Avanza), **Santiago de Compostela** (4/day, 9 hours, includes 1 night bus, Alsa), and **Granada** (nearly hourly, 5-6 hours, Alsa). The station sits squarely on top of the Méndez Álvaro Metro (has TI, tel. 914-684-200, www.estacionautobuses-madrid.com).

Moncloa Station: This station, in the Moncloa Metro station, serves **Santiago de Compostela** (3/day, 9 hours, Alsa), **El Escorial** (4/hour, fewer on weekends, 1 hour), and **Segovia** (about 2/hour). To reach the **Valley of the Fallen,** it's best to connect via El Escorial.

Avenida de América Station: Served by Alsa. Located at the Avenida de América Metro, buses go to **Granada** (3/day, 6 hours) and **Pamplona** (nearly hourly, 6 hours).

Consider several fine side-trips northwest of Madrid, all conveniently reached by car or public transit. An hour from Madrid, tour the imposing palace at **El Escorial**, headquarters of the Spanish Inquisition. Nearby, at the awe-inspiring **Valley of the Fallen,** pay tribute to the countless victims of Spain's bloody civil war. **Segovia,** an altogether lovely burg with a remarkable Roman aqueduct, fine cathedral, and romantic castle, is another worthwhile destination. Lively **Salamanca** has a youthful vibe, a pair of cathedrals, and a marvelous town square.

History buffs can see El Escorial and the Valley of the Fallen in less than a day. By bus, visit them as a day trip from Madrid; by car, see them en route to Segovia, which itself is worth a half-day of sightseeing. Thanks to speedy train connections, it's also possible to take in Segovia on the way from Madrid to Salamanca.

Salamanca makes for a long but doable day trip from Madrid (1.5 hours via train). Here's a possible two-day

option for combining Salamanca and Segovia: Bus to Salamanca in the morning, spend the night (enjoying the nightlife), bus to Segovia the next morning, and return to Madrid that evening.

El Escorial

The Monasterio de San Lorenzo de El Escorial, worth ▲▲, is a symbol of power rather than elegance. To its builder, King Philip II, El Escorial embodied the wonders of Catholic learning, spirituality, and arts. To architects, the building—built on the cusp between styles—exudes both Counter-Reformation grandeur and understated Renaissance simplicity. Today it's a time capsule of Spain's Golden Age, giving us a better feel for the Counter-Reformation and the Inquisition than any other building.

Getting There

Buses to El Escorial leave from Madrid's Moncloa bus station (#664 and #661, 4/ hour, fewer on weekends, 1 hour, €4.20 one-

El Escorial Palace

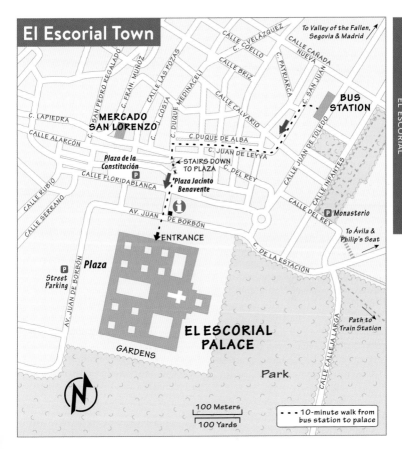

El Escorial Town

To Valley of the Fallen,
Segovia & Madrid

CALLE VELÁZQUEZ

C. COELLO

CALLE CAÑADA NUEVA

CALLE BRIZ

C. PATRIARCA

C. SAN JUAN

CALLE FRAN. MUÑOZ

C. SAN PEDRO REGALADO

CALLE LAS POZAS

C. COSTA

C. DUQUE MEDINACELI

CALLE CALVARIO

BUS STATION

CALLE JUAN DE TOLEDO

C. LAPIEDRA

MERCADO SAN LORENZO

CALLE ALARCÓN

C. DUQUE DE ALBA

C. JUAN DE LEYVA

CALLE INFANTES

Plaza de la Constitución

←STAIRS DOWN TO PLAZA

C. DEL REY

CALLE FLORIDABLANCA

↓**Plaza Jacinto Benavente**

CALLE RUBIO

CALLE SERRANO

AV. JUAN DE BORBÓN

CALLE DEL REY

Monasterio

To Ávila &
Philip's Seat

↓**ENTRANCE**

C. DE LA ESTACIÓN

Plaza

Street Parking

AV. JUAN DE BORBÓN

EL ESCORIAL PALACE

GARDENS

Park

Path to
Train Station

CALLE CALLEJA LARGA

100 Meters

100 Yards

- - - 10-minute walk from
bus station to palace

way, www.alsa.es). Either bus drops you downtown in San Lorenzo de El Escorial, a pleasant 10-minute stroll from the palace.

Local **trains** (*cercanías* line C-8A) run at least twice an hour from Madrid's Atocha and Chamartín stations to the El Escorial station. The palace is a 20-minute walk away (straight uphill through Casita del Príncipe park). Or take a shuttle bus (L1, 2/hour, €1.30) or taxi (€7.50) to the town center and the palace.

By car from Madrid, head out on highway A-6, exiting at kilometer 47 (following signs toward *El Escorial/Guadarrama/M-600*). You'll find several options for parking near the monastery.

Orientation

Cost and Hours: €10, Tue-Sun 10:00-20:00, Oct-March until 18:00, closed Mon year-round, last entry one hour before closing, tel. 918-905-904, www.patrimonio nacional.es.

Tours: For an extra €4, a 1.5-hour **guided tour** takes you through the complex, but there are few tours in English; otherwise, rent the €3 **audioguide**, or download the El Escorial **app** from the palace website.

Eating: El Escorial doesn't even have a simple café; for food or drinks, you must venture across the street, into town.

⊙ Visiting the Palace

The giant, gloomy building appears confusing at first—mostly because of the pure magnitude of this stone structure—but the *visita* arrows and signs help guide you through one continuous path. As you tour, look for these highlights.

Royal Library: Before you enter the library, pause and look at the top of the fancy wooden doorframe outside. The plaque warns *"Excomunión..."*—you'll be excommunicated if you take a book without checking it out. El Escorial was a place of learning—Catholic learning, of course, which meant that books held a special place. The armillary sphere in front of you—an elaborate model of the solar system—looks like a giant gyroscope, revolving unmistakably around Earth, with a misshapen, underexplored North America.

Basilica: The basilica is the spiritual centerpiece of this church/palace/fortress. Flanking the altar are two sets of golden statues honoring two great Spanish kings: on the left, Charles V (the first Habsburg ruler, who joined the mighty empires of Spain and Austria); and on the right, his son, Philip II, who built El Escorial.

Chapter Houses: These rooms are where the monks met to do church business. As you enter, you're face-to-face with the most significant painting in El Escorial, El Greco's *Martyrdom of St. Maurice and the Theban Legion* (1580-82). In the room on the left, look for Titian's *Last Supper*.

Pantheon of the Princes: El Escorial's middle level is for the church. The upper level is for royal residences. And the lower level is for the dead. These corridors are filled with the tombs of lesser royals. Partway through the pantheon is the evocative Pantheon of Royal Children, which holds the remains of various royal children.

Royal Pantheon: This is the gilded resting place of 26 kings and queens...four centuries' worth of Spanish monarchy in uniform gray, marble coffins, labeled with bronze plaques. All the kings are here—but the only queens allowed are mothers of kings.

Charles V and his Queen Isabel (labeled in German, *Elisabeth*), flank the altar on the top shelf. Their son Philip II rests below Charles and opposite (only) one of Philip's four wives.

Habsburg Palace: This wing is named for the Habsburg monarchs who built El Escorial. The palace is like Philip: austere. Notice the simple floors, plain white walls, and bare-bones decor. A highlight of this wing is the **Hall of Battles**, with paintings celebrating Spain's great military victories—including the Battle of San Quentin over France (1557) on St. Lawrence's feast day, which inspired the construction of El Escorial.

Valley of the Fallen

Six miles from El Escorial, high in the Sierra de Guadarrama Mountains, is the Valley of the Fallen (Valle de los Caídos). A 500-foot-tall granite cross marks this immense and powerful underground monument to the victims of the Spanish Civil War (1936-1939).

Valley of the Fallen

Getting There

Drivers find it easy to reach (take exit 47 off A-6; after one-half mile, it's on your right). Without wheels, negotiate a deal with a taxi to take you from El Escorial to Valley of the Fallen, wait 30-60 minutes, and then head back to El Escorial (about €45).

Orientation

Cost and Hours: €9, Tue-Sun 10:00-19:00, Oct-March until 18:00, closed Mon year-round, last entry one hour before closing, tel. 918-905-611, www.valledeloscaidos.es.

Mass: One-hour services run Tue-Sat at 11:00 and Sun at 11:00, 13:00, and 17:30 (17:00 in winter).

❂ Visiting the Basilica

In 1940, prison workers dug 220,000 tons of granite out of the hill beneath the cross to form an underground basilica, then used the stones to erect the cross (built like a chimney, from the inside). The emotional pietà draped over the basilica's entrance is huge—you could sit in the palm of Christ's hand.

A solemn silence and a stony chill fill the basilica. After walking through the two long vestibules, stop at the iron gates of the actual basilica. The line of torch-like lamps adds to the shrine-like ambience. The sides of the monument are lined with copies of 16th-century Brussels tapestries of the Apocalypse, and alabaster statues of the Virgin Mary perch above the arches of the side chapels.

Take the long walk down the nave, then up 10 steps into the main part of the church. Under a glittering mosaic dome is the high altar. At the base of the dome, four gigantic bronze angels look down over you.

Interred behind the high altar and side chapels (marked "RIP, 1936-1939, died for God and country") are the remains of approximately 34,000 people, both Franco's Nationalists and the anti-Franco Republicans (about 12,000), who lost their lives in the war. Franco's grave, strewn with flowers, lies behind the high altar. Today, families of the buried Republicans remain upset that their kin are lying with Franco and his Nationalists.

Segovia

A beautiful city built along a ridge, Segovia boasts a thrilling Roman aqueduct, a grand cathedral, and a historic castle. It's a fun place to simply hang out and enjoy some low-impact sightseeing.

Day Plan

Segovia is a medieval "ship" ready for your inspection. Start at the stern—the aqueduct—and stroll up Calle de Cervantes and Calle Juan Bravo to the prickly Gothic masts of the cathedral. Visit the cathedral, enjoy playful Plaza Major, explore the tangle of narrow streets around the square, then descend to the Alcázar at the bow.

With more time, experience Segovia's charming evening scene and stay the night. You'll pay less for a hotel here than you would in Madrid.

Orientation

Tourist Information: There's a TI at Plaza del Azoguejo, at the base of the aqueduct (daily, tel. 921-466-720, www.turismodesegovia.com) and on Plaza Mayor (at #10; daily, www.turismocastillayleon.com).

Local Guide: Consider Elvira Valderrama Rascon (€115/3 hours, elvisvalrras@yahoo.es).

Getting There

Given the easy train and bus connections, Segovia makes a fine day trip from Madrid. The AVE train goes between Madrid's Chamartín station and Segovia's Guiomar station in 30 minutes (8-10/day). From Guiomar, ride bus #11 for 20 minutes to the base of the aqueduct. Buses run to Segovia from Madrid's Moncloa station (2/hour, 1.5 hours, www.lasepulvedana.es). It's a 10-minute walk on Avenida Fernández Ladreda from the bus station to the aqueduct.

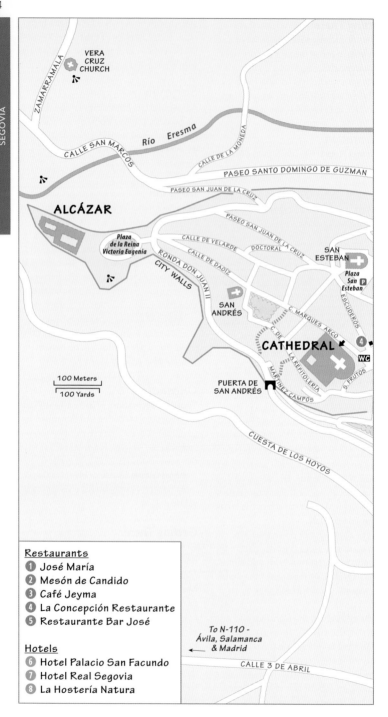

VERA
CRUZ
CHURCH

ZAMARRAMALA

CALLE SAN MARCOS

Río Eresma

CALLE DE LA MONEDA

PASEO SANTO DOMINGO DE GUZMAN

PASEO SAN JUAN DE LA CRUZ

ALCÁZAR

Plaza
de la Reina
Victoria Eugenia

PASEO SAN JUAN DE LA CRUZ

CALLE DE VELARDE

DOCTORAL

SAN
ESTEBAN

CALLE DE DAOÍZ

RONDA DON JUAN II

CITY WALLS

Plaza
San
Esteban

ESCUDEROS

SAN
ANDRÉS

C. MARQUES ARCO

C. DE LA REFITOLERIA

CATHEDRAL

4

WC

S. FRUTOS

100 Meters
100 Yards

PUERTA DE
SAN ANDRÉS

MARTINEZ CAMPOS

CUESTA DE LOS HOYOS

Restaurants
1 José María
2 Mesón de Candido
3 Café Jeyma
4 La Concepción Restaurante
5 Restaurante Bar José

Hotels
6 Hotel Palacio San Facundo
7 Hotel Real Segovia
8 La Hostería Natura

To N-110 -
Ávila, Salamanca
& Madrid

CALLE 3 DE ABRIL

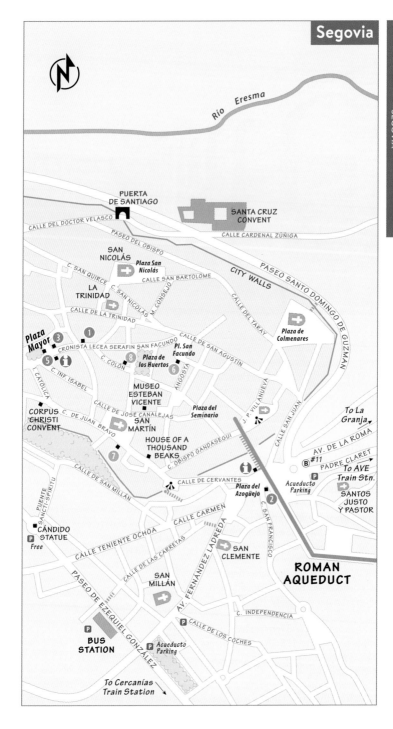

Segovia

Río Eresma

PUERTA DE SANTIAGO

SANTA CRUZ CONVENT

CALLE DEL DOCTOR VELASCO

PASEO DEL OBISPO

CALLE CARDENAL ZÚÑIGA

PASEO SANTO DOMINGO DE GUZMAN

SAN NICOLÁS

Plaza San Nicolás

C. SAN QUIRCE

CALLE SAN BARTOLOMÉ

CITY WALLS

LA TRINIDAD

C. SAN NICOLÁS

M. CONSEJO

CALLE DE LA TRINIDAD

CALLE DEL TARAY

Plaza de Colmenares

Plaza Mayor ❸

❶

CRONISTA LECEA SERAFIN SAN FACUNDO

CALLE DE SAN AGUSTÍN

❺ ℹ️

C. COLÓN

❽ Plaza de los Huertos

Pl. San Facundo

C. INF. ISABEL

ANGOSTA

❻

I. CATÓLICA

MUSEO ESTEBAN VICENTE

Plaza del Seminario

CORPUS CHRISTI CONVENT

C. DE JUAN BRAVO

CALLE DE JOSE CANALEJAS

SAN MARTÍN

J. P. VILLANUEVA

CALLE SAN JUAN

To La Granja

HOUSE OF A THOUSAND BEAKS

❼

C. OBISPO GANDASEGUI

AV. DE LA ROMA

PADRE CLARET

Ⓑ #11

To AVE Train Stn.

PUENTE SANCTI-SPIRITU

CALLE DE SAN MILLÁN

CALLE DE CERVANTES

🅿 Acueducto Parking

SANTOS JUSTO Y PASTOR

CÁNDIDO STATUE

🅿 Free

Plaza del Azoguejo

❷

C. SAN FRANCISCO

CALLE CARMEN

ROMAN AQUEDUCT

CALLE TENIENTE OCHOA

CALLE DE LAS CARRETAS

AV. FERNANDEZ LADREDA

SAN CLEMENTE

PASEO DE EZEQUIEL GONZÁLEZ

SAN MILLÁN

C. INDEPENDENCIA

🅿 BUS STATION

🅿 Acueducto Parking

CALLE DE LOS COCHES

To Cercanías Train Station

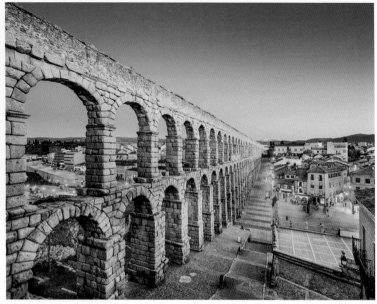

Roman aqueduct at Segovia

It's best not to **drive** into the heart of town. Instead, park in the free lot northwest of the bus station (along Paseo de Ezequiel González) or pay to park at the Acueducto Parking underground garage near the bus station.

Sights

▲▲ROMAN AQUEDUCT

Plaza del Azoguejo is dominated by Segovia's defining feature: its 2,000-year-old, hundred-foot-high *acueducto romano*. The ancient city was approximately the same size as today's Segovia—with some 50,000 inhabitants, including soldiers at a military base, all of whom needed a reliable water supply. Emperor Trajan's engineers built a nine-mile aqueduct to channel water to the city. The exposed section of the aqueduct that you see here is 2,500 feet long and 100 feet high, has 118 arches, was made from 20,000 granite blocks without any mortar, and can still carry a stream of water.

From the square, a grand stairway leads from the base of the aqueduct to the top—offering close-up looks at the imposing work.

▲▲SEGOVIA CATHEDRAL (CATEDRAL DE SEGOVIA)

Segovia's cathedral, built from 1525 through 1768, was Spain's last major Gothic building. Embellished to the hilt with pinnacles and flying buttresses, the exterior is a great example of the final, overripe stage of Gothic, called Flamboyant. Yet the Renaissance arrived before it was finished—as evidenced by the fact that the cathedral is crowned not by a spire, but by a dome.

Cost and Hours: Cathedral-€3, free Sun 9:30-10:30, Nov-March until 13:15 (cathedral access only—no cloisters); open daily 9:30-21:30, Nov-March until 18:30; tower-€5 (visits by guided tour only), combo-ticket for cathedral and tower-€7.

▲▲ALCÁZAR

In the Middle Ages, this fortified palace was one of the favorite residences of the monarchs of Castile and a key fortress

Segovia's Alcázar

for controlling the region. The Alcázar grew through the ages, and its function changed many times: After its stint as a palace, it was a prison for 200 years, and then a royal artillery school. It burned in 1862, after which it was remodeled in the eye-pleasing style you see today. First ogle the exterior. Then visit the finely decorated interior and view terrace. And finally—if you don't mind the steps—you can climb to the top of the tower for the only 360-degree city view in town.

Cost and Hours: Palace–€5.50, daily 10:00-20:00, Nov-March until 18:00, €3 audioguide describes each room; tower–€2.50, same hours as palace except closed third Tue of month and in windy, rainy weather; www.alcazardesegovia.com.

Eating

To sample Segovia's culinary claim to fame, roast suckling pig it's smart to reserve ahead at either **$$$$ José María** (daily, a block off Plaza Mayor at Cronista Lecea 11, www.restaurantejosemaria. com) or **$$$$ Mesón de Cándido** (daily,

Plaza del Azoguéjo 5, under aqueduct, www.mesondecandido.es). Plaza Mayor provides a great backdrop for a meal—good options include **$$$ Café Jeyma, $$$ La Concepción Restaurante,** and **$$$ Restaurante Bar José.**

Sleeping

Places in the center include the luxuriously modern **$$$ Hotel Palacio San Facundo** (Plaza San Facundo 4, www. hotelpalaciosanfacundo.com), the classic **$$ Hotel Real Segovia** (Juan Bravo 30, www.hotelrealsegovia.com), and the colorful **$ La Hostería Natura** (Calle Colón 5www.naturadesegovia.com).

Salamanca

This sunny sandstone city boasts Spain's grandest plaza, its oldest university, and a fascinating history, all swaddled in a strolling, college-town ambience. Salamanca is home to a fine ensemble of monuments, a pair of buttress-sharing cathedrals from different centuries, clusters of cloisters, and some surprisingly good museums.

Day Plan

Head straight to Plaza Mayor and wander the square. Visit the cathedrals and university. Sample tapas at bars as needed. Visit the square again; linger over a drink or meal. It's fun to just get lost browsing the beautiful, mostly traffic-free back lanes of Salamanca's old town. The pedestrian-only Roman Bridge has one of the city's best paseo scenes on a warm evening.

Orientation

Salamanca's sights cluster in a barbell shape, with its magnificent Plaza Mayor at the north end, and the cathedrals and university a 10-minute walk south. The surrounding streets are lively with eateries, shops, and people.

Tourist Information: The TI is on Plaza Mayor (daily, Plaza Mayor 32, tel. 923-218-342, www.salamanca.es).

Local Guide: Ines Criado Velasco will tailor a town walk to your interests (€100/3 hours, more on weekends, icriadovelasco@gmail.com).

Getting There

Salamanca is feasible as a long day-trip from Madrid (1.5 hours via high-speed train, 4/day from Madrid Chamartín station). By car or bus (hourly express from Estación Sur, www.avanzabus.com), it's 2.5 hours from Madrid.

From either Salamanca's train or bus station to Plaza Mayor, it's a 25-minute walk, an easy bus ride (€1.05, pay driver), or a €7 taxi trip. The train station has no lockers; day-trippers can store bags at the bus station. The old center is ringed by underground parking garages (around €15/day).

Sights

▲▲▲PLAZA MAYOR

Built between 1729 and 1755 by brothers Alberto and Nicolas Churriguera, Spain's ultimate plaza is a lovely place to enjoy a cup of coffee (try Café Novelty), and watch the world go by. This square has long been Salamanca's community living room. Old-timers remember an earlier

Salamanca's Plaza Mayor

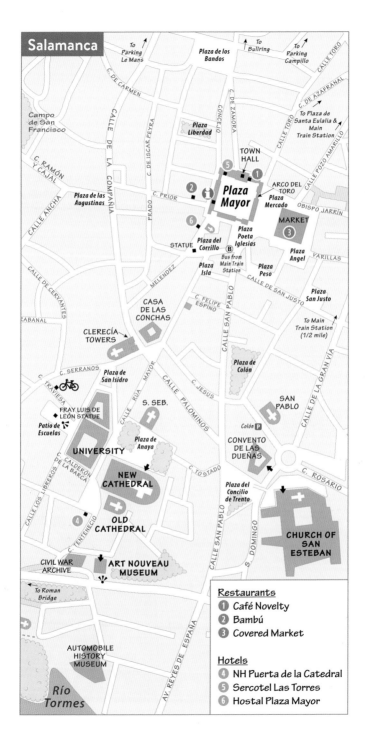

Salamanca

To Parking Le Mans — To Bullring — To Parking Campillo

CALLE TORO

Plaza de los Bandos

C. DE CARMEN

C. DE AZAFRANAL

Campo de San Francisco

C. DE ISCAR PEYRA

CALLE DE LA COMPAÑIA

CONCEJO

C. DE ZAMORA

CALLE TORO

C. DE AZAFRANAL

Plaza Liberdad

To Plaza de Santa Eulalia & Main Train Station

C. RAMÓN Y CAJAL

CALLE ANCHA

C. PRIOR

C. PRIOR

TOWN HALL

CALLE POZO AMARILLO

Plaza de las Augustinas

PRADO

Plaza Mayor

ARCO DEL TORO

OBISPO JARRIN

Plaza Mercado

MARKET

STATUE

Plaza del Corrillo

Plaza Poeta Iglesias

Plaza Angel

VARILLAS

MELENDEZ

Bus from Main Train Station

Plaza Isla

Plaza Peso

CALLE DE SAN JUSTO

Plaza San Justo

CABANAL

CALLE DE CERVANTES

CASA DE LAS CONCHAS

C. FELIPE ESPINO

CALLE SAN PABLO

To Main Train Station (1/2 mile)

CLERECÍA TOWERS

C. SERRANOS

Plaza de San Isidro

CALLE RÚA MAYOR

CALLE PALOMINOS

C. JESUS

Plaza de Colón

CALLE DE LA GRAN VIA

C. TRAVIESA

FRAY LUIS DE LEÓN STATUE

Patio de Escuelas

S. SEB.

SAN PABLO

Colón P

Plaza de Anaya

CONVENTO DE LAS DUEÑAS

C. ROSARIO

UNIVERSITY

C. CALDERON DE LA BARCA

NEW CATHEDRAL

C. TOSTADO

Plaza del Concilio de Trento

CALLE LOS LIBREROS

OLD CATHEDRAL

C. TENTENECIO

CALLE SAN PABLO

S. DOMINGO

CHURCH OF SAN ESTEBAN

CIVIL WAR ARCHIVE

ART NOUVEAU MUSEUM

To Roman Bridge

AUTOMOBILE HISTORY MUSEUM

AV. REYES DE ESPAÑA

Río Tormes

Restaurants
1 Café Novelty
2 Bambú
3 Covered Market

Hotels
4 NH Puerta de la Catedral
5 Sercotel Las Torres
6 Hostal Plaza Mayor

era, when teenage girls would promenade clockwise around the colonnade while the boys cruised counterclockwise. Today, if you're lucky, you may find local student musicians performing on the square. Perhaps the best time for people-watching is Sunday after Mass (13:00-15:00), when the grandmothers gather here in their Sunday best.

Rick's Tip: *On summer weeknights, you may encounter students—dressed in traditional black capes and leggings—serenading the public in the bars on and around Plaza Mayor. Their music is named* **tuna,** *which has nothing to do with fish, but refers to a vagabond student lifestyle.*

Notice the square's perfectly symmetrical arches (hiding a pleasantly shaded arcade), three levels of charming little balconies with matching shutters, and artful lampposts. While most European squares honor a single king or a saint, Plaza Mayor—ringed by famous Castilians—is for all the people. The medallions above the colonnade surrounding the plaza depict writers (Miguel de Cervantes), heroes, and conquistadors (Christopher Columbus and Hernán Cortés), as well as numerous kings.

Rick's Tip: *The* **University of Salamanca,** *the oldest in Spain (est. 1218), was one of Europe's leading centers of learning (Columbus came here for travel tips). While you can pay to enter its historic lecture halls, its most interesting feature—the* **ornately decorated entrance** *facade (on Patio de Escuelas)—is free to view.*

▲▲SALAMANCA CATHEDRAL (CATEDRAL DE SALAMANCA)

Salamanca's cathedral is a two-fer: When constructing a spacious new cathedral (built 1513-1733), Church fathers put it right next to the town's 12th-century Romanesque church. The "New Cathedral," a towering mix of Gothic, Renaissance, and Baroque, actually shares buttresses with its older partner.

The towering New Cathedral interior

Cost and Hours: €5, includes audioguide; daily 10:00-20:00, Oct-March until 18:00, last entry 45 minutes before closing; tower-€3.75, daily 10:00-20:00, Jan-Feb until 18:00; last entry one hour before closing; www.catedralsalamanca.org.

Visiting the Cathedrals: To get to the old, you have to walk through the new. The interior of the New Cathedral (Catedral Nueva) is vast and majestic—architecturally rivaling any in Spain. The or choir, blocks up half of the church, but its wood carving is sumptuous; look up to see the recently restored, elaborate organ.

You'll enter the Old Cathedral (Catedral Vieja) through the San Lorenzo Chapel (to the left of the New Cathedral's main door). Sit in a front pew to study the altarpiece's 53 scenes from the lives of Mary and Jesus (by the Italian Florentino, 1445) surrounding a precious 12th-century statue of the Virgin of the Valley. High above, notice the dramatic Last Judgment fresco of Jesus sending condemned souls into the literal jaws of hell.

For a fantastic view of the upper floors and terraces of both cathedrals, visit the tower (entrance to the right as you exit the Old Cathedral).

▲▲ART NOUVEAU MUSEUM (MUSEO ART NOUVEAU Y ART DECO)

Located in the turn-of-the-century Casa Lis, this museum displays a stunning collection of stained glass, paintings, vases, furniture, jewelry, cancan statuettes, and toy dolls. Nowhere else in Spain will you enjoy an Art Nouveau collection in a building from the same era.

Cost and Hours: €4, free Thu 11:00-14:00; open daily 11:00-20:00, shorter hours and closed Mon mid-Nov-mid-March; between the cathedrals and the river at Calle Gibraltar 14, tel. 923-121-425, www.museocasalis.org.

▲AUTOMOBILE HISTORY MUSEUM (MUSEO DE HISTORIA DE LA AUTOMOCIÓN)

This museum—worth ▲▲▲ for gearheads—has three floors showcasing about 100 vehicles in chronological order from 1886 to the present. There's no posted English information, but at least you'll know the make, model, and year of each automobile (and you can download a free audioguide using the on-site Wi-Fi). Begin in the basement, then work your way up.

Cost and Hours: €4, Tue-Sun 10:00-14:00 & 17:00-20:00, longer afternoon hours July-Aug, closed Mon year-round, Plaza del Mercado Viejo, near the river immediately below the Art Nouveau Museum, tel. 923-260-293, www.museoautomocion.com.

Eating

At one of the casual eateries on Plaza Mayor you can savor some of Europe's best people-watching. The places here are basically interchangeable—just find the view you like best and don't expect high cuisine. For dessert, stroll with an ice-cream cone from **$$ Café Novelty,** the oldest café in Salamanca (daily). Just off the square, you'll find the bright, energetic, and modern **$$ Bambú,** serving delicious tapas (daily, Calle Prior 4).

For **picnic food,** head to the beautiful covered market on Plaza Mercado (closed Sun, east side of Plaza Mayor).

Sleeping

At **$$$ NH Puerta de la Catedral,** it's worth the extra euros for a room with a great view of the cathedral (Plaza de Juan XXIII 5, www.nh-hotels.com). **$$ Sercotel Las Torres** is located right on Plaza Mayor (Calle Concejo 4, www.sercotelhoteles.com). **$ Hostal Plaza Mayor** has a homey feel (Plaza del Corrillo 20, www.hostalplazamayor.es).

Toledo

About an hour south of Madrid, Toledo teems with tourists, souvenirs, and great art by day, and delicious dinners, echoes of El Greco, and medieval magic by night. Incredibly well preserved and full of cultural wonder, the entire city has been declared a national monument.

Toledo was once Spain's capital and packs 2,500 years of tangled history—Roman, Jewish, Visigothic, Moorish, and Christian—onto a rocky perch protected on three sides by the Tajo River. The rich mix of Jewish, Moorish, and Christian heritages makes Toledo one of Europe's cultural highlights and a great way to sample Spain's cultural mix.

Today, Toledo thrives as a provincial capital and tourist destination—it's a slick 30-minute train ride from Madrid. And whether you arrive by car, train, or bus, getting into town is easy by public transportation or on foot (thanks to handy escalators). You'll find an old city center that's largely traffic-free.

Toledo sits enthroned on its history, much as it was when Europe's most powerful monarch, the Holy Roman Emperor Charles V (King Charles I in Spain), and its most famous resident artist, El Greco, called it home. Be sure to get off the main walkways and explore some of the back streets. In just a few steps, you'll find a corner of Toledo all your own.

TOLEDO IN 2 DAYS

You'll need at least two nights and a day to see Toledo's sights and experience its medieval atmosphere, especially after dark. Spending two days is more relaxing. Keep in mind that day-trippers and commuters can fill up early and late trains; it's best to purchase tickets in advance.

Day 1: Upon arrival, head to the main square, Plaza de Zocodover, and get oriented by following my self-guided walk. Then visit the cathedral interior and the finest El Greco, inside Santo Tomé.

Evening: Wander the back lanes, sample sweet *mazapán*, people-watch at Plaza de Zocodover, and dine well—*carcamusas* (pork stew), anyone?

Day 2: Consider the Army Museum (for history aficionados), the Santa Cruz Museum (for art lovers), the El Greco Museum (the artist's life and times), a remarkably well-preserved historic Mudejar synagogue (Tránsito), or the royal burial church at San Juan de los Reyes. If you want to cut your visit short, you could travel to your next destination later today (you'll likely transfer in Madrid, the nearest major hub).

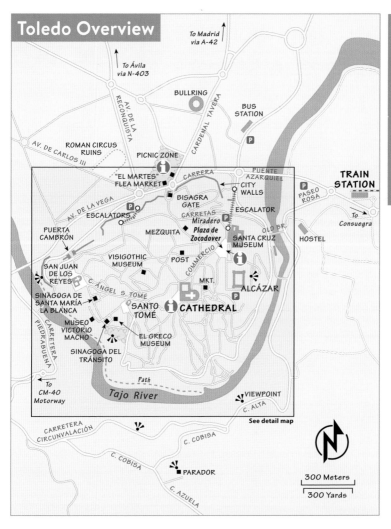

Toledo Overview

To Madrid
via A-42

To Ávila
via N-403

AV. DE LA RECONQUISTA

BULLRING

BUS STATION

CARDENAL TAVERA

ROMAN CIRCUS RUINS

AV. DE CARLOS III

PICNIC ZONE

CARRERA

PUENTE AZARQUIEL

"EL MARTES" FLEA MARKET

CITY WALLS

TRAIN STATION

BISAGRA GATE

ESCALATORS

AV. DE LA VEGA

CARRETAS

ESCALATOR

PASEO ROSA

PUERTA CAMBRÓN

MEZQUITA

Miradero

Plaza de Zocodover

SANTA CRUZ MUSEUM

OLD BR.

To Consuegra

HOSTEL

VISIGOTHIC MUSEUM

POST

COMMERCIO

SAN JUAN DE LOS REYES

C. ÁNGEL S. TOMÉ

MKT.

ALCÁZAR

SINAGOGA DE SANTA MARÍA LA BLANCA

SANTO TOMÉ

CATHEDRAL

CARRETERA PIEDRABUENA

MUSEO VICTORIO MACHO

EL GRECO MUSEUM

SINAGOGA DEL TRÁNSITO

Path

To CM-40 Motorway

Tajo River

VIEWPOINT

C. ALTA

See detail map

CARRETERA CIRCUNVALACIÓN

C. COBISA

C. COBISA

PARADOR

C. AZUELA

300 Meters

300 Yards

N

ORIENTATION

Toledo sits atop a circular hill, with the cathedral roughly dead-center. Lassoed into a tight tangle of streets by the sharp bend of the Tajo River, Toledo has Spain's most confusing medieval street plan. But it's a small town within its walls, with only 10,000 inhabitants (84,000 live in greater Toledo, including its modern suburbs). The major sights are well signed, and locals will politely point you in the right direction. (You are, after all, the town's bread and butter.)

The top sights stretch from the main square, Plaza de Zocodover (zoh-koh-doh-VEHR), southwest along Calle del Comercio (nicknamed Calle Ancha, "Wide Street") to the cathedral, and beyond that to Santo Tomé and more. The visitor's city lies basically along this small but central street, and most tourists never stray from this axis. Make a point to get lost. The town is compact. When

TOLEDO AT A GLANCE

▲▲▲**Toledo Cathedral** One of Europe's best, with a marvelously vast interior and great art. **Hours:** Mon-Sat 10:00-18:30, Sun from 14:00. See page 235.

▲▲**Santo Tomé** Simple chapel with El Greco's masterpiece, *The Burial of the Count of Orgaz.* **Hours:** Daily 10:00-18:45, until 17:45 mid-Oct-Feb. See page 242.

▲**Army Museum** Covers all things military; located in the imposing fortress, the Alcázar. **Hours:** Tue-Sun 10:00-17:00, closed Mon. See page 235.

▲**Santa Cruz Museum** Renaissance building housing wonderful artwork, including eight El Grecos. **Hours:** Mon-Sat 9:30-18:30, Sun 10:00-14:00. See page 234.

▲**El Greco Museum** Small collection of paintings, including the *View and Plan of Toledo,* El Greco's panoramic map of the city. **Hours:** Tue-Sat 9:30-19:30—Nov-Feb until 18:00, Sun 10:00-15:00, closed Mon. See page 243.

▲**Tránsito Synagogue and Jewish Museum** Museum of Toledo's Jewish past. **Hours:** Tue-Sat 9:30-19:30—until 18:00 off-season, Sun 10:00-15:00, closed Mon. See page 244.

▲**Victorio Macho Museum** Collection of 20th-century Toledo sculptor's works, with expansive river-gorge view. **Hours:** Mon-Fri 10:00-14:00 & 17:00-19:00, closed Sat-Sun. See page 245.

▲**San Juan de los Reyes Monasterio** Church/monastery intended as final resting place of Isabel and Ferdinand. **Hours:** Daily 10:00-18:45, until 17:45 mid-Oct-March. See page 245.

▲**Visigothic Museum** Romanesque church housing the only Visigothic artifacts in town. **Hours:** Tue-Sat 9:45-14:15 & 16:00-18:30, Sun 10:00-14:00, closed Mon. See page 241.

Toledo's History

Perched strategically in the center of Iberia, Toledo was for centuries a Roman transportation hub with a thriving Jewish population. After Rome fell, the city became a Visigothic capital (AD 554). In 711 the Moors (Muslims) made it a regional center. Because of its importance, Toledo was the first city in the cross-hairs of Christian forces. It fell in 1085, marking the beginning of the end of Muslim Spain, which culminated in the fall of Granada four centuries later. A local saying goes, "A carpet frays from the edges, but the carpet of Al-Andalus (Muslim Spain) frayed from the very center"...Toledo.

Though the city was then dominated by Christians, many Moors remained in Toledo, tolerated and respected as scholars and craftsmen. During its medieval heyday (c. 1350), Toledo was a city of the humanities, where God was known by many names. In this haven of cultural diversity, people of different faiths lived in harmony, and the Jewish community—educated, wealthy, and cosmopolitan—thrived (relatively speaking) from the city's earliest times. Jews of Spanish origin are called Sephardic Jews.

The city reached its peak in the 1500s, when Spain was in its Golden Age, Toledo's bishops wielded vast political power, Emperor Charles V made it his "Imperial City," and artists like El Greco called it home. All of Spain considered Toledo to be the heart of what was becoming a budding nation-state.

Then suddenly, in 1561, Philip II decided to move the capital to a small town north of here—Madrid. Some say that Madrid was the logical place for a capital in the geographic center of newly formed *España*. Others think Philip wanted more room to grow, or to separate politics from religion. Whatever the reason, Toledo—though still Spain's religious capital—began a slow decline. Its medieval structures were never rebuilt, leaving it mothballed. In the 19th century, Romantic travelers rediscovered it and wrote of it as a mystical place, which it remains today.

it's time to return to someplace familiar, pull out the map or ask, *"¿Para Plaza de Zocodover?"* From the far end of town, handy bus #12 circles back to Plaza de Zocodover.

Although the city is very hilly (in Toledo, they say, everything's uphill—it certainly feels that way), nothing is more than a short hike away.

Tourist Information

Toledo has four TIs: at the **train station** (daily 9:30-15:00, tel. 925-239-121), at **Bisagra Gate,** in a freestanding building in the park just across from the gate (Mon-Sat 10:00-18:00, Sun until 14:00, tel. 925-

211-005); on **Plaza del Ayuntamiento,** facing the cathedral (daily 10:00-18:00, WC, tel. 925-254-030); and at **Plaza de Zocodover** (Mon-Sat 10:00-18:00, Sun until 14:00). All locations share a website (www.toledo-turismo.com).

Sightseeing Passes: Skip the **Toledo Pass** or **Toledo Card**—neither saves you money over individual tickets. The **Pulsera Turística** wristband (€9, sold at participating sights) only makes sense if you plan to see at least four of the monuments and churches it covers: Santo Tomé, Sinagoga de Santa María la Blanca, San Juan de los Reyes Monasterio, Mezquita del Cristo de la Luz, Church

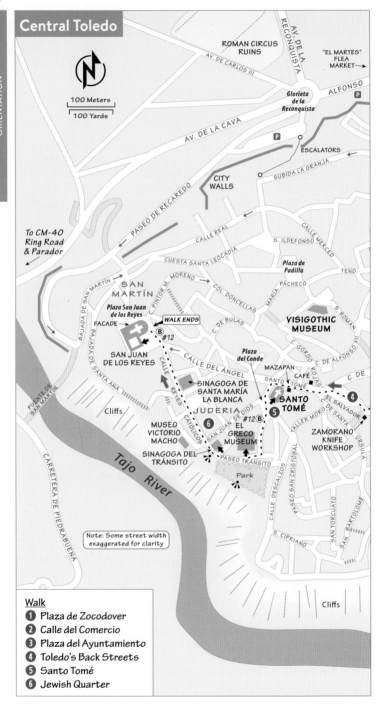

Central Toledo

ROMAN CIRCUS RUINS

AV. DE LA RECONQUISTA

AV. DE CARLOS III

"EL MARTES" FLEA MARKET →

Glorieta de la Reconquista

ALFONSO

P

N

100 Meters
100 Yards

AV. DE LA CAVA

P

ESCALATORS

SUBIDA LA GRANJA

CITY WALLS

PASEO DE RECAREDO

To CM-40 Ring Road & Parador

CALLE REAL

S. ILDEFONSO

CALLE MERCED

CUESTA SANTA LEOCADIA

Plaza de Padilla

TEND.

SAN MARTÍN

C. PINTOR M. MORENO

COL. DONCELLAS

MARÍA PACHECO

S. ROMÁN

Plaza San Juan de los Reyes

C. DE BULAS

VISIGOTHIC MUSEUM

BAJADA DE SAN MARTÍN

FACADE

WALK ENDS

B #12

C. GORDO

C. DE ALFONSO XII

SAN JUAN DE LOS REYES

CALLE DEL ÁNGEL

Plaza del Conde

MAZAPÁN

ROJAS

C. DE

BAJADA DE SANTA ANA

PUENTE DE SAN MARTÍN

Cliffs

SINAGOGA DE SANTA MARÍA LA BLANCA

JUDERÍA

SANTO TOMÉ

CAFÉ

SANTO TOMÉ

4

EL SALVADOR

C. DE

CALLE REYES CATÓLICOS

MUSEO VICTORIO MACHO

SINAGOGA DEL TRÁNSITO

SAN JUAN DE DIOS

6

5

EL GRECO MUSEUM

#12 B

TALLER MORO

DE SANTA ÚRSULA

ZAMORANO KNIFE WORKSHOP

Tajo River

PASEO TRANSITO

Park

CARRETERA DE PIEDRABUENA

CALLE DESCALZOS

PASEO SAN CRISTÓBAL

SAN TORCUATO

SAN BARTOLOME

Note: Some street width exaggerated for clarity

S. CIPRIANO

Cliffs

Walk

1 Plaza de Zocodover
2 Calle del Comercio
3 Plaza del Ayuntamiento
4 Toledo's Back Streets
5 Santo Tomé
6 Jewish Quarter

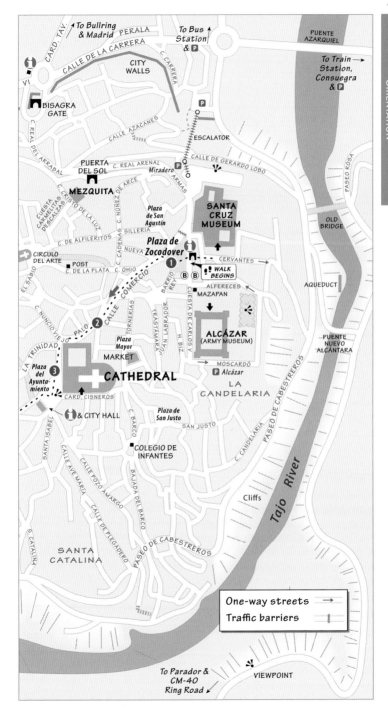

To Bullring
& Madrid
CARD. TAV.
PERALA
CALLE DE LA CARRERA
C. CARRERA
CITY
WALLS
VI
BISAGRA
GATE
C. REAL DEL ARRABAL
CALLE AZACANES
To Bus
Station
& P
PUENTE
AZARQUIEL
To Train →
Station,
Consuegra
& P
P
ESCALATOR
PASEO ROSA
PUERTA
DEL SOL
C. REAL ARENAL
Miradero
CALLE DE GERARDO LOBO
MEZQUITA
CUESTA CARMELITAS DESCALZAS
C. CRISTO DE LA LUZ
Plaza
de San
Agustín
C. NÚÑEZ DE ARCE
ARMAS
P
SANTA
CRUZ
MUSEUM
OLD
BRIDGE
C. DE ALFILERITOS
C. CADENAS
SILLERIA
NUEVA
Plaza de
Zocodover
CERVANTES
AQUEDUCT
CÍRCULO
DEL ARTE
POST
C. DE LA PLATA
C. OHIO
EL SABIO
BARRIO REY
WALK
BEGINS
B B
ALFERECES
MAZAPAN
C. NUNCIO VIEJO
PALO
CALLE COMERCIO
TORNERÍAS
TRASTAMARA
JUAN LABRADOR
H. BIZ
CUESTA DE CARLOS V
ALCÁZAR
(ARMY MUSEUM)
PUENTE
NUEVO
ALCÁNTARA
LA
TRINIDAD
Plaza
Mayor
MARKET
MOSCARDÓ
P Alcázar
PASEO DE CABESTREROS
Plaza
del
Ayunta-
miento
CATHEDRAL
LA
CANDELARIA
CARD. CISNEROS
& CITY HALL
Plaza de
San Justo
SAN JUSTO
C. BARCO
C. CANDELARIA
SANTA ISABEL
CALLE AVE MARIA
CALLE POZO AMARGO
BAJADA DEL BARCO
COLEGIO DE
INFANTES
CALLE DE PLEGADERO
PASEO DE CABESTREROS
Cliffs
Tajo River
S. CATALINA
SANTA
CATALINA
PASEO DE CABESTREROS
To Parador &
CM-40
Ring Road
VIEWPOINT

One-way streets →
Traffic barriers

of El Salvador, Real Colegio de Doncel-las Nobles, and Church of San Ildefonso/Jesuitas.

Helpful Hints

Useful App: Toledo Be Your Guide is a simple but useful free travel app. Ignore the sections on restaurants, shopping, and nightlife; instead select "Attractions" for info on sights around town.

Local Guidebook: Consider the read-able *Toledo: Its Art and Its History* (sold all over town). It explains all the sights (which often lack on-site information) and gives you a photo to point at and say, *"¿Dónde está...?"*

Tours

The main reason to take a tour is to reach the viewpoint made famous by El Greco, on a hilltop adjacent to the old town.

TOURIST TRAIN

For a pleasant city overview, take the **TrainVision Tourist Train**—a 45-minute putt-putt through Toledo and around the Tajo River Gorge. It's a cheesy but fine way for nondrivers to enjoy views of the city from across the Tajo Gorge (€6.50, buy ticket from kiosk on Plaza de Zoco-dover, leaves Plaza de Zocodover daily 1-2/hour 10:00-18:30, later in summer, recorded English/Spanish commentary, tel. 625-301-890).

PUBLIC BUSES

For the cheapest tour, use public trans-portation. Take my "Bus #12 Self-Guided Tour" through town (see page 245). Or, for a "gorge-ous" loop trip, try bus #71, which leaves from opposite the entrance of the Alcázar (hourly 7:45-21:45); its route circles around to El Greco's famous viewpoint, where you can get off and snap some pho-tos, then wait about an hour at the same stop for the next bus to take you back.

LOCAL GUIDE

Juan José Espadas (a.k.a. Juanjo) is a good guide who enjoys sharing his home-town in English (€150/3 hours, tel. 667-780-475, juanjo@guiadetoledo.es).

TOLEDO WALK

This walk snakes through the center of town from Plaza de Zocodover to the cathedral and Santo Tomé and then down to the Jewish Quarter, linking all of Tole-do's top sights (described in more detail under "Sights"). To trace the route, see the "Central Toledo" map.

◉ Self-Guided Walk

• *Begin at Toledo's main square.*

❶ *Plaza de Zocodover*

Position yourself in the middle of the square and survey the scene. Plaza de Zocodover was once the scene of Inquisi-tion judgments and bullfights, but it's now a lot more peaceful.

The tourist train to the panoramic viewpoint made famous by El Greco leaves from here. Just uphill, near the taxi stand, is the stop for bus #12, which trav-els around the old town to Santo Tomé (and works as a good self-guided tour—described at the end of the "Sights" sec-tion), and for bus #71, which heads out to the El Greco viewpoint.

The "square" has an oddly triangular footprint. In the 16th century, King Philip II tried in vain to knock down some build-ings and create a more typical square. But key buildings were owned by the Church, which refused to grant permission. The cathedral in Toledo—Spain's most important—has always exerted an over-sized influence on civic life. And that's one of the many reasons Philip II decided to relocate his capital (in 1561) to Madrid, where he could build whatever he liked.

Now walk to the edge of the square along the busy street and face a big gov-ernmental building. Look uphill to your right to see two of the four corner turrets of the **Alcázar**—the mighty fortress that was for a time (in the 16th century, before

Plaza de Zocodover

Philip left in a huff) Spain's seat of power. During the Spanish Civil War, Franco's Nationalists holed up inside the Alcázar, and the Republicans laid siege to the fortress. Most of the area around the Alcázar was destroyed—this part of town, including much of Plaza de Zocodover, has been rebuilt (notice the *Restaurado 1945* sign on the governmental building). Today the Alcázar houses the Army Museum, a sprawling exhibit on Spain's military history.

Dodge buses as you cross the street and look right to see an outpost of **Santo Tomé,** one of Toledo's top shops for the delicious almond candy called *mazapán.* If you're ready for a treat, stop in and buy an assortment to munch.

Continue down the stairs straight past the *mazapán* shop and head through the arch. Notice that the archway you just came through has a distinctive keyhole shape—a classic feature of **Mudejar** architecture, the hybrid Moorish/Gothic style of Muslim craftspeople who stayed behind after the Moors were forced out of Spain. Toledo—which was the first major town retaken by the Reconquista, in 1085—is *the* top Mudejar city in Spain. In

many ways, Toledo is a hinge between the Moorish-flavored south and the distinctly Christian north.

Look right up the street to the big, blocky building. This is the entrance to the **Army Museum,** inside the Alcázar fortress. Then continue 30 paces straight ahead (downhill on Cervantes Street) and look left to see the frilly Plateresque entrance to the **Santa Cruz Museum,** with a fine collection of art, including some top El Grecos. (For details on both, see "Sights," later).

• *Retrace your steps back up through that keyhole arch, and cross the street into Plaza de Zocodover. Continue straight through the middle of the square and carry on (past Hostal Centro) along Toledo's main shopping artery, the aptly named...*

❷ *Calle del Comercio*

This main drag, connecting Plaza de Zocodover with the cathedral, is jammed with day-trippers. But *Toledanos* still shop here, too. Many visitors never break free of this gauntlet, but make sure you do— some of Toledo's most appealing back streets lie just above and below here.

Calle del Comercio

City Hall

Walk a few blocks along Calle de Comercio as it winds through the heart of town. Where the street widens, take the right fork (Calle del Hombre del Palo). Soon you're walking along the bulky wall of the **cathedral** complex, on your left. At the next fork—at the lovely building with the double-headed eagle on top—take a sharp left and continue downhill alongside the cathedral.

As you walk along the cathedral, look about 20 feet up to see metal girders. These support priceless Flemish tapestries—some dating back to the 16th century—during the annual celebration of **Corpus Christi,** 60 days after Easter. On that day, the communion host is paraded around town in a gigantic gold monstrance (you can see it inside the cathedral).

You'll pass under a skybridge that connects the cathedral to the bishop's palace—the gigantic, hulking building on your right.

• *Just below that, you pop out into the square called...*

❸ *Plaza del Ayuntamiento*

This square is named for Toledo's **City Hall**—the mini Alcázar straight ahead.

Now turn around to appreciate the **view of the cathedral**. The tower rocketing up is capped with three crowns—signifying this cathedral's primacy over all other Spanish churches. On the right side, notice the stubby base of what was planned to be a matching second steeple. As work progressed, the foundation began to crumble (you can see the damage)—it was being built on the artificially leveled-out square rather than the angled rock at the base of the existing tower. So plans were scaled back and the area was topped with a chapel instead.

Study the **facade.** The tympanum (over the door) illustrates the founding story of the cathedral: In the seventh century, the local Bishop Ildefonso wrote a book about the Virgin Mary—who rewarded him by miraculously appearing and offering him a holy vestment, legitimizing Toledo as the leading Christian city of Spain. The original carvings in soft, white limestone were later protected by a harder layer of gray granite carvings.

The **cathedral interior** is undoubtedly the top sight in town. To enter, head up the lane on the right side of the cathedral. The ticket office is on the right side of the

Toledo's back streets

street. (A self-guided tour of the interior is outlined later, under "Sights.")
• *When you're ready to move on, we'll take a stroll through...*

❹ Toledo's Back Streets

Leave Plaza del Ayuntamiento on the narrow, uphill lane to the right of the City Hall. Continuing straight ahead, you'll go under an arch, then through a little passage and out a door on the other side.

You'll exit to a fine little square. Straight ahead through the square, in the corner, is one of Toledo's most interesting knife shops, **Fabrica Zamorano.** Why are knives such a big deal in Toledo? In the Middle Ages, Toledo made the very best steel—using know-how imported from the Middle East via Mudejar craftsmen.

From where you came through the door, turn right, then right again, and curl steeply uphill. You'll be walking along the apse (on your left) of the Mudejar-style Santa Ursula convent from the 13th century (notice the keyhole arches).

Cresting the hill on Camino el Salvador, notice the wide-open space on your right. In Toledo's medieval cityscape—where streets are tight and buildings are

close together—open space like this is a sure sign that something once here is now gone. Sure enough, this was a site of yet another monastery, which collapsed. Now it's a rare park.

Reaching the end of the park, jog left slightly to continue along Calle Santo Tomé—toward the rectangular steeple. At the start of this street are two more opportunities to sample *mazapán*. On the right is the endearing **El Café de las Monjas,** which sells desserts created by nuns living in Toledo's convents. Across the street, ahead on the left, is the original branch of the **Santo Tomé *mazapán* shop** that we saw on Plaza de Zocodover.
• *Continue on Calle Santo Tomé. When you reach the tall, rectangular tower, turn left down the narrow lane just past it. You'll emerge at the long square marking...*

❺ Santo Tomé

This otherwise unexceptional church is home to the masterpiece of Toledo's great medieval painter, El Greco. *The Burial of the Count of Orgaz* illustrates the attendants of a local bigwig's funeral, both in heaven and here on earth. You'll likely see a line at the ticket office (facing the long square), but the wait is worth it. (For details, see the "Santo Tomé" listing under "Sights.")

The square extending behind Santo Tomé—**Plaza del Conde**—is the terminus for handy bus #12 (bus stop at far end of square). This marks the end of the first half of this walk. If your time in Toledo is short, visit San Tomé, then hightail it back to Plaza Zocodover on the bus (or walk back via the back streets instead of the clogged Calle del Comercio).
• *With more time, keep going to visit a string of worthwhile sights between here and the river.*

❻ Toledo's Jewish Quarter

You've already entered Toledo's former Jewish Quarter. In 1492, Isabel and Ferdinand expelled the Jews (except for those who converted to Christianity).

Most synagogues and other Jewish institutions were destroyed or repurposed as churches, but one very rare synagogue building survived.

To reach the heart of the Jewish quarter—and that synagogue (described later, under "Sights")—continue steeply downhill on the cobbled street past the Santo Tomé ticket office. Stay on this lane as it curves sharply left, descending below the bottom end of Plaza del Conde.

In a few minutes, the lane takes you past the entrance of the **El Greco Museum** (on your right). While the best paintings by El Greco are displayed elsewhere—this museum offers a more in-depth look at the painter's life and times.

Across the street from the El Greco Museum is a big park. Turn right here, and in 100 yards you'll run right into the entrance to the **Tránsito Synagogue** building, which offers a very rare-in-Spain look inside a historic synagogue and also houses a fine museum.

Continue past the Tránsito Synagogue on Calle de los Reyes Católicos, which links up several more sights. A block past the synagogue, a side-street on the left leads to the **Museo Victorio Macho,** with works by Spain's most important 20th-century sculptor (watch for signs to *Real Fundación de Toledo*).

Farther along, Calle de los Reyes Católicos passes the huge **San Juan de los Reyes Monastery** complex, originally designed to be the final resting place for Isabel and Ferdinand. At the very end of the street, the castle-like church exterior displays a variety of chains that were supposedly used by the Moors to shackle Christians in Granada before the Reconquista. The interior of the monastery and its chapel are also worth a look.

• *Our walk is finished. Across the street from the San Juan de los Reyes Monastery is another stop for bus #12, which you can take on a scenic ride outside Toledo's walls and then back up to Plaza de Zocodover. See the end of the "Sights" section for details.*

SIGHTS

Near Plaza de Zocodover

▲SANTA CRUZ MUSEUM (MUSEO DE SANTA CRUZ)

This stately Renaissance building, formerly an orphanage and hospital, has a good permanent collection (with eight El Grecos) about Spain under Charles V and his offspring, a peaceful cloister with a good ceramics collection, and temporary exhibits.

The building's facade still wears bullet scars from the Spanish Civil War. The frilly decorations around the main entrance (as well as the cloister arches and stairway leading to the upper cloister) are fine examples of the Plateresque style, an ornate strain of Spanish Renaissance named for the detailed work of silversmiths of the 16th century. The highlight of the museum is the dozen or so El Greco paintings (a rotating display of some permanent, some on loan). El Greco's specialty was capturing ascetic Christian saints in voluminous robes experiencing their moment of epiphany. They tilt their faces heavenward or express their

Santa Cruz Museum

deep feelings with a simple hand gesture. The scenes are rendered in bright, almost florescent colors that give these otherwise ordinary humans a heavenly aura.

Cost and Hours: €4, more with special exhibits, free on Sun; open Mon-Sat 9:30-18:30, Sun 10:00-14:00; from Plaza de Zocodover, go through arch to Calle Miguel de Cervantes 3; tel. 925-221-402, www.patrimoniohistoricoclm.es.

▲ARMY MUSEUM (MUSEO DEL EJÉRCITO)

Much of Spain's history is military. This museum—housed in the mighty Alcázar fortress that caps Toledo—tells that part of Spain's story from 1492 to the 20th century. You'll see numerous rooms of Spanish military collections of armor, uniforms, cannons, guns, paintings, and models. The posted English information is excellent, and the audioguide is a worthwhile supplement. The museum has one major flaw: its skimpy coverage of the Spanish Civil War (1936-1939). One of Europe's top military museums, the Army Museum is worth ▲▲ and at least three hours for military history buffs. Those bored by weapons and war can skip it.

Army Museum

Cost and Hours: €5, free on Sun, great audioguide-€3; free to enter temporary exhibits and archaeological ruins—ask for pass at ticket office; open Tue-Sun 10:00-17:00, closed Mon; café/restaurant and view terrace, tel. 925-238-800, www.museo.ejercito.es.

Visiting the Museum: The permanent exhibits fill four floors: thematic exhibits on T1 and T2, and a chronological sweep through Spanish military history on H1 and H2.

One highlight is the **Moscardó Room**. In 1936, in the midst of the Spanish Civil War, Toledo's Alcázar was under siege. This office was the headquarters of Toledo's Fascist forces, holding out against the Republicans. The room is preserved as it was by the end, battered and bullet-ridden. For Americans, another highlight is a series of rooms on the **"Liberal State,"** when Spain was in decline and her monarchs battled the US (1898) over **Cuba and the Philippines** (see US Army gear, a video on the sinking of the *Maine,* and insignia from Teddy Roosevelt's charge up San Juan Hill). Also look for "The 20th Century" and the **Spanish Civil War.** You'll find some timelines and maps, a script of Franco's victory speech, and objects rescued from the rubble of the Alcázar—a motorcycle, a telephone, and a daily ration of bread.

Rick's Tip: *Many of Toledo's* **sights have free audioguides** *that you can download or listen to while you're at the sight (using free Wi-Fi networks). When buying your ticket, look for signs—or ask—about how this works.*

The Cathedral and Nearby

▲▲▲TOLEDO CATHEDRAL

Holy Toledo! Spain's leading Catholic city has a magnificent cathedral. For more than 1,500 years, the people of Toledo have worshipped on this spot. The first

Toledo Cathedral

were Visigoth Christians, in a small church. Around 711, Islamic Moors conquered the city, tore down that church, and built a magnificent mosque. When Toledo was reconquered (in 1085), Christians started using the mosque for their own services. But in 1226, the now-crumbling structure was dismantled, and construction began on the current cathedral. With its long history, Toledo's cathedral is still considered the spiritual heart of Spain.

Over the centuries, the church was decorated with the sights we see today: a five-story Gothic altarpiece, Renaissance-era frescoes, a one-of-a-kind Baroque skylight, a 10-foot-tall golden monstrance, and museum-worthy paintings by El Greco and others. Shoehorned into the old center, the cathedral's exterior is hard to appreciate. But its rich and lofty interior will have you wandering around like a Pez dispenser stuck open, whispering "Wow."

Cost and Hours: €10 ticket includes audioguide; €12.50 ticket adds trip up bell tower at assigned times; cash only, tickets sold in shop opposite church entrance on Calle Cardenal Cisneros; open Mon-Sat 10:00-18:30, Sun from 14:00, open earlier for prayer only; tel. 925-222-241.

➲ SELF-GUIDED TOUR

Wander among the pillars, thick and sturdy as a redwood forest. Sit under one and imagine a time when the lightbulbs were candles and the tourists were pilgrims—when every window provided spiritual as well as physical light. This cathedral is Spain's purest example of the Gothic style. Enjoy the soaring crisscross ceiling, elaborate wrought-iron work, lavish wood carvings, and windows of 500-year-old stained glass.

• Head for the...

High Altar: Climb two steps and grip the iron grille as you marvel at one of the most stunning altarpieces in Spain. Eighty feet tall and made of real gold on wood, it's one of the country's best pieces of Gothic art. Twenty-seven Flemish, French, and local artists labored on it for seven years. The images seem to celebrate the colorful Assumption of Mary (upper center), with Mary escorted by six upwardly mobile

The cathedral entrance

High altar

Toledo Cathedral

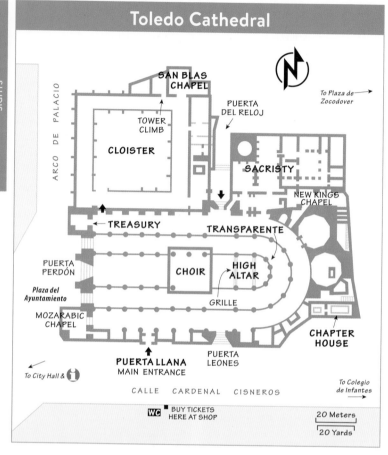

SAN BLAS
CHAPEL

ARCO DE PALACIO

TOWER
CLIMB

CLOISTER

PUERTA
DEL RELOJ

SACRISTY

NEW KINGS
CHAPEL

To Plaza de
Zocodover →

TREASURY

TRANSPARENTE

PUERTA
PERDÓN

Plaza del
Ayuntamiento

MOZARABIC
CHAPEL

CHOIR

HIGH
ALTAR

GRILLE

CHAPTER
HOUSE

PUERTA LLANA
MAIN ENTRANCE

PUERTA
LEONES

To City Hall & 🛈

CALLE   CARDENAL   CISNEROS

To Colegio
de Infantes →

WC ▪ BUY TICKETS
HERE AT SHOP

20 Meters

20 Yards

angels. The crucified Christ on top is nine feet tall—taller than the lower statues—to keep this towering altar approachable. Don't miss the finely worked, gold-plated iron **grille** itself—considered to be the best from the 16th century in Spain.

• About-face to the...

Choir: This intimate space, lined with 120 carved-wood stalls, is where VIPs and hymn-singing musicians (hence the name "choir") can celebrate Mass near the high altar. Stepping inside, you're greeted by a 700-year-old statue of the **Virgin and Child.** This "White Virgin" is thought to be a gift from the French king to Spain.

Rick's Tip: The choir is ringed by **stone statues**—*an alabaster genealogy of Christ—starting with Adam and Eve and working counterclockwise to Joseph and "S. M. Virgo Mater" (St. Mary the Virgin Mother). The focal point is the archbishop's throne, in the center of the far wall. Get close and find the fine alabaster relief just above the throne. It shows the miraculous event that put this cathedral on the map: In the seventh century, Mary came down from heaven to the cathedral to give Toledo's bishop, Saint Ildefonso, a holy robe. This legitimized Toledo as the spiritual capital (and therefore political capital) of the budding nation of Spain.*

Now turn to the richly carved wooden **stalls**. The carvings depict scenes of the Christian Reconquista, specifically the steady one-city-at-a-time finale—the retaking of the towns around Granada. Each castle represents a different town, labeled with its name, besieged by valiant Christian armies. The assault culminates at the archbishop's throne (the two reliefs to either side), with the final victory at Granada in 1492. The soldiers' clothing, armor, and weaponry are so detailed that historians have studied them to learn the evolution of weaponry.

Also check out the **seat backs,** made of carved walnut and featuring New Testament figures—including Peter (key) and Paul (sword) alongside the archbishop himself. Now turn to the stalls' misericords—the tiny seats that allowed tired worshippers to lean while they "stand." These carvings depict various sins and proverbs. They feature folksy, sexy, secular scenes: animals, mermaids, unicorns, and common laborers. Apparently, since you sat on it, it could never be sacred anyway.

Before leaving the choir, take a moment to absorb the marvelous complexity, harmony, and cohesiveness of the art around you. Look up. There are two fine **pipe organs:** one (frilly, on the left) is early-18th-century Baroque, and the other (austere and pointy, on the right) is late-18th-century Neoclassical.

• *Face the huge altarpiece and go around it to your right to the...*

Chapter House (Sala Capitular): Under a lavish ceiling, a **fresco** celebrates the humanism of the Italian Renaissance. There's a Deposition (taking crucified Jesus off the cross), a pietà, and a Resurrection on the front wall; they face a fascinating Last Judgment, where the seven sins are spelled out in the gang going to hell: arrogance (the guy striking a pose), avarice (holding his bag of coins), lust (the easy woman with the lovely hair and fiery crotch), anger (shouting at lust), gluttony (the fat guy), envy, and laziness. Think about how instructive this was in 1600.

Below the fresco, a pictorial review of 1,900 years of Toledo archbishops circles the room. The upper row of **portraits** dates from the 16th century. Except for the last two, these were not painted from

Chapter House

life (the same face seems to be recycled over and over). The lower portraits were added one at a time from 1515 on and are of more historic than artistic interest. Imagine sitting down to church business surrounded by all this tradition and theology.

As you leave, notice the iron-pumping cupids carved into the pear-tree panels lining the walls.

• *Go behind the high altar to find the...*

Transparente: The Transparente—a towering white, red, and gold altarpiece bursting with statues—is a unique feature of the cathedral. But that's just half of this multimedia extravaganza. Look up. In the 1700s, a hole was cut in the ceiling. The opening faces east, and each morning the sun sends a beam into the church to strike the altarpiece, lighten this space for worship, and remind all that God is light. Put these elements together, and the result is a Baroque masterpiece. Gape up at this riot of angels doing flip-flops, babies breathing thin air, bottoms of feet, and gilded sunbursts. Carved out of marble from Italy, it's bursting with motion and full of energy. Appreciate those tough little cherubs who are supporting the whole

Transparente altarpiece

thing—they've been waiting for help for about 300 years now.

• *Continue around the apse. On the right, enter the...*

Chapel of the New Kings (Capilla de Reyes Nuevos): These reclining statues mark the tombs of just some of the monarchs buried in this venerable cathedral. In the 16th century, Emperor Charles V moved these eight tombs of medieval-era kings here.

• *Back in the apse, the next door on your right takes you into the...*

Sacristy: The cathedral's sacristy is a mini Prado, with 19 El Grecos and masterpieces by Francisco de Goya, Titian, Diego Velázquez, Caravaggio, and Giovanni Bellini. First, notice the fine perspective work on the **ceiling,** painted by Neapolitan artist Luca Giordano around 1690. (You can see the artist himself—with his circa-1690 spectacles—in the far-left corner.)

The most important painting in the collection—framed by marble columns—is **El Greco's *The Spoliation*** (a.k.a. *Christ Being Stripped of His Garments,* 1579). The great Spanish painter was Greek, and this is the first masterpiece he created after arriving in Toledo. It hangs exactly where he intended it to—in the room where priests donned their sacred robes for Mass.

El Greco shows Jesus surrounded by a sinister mob and suffering the humiliation of being stripped in public before his execution. His scarlet robe is about to be yanked off; the women (lower left) avert their eyes, turning to watch a carpenter at work (lower right) boring the holes for nailing Jesus to the cross. While the carpenter bears down, Jesus—the other carpenter—looks up to heaven. The contrast between the motley crowd gambling for his clothes and Jesus' noble face underscores the quiet dignity with which he endures this ignoble treatment. Jesus' delicate white hand stands out from the flaming red tunic with an odd gesture that's common in El Greco's paintings. Some say this was the way Christians of the day swore they were true believers, not merely Christians-in-name-only, such as former Muslims or Jews who converted to survive.

Other El Grecos adorn the room. His various saints show his trademark style: thin, solemn, weathered men on a neutral background, with simple expressive gestures. Close to the entrance is a scene rarely painted: **St. Joseph and the Christ Child.** Joseph is walking with Jesus, just as El Greco enjoyed walking around the Toledo countryside with his sons. Notice Joseph's gentle expression—and the Toledo views in the background.

To the right of *The Spoliation* is a more down-to-earth depiction of Christ's Passion: Francisco de Goya's **Betrayal of Christ.** It shows Judas preparing to kiss Jesus, thus identifying him to the Roman soldiers.

In an adjoining room are more treasures by master artists, including Titian's probing portrait of Pope Paul III (a friend of Michelangelo) and Cardinal Mendoza's cross.
• *As you step out of the sacristy, glance high up to your right at a beautiful* **rose window***—the oldest stained glass in the church (14th century). Now locate our final stops: The Treasury is in a chapel straight ahead. The cloister is through doors near the Treasury. Step outside into...*

The Cloister: The cloister is worth a visit for its finely carved colonnade. Take a peaceful detour to the funerary San Blas Chapel. The ceiling fresco over the alabaster tomb of a bishop is by a student of the 14th-century Italian Renaissance master Giotto.
• *Returning to the cathedral the same way you came in, turn right to find the...*

Treasury: The star attraction here is a 10-foot-high, 430-pound gold-and-silver **monstrance**—the ceremonial tower designed to hold the Holy Communion wafer (the host) that every year is paraded atop a float through the city during the festival of Corpus Christi ("body of Christ"). Built in 1517 by Enrique de Arfe, it's made of 5,000 pieces held together by 12,500 screws. There are dia-

Cathedral cloister

monds, emeralds, rubies, and 400 pounds of gold-plated silver. The inner part (which is a century older) is 40 pounds of solid gold. Yeow.

This precious and centuries-old monstrance is still a vital part of civic life, a testament to the Toledo Cathedral's unique position as the religious center of Spain.
• *Your essential cathedral tour is over, but there is one other sight to consider.*

Bell Tower: If you paid for the bell tower, meet just to the left of the San Blas Chapel at your assigned time. You'll climb several sections of tight spiral staircases (about 200 stairs in all) to reach panoramic views of Toledo and the largest, though cracked, bell in Spain.

▲VISIGOTHIC MUSEUM IN THE CHURCH OF SAN ROMÁN (MUSEO DE LOS CONCILIOS Y DE LA CULTURA VISIGODA)

Though small, this sight offers a thought-provoking collection of artifacts from Toledo's infancy, displayed in a colorfully decorated church in an untouristed part of Toledo. Built by Visigoth Christians in the seventh century atop one of Toledo's highest hills, the church was con-

Church of San Román

verted to a mosque in the 10th century, then transformed back to a church in the 13th century. Elements of all three remain.

Cost and Hours: €2, buy at ticket machine, Tue-Sat 9:45-14:15 & 16:00-18:30, Sun 10:00-14:00, closed Mon, no English information, west of the cathedral at Plaza San Román, tel. 925-227-872.

Visiting the Museum: Start with the church interior. A few Visigoth capitals from the original church were reused and placed atop columns in the nave. The keystone arches and lobed windows date from the mosque. The Christian-themed murals were painted to cover up Islamic imagery. This mix of Christian and Islamic (called Mudejar) represents how each culture both conquered and celebrated their predecessors. Now turn to the Visigoth artifacts from the *"Siglo VII"*—the seventh century. (Some are 1,400-year-old originals; some are replicas.) A carved relief depicts a row of robed saints and naked Adam and Eve. You'll see early Christian symbols: crosses, doves, and olive branches. The X-shaped symbol flanked by the Greek letters alpha and omega represents how Christ (the X) is the beginning and end of all.

The Visigoths reigned supreme until the year 711, when the Islamic Moors invaded. Because Toledo was the political, cultural, and spiritual head of Spain, by decapitating Toledo, the Moors quickly took the entire peninsula. They made this Visigoth church a mosque, which was, in turn, incorporated into the church we see today. Now artifacts from Visigothic times are on display, bringing the story full circle.

Southwest Toledo

These sights cluster at the southwest end of town. For efficient sightseeing, visit them in this order, then return to the center on bus #12 (listed at the end of this section).

▲▲SANTO TOMÉ

A simple chapel on Plaza del Conde holds El Greco's most beloved painting—*The Burial of the Count of Orgaz*—which couples heaven and earth in a way only The Greek could. It feels so right to see a painting in the same church where the artist placed it 400 years ago (though moved slightly to accommodate modern crowds). This 15-foot-tall masterpiece, painted at the height of El Greco's powers, is the culmination of his unique style.

Cost and Hours: €2.80, daily 10:00-18:45, until 17:45 mid-Oct-Feb, audioguide-€1, tel. 925-256-098. There's often a line to get in; try going early or late to avoid tour groups.

Visiting the Chapel: Take this slow. Stay for a while—let it perform. The year is 1323. Count Don Gonzalo Ruiz of Orgaz, the mayor of Toledo, has died. You're at his burial right here in the chapel that he himself had ordered built. The good count was so holy, even saints Augustine and Stephen have come down from heaven to lower his body into the grave. (The painting's subtitle is "Such is the reward for those who serve God and his saints.")

More than 250 years later, in 1586, a local priest (depicted on the far right, reading the Bible) hired El Greco to make a painting of the burial to hang over the count's tomb. The funeral is attended by Toledo's most distinguished citizens. (El Greco used local nobles as models.) The serene line of noble faces divides the painting into two realms—heaven above and earth below.

El Greco (1541-1614)

Born on Crete and trained in Venice, Doménikos Theotokópoulos (tongue-tied friends just called him "The Greek") came to Spain to get a job decorating El Escorial. He failed there, but succeeded in Toledo, where he spent the last 37 years of his life. He mixed all three regional influences into his palette. From his Greek homeland, he absorbed the solemn, abstract style of icons. In Italy, he learned the bold use of color, elongated figures, twisting poses, and dramatic style of the later Renaissance. These elements were then fused in the fires of fanatic Spanish-Catholic devotion.

Not bound by the realism so important to his fellow artists, El Greco painted dramatic visions of striking colors and figures—bodies unnatural and lengthened as though stretched between heaven and earth. He painted souls, not faces. His work is on display at nearly every sight in Toledo. Thoroughly modern in his disregard for realism, he didn't impress the austere Philip II. But his art still seems as fresh as contemporary art does today. El Greco was essentially forgotten through the 18th and most of the 19th centuries. Then, with the Romantic movement (and the discovery of Toledo by Romantic-era travelers, artists, and poets), the paintings of El Greco became the hits they are today.

Above the faces, the count's soul, symbolized by a little baby, rises up through a mystical birth canal to be reborn in heaven, where he's greeted by Jesus, Mary, and all the saints. A spiritual wind blows through as colors change and shapes stretch. This is Counter-Reformation propaganda—notice Jesus pointing to St. Peter, the symbol of the pope in Rome, who controls the keys to the pearly gates.

El Greco considered this to be one of his greatest works. It's a virtual catalog of his lifelong techniques: elongated bodies, elegant hand gestures, realistic faces, surreal colors, voluminous robes, and a mix of heaven and earth. The boy in the foreground—pointing to the two saints as if to say, "One's from the first century, the other's from the fourth...it's a miracle!"—is El Greco's own son. On the handkerchief in the boy's pocket is El Greco's signature, written in Greek. The only guy in this whole scene who doesn't seem to be completely engaged in the burial is the seventh figure from the left, looking directly out at the viewer—El Greco himself.

▲EL GRECO MUSEUM (MUSEO DEL GRECO)

Housed in a faux 16th-century villa located near the site of El Greco's actual home, this museum offers a look at the genius of his art and Toledo in his day. While you won't find many great works by El Greco here (for those, visit Santo Tomé, the cathedral, and the Santa Cruz Museum), there are a few good ones,

El Greco, The Burial of the Count of Orgaz

along with thoughtful exhibits. Come here if you've developed an affinity for El Greco and want to know more about his life and work. You'll learn about his upbringing in Crete, his training in Venice and Rome, and his arrival in Toledo—each step spurring his style to evolve. One highlight is the long hall lined with portraits of the 12 apostles, plus Jesus. At the end of the hall is the remarkable *View and Plan of Toledo,* a panoramic map showing the city in 1614. The exhibit wraps up with a description of El Greco's workshop, creative process, and some of his talented students, including his son Jorge Manuel—the kid in the *Burial of Count Orgaz.*

Cost and Hours: €3, €5 combo-ticket with Sinagoga del Tránsito, free Sat afternoon from 14:00 and all day Sun; open Tue-Sat 9:30-19:30, Nov-Feb until 18:00, Sun 10:00-15:00, closed Mon; next to Sinagoga del Tránsito on Calle Samuel Leví, tel. 925-223-665.

▲TRÁNSITO SYNAGOGUE AND JEWISH MUSEUM (SINAGOGA DEL TRÁNSITO Y MUSEO SEFARDÍ)

Built in 1361, this is the best surviving slice of Toledo's Jewish past. The austere interior rewards patient visitors with its fine details. Serving as Spain's national Jewish museum, the building also displays a modest selection of Jewish artifacts, including traditional costumes, menorahs, and books. Paltry English sheets in each room explain the museum; for more detail, get the audioguide.

Cost and Hours: €3, €5 combo-ticket with El Greco Museum, free Sat afternoon from 14:00 and all day Sun; open Tue-Sat 9:30-19:30 (off-season until 18:00), Sun 10:00-15:00, closed Mon; audioguide-€2 (or use free Wi-Fi version); near El Greco Museum on Calle de los Reyes Católicos, tel. 925-223-665.

Visiting the Synagogue: This 14th-century synagogue was built at the peak of Toledo's enlightened tolerance—constructed for Jews with Christian approval by Muslim craftsmen. Nowhere else in the

Sinagoga del Tránsito

city does Toledo's three-culture legacy shine brighter than at this place of worship. But in 1391, just a few decades after the synagogue was built, the Church and the Spanish kings began a violent campaign to unite Spain as a Christian nation, forcing Jews and Muslims to convert or leave. In 1492 Ferdinand and Isabel exiled Spain's remaining Jews, and although a third of them left, others converted to Christianity to remain in the country.

What makes this synagogue unique is that its interior decor looks more Muslim than Jewish. After Christians reconquered the city in 1085, many Moorish workmen stayed on, beautifying the city with the style called Mudejar. The synagogue's intricate, geometrical carving in stucco—nearly all original, from 1360—features leaves, vines, and flowers; there are no human shapes, which are forbidden by the Torah—like the Quran—as being potential objects of idolatry. In the frieze (running along the upper wall, just below the ceiling), the Arabic-looking script is actually Hebrew, quoting psalms (respected by all "people of the book"—Muslims, Jews, and Christians alike).

Move up to the front. Stand close to the holy wall and study the exquisite workmanship (with reminders of all three religions: the coat of arms of the Christian king, Hebrew script, and Muslim decor). Look down. The small rectangular patch of the original floor survived only because the Christian altar table sat there.

Then head into the **side hall,** with displays about the history of Toledo's Jews and the development of the Jewish quarter. The Memorial Garden displays Jewish tomb markers from around Spain.

▲VICTORIO MACHO MUSEUM (MUSEO VICTORIO MACHO)

Overlooking the gorge and Tajo River, this small and attractive museum— once the home and workshop of the early-20th-century sculptor Victorio Macho—offers a delightful collection of

San Juan de los Reyes cloister

his bold Art Deco-inspired work. Macho (1887-1966) was Spain's first great modern sculptor. When his left-wing Republican (say that three times) politics made it dangerous for him to stay in Franco's Spain, he fled to the USSR, then to Mexico and Peru, where he met his wife, Zoila. They later returned to Toledo. The house and its garden are a cool oasis of calm in the city. Inside, you'll find a single room, marked *Museo*, filled with Macho's art. A pietà is carved expressively in granite. Other statues show the strength of the people's spirit as leftist Republicans stood up to Franco's fascist forces, and Spain endured its 20th-century bloodbath. The highlight is *La Madre* (from 1935), Macho's life-size sculpture of his mother sitting in a chair. It illustrates the sadness and simple wisdom of Spanish mothers who witnessed so much suffering.

Cost and Hours: €3, Mon-Fri 10:00-14:00 & 17:00-19:00, closed Sat-Sun, Plaza de Victorio Macho 2, ring doorbell to enter, tel. 925-284-225.

▲MONASTERY OF SAN JUAN DE LOS REYES (SAN JUAN DE LOS REYES MONASTERIO)

"St. John of the Monarchs" is a grand Franciscan monastery, impressive church, and delightful "Isabeline" cloistered courtyard. The style is late Gothic, contemporaneous with Portugal's Manueline (c. 1500) and Flamboyant Gothic elsewhere in Europe. It was the intended burial site of the Catholic Monarchs, Isabel and Ferdinand. But after the Moors were expelled in 1492 from Granada, their royal bodies were planted there to show Spain's commitment to maintaining a Moor-free peninsula.

Cost and Hours: €2.80, daily 10:00-18:45, mid-Oct-March until 17:45, free Wi-Fi audioguide, San Juan de los Reyes 2, tel. 925-223-802.

▲BUS #12 SELF-GUIDED TOUR

When you're finished with the sights at the Santo Tomé end of town, you can hike all the way back to Plaza de Zocodover (not fun), or simply catch bus #12 (fun!). The ride offers tired sightseers an interesting 15-minute look at the town walls. You can catch the bus from Plaza del Conde in front of Santo Tomé. This is the end of the line, so buses wait to depart from here twice hourly (at :25 and :55, until 21:25, pay driver €1.40). You can catch the same bus a few stops downhill, at the very bottom of Toledo's sightseeing spine, across the street from the San Juan de los Reyes ticket entrance (a few minutes after it leaves Plaza del Conde).

◐ **Self-Guided Tour:** Leaving Plaza del Conde, you'll first ride through Toledo's Jewish section. On the right, you'll pass the El Greco Museum, Sinagoga del Tránsito, and—on your left—the ornate Flamboyant Gothic facade of San Juan de los Reyes Monasterio. After squeezing through the 16th-century city gate, the bus follows along the outside of the mighty 10th-century wall.

Just past the big escalator (which brings people up from parking lots into the city) and Hotel del Cardenal, the wall gets fancier, as demonstrated by the little old Bisagra Gate. Soon after, you see the big new Bisagra Gate, the main entry into the old town. While the city walls date from the 10th century, this gate was built as an arch of triumph in the 16th century. The massive coat of arms of Emperor Charles V, with the double eagle, reminded people that he ruled a unified Habsburg empire. Just outside the big gate is a well-maintained and shaded park—a picnic-perfect spot and one of Toledo's few green areas.

After a detour to the bus station basement to pick up people arriving from Madrid, you swing back around Bisagra Gate. As an example of how things have changed in the last generation, as recently as 1960, all traffic into the city at this point had to pass through this gate's tiny original entrance.

As you climb back into the old town, you'll pass the fine 14th-century Moorish Puerta del Sol (Gate of the Sun) on your right. Then, on your left, is the modern Palacio de Congresos Miradero convention center, which is artfully incorporated into the more historic cityscape. Within moments you pull into Plaza de Zocodover.

EXPERIENCES

Shopping

Toledo is *the* place to buy medieval-looking swords, armor, maces, three-legged stools, lethal-looking letter-openers, and other nouveau antiques. It's also Spain's damascene center, where, for centuries, craftspeople have inlaid black steel with gold, silver, and copper wire. Spain's top bullfighters wouldn't have their swords made anywhere else.

Knives: At the workshop of English-speaking **Mariano Zamorano,** you can see swords and knives being made. His family has been putting its seal on hand-crafted knives since 1890. Judging by what's left of Mariano's hand, his knives are among the sharpest (Mon-Fri 10:00-14:00 & 16:00-19:00, Sat-Sun 10:30-14:00—although you may not see work done on weekends, 10 percent discount with this book, behind Ayuntamiento/City Hall at Calle Ciudad 19, don't confuse the Zamorano shop—tucked back in the corner—with their bigger neighbor, tel. 925-222-634, www.marianozamorano.com).

Damascene: You can find artisans all over town pounding gold and silver threads into a steel base to create shiny inlaid plates, decorative wares, and jewelry. The damascene is a real tourist racket, but it's fun to pop into a shop and see the intricate handiwork in action.

El Martes: Toledo's colorful outdoor market is a lively scene on Tuesdays at

Toledo souvenirs

Paseo de Merchan, better known to locals as "La Vega" (9:00-14:00, outside Bisagra Gate near TI).

Nightlife

Toledo is sleepy after dark. If there's something going on, it's likely at **Círculo del Arte,** a bar and music venue that fills a jaw-dropping 12th-century Mudejar hall—with keyhole brick arches—hiding in back streets near the top of town. It offers a diverse slate of musical events—some free, others with a cover—and on weekends, the action can continue late into the night (schedule at www.circuloartetoledo.org, Plaza San Vicente 2, tel. 925-256-653).

EATING

Typical Toledo dishes include partridge (*perdiz*), venison (*venado*), wild boar (*jabalí*), roast suckling pig (*cochinillo asado*), or baby lamb (*cordero*—similarly roasted after a few weeks of mother's milk). Also popular is the flavorful pork stew called *carcamusas*—everyone seems to have their own recipe. After dinner, find a *mazapán* place for dessert.

Memorable Dining

$$$ Los Cuatro Tiempos Restaurante ("The Four Seasons") specializes in local game and roasts, proficiently served in a tasteful and elegant setting—a mix of traditional and modern. They offer spacious dining with an extensive and inviting Spanish wine list (Mon-Sat 13:00-16:00 & 20:30-23:00, Sun 13:00-16:00 only, at downhill corner of cathedral, Calle Sixto Ramón Parro 5, tel. 925-223-782).

$$$ El Botero Taberna is a delightful little hideaway. The barman downstairs serves mojitos, fine wine, and exquisite tapas that are well priced and described. Upstairs is an intimate, seven-table restaurant with romantic, white-table-cloth ambience and modern Mediterranean dishes (Wed-Sun 13:30-16:00 &

21:00-23:30, Mon 13:30-16:00 only, closed Tue, a block from cathedral at Calle de la Ciudad 5, tel. 925-229-088).

$$$ Colección Catedral is the wine bar of local chef Adolfo, who, with his brother Carlos, cooks up a somewhat pricey list of gourmet plates, including some traditional local dishes done with a modern spin. Some dishes can be modified to suit vegetarians and vegans (daily 12:00-16:00 & 20:30-23:30, across from cathedral at Calle Nuncio Viejo 1, tel. 925-224-244).

$$ Mercado San Agustín is part of a trend to create a space for several different eateries under one roof. It offers four levels of eating choices, including tapas and *pintxos,* gourmet cheeses, organic hamburgers, Japanese cuisine, coffee, and sweet delights. Find a table on any of the levels to dig in, or go to the rooftop terrace for a cocktail (Tue-Sun 10:00-24:00, closed Mon, at Calle Cuesta de Águila 1 right off of Plaza San Agustín—just a block off Plaza de Zocodover, tel. 925-215-898).

Restaurants with Character

These places are listed roughly in geographical order from Plaza de Zocodover to Santo Tomé. Plaza de Zocodover is busy with eateries serving edible food at affordable prices, and its people-watching scene is great. But my recommended eateries are on side streets a bit off the main drag. It's worth a few extra minutes to find places where you'll be eating with locals as well as with tourists. Toledo also has a lively midday tapas scene, and almost every bar you pop into for a stand-up drink will come with a small plate of something to nibble.

$$ El Trébol, tucked peacefully away just a few steps off Plaza de Zocodover, is the place to dine with younger Spaniards. Locals enjoy their *pulgas* (sandwiches), and their mixed grill can feed two (daily 9:00-24:00, Calle de Santa Fe 1, tel. 925-281-297).

$$ Restaurante Ludeña is a classic eatery with a dive bar up front, a well-worn dining room in back, and a handful of tables on a sunny courtyard. They serve up big, stick-to-your-ribs portions of traditional comfort food, including a rich, bright-red *carcamusas* pork stew; their filling fixed-price meals are a good value (Plaza de la Magdalena 10, tel. 925-223-384).

$$ Madre Tierra Restaurante Vegetariano is Toledo's answer to a vegetarian's prayer. Bright, spacious, classy, air-conditioned, and tuned in to the healthy eater's needs, its appetizing dishes are based on both international and traditional Spanish cuisine (good tea selection, great veggie pizzas, Wed-Sun 13:00-16:00 & 20:30-23:00, Mon 13:00-16:00 only, closed Tue, 20 yards below La Posada de Manolo just before reaching Plaza de San Justo, Bajada de Tripería 2, tel. 925-223-571).

$$ Restaurante Placido, run by high-energy Anna and *abuela* (grandma) Sagradio, serves traditional family-style cuisine on a shady terrace or in a wonderful Franciscan monastery courtyard (open daily for lunch and dinner in summer, lunch only in winter, about a block uphill from Santo Tomé at Calle Santo Tomé 2, tel. 925-222-603).

Picnics: Picnics are best assembled at the humble city market, **Mercado Municipal,** on Plaza Mayor (on the Alcázar side of cathedral, with a supermarket inside open Mon-Sat 9:00-14:30 & 17:00-20:00 and stalls open mostly in the mornings until 14:00, closed Sun). **Supermarket Suma,** on Plaza de la Magdalena, has groceries and lots of other stuff at good prices (daily 9:30-22:00, just below Plaza de Zocodover). For a picnic with people-watching on an atmospheric square, consider Plaza de Zocodover or Plaza del Ayuntamiento.

Dessert

Toledo's famous almond-fruity-sweet *mazapán* is sold all over town. If you can't

Mazapán *confections*

track down a convent selling sweets in the labyrinth of Holy Toledo, visit **El Café de las Monjas,** a pastry and coffee shop around the corner from the Santo Tomé church that brings in *mazapán* from local convents (daily 9:00-21:00, Calle Santo Tomé 2).

The big *mazapán* producer is **Santo Tomé** (several outlets, including near Plaza de Zocodover and at Calle Santo Tomé 3, daily 9:00-22:00). They sell *mazapán* goodies individually (*sin relleno*—without filling—is for purists, *de piñon* has pine nuts, *imperiales* is with almonds, others have fruit fillings). Boxes are good for gifts, but if you want an assortment, tell them what you want à la carte. Their *Toledana* is a bigger, nutty, crumbly, not-too-sweet cookie with a subtle thread of squash filling.

Rick's Tip: *For a* **sweet and romantic evening moment,** *pick up a few pastries and head down to the cathedral. Sit on the Plaza del Ayuntamiento's benches. A fountain is on your right, Spain's best-looking City Hall is behind you, and before you is the cathedral—built back when Toledo was Spain's capital—shining brightly against the black night sky.*

SLEEPING

Day-trippers darken the sunlit cobbles, but few stay to see Toledo's medieval moonrise. Spend the night. Most hotels have a two-tiered price system, with prices at least 20 percent higher on Friday and Saturday (I've based my rankings on weekday prices). Spring and fall are high season; rooms are scarce and prices go up during the Corpus Christi festival as well (usually late May or early June).

Near the Cathedral

$ Hotel Santa Isabel, in a 15th-century building two blocks from the cathedral, has 41 clean, modern, and comfortable rooms and squeaky tile hallways (some view rooms, elevator, scenic roof terrace, pay parking—call same day to reserve, drivers enter from Calle Pozo Amargo, Calle Santa Isabel 24, tel. 925-253-120, www.hotelsantaisabeltoledo.es, info@hotelsantaisabeltoledo.es).

$ La Posada de Manolo rents 14 tight, rustic, cozy rooms across from the downhill corner of the cathedral. Manolo Junior (and wife Almudena) opened this hostal according to his father's vision: a place with each of its three floors themed differently—Moorish, Jewish, and Christian. The place has its quirks, and noise carries through its tiled halls, but it has personality and is popular with European tourists (RS%, two nice view terraces, Calle Sixto Ramón Parro 8, tel. 925-282-250, www.laposadademanolo.com, toledo@laposadademanolo.com).

$ Hotel Eurico cleverly fits 23 dated, simple, but well-priced and well-located rooms into a medieval building buried deep in the old town (air-con, Calle Santa Isabel 3, tel. 925-284-178, www.hoteleurico.com, reservas@hoteleurico.com).

Near Plaza de Zocodover

$ Antidoto Rooms' owner was looking to create an antidote to the epidemic of same-old, same-old hotels in Toledo. He

succeeded, crafting 10 modern rooms with concrete floors and pops of color, each with a tiny balcony. It's ideally located on a back street just a short stroll from Plaza de Zocodover (elevator, air-con, Calle Recoletos 2, tel. 925-228-851, www.antidotorooms.com).

$ Hotel Toledo Imperial, sitting efficiently above Plaza de Zocodover, rents 29 nondescript rooms (air-con, elevator, Calle Horno de los Bizcochos 5, tel. 925-280-034, www.hoteltoledoimperial.com, reservas@hoteltoledoimperial.com).

$ Hotel La Conquista de Toledo, with 35 dated but well-priced rooms, gleams with marble—it almost feels more like a hospital than a hotel (family rooms, air-con, elevator, Juan Labrador 8, tel. 925-210-760, www.hotelconquistadetoledo.com, conquistadetoledo@yithoteles.com).

In the Jewish Quarter

$$ Hotel Pintor El Greco is a chain hotel with 56 modern, colorful rooms across the street from the El Greco Museum (elevator, air-con, pay parking, Calle Alamillos del Tránsito 13, tel. 925-285-191, www.hotelpintorelgreco.com).

$$ Hotel San Juan de los Reyes fills a historic old 19th-century brick factory building with 35 cookie-cutter, characterless, but predictably comfortable rooms, on the road between its namesake monastery and the Tránsito synagogue (elevator, air-con, pay parking, Calle Reyes Católicos 5, tel. 925-283-535, www.hotelsanjuandelosreyes.com).

Near Bisagra Gate

$$ Hacienda del Cardenal, a 17th-century cardinal's palace built into Toledo's wall, is quiet and elegant, with 27 rooms, a cool garden, and a stuffy restaurant. This poor man's parador—a pleasant oasis next to the dusty old gate of Toledo—is close to the station, but below all the old-town action (elevator, air-con, enter through town wall 100 yards below Bisagra Gate, Paseo de Recaredo 24, tel. 925-

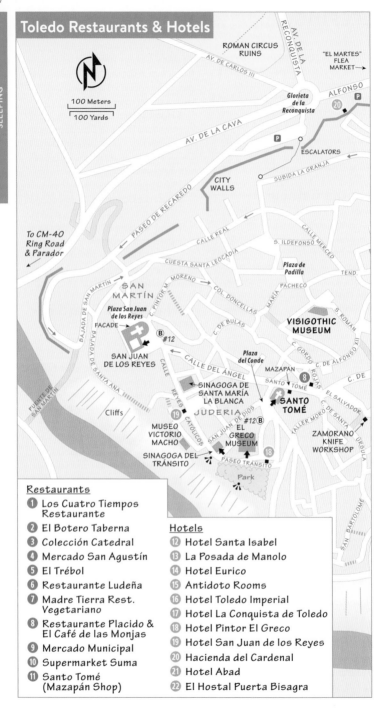

Toledo Restaurants & Hotels

Restaurants

1 Los Cuatro Tiempos Restaurante
2 El Botero Taberna
3 Colección Catedral
4 Mercado San Agustín
5 El Trébol
6 Restaurante Ludeña
7 Madre Tierra Rest. Vegetariano
8 Restaurante Placido & El Café de las Monjas
9 Mercado Municipal
10 Supermarket Suma
11 Santo Tomé (Mazapán Shop)

Hotels

12 Hotel Santa Isabel
13 La Posada de Manolo
14 Hotel Eurico
15 Antidoto Rooms
16 Hotel Toledo Imperial
17 Hotel La Conquista de Toledo
18 Hotel Pintor El Greco
19 Hotel San Juan de los Reyes
20 Hacienda del Cardenal
21 Hotel Abad
22 El Hostal Puerta Bisagra

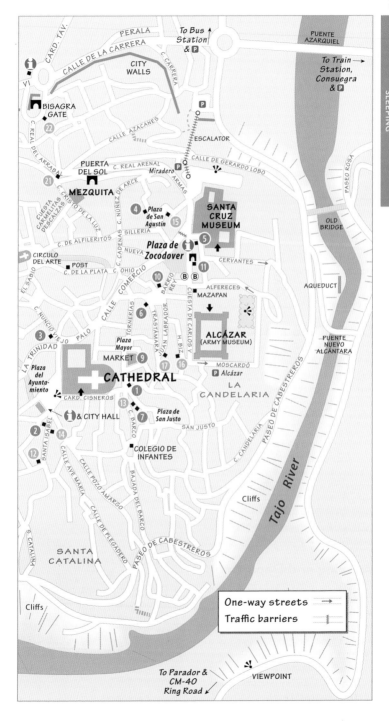

PERALA

CALLE DE LA CARRERA

CARD. TAV.

C. CARRERA

CITY
WALLS

To Bus
Station
& P

PUENTE
AZARQUIEL

To Train →
Station,
Consuegra
& P

BISAGRA
GATE

22

CALLE AZACANES

C. REAL DEL ARRABAL

ESCALATOR

CALLE DE GERARDO LOBO

PASEO ROSA

PUERTA
DEL SOL

C. REAL ARENAL

Miradero

21

MEZQUITA

C. CRISTO DE LA LUZ

CUESTA CARMELITAS DESCALZAS

C. NUÑEZ DE ARCE

ARMAS

SANTA
CRUZ
MUSEUM

OLD
BRIDGE

4

Plaza
de San
Agustín

15

C. DE ALFILERITOS

SILLERIA

C. CADENAS

NUEVA

Plaza de
Zocodover

5

AQUEDUCT

CÍRCULO
DEL ARTE

POST

EL SABIO

C. DE LA PLATA

C. OHIO

COMERCIO

CALLE

BARRIO REY

11

CERVANTES

10

B B

ALFERECES

MAZAPAN

C. NUNCIO VIEJO

PALO

3

TORNERIAS

6

TRASTAMARA

CUESTA DE CARLOS V

ALCÁZAR
(ARMY MUSEUM)

PUENTE
NUEVO
ALCÁNTARA

Plaza
Mayor

JUAN LABRADOR

LA TRINIDAD

Plaza
del
Ayunta-
miento

MARKET

9

H. BIZ.

17 16

MOSCARDÓ

P Alcázar

LA
CANDELARIA

CATHEDRAL

1

CARD. CISNEROS

13

& CITY HALL

C. BARCO

7

Plaza de
San Justo

SAN JUSTO

2

14

Santa Isabel

12

CALLE AVE MARIA

CALLE POZO AMARGO

COLEGIO DE
INFANTES

BAJADA DEL BARCO

PASEO DE CABESTREROS

C. CANDELARIA

Cliffs

Tajo River

S. CATALINA

SANTA
CATALINA

CALLE DE PLEGADERO

PASEO DE CABESTREROS

One-way streets →

Traffic barriers

Cliffs

VIEWPOINT

To Parador &
CM-40
Ring Road ↙

224-900, www.haciendadelcardenal.com, hotel@haciendadelcardenal.com).

$ Hotel Abad, just a block inside the Bisagra Gate (next to the Puerta del Sol), feels more stylish than the Toledo norm. They rent 28 trendy-rustic rooms with stone walls, wooden rafters, and contemporary furnishings at the higher end of this price range (air-con, elevator, Calle Real del Arrabal 1, tel. 925-283-500, www.hotela-badtoledo.com, reservas@hotelabad.com).

$ El Hostal Puerta Bisagra, in a sprawling old building, is fresh and modern inside. It's picturesquely located right next to Bisagra Gate, with 38 comfortable rooms at a good value (air-con, elevator, Calle del Potro 5, tel. 925-285-277, www.puertabisagra.com, elhostal@puertabisagra.com).

TRANSPORTATION

Getting Around Toledo

You can walk anywhere within the town walls in small, hilly Toledo, but buses can also come in handy. Bus #12 gets you across town and back—running between Plaza de Zocodover and Santo Tomé (€1.40, pay driver; see my "Bus #12 Self-Guided Tour" on page 245). To get to the famous viewpoint across the gorge, see "Tours," near the beginning of this chapter. As for taxis, you'll find stands at the train station, bus station, and in the old town (Plaza de Zocodover, Bisagra Gate, and Santo Tomé). For around €15, taxis routinely give visitors scenic circles around town with photo stops.

Arriving and Departing

"Arriving" in Toledo means getting uphill to Plaza de Zocodover. Since the bus and train stations are below the town center and parking can be a challenge, this involves a taxi, a city bus, or a walk plus a ride up a series of escalators.

Toledo and Madrid are easily and frequently connected by AVE train (30 minutes) and buses (1 hour).

By Train

Toledo's early-20th-century train station is Neo-Moorish and a national monument itself for its architecture and art, both of which celebrate the three cultures that coexisted here.

Early and late trains can sell out; reserve ahead. If you haven't yet bought a ticket for your departure from Toledo (even for the next day), get it before you leave the Toledo station. Choose a specific time rather than leave it open-ended. (If you prefer more flexibility, take the bus—see "By Bus" later.)

From the train station to Plaza de Zocodover, a **taxi** is about €5 (the ride to individual hotels is metered). It's easy to take **city bus** #5, #11, #61, or #62; leaving the station, you'll see the bus stop 30 yards to the right (€1.40, pay on bus, confirm by asking, *"¿Para Plaza de Zocodover?"*). Skip the red-and-purple tourist buses that meet arriving day-trippers in front of the station—they're a bad value.

To **walk** into town, allow 25 minutes and turn right as you leave the station and follow the fuchsia line on the sidewalk labeled *Up Toledo, Follow the Line.* Track this line (and periodic escalator symbols) past a bus stop, over the bridge, around the roundabout to the left, and into a bus parking area. From here, go up a series of escalators that take you to the center of town: You'll emerge about a block downhill from Plaza de Zocodover.

Toledo's train station

From Toledo by Train to: Madrid
(nearly hourly, 30 minutes by AVE or
Avant to Madrid's Atocha station, www.
renfe.com). To get to **Granada, Sevilla,**
and elsewhere in Spain, assume you'll
have to transfer in Madrid. See "Transportation" at the end of the Madrid chapter for information on reaching various
destinations.

By Bus

At the bus station, buses park downstairs. Luggage lockers and a small
bus-information office—where you can
buy locker tokens—are upstairs, opposite the cafeteria. From the bus station,
Plaza de Zocodover is a €4.50 **taxi** ride
or a short **bus** ride away (catch #5 or #12
downstairs; €1.40, pay on bus). It's also
possible to **walk:** Exit the bus station, go
straight through the roundabout, and
continue straight ahead. Look for a tunnel burrowed into the cliff (below the
big, blocky convention center), where
you can ride a series of escalators into
town, letting you off just below Plaza
de Zocodover.

Before leaving the station, confirm
your departure time (around 2/hour to
Madrid). Buses don't often book up, and
you can put off buying a return ticket until
just minutes before you leave Toledo.
Specify that you'd like a *directo* bus
(1-hour trip). If you miss the *directo* bus
(or if it's sold out), the 1.5-hour *ruta* option
takes only 30 minutes more and offers a
peek of Madrid suburbia.

From Toledo by Bus to: Madrid (2/
hour, 1-1.5 hours, directo is faster than

ruta, bus drops you at Madrid's Plaza Elíptica Metro stop, Alsa, www.alsa.es).

By Taxi

While it may seem extravagant, if you
have limited time, lots of luggage, and
a small group, simply taking a taxi from
your Toledo hotel to your Madrid hotel is
breathtakingly efficient (€90, one hour
door-to-door, tel. 925-255-050 or 925-
227-070). You can ask several cabbies for
their best "off the meter" rate. A taxi to
the Madrid airport costs €110 (find one
who will go "off the meter") and takes
an hour.

By Car

A car is useless within Toledo's city walls,
where the narrow, twisting streets are no
fun to navigate (watch your mirrors). But
if you're arriving or leaving by car, you can
enjoy a scenic big-picture orientation by
following the *Ronda de Toledo* signs on a
circular drive around the city. You'll see
the city from many angles along the Circunvalación road across the Tajo Gorge.
Stop at a viewpoint (best at sunset).

Many hotels offer discounted parking rates at nearby garages; ask when
making your reservation. The most convenient place to park is the big underground **Miradero Garage** at the convention center (€16/day; drive through Bisagra Gate, go uphill half a mile, look for
sign on the left directing you to *Plaza del
Miradero*). Farther into town, there's parking at the **Alcázar Garage** (just past the
Alcázar—€2/hour, €20/day).

Granada

Granada was once the grandest city in Spain. Its magnificent Alhambra fortress represented the power of the Moorish kingdom—until it became its last stronghold. After the Christians retook Granada in 1492 and drove out the Moors, the city settled into a long slumber. Today, the city's evocative history and diverse North African-flavored culture make it worldly, while its large student population lends it a youthful zest.

A Spanish poet once wrote that "there is nothing worse in this life than to be blind in Granada." The city has much to see, and reveals itself in unpredictable ways. Peer through the intricate lattice of a Moorish window. Hear water burbling unseen among the labyrinthine hedges of the Generalife Gardens. Listen to a flute trilling deep in the swirl of alleys around the cathedral. Wander the angled Moorish quarter, the Albayzín. Don't be blind in Granada—open all your senses.

GRANADA IN 2 DAYS

Be sure to make reservations for the Alhambra in advance; this plan assumes you're touring it on Day 2.

Day 1: Stroll the Alcaicería market streets and follow my self-guided tour of the old town, including a visit to the cathedral and its Royal Chapel. Enjoy the vibe at Plaza Nueva, the town's main square. Wander into the Albayzín Moorish quarter, stopping by a funky teahouse along the way. End your day at the San Nicolás viewpoint—the golden hour before sunset is best, when the Alhambra seems to glow with its own light.

On any evening: Tapa-hop for dinner (consider Gayle's Granada Tapas Tours) or splurge on fine dining at a *carmen*. When the evening cools down, join the paseo. Take in a *zambra* dance in the Sacromonte district. Relax in an Arab bath (Hammam al Andalus) or a *tetería* (tea shop), or both. Slow down and smell the incense.

Day 2: Follow my self-guided tour of the Alhambra; you'll see the elaborate and many-roomed Palacios Nazaríes, Charles V's Palace, the refreshing Generalife Gardens, and more.

Rick's Tip: *If you're not prepared, you could become one of the untold number of tourists who show up in Granada and never see its main sight. To ensure that you can get into the Alhambra's Palacios Nazaríes during your stay, make an* **advance reservation** *online.*

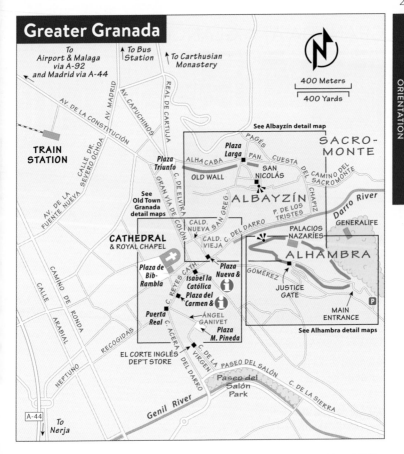

Greater Granada

To Airport & Malaga via A-92 and Madrid via A-44

To Bus Station

To Carthusian Monastery

400 Meters
400 Yards

TRAIN STATION

AV. DE LA CONSTITUCIÓN

AV. MADRID

AV. CAPUCHINOS

REAL DE CARTUJA

CALLE DR. SEVERO OCHOA

AV. DE LA FUENTE NUEVA

GRAN VÍA DE COLÓN

C. DE ELVIRA

Plaza Triunfo

See Old Town Granada detail maps

See Albayzín detail map

Plaza Larga

ALHACABA

OLD WALL

SAN NICOLÁS

PAGÉS

PAN.

CUESTA DEL CHAPIZ

CAMINO DEL SACROMONTE

SACRO-MONTE

ALBAYZÍN

P. DE LOS TRISTES

Darro River

GENERALIFE

CALD. NUEVA

SAN GREG.

C. DEL DARRO

CALD. VIEJA

PALACIOS NAZARÍES

CATHEDRAL & ROYAL CHAPEL

Plaza de Bib-Rambla

C. REYES CATH.

Plaza Nueva &

GOMÉREZ

ALHAMBRA

JUSTICE GATE

Isabel la Católica

Plaza del Carmen &

ÁNGEL GANIVET

Puerta Real

C. ACERA DEL DARRO

Plaza M. Pineda

MAIN ENTRANCE

See Alhambra detail maps

CAMINO DE RONDA

CALLE ARABIAL

RECOGIDAS

NEPTUNO

EL CORTE INGLÉS DEP'T STORE

C. DE LA VIRGEN

PASEO DEL SALÓN

Paseo del Salón Park

C. DE LA SIERRA

Genil River

A-44

To Nerja

ORIENTATION

Modern Granada sprawls (235,000 people), but its main sights are all within a 20-minute walk of Plaza Nueva, where dogs wag their tails to the rhythm of modern hippies and street musicians. Most of my recommended hotels are within a few blocks of the main square, Plaza Nueva. Make this the hub of your Granada visit.

Plaza Nueva sits between two hills. On one hill is the great Moorish palace, the Alhambra, and on the other is the best-preserved Moorish quarter in Spain, the Albayzín. To the southwest are the cathedral, Royal Chapel, and Alcaicería (Moorish market), where the city's two main drags—Gran Vía de Colón (often just called "Gran Vía" by locals) and Calle Reyes Católicos—lead away into the modern city.

Tourist Information

The Granada TI is inside City Hall on Plaza del Carmen, a short walk from the cathedral (Mon-Sat 9:00-18:00, Sun until 14:00, longer hours in summer, tel. 958-248-280, http://en.granadatur.com). Another TI, tucked away just above Plaza Nueva near the Santa Ana Church, covers not only Granada but also Andalucía, with good, free maps for destinations across the region. This TI also posts all of Granada's bus departures (Mon-Fri 9:00-19:30, Sat-Sun 9:30-15:00, tel. 958-575-202).

GRANADA AT A GLANCE

▲▲▲**Alhambra** The last and finest Moorish palace in Iberia, highlighting the splendor of that civilization in the 13th and 14th centuries. **Hours:** Daily 8:30-20:00, mid-Oct-March until 18:00; also Tue-Sat for nighttime visits (Fri-Sat only in off-season). See page 266.

▲▲**Royal Chapel** Lavish 16th-century chapel with the tombs of Queen Isabel and King Ferdinand. **Hours:** Mon-Sat 10:15-18:30, Sun 11:00-18:00. See page 280.

▲▲**San Nicolás Viewpoint** Breathtaking vista over the Alhambra and the Albayzín. **Hours:** Best at sunset. See page 287.

▲**Granada Cathedral** The second-largest cathedral in Spain, unusual for its bright Renaissance interior. **Hours:** Mon-Sat 10:00-19:00, Sun 15:00-18:00. See page 283.

▲**Albayzín** Spain's best old Moorish quarter. See page 286.

▲**Great Mosque of Granada** Islamic house of worship featuring a minaret with a live call to prayer and a courtyard with commanding views. **Hours:** Daily 11:00-14:00 & 18:00-21:00, shorter hours in winter. See page 288.

Sightseeing Pass: The €40 **Granada Card** covers the Alhambra and may get you a reservation when the main Alhambra website is sold out. It includes the "Alhambra General" ticket (see "Alhambra Tour," later), entry to the main sights in town (the cathedral, Royal Chapel, Carthusian Monastery), plus bus rides and a few other admissions and discounts—and it's good for five days. It's best purchased online in advance (http://en.granadatur.com/granada-card).

Helpful Hints

Theft Alert: Be on guard for pickpockets wherever there's a crowd, and especially late at night in the Albayzín. Your biggest threat is being conned while enjoying drinks and music in Sacromonte. Pushy women, usually hanging out near the cathedral and Alcaicería, may accost you with sprigs of rosemary, then demand payment for fortune-telling services—just say, *"No, gracias."*

Laundry: La Colada is closest to my recommended hotels north of Plaza Nueva (daily 10:30-21:30, self-service, Calle de Elvira 85, mobile 637-834-997).

Tours

HOP-ON, HOP-OFF TOURIST TRAIN

For a relaxing and scenic loop through the old town, the touristy hop-on, hop-off train can be time and money well spent (€8/24 hours, daily 9:30-23:00, Nov-March until 19:30, leaves every 20 minutes, includes Alhambra and Albayzín quarter, recorded English narration, www.granada.city-tour.com).

WALKING TOURS

Cicerone offers informative and spirited two-hour city tours daily at 10:30; reservations are encouraged but not required (€18, RS%—show this book; basic Granada tours leave from Calle San Jerónimo 10, tel. 958-561-810 or mobile 607-691-676, www.ciceronegranada.com, reservas@ciceronegranada.com). They

also offer small group tours of the Alhambra that include an entry time to Palacios Nazaríes—handy if you have trouble getting a reservation on your own.

"FREE" (TIP-BASED) WALKING TOURS

Students who've memorized a script lead entertaining walks through the historic town center. While you won't get the quality of a licensed guide, the price is right: Just show up, have fun, and tip what you like. With competing advertising umbrellas and enthusiastic welcomes, groups offering these tours gather daily at Plaza Nueva and at Plaza Isabel La Católica.

LOCAL GUIDES

Margarita Ortiz de Landazuri (mobile 687-361-988, www.alhambratours.com, info@alhambratours.com) and **Miguel Ángel** (mobile 617-565-711, miguelangelalhambratours@gmail.com) are both good, licensed private guides (€130/3 hours, €260/day).

GAYLE'S GRANADA TAPAS TOURS

Having lived in Granada since 1996, Scottish-born Gayle Mackie knows where to find the best food. She and her team take small groups off the beaten path to characteristic tapas bars, providing cuisine tips and fascinating insights into Granada (2.5 hours, €40/person, tours for 2-6 people, daily at 13:00 or 20:00, mobile 619-444-984, www.granadatapastours.com).

GRANADA OLD TOWN WALK

This short self-guided walk covers all the essential old town sights. Along the way, we'll see vivid evidence of the dramatic Moorish-to-Christian transition brought about by the Reconquista—the long and ultimately successful battle to retake Spain from the Muslim Moors and reestablish Christian rule.

❯ Self-Guided Walk

• *Start at Corral del Carbón, near Plaza del Carmen.*

❶ *Corral del Carbón*

A caravanserai (of Silk Road fame) was a protected place for merchants to rest their animals, spend the night, get a bite to eat, and spin yarns. This, the only surviving caravanserai of Granada's original 14, was just a block away from the silk market (Alcaicería; the next stop on this walk). Stepping through the caravanserai's grand Moorish door, you find a square with 14th-century Moorish brickwork surrounding a water fountain. This plain-yet-elegant structure evokes the times when traders would gather here with exotic goods and swap tales from across the Muslim world.

It's a common mistake to think of the Muslim Moors as somehow not Spanish. They lived here for seven centuries and were really just as "indigenous" as the Romans, Goths, and Celts. While the Moors were Muslim, they were no more connected to Arabia than they were to France.

After the Reconquista, this space was used as a coal storage facility (hence "del Carbón"). These days it houses two offices where you can buy tickets for musical events. There is a handy public WC to the right as you enter and sometimes an Alhambra tourist info office to the left.

• *From the caravanserai, exit straight ahead down Puente del Carbón to the big street named Calle Reyes Católicos. The street covers a river that once ran openly here. Cross here and continue one block farther to the horseshoe-shaped gate marked **Alcaicería**. The pedestrian street you're crossing, Zacatín, was the main drag, which ran parallel to the river before it was covered in the 19th century. Today it's a favorite paseo destination, busy each evening with strollers. Pass through the Alcaicería gate and walk 20 yards into the old market to the first intersection at Calle Ermita.*

❷ *Alcaicería*

Originally a Moorish silk market with 200 shops, the Alcaicería (al-kai-thay-REE-ah) was filled with precious silver, spices, and silk. It had 10 armed gates and its own guards. Silk was huge in Moorish times, and silkworm-friendly mulberry trees flourished in the countryside. It was such an important product that the sultans controlled and guarded it by constructing this fine, fortified market. After the Reconquista, the Christians realized this market was good for business and didn't mess with it. Later, the more zealous Philip II had it shut down. A terrible fire in 1850 destroyed what was left. Today's Alcaicería is an "authentic fake"—rebuilt in the late 1800s as a tourist souk (marketplace) to complement the romantic image of Granada popularized by the writings of Washington Irving.

Explore the mesh of tiny shopping lanes: overpriced trinkets, popcorn

Corral del Carbón

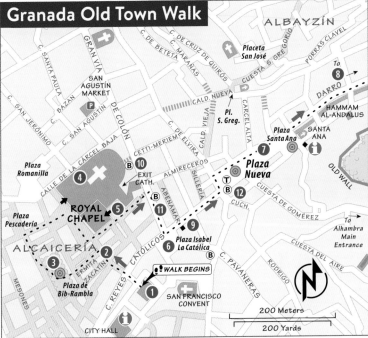

Granada Old Town Walk

Walk
1. Corral del Carbón
2. Alcaicería
3. Plaza de Bib-Rambla
4. Granada Cathedral
5. Royal Chapel Square
6. Plaza Isabel La Católica (Bus to Alhambra)
7. Plaza Nueva
8. To Paseo de los Tristes & Hammam El Bañuelo

Other
9. Alhambra Bookstore
10. Gran Vía Cathedral Bus Stop (from Train & Bus Stations)
11. Gran Vía del Colón Bus Stop (to Train & Bus Stations)
12. Plaza Nueva Bus Stop (to Albayzín & Sacromonte)

machines popping, balloon vendors, leather goods spread out on streets, kids playing soccer, barking dogs, dogged shoe-shine boys, and the whirring grind of bicycle-powered knife sharpeners.

• Turn left down Calle Ermita. After 50 yards, you'll leave the market via another fortified gate and enter a big square crowded with outdoor restaurants. Skirt around the tables to the Neptune fountain, which marks the center of the...

❸ Plaza de Bib-Rambla

This exuberant square was once the center of Moorish Granada. While Moorish rule of Spain lasted 700 years, the last couple of those centuries were a period of decline as Muslim culture split under weak leadership and Christian forces grew more determined. The last remnants of the Moorish kingdom united and ruled from Granada. As Muslims fled south from reconquered lands, Granada was

1 *Alcaicería entrance*
2 *Plaza Isabel La Católica*
3 *Plaza de Bib-Rambla*
4 *Cathedral*

flooded with refugees. By 1400, Granada had an estimated 100,000 people—huge for medieval Europe. This was the main square, the focal point for markets and festivals, but it was much smaller than now, pushed in by the jam-packed city.

Under Christian rule, Moors were initially tolerated (as they were considered good for business), and this area became the Moorish ghetto. Then, with the Inquisition (under Philip II, c. 1550), ideology trumped pragmatism, and Jews and Muslims were evicted or forced to convert. The elegant square you see today was built, and built big. In-your-face Catholic processions started here. To assert Christian rule, all the trappings of Christian power were layered upon what had been the trappings of Moorish power. Between here and the cathedral were the Christian University (the big orange building) and the adjacent archbishop's palace.

Today Plaza de Bib-Rambla is good for coffee or a meal amid the color and fragrance of flower stalls and the burbling of its Neptune-topped fountain. It remains a multigenerational hangout, where it seems everyone is enjoying a peaceful retirement.

With Neptune facing you, leave the plaza by the left corner (along Calle Pescadería) to reach a smaller, similarly lively square—little Plaza Pescadería, where families spill out to enjoy its many restaurants. For a quick snack, drop into tiny **Cunini Pescadería**—just beyond its namesake restaurant—for a takeaway bite of *pescaito frito*—fried fish.

• *Leave Plaza Pescadería on Calle Marqués de Gerona; within one block, you'll come to a small square fronting a very big church.*

❹ Granada Cathedral (Catedral de Granada)

Wow, the cathedral facade just screams triumph. That's partly because its design is based on a triumphal arch, built over a destroyed mosque. Five hundred yards away, there was once open space outside the city wall with good soil for a foundation. But the Christian conquerors said, "No way." Instead, they destroyed the mosque and built their cathedral right here on difficult, sandy soil. This was the place where the people of Granada traditionally worshipped—and now they would worship as Christians.

The church—started in the early 1500s and not finished until the late 1700s—has a Gothic foundation and was built mostly in the Renaissance style, with its last altars done in Neoclassical style. Hometown artist Alonso Cano (1601-1667) finished the building, at the king's request, in Baroque. Accentuating the power of the Roman Catholic Church, the emphasis here is on Mary rather than Christ. The facade declares *Ave Maria.* (This was Counter-Reformation time, and the Church was threatened by Protestant Christians. Mary was also more palatable to Muslim converts, as she is revered in the Quran.)

• *To tour the cathedral now, you can enter here (the interior is described in more detail on page 283). You'll exit on the far side, near the big street called Gran Vía de Colón.*

If you're skipping the cathedral interior for now, circle around the cathedral to the right, keeping the church on your left, until you reach the small square facing the Royal Chapel.

❺ Royal Chapel Square

This square was once ringed by important Moorish buildings: a hammam (public bath), a caravanserai (Days Inn), the silk market, the leading mosque, and a madrassa (school).

With Christian rule, the **Palacio de la Madraza** (its facade painted in 3-D Baroque style with faux gray stonework) became Granada's first City Hall. It's worth a quick look (€2, daily 10:30-20:00). Five hundred years ago, this was a Quranic school (if you want to know God, knowledge will wash your sins away). Your admission gets you a peek at an ornate-as-the-Alhambra mini prayer room on the ground level and, upstairs, a modern university lecture room with a circa 1500 Mudejar interlocking wood ceiling, finely painted and circled by a script celebrating the Christian conquest.

Also on this square is the entrance to the Royal Chapel, where the coffins of Ferdinand and Isabel were moved in 1521 from the Alhambra.

• *Continue up the cobbled, stepped lane to Gran Vía. Turn right and walk toward the big square just ahead (near where minibuses to the Alhambra stop), across the busy Calle Reyes Católicos.*

❻ *Plaza Isabel La Católica*

Granada's two grand boulevards, Gran Vía and Calle Reyes Católicos, meet here at Plaza Isabel La Católica. Above the fountain, a beautiful statue shows Columbus unfurling a long contract with Isabel. It lists the terms of Columbus' MCCCCLXXXXII voyage: "For as much as you, Columbus, are going by our command to discover and subdue some Islands and Continents in the ocean...." Two reliefs below the figures show the big events in Granada of 1492: Isabel and Ferdinand accepting Columbus' proposal, and a stirring battle scene (which never happened) at the walls of the Alhambra.

Isabel was driven by her desire to spread Catholicism. Spain, needing an alternate trade route to the Orient's spices after the Ottoman Empire cut off the traditional overland routes, was driven by trade. And Columbus was driven by his desire for money. As a reward for adding territory to Spain's Catholic empire, Isabel promised Columbus the ranks of Admiral of the Oceans and Governor of the New World. To sweeten the pot, she tossed in one-eighth of all the riches he brought home. Isabel died thinking that Columbus had found India or China. Columbus died poor and disillusioned.

Look back at the fine buildings flanking the start of Gran Vía. With the arrival of cars and the modern age, the people of Granada wanted a Parisian-style boulevard. In the early 20th century, they mercilessly cut through the old town and created Gran Vía—in the process destroying everything in its path, including many historic convents. Elegant facades—like the two circa-1910 Paris-inspired buildings facing the square—once ornamented the entire Gran Vía.

• *Follow Calle Reyes Católicos uphill (to the left) for a couple of blocks until you reach...*

❼ *Plaza Nueva*

Plaza Nueva is dominated at the far end by the regional Palace of Justice (grand Baroque facade with green Andalusian flag). The fountain is capped by a stylized pomegranate—the symbol of the city, always open and fertile. The main action here is the comings and goings of the busy little shuttle buses serving the Albayzín. The local hippie community, nicknamed the *pies negros* (black feet) for obvious reasons, hangs out here and on Calle de Elvira. They squat—with their dogs and guitars—in abandoned caves above those the Roma (Gypsies) occupy in Sacromonte. Many are the children of rich Spanish families from the north, hellbent on disappointing their high-achieving parents.

• *Our tour continues with a stroll up Carrera del Darro. Leave Plaza Nueva opposite where you entered, on the little lane that runs alongside the Darro River. This is particularly enjoyable in the cool of the evening.*

Plaza Nueva

❽ *Paseo de los Tristes*

This stretch of road is also called Paseo de los Tristes—"Walk of the Sad Ones." It was once the route of funeral processions to the cemetery at the edge of town. As you leave Plaza Nueva, notice the small Church of Santa Ana on your right. This was originally a mosque—the church tower replaced a minaret. Notice the ceramic brickwork. This is Mudejar art by Moorish craftsmen, whose techniques were later employed by Christians.

Follow Carrera del Darro along the Darro River, which flows around the base of the Alhambra (look down by the river for a glimpse of feral cats). Six miles upstream, part of the Darro is diverted to provide water for the Alhambra's many fountains—a remarkable feat of Moorish engineering in 1238.

After passing two small, picturesque bridges, the road widens slightly for a bus stop. Here you'll see the broken nub of a once-grand 11th-century bridge that led to the Alhambra. Notice two slits in the column: One held an iron portcullis to keep bad guys from entering the town via the river. The second held a solid door that was lowered to build up water, then released to flush out the riverbed and keep it clean.

• *Across from the remains of the bridge is the brick facade of an evocative Moorish bath.*

Hammam El Bañuelo (Moorish Baths)

In Moorish times, hammams were a big part of the community (working-class homes didn't have bathrooms). Baths were strictly segregated and were more than places to wash: These were social meeting points where business was done. In Christian times it was assumed that conspiracies brewed in these baths— therefore, only a few of them survive. This place gives you the chance to explore the stark but evocative ruins of an 11th-century Moorish public bath.

Cost and Hours: €5, covered by Dobla de Ora card (described under "Alhambra Tour," later); daily 9:30-14:30 & 17:00-21:00, mid-Sept-March 10:00-17:00; Carrera del Darro 31, tel. 958-027-800.

Visiting the Baths: Upon entering, you pass the house of the keeper and the foyer, then visit the cold room, the warm room (where services like massage were offered), and finally the hot, or steam, room. Beyond that, you can see the oven that generated the heat, which flowed under the hypocaust-style floor tiles (the ones closest to the oven were the hottest). The romantic little holes in the ceiling once had stained-glass louvers that attendants opened and closed with sticks to regulate the heat and steaminess. Whereas Romans soaked in their pools, Muslims just doused. Rather than being totally immersed, people scooped and splashed water over themselves. Imagine attendants stoking the fires under the metal boiler...while people in towels and wooden slippers (to protect their feet from the heated floors) enjoyed all the spa services you can imagine as beams of light slashed through the mist.

• *Just across from the baths is a stop for minibus #C31 and #C32—the easy way to*

Hammam El Bañuelo

*head up to the **Albayzín**. Otherwise, continue straight ahead to the end of this walk, at the Paseo de los Tristes—with its restaurant tables spilling out under the floodlit Alhambra.*

ALHAMBRA TOUR

The last and greatest Moorish palace, the Alhambra is one of Europe's top sights and worth ▲▲▲. Attracting 8,000 visitors a day, it's the reason most tourists come to Granada. Nowhere else does the splendor of Moorish civilization shine so beautifully.

The last Moorish stronghold in Europe is, with all due respect, really a symbol of retreat. For centuries, Granada was merely a regional capital. Gradually the Christian Reconquista moved south, taking Córdoba (1237) and Sevilla (1248). The Nazarids, one of the many diverse ethnic groups of Spanish Muslims, held together the last Moorish kingdom, which they ruled from Granada until 1492. As you tour their grand palace, remember that while Europe slumbered through the Dark Ages, Moorish magnificence blossomed—ornate stucco, plaster "stalactites," colors galore, scalloped windows framing Granada views, exuberant gardens, and water, water everywhere. Water—so rare and precious in most of the Islamic world—was the purest symbol of life to the Moors. The Alhambra is decorated with water: standing still, cascading, masking secret conversations, and drip-dropping playfully.

The Alhambra consists of four sights clustered together atop a hill, all covered by the following self-guided tour:

Palacios Nazaríes: Exquisite Moorish palace, the Alhambra's must-see sight.

Charles V's Palace: Christian Renaissance palace, with the fine Alhambra Museum inside.

Generalife Gardens: Fragrant, lovely manicured gardens with a small summer palace.

Alcazaba Fort: Empty but evocative old fort with tower and views.

Getting There

There are two entrances to the sprawling Alhambra: the Justice Gate, nearest the Palacios Nazaríes, and the main entrance, 400 yards farther along at the top. Go directly to the Justice Gate, which is for those with tickets in hand or on their phone. You have four options for getting there:

On Foot: From Plaza Nueva, hike 20 minutes up Cuesta de Gomérez. Keep going straight—you'll see the Alhambra high on your left. After about 10 minutes, you'll see the Justice Gate, which leads to the Palacios Nazaríes.

By Bus: Just uphill from Plaza de Isabel La Católica, catch the red #C30 or #C32 minibus, marked *Alhambra* (€1.40 per trip). Stops are shown on "The Alhambra" map: Generalife (main ticket office and the gardens), Charles V, and Justice Gate.

By Taxi: It's a €6 ride from Plaza Nueva.

By Car: If you have a car in town, do not use it to go to the Alhambra. But if you're coming from outside the city, you can drive here without passing through Granada's historic center. From the freeway, take the exit marked *Alhambra*. Signs lead you to a public parking lot, located at the top of the Alhambra (€2.70/hour). Overnight and multiday parking is permissible (€19/24 hours, guarded at night).

Planning Your Time

"Alhambra General" tickets come with a 30-minute time slot for admission to the Palacios Nazaríes (first entry to palaces at 8:30, last entry one hour before closing). You must enter the Palacios Nazaríes within the 30-minute window, but once inside, you can linger as long as you like. You can see the other Alhambra sights any time during that single day.

Don't miss your appointed time. Ticket checkers at the Palacios Nazaríes are strict. If you're seeing the Generalife Gardens first, you're a 15-minute walk away from Palacios Nazaríes at the other end. Plan accordingly.

Although you can see the sights in any order, to minimize walking, see the three sights at the lower end first (Charles V's Palace and the Alcazaba fort), then visit Palacios Nazaríes. When you finish touring the palace, you'll leave through the Partal Gardens, a pleasant 15-minute gradual uphill stroll to the Generalife Gardens. If you have a long time to wait for your Palacios Nazaríes appointment, you could do the gardens first, then head down to the other three. Or you can kill time luxuriously on the breezy view terrace of the parador bar (within the Alhambra walls).

Orientation

While this ticket information was accurate when this edition went to press, changes are likely; confirm details at www.tickets. alhambra-patronato.es.

Cost: There are many versions of the "Alhambra" ticket: Be sure to purchase a ticket that includes the Palacios Nazaríes.

- **Alhambra General:** €15, covers the Palacios Nazaríes, the Alcazaba fort, and Generalife Gardens.

- **Alhambra Gardens (Generalife and Alcazaba):** €7, covers daytime admission to almost everything—but not the Palacios Nazaríes.
- **Alhambra Night Visit—Palacios Nazaríes:** €8, nighttime-only visit to the Palacios Nazaríes.
- **Alhambra Night Visit—Generalife:** €8, nighttime-only visit to the gardens.
- **Alhambra Experiences:** €15, nighttime visit to Palacios Nazaríes, then next-day entry to the Alcazaba fort and Generalife Gardens.
- **Dobla de Oro General Card:** €21, valid for three days, includes Alhambra General ticket (with a timed-entry to Palacios Nazaríes) and several minor Albayzín sights.
- **Children's Tickets:** Children under 12 are free, but still need a reservation booked online in their name.

Hours: The entire Alhambra complex is open April-mid-Oct daily 8:30-20:00, mid-Oct-March until 18:00. Last entry is one hour before closing

Evening Hours: The Palacios Nazaríes and Generalife Gardens are also open and nicely lit some evenings. Note that night tickets include the palace or the gardens,

The Alhambra

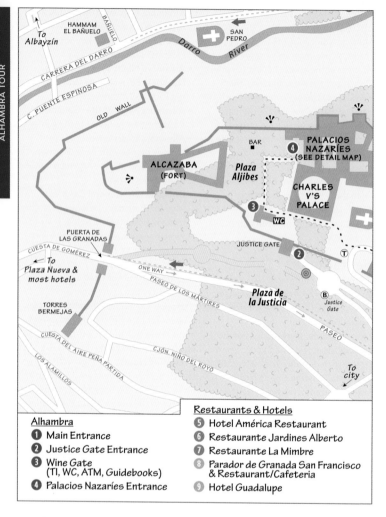

Alhambra
1. Main Entrance
2. Justice Gate Entrance
3. Wine Gate
   (TI, WC, ATM, Guidebooks)
4. Palacios Nazaríes Entrance

Restaurants & Hotels
5. Hotel América Restaurant
6. Restaurante Jardines Alberto
7. Restaurante La Mimbre
8. Parador de Granada San Francisco
   & Restaurant/Cafeteria
9. Hotel Guadalupe

never both. These tickets are not timed, and it's extremely crowded when the doors open; you must enter no later than one hour before closing.

Information: Tel. 958-027-971, www.tickets.alhambra-patronato.es.

Reservations: Buy tickets online. Select a ticket, choose a date, then select an entry time for Palacios Nazaríes (you'll have a 30-minute window to enter). You can either print the ticket or show the bar code on your mobile phone as you enter, along with a photo ID.

Without Reservations: If you arrive in Granada without a reservation for the Palacios Nazaríes, you have a few options:

- Pay for a tour that includes admission (recommended Cicerone has Alhambra tours that can be booked 3-4 days ahead—see listing under "Tours" at the beginning of this chapter).
- Try to book a ticket online one minute after midnight Spain time, when unclaimed tickets for that day are released.

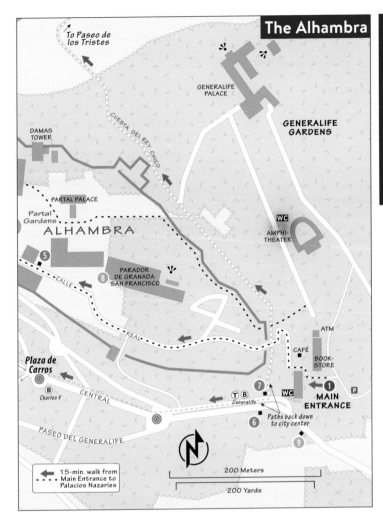

The Alhambra

• Buy a Granada Card sightseeing pass that covers the Alhambra and may score you a reservation when the main Alhambra website is sold out; see "Tourist Information" at the beginning of this chapter.

• Get used to the reality that you will not see Palacios Nazaríes, and enjoy the rest, either with a ticket to the fortress (Alcazaba) and gardens (Generalife) or even just walking the grounds (including Charles V's Palace and the parador).

Alhambra Ticket Info: The TI and hotels are adept at Alhambra issues. There's also a helpful info desk at the top of the Alhambra near the Wine Gate (daily, 8:00-20:00) and sometimes one inside the Corral del Carbón (in the town center, daily 9:00-19:00, tel. 958-575-131).

Ticket Hints: Except for the Palacios Nazaríes, if you have your ticket QR code (printed or on your phone), you can re-enter as you like for one day; otherwise, check in at the ticket center. Keep your ticket until the end of your visit. Have a photo ID ready for random checks.

Tours: The Alhambra's excellent €6 tablet audioguide covers the entire complex very well. Rentals are at both entrances, but you must return the audioguide to the same location.

Services: A service center, with bag check (free for ticket holders only), WCs, and water and snack machines, is at each entrance. There are no WCs inside the Palacios Nazaríes. Day packs must be worn in front or carried by hand.

Eating: Within the Alhambra walls, food options are limited and generally overpriced. Choose between the restaurant or the cafeteria at the **$$$ parador;** the peaceful ambience of the courtyard at **$$$ Hotel América** (Sun-Fri 12:30-16:30, closed Sat); a small **$ bar-café kiosk** in front of the Alcazaba fort (basic sandwiches and other snacks); and **vending machines** (at the WC) next to the Wine Gate, near Charles V's Palace. You're welcome to bring in a **picnic** as long as you eat it outside ticketed areas.

For better-value (but still touristy) options, head outside to the area around the parking lot and ticket booth at the top of the complex, where there's a strip of handy eateries.

$$$ Restaurante Jardines Alberto, across from the main entrance, has a nice courtyard and offers a charming setting (daily 12:00-23:30, off-season until 18:00; Paseo de la Sabica 1, tel. 958-221-661, climb the stairs from the street). The breezy **$$$ Restaurante La Mimbre** offers shade and a break from the crowds. They also serve breakfast (daily 9:30-23:00, Paseo del Generalife 18, tel. 958-222-276).

City Tour from Alhambra Exit: The hop-on, hop-off tourist train leaves from the top of the Alhambra, offering a convenient hour-long sightseeing tour on the way back to town (see "Tours," earlier.)

⊘ Self-Guided Tour

I've listed the Alhambra sights in the order you're likely to visit them. The first three cluster at the bottom end of the complex, while the Generalife Gardens are about a 15-minute walk away, at the top.

▲▲ Charles V's Palace

While it's only natural for a conquering king to build his own palace over his foe's palace, the Christian Charles V (the Holy Roman Emperor, who ruled as Charles I over Spain) respected the splendid Moorish palace. And so, to make his mark, he built a modern Renaissance palace for official functions and used the existing Palacios Nazaríes as a royal residence. With a unique circle-within-a-square design by Pedro Machuca, a pupil of Michelangelo, this is Spain's most impressive Renaissance building. Stand in the circular courtyard surrounded by mottled marble columns, then climb the stairs. Perhaps Charles' palace was designed to have a dome, but it was never finished—his son, Philip II, abandoned it to build his own, much more massive palace outside Madrid, El Escorial (the final and most austere example of Spanish Renaissance architecture). Even without a dome, acoustics are perfect in the center—stand in the middle and sing your best aria.

▲ Alhambra Museum

On the ground floor of Charles V's Palace, this museum (Museo de la Alhambra) shows off some of the Alhambra's best surviving Moorish art. Its beautifully displayed and well-described artifacts—including tiles, characteristic green, blue, and black pottery, lion fountains, and a beautiful carved-wood door—help humanize the Alhambra (free, Wed-Sat 8:30-20:00, Sun and Tue until 14:30, shorter hours off-season, closed Mon year-round). The **Fine Arts Museum** (Museo de Bellas Artes, upstairs in

Charles V's Palace and the Alhambra Museum

Alcazaba

Charles V's Palace, free) has Christian-era paintings and statues and is of little interest to most.

• *From the front of Charles V's Palace (as you face the Alcazaba fort), the entrance to Palacios Nazaríes is to the right, while the Alcazaba is the towering brick structure across a moat straight ahead.*

Alcazaba

This fort—the original "red castle" ("Alhambra")—is the oldest and most ruined part of the complex. What you see is from the mid-13th century, but there was probably a fort here in Roman times. Once upon a time, this tower defended a medina (town) of 2,000 Muslims living within the Alhambra walls. It's a huge, sprawling complex—wind your way through passages and courtyards, over uneven terrain, to reach the biggest tower at the tip of the complex. Then climb stairs steeply up to the very top. From there (looking north), find Plaza Nueva and the San Nicolás viewpoint in the Albayzín. To the south are the Sierra Nevada Mountains.

Imagine that day in 1492 when the Christian cross and the flags of Aragon and Castile were raised on this tower, and (according to a probably fanciful legend) the fleeing Moorish king Boabdil (Abu Abdullah) looked back and wept. With this defeat, more than seven centuries of Muslim rule in Spain came to an end.

• *If you're going from the Alcazaba to Palacios Nazaríes, backtrack toward Charles V's Palace and join the line to the left.*

▲▲▲Palacios Nazaríes

During the 30-minute entry time stamped on your ticket, enter the jewel of the Alhambra: the Moorish royal palace. Once inside, relax. You're no longer under any time constraints. You'll walk through three basic sections: royal offices, ceremonial rooms, and private quarters. Built mostly in the 14th century, this palace offers your best possible look at the refined, elegant Moorish civilization of Al-Andalus (the Moorish-controlled Iberian Peninsula).

You'll visit rooms decorated from top to bottom with carved wood ceilings, stucco "stalactites," ceramic tiles, molded-plaster walls, and filigree windows. Open-air courtyards feature fountains with bubbling water. A garden enlivened by lush vegetation and peaceful pools is the Quran's symbol of heaven. The palace is well-preserved and well-restored, but the trick to fully appreciating it is to imagine it furnished and filled with Moorish life...sultans with hookah pipes lounging on pillows upon Persian carpets, heavy curtains on the windows, and ivory-studded wooden furniture. The whole place was painted with bright colors, many suggested by the Quran—red (blood), blue (heaven), green (oasis), and gold (wealth).

Throughout the palace, walls, ceilings, vases, carpets, and tiles were covered with decorative patterns and calligraphy, mostly poems and verses of praise from the Quran and from local poets. Much of what is known about the Alhambra is known simply from reading the inscriptions that decorate its walls.

• *Begin by walking through a few administrative rooms with a stunning Mecca-oriented prayer room (the oratorio, with a niche on the right facing Mecca, and lacy windows filling it with light and great views) and a small courtyard with a round fountain. Eventually you hit the big rectangular courtyard with a fish pond lined by two myrtle-bush hedges.*

❶ **Courtyard of the Myrtles** (Patio de Arrayanes): The standard palace design included a central courtyard like this. Moors loved their patios—with a garden and water, under the sky. The apartments of the sultan's women looked over this courtyard: two apartments for wives on either side (four was the maximum allowed), and a dorm for the concubines at the far end (a man could have "as many concubines as he could maintain with dignity"). In accordance with medieval Moorish mores, women rarely went out, so they stayed in touch with nature in courtyards like the Courtyard of the Myrtles—named for the two fragrant myrtle hedges that added to the courtyard's charm. Notice the wooden screens ("jalousies" erected by jealous husbands) that allowed the cloistered women to look out without being clearly seen.

• *Head left from the entry through gigantic wooden doors into the long narrow antechamber to the throne room, called the...*

❷ **Ship Room** (Sala de la Barca): It's understandable that many think the Ship Room is named for the upside-down-hull shape of its fine cedar ceiling. But the name is actually derived from the Arab word *baraka*, meaning "divine blessing and luck." As you passed through this room, blessings and luck are exactly what you'd need—because in the next room, you'd be face-to-face with the sultan.

• *Oh, it's your turn. Enter the ornate throne room.*

Courtyard of the Myrtles, Palacios Nazaríes

The Alhambra's Palacios Nazaríes

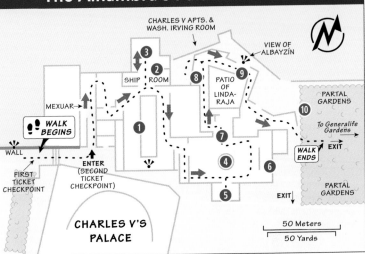

1 Courtyard of the Myrtles
2 Ship Room
3 Grand Hall of the Ambassadors
4 Courtyard of the Lions
5 Hall of the Abencerrajes
6 Hall of the Kings
7 Hall of Two Sisters
8 Washington Irving Room
9 Hallway with a View
10 Partal Gardens

3 Grand Hall of the Ambassadors
(Gran Salón de los Embajadores): The palace's largest room, also known as the Salón de Comares, functioned as the throne room. It was here that the sultan, seated on a throne opposite the entrance, received foreign emissaries. Ogle the room—a perfect cube—from top to bottom. The star-studded, domed wooden ceiling (made from 8,017 inlaid pieces like a giant jigsaw puzzle) suggests the complexity of Allah's infinite universe. Wooden "stalactites" form the cornice, running around the entire base of the ceiling. The stucco walls, even without their original paint and gilding, are still glorious. The filigree windows once held stained glass and had heavy drapes to block out the heat. Some precious 16th-century tiles survive in the center of the floor.

A visitor here would have stepped from the glaring Courtyard of the Myrtles into this dim, cool, incense-filled world, to meet the silhouetted sultan. Imagine the alcoves functioning busily as work stations, and the light at sunrise or sunset, rich and warm, filling the room.

Let your eyes trace the finely carved Arabic script. Muslims avoided making images of living creatures—that was God's work. But they could carve decorative religious messages. One phrase—"only Allah is victorious"—is repeated 9,000 times throughout the palace. Find the character for "Allah"—it looks like a cursive W with a nose on its left side, with a vertical line to the right. The swoopy toboggan blades underneath are a kind of artistic punctuation used to set off one phrase.

In 1492, two historic events likely took place in this room. Culminating a 700-year-long battle, the Reconquista

Islamic Art

Rather than making paintings and statues, Islamic artists expressed themselves with beautiful but functional objects. Ceramics (most of them blue and white, or green and white), carpets, glazed tile panels, stucco-work ceilings, and glass tableware are covered with complex patterns. The intricate interweaving, repetition, and unending lines suggest the complex, infinite nature of God, known to Muslims as Allah.

You'll see few pictures of humans, since Islamic doctrine holds that the creation of living beings is God's work alone. However, secular art by Muslims for their homes and palaces was not bound by this restriction; you'll get an occasional glimpse of realistic art featuring men and women enjoying a garden paradise, a symbol of the Muslim heaven.

Look for floral patterns (twining vines, flowers, and arabesques) and geometric designs (stars and diamonds). The decorative motifs (Arabic script, patterns, flowers, shells, and so on) that repeat countless times throughout the palace were made by pressing wet plaster into molds. The most common pattern is calligraphy—elaborate lettering of an inscription in Arabic, the language of the Quran. A quote from the Quran on a vase or lamp combines the power of the message with the beauty of the calligraphy.

was completed here as the last Moorish king, Boabdil, signed the terms of his surrender before eventually leaving for Africa.

And it was here that Columbus made one of his final pitches to Isabel and Ferdinand to finance a sea voyage to the Orient. Imagine the scene: The king, the queen, and the greatest minds from the University of Salamanca gathered here while Columbus produced maps and pie charts to make his case that he could sail west to reach the East. Ferdinand and the professors laughed and called Columbus mad—not because they thought the world was flat (most educated people knew otherwise), but because they thought Columbus had underestimated the size of the globe, and thus the length and cost of the journey.

But Isabel said, *"Sí, señor."* Columbus fell to his knees (promising to pack light, wear a money belt, and use the most current guidebook available).

Opposite the Ship Room entrance,

photographers pause for a picture-perfect view of the tower reflected in the Courtyard of the Myrtles pool. This was the original palace entrance (before Charles V's Palace was built).

• *Continue deeper into the palace, to a courtyard where, 600 years ago, only the royal family and their servants could enter. It's the much-photographed...*

❹ **Courtyard of the Lions** (Patio de los Leones): This delightful courtyard is named for the famous fountain at its center with its ring of 12 marble lions—originals from the 14th century. Conquering Christians disassembled the fountain to see how it worked, rendering it nonfunctional; it finally flowed again in 2012. From the center of the courtyard, four channels carry water outward—figuratively to the corners of the earth and literally to various more private apartments of the royal family. The arched gallery that surrounds the courtyard is supported by 124 perfectly balanced columns. The craftsmanship is first-class. For example, the lead fittings between

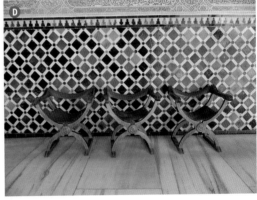

🅐 *Courtyard of the Myrtles*

🅑 *Courtyard of the Lions*

🅒 *Grand Hall of the Ambassadors*

🅓 *Alhambra tilework*

🅔 *Washington Irving Room*

the precut sections of the columns allow things to flex during earthquakes, preventing destruction during shakes.

Six hundred years ago, the Muslim Moors could read the Quranic poetry that ornaments this court, and they could understand the symbolism of this lush, enclosed garden, considered the embodiment of paradise or truth. ("How beautiful is this garden/where the flowers of Earth rival the stars of Heaven./What can compare with this alabaster fountain, gushing crystal-clear water?/Nothing except the fullest moon, pouring light from an unclouded sky.")

• *On the right, off the courtyard, the only original door still in the palace leads into a square room called the...*

❺ Hall of the Abencerrajes (Sala de los Abencerrajes): This was the sultan's living room, with an exquisite ceiling based on the eight-sided Muslim star.

The name of the room comes from a bloody event of the 16th century. The father of Boabdil took a new wife and wanted to disinherit the children of his first marriage—one of whom was Boabdil. To deny power to Boabdil and his siblings, the sultan killed nearly all the pre-Boabdil Abencerraje family members. He thought this would pave the way for the son of his new wife to be the next sultan. He is said to have stacked 36 Abencerraje heads in the pool, under the sumptuous honeycombed stucco ceiling in this hall. But his scheme failed, and Boabdil ultimately assumed the throne.

• *At the end of the court opposite where you entered is the...*

❻ Hall of the Kings (Sala de los Reyes): This hall is famous for its paintings on the goat-leather ceiling depicting scenes of the sultan and his family. The center room's group portrait shows the first 10 of the Alhambra's 22 sultans. The scene is a fantasy, since these people lived over a span of many generations. The two end rooms display scenes of princely pastimes, such as hunting and shooting skeet. In a palace

otherwise devoid of figures, these offer a rare look at royal life in the palace.

• *Continue around the lion fountain. Before entering the next room, you'll pass doors leading right and left to a 14th-century WC plumbed by running water and stairs up to the harem. Next is the...*

❼ Hall of Two Sisters (Sala de Dos Hermanas): This is another royal reception hall, with alcoves for private use and a fountain. Running water helped cool and humidify the room but also added elegance and extravagance, as running water was a luxury most could only dream of.

The room features geometric patterns and stylized Arabic script quoting verses from the Quran. If the inlaid color tiles look "Escher-esque," you've got it backward: Escher is Alhambra-esque. M. C. Escher was inspired by these very patterns on his visit. Study the patterns—they remind us of the Moorish expertise in math. The sitting room (farthest from the entry) has low windows, because Moorish people sat on the floor. Some rare stained glass survives in the ceiling.

• *That's about it for the palace. From here, we enter the later, 16th-century Christian section, and wander past the domed roofs of the old baths down a hallway to a pair of rooms decorated with mahogany ceilings. Marked with a large plaque is the...*

❽ Washington Irving Room: While living in Spain in 1829, Washington Irving stayed in the Alhambra, and he wrote *Tales of the Alhambra* in this room. His "tales" rekindled interest in the Alhambra, causing it to be recognized as a national treasure. A plaque on the wall thanks Irving, who later served as the US ambassador to Spain (1842-1846). Here's a quote from Irving's *The Alhambra by Moonlight*: "On such heavenly nights I would sit for hours at my window inhaling the sweetness of the garden, and musing on the checkered fortunes of those whose history was dimly shadowed out in the elegant memorials around."

• *As you leave, stop at the open-air...*

Hall of Two Sisters

❾ Hallway with a View: Here you'll enjoy the best-in-the-palace view of the labyrinthine Albayzín—the old Moorish town on the opposite hillside. Find the famous San Nicolás viewpoint (below where the white San Nicolás church tower breaks the horizon). Green patches are the gardens of *carmens* (old noble farms, many that are now romantic restaurants). Below is the river and the Paseo de los Tristes (with its square filled with inviting restaurants). Creeping into the mountains on the right are the Roma neighborhoods of Sacromonte.

The Patio de Lindaraja (with its garden of maze-like hedges) marks the end of the palace visit.

• *Step outside into our last stop...*

❿ The Partal Gardens (El Partal): The Partal Gardens are built upon the ruins of the Partal Palace. Imagine a palace like the one you just toured, built around this reflecting pond. A fragment of it still stands—once the living quarters—on the cooler north side. Its Mecca-facing oratory (the small building a few steps above the pool) survives. The Alhambra was the site of seven different palaces in 150 years. You have toured parts of just two or three.

• *Leaving the palace, climb a few stairs, continue through the gardens, and follow signs directing you left to the Generalife Gardens or right to the Alcazaba (and the rest of the Alhambra grounds).*

The path to the Generalife Gardens is a delightful 15-minute stroll—just follow signs for Generalife. Just before reaching the Generalife, you'll cross over a bridge and look down on the dusty lane called Cuesta del Rey Chico (a handy shortcut for returning to downtown later).

▲▲Generalife Gardens

The sultan's vegetable and fruit orchards and summer palace retreat, called the Generalife (heh-neh-rah-LEE-fay), was outside the protection of the Alhambra wall—and, today, a short hike uphill past the main entrance. The thousand-or-so residents of the Alhambra enjoyed the fresh fruit and veggies grown here. But most important, this little palace provided the sultan with a cool and quiet summer escape.

The Generalife

The Alhambra Grounds

As you wander the grounds, remember that the Alhambra was once a city of a thousand people fortified by a 1.5-mile rampart and 30 towers. The zone within the walls was the **medina,** an urban town. As you stroll from the main entrance down the garden-like Calle Real de la Alhambra to the palace, you're walking through the ruins of the medina (destroyed by the French in 1812). This path traces the wall, with its towers on your left. In the distance are the snowcapped Sierra Nevada peaks—the highest mountains in Iberia. The Palacios Nazaríes, Alcazaba fort, and Generalife Gardens all have entry fees and ticket checkpoints. But the medina—with Charles V's Palace, a church, a line of shops showing off traditional woodworking techniques, and the fancy Alhambra parador—is wide open and free to everyone.

It's especially fun to snoop around the historic **Parador de Granada San Francisco,** which—as a national monument—is open to the public. Once a Moorish palace within the Alhambra, it was later converted into a Franciscan monastery, with a historic claim to fame: Its church is where the Catholic Monarchs (Ferdinand and Isabel) chose to be buried. For a peek, step in through the front door leading to a small garden area and reception. Continue straight to see the burial place, located in the open-air ruins of the church (passing the reception-desk area and a delightful former cloister; the history is described in English). The slab on the ground near the altar—a surviving bit from the mosque that was here before the church—marks the place where the king and queen rested until 1521 (when they were moved to the Royal Chapel downtown). Now a hotel, the parador has a restaurant and terrace café—with lush views of the Generalife—open to nonguests.

The medina's main road dead-ended at the **Wine Gate** (Puerta del Vino), which protected the fortress. When you pass through the Wine Gate, you enter a courtyard that was originally a moat, then a reservoir (in Christian times). The well—now encased in a bar-kiosk—is still a place for cold drinks. If you're done with your Alhambra visit, you can exit down to the city from the Wine Gate via the Justice Gate, immediately below. From there you'll walk past a Renaissance fountain and pass through the **Pomegranate Gate** (Puerta de las Granadas) into the modern city, close to Plaza Nueva.

Follow the simple one-way path through the sprawling gardens. You'll catch glimpses of a sleek, modern outdoor theater, built in the 1950s. It continues to be an important concert venue for Granada.

From the head of the theater, signs will lead you through manicured-hedge gardens, along delightful ponds and fountains, to the sultan's small summer palace.

Before arriving at the bright white palace, pass through the dismounting room (imagine dismounting onto the helpful stone ledge, and letting your horse drink from the trough here). Enter the most accurately re-created Arabian garden in Andalucía.

Here in the retreat of the Moorish kings, this garden is the closest thing on earth to the Quran's description of heaven. It was planted more than 600 years ago—that's remarkable longevity for a European garden. While there were originally only eight water jets, most of the details in today's garden closely match those lovingly described in old poems. The flowers, herbs, aromas, and water are exquisite...even for a sultan. Up the Darro River, the royal aqueduct diverted a life-giving stream of water into the Alhambra. It was channeled through this extra-long decorative fountain to irrigate the bigger garden outside, then along an aqueduct into the Alhambra for its thirsty residents. And though the splashing fountains are a delight, they are a 19th-century addition. The Moors liked a peaceful pond instead.

At the end of the pond, you enter the sultan's tiny three-room summer retreat. From the last room, climb 10 steps into the upper Renaissance gardens (c. 1600). The ancient tree rising over the pond inspired Washington Irving, who wrote that this must be the "only surviving witness to the wonders of that age of Al-Andalus."

Climbing up and going through the turnstile, you enter the Romantic 19th-century garden. Your visit to the Alhambra is complete, and you've earned your reward. "Surely Allah will make those who believe and do good deeds enter gardens beneath which rivers flow; they shall be adorned therein with bracelets of gold and pearls, and their garments therein shall be of silk" (Quran 22.23).

• *If you're exhausted, just head to the right and follow* salida *signs toward the gardens' exit (next to the Alhambra's main entrance). The #C30 and #C32 minibuses leave from here back to Plaza Isabel La Católica.*

But if you want a little more exercise (and views), turn left at the sign for "continuación de la visita," *and take the half-mile loop up and around to see the staircase called Escalera del Agua, which has banisters that double as little water canals. From the top, you'll have a chance to enter the "Romantic Viewpoint"—a top-floor view over the gardens. Then hike back down through the garden and follow* salida *signs to the exit.*

There are two direct and **scenic routes to town.** *One is the easily overlooked Cuesta del Rey Chico pathway. It starts under the two stone arches not far from the main entrance, by Restaurante La Mimbre and the minibus stop—a sign just past the restaurant entrance will confirm you're on the right path. You'll walk downhill on a peaceful, cobbled lane scented with lavender and rock rose, beneath the Alhambra ramparts and past the sultan's horse lane leading up to Generalife Gardens. In 15 minutes you're back in town at Paseo de los Tristes.*

The other route is the shortest and most common: a straight walk along the main road and the base of the fortress wall until you reach a fountain on the left. Follow the shady canopy of trees down, down, down until reaching Cuesta de Gomérez and Plaza Nueva.

MORE SIGHTS IN GRANADA

In the Old Town

▲▲ROYAL CHAPEL (CAPILLA REAL)

Without a doubt Granada's top Christian sight, this lavish chapel in the old town holds the dreams—and bodies—of Queen Isabel and King Ferdinand. The Catholic Monarchs were all about the Reconquista. Their marriage united the Aragon and Castile kingdoms, allowing an acceleration of the Christian and Spanish push south. Symbolic of Ferdinand and Isabel's eventual victory, Granada—the last Moorish capital—was their chosen burial place. This chapel, while smaller and less architecturally striking than Granada's cathedral, is far more historically significant.

Cost and Hours: €5, includes audioguide, Mon-Sat 10:15-18:30, Sun 11:00-18:00; entrance on Calle Oficios, just off Gran Vía del Colón—go through iron gate, tel. 958-227-848, www.capillarealgranada.com.

Visiting the Chapel: In the lobby, before you enter the chapel, notice the

Royal Chapel and Cathedral

painting of Boabdil (on the black horse) giving the key of Granada to the conquering King Ferdinand. Boabdil wanted to fall to his knees, but the Spanish king, who had great respect for his Moorish foe, embraced him instead. Ferdinand is in red, and Isabel is behind him wearing a crown.

Isabel decided to make Granada the capital of Spain (and burial place for Spanish royalty) for three reasons: 1) With the conquest of this city, Christianity had finally overcome Islam in Europe; 2) her marriage with Ferdinand, followed by the conquest of Granada, had marked the beginning of a united Spain; and 3) in Granada, she agreed to sponsor Columbus.

Step into the **chapel**. It's Plateresque Gothic—light and lacy silver-filigree style, named for and inspired by the fine silverwork of the Moors. The chapel's interior was originally austere, with fancy touches added later by Ferdinand and Isabel's grandson, Emperor Charles V. Five hundred years ago, this must have been the most splendid space imaginable. Because of its speedy completion (1506-1521), the Gothic architecture is unusually harmonious.

In the center of the chapel (in front of the main altar), the **four royal tombs** are Renaissance-style. Carved in Italy in 1521 from Carrara marble, they were sent by ship to Spain. The faces—based on death masks—are considered accurate. **Ferdinand** and **Isabel** are the lower, more humble of the two couples. (Isabel fans attribute the bigger dent she puts in the pillow to the weight of her larger brain.) Isabel's contemporaries described the queen as being of medium height, with auburn hair and blue eyes, and possessing a serious, modest, and gentle personality. (Compare Ferdinand and Isabel's tomb statues with the painted and gilded wood statues of them kneeling in prayer, flanking the altarpiece.)

Philip the Fair and **Juana the Mad** (who succeeded Ferdinand and Isabel) lie on the left. Philip was so "Fair" that it drove the insanely jealous Juana "Mad." Philip died young, and Juana, crazy like a fox, used her "grief" over his death to forestall a second marriage, thereby ensuring that their son Charles would inherit the throne. Charles was a key figure in European history, as his coronation merged the Holy Roman Empire (Philip the Fair's Habsburg domain) with Juana's Spanish empire.

Granada lost power and importance when Philip II, the son of Charles V, built his El Escorial palace outside Madrid, establishing that city as the single capital of a single Spain. This coincided with the beginning of Spain's decline, as the country squandered its vast wealth trying to maintain an impossibly huge empire. Spain's rulers were defending the romantic, quixotic dream of a Catholic empire—ruled by one divinely ordained Catholic monarch—against an irrepressible tide of nationalism and Protestantism that was sweeping across the vast Habsburg holdings in Central and Eastern Europe.

Look at the intricate **carving** on the Renaissance tombs. Dating from around 1520, it's a humanistic statement, with these healthy, organic, realistic figures rising out of the Gothic age. Charles V thought the existing chapel wasn't dazzling enough to honor his grandparents' importance, so he funded decorative touches like the iron screen and the fine 16th-century copy of the Rogier van der Weyden painting *The Deposition* (to the left after passing through the screen; the original is at the Prado in Madrid). Immediately to the right of the painting, with the hardest-working altar boys in Christendom holding up gilded Corinthian columns, is a chapel with a locked-away relic (an arm) of John the Baptist.

From the feet of the marble tombs, step downstairs to see the actual **coffins.** They are plain. Ferdinand and Isabel were originally buried in the Franciscan monastery (in what is today the parador, up at the Alhambra). You're standing in front of the two people who created Spain. The fifth coffin (on right, marked *Príncipe Miguel*) belongs to a young Prince Michael, who would have been king of a united Spain and Portugal. (A sad—but too-long—story...)

The **high altar** is one of the finest Renaissance works in Spain. It's dedicated to two Johns: the Baptist and the Evangelist. In the center you can see the Baptist and the Evangelist chatting as if over tapas—an appropriately humanistic scene. Flanking both Johns, statues of Ferdinand and Isabel kneel in prayer. A colorful series of reliefs at the bottom level recalls the Christian conquest of the Moors (left to right): a robed processional figure, Boabdil with army and key to Alhambra, Moors expelled from Alhambra, conversion of Muslims by tonsured monks (two panels, right of altar table), and another robed figure.

A finely carved Plateresque arch, with the gilded royal initials *F* and *Y,* leads from the chapel into the sacristy/treasury/museum, where you'll see Queen Isabel's silver crown ringed with pomegranates (symbolizing Granada), her scepter, and King Ferdinand's sword. Do a counterclockwise spin around the room to see it

Painting of Boabdil

Royal tombs

all: the devout Isabel's prayer book, the fancy box Isabel filled with jewels and gave to bankers as collateral for the cash to pay Columbus, Isabel's simple rosary, and other personal items.

The next zone of this grand hall holds the first great **art collection** established by a woman. Queen Isabel amassed more than 200 important paintings. After Napoleon's visit, only 31 remained. Even so, this is an exquisite collection, all on wood, featuring works by Sandro Botticelli, Pietro Perugino, the Flemish master Hans Memling, and some less-famous Spanish masters.

▲GRANADA CATHEDRAL (CATEDRAL DE GRANADA)

One of only two Renaissance churches in Spain (the other is in Córdoba), Granada's cathedral is the second-largest church in the country (after Sevilla's). While it was started as a Gothic church, it was built using Renaissance elements, and then decorated in Baroque style.

Cost and Hours: €5, includes audioguide, Mon-Sat 10:00-19:00, Sun 15:00-18:00, tel. 958-222-959, www.catedraldegranada.com.

Visiting the Cathedral: Enter the church from Plaza de las Pasiegas. Before exploring the interior, step into the cathedral's little **museum** (tucked into the corner behind the ticket counter). Filling the ground floor of the big bell tower, it's worth seeking out for two pieces of art: a Gothic, hexagonal-shaped monstrance with a Renaissance-era base given to the cathedral by Isabel, and a beautiful sculpture of San Pablo (Paul, with a flowing beard, carved in wood and painted)—a self-portrait by hometown great Alonso Cano.

Leave the museum and stand in the back of the **nave** for an overview. Survey the church. It's huge. It was designed to be the national church when Granada was the capital of a newly reconquered-from-the-Muslims Spain. High above the main altar are square niches originally intended

Granada Cathedral

The cathedral's Baroque interior

for the burial of Charles V and his family. But King Philip II changed focus and abandoned Granada for El Escorial, so the niches are now plugged with paintings depicting the Doctors of the Church. High above under the stained glass are paintings by Alonso Cano—seven scenes from the life of Mary.

The cathedral's cool, spacious interior is mostly Renaissance—a refreshing break from the closed-in, dark Gothic of so many Spanish churches. In a move that was modern back in the 18th century, the walls of the choir (the big, heavy wooden box that dominates the center of most Spanish churches) were taken out so that people could be involved in the worship. Notice that the two rear chapels (sand-colored, on right and left) are Neoclassical in style—a reminder that the church took 300 years to finish. As you explore, remember that the abundance of Marys is all part of the Counter-Reformation. Most of the side chapels are decorated in Baroque style.

As you walk to the front for a closer look at the **altar,** take a small detour to the scale model of the entire complex (left of pews). Examine the cathedral's immensity. Standing before the altar, notice the abundance of gold leaf. It's from Spain's Darro River, which originally attracted Romans here for its gold. As this is a seat of the local bishop, there's a fine wooden bishop's throne on the right.

Between the pairs of Corinthian columns on both sides of the altar are **sculptures** with a strong parenting theme: Inside the thick, round frames at the top are busts of Adam and Eve, from whom came mankind. Around them are the four gold-covered evangelists, who—with the New Testament—brought the Good News of salvation to believers. Completing the big parenting picture (under Adam and Eve) are Ferdinand and Isabel, kneeling in prayer, who brought Catholicism to the land. Their complex coat of arms (beneath each respective statue) celebrates how their marriage united two influential kingdoms to create imperial Spain.

Strolling behind the altar, look for the **giant music sheets:** They're mostly 16th-century Gregorian chants. Notice the sliding C clef. Rather than a fixed G or F clef, the monks knew that this clef—which could be located wherever it worked best on the staff—marked middle C, and they chanted to notes relative to that. Go ahead—try singing a few verses of the Latin.

Step to the center to view the high altar from the rear. The giant four-sided swiveling music rack held these huge sheets, allowing monks to sign in unison in the days before printed hymnals. Look up at the paintings in the dome: Church fathers plugging the planned royal tombs and, above those, the Cano scenes of Mary's life.

The **sacristy** (between the exit and the St. James altarpiece, in the right corner)—filled with closets and drawers for the robes and garments necessary for the high Church pageantry—is worth a look. It's lush and wide open; its gilded ceilings, mirrors, and wooden cabinets give it a light, airy feel. Two grandfather clocks made in London (one with Asian motifs) ensured that everyone got dressed on time. The highlight of this room is a work by Cano—a small, delicate painted wood statue of the *Immaculate Conception,* under the Crucifixion.

Exit the cathedral through its little **shop** (with a nicely curated selection of religious and secular souvenirs). If you walk straight out, you'll come directly to Gran Vía and the stop for minibus #C32 for the Albayzín.

The Albayzín

Spain's best old Moorish quarter, with countless colorful corners, flowery patios, and shady lanes, is worth ▲. While the city center of Granada feels more or less like many other pleasant Spanish cities, the Albayzín is unique. You can't say you've really seen Granada until you've at least strolled a few of its twisty lanes. Climb high to the San Nicolás church for the best view of the Alhambra. Then wander through the mysterious back streets.

Getting to the Albayzín: Ride the bus, hike up, or take a taxi (€5) to the San Nicolás viewpoint. The handy Albayzín **minibus #C31** makes a 20-minute loop through the quarter, getting you scenically and sweatlessly to the San Nicolás viewpoint (departs about every 10 minutes from the Cathedral/Gran Vía or Plaza Nueva).

The Albayzín

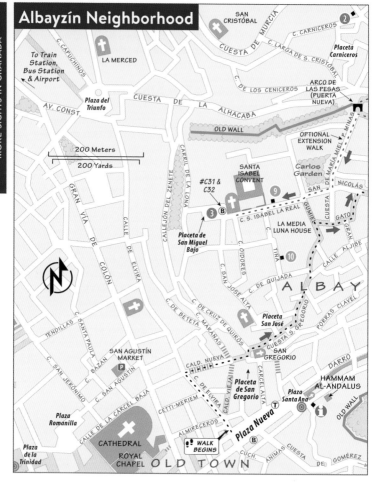

Albayzín Neighborhood

SAN
CRISTÓBAL

CUESTA DE MURCIA
C. CARNICEROS
C. LARGA DE S. CRISTÓBAL
Placeta
Carniceros

To Train
Station,
Bus Station
& Airport
C. CAPUCHINOS
LA MERCED

C. DE LOS CENICEROS
ARCO DE
LAS PESAS
(PUERTA
NUEVA)

AV. CONST.
Plaza del
Triunfo
CUESTA DE LA ALHACABA

OLD WALL

OPTIONAL
EXTENSION
WALK

Carlos
Garden

200 Meters
200 Yards

SANTA
ISABEL
CONVENT
#C31 &
C32

NICOLÁS

GAT O

CUESTA DE MARIA MIEL Y. MINAS

GRAN VIA DE
CALLE DE COLÓN
CALLEJÓN DEL ZENETE
CARRIL DE LA LONA

3

C. S. ISABEL LA REAL

9

LA MEDIA
LUNA HOUSE

Placeta de
San Miguel
Bajo

C. OIDORES
C. TINA
10

CALLE ALJIBE

CUESTA DE GUINEO

CALLE DE ELVIRA

C. SAN JOSÉ ALTA
C. DE QUIJADA
A L B A Y

C. DE CRUZ DE QUIROS
C. DE BETETA
C. MARARAS
Placeta
San José
PORRAS CLAVEL

TENDILLAS
SANTA PAULA
C. BAZÁN
SAN AGUSTÍN
MARKET
P
CUESTA S. GREGORIO
SAN
GREGORIO
DARRO

C. SAN JERÓNIMO
C. SAN AGUSTÍN
CALD. NUEVA
CARCEL ALTA
HAMMAM
AL-ANDALUS

Plaza
Romanilla
CALLE DE LA CÁRCEL BAJA
C. DE ELVIRA
CALD. VIEJA
Placeta
de San
Gregorio
Plaza
Santa Ana
OLD WALL

CETTI-MERIEM
Plaza Nueva

Plaza
de la
Trinidad
ALMIRECEROS
WALK
BEGINS
B
T
i

CATHEDRAL
ROYAL
CHAPEL
O L D   T O W N
CUCH.
ÁNIMAS CUESTA
DEL
GOMÉREZ

▲ALBAYZÍN WALK

It's a steep but fascinating 30-minute walk up from Plaza Nueva to the San Nicolás viewpoint (see route on "Albayzín Neighborhood" map). Leave the west end of Plaza Nueva on Calle de Elvira. When you see a tiny signal light, turn uphill (90 degrees, right) on Calle Calderería Nueva. Follow this stepped street—a virtual tunnel of hippie souvenirs leading to a stretch of Moroccan eateries and pastry shops, vendors of imported North African goods, halal butchers, and inviting *teterías* (Moorish tearooms). Ahead is the tiny

square and Church of San Gregorio.

Placeta de San Gregorio, the tiny junction at the top of Calle Calderería Nueva, has a special hang-loose character. Grab a rickety seat here at Bar las Cuevas, under the classic church facade with potted plants and a commotion of tiled roofs, and enjoy the steady stream of hippies (and wannabe hippies) flowing by. Another fine perch a few steps higher up is Taverna 22, great for a Reserva 1925 (Granada's best craft beer), *vermut de la casa,* or a sweet sherry (*jerez*).

The **Church of San Gregorio** is the

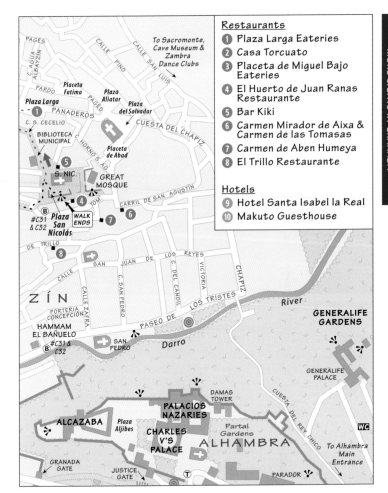

Restaurants
1. Plaza Larga Eateries
2. Casa Torcuato
3. Placeta de Miguel Bajo Eateries
4. El Huerto de Juan Ranas Restaurante
5. Bar Kiki
6. Carmen Mirador de Aixa & Carmen de las Tomasas
7. Carmen de Aben Humeya
8. El Trillo Restaurante

Hotels
9. Hotel Santa Isabel la Real
10. Makuto Guesthouse

domain of a small group of Franciscan sisters. For a bit of tranquility, step inside. One of the sisters, dressed in glorious white, is kneeling at the altar in prayer all day, every day.

Continue your climb up Cuesta de San Gregorio. When you reach the big brick tower of a Moorish-style house, La Media Luna (with the tall palm trees and key-hole-style doorway), stop for a photo and a breather, then follow the wall, continuing uphill. At the T-intersection (with the painted black cats on the wall), turn right on Aljibe del Gato. A bit farther on, take

the first left onto the stepped Cuesta de María de la Miel. Keep going up, up, up. Take the first right, on Camino Nuevo de San Nicolás, then walk to the street that curves up and left. Continue up the curve, and soon you'll see feet hanging from the plaza wall. More steps lead up to the viewpoint. Whew! You made it!

The ▲▲ San Nicolás viewpoint (mirador de San Nicolás) is one of Europe's most romantic spots. If you can, be here at sunset, when the Alhambra glows red and Albayzín widows share the benches with local lovers, hippies, and tourists. For

San Nicolás viewpoint at sunset

an overpriced drink with the same million-euro view, step into the El Huerto de Juan Ranas Bar (just below and to the left, at Calle de Atarazana 8). Enjoy the Roma musicians who perform here for tips. Order a drink, tip them, settle in, and consider it a concert.

Just next to the viewpoint (to your left as you face the Alhambra) is the striking and inviting ▲ **Great Mosque of Granada** (Mezquita Mayor de Granada). Built in 2003, it has a peaceful view courtyard and a minaret that comes with a live call to prayer five times a day (printed schedule inside). It's stirring to hear the muezzin holler "God is Great" from the minaret. Visitors are welcome in the courtyard, which offers Alhambra views without the hedonistic ambience of the more famous San Nicolás viewpoint (free, daily 11:00-14:00 & 18:00-21:00, shorter hours in winter, www.mezquitadegranada.com).

Optional Albayzín Walk Extension: From the San Nicolás viewpoint and the Great Mosque, you're at the edge of a hilltop neighborhood even the people of Granada recognize as a world apart. With

another 20 minutes or so, you can dive in.

From the viewpoint, turn your back to the Alhambra and walk north (passing the church on your right and, further on, the Biblioteca Municipal on your left). The small lane Callejón San Cecilio leads past a white brick arch (on your right)—now a chapel built into the old Moorish wall. You're walking by the scant remains of the pre-Alhambra fortress of Granada. At the end of the lane, step down to the right through the 11th-century "New Gate" (Puerta Nueva—older than the Alhambra) and into **Plaza Larga.** In medieval times, this tiny square (called "long," because back then it was) served as the local marketplace. It still is a busy market each morning. Casa Pasteles, at the near end of the square, serves good coffee and cakes.

From Plaza Larga look up **Calle Agua de Albayzín** (as you face Casa Pasteles, it's to your right). The street, named for the public baths that used to line it, shows evidence of the Moorish plumbing system: gutters. Back when Europe's streets were filled with muck, Granada had gutters with drains leading to clay and lead pipes.

Safety in the Albayzín

With tough economic times, young ruffians are hanging out in the dark back lanes of the labyrinthine Albayzín quarter. While this charming Moorish district is certainly safe by day, it can be edgy after dark. Most of the area is fine to wander, though many streets are poorly lit, and the maze of lanes can make it easy to get lost and wind up somewhere you don't want to be. Some nervous travelers choose to avoid the neighborhood entirely after dark, but I recommend venturing into the Albayzín to enjoy its restaurants, ideal sunset views, and charming ambience. Just exercise normal precautions: Leave your valuables at your hotel, stick to better-lit streets, and take a minibus or taxi home if you're unsure of your route. Violent crime is rare, but pickpocketing is common.

You're in the heart of the Albayzín. Explore. Poke into an old church. They're plain by design to go easy on the Muslim converts, who weren't used to being surrounded by images as they worshipped. You'll see lots of real Muslim culture living in the streets. When you are finished exploring, walk back down Placeta de las Minas (which becomes Cuesta de María de la Miel) to Camino Nuevo de San Nicolás, where you walked up. Turn right, and wander to **Placeta de San Miguel Bajo,** where you can stop for a meal or a refreshing snack (see "Eating," later) before catching minibus #C31 or #C32 back into town.

EXPERIENCES

Arab Baths

For an intimate and subdued experience, consider some serious relaxation at **Hammam al Andalus,** where you can enjoy three different-temperature pools and a steam room. Up to 35 people are allowed in the baths at one time.

Cost and Hours: €30 for 90-minute soak in the baths (more if you add a massage), daily 10:00-24:00, appointments scheduled every even-numbered hour, coed with mandatory swimsuits, quiet atmosphere encouraged, free lockers and towels available, no loaner swimsuits but you can buy one, just off Plaza Nueva—follow signs a few doors down from the TI to Santa Ana 16, paid reservation required (refunded if cancelled up to 48 hours before the appointment), tel. 958-229-978, www.hammamalandalus.com.

Paseo Without the Tourists

While Granada's old town is great for strolling, it's also fun to just be in workaday Granada with everyday locals. A five-minute walk from Plaza Nueva gets you into a delightful and untouristy urban slice of Andalucía. To enjoy an evening paseo without tourists (worth ▲▲), start with a tapas crawl along any of the streets beyond Plaza del Carmen (see under "Eating," later), then stroll down Carrera de la Virgen, off Plaza del Campillo, where there's always something cultural happening. Carrera de la Virgen leads gracefully down to the Paseo del Salón riverbank park, passing the El Corte Inglés department store.

Zambra Dance

A long flamenco tradition exists in Granada, and the Roma of Sacromonte are credited with developing this city's unique flavor of the Andalusian art form. Sacromonte is a good place to see *zambra,* a flamenco variation in which the singer also dances. A half-dozen cave-bars offering *zambra* in the evenings line Sacromonte's main drag. Hotels are happy to book you a seat and arrange the included transfer. Experiencing flamenco in a Roma cave is like seeing art in situ.

Zambra *dance*

Two well-established venues are **Zambra Cueva de la Rocio** (€30, includes a drink and bus ride from and back to your hotel, €20 without transport, daily show at 22:00, 1 hour, Camino del Sacromonte 70, tel. 958-227-129, www.cuevalarocio. es) and **María la Canastera,** an intimate venue where the Duke of Windsor and actor Yul Brynner came to watch *zambra* (€28, includes drink and bus from hotel, €22 without transport, daily show at 22:00, 1 hour, Camino del Sacromonte 89, tel. 958-121-183, www.marialacanaster.com). The biggest operation here is the restaurant **Venta El Gallo,** which has performances of more straightforward flamenco (not specifically *zambra*, €33 with bus from hotel, €26 without transport, daily shows at 21:00 and 22:30, dinner possible beforehand on outdoor terrace, Barranco de los Negros 5, tel. 958-228-476, www.ventaelgallo.com).

If you don't want to venture to Sacromonte, try **Casa del Arte Flamenco,** which performs one-hour shows just off Plaza Nueva (€18, €3 discount for booking online, at 19:30 and 21:00, Cuesta de Gomérez 11, tel. 958-565-767, www.casadelarteflamenco.com).

EATING

Granada's bars pride themselves on serving a small tapas plate free with any beverage—a tradition that's dying out in most of Spain. Save on your food expenses by doing a tapas crawl (but avoid touristy Calle Navas, right off Plaza del Carmen) and claim your "right" to a free tapa with every drink. Order your drink and wait for the free tapa before ordering food.

For more budget-eating thrills, buy picnic supplies near Plaza Nueva, and schlep them up into the Albayzín. This makes for a great cheap date at the San Nicolás viewpoint or on one of the scattered squares and lookout points.

Rick's Tip: *In search of an* **edible memory***? Berenjenas fritas (fried eggplant) and habas con jamón (fava beans cooked with cured ham) are worth seeking out. Tinto de verano—a red-wine spritzer with lemon and ice—is refreshing on a hot evening.*

In the Albayzín

Plaza Larga is extremely characteristic, with tapas bar tables spilling out onto the square, a morning market, and a much-loved pastry shop. A few blocks beyond Plaza Larga, **$$ Casa Torcuato** is a hard-working eatery serving creative food in a smart upstairs dining room. Or grab a table on the little square out front or in the downstairs bar. They serve a good fixed-price lunch, plates of fresh fish, and prizewinning, thick, *salmorejo*-style gaz-pacho (closed Sun night and Wed, Calle Pagés 31, tel. 958-202-818). Minibus #C34 stops right in front of the restaurant or it's only €5 by taxi from Plaza Nueva.

Placeta de Miguel Bajo, the farthest hike into the Albayzín, boasts a spirited local scene—kids kicking soccer balls, old-timers warming benches, and women gossiping under the facade of a humble church. It's circled by half a dozen inviting little bars and restaurants—each very competitive with cheap lunch deals. In the evening, the most serious restaurant is **$ Bar Lara,** with nice traditional plates (€10), salads, paellas, and fish (closed Wed, Placeta de Miguel Bajo 4, tel. 958-209-466). This square is a nice spot to end your Albayzín visit, as there's a viewpoint overlooking the modern city a block beyond the square. Minibus #C31 rumbles by every few minutes, ready to zip you back to Plaza Nueva. Or just walk 10 minutes downhill.

Near the San Nicolás Viewpoint

$$$ El Huerto de Juan Ranas Restaurante is a stuffy restaurant below a popular rooftop bar. Packed with a commotion of people shooting selfies, sipping cocktails, and paying too much for tapas, it's immediately below the San Nicolás viewpoint and has amazing Alhambra views (daily 11:30-24:00, Calle de Atarazana 8, tel. 958-286-925).

$$ Bar Kiki, a laid-back and popular bar-restaurant, is on an unpretentious square with no view but plenty of people-watching. They serve simple dishes outside on rickety tables and plastic chairs. Try their tasty fried eggplant (Thu-Tue 9:00-24:00, closed Wed, just behind viewpoint at Plaza de San Nicolás 9, tel. 958-276-715).

Romantic Carmenes

For dinner in a dressy setting with romance and a dreamy Alhambra view, consider dining in a *carmen,* a typical Albayzín house with a garden (buzz to get in).

$$$ Carmen Mirador de Aixa is small and elegant. You'll pay a little more, but the food is exquisitely presented and the view makes the price worthwhile. Try the codfish or ox (Tue-Sat 20:00-23:00, also open for lunch Wed-Sun 13:30-15:30, closed Mon all day; next to Carmen de las Tomasas at Carril de San Agustín 2, tel. 958-223-616, www.miradordeaixa.com).

$$$ Carmen de las Tomasas serves thoughtfully presented gourmet Andalusian cuisine with killer views on three terraces. The service is friendly if slightly formal (mid-June-mid-Oct Tue-Sat 20:30-24:00, closed Sun-Mon; off-season also open for lunch, closed Mon; reservations required, Carril de San Agustín 4, tel. 958-224-108, www.lastomasas.com, Joaquín).

$$ Carmen de Aben Humeya, with outdoor-only seating, is another smart option (daily 12:00-16:00 & 19:00-23:00, reservations required, Cuesta de las Tomasas 12, tel. 958-228-345, www.abenhumeya.com).

$$ El Trillo Restaurante is homey, without pretense or big groups. Most tables are in a tranquil garden (with trees but no view); several tables upstairs with good Alhambra views have the ambience of eating on a wealthy friend's balcony. When it's cold, meals are served in their vintage dining room. The menu of modern Mediterranean and Spanish dishes is fun and creative, often with a surprising twist (daily 13:00-16:00 & 19:00-23:00, when reserving ask for garden or terrace; tricky to find—three levels below San Nicolás viewpoint, Calle Aljibe de Trillo 3, tel. 958-225-182, www.restaurante-eltrillo.com).

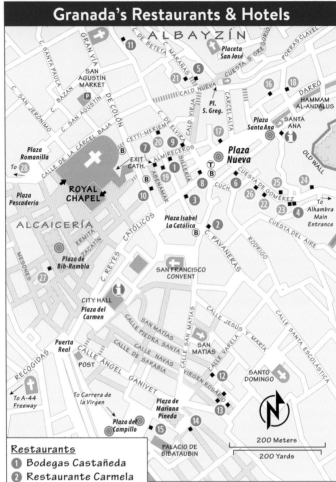

Granada's Restaurants & Hotels

Restaurants
1. Bodegas Castañeda
2. Restaurante Carmela
3. La Cueva de 1900
4. Cafetería Landazuri
5. Arrayanes
6. Los Diamantes
7. Café Bernina
8. Greens & Berries
9. Papas Elvira
10. Los Italianos Ice Cream
11. Supermarket
12. La Botillería
13. Taberna La Tana, Bar Los Diamantes II & Taberna de JAM
14. Café Fútbol & La Esquinita de Javi
15. Restaurante Chikito

Hotels
16. Hotel Casa 1800 Granada
17. Hotel Maciá Plaza
18. Casa del Capitel Nazarí
19. Hotel Anacapri
20. Hotel Inglaterra
21. Oasis Hostel Granada
22. Hotel Puerta de las Granadas
23. Pensión Landazuri
24. Pensión Al Fin
25. Hostal Navarro Ramos
26. Pensión Austria
27. Hotel Los Tilos
28. To Hotel Reina Cristina, Hostals Lima & Rodri; Pensión Zurita

Near Plaza Nueva

For people-watching, consider the many restaurants on Plaza Nueva or Plaza de Bib-Rambla. For a happening scene, check out the bars on and around Calle de Elvira. For views, try Paseo de los Tristes—like a stage set of outdoor bars on a terrace over the river gorge: cool, with the floodlit Alhambra high above and a happy crowd of locals enjoying a meal or drink out.

$$ Bodegas Castañeda, just a block off Plaza Nueva, is the best mix of lively, central, and cheap among the tapas bars I visited. When it's crowded, you need to power your way to the bar to order. When it's quiet, you can order at the bar and grab a little table (same prices). Consider their *tablas combinadas*—variety plates of cheese, meat, and *ahumados* (four varieties of smoked fish)—and tasty *croquetas de jamón* (breaded and fried béchamel sauce with cured ham). Order a glass of gazpacho. The big kegs tempt you with local vermouths, and wine comes with a free tapa (daily 11:30-16:30 & 19:00-24:00, Calle Almireceros 1, tel. 958-215-464).

$$ Restaurante Carmela, with a sloppy ambience, is respected for its creative tapas, best enjoyed family-style. You can eat on the outside terrace or take a table in the modern interior (daily 8:00-24:00, just up from Plaza Isabel La Católica at Calle Colcha 13, tel. 958-225-794).

$$ La Cueva de 1900, a family-friendly chain on the main drag, is appreciated for its simple dishes and quality ingredients. Though it lacks character, it's reliable and low-stress. They're proud of their homemade hams, sausages, and cheeses—sold in 100-gram lots and served on grease-proof paper (daily 8:00-23:00, Calle Reyes Católicos 42, tel. 958-229-327).

$ Cafetería Landazuri, connected to the recommended Pensión Landazuri, is a smart option for travelers walking down from the Alhambra and anyone who wants quality food at a bargain basement price. Manolo cooks to order; his individ-ual-sized *tortilla española* and salads are good and filling (daily 7:00-16:00, Cuesta de Gomérez 24, tel. 958-221-406).

$$ Arrayanes is a good Moroccan restaurant a world apart from my other listings. Brothers Mostafa and Ibrahím treat guests like old friends and will help you choose among the many salads, the *briwat* (a chicken-and-cinnamon pastry appetizer), the *pastela* (a first-course version of *briwat*), the couscous, or *tajin* dishes. The homemade lemonade with mint pairs well with everything (daily 13:30-16:30 & 19:30-23:30, two locations, just off of Calle Calderería Nueva—from Church of San Gregorio, walk one block and take first right, uphill to Cuesta Marañas 4 and 7, tel. 958-228-401).

$$ Los Diamantes is a modern, packed, high-energy local favorite for fresh seafood (free tapa with drink, only *raciones* and half-*raciones* on the menu, same price for picnic-bench seating or bar, daily 12:00-24:00, facing Plaza Nueva at #13, tel. 958-075-313).

$ Café Bernina is a hardworking, bright, and basic diner serving locals since 1930. It feels like a café/bakery (but with plenty of alcohol) and serves hearty salads, sandwiches, and muffins; tapas are served only at the bar. Indoor dining prices are lower than on the terrace. It's great for breakfast (daily 7:30-24:00, air-con, free Wi-Fi, Almireceros 4—just behind Puerta & Bernina, facing Gran Vía but 30 yards off the big street opposite cathedral; tel. 958-050-908).

CHEAP TO-GO OPTIONS

A strip of dirt-cheap eateries (including pizza and kebab shops) lines the bottom end of Plaza Nueva. Some have stools, or get your food to go and enjoy it on a sunny plaza bench on the square.

$ Greens and Berries serves fresh salads, sandwiches, and real fruit smoothies to take away (there's no seating). Try one of their combos, such as the *queso de cabra y tomate* sandwich (goat cheese and tomato with caramelized onions) paired with a Caribbean smoothie (daily 9:00-22:00, Plaza Nueva 1, tel. 633-895-086).

$ Papas Elvira is a hole-in-the-wall with fast, cheap Moroccan food (daily until 24:00, Calle de Elvira 9).

Ice Cream: Italian-run and teeming with locals, popular **Los Italianos** serves ice cream, *horchata* (chufa-nut drink), and shakes. For something special, try their *cassata,* a slice (not scoop) of Neapolitan with frozen fruit in a cone. Their photo menu is helpful (daily 9:00-24:00, shorter hours and sometimes closed off-season, across the street from cathedral and Royal Chapel at Gran Vía 4, tel. 958-224-034).

Supermarket: Covirán Supermercado is a handy option near Plaza Nueva and the cathedral (daily 9:00-14:00 & 17:00-24:00, Calle de Elvira 52).

Beyond Plaza del Carmen

TAPAS BARS

Granada is a wonderland of happening little tapas bars. As the scene changes from night to night, it's best to simply wander and see what appeals. Remember, it's fun to join the paseo around here (best around 19:00, see "Paseo Without the

Tourists," earlier).

From Plaza del Carmen, wander through the gauntlet of touristy places along Calle Navas, which eventually becomes Calle Virgen del Rosario, with a cluster of fun tapas spots. Consider these places (all within a block of each other):

$$ La Botillería is more relaxed than the standard tapas bar. It has a dressy zone (with nicer tables but the same menu) along with a fun bar scene and tables on a quiet little square. They serve good salads, tasty pork cheeks, and wine by the glass (daily 12:00-24:00, Calle Varela 10, tel. 958-224-928).

$$ Taberna La Tana is a tight, intensely Andalusian place with tiny tables and people hanging out in the street. It's well-known for its fine tapas, wine, and classic *raciones* (daily 13:00-16:30 & 20:30-24:00, Placeta del Agua 3, tel. 958-225-248).

$$ Bar Los Diamantes II is famous for its seafood and happy energy. The menu is easy, prices are great, and locals appreciate fish fried in fresh olive oil. Portions can be huge; prices are the same at the bar, tables, and terrace. The seating in back feels like a fish-and-chips joint. I'd go for the *surtido de pescado* with five kinds

of fish (daily 13:00-16:00 & 20:00-23:00, Calle Rosario 12, mobile 619-787-828).

$$ Taberna de JAM (pronounced "hahm") is a play on the word *jamón* and the initials of the renowned owner/*cortador* (one who cuts ham)—José Angel Muñoz. The extensive menu with traditional and innovative dishes is worthwhile, but this is *the* place for a plate of exquisite *jamón* matched with red wine—try sharing the *cata vertical*—a tasting menu with four types of ham (Mon-Sat 9:00-16:00 & 20:00-24:00, closed Sun; at the top of Calle Virgen del Rosario at Plaza los Campos 1, tel. 958-225-770).

$$ Café Fútbol is an old-school classic with an Art Deco vibe, serving basic Spanish dishes. It's the best place in town to finish your pub crawl (or start your day) with a dessert of chocolate and *churros;* a *media ración* (half-portion) is plenty for two (daily 7:00-24:00, Plaza de Mariana Pineda 6, tel. 958-226-662).

RESTAURANTS FOR FULL MEALS

$$ Restaurante Chikito, a venerable classic on a leafy square at the top of a strolling boulevard, serves big plates *(para compartir)* designed to split. Its conservative local clientele appreciates the traditional Spanish cuisine and good prices; Sinatra would enjoy its tapas bar. You can dine in its dressy, white-tablecloth interior or on the square (Thu-Tue 12:30-16:30 & 20:00-23:30, closed Wed, Plaza del Campillo 9, tel. 958-223-364).

$$ La Esquinita de Javi has the same "crank-out-the-fresh-seafood" formula and is run by the same family as Diamantes (listed earlier), but it's less crazy and more like a normal sit-down restaurant. It has a family-friendly conviviality and an easy menu served in its well-lit, spacious interior and at pleasant tables on the square—where you'll pay 20 percent more (Tue-Sat 13:00-16:00 & 20:30-23:00, Sun 13:00-16:00, closed Mon, two locations on Plaza Mariana Pineda—the better one is adjacent to Café Fútbol on downhill side, tel. 958-049-142).

SLEEPING

On or near Plaza Nueva

$$$ Hotel Casa 1800 Granada sets the bar for affordable class. Its 25 rooms face the beautiful, airy courtyard of a 17th-century mansion in the lower part of the Albayzín (just steps above Plaza Nueva). Tidy, friendly, and well-run, it has a free, 24-hour refreshments bar and complimentary tea each afternoon (pricier rooms not much different except for the Alhambra views and patios, air-con, elevator, Benalúa 11, tel. 958-210-700, www.hotelcasa1800granada.com, info@hotelcasa1800granada.com).

$$$ Hotel Maciá Plaza, right on the colorful Plaza Nueva, has 44 smallish, clean rooms, dressed in modern veneers over dated "bones." Choose between an on-the-square Alhambra view or a quieter interior room (RS%, air-con, elevator, Plaza Nueva 5, tel. 958-227-536, www.maciahoteles.com, maciaplaza@macia-hoteles.com, friendly Pedro).

$$ Casa del Capitel Nazarí, just off the church end of Plaza Nueva, is a restored 16th-century Renaissance manor with 23 tastefully down-to-earth rooms that are intimate, bright, and spacious, most facing a courtyard that hosts art exhibits (some view rooms, afternoon tea/coffee, air-con, elevator, loaner laptop, pay parking, Cuesta Aceituneros 6, tel. 958-215-260, www.hotelcasacapitel.com, info@hotelcasacapitel.com). Their connected annex, **$$$ Mariana Pineda,** has five exquisitely decorated rooms in a former palace.

$$ Hotel Anacapri is a bright, cool marble oasis with 53 vibrantly colored rooms and a comfortable lounge (family rooms, air-con, elevator, pay parking, 2 blocks toward Gran Vía from Plaza Nueva at Calle Joaquín Costa 7, just a block from cathedral bus stop, tel. 958-227-477, www.hotelanacapri.com, reservas@hotelanacapri.com).

$ Hotel Inglaterra, with 36 basic rooms, is a little rough around the edges and feels institutional but is in an ideal location. Exterior rooms come with some noise from the popular bars below (air-con, elevator to third floor only, pay parking, Cetti Merien 6, tel. 958-221-559, www.hotelinglaterragranada.com, info@ hotel-inglaterra.es).

$ Oasis Hostel Granada offers a communal terrace, the scent of fried food, and lots of backpacker bonding, including daily tours and activities on request. It's just a block above the lively Moorish-flavored tourist drag (includes welcome drink with direct booking, pay parking, at the top end of Placeta Correo Viejo at #3, tel. 958-215-848, www.oasisgranada.com, granada@hostelsoasis.com).

Cheap Sleeps on Cuesta de Gomérez

$ Hotel Puerta de las Granadas rents 16 crisp, clean rooms with an Ikea vibe. It has a courtyard, public areas with views, and a handy location (RS%, air-con, elevator, free tea and coffee in cafeteria all day, pay parking, Cuesta de Gomérez 14, tel. 958-216-230, www.hotelpuertadelasgranadas. com, reservas@hotelpuertadelasgranadas. com).

$ Pensión Landazuri is run by friendly English-speaking Matilde Landazuri, her son Manolo, and daughters Margarita and Elisa. Their characteristic old house has 18 well-worn rooms. It boasts hardworking, helpful management and a great roof garden with a splendid Alhambra view (family rooms, no elevator or air-con, pay parking, Cuesta de Gomérez 24, tel. 958-221-406, www.pensionlandazuri. com, info@pensionlandazuri.com). The Landazuris also run a good, cheap café open for breakfast and lunch, next door.

$ Pensión Al Fin is located just up the street from Pensión Landazuri and run by the same family. Its five high-ceilinged rooms, with antique wooden beams and marble columns, are colorful and stylish, with Cuban flair. A glass floor in the lobby lets you peer into a well from an ancient house (some rooms with balconies, pay parking, reception at Pensión Landazuri, Cuesta de Gomérez 31, tel. 958-221-406, www.pensionalfin.com, info@pension alfin.com).

¢ Hostal Navarro Ramos is a small cheapie, renting seven quiet, clean rooms (5 with private baths) facing away from the street (no elevator, Cuesta de Gomérez 21, tel. 958-250-555, www.pensionnavarroramos.com, info@pensionna-varroramos.com, Carmen).

¢ Pensión Austria rents 15 charmingly dated-but-tidy, backpacker-type rooms (family rooms, air-con, Cuesta de Gomérez 4, tel. 958-227-075, www.pensionaustria.com, pensionaustria@pensionaustria.com).

Near the Cathedral

$ Hotel Los Tilos offers 30 comfortable, business-like rooms (some with balconies) on the charming, traffic-free Plaza de Bib-Rambla. Guests are welcome to use the fourth-floor terrace with views of the cathedral and the Alhambra (RS%—free breakfast for readers with this book, air-con, pay parking, Plaza de Bib-Rambla 4, tel. 958-266-712, www.hotellostilos.com, clientes@ hotellostilos.com, friendly José María).

On or near Plaza de la Trinidad

$$ Hotel Reina Cristina has 55 quiet, homey rooms a few steps off Plaza de la Trinidad. Check out the great Mudejar ceiling at the top of the stairwell. The famous Spanish poet Federico García Lorca hid out in this house before being captured and executed by the Guardia Civil during the Spanish Civil War (includes breakfast, cheaper rate without breakfast, air-con, elevator, pay parking, near Plaza de la Trinidad at Tablas 4, tel. 958-253-211, www.hotelreinacristina.com, clientes@hotelreinacristina.com).

$ Hostal Lima, run with class by Manolo and Carmen, has 25 well-appointed rooms (some small) in two buildings a block off the square. The public areas and rooms are flamboyantly decorated with medieval flair—colorful tiles, wood-carved life-sized figures, and swords (home-cooked dinner available—book in advance, air-con, elevator in one building only, pay parking, Laurel de las Tablas 17, tel. 958-295-029, www.hostallimagranada.eu, info@hostal-limagranada.eu).

$ Hostal Rodri, run by Manolo's brother José, has 10 similarly good rooms a few doors down that feel new and classy for their price range. Take in the sun on an "L"-shaped terrace (air-con, elevator, pay parking, Laurel de las Tablas 9, tel. 958-288-043, www.hostalrodri.com, info@hostalrodri.com).

$ Pensión Zurita, well-run by personable Francisco and Loli, faces Plaza de la Trinidad. Twelve of the 14 rooms have modern, in-room baths and small exterior balconies. Even with double-pane windows, some rooms may come with night noise from cafés below (air-con, kitchen nook available for guest use, pay parking, Plaza de la Trinidad 7, tel. 958-275-020, mobile 685-843-745, www.pensionzurita.es, pensionzurita@gmail.com).

In the Albayzín

$$$ Hotel Santa Isabel la Real, a handsome 16th-century edifice, has 11 rooms ringing a charming courtyard. Each room is a bit different; basic rooms look to the patio, while pricier rooms have better exterior views. The owners' antiques accentuate the Moorish ambience (breakfast included, air-con, elevator, pay parking, midway between San Nicolás viewpoint and Placeta de San Miguel Bajo on Calle Santa Isabel la Real, minibus #C31 stops near hotel, tel. 958-294-658, www.hotelsantaisabellareal.com, info@hotelsantaisabellareal.com).

¢ Makuto Guesthouse, a hostel tucked deep in the Albayzín, feels like a hippie commune you can pay to join for a couple of days. With 39 beds in eight compact rooms clustered around a lush garden courtyard that's made for hanging out—including several hammock-and-lounge-sofa "hang-out zones"—it exudes a young, easygoing Albayzín vibe (private rooms available, includes breakfast, communal kitchen, Calle Tiña 18, tel. 958-805-876, www.makutohostel.com, info@makutohostel.com). From the minibus stop on Calle Santa Isabel la Real, it's a long block down Calle Tiña and on the left.

In and near the Alhambra

$$$$ Parador de Granada San Francisco offers 40 designer rooms in a former Moorish palace that was later transformed into a 15th-century Franciscan monastery. It's considered Spain's premier parador—and that's saying something (air-con, free parking, Calle Real de la Alhambra, tel. 958-221-440, www.parador.es, granada@parador.es). You must book months ahead to spend the night in this lavishly located, stodgy, and historic palace. Any peasant, however, can drop in for a coffee, drink, snack, or meal.

$ Hotel Guadalupe, big and modern with 58 sleek rooms, is quietly and conveniently located overlooking the Alhambra parking lot. While it's a 30-minute hike above the town, many—especially drivers—find this to be a practical option (air-con, elevator, special parking rate in Alhambra lot, Paseo de la Sabica 30, tel. 958-225-730, www.hotelguadalupe.es, info@hotelguadalupe.es).

TRANSPORTATION

Getting Around Granada

With cheap taxis, frisky minibuses, good city buses, and nearly all points of interest an easy walk from Plaza Nueva, you'll get around Granada easily.

Tickets for minibuses and city buses cost €1.40 per ride (buy from curbside machines or driver; must use machine for #4 bus tickets). For schedules and routes, see www.transportesrober.com.

Credibús cards save you money if you'll be riding often—or, since they're share-able, if you're part of a group (per-ride price drops to €0.80; can be loaded with €5, €10, or €20). To get a €5 card—likely all you'll need—ask for *"un bono de cinco."* These are valid on all buses (no fee for connecting bus if you transfer within 45 minutes).

By Minibus: Handy little made-for-tourists red minibuses—which cover the city center—depart every few minutes from Plaza Nueva, Plaza Isabel La Católica, and Gran Vía (Catedral stop) until late in the evening. Here are handy minibus routes to look for:

Bus #C30 is the best for a trip up to the Alhambra, departing 30 yards uphill from Plaza Isabel La Católica, with Alhambra stops at the main entrance and the shortcut Justice Gate (Puerta de la Justicia) entrance (every 5-7 minutes, 7:00-23:00).

Bus #C31 departs from Plaza Nueva and circles counterclockwise around the Albayzín quarter, navigating the narrow one-way lanes (every 8-10 minutes, 7:00-23:00).

Bus #C32 connects the Alhambra to the Albayzín quarter and goes through the city center (7:00-23:00).

Bus #C34 runs from Plaza Nueva to Sacromonte (8:00-22:00).

Arriving and Departing
By Plane
Though Granada airport—officially Federico García Lorca Granada-Jaén Airport—is far from the city center, it still provides faster connections to Spain's big cities than current train and bus services. Iberia and low-cost carrier Vueling offer several direct flights daily to Madrid and Barcelona (code: GRX, tel. 902-404-704, www.aena.es, select "Granada-Jaén F.G.L.").

To get between the airport and downtown, you can take a taxi (€35) or the much cheaper airport bus, timed to leave from directly outside the terminal when flights arrive and depart (€3, 16/day, 45 minutes). Get off at the Cathedral stop. To reach the airport from the town center, use the Cathedral bus stop at the end of Gran Vía.

By Train
Granada's modest train station is connected to the center by frequent buses, a €6 taxi ride, or a 30-minute walk down Avenida de la Constitución and Gran Vía. The train station does not have luggage storage.

Taxis wait out front. It's a two-minute walk to reach the bus stop: Exiting the train station, walk straight ahead up tree-lined Avenida Andaluces (following the Metro tracks). At the first major intersection, find a covered bus stop to the right on Avenida de la Constitución. The #4 bus heads down Avenida de la Constitución to Gran Vía and stops at the cathedral (Catedral)—the nearest stop to Plaza Nueva and most of my recommended hotels (stops are shown on monitors).

TRAIN CONNECTIONS
Although tracks are laid, high-speed train service from Granada isn't running yet. Instead, you'll go by bus to Antequera (1.25 hours), then continue on the AVE train. Expect to take a bus to Antequera and transfer there, regardless of your destination.

From Granada by Train to: Barcelona (2/day, 8 hours), **Madrid** (5/day, 4 hours), **Toledo** (all service is via Madrid, with nearly hourly AVE connections to Toledo), **Algeciras** (3/day, 4-5 hours), **Ronda** (3/day, 3 hours), **Sevilla** (4/day, 3.5 hours), **Córdoba** (7/day, 2 hours), **Málaga** (6/day, 2.5 hours with 1 transfer—bus is better). Many of these connections have a more frequent (and sometimes much faster) bus option—see next.

By Bus
Located on the city outskirts, Granada's bus station (*estación de autobuses*) has a good and cheap cafeteria, ATMs, luggage lockers,

and a privately run tourist agency masquerading as an official TI. All of these services are downstairs, where you exit the buses.

Upstairs is the main arrivals hall with ticket windows, ticket machines, and a helpful information counter in the main hall that hands out printed schedules for each route. All buses are operated by Alsa (tel. 902-422-242, www.alsa.es).

To get from the bus station to the city center, it's either a 10-minute taxi ride (€8) or a 25-minute ride on bus #33 (€1.40, pay driver). For Plaza Nueva, get off on Gran Vía at the Catedral stop (check monitors), a half-block before the grand square called Plaza Isabel La Católica.

BUS CONNECTIONS
From Granada by Bus to: Nerja (6/day, 2.5 hours), **Sevilla** (7/day to Plaza de Armas station, 2/day to El Prado station, 3 hours *directo*), **Córdoba** (6/day *directo*, 3 hours), **Madrid** (hourly, 5-6 hours; most to Estación Sur, a few to Avenida de América, 2 direct to T4 Barajas Airport), **Málaga** (hourly, 2 hours, several direct to Málaga airport, change here to continue to La Línea de la Concepción/Gibraltar), **Algeciras** (4/day, 4 hours), **Barcelona** (4/day, 14 hours). To reach **Ronda,** change in Málaga or Antequera (train is direct and better option).

By Car
Driving in Granada's historic center is restricted to buses, taxis, and tourists with hotel reservations. Hidden cameras snap a photo of your license plate as you enter the restricted zone. If you have a reservation, simply drive past the sign and make sure your hotel registers you with the local traffic police (this is routine for them, but if they don't do it within 48 hours, you'll be stuck with a steep ticket). Hotels provide parking or have a deal with a central-zone garage (such as Parking San Agustín, just off Gran Vía del Colón, €25/day).

If you're driving and don't have a hotel reservation in the center, park outside the prohibited zone. The Alhambra, above the old town, has a huge lot where you can park for €18 per 24 hours (walk, catch the minibus, or taxi into the center). There are also garages just outside the restricted zone: the Triunfo garage to the east (€23/day, Avenida de la Constitución 5) or the Neptune garage to the south (Centro Comercial Neptuno, €17/day, on Calle Neptuno). To reach the city center from either parking garage, catch the articulated #4 bus nearby (on Avenida de la Constitución) and get off at the Catedral stop.

Andalucía's
White Hill Towns

The American image of Spain is Andalucía. This is the home of bullfights, flamenco, gazpacho, and a charm bracelet of pristine whitewashed villages perched in the sierras.

Following the Route of the White Hill Towns (Ruta de los Pueblos Blancos) gives you wonderfully untouched Spanish culture. The romantic queen of the white towns is sleepy Arcos de la Frontera. (Towns with "de la Frontera" in their names were established on the front line of the centuries-long fight to recapture Spain from the Muslims, who were slowly pushed back into Africa.) Farther east is the bigger, livelier town of Ronda, stunning visitors with its breathtaking setting—straddling a gorge that thrusts deep into the Andalusian bedrock.

Between Arcos and Ronda is the Pileta Cave, with prehistoric art, and two cute hill towns—Zahara and Grazalema. As a whole, the hill towns—no longer strategic, no longer on any frontier—are now just passing time peacefully. Join them.

Nearby is the workaday town of Jerez, a transit hub for the region; it's easy to visit on your way to or from the hill towns. Jerez is known for horse shows and sherry tastings; a well-timed visit can include both.

WHITE HILL TOWNS IN 2 DAYS

The most substantial and entertaining home base is Ronda. Small, sleepy Arcos is best early or late—good for a short visit or an overnight stop. Both towns have bus connections with surrounding towns, and Ronda is on a train line.

To help you experience both towns, the following plan includes stays in each:

Day 1: Arrive in Ronda early in the morning (or settle in the night before). Spend the day enjoying Ronda: bridge, bullring, sights, and tapas scene. You could taxi (or drive) to Pileta Cave.

Day 2: Head to Arcos. Drivers could leave early, choosing from these stops en route: Pileta Cave, Grazalema, and Zahara. If you're taking public transportation, linger in Ronda (maybe taxi to Pileta Cave), and bus to Arcos later in the day.

Day 3: In the morning, leave Arcos by car or bus for Jerez (horse and sherry action). Or head to Sevilla instead.

Note that you could easily reverse this plan to start in Jerez, overnight in Arcos, then head to Ronda.

WHITE HILL TOWNS AT A GLANCE

▲▲▲ **Ronda** Midsize town dramatically overhanging a deep gorge, and home to Spain's oldest bullring, with nearby prehistoric paintings at Pileta Cave. See page 313.

▲▲ **Arcos de la Frontera** Queen of the Andalusian hill towns, with a cliff-perched old town that meanders down to a vibrant modern center. See page 304.

▲ **Jerez de la Frontera** Proud equestrian mecca and birthplace of sherry, with plenty of opportunities to enjoy both in a relatively urban setting. See page 325.

Zahara de la Sierra Tiny whitewashed village scenically set between a rocky Moorish castle and a turquoise reservoir. See page 312.

Grazalema Bright-white town nestled in the green hills of the Sierra de Grazalema Natural Park. See page 313.

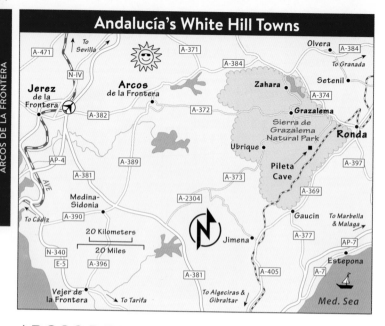

Andalucía's White Hill Towns

ARCOS DE LA FRONTERA

Arcos smothers its long, narrow hilltop and tumbles down the back of the ridge like the train of a wedding dress. It's larger than most other Andalusian hill towns, but equally atmospheric. The old center is a labyrinthine wonderland, a photographer's feast. Viewpoint-hop through town. Feel the wind funnel through the narrow streets as cars inch around tight corners. Join the kids' soccer game on the churchyard patio. Enjoy the moonlit view from the main square. You can arrive late and leave early and still see it all.

Orientation
Tourist Information

The **main TI** is on the skinny one-way road leading up into the old town (Mon-Sat 9:30-14:00 & 15:00-19:30, Sun 10:00-14:00; Cuesta de Belén 5, tel. 956-702-264, www.turismoarcos.com).

Rick's Tip: *There are* **no ATMs in the old town.** *You'll find several ATMs in the new town along Calle Corredera and near the Paseo de Andalucía underground parking lot.*

○ Arcos Old Town Walk

This self-guided walk will introduce you to virtually everything worth seeing in Arcos. (Avoid this walk during the hot midday siesta.)

• *Start at the top of the hill, in the main square dominated by the church.*

Plaza del Cabildo

Stand at the viewpoint opposite the church on the town's main square. Survey the square, which in the old days doubled as a bullring. On your right is the parador, a former palace of the governor. It flies three flags: green for Andalucía, red-and-yellow for Spain, and blue-and-yellow for the European Union. On your left is City Hall, below the 11th-century Moorish castle where Ferdinand and Isabel held Reconquista strategy meetings.

Now belly up to the railing and look down at the dramatic view. The people of Arcos boast that only they see the backs of the birds as they fly. Ponder the parador's erosion concerns (it lost part of its lounge in the 1990s when it dropped right off), the orderly orange groves, and the fine views toward the southernmost part of Spain. You're 300 feet above the Guadalete River. This is the town's suicide departure point for men (women jump from the other side).

• *Looming over the square is the...*

Church of Santa María

After Arcos was retaken from the Moors in the 13th century, this church was built atop a mosque. Notice the church's fine but chopped-off bell tower. The old one fell in the earthquake of 1755 (famous for destroying Lisbon). The replacement was intended to be the tallest in Andalucía after Sevilla's—but money ran out.

Cost and Hours: €2, €3 combo-ticket includes Church of San Pedro, Mon-Fri 10:00-13:00 & 16:00-19:00, Sat 10:00-14:00, shorter hours in winter, closed Sun and Jan-Feb.

Visiting the Church: Work your way between the pews to examine the beautifully carved choir. Its organ was built in 1789 with that many pipes. At the very front of the church, the nice Renaissance high altar—carved in wood—covers up a Muslim prayer niche that survived from the older mosque. The altar shows God with a globe in his hand (on top), and scenes from the life of Jesus (on the right) and Mary (left). To the left of the altar is a fine surviving 14th-century Andalusian Gothic fresco.

Continue circling the church and notice the elaborate chapels. Although most of the architecture is Gothic, the chapels are decorated in the Baroque and Rococo styles that were popular when the post-earthquake remodel began. The ornate statues are used in Holy Week

processions. Sniff out the "incorruptible body" (miraculously never rotting) of St. Felix—a third-century martyr (directly across from the entry). Felix may be nicknamed "the incorruptible," but take a close look at his knee. He's no longer skin and bones...just bones and the fine silver mesh that once covered his skin. Rome sent his body here in 1764, after recognizing this church as the most important in Arcos. In the back of the church, near a huge fresco of St. Christopher (carrying his staff and Baby Jesus), is a gnarly Easter candle from 1767.

• *Back outside, circle clockwise around the church and examine the church exterior...*

Down four steps, find the third-century Roman votive altar with a carving of the palm tree of life directly in front of you. Though the Romans didn't build this high in the mountains, they did have a town and temple at the foot of Arcos. This carved stone was discovered in the foundation of the original Moorish mosque, which stood here before the first church was built. This has long been considered a fertility stone (women would come here to help with pregnancy).

Head down a few more steps and come to the main entrance (west portal) of the church. This is a good example of Plateresque Gothic—Spain's last and most ornate kind of Gothic.

In the pavement, notice the 15th-century magic circle with 12 red and 12 white stones—the white ones have various "constellations" marked (though they don't resemble any of today's star charts). When a child would come to the church to be baptized, the parents stopped here first for a good Christian exorcism. While locals no longer do this (and a modern rain drain now marks the center), many Sufi Muslims still come here in a kind of pilgrimage every November. (Down a few more steps, you can catch the public minibus for a circular joyride through Arcos.)

Go down the next few stairs to the street and circle right. Just past the rec-

Arcos de la Frontera

Restaurants
1 Mesón Los Murales
2 Taberna Jóvenes Flamencos
3 Bar La Cárcel
4 Alcaraván

Hotels
5 Parador de Arcos de la Frontera
6 Hotel El Convento
7 La Casa Grande
8 Casa Mirador San Pedro
9 Rincón de las Nieves
10 Hostal El Patio
11 Hostal & Bar San Marcos

ommended Hostal El Patio, peer down a narrow path called Cuesta de las Monjas. The security grille (over the window above) protected cloistered nuns when this building was a convent. Look at the arches that prop up the houses downhill; all over town, arches support earthquake-damaged structures.

Continue straight under the **flying buttresses.** Notice the scratches of innumerable car mirrors on each wall (and be glad you're walking). The buttresses were built to shore up the church when it was dam-

aged by an earthquake in 1699. (Thanks to these supports, most of the church survived the bigger earthquake of 1755.)
• *Now make your way...*

From Santa María to the Church of San Pedro

Completing your circle around the Church of Santa María (huffing back uphill), turn left under more arches built to repair earthquake damage and walk east down the bright, white Calle Escribanos ("Street of the Scribes"). Although it

Church of Santa María

A typical Arcos side street

changes names, you'll basically follow this lane until you come to the town's second big church (San Pedro's).

After a block, you hit Plaza Boticas. On your right is the last remaining **convent** in Arcos. Notice the no-nunsense, spiky window grilles high above, with tiny peepholes in the latticework for the cloistered nuns to see through. If you're hungry, check out the list and photos of the treats the nuns provide. Then step into the lobby under the fine portico to find their one-way mirror and a spinning cupboard that hides the nuns from view. Push the buzzer, and one of the eight sisters (several are from Kenya and speak English well) will spin out some boxes of excellent, freshly baked cookies—made from pine nuts, peanuts, almonds, and other nuts—for you to consider (€7-8, open daily but not reliably 8:30-14:30 & 17:00-19:00). If you ask for *magdalenas,* bags of cupcakes will swing around (€3.50). These are traditional goodies made from natural ingredients. Buy some treats to support their church work, and give them to kids as you complete your walk.

• *As you exit the convent, turn right and go right again down Calle Botica.*

As you continue straight, notice that the walls are scooped out on either side of the windows. These are a reminder of the days when women stayed inside but wanted the best possible view of any action in the streets. These "window ears" also enabled boys in a more modest age to lean inconspicuously against the wall to chat up eligible young ladies.

Across from the old chapel facade ahead, find the **Palace del Mayorazgo,** which houses the Association of San Miguel. Duck right, past a bar, into one of the oldest courtyards in town—you can still see the graceful Neo-Gothic lines of this noble home from 1850. Enjoy any art exhibits and the garden. The bar is a club for retired men—always busy when a bullfight's on TV or during card games.

• *Just beyond, facing the elegant front door of that noble house, is Arcos' second church...*

Church of San Pedro

Enter through the small door to the left of the main entrance (€2, €3 combo-ticket includes Church of Santa María, same hours as Church of Santa María). You know it's the Church of San Pedro because San Pedro, mother of God, is the centerpiece of the facade. It really is the town's second church, having had an extended battle with Santa María for papal recognition as the leading church in Arcos. When the pope finally favored Santa María (he declared it a minor basilica in 1993), the parishioners at this church changed their prayers. Rather than honoring "María," they wouldn't even say her name. They prayed "San Pedro, mother of God." Like Santa María, it's a Gothic structure, filled with Baroque decor (including a stunning organ covered with cherubs), many Holy Week procession statues, and humble English descriptions. Santa María may have won papal recognition, but this church has more relic skeletons in glass caskets (flanking both sides of the main altar are St. Fructuoso

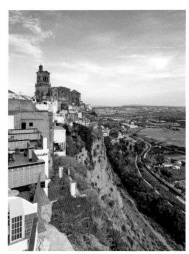

Arcos clings to its hilltop.

and St. Víctor, martyrs from the third century AD). The music stand in the choir illustrates how the entire chorus can sing from just four hymnals.

• *Back outside, explore...*

Back Lanes, Artisan Workshops, and Courtyards

Twenty yards beyond the church, step into the humble **Galería de Arte San Pedro,** featuring artisans in action and their reasonably priced paintings, engravings, and pottery (Mon-Fri 10:00-21:00, Sat-Sun until 19:00, shorter hours in winter).

Crossing behind the church to the next lane, signs direct you to a **mirador**—a tiny square 100 yards downhill that affords a commanding view of Arcos. The reservoir you see to the northeast of town is used for water sports in the summertime. Looking south, among the rolling fields you'll see a power plant that local residents protested—to no avail—based on environmental concerns. Wind-driven generators blink along the horizon at night. Relax on a bench and take in this spectacular view.

• *Return to the Church of San Pedro, then circle down and right along Calle Maldonado as we head back toward the main square.*

Just below San Pedro's is a delightful little **Andalusian garden** (formal Arabic style, with aromatic plants such as jasmine, rose, and lavender, and water in the center). About 100 yards farther along on Maldonado (on the right after the dip), peek into the **Belén Artístico,** a little cave-like museum, which highlights a popular Spanish tradition of setting up a Nativity scene during Christmas using miniature figures (free but donations accepted, generally Mon-Sat 10:30-13:30, closed Sun).

• *This street eventually leads you back to Plaza Boticas (and those cloistered nuns selling cookies).*

The lanes that run steeply down behind Plaza Boticas and the Church of Santa María offer both exercise and a chance to see into **Arcos' lovely courtyards.** The lane called Higinio Capote is particularly picturesque with its many geraniums. Peek discreetly into the private patios. These wonderful, cool-tiled courtyards filled with plants, pools, furniture, and happy family activities are typical of Arcos. Except in the mansions, these patios are generally shared by several families. Originally, each courtyard served as a catchment system, funneling rainwater to a drain in the middle, which filled the well. You can still see tiny wells in wall niches with now-decorative pulleys for the bucket.

Eating
View Dining

\$\$\$ The **Parador** hotel has a formal restaurant and a cafeteria with a cliff-edge setting. Its tapas and *raciones* are reasonably priced, and even just a drink and a snack on the million-dollar-view terrace at sunset is a nice experience (daily 13:00-16:00 & 20:00-23:00, shorter hours off-season, on main square, tel. 956-700-500).

Cheaper Eating in the Old Town

Several decent, rustic bar-restaurants are in the old town, within a block or two of the main square and church. Most serve tapas and *raciones* both at the bar and at their tables.

$$ Mesón Los Murales serves tasty, affordable tapas, *raciones*, and fixed-price meals in their simple bar or at tables in the square outside (Fri-Wed 10:00-24:00, closed Thu, Plaza Boticas 1, tel. 956-700-607).

$$ Taberna Jóvenes Flamencos offers a fun and accessible menu and is high-energy for Arcos. Try their specialties—*abajao,* an egg-and-asparagus dish, and *perolitos,* an egg scramble in a mini pan (Thu-Tue 12:00-24:00, closed Wed, Calle Dean Espinosa 11, tel. 657-133-552).

$$ Bar La Cárcel ("The Prison"), next door, celebrates seafood and local meats (Tue-Sun 12:00-24:00, closed Mon, Calle Dean Espinosa 18, tel. 956-700-410).

$$ Alcaraván, run by the same owners as La Cárcel, tries to be a bit trendier yet *típico.* A funky and fun ambience fills its medieval vault in the castle's former dungeon. This place attracts French and German tourists who give it a cooler vibe (Wed-Sun 12:00-17:00 & 18:00-23:00, closed Mon-Tue, Calle Nueva 1, tel. 956-703-397).

$$ Bar San Marcos is a tiny, homey bar with five tables and an easy-to-understand menu offering hearty, simple home cooking (Sun-Mon 9:00-16:30, Tue-Sat 8:00-24:00, Marqués de Torresoto 6, tel. 956-700-721).

Sleeping

Hotels in Arcos consider April, May, August, September, and October to be high season. Note that some hotels double their rates during the motorbike races in nearby Jerez de la Frontera (usually April or May) and during Holy Week before Easter.

In the Old Town

Drivers should obtain a parking pass from their hotel to park overnight on the main square. (The pass does not exempt you from daytime rates.) Otherwise, park in the Paseo de Andalucía lot at Plaza de España in the new town and walk or catch a taxi or the shuttle bus up to the old town.

$$$ Parador de Arcos de la Frontera is royally located, with 23 elegant and reasonably priced rooms (eight have balconies). The terraces offer splendid views of the town and the valley below (air-con, elevator, Plaza del Cabildo, tel. 956-700-500, www.parador.es, arcos@parador.es).

$$ Hotel El Convento, deep in the old town just beyond the parador, is the best value in town. Run by a hardworking family and their wonderful staff, this cozy hotel offers 13 delicately romantic rooms—all with great views, most with balconies. In 1998 I enjoyed a big party here with most of Arcos' big shots as they dedicated a fine room with a grand-view balcony to "Rick Steves, Periodista Turístico." Guess where I sleep when in Arcos...(RS%, communal terrace, usually closed Nov-Feb, Maldonado 2, tel. 956-702-333, www.hotelelconvento.es, reservas@hotelelconvento.es).

$$ La Casa Grande is a lovingly appointed *Better Homes and Moroccan Tiles* kind of place that rents eight rooms with big-view windows. As in a lavish yet authentic old-style inn, you're free to enjoy its fine view terrace and homey library, or have a traditional breakfast (extra) on the atrium-like patio. They also offer massage services (family rooms, air-con, Wi-Fi in public areas only, Maldonado 10, tel. 956-703-930, www.lacasagrande.net, info@lacasagrande.net, Elena).

$$ Casa Mirador San Pedro, in the shadow of the Church of St. Peter, has seven rustically cozy rooms and a whimsical rooftop terrace with great Arcos views. The windows are single pane, but the street noise quiets down in the evening (apartment available, air-con, El Juan de Cuenca 2—around the corner from Taberna San Pedro, tel. 635-189-005, miradorjuandecuenca@hotmail.com).

$ Rincón de las Nieves, with simple Andalusian charm, has a cool inner courtyard filled with plants and ceramics surrounded by three rooms. Two rooms have their own outdoor terraces with obstructed views, and all have high ceilings and access to the rooftop terrace (the highest in town) with nearly 360-degree views (air-con, Boticas 10, also rents an apartment, tel. 956-701-528, mobile 656-886-256, www.rincondelas-nieves.com, rincondelasnieves@gmail.com, Paqui).

¢ **Hostal El Patio** offers the best cheap beds in the old town. With a tangled floor plan and eight simple rooms, it's on a sometimes-noisy street behind the Church of Santa María (air-con, Calle Callejón de las Monjas 4, tel. 956-702-302, mobile 605-839-995, www.elpatio-arcos.com, reservas@elpatio-arcos.com, staff speak a bit of English). The bar-restaurant with bullfighting posters in the cellar serves affordable breakfast, tapas, and several fixed-priced meals.

¢ **Hostal San Marcos,** above a neat little bar in the heart of the old town, offers four air-conditioned rooms and a great sun terrace with views of the reservoir (air-con, Marqués de Torresoto 6, best to reserve by phone at tel. 956-105-429, mobile 675-459-106, reservas@elpatio-arcos.com, José Luis speaks some English).

In the New Town

$$ **Hotel Los Olivos** is a bright, cool, and airy place with 19 rooms, an impressive courtyard, roof garden, generous public spaces, bar, view, friendly folks, and easy pay parking. The four view rooms can be a bit noisy in the afternoon, but—with double-pane windows—are usually fine at night (RS%, includes breakfast, Paseo de Boliches 30, tel. 956-700-811, www.hotel-losolivos.es, reservas@hotel-losolivos.es, Raquel, Marta, and Miguel Ángel).

Transportation
Getting Around Arcos

The old town is easily walkable, but it's fun to take a circular ramble on the **shuttle bus.** The minibus constantly circles through the town's one-way system and around the valley (see next section). For a 30-minute tour, just hop on. In the old town, you can catch it just below the main church near the mystical stone circle (generally departs at :20 and :50 past the hour). Sit in the front seat for the best view of the tight squeezes and the school kids hanging out in the plazas. After passing under a Moorish gate, you enter a modern residential neighborhood, circle under the eroding cliff, and return to the old town by way of the bus station and Plaza de España.

Arriving and Departing

BY BUS

The bus station is on Calle Corregidores, at the foot of the hill. To get up to the old town, catch the **shuttle bus** marked *Centro* from the bus stalls behind the station. Tell the driver the name of your hotel and he'll bring you to the closest stop (€1, pay driver, generally departs at :15 and :45 past the hour, runs roughly Mon-Fri 7:45-21:15, Sat until 14:15, none on Sun). Alternately, hop a taxi (€5 fixed rate; if none are waiting, call 956-704-640), or hike 15 uphill minutes.

Leaving Arcos by bus can be frustrating—buses generally leave late, the schedule information boards are often inaccurate, and the ticket window usually isn't open (luckily, you can buy tickets onboard). Buses run less frequently on weekends. The closest train station to Arcos is Jerez.

Two bus companies—Damas (www.damas-sa.es) and Comes (www.tgcomes.es)—share the Arcos bus station. If your Spanish is good, you can call for departure times—otherwise ask your hotelier or the TI for help. Also try Movelia.es for bus schedules and routes.

From Arcos by Bus to: Jerez (hourly, 40 minutes), **Ronda** (2/day, 2 hours), **Sevilla** (1-2/day, 2 hours, more departures with transfer in Jerez).

Rick's Tip: *For drivers,* **the best town overlook** *is from a tiny park just beyond the new bridge on the El Bosque road.*

BY CAR

The old town is a tight squeeze with a one-way traffic flow from west to east (coming from the east, circle south under town). The TI and my recommended hotels are in the west. If you miss your target, you must drive out the other end, double back, and try again. Driving in Arcos is like threading needles (many drivers pull in their side-view mirrors to buy a few extra precious inches). Turns are tight, parking is frustrating, and congestion can lead to long jams.

It's less stressful to park in the modern Paseo de Andalucía underground pay lot (€15/day) at Plaza de España in the new town and **hike** 15 uphill minutes to the old town. Or catch a **taxi** or the *Centro* **shuttle bus**—see "By Bus" earlier (as you're looking uphill, the bus stop is to the right of the traffic circle). Many hotels offer discounts at this lot; inquire when booking your room.

Small cars capable of threading the narrow streets of the old town can pay to park in the main square at the top of the hill (Plaza del Cabildo; buy a ticket from the machine). Hotel guests parking here overnight must obtain a €5 dashboard pass from their hotelier; daytime parking charges still apply.

ZAHARA & GRAZALEMA

If you're connecting Arcos and Ronda by car, you'll drive through Zahara de la Sierra and Grazalema, two of my favorite white hill towns. Either or both villages make a pleasant stop for a meal or a stroll. Public transportation is frustrating, so I'd only visit these villages by car.

Zahara de la Sierra

This tiny town in a tingly setting under a Moorish castle has a spectacular view over a turquoise reservoir. While the big church facing the town square is considered one of the richest in the area, the smaller church has the most-loved statue. The Virgin of Dolores is Zahara's answer to Sevilla's Virgin of Macarena (and is similarly paraded through town during Holy Week).

Drivers can park for free in the main plaza, or continue up the hill to the parking lot at the base of the castle, just past the recommended Hotel Arco de la Villa. It's one way up and one way down, so follow *salida* signs to depart.

Zahara de la Sierra

Tourist Information

The TI is located in the main plaza (closed Mon, gift shop, Plaza del Rey 3, tel. 956-123-114, www.zaharadelasierra.es). Upstairs from the TI are Spanish-only displays about the flora and fauna of nearby Sierra de Grazalema Natural Park. A map posted nearby shows the tour and trail system.

Sights

During Moorish times, Zahara lay within the fortified castle walls above today's town. It was considered the gateway to Granada and a strategic stronghold for the Moors by the Christian forces of the Reconquista. Locals tell of the Spanish conquest of the Moors' castle (in 1482) as if it happened yesterday. Skip the church, but it's a fun 15-minute climb up to the remains of the **castle** (free, tower always open). Start at the paved path across from the town's upper parking lot.

Eating and Sleeping

$ Hotel Arco de la Villa is the town's only real hotel (16 small modern rooms, Wi-Fi in common areas only, tel. 956-123-230, www.tugasa.com, arco-de-la villa@tugasa.com). Its very good **$ restaurant** offers a reasonably priced menú del día, along with reservoir and mountain views.

Grazalema

A beautiful postcard-pretty hill town, Grazalema offers a royal balcony for a memorable picnic, a square where you can watch old-timers playing cards, and plenty of quiet whitewashed streets and shops to explore. Situated within Sierra de Grazalema Natural Park, Grazalema is graced with lots of scenery and greenery.

A tiny lane leads a block from the center rear of the square to Plaza de Andalucía (filled by the tables of a commotion of tapas bars). Shops sell the town's beautiful and famous handmade wool blankets and good-quality leather items from nearby Ubrique. A block farther uphill takes you to the main square with the church, Plaza de España. A coffee on the square here is a joy. Small lanes stretch from here into the rest of the town.

Tourist Information

The bare-bones **TI** is located at the car park at the cliffside viewpoint, Plaza de los Asomaderos. Depending on the day, it could be staffed with Spanish-only speakers who can give you a town map and not much else (closed Mon and some holidays, tel. 956-132-052, better info online at www.grazalemaguide.com).

Eating

Tiny Plaza de Andalucía has several good **$$** bars for tapas, including **Zulema**, **La Posadilla,** and **La Cidulia.** To pick up picnic supplies, head to the **Día** supermarket (Mon-Sat 9:00-14:00 & 17:00-21:00, Sun 9:00-14:00, on Calle Corrales Terceros 3).

RONDA

With more than 34,000 people, Ronda (rated ▲▲▲) is one of the largest white hill towns. It's also one of the most spectacular, thanks to its gorge-straddling setting. Approaching the town from the train or bus station, it seems flat...until you reach the New Bridge and realize that it's clinging to the walls of a canyon. During Moorish times, this was a tight, fortified town of 9,000—a bastion second only to Granada during the last years of Moorish rule in southern Spain. (It fell to Christian forces only in 1485—seven years before Granada.)

Ronda's main attractions are its gorge-spanning bridges and the oldest bullring in Spain (it's known as the cradle of modern bullfighting and the romantic home of 19th-century bandoleros). But the real joy of Ronda lies in exploring its back streets and taking in its beautiful balconies, exuberant flowerpots, and panoramic views.

Day-trippers clog Ronda's streets during the day, but locals retake the town in the early evening, making nights peaceful. Since it's served by train and bus, Ronda makes a relaxing break for nondrivers traveling between Granada, Sevilla, and Córdoba. Drivers can use Ronda as a convenient base from which to explore many of the other *pueblos blancos*.

Orientation

Ronda's breathtaking ravine divides the town's labyrinthine Moorish quarter and its new, noisier, and more sprawling Mercadillo quarter. A massive-yet-graceful 18th-century bridge connects these two neighborhoods. Most things of touristic importance (TI, hotels, bullring) are clustered within a few blocks of the bridge. The paseo (early evening stroll) happens in the new town, on Ronda's major pedestrian and shopping street, Carrera Espinel.

Tourist Information

Ronda's hardworking TI, across the square from the bullring, covers not only the town but all of Andalucía. It gives out good, free maps of the town, Andalusia's roads, Granada, Sevilla, and the Route of the White Towns. The TI also organizes a creative array of activities such as tours, concerts, and walks, all described in helpful lists (Mon-Fri 10:00-19:00, Sat until 17:00, Sun until 14:30, shorter hours Oct-late March, Paseo Blas Infante, tel. 952-187-119, www.turismoderonda.es).

Sightseeing Pass: The €8 **Bono Turístico** city pass gets you into four sights—the Arab Baths, Joaquín Peinado Museum, Mondragón Palace, and the New Bridge Interpretive Center.

Helpful Hints

Laundry: HigienSec has self- and full-service options (closed Sun, two blocks east of the bullring at Calle Molino 6, tel. 952-875-249).

Local Guide: Energetic and knowledgeable **Antonio Jesús Naranjo** will take you on a two-hour walking tour of the city's sights (€125, reserve early, mobile 639-073-763, www.guiaoficialderonda.com, guiajesus@yahoo.es).

Ronda's dramatic gorge and New Bridge

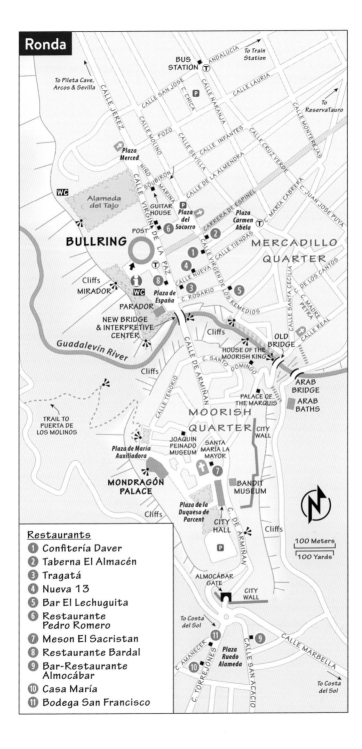

Ronda

To Pileta Cave, Arcos & Sevilla

BUS STATION

To Train Station

To ReservaTauro

Plaza Merced

Alameda del Tajo

WC

GUITAR HOUSE

POST

Plaza del Socorro

Plaza Carmen Abela

BULLRING

MERCADILLO QUARTER

Cliffs

MIRADOR

WC

Plaza de España

PARADOR

NEW BRIDGE & INTERPRETIVE CENTER

Guadalevín River

Cliffs

Cliffs

OLD BRIDGE

HOUSE OF THE MOORISH KING

ARAB BRIDGE

ARAB BATHS

PALACE OF THE MARQUIS

MOORISH QUARTER

CITY WALL

TRAIL TO PUERTA DE LOS MOLINOS

JOAQUIN PEINADO MUSEUM

SANTA MARÍA LA MAYOR

Plaza de María Auxiliadora

MONDRAGÓN PALACE

BANDIT MUSEUM

Plaza de la Duquesa de Parcent

CITY HALL

Cliffs

N

100 Meters
100 Yards

ALMOCÁBAR GATE

CITY WALL

To Costa del Sol

Plaza Ruedo Alameda

CALLE MARBELLA

To Costa del Sol

Restaurants

1 Confitería Daver
2 Taberna El Almacén
3 Tragatá
4 Nueva 13
5 Bar El Lechuguita
6 Restaurante Pedro Romero
7 Meson El Sacristan
8 Restaurante Bardal
9 Bar-Restaurante Almocábar
10 Casa María
11 Bodega San Francisco

Sights
In the New Town
▲▲▲THE GORGE AND NEW BRIDGE (PUENTE NUEVO)

The ravine, called El Tajo—over 300 feet deep and just about 200 feet wide— divides Ronda into the whitewashed old city (Moorish Quarter) and the new town (El Mercadillo) that was built after the Christian reconquest in 1485. The New Bridge mightily spans the gorge. A different bridge was built here in 1735, but it fell after six years. This one was built from 1751 to 1793. Look down from the bridge viewpoint. Spit.

You can see the foundations of the original bridge and a super view of the New Bridge from the walkway between the gorge and the parador—the town's former town hall-turned-hotel—which overlooks the gorge and bridge from the new-town side.

From the new-town side of the bridge (just outside the parador), you'll see the entrance to the **New Bridge Interpretive Center,** where you can pay to climb down and enter the structure of the bridge itself (€2; Mon-Fri 10:00-19:00, Sat-Sun until 15:00, closes earlier off-season). Inside the empty-feeling hall are modest audiovisual displays about the bridge's construction and the famous visitors to Ronda—worth a quick look only if you have the Bono Turístico pass. The views of the bridge and gorge from the outside are far more thrilling than anything you'll find within.

▲▲BULLRING (REAL MAESTRANZA DE CABALLERÍA DE RONDA)

Ronda is the birthplace of modern bullfighting, and this was the first great Spanish bullring. Philip II initiated bullfighting as war training for knights in the 16th century. Back then, there were two kinds of bullfighting: the type with noble knights on horseback, and the coarser, man-versus-beast entertainment for the commoners (with no rules...much like when WWF wrestlers bring out the folding chairs). Ronda practically worships Francisco Romero, who melded the noble and chaotic kinds of bullfighting with rules to establish modern bullfighting right here in the early 1700s. He introduced the scarlet cape, held unfurled with a stick. His son Juan further developed the ritual, and his grandson Pedro was one of the first great matadors (killing nearly 6,000 bulls in his career).

Ronda's bullring and museum rivals Sevilla's as Spain's most interesting. To tour the ring, stables, chapel, and museum, buy a ticket at the back of the bullring.

Cost and Hours: €7, daily April-Sept 10:00-20:00, March and Oct until 19:00, Nov-Feb until 18:00, tel. 952-874-132, www.rmcr.org. The excellent €1.50 audioguide describes everything and is essential to fully enjoy your visit (drop it at the gift shop as you leave).

Bullfights: Bullfights are scheduled only

Ronda's historic bullring

Bullfighting Museum

for the first weekend of September during the *feria* (fair). Whereas every other *feria* in Andalucía celebrates a patron saint, the Ronda fair glorifies legendary bullfighter Pedro Romero. (As these fights are so limited and sell out immediately, Sevilla and Madrid are more practical places for a tourist to see a bullfight.)

◯ **Self-Guided Tour:** I'd visit in this order. Disobey *exit* signs and enter directly to the right to see the bullfighters' **chapel.** Before going into the ring, every matador would stop here to pray to Mary for safety—and hope to see her again.

• *Just beyond the chapel are the doors to the museum exhibits filling two long hallways: horse gear on the left, and the story of bullfighting on the right, all with English translations.*

The **horse gear exhibit** makes the connection with bullfighting and the equestrian upper class. As throughout Europe, "chivalry" began as a code among the sophisticated, horse-riding gentry. (In Spanish, the word for "gentleman" is the same as the word for "horseman"—*caballero*.)

Return to the hallway behind the chapel for the **history exhibit.** It's a shrine to bullfighting and the historic Romero family. First it traces the long history of bullfighting, going all the way back to the ancient Minoans on Crete. Historically, there were only two arenas built solely for bullfighting: in Ronda and Sevilla. Elsewhere, bullfights were held in town squares—you'll see a painting of Madrid's Plaza Mayor filled with spectators for a bullfight. (For this reason, to this day, even a purpose-built bullring is generally called *plaza de toros*—"square of bulls.") You'll also see stuffed bull heads, photos, "suits of light" worn by bullfighters, and capes (bulls are colorblind, but the traditional red cape was designed to disguise all the blood). One section explains some of the big "dynasties" of fighters. At the end of the hall are historical posters from Ronda's bullfights (all originals except the Picasso). Running along the left wall are various examples of artwork glorifying bullfighting, including original Goya engravings.

• *Exit at the far end of the bullfighting history exhibit into the arena.*

Here's your chance to play *toro*, surrounded by 5,000 empty seats. The two-tiered **arena** was built in 1785—on the 300th anniversary of the defeat of the Moors in Ronda. As you leave the museum and walk out on the sand, look ahead to see the ornamental columns and painted doorway marking the royal box where the king and dignitaries sit (over the gate where the bull enters). Opposite the VIP box is the place for the band (marked *música*), which, in the case of a small town like Ronda, is most likely a high school band. Notice the 136 classy columns, creating a kind of 18th-century theater. Lovers of the "art" of bullfighting will explain that the event is much more than the actual killing of the bull. It celebrates noble heritage and Andalusian horse culture.

• *Just beyond the arena are more parts of the complex. Find the open gate beneath the VIP seats.*

Walk through the bulls' entry into the bullpen and the **stables.** There are six bulls per fight (plus two backups)—and three matadors. Before the fight, the bulls are penned up in this bovine death row, and ropes and pulleys safely open the right door at the right time. Climb the skinny staircase and find the indoor arena (*picadero*) and see Spanish thoroughbred horses training from the **Equestrian School** of the Real Maestranza (often during weekdays). Explore the spectators' seating before exiting through the gift shop.

• *From the bullring you can walk out to the* **Mirador de Ronda** *viewpoint and along the cliffside walkway to the New Bridge.*

Nearby: One block away from the bullring, breezy Alameda del Tajo Park is a great place for a picnic lunch or people-watching. Don't miss its balcony overlooking the scenic Serranía de Ronda mountains.

In the Old Town

▲ CHURCH OF SANTA MARÍA LA MAYOR (IGLESIA DE SANTA MARÍA)

This church (built from the 15th to the 17th centuries) has a fine Mudejar bell tower and shares a parklike square with orange trees and City Hall. It was built on and around the remains of Moorish Ronda's main mosque (which was itself built on the site of an ancient Roman temple to Julius Caesar). With a pleasantly eclectic interior that features some art with unusually modern flair, and a good audioguide to explain it all, it's worth a visit.

Cost and Hours: €4.50, daily April-Sept 10:00-20:00, closed Sun 13:00-14:00 for Mass, may close earlier off-season, includes audioguide, Plaza Duquesa de Parcent in the old town.

Visiting the Church: In the room where you purchase your ticket, look for the rare surviving door to the Moorish mosque (that's a mirror; look back at the actual door). Partially destroyed by an earthquake, the church was reconstructed with the fusion (or confusion) of Moorish, Gothic, Renaissance, and Baroque styles you see today.

Inside the church, marvel at the magnificent Baroque **Altar del Sagrario** with a statue of the Immaculate Conception in the center. The smaller altar (adjacent on the right) is a good example of Churrigueresque architecture, a kind of Spanish Rococo in which the decoration consumes the architecture—notice that you can hardly make out the souped-up columns. The big fresco of St. Christopher with Baby Jesus on his shoulders (left, above the door where you entered) shows the patron saint both of Ronda and of travelers.

In the center of the church is an elaborately carved **choir** with a series of modern reliefs depicting scenes from the life of the Virgin Mary. Similar to the Via Crucis (Way of the Cross), this is the Via Lucis (Way of the Light), with 14 stations focusing on the Resurrection and its aftermath (such as #13—the Immaculate Conception, and #14—Mary's assumption into heaven) that serve as a worship aid to devout Catholics.

Church of Santa María la Mayor

Mondragón Palace

Head to the left around the choir, noticing the bright **paintings** along the wall by French artist Raymonde Pagegie. He gave sacred scenes a fresh twist—like the Last Supper attended by female servants, or (opposite) the scene of Judgment Day, when the four horsemen of the apocalypse pause to adore the Lamb of God.

The **treasury** (at the far-right corner, with your back to the choir) displays vestments that look curiously like matadors' brocaded outfits. Before exiting the treasury, find a spiral staircase. Climb the 73 steps to a U-shaped **terrace** around the church's rooftop. Survey the entire deck (ducking under the buttresses) for great views. The highlight is actually inside: Find a tiny door that leads to a breathtaking perch high above the elaborate main altar.

MONDRAGÓN PALACE CITY MUSEUM (PALACIO DE MONDRAGÓN)

This beautiful Moorish building was erected in the 14th century and restored in the 16th century (notice the Mudejar tiled courtyard). Upstairs is Ronda's Municipal Museum, focusing on prehistory and geology. Its kid-friendly rooms have exhibits on Neolithic toolmaking and early metallurgy (like a seventh-century BC mold for making a sword from molten metal). If you plan to visit the Pileta Cave, find the panels that describe the cave's formation and shape. Linger in the two small gardens with wonderful panoramic views.

Cost and Hours: €3.50; Mon-Fri 10:00-19:00, Sat-Sun until 15:00, closes earlier off-season; on Plaza Mondragón, tel. 952-870-818.

Rick's Tip: *Plaza de María Auxiliadora leads to the best Ronda view at sunset. Look for the tiled Puerta de los Molinos sign and head down, down, down. Wait until just before sunset for the best light and cooler temperatures.*

▲JOAQUÍN PEINADO MUSEUM (MUSEO JOAQUÍN PEINADO)

Housed in an old palace, this fresh museum features an overview of the life's work of Joaquín Peinado (1898-1975), a Ronda native and pal of Picasso. Because Franco killed creativity in Spain for much of the last century, nearly all of Peinado's creative work was done in Paris. His style evolved through the big "isms" of the 20th century, ranging from Expressionism to Cubism, and even to eroticism. The short movie that kicks off the display is only in Spanish, though there are good English explanations throughout the museum. Find a famous Cubist version of Don Quixote upstairs and a few Picasso pieces downstairs. It's an interesting modern art experience with no crowds, and fun to be exposed to a lesser-known but very talented artist in his hometown.

Cost and Hours: €4, Mon-Fri 10:00-17:00, Sat until 15:00, closed Sun, Plaza del Gigante, tel. 952-871-585, www.museojoaquinpeinado.com.

▲▲CONCERT AT RONDA GUITAR HOUSE

Local Spanish guitar artist Paco Seco performs a 45-minute solo concert in a 50-seat theater in the back of his shop nearly every night at 19:00. It's an intimate affair with Paco describing his three guitars (historic, classical, and flamenco) and the pieces he performs. Travelers who show this guidebook get a free glass of Ronda wine to enjoy during the show (be sure to ask, as Paco's wife Lucy is happy to provide this to Rick Steves travelers). Seating is first-come, first-seated (Lucy puts your name on the chair). Buy tickets in person, by phone, or from the TI. The Ronda Guitar House is a half-block from the city park at Calle Mariano Soubiron 4 (concert-€15, shop open 10:00-21:00, closed in July, tel. 951-916-843, www.rondaguitarhouse.com).

Near Ronda

▲PILETA CAVE (CUEVA DE LA PILETA)

The Pileta Cave, set in a dramatic, rocky limestone ridge at the eastern edge of Sierra de Grazalema Natural Park (and about 14 miles from Ronda), offers Spain's most intimate look at Neolithic and Paleolithic paintings. The caves are open only to escorted groups, as guides (speaking English and Spanish) take up to 25 visitors at a time deep into the mountain. Because the number of cave visitors is strictly limited, Pileta's rare paintings are among the best-preserved in the world.

Cost and Hours: €10; tours run year-round Mon-Fri at 11:30, 13:00, and 16:30; Sat-Sun at 11:00, 12:00, 13:00, 16:00, and 17:00; also at 18:00 daily April-early Oct; €3 interpretive map, €10 guidebook, mobile 687-133-338, www.cuevadelapileta.org.

Reservations and Getting In: Call or email at least a day ahead to see if there's a tour and space available at the time you want. Arrive at least 15 minutes before your reserved time, and budget in a 10-minute steep hike to the ticket booth from the parking lot.

Getting There: From Ronda, you can get to the cave by taxi—it's about a half-hour drive on twisty roads—and have the driver wait (€70 round-trip). If you're driving, it's easy: Leave Ronda through the new part of town, and take A-374 toward Sevilla. After a few miles, exit left toward Benaoján on MA-7401. Go through Benaoján (MA-7401 changes names to MA-8400), then take a sharp left onto MA-8401 and follow signs (reading *Cueva de la Pileta*) to the cave.

Visiting the Cave: Arrive early, and be flexible. Bring a sweater and sturdy shoes. You need a good sense of balance to take the tour. The 10-minute hike from the parking lot up a stone-stepped trail to the cave entrance is moderately steep. Inside the cave, it can be difficult to keep your footing on the slippery, uneven floor while being led single-file, with only a lantern light illuminating the way.

As you walk the cool half-mile, your guide explains the black, ochre, and red drawings, which are more than 30,000 years old—that's five times as old as the Egyptian pyramids. Among other animals, you'll see horses, goats, cattle, and a rare giant fish, made from a mixture of clay and fat by finger-painting prehistoric *hombres*. Surprisingly, the plain-looking stick drawings in black are more recent than the discernible animal shapes. The 200-foot main hall is cavernous and feels almost sacred. Throughout the site, mineral monoliths look adorned in lace and drapery. Stalagmites and stalactites reach toward one another as they have for a million years or so in these caves, and some formations lend themselves to appropriate names like "The Organ" and "The Castle."

▲RESERVATAURO

As the birthplace of modern bullfighting, Ronda attracts plenty of *aficionados* and even bullfighters themselves. Rafael Tejada worked as an engineer for many years but eventually switched gears to train as a bullfighter. In 2011, he bought land in the nearby *serranía* to raise horses, cows, and stud bulls, and now welcomes visitors to experience his working farm. A visit here allows you to get up close and personal with bulls and horses, as well as try out some matador skills in a practice ring (no bulls, no worries...just the capes). The two-hour option lets you also help the herdsman in one of his daily tasks, such as feeding the free-range bulls, and concludes with local wine and tapas.

Cost and Hours: €25/person for 70 minutes, €40/person for 2 hours; daily 10:00-19:00, until 18:00 off-season; reservations recommended, tel. 951-166-008, www.reservatauro.com.

Getting There: Drivers should leave Ronda through the new part of town, and take A-367 (Carretera Ronda-Campillos) towards Campillos. After about 5.5 miles, turn right into a stone gate marked by a small black-and-white, arrow-shaped sign labeled *RESERVATAURO*. If you're visiting without a car, request a special taxi (€24) for round-trip transportation when you book your tour by phone or email.

Eating

Plaza del Socorro, a block in front of the bullring, is an energetic scene, bustling with tourists and local families enjoying the square and its restaurants. The pedestrian-only **Calle Nueva** is lined with hardworking eateries. To enjoy a drink or a light meal with the best view in town, consider the terraces of Hotel Don Miguel just under the bridge.

For coffee and pastries, locals like the elegant little **$ Confitería Daver,** where they say, "Once you step inside...it's too late" (café open daily 8:00-20:30, Calle Virgen de los Remedios 6).

Tapas in the City Center

Ronda has a fine tapas scene. You won't get a free tapa with your drink as in some other Spanish towns, but these bars have accessible tapas lists, and they serve bigger plates. Each of the following places could make a fine solo destination for a meal, but they're close enough that you can easily try more than one.

$$ Taberna El Almacén offers a modern take on traditional tapas from many Spanish regions in an industrial chic setting. Friendly, approachable staff can explain the day's specials that are *fuera de carta* (not listed on the menu). Even veggie haters rave over their *pisto*—a type of ratatouille where all ingredients are first cooked separately, then mixed together and served with a fried egg on the side. This is a good spot to try local wines as well (Tue-Sat 13:00-16:00 & 20:30-23:00, Sun 13:00-16:00, closed Mon, Calle Virgen de los Remedios 7, tel. 951-489-818).

$$ Tragatá serves creative and tasty tapas in a stainless-steel minimalist bar. You'll pay more for it, but if you want to sample Andalusian gourmet (such as asparagus on a stick sprinkled with grated manchego cheese), this is the place to do it (daily 13:00-16:00 & 20:00-23:00, Calle Nueva 4, tel. 952-877-209).

$$ Nueva 13 serves up admirable and affordable *raciones*. Specials such as *rabo de toro* (bull's-tail stew) and *calamares* (squid) are listed on the giant blackboard inside. Tables spill onto the pedestrian lane—those with tablecloths are for the full menu, and the rest are for the bar menu (Tue-Sat 12:00-16:00 & 19:00-23:00, Sun 12:00-16:00, closed Mon, Calle Nueva 13, tel. 952-190-090).

$ Bar El Lechuguita, a traditional hit with locals, serves a long and tasty list of €1 tapas. Don't miss the bar's namesake, *lechuguita* (#16, a wedge of lettuce with vinegar, garlic, and a secret ingredient). This place is small—just a bar and some stand-up ledges along the wall, plus some rustic tables with stools outside. Ideally, be there when the doors open and grab a spot at the bar (Mon-Sat 13:00-15:00 & 20:15-23:30, closed Sun, Calle Virgen de los Remedios 35).

Dining in the City Center

$$$ Restaurante Pedro Romero, though touristy and overpriced, is a venerable institution in Ronda. Assuming a shrine to bullfighting draped in *el toro* memorabilia doesn't ruin your appetite, rub elbows with the local bullfighters or dine with the likes (well, photographic likenesses) of Orson Welles, Ernest Hemingway, and Francisco Franco (daily 12:00-16:00 & 19:30-23:00, across from bullring at Calle Virgen de la Paz 18, tel. 952-871-110).

$$$ Meson El Sacristan is a well-respected restaurant serving classical and innovative dishes with a focus on meat (many prepared in the wood-fired oven). Their 12-hour *rabo de toro* oxtail stew is a favorite. Their tasting menus are enticing, and the savory homemade *croquetas* are exceptional (Thu-Mon 11:30-23:00, Tue until 17:00, closed Wed and in extreme summer heat, reservations smart, Plaza Duquesa Parcent 14, tel. 952-875-684).

$$$$ Restaurante Bardal has the only Michelin star in town. Local-wonder chef Benito Gómez serves two tasting menus (16 tiny courses-€85, 20 courses-€100, wine extra). Benito serves about 20 people each lunch and dinner, and all are treated like VIPs (Tue-Sat 12:00-16:30 & 20:00-23:30, closed Sun-Mon, reserve ahead, Calle José Aparicio 1, tel. 951-489-828, www.restaurantebardal.com).

Outside the Almocábar Gate

To entirely leave the quaint old town and bustling city center with all of its tourists and grand gorge views, hike 10 minutes out to the far end of the old town, past City Hall, to a big workaday square that goes about life as if the world didn't exist outside Andalucía.

$$ Bar-Restaurante Almocábar is a favorite eatery for many Ronda locals. Its restaurant—a cozy eight-table room with Moorish tiles and a window to the kitchen—serves up tasty, creative, well-presented meals. Many opt for the good salads—rare in Spain. At the bar up front, choose from gourmet tapas like the *serranito* (a pork, roast pepper, and tomato mini sandwich) or you can order from the dining-room menu (Wed-Mon

13:00-16:00 & 19:30-23:00, closed Tue, reservations smart, Calle Ruedo Alameda 5, tel. 952-875-977).

$$$ Casa María is a delightful, family-run place. There's no menu—only the promise of a wonderful meal. Just sit down, and for €30 you'll be treated to a full home-cooked feast: salad, vegetables, fish, meat, and dessert. It's worth making a reservation for this adventure (Wed-Mon 12:00-15:00 & 19:30-22:30, closed Tue, facing Plaza Ruedo Alameda at #27, tel. 951-083-663).

$$ Bodega San Francisco is a rustic bar with homey restaurant seating upstairs and tables out front and on the square. They offer an accessible list of *raciones* and tapas, as well as serious plates and big splittable portions (long hours, closed Thu, same menu in bar and restaurant, Ruedo de Alameda 32, tel. 952-878-162).

Sleeping

Ronda has plenty of reasonably priced, decent-value accommodations. It's crowded only during Holy Week (the week leading up to Easter) and the first week of September (for bullfighting season). Most of my recommendations are in the new town, a short stroll from the New Bridge and about a 10-minute walk from the train station. In cheaper places, ask for a room with a *ventana* (window) to avoid the few interior rooms. Breakfast is usually not included. If arriving by car, email your hotel for driving and parking instructions. For locations, see map on page 323.

In the Old Town

Clearly the best options in town, these hotels are worth reserving early. All are right in the heart of the old town.

$$ Hotel San Gabriel has 22 pleasant rooms, a kind staff, public rooms filled with art and books, a cozy wine cellar, and a fine garden terrace. It's a large 1736 labyrinth of a townhouse, once the family's home, that's been converted into a characteristic hotel, marinated in history. If

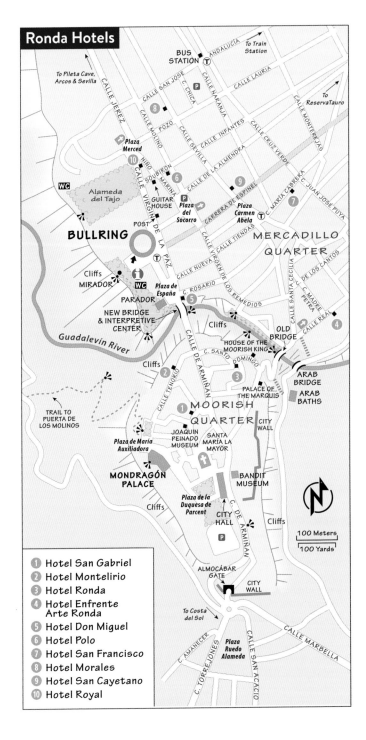

Ronda Hotels

To Pileta Cave,
Arcos & Sevilla

To Train
Station

To ReservaTauro

BUS STATION

Plaza Merced

WC

Alameda del Tajo

GUITAR HOUSE

Plaza del Socorro

Plaza Carmen Abela

MERCADILLO QUARTER

BULLRING

POST

Cliffs

MIRADOR

WC

PARADOR

Plaza de España

NEW BRIDGE & INTERPRETIVE CENTER

Guadalevín River

Cliffs

Cliffs

HOUSE OF THE MOORISH KING

OLD BRIDGE

ARAB BRIDGE

ARAB BATHS

PALACE OF THE MARQUIS

MOORISH QUARTER

CITY WALL

TRAIL TO PUERTA DE LOS MOLINOS

JOAQUIN PEINADO MUSEUM

SANTA MARÍA LA MAYOR

Plaza de María Auxiliadora

MONDRAGÓN PALACE

BANDIT MUSEUM

Cliffs

Plaza de la Duquesa de Parcent

CITY HALL

Cliffs

N

100 Meters
100 Yards

ALMOCÁBAR GATE

CITY WALL

To Costa del Sol

Plaza Ruedo Alameda

CALLE MARBELLA

1 Hotel San Gabriel
2 Hotel Montelirio
3 Hotel Ronda
4 Hotel Enfrente Arte Ronda
5 Hotel Don Miguel
6 Hotel Polo
7 Hotel San Francisco
8 Hotel Morales
9 Hotel San Cayetano
10 Hotel Royal

you're a cinephile, kick back in the charming TV room—with seats from Ronda's old theater and a collection of DVD classics—then head to the breakfast room to check out photos of big movie stars (and, ahem, a certain travel writer) who have stayed here (RS%, air-con, incognito elevator, Calle Marqués de Moctezuma 19 at Plaza del Gigante, tel. 952-190-392, www.hotelsangabriel.com, info@hotelsangabriel.com, family-run by siblings José Manuel and Ana).

$$$ Hotel Montelirio perches on the cliffs of the western side of the Moorish quarter with dramatic views of the valley and the new town. The former 17th-century palace of a count, it feels both traditional and plush with its 15 classically tasteful rooms (the view rooms are worth the splurge) and its elegant common areas (air-con, elevator, pool, sun deck, terrace dining, Tenorio 8, tel. 952-873-855, www.hotelmontelirio.com, recepcion@hotelmontelirio.com).

$ Hotel Ronda provides an interesting mix of minimalist and traditional Spanish decor in this refurbished mansion, which is both quiet and homey. Although its five rooms are without views, the small, lovely rooftop deck overlooks the town (air-con, Ruedo Doña Elvira 12, tel. 952-872-232, www.hotelronda.net, reservas@hotelronda.net, some English spoken by kind and gentle Sra. Nieves).

In the New Town
More convenient than charming (except the Hotel Enfrente Arte Ronda—in a class all its own), these hotels put you in the thriving new town.

$$ Hotel Enfrente Arte Ronda, on the edge of things a steep 10- to 15-minute walk below the heart of the new town, is relaxed and funky. The 12 rooms are spacious and exotically decorated. It features a sprawling maze of public spaces, a peaceful bamboo garden, small swimming pool, sauna, and terraces with sweeping countryside views. Guests can help themselves to free drinks from the self-sevice bar or have their feet nibbled for free by "Dr. Fish." This one-of-a-kind place is in all the guidebooks, so reserve early (includes buffet breakfast with home-baked bread, air-con, elevator, Calle Real 40, tel. 952-879-088, www.enfrentearte.com, reservations@enfrentearte.com).

$$ Hotel Don Miguel, facing the gorge next to the bridge, can seem like staying in a cave, but it couldn't be more central. Of its 30 sparse but comfortable rooms, 20 have gorgeous views. Street rooms come with a little noise (air-con, elevator, pay parking a block away, Plaza de España 4, tel. 952-877-722, www.hoteldonmiguel-ronda.com, reservas@dmiguel.com).

$ Hotel Polo is a boutique gem run by the Puya family in the heart of the new town. Each of its 36 bright and spacious rooms features a watercolor painted by Miguel Puya. Inviting common spaces like the social "Food Corner" and the vast roof-top terrace provide a tranquil respite and cool views (family rooms, air-con, elevator, honesty bar, pay parking, Padre Mariano Souvirón 8, tel. 952-872-447, www.hotelpolo.net, reservas@hotelpolo.net).

$ Hotel San Francisco offers 27 small, nicely decorated rooms and rooftop terrace a block off the main pedestrian street in the town center. Their public cafeteria doubles as the breakfast room (family rooms available, air-con, elevator, pay parking, María Cabrera 20, tel. 952-873-299, www.hotelsanfrancisco-ronda.com, recepcion@hotelsanfrancisco-ronda.com).

$ Hotel Morales has 18 simple but prim-and-proper rooms, and friendly Lola helps you feel right at home. Interior rooms can be a bit dark, so request to be streetside. There's little traffic at night (air-con, elevator, pay parking nearby, Sevilla 51, tel. 952-871-538, www.hotelmorales.es, reservas@hotelmorales.es).

$ Hotel San Cayetano puts you in the heart of the evening paseo. With 22 basic, traditional Mediterranean rooms, it provides easy access to recommended restaurants on a pedestrian offshoot of the main drag (air-con, elevator, pay parking nearby, Sevilla 16, tel. 952-161-212, www.hotelsancayetano.com, reservas@ hotelsancayetano.com).

¢ **Hotel Royal** has a dark reception hall but friendly staff and 29 clean, spacious, simple rooms—many on the main street that runs between the bullring and bridge. Thick glass keeps out most of the noise, while the tree-lined Alameda del Tajo park is just across the way (air-con, pay parking, Calle Virgen de la Paz 42, tel. 952-871-141, www.hotelroyalronda.es, hroyal@ ronda.net).

Transportation
Arriving and Departing
Note that some destinations are linked with Ronda by both bus and train. Direct bus service to other hill towns can be sparse (as few as one per day), and train service usually involves a transfer in Bobadilla. It's worth spending a few minutes in the bus or train station on arrival to compare schedules and plan your departure (or pick up timetables at the TI).

BY TRAIN
The small station has ticket windows, a train information desk, and a café, but no lockers (there's storage at the nearby bus station).

From the station, it's a 15-minute **walk** to the center: Exit the station, turn right onto Avenida de Andalucía, and walk to the large roundabout (you'll see the bus station on your right). Continue straight down the street (now called San José) until you reach its end at Calle Jerez. Turn left and walk downhill past a church and the Alameda del Tajo park. Keep going, passing the bullring, to reach the TI and the famous bridge.

From Ronda by Train to: **Algeciras** (5/ day, 1.5 hours), **Málaga** (1/day, 2 hours, 2 more with transfer in Bobadilla), **Sevilla** (4/day, 3 hours, transfer in Bobadilla, Córdoba, or Antequera), **Granada** (3/day, 3

hours, transfer to bus in Antequera due to AVE construction, buses will wait for you), **Córdoba** (2/day direct, 2 hours; 2 more with transfer in Antequera, 2 hours), **Madrid** (2/day direct, 4 hours; more with transfer in Antequera).

BY BUS
To get to the center from the bus station, leave the station walking to the right of the roundabout, then follow the directions for train travelers described above. Baggage storage is available. Bus info: Damas (www.damas-sa.es), Avanza (www.avanzabus.com), Portillo (http:// portillo.avanzabus.com), and Comes (www.tgcomes.es).

From Ronda by Bus to: **Algeciras** (1/ day, 3.5 hours, Comes), **La Línea/Gibraltar** (2/hour, 45 minutes, Comes), **Arcos** (2/day, 2 hours, Comes), **Grazalema** (2/ day, 1 hour, Damas), **Zahara** (2/day, Mon-Fri only, 45 minutes, Comes), **Sevilla** (7/day, 2.5 hours, fewer on weekends, Damas), **Málaga** (*directo* 15/day Mon-Fri, 8-10/day Sat-Sun, 2 hours, Damas), **Nerja** (4 hours, transfer in Málaga).

BY CAR
Street parking away from the center is often free. The handiest place for paid parking is the underground lot at Plaza del Socorro (one block from the bullring). Narrow lanes and tight turns can be challenging for even medium-sized vehicles, and some access is restricted for nonresidents. Be sure to get driving and parking instructions from your hotel.

JEREZ DE LA FRONTERA

With more than 200,000 people, Jerez de la Frontera is your typical big-city mix of industry and dusty concrete suburbs, but it has a lively old center and two claims to touristic fame: horses and sherry. Jerez is ideal for a noontime visit on a weekday. See the famous horses, sip some sherry, wander through the old quarter, and swagger out. For the most efficient visit if arriving by bus or train, taxi from the train station right to the Royal Andalusian School for the equestrian performance, then walk around the corner to Sandeman's for the next sherry tour.

Orientation

Thanks to its complicated medieval street plan, there is no easy way to feel oriented in Jerez—so ask for directions liberally.

Tourist Information

The helpful **TI** is on Plaza del Arenal (Mon-Fri 9:00-16:30, Sat-Sun 9:30-14:30, tel. 956-338-874, www.turismojerez.com).

Sights

▲▲ROYAL ANDALUSIAN SCHOOL OF EQUESTRIAN ART

If you're into horses, a performance of the Royal Andalusian School of Equestrian Art (Fundación Real Escuela Andaluza del Arte Ecuestre) is a must. Even if you're not, this is art like you've never seen.

Getting There: From the bus or train stations to the horses, it's about a €7 **taxi** ride. Taxis wait at the exit of the school for the return trip. One-way streets mean there is only one way to arrive by **car:** Follow signs to *Real Escuela de Arte Ecuestre*. Expect to make at least one wrong turn, so allow a little extra time. You'll find plenty of free parking behind the school.

EQUESTRIAN PERFORMANCES

This is an equestrian ballet with choreography, purely Spanish music, and costumes from the 19th century. The stern riders and their talented, obedient steeds prance, jump, hop on their hind legs, and do-si-do in time to the music.

The riders cue the horses with subtle dressage commands, either verbally or with body movements. You'll see both purebred Spanish horses (with long tails and good jumping ability) and the larger mixed breeds (with short tails and a walking—not prancing—gait). The horses must be three years old before their three-year training begins, and most performing horses are

Royal Andalusian School of Equestrian Art

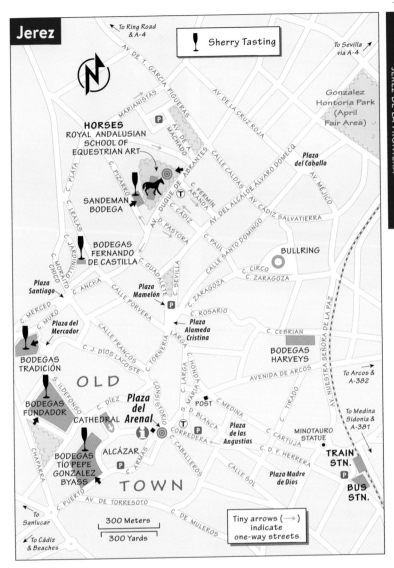

Jerez

Sherry Tasting

To Ring Road & A-4

To Sevilla via A-4

AV. DE T. GARCIA FIGUERAS

MARIANISTAS

HORSES
ROYAL ANDALUSIAN SCHOOL OF EQUESTRIAN ART

AV. DE LA CRUZ ROJA

Gonzalez Hontoria Park (April Fair Area)

Plaza del Caballo

C. PLATA

C. LEALAS

C. PIZARRO

C. JARDINILLO

C. MORCITO

DUQUE DE ABRANTES

C. FERMÍN ARANDA

C. CADIZ

AV. DE A. MACHADO

CALLE CALDAS

AV. DEL ALCALDE ALVARO DOMECQ

AV. CADIZ SALVATIERRA

AV. MÉJICO

SANDEMAN BODEGA

AV. P. PASTORA

C. PAUL

CALLE SANTO DOMINGO

BODEGAS FERNANDO DE CASTILLA

C. GUADALETE

C. SEVILLA

BULLRING

C. CIRCO

C. ZARAGOZA

Plaza Santiago

C. MERCED

C. MURO

C. ANCHA

CALLE PORVERA

Plaza Mamelón

C. ZARAGOZA

Plaza del Mercado

CALLE FRANCOS

C. J. DIOS LACOSTE

CALLE LARGA

TORNERIA

C. ROSARIO

Plaza Alameda Cristina

C. CEBRIAN

BODEGAS HARVEYS

BODEGAS TRADICIÓN

S. ILDEFONSO

O L D

C. DIEZ

CONSISTORIO

C. LARGA

MARIANON

AVENIDA DE ARCOS

To Arcos & A-382

AV. NUESTRA SEÑORA DE LA PAZ

BODEGAS FUNDADOR

CHAPARRA

CATHEDRAL

Plaza del Arenal

CORREDERA

D. BLANCA

POST

C. MEDINA

Plaza de las Angustias

C. TIRADO

C. CARTUJA

To Medina Sidonia & A-381

MINOTAURO STATUE

BODEGAS TÍO PEPE GONZALEZ BYASS

ALCÁZAR

C. ARMAS

C. CABALLEROS

C. D. F. HERRERA

CALLE SOL

TRAIN STN.

T O W N

C. PUERTO

AV. DE TORRESOTO

C. DE MULEROS

Plaza Madre de Dios

BUS STN.

To Sanlucar

To Cádiz & Beaches

300 Meters
300 Yards

Tiny arrows (→) indicate one-way streets

male (stallions or geldings), since mixing the sexes brings problems.

The equestrian school is a university. Professors often team with students and evaluate their performance during the show. Tightly fitted mushroom hats are decorated with different stripes to show each rider's level.

Cost and Hours: €21 general seating, €27 "preference" seating; 1.5-hour show at 12:00 every Thu, March-Dec also on Tue, Aug-Oct also on Fri, additional Sat show once per month year-round; tel. 956-318-008, best to purchase in advance online at www.realescuela.org. General seating is fine; some "preference" seats are too

Equestrian performance

Sherry bodega tour

close for good overall views. The show explanations are in Spanish.

TRAINING SESSIONS

The public can get a sneak preview at training sessions on nonperformance days. Afterward, you can take a 1.5-hour guided tour of the stables, horses, multimedia and carriage museums, tack room, gardens, and horse health center. Sip sherry in the arena's bar to complete this Jerez experience.

Cost and Hours: €11, Mon 10:00-14:00 plus Wed and Fri Nov-July and Tue mid-Dec-Feb, last entry at 12:00, tours depart when a large enough group forms. A shorter €6.50 tour covers only the museums and saddlery.

▲▲SHERRY BODEGA TOURS

Spain produces more than 10 million gallons per year of the fortified wine known as sherry. The name comes from English attempts to pronounce Jerez. Your tourist map of Jerez is speckled with *venencia* symbols, each representing a sherry bodega that offers tours and tasting.

(*Venencias* are specially designed ladles for dipping inside the sherry barrel.) For all the bodegas, it's smart to confirm tour times before you go, as schedules can be changeable.

Just around the corner from the equestrian school is the venerable Sandeman winery, founded in 1790 and the longtime drink of English royalty. This tour is the aficionado's choice for its knowledgeable guides and their quality explanations of the process. Each stage is explained in detail (€8 for regular sherries, €15 for rare sherries, €8 adds tapas to the tasting, tour/tasting lasts 1-1.5 hours; English tours Mon, Wed, and Fri at 11:30, 12:30, and 13:30 plus April-Oct also at 14:30; Tue and Thu at 10:30, 12:00, 13:00, and 14:15; Sat by appointment only, closed Sun; fewer tours in winter; reservations not required, tel. 675-647-177, www.sandeman.com).

Rick's Tip: *It looks tempting, but* **don't bother with** *Jerez's gutted* **Alcázar castle.**

Transportation
Arriving and Departing

The bus and train stations are located side by side, near the Plaza del Minotauro (with enormous headless statue). Unfortunately, you can't store luggage at either one.

Rick's Tip: *You can* **stow bags for free** *in the Royal Andalusian School's coatroom if you attend their equestrian performance, but only for the duration of the show.*

Cheap and easy **taxis** wait in front of the train station (€5 to TI; about €7 to the horses). Otherwise, it's a 20-minute **walk** from the stations to the center of town and the TI: Angle across the brick plaza (in front of the stations, with two black smokestacks) to find Calle Diego Fernández de Herrera. Follow this street for several blocks until you reach a little square (Plaza de las Angustias). Leave the square at the far left side down Calle Corredera. In a few minutes you'll arrive at Plaza del Arenal (ringed with palm trees, with a large fountain in the center)—the TI is in the arcaded building across the plaza.

BY BUS

Jerez's bus station is shared by multiple bus companies, each with its own schedule (Damas, www.damas-sa.es; Comes, www.tgcomes.es; Autocares Valenzuela, www.grupovalenzuela.com). Shop around for the best departure time and most direct route. While here, clarify routes for any further bus travel you may be doing in Andalucía—especially if you're going through Arcos de la Frontera, where the ticket office is often closed. Also try Movelia.es for bus schedules and routes.

From Jerez by Bus to: Arcos (4/day, 40 minutes), **Ronda** (2/day, 2.5-3 hours), **La Línea/Gibraltar** (1/day, 2.5 hours), **Sevilla** (hourly, 1-1.5 hours), **Granada** (1/day, 4.5 hours).

BY TRAIN

From Jerez by Train to: Sevilla (hourly, 1 hour), **Madrid** (3-4/day direct, 4 hours; nearly hourly with change in Sevilla, 4 hours), **Barcelona** (nearly hourly, 7-8 hours, all with change in Sevilla and/or Madrid). Train info: tel. 912-320-320, www.renfe.com.

BY CAR

Driving in Jerez can be frustrating. The outskirts are filled with an almost endless series of roundabouts. Continue straight through each one (you'll see a rail bridge) and follow traffic and signs to *Centro Ciudad*. The circuitous route will ultimately take you into Plaza Alameda Cristina; park in one of the many underground garages and catch a cab or walk.

Sevilla

Flamboyant Sevilla (seh-VEE-yah) thrums with flamenco music, sizzles in the summer heat, and pulses with passion. As the capital of Andalucía, Sevilla offers a sampler of every Spanish icon, from sherry to matadors to Moorish heritage to flower-draped whitewashed lanes.

As the gateway to the New World in the 1500s, Sevilla boomed when Spain did. Explorers Amerigo Vespucci and Ferdinand Magellan sailed from its great river harbor, discovering new trade routes and abundant sources of gold, silver, cocoa, and tobacco. By the 1600s, Sevilla had become Spain's largest and wealthiest city, home to artists like Diego Velázquez and Bartolomé Murillo, who made it a cultural center. But by the 1700s, Sevilla's Golden Age was ending, as trade routes shifted, the harbor silted up, and the Spanish empire crumbled.

Today, Spain's fourth-largest city (pop. 700,000) buzzes with guitars, castanets, and street life. It's home to the world's largest Gothic cathedral, and the Alcázar is a fantastic royal palace and garden, ornamented with Islamic flair. But the real magic is the city itself, with its tangled former Jewish Quarter, riveting flamenco shows, thriving bars, and teeming evening paseo. As James Michener wrote, "Sevilla doesn't *have* ambience, it *is* ambience."

SEVILLA IN 2 DAYS

Day 1: Take Concepción Delgado's city walk. In the afternoon, tour the cathedral (book in advance) and climb its Giralda bell tower. With extra time, visit another sight, such as the Hospital de la Caridad nearby.

On any evening: Take my Barrio Santa Cruz neighborhood walk (best about 18:00). Attend a flamenco concert, show, or class. Stroll along the northern bank of the Guadalquivir River, or cross the river to explore the Triana neighborhood and savor cityscape views. Stay out late at least once to appreciate Sevilla on a warm night—one of its major charms.

Day 2: Tour the Royal Alcázar in the morning (before 13:30 at the latest, if you want to see the Upper Royal Apartments—must reserve entry time online). In the afternoon, take your pick among the Bullfight Museum, Flamenco Dance Museum, Museo de Bellas Artes (Fine Arts Museum), suggested Shopping Paseo, or, farther from the center, the Basílica de la Macarena.

Day Trip: For Moorish sights, stay another day to make a quick trip to Cór-

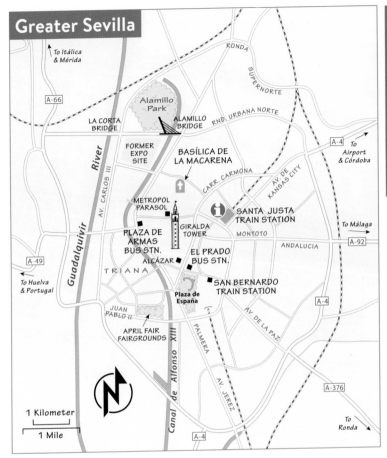

Greater Sevilla

To Itálica & Mérida

RONDA

SUPER NORTE

A-66

La Corta Bridge

Alamillo Park

Alamillo Bridge

RND. URBANA NORTE

A-4 To Airport & Córdoba

FORMER EXPO SITE

BASÍLICA DE LA MACARENA

CARR. CARMONA

AV. DE KANSAS CITY

River

AV. CARLOS III

METROPOL PARASOL

SANTA JUSTA TRAIN STATION

To Málaga

GIRALDA TOWER

MONTOTO

A-92

Guadalquivir

PLAZA DE ARMAS BUS STN.

ANDALUCIA

A-49

ALCÁZAR

EL PRADO BUS STN.

To Huelva & Portugal

TRIANA

SAN BERNARDO TRAIN STATION

A-4

Plaza de España

JUAN PABLO II

AV. DE LA PAZ

APRIL FAIR FAIRGROUNDS

Canal de Alfonso XIII

PALMERA

1 Kilometer

AV. JEREZ

A-376

1 Mile

A-4

To Ronda

doba (45 minutes on AVE high-speed train).

ORIENTATION

For the tourist, this big city is small. The bull's-eye on your map should be the cathedral and its Giralda bell tower, which can be seen from all over town. Nearby are Sevilla's other major sights, the Alcázar (palace and gardens) and the lively Barrio Santa Cruz district. The central north-south pedestrian boulevard, Avenida de la Constitución, stretches north a few blocks to Plaza Nueva, gateway to the shopping district. A few blocks

west of the cathedral are the bullring and the Guadalquivir River, while Plaza de España is a few blocks south. The colorful Triana neighborhood, on the west bank of the Guadalquivir River, has a thriving market and plenty of tapas bars, but no major tourist sights. While most sights are within walking distance, don't hesitate to hop in a taxi to avoid a long, hot walk (they are plentiful and cheap).

Tourist Information

Sevilla has tourist offices at **Santa Justa train station** (just inside the main entrance, Mon-Sat 9:00-19:30, Sun 9:30-15:00, tel. 954-782-002), near the cathedral on **Plaza**

SEVILLA AT A GLANCE

▲▲▲**Flamenco** Flamboyant, riveting music-and-dance performances, offered at clubs throughout town. See page 373.

▲▲**Sevilla Cathedral** The world's largest Gothic church, with Columbus' tomb, and climbable bell tower. **Hours:** Tue-Sat 11:00-17:00, Sun 14:30-18:00, Mon 10:30-16:00 (open later July-Aug). See page 345.

▲▲**Royal Alcázar** Palace built by the Moors in the 10th century, revamped in the 14th century, and still serving as royal digs. **Hours:** Daily 9:30-19:00, Oct-March until 17:00. See page 352.

▲▲**Hospital de la Caridad** Former charity hospital (funded by likely inspiration for Don Juan) with gorgeously decorated chapel. **Hours:** Daily 10:30-19:30. See page 360.

▲▲**Church of the Savior** Sevilla's second-biggest church and home to some of its most beloved statues used for religious festivals. **Hours:** Mon-Sat 11:00-18:00 (July-Aug from 10:00), Sun 15:00-19:30. See page 362.

▲▲**Basílica de la Macarena** Church and museum with much-venerated Weeping Virgin statue and Holy Week floats. **Hours:** daily 9:00-14:00 & 18:00-21:30, shorter evening hours mid-Sept-May. See page 365.

▲▲**Triana** Energetic, colorful neighborhood on the west bank of the river. See page 367.

▲▲**Bullfight Museum** Guided tour of the bullring and its museum. **Hours:** Daily 9:30-21:00, Nov-March until 19:00, until 15:00 on fight days. See page 370.

▲▲**Evening Paseo** Locals strolling in various zones around the city. **Hours:** Spring through fall; best paseo scene 18:00-20:00, until very late in summer. See page 373.

▲**Flamenco Dance Museum** High-tech museum on the history and art of flamenco. **Hours:** Daily 10:00-19:00. See page 362.

▲**Museo de Bellas Artes** Andalucía's top paintings, including works by Murillo and Zurbarán. **Hours:** Tue-Sat 9:00-20:00, until 15:00 on Sun and in summer, closed Mon year-round. See page 362.

▲**Bullfights** Some of Spain's best bullfighting, held at Sevilla's arena. **Hours:** Fights generally at 18:30 on most Sundays in May and June, on Easter and Corpus Christi, and daily through the April Fair and in late September. See page 369.

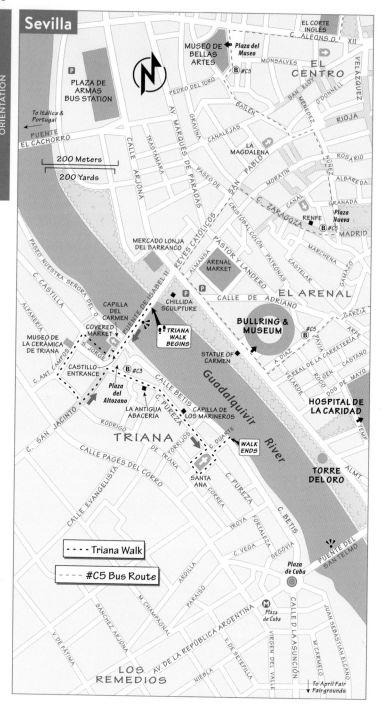

Sevilla

EL CORTE INGLÉS

C. ALFONSO XII

MUSEO DE BELLAS ARTES

Plaza del Museo

MONSALVES

EL CENTRO

B #C5

VELÁZQUEZ

PLAZA DE ARMAS BUS STATION

PEDRO DEL TORO

SAN ELOY

O'DONNELL

SAN MENENDEZ

RIOJA

To Itálica & Portugal

PUENTE EL CACHORRO

CALLE ARJONA

TRASTÁMARA

AV. MARQUÉS DE PARADAS

GRAVINA

CANALEJAS

BAILÉN

LA MAGDALENA

SAN PABLO

MORATÍN

ROSARIO

NÚÑEZ

ALBAREDA

200 Meters

200 Yards

C. CASTILLA

PASEO NUESTRA SEÑORA DEL O

ALFARERIA

C. ANT. CAMPOS

C. SAN JACINTO

PASEO DE CRISTÓBAL COLÓN

REYES CATÓLICOS

MERCADO LONJA DEL BARRANCO

PASTOR Y LANDERO

ALMANSA

ARENAL MARKET

CASTELAR

C. ZARAGOZA

CANAL

GRANADA

RENFE

Plaza Nueva

B #C5

MADRID

MARCHENA

GAMAZO

EL ARENAL

CALLE DE ADRIANO

CHILLIDA SCULPTURE

CAPILLA DEL CARMEN

COVERED MARKET

PUENTE DE ISABEL II

S. JORGE

TRIANA WALK BEGINS

BULLRING & MUSEUM

GARCÍA

#C5

B

ARFE

PAVIA

MUSEO DE LA CERÁMICA DE TRIANA

CASTILLO ENTRANCE

B #C5

Plaza del Altozano

CALLE BETIS

C. PUREZA

STATUE OF CARMEN

A. DIAZ

REAL DE LA CARRETERIA

VELARDE

RODO

GEN. CASTAÑO

DOS DE MAYO

HOSPITAL DE LA CARIDAD

TEMP.

LA ANTIGUA ABACERÍA

TRIANA

RODRIGO DE TRIANA

CAPILLA DE LOS MARINEROS

C. DUARTE

WALK ENDS

Guadalquivir River

TORRE DEL ORO

ALMT.

CALLE PAGÉS DEL CORRO

SANTA ANA

C. PUREZA

CORREA

C. SAN JACINTO

CALLE EVANGELISTA

TROYA

FORTALEZA

C. VEGA

SEGOVIA

C. BETIS

PUENTE DE SAN TELMO

SÁNCHEZ ARJONA

V. DE FÁTIMA

M. CHAMPAGNAT

PARAÍSO

ARDILLA

AV. DE LA REPÚBLICA ARGENTINA

NIEBLA

V. DE SETEFILLA

VIRGEN DEL VALLE

CALLE D. LA ASUNCIÓN

Plaza de Cuba

Plaza de Cuba

JUAN SEBASTIÁN ELCANO

M. CARMELO

LOS REMEDIOS

To April Fair Fairgrounds

- - - - Triana Walk

- - - - #C5 Bus Route

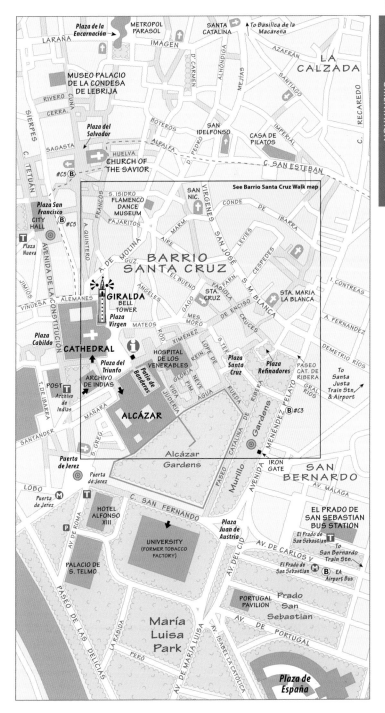

Plaza de la Encarnación

METROPOL PARASOL

LARAÑA

IMAGEN

SANTA CATALINA

To Basílica de la Macarena

D.ª CARMEN

AZAFRÁN

LA CALZADA

ALHÓNDIGA

MEJÍAS

SANTIAGO

C. RECAREDO

MUSEO PALACIO DE LA CONDESA DE LEBRIJA

RIVERO

CERRA.

CUNA

SIERPES

SAGASTA

C. TETUÁN

BOTEROS

SAN IDELFONSO

IMPERIAL

CASA DE PILATOS

Plaza del Salvador

ALFALFA

D. PEDRO

HUELVA

CHURCH OF THE SAVIOR

C. SAN ESTEBAN

#C5 B

Plaza San Francisco

CITY HALL

B #C5

A. QUINTERO

S. ISIDRO

FLAMENCO DANCE MUSEUM

PAJARITOS

SAN NIC.

VÍRGENES

CONDE

DE

IBARRA

Plaza Nueva

T

AVENIDA DE LA CONSTITUCIÓN

A. DE MOLINA

GUZ.

MARM.

AIRE

SAN JOSÉ

LEVIES

CÉSPEDES

JIMIOS

VINUESA.

ALEMANES

BARRIO SANTA CRUZ

EL BUENO

GAGO

FABIOLA

S. M. BLANCA

I. CONTRERAS

Plaza Cabildo

GIRALDA BELL TOWER

Plaza Virgen

ÁNGELES

STA. CRUZ

STA. MARÍA LA BLANCA

A. FERNÁNDEZ

MATEOS

MES. MORO

DE ENCISO

CATHEDRAL

ROD.

JIMÉNEZ

CRUCES

DEMETRIO RÍOS

Plaza del Triunfo

HOSPITAL DE LOS VENERABLES

REINE DE

S. TER.

Plaza Santa Cruz

Plaza Refinadores

PASEO CAT. DE RIBERA

To Santa Justa Train Stn. & Airport

POST

ARCHIVO DE INDIAS

T

T. DE IBARRA

Archivo de Indias

Patio de Banderas

GLORIA

PIM.

VIDA

JUDERÍA

AGUA

NEVE

RUEDA

DE RIBERA

GRAL. RÍOS

MENÉNDEZ PELAYO

B #C3

SANTANDER

MAÑARA

S. GREG.

ALCÁZAR

Puerta de Jerez

Puerta de Jerez

LOBO

M

Puerta de Jerez

Alcázar Gardens

Gardens

IRON GATE

SAN BERNARDO

AV. MÁLAGA

Alcázar Gardens

AV. DE ROMA

P

HOTEL ALFONSO XIII

C. SAN FERNANDO

Plaza Juan de Austria

EL PRADO DE SAN SEBASTIAN BUS STATION

El Prado de San Sebastián

T

To San Bernardo Train Stn.

PALACIO DE S. TELMO

UNIVERSITY (FORMER TOBACCO FACTORY)

AV. DEL CID

AV. DE CARLOS V

El Prado de San Sebastián

M

B

EA Airport Bus

PASEO DE LAS DELICIAS

LA RÁBIDA

PERÓ

AV. DE MARÍA LUISA

AV. ISABEL LA CATÓLICA

PORTUGAL PAVILION

Prado San Sebastian

AV. DE PORTUGAL

María Luisa Park

Plaza de España

See Barrio Santa Cruz Walk map

del Triunfo (Mon-Fri 9:00-19:30, Sat-Sun from 9:30, tel. 954-210-005), and at the airport (same hours as station TI).

At any TI, ask for the English-language magazine *The Tourist* (also available at www.thetouristsevilla.com) and a current listing of sights with opening times. Helpful websites are www.turismosevilla.org and www.andalucia.org. Steer clear of the "visitors centers" on Avenida de la Constitución and at Santa Justa train station (overlooking tracks 6-7), which are private enterprises.

Helpful Hints

Festivals: Sevilla's peak season is April and May, and it has two one-week spring festival periods when the city is packed: Holy Week and April Fair. Book rooms well in advance for these festival times. Prices can go sky-high and many hotels have four-night minimums.

Rosemary Scam: In the city center—especially near the cathedral—you may encounter women thrusting sprigs of rosemary into the hands of passersby, grunting, *"Toma! Es un regalo!"* ("Take it! It's a gift!"). The twig is free...and then they grab your hand and read your fortune for a tip. Coins are "bad luck," so the minimum payment they'll accept is €5. You don't need to take their demands seriously—don't make eye contact, don't accept a sprig, and say firmly but politely, *"No, gracias."*

Laundry: Lavandería Tintorería Roma offers quick and economical drop-off service (Mon-Fri 10:00-14:00 & 17:30-20:30, Sat 10:00-14:00, closed Sun, a few blocks west of the cathedral at Calle Arfe 22, tel. 954-210-535, shown on "Sevilla Hotels" map, later).

Tours

SEVILLA WALKING TOURS

Concepción Delgado, an enthusiastic teacher, takes small groups on English-only walks. Although you can just show up, it's smart to confirm departure times and reserve a spot (4-person minimum, none on Sun or holidays, tel. 902-158-226, www.sevillawalkingtours.com, info@sevillawalkingtours.com). Her fine two-hour **City Walk** skips the famous monuments and shares intimate insights the average visitor misses (€15/person, Mon-Sat at 10:30, check website for schedule in Dec-Feb and Aug, meet at statue in Plaza Nueva). Concepción also offers 75-minute visits to the **cathedral** (€12 plus admission) and the **Alcázar** (€26 including admission, must book in advance)—they're designed to fit efficiently after the City Walk (€2 discount if combined; cathedral tours—Mon, Wed, and Fri; Alcázar tours—Tue, Thu, and Sat; meet at 13:00 at the statue in Plaza del Triunfo).

ALL SEVILLA GUIDED TOURS

This group of three licensed guides (Susana, Jorge, and Elena) offers quality private tours (€160/3 hours). They also run a Monuments Tour covering the Sevilla basics: cathedral, Alcázar, and Barrio Santa Cruz (€25/person plus admissions, Mon-Sat at 14:00, 2.5 hours, leaves from Plaza del Triunfo, mobile 606-217-194; www.allsevillaguides.com, info@allsevillaguides.com).

REALLY DISCOVER SEVILLE

Sevillian Luis Salas is a smart local guide offering private tours of both the big monuments and the hidden gems (€155/2.5 hours, €200/3.5 hours, tel. 628-946-645, www.reallydiscover.com, luissalas@reallydiscover.com).

HORSE-AND-BUGGY TOURS

A carriage ride is a classic, popular way to survey the city and a relaxing way to enjoy María Luisa Park (€45 for a 45-minute clip-clop, much more during Holy Week and the April Fair, find a likable English-speaking driver for better narration). Look for rigs at Plaza de América, Plaza del Triunfo, the Torre del Oro, the Alfonso XIII Hotel, and Plaza de España.

Holy Week (Semana Santa)

Holy Week—the week between Palm Sunday and Easter—is a major holiday throughout the Christian world, but nowhere is it celebrated with as much fervor as in Sevilla.

Holy Week is all about the events of the Passion of Jesus Christ: his entry into Jerusalem, his betrayal by Judas and arrest, his crucifixion, and his resurrection. Each day throughout the week, 60 neighborhood groups parade from their churches to the cathedral with floats depicting some aspect of the Passion story. (This amazing event was featured in my *Rick Steves' European Easter* public television special, viewable and free at www.ricksteves.com/watch-read-listen.)

Visitors pour into town, grandstands are erected along parade routes, and TV stations anxiously monitor the weather report. (The floats are so delicate that rain can force the processions to be called off—a crushing disappointment.) By midafternoon, thousands line the streets and the parade begins. First comes a line of "penitents" carrying a big cross, candles, and incense. They perform their penance publicly but anonymously, their identities obscured by pointy, hooded robes (the garb has been worn for centuries—long before it became associated with racism in the American South). Some processions are silent, but others are accompanied by beating drums, brass bands, or wailing singers.

A hush falls over the crowd as the floats approach. First comes a Passion float, showing Christ in some stage of the drama—being whipped, appearing before Pilate, or carrying the cross to his execution. More penitents follow—with hundreds or even thousands of participants, a procession can stretch out over a half-mile. All this sets the stage for the finale—typically a float of the Virgin Mary, who represents the hope of resurrection.

The elaborate floats feature carved wooden religious sculptures, most embellished with gold leaf and silverwork. They can be adorned with fresh flowers, rows of candles, and even jewelry on loan from the congregation. Each float is carried by 30 to 50 men, who labor unseen—although you might catch a glimpse of their shuffling feet. The bearers wear turban-like headbands to protect their heads and necks from the crushing weight (the floats can weigh as much as three tons). Two "shifts" of float carriers rotate every 20 minutes.

As the procession nears the cathedral, many pass through the square called La Campana, south along Calle Sierpes, and through Plaza de San Francisco. It's a remarkable spectacle, but it's extremely crowded. Parade routes can block your sightseeing for hours. If you do find a procession blocking your way, look for a crossing point marked by a red-painted fence, or ask a guard. Even if all you care about on Easter is a chocolate-bearing bunny, the intense devotion of the Andalusian people during their Holy Week traditions is an inspiration to behold.

Rick's Tip: *Sevilla is an extremely* **biker-friendly city,** *with designated bike lanes and a public bike-sharing program. Ask the TI about this and other bicycle-rental options.*

BARRIO SANTA CRUZ WALK

The soul of Sevilla is best found in the narrow lanes of its oldest quarter—the Barrio Santa Cruz. Of Sevilla's once-thriving Jewish Quarter, only the tangled street plan and a wistful Old World ambience survive. This classy maze of lanes (too tight for most cars), small plazas, tile-covered patios, and whitewashed houses with wrought-iron latticework draped in flowers is a great refuge from the summer heat and bustle of Sevilla. The streets are narrow—some with buildings so close they're called "kissing lanes." A happy result of the narrowness is shade: Locals claim the Barrio Santa Cruz is three degrees cooler than the rest of the city.

When to Go: Tour groups often trample the *barrio*'s charm in the morning. I find that early evening—around 18:00—is the ideal time to explore the quarter.

❷ Self-Guided Walk

• *Start in the square in front of the cathedral, at the lantern-decked fountain in the middle that dates from Expo '29.*

❶ Plaza de la Virgen de los Reyes

Do a 360-degree spin and take in some of Sevilla's signature sights. There's the gangly cathedral with its soaring Giralda bell tower. To the right is the ornate red Archbishop's Palace, a center of power since Christians first conquered the city from the Moors in 1248. The next building is almost a cliché of 19th-century (and now government-protected) Sevillian architecture—whitewashed with goldenrod trim and ironwork balconies. The street stretching away from the cathedral is lined with another Sevillian trademark—tapas bars. Continuing your spin, there's a row of Sevilla's signature orange trees. Hiding in the orange trees is a statue of Pope John Paul II, who performed Mass here before a half-million faithful Sevillians during a 1982 visit. Finally, you return to the Giralda bell tower.

The Giralda encapsulates Sevilla's 2,000-year history. The large blocks that form the very bottom of the tower date from when Sevilla was a Roman city. The tower's main trunk, with its Islamic patterns and keyhole arches, was built by the Moors (with bricks made of mud from the river) as a call-to-prayer tower for a mosque. The top (16th-century Renaissance), with its bells and weathervane figure representing Faith, was added after Christians reconquered Sevilla, tore down the mosque, built the sprawling cathedral—and kept the minaret as their bell tower.

This square is dedicated to that Christian reconquest, and to the Virgin Mary. Turn 90 degrees to the left as you face the cathedral and find (hiding behind the orange trees) the Virgin of the Kings (see her blue-and-gold tiled plaque on the white wall). This is one of the many different versions of Mary you'll see around town—some smiling, some weeping, some triumphant—each appealing to a different type of worshipper.

• *Facing the cathedral, turn left and walk toward the next square to find some...*

❷ Nun Goodies

The white building on your left was an Augustinian convent. Step inside the door at #3 to meet (but not see) a cloistered nun behind a fancy *torno* (a lazy Susan the nuns spin to sell their goods while staying hidden). The sisters raise money by selling rosaries, prayer books, and communion wafers (*tabletas*—bland, but like sin-free cookies). Consider buying something here just as a donation. The sisters, who speak only Spanish, have a sense of humor—

Barrio Santa Cruz Walk

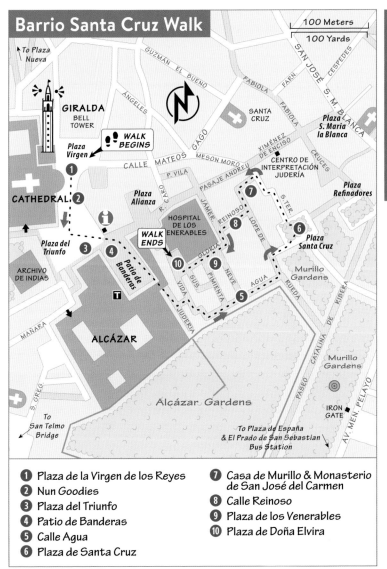

1. Plaza de la Virgen de los Reyes
2. Nun Goodies
3. Plaza del Triunfo
4. Patio de Banderas
5. Calle Agua
6. Plaza de Santa Cruz
7. Casa de Murillo & Monasterio de San José del Carmen
8. Calle Reinoso
9. Plaza de los Venerables
10. Plaza de Doña Elvira

have fun practicing your Spanish with them (Mon-Sat 9:15-13:00 & 16:45-18:15, Sun 10:00-13:00).

• Step into the square marked with a statue of the Virgin atop a pillar. This is...

❸ Plaza del Triunfo

Bordered by three of Sevilla's most

important buildings—the cathedral, the walled Alcázar, and the Archivo General de Indias (filled with historic papers)—this place was the center of the action during the Golden Age of the 16th and 17th centuries. Businessmen from all over Europe gathered here to trade in the exotic goods pouring in from the New

World. That wealth produced a flowering of culture, including Sevilla's most beloved painter, Bartolomé Murillo, who is honored at the base of the pillar. The "Plaza of Triumph" is named for yet another Virgin statue atop a smaller pillar at the far end of the square. This Virgin helped the city miraculously "triumph" over the 1755 earthquake that destroyed Lisbon but only rattled Sevilla.

• *Pass through the arched opening in the Alcázar's spiky, crenellated wall. You'll emerge into a white-and-goldenrod courtyard called the...*

❹ Patio de Banderas

The Banderas Courtyard was part of the Alcázar, the Spanish king's residence when he was in town. This square was a military parade ground, and the barracks surrounding it housed the king's bodyguards. Before the Alcázar was the palace of the Christian king, it was the palace of the Muslim Moors who ruled Sevilla. Archaeologists found remains of this palace (as well as 2,000-year-old Roman ruins) beneath the courtyard.

Orange trees abound. Because they never lose their leaves, they provide constant shade. When they blossom (for three weeks in spring, usually in April), the aroma is heavenly.

Head for the far-left (downhill) corner of this square, do a 180, and enjoy the stunning view of the Giralda bell tower.

• *Exit the courtyard at this far-left corner, through the Judería arch. Go down the long, narrow passage still paved with its original herringbone brickwork. Emerging into the light, you'll be walking alongside the red Alcázar wall. Take the first left at the corner lamppost and you'll pass another gate. A gate here was locked each evening—at first to protect the Jewish community (when they were the privileged elite—bankers, merchants, tax collectors) and later during times of persecution to isolate them (until they were finally expelled in 1492). Passing the gate, go right, through a small square, and follow the long narrow alleyway called...*

Plaza de la Virgen de Los Reyes

❺ Calle Agua

This narrow lane is typical of the *barrio*'s tight quarters, born when the entire Jewish community was forced into a small segregated ghetto. As you walk, on your right is one of the older walls of Sevilla, dating back to Moorish times. Glancing to the left, peek through iron gates for occasional glimpses of the flower-smothered patios of restaurants and exclusive private residences (sometimes open for viewing).

The plaque above and to the left of #1 remembers Washington Irving. He and Romantic novelists, poets, and painters of his era inspired early travelers and popularized the Grand Tour. Aristocrats back in the 19th century had their favorite stops as they gallivanted around Europe, and Sevilla—with its operettas (like *Carmen*), bullfighting, and flamenco—was hard to resist.

Emerging at the end of the street, turn around and look back at the openings of two old pipes built into the wall. These 12th-century Moorish pipes once carried fresh spring water to the Alcázar. They were part of a 10-mile-long aqueduct system that was originally built by the ancient Romans and expanded by the Moors, serving some parts of Sevilla until the 1600s. You're standing at an entrance into the pleasant Murillo Gardens (through the iron gate), formerly the fruit-and-vegetable gardens for the Alcázar.

• *Don't enter the gardens now, but instead cross the square diagonally, and continue 20 yards down a lane to the...*

🅐 *Patio de Banderas*

🅑 *Washington Irving plaque on Calle Agua*

🅒 *Calle Reinoso*

🅓 *Side street off Plaza de la Alianza*

❻ Plaza de Santa Cruz

Arguably the heart of today's *barrio*, this pleasant square encapsulates the history of the neighborhood. In early medieval times, it was the *Judería*, with a synagogue standing where the garden is today. When the Jews were rousted in the 1391 pogrom, the synagogue was demolished, and a Christian church was built on the spot (the Church of Santa Cruz). It was the neighborhood church of the Sevillian painter Bartolomé Murillo (and later

his burial site). But when the French (under Napoleon) invaded, the church was demolished. A fine 17th-century iron cross in the center of the square now marks the former site of the church. This "holy cross" (*santa cruz*) has inspired similar-looking crosses still carried in Holy Week processions, and gave this former Jewish Quarter its Christian name.

• *Exit the square left of the French consulate, going uphill (north) on Calle Santa Teresa. After the bend in the road, find #8 (on the left).*

❼ Casa de Murillo and Monasterio de San José del Carmen

Sevilla's famous painter, Bartolomé Esteban Murillo, lived here in the 17th century. Born and raised in Sevilla, Murillo spent his final years here, soaking in the ambience of street life and reproducing it in his paintings. He also painted iconic versions of local saints, and took Sevilla's devotion to the Virgin to another level with his larger-than-life Immaculate Conceptions.

Directly across from Casa de Murillo is the enormous wooden doorway of the Monasterio de San José del Carmen. This convent was founded by the renowned mystic, St. Teresa of Ávila. Today, the Baroque convent keeps some of Teresa's artifacts and spiritual manuscripts, but it's closed to the public except for early morning Mass (Mon-Fri at 8:45 and Sun at 9:00).

• *Continue north on Calle Santa Teresa, then take the first left on Calle Lope de Rueda (just before the popular Las Teresas café). Here you enter a series of very narrow lanes. Take a left again, then right on...*

❽ Calle Reinoso

This street—so narrow that the buildings almost touch—is one of the *barrio's* "kissing lanes." A popular explanation suggests the buildings were so close together to provide maximum shade. But the history is

more complex than that: This labyrinthine street plan goes back to Moorish times, when this area was a tangled market.

• *Leaving the "kissing zone," just to the left, the street spills onto...*

❾ Plaza de los Venerables

This tiny square is another candidate for "heart of the *barrio*," as it captures the romantic ambience that inspired so many operettas in Sevilla (from *Don Giovanni* and *Carmen* to *The Barber of Seville* and *The Marriage of Figaro*). With its vibrant buildings and visitor-oriented businesses, it typifies the *barrio* today: traditional and touristy at the same time. The harmonious red-and-white Sevillian-Baroque Hospital de los Venerables (1675) was once a retirement home for old priests (the "venerables"). It's now a cultural foundation worth visiting for its ornate church and small but fine collection of Sevillian paintings (www.focus.abengoa.es).

• *Pass through the square. On Calle de Gloria is an interesting tile map of the Jewish Quarter. (Find yourself in the lower left, second row up, third tile from the left.) Now continue west on Calle de Gloria, where you'll soon emerge into...*

❿ Plaza de Doña Elvira

This square sums up our *barrio* walk. Shops sell work by local artisans, such as ceramics, embroidery, and fans. In the 19th century, aristocrats flocked here to see the supposed home of the legendary lady love of the legendary Don Juan. At night, with candlelight and Spanish guitars playing, this is indeed a romantic place to dine.

But the plaza we see today reflects the fate of much of the *barrio*. After the neighborhood's Jews were expelled in 1492, the area went into slow decline. By the early 1900s it was deserted and run down. Sevilla began an extensive urban renewal project, which culminated in the 1929 world's fair. They turned much of the *barrio*, including this plaza, into a showcase of Andalusian style. Architects renovated with traditional-style railings, tile work, orange trees, and other too-cute, Epcot-like adornments. The Barrio Santa Cruz may not be quite as old as it appears, but the new and improved version respects tradition while carrying the neighborhood's 800-year legacy into the future.

• *Our walk is over. To return to the area near the start of this walk, cross the plaza and head north along Calle Rodrigo Caro; keep going until you enter the large Plaza de la Alianza. From here, a narrow lane (Calle Joaquín Romero Murube) leads left back to the Alcázar.*

SIGHTS

▲▲SEVILLA CATHEDRAL

Sevilla's cathedral is the third-largest church in Europe (after St. Peter's at the Vatican in Rome and St. Paul's in London) and the largest Gothic church anywhere. When they ripped down a mosque of brick on this site in 1401, the Reconquista Christians vowed they'd build a cathedral so huge that "anyone who sees it will take us for madmen." When it was finished in

1528, it was indeed the world's biggest, and remained so for a century until St. Peter's came along. Even today, the descendants of those madmen proudly point to a *Guinness Book of Records* letter certifying, "Santa María de la Sede in Sevilla is the cathedral with the largest area."

Cost and Hours: €9 combo-ticket includes Giralda bell tower and entry to the Church of the Savior, Tue-Sat 11:00-17:00 (July-Aug until 18:00), Sun 14:30-18:00 (July-Aug 14:00-19:00), Mon 10:30-16:00; last entry to cathedral one hour before closing.

Information: Tel. 954-214-971, www.catedraldesevilla.es.

Rick's Tip: Buy your cathedral ticket online *(available starting three weeks in advance) or buy a combo-ticket at the Church of the Savior, then boldly walk to the front of the line to find the special entry for smart travelers.*

Tours: The €3 audioguide is excellent. Or consider joining Concepción Delgado's

Sevilla Cathedral

guided tour instead (see "Tours," earlier). The cathedral offers a 90-minute **guided rooftop visit** (€15, includes cathedral entrance, book online, English tours daily June-Sept at 10:30 and 18:00, Oct-May at 12:00 and 16:30, meet at west facade 15 minutes before tour. If you do this tour, you can skip the Giralda tower climb.

⊘ SELF-GUIDED TOUR

On this tour, we'll marvel at the vast interior, over-the-top altars, world-class art, a stuffed crocodile, and the final resting place of Christopher Columbus.

• *You'll enter the church at the south facade (closest to the Alcázar). But before you head inside, take time to circle clockwise around the exterior.*

❶ **Exterior:** Sevilla's cathedral has an odd exterior that is hard to fully appreciate. As the mosque was square and the cathedral was designed to entirely fill its footprint, the transepts don't show from the outside. And with no great square leading to the church, you hardly know where the front door is (it's on the west side). Today's tourists enter through the south facade, which is 19th-century Neo-Gothic and unfinished—notice the empty niches that never got their statues.

The west facade faces the trams, horses, and commotion of Avenida de la Constitución. The central door shows the Assumption of Mary, with the beloved Virgin rocketing up to heaven to be crowned by God with his triangular halo (reminding all of the Trinity). While this part wasn't finished until the 19th century, the side doors—with their red terra-cotta saints—date from the 15th century.

Continuing around the huge cathedral, at the next corner (across from Starbucks) you'll see animal-blood graffiti from 18th-century students celebrating their graduation—revealed in a recent cleaning project. On the north side, the Puerta del Perdón was once the entry to the mosque's courtyard. But, as with much of the Moorish-looking art in town,

it's now actually Christian—the two coats of arms are a giveaway.

• *Circle back to the south facade and enter the cathedral. You'll pass through the...*

❷ **Art Pavilion:** This room features paintings that once hung in the church. You'll likely see a few by Sevilla's 17th-century master, Bartolomé Murillo, including paintings of beloved local characters who'll crop up again on our tour. King (and saint) Ferdinand III—usually shown with sword, crown, globe, and ermine robe—is the man who took Sevilla from the Moors and made this church possible. Santa Justa and Santa Rufina—Sevilla's patron saints—represent the city's ongoing 2,000-year Christian tradition. They were killed in ancient Roman times for their Christian faith. Potters by trade, they're easy to identify by their palm branches (symbolic of their martyrdom), their pots (at their feet or in their hands), and the Giralda bell tower symbolizing the town they protect.

• *Now enter the actual church and take in the...*

❸ **View of the Nave:** The church is more than two acres, the size of an entire city block in downtown Manhattan. Measured by area, this is still the world's largest church. While most Gothic churches are long and tall, this nave is square and compressed. The pillars are massive. Like other Spanish churches, this nave is clogged in the middle by the huge rectangular enclosure called the choir.

• *Walk up the nave, past the choir, to the center of the church, where you can enjoy a view of the main altar. Look through the wrought-iron Renaissance grille at the...*

❹ **High Altar:** This dazzling 80-foot wall of gold covered with statues is considered the largest altarpiece ever made. Carved from walnut and chestnut, and blanketed by a staggering amount of gold leaf, it took three generations to complete (1481-1564). Its 44 scenes tell the story of Jesus and Mary—left to right, bottom to top. Focus on the main spine of scenes

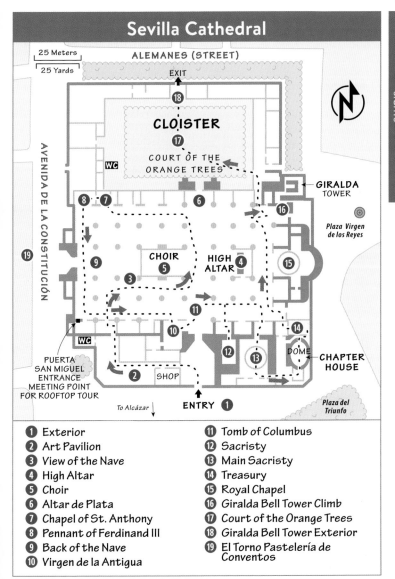

Sevilla Cathedral

| 25 Meters |
| 25 Yards |

ALEMANES (STREET)

EXIT

18

CLOISTER

17

COURT OF THE
ORANGE TREES

WC

GIRALDA
TOWER

8 7   6   16

Plaza Virgen
de los Reyes

AVENIDA DE LA CONSTITUCIÓN

19

CHOIR   HIGH
5   ALTAR   4

9   15

3

11

10

WC

PUERTA
SAN MIGUEL
ENTRANCE
MEETING POINT
FOR ROOFTOP TOUR

2   SHOP

14

12   13   DOME   CHAPTER
HOUSE

To Alcázar   ENTRY 1

Plaza del
Triunfo

1 Exterior
2 Art Pavilion
3 View of the Nave
4 High Altar
5 Choir
6 Altar de Plata
7 Chapel of St. Anthony
8 Pennant of Ferdinand III
9 Back of the Nave
10 Virgen de la Antigua

11 Tomb of Columbus
12 Sacristy
13 Main Sacristy
14 Treasury
15 Royal Chapel
16 Giralda Bell Tower Climb
17 Court of the Orange Trees
18 Giralda Bell Tower Exterior
19 El Torno Pastelería de
    Conventos

running up the center. At the bottom sits a 750-year-old silver statue of Mary and Baby Jesus, the cathedral's patroness since Christians first worshipped here in the old converted mosque. Above Mary, find the scene of Baby Jesus being born in a manger. Above that, Mary is assumed into heaven. Above that, a shirtless, flag-waving Jesus stands atop his coffin, having been resurrected. And above that, he ascends past his disciples into heaven. Look way up to the tippy-top, where a Crucifixion adorns the dizzying summit: That teeny figure is six feet tall.

Now crane your neck skyward to admire the elaborate **ceiling** with its intricate interlacing arches. Though done in the 16th-century Spanish Renaissance style, this stonework is only about 100 years old.

• *Turn around and check out the...*

❺ **Choir:** A choir area like this one—enclosed within the cathedral for more intimate services—is common in Spain and England, but rare in churches elsewhere. They're called choirs because singers were also allowed here to accompany services. This one features an organ of more than 7,000 pipes (played Mon-Fri at the 10:00 Mass, Sun at the 10:00 and 13:00 Mass, not in July-Aug, free entry for worshippers). The big, spinnable book holder in the middle of the room held giant hymnals—large enough for all to chant from in an age when there weren't enough books to go around.

• *Now turn 90 degrees to the right to take in the enormous silver sunburst of the...*

❻ **Altar de Plata:** This gleaming silver altarpiece is meant to resemble a monstrance—that's the ceremonial vessel that displays a communion wafer in the center. This one is gargantuan—it's made from more than 5,000 pounds of silver looted from Mexico by Spanish conquistadores in the 16th century. Amid the gleaming silver is a colorful statue of the Virgin.

• *From here, we'll tour some sights going counterclockwise around the church. Head left from the Altar de Plata, pass a few chapels where people come to pray to their chosen saint, and keep going to the last chapel on the right (with the big, marble baptismal font).*

❼ **Chapel of St. Anthony:** This chapel holds a special place in the hearts of Sevillians. Many were baptized in the big Renaissance-era font with the delightful carved angels dancing along its base. The chapel is also special for Murillo's tender painting of the *Vision of St. Anthony* (1656). The saint kneels in wonder as Baby Jesus comes down surrounded by a choir of angels. Anthony is the patron saint of lost things—so people come here

Bartolomé Murillo (1617-1682)

The son of a barber of Seville, Bartolomé Murillo (mur-EE-oh) got his start selling paintings meant for export to the frontier churches of the Americas. In his 20s, he became famous after he painted a series of saints for Sevilla's Franciscan monastery. By about 1650, Murillo's sugary, simple, and accessible religious style was spreading through Spain and beyond.

Murillo painted street kids with cute smiles and grimy faces, and radiant young Marías with Ivory-soap complexions and rapturous poses (Immaculate Conceptions). His paintings view the world through a soft-focus lens, wrapping everything in warm colors and soft light, with a touch (too much, for some) of sentimentality.

Murillo became a rich, popular family man, and the toast of Sevilla's high society. In 1664, his wife died, leaving him heartbroken, but his last 20 years were his most prolific. At age 65, Murillo died after falling off a scaffold while painting. His tomb is lost somewhere under the bricks of Plaza de Santa Cruz.

to pray for his help in finding jobs, car keys, and life partners. Above the *Vision is The Baptism of Christ,* also by Murillo. The stained glass dates from 1685, and by now you must know who the women are—Santa Justa and Santa Rufina, the third-century Roman sisters eaten by lions at Itálica because of their faith.

• *Exiting the rear of the chapel, look for the enormous glass display case with the...*

❽ **Pennant of Ferdinand III:** This 800-year-old battle flag shows the castle of Castile and the lion of León—the two kingdoms Ferdinand inherited, forming the nucleus of a unified, Christian Spain.

Ⓐ *High Altar*

Ⓑ *Nave and Plateresque ceiling*

Ⓒ *Tomb of Columbus*

Ⓓ *Virgen de la Antigua*

This pennant was raised here over the minaret of the mosque on November 23, 1248, as Christian forces finally expelled the Moors from Sevilla. For centuries afterward, it was paraded through the city on special days.

• *Continuing on, stand at the...*

❾ **Back of the Nave:** Face the choir and appreciate the ornate immensity of the church. On the floor before you (breaking the smooth surface) is the gravestone of Ferdinand Columbus (Hernando Colón), Christopher's second son. Having given the cathedral his collection of 6,000 precious books, he was rewarded with this prime burial spot. Behind you (behind an iron grille) is Murillo's *Guardian Angel* pointing to the light and showing an astonished child the way.

• *Continue counterclockwise, passing a massive wooden candlestick from 1560. That's old, but there's even older stuff here. Find a chapel (opposite the towering organ) with a big wall of statues whose centerpiece is a golden fresco of Mary and Baby Jesus.*

❿ **Virgen de la Antigua:** In this gilded fresco, the Virgin delicately holds a rose while the Christ Child holds a bird. It's some of the oldest art here (from the 1300s), even older than the cathedral itself. This chapel was once the site of the mosque's mihrab—the horseshoe-shaped prayer niche that points toward Mecca. When Christians moved in (1248), they initially used the mosque for their church services, covering the mihrab with this Virgin. The mosque served as a church for about 120 years—until it was completely torn down and replaced by today's cathedral. But the Virgin stayed, thanks to her beauty and her role as protector of sailors—crucial in this port city.

• *Just past the Virgen de la Antigua chapel is the...*

⓫ **Tomb of Columbus:** It's appropriate that Columbus is buried here. His 1492 voyage departed just 50 miles away, and the port of Sevilla became the exclusive entry point for all the New World plunder that made Spain rich. Columbus' pallbearers represent the traditional kingdoms that formed the core of Spain: Castile, Aragon, León, and Navarre. The last kingdom, Granada, is also represented: Notice how Señor León's pike is stabbing a pomegranate, the symbol of Granada—the last Moorish-ruled city to succumb to the Reconquista in that momentous year of 1492.

Columbus didn't just travel a lot while alive—he even kept it up posthumously. He died in 1506 in northwestern Spain (in Valladolid) where he was also buried. His remains were then moved to a monastery here in Sevilla, then to what's now the Dominican Republic (as he'd requested), then to Cuba. Finally—when Cuba gained independence from Spain in 1902—his remains sailed home again to Sevilla. After all that, are these really his remains? In 2006, a DNA test matched the bones of his son (buried just a few steps from here), giving Sevillians some evidence to substantiate their proud claim.

Columbus' tomb stands, appropriately, at the church entrance reserved for pilgrims, near a 1584 mural of St. Christopher, patron saint of travelers. The clock above has been ticking since 1788.

• *From here, our tour focuses on some of the artistic treasures of this rich church. For centuries, the faithful have donated their time and money to beautify their cathedral. The next chapel is the...*

⓬ **Sacristy:** This space is where the priests get ready each morning before Mass. The Goya painting above the altar was specifically painted for this room, and it features our old friends Justa and Rufina. Here they're bathed in a heavenly light, triumphing over a broken pagan statue, while the lion who was supposed to attack meekly licks their toes.

• *Two chapels farther along is the entrance to the...*

⓭ **Main Sacristy:** Marvel at the ornate, 16th-century dome of the main room, a grand souvenir from Sevilla's Golden

Age. The intricate masonry, called Plateresque, resembles lacy silverwork. God is way up in the cupola. The three layers of figures below him show the heavenly host; relatives in purgatory—hands folded in prayer—looking to heaven in hope of help; and the wretched in hell, including naked sinners engulfed in flames and teased cruelly by pitchfork-wielding monsters. Dominating the room is a nearly 1,000-pound, silver-plated monstrance used to parade the holy host through town during Corpus Christi festivities.

• *The next door down leads you through a few rooms, including one with a unique oval dome—the 16th-century chapter house with Murillo's* **The Immaculate Conception** *high above the bishop's throne. Now enter the...*

⑭ Treasury: This wood-paneled Room of Ornaments shows off gold and silver reliquaries, which hold hundreds of holy body parts and splinters of the true cross. The star of the collection is Spain's most valuable crown—the Corona de la Virgen de los Reyes. Made in 1904, it sparkles with nearly 12,000 precious stones, including the world's largest pearl—used as the torso of an angel.

• *Leave the treasury and continue around, passing (directly behind the high altar) the closed-to-tourists* **⑮ Royal Chapel.** *Though it's only open for worship (access from outside), it's the holy-of-holies of Sevillian history, with the tombs of Sevilla's founder Ferdinand III, his enlightened successor Alfonso the Wise, and Pedro I, who built the Alcázar. In the far corner is the entry to the Giralda bell tower. It's time for some exercise (unless you're touring the rooftop later—then you can skip it).*

⑯ Giralda Bell Tower Climb: Notice the beautiful Moorish simplicity as you climb to the top of this former minaret, 330 feet up (35 ramps plus 17 steps) with a grand city view. The graded ramp was designed to accommodate a donkey-riding muezzin, who clip-clopped up five times a day to give the Muslim call to prayer back when a mosque stood

Ⓐ *Corona de la Virgen de los Reyes*
Ⓑ *View from the Bell Tower*
Ⓒ *Moorish-style doorway*
Ⓓ *Court of the Orange Trees*

here. Along the way, stop at balconies for expansive views over the entire city.

• *Back on the ground, head outside. As you cross the threshold, look up. Why is a* **crocodile** *hanging here? It's a reminder of the live crocodile given by the Islamic sultan of Egypt (in 1260) to the Christian king Alfonso the Wise as a show of goodwill. Alfonso proudly showed his croc off, and when it died he had the body stuffed for display. When that rotted, it was replaced with this wooden replica.*

You're now in an open-air courtyard (with WCs at the far end). This is the...

⑰ Court of the Orange Trees: Back when this was a mosque, this courtyard—one of the few things remaining from the original mosque—was the place for ritual ablutions. Another remnant is the Puerta del Perdón ("Door of Forgiveness"), the keyhole-arch entrance (and now tourist exit), with its original green doors of finely wrought bronze-covered wood. The lanes between the courtyard bricks were once irrigation streams—a reminder that the Moors introduced irrigation to Iberia. Otherwise, the Christians completely leveled the site and turned a mosque of brick into a cathedral of stone.

• *The biggest remnant of the original mosque ended up becoming the symbol of Sevilla itself—the Giralda bell tower. Find a spot near the Puerta del Perdón where you can look back and take in the tower.*

⑱ Giralda Bell Tower Exterior: This was the mosque's minaret from which Muslims were called to prayer. After the Reconquista, it still called the faithful to prayer...but as a Christian bell tower (see a full description in my Barrio Santa Cruz Walk, earlier).

Take in the whole scene—Giralda tower, courtyard, and the church with its flying buttresses and magnificent Gothic doorways. Appreciate the significance of this site that was sacred to two great world religions.

• *Your cathedral tour is finished. For a truly religious experience, consider one more stop. After exiting the cathedral, make a U-turn left onto Avenida de la Constitución. At #24 (directly across from the church door), enter the passageway marked* **Plaza del Cabildo,** *which leads into a quiet courtyard with a humble little hole-in-the-wall shop.*

⑲ El Torno Pastelería de Conventos: Here, nuns sell handicrafts (such as baptismal dresses for babies) and baked goods (Mon-Fri 10:00-13:30 & 17:00-19:30, Sat-Sun 10:30-14:00, closed Aug). The pastries they make are heavenly—Sevilla's best cookies, bar nun.

▲▲▲ROYAL ALCÁZAR

This palace has been a lavish residence for Spain's rulers for a thousand years. Originally a 10th-century palace built for the governors of the local Moorish state, it still functions as one of the royal family's homes—the oldest in Europe that's still in use. The core of the palace features an extensive 14th-century rebuild, done by Muslim workmen for the Christian king, Pedro I (1334-1369). Pedro was nicknamed either "the Cruel" or "the Just," depending on which end of his sword you were on. Pedro's palace embraces both cultural traditions. Today, visitors can enjoy several sections of the Alcázar (Real Alcázar).

Royal Alcázar

Spectacularly decorated halls and court-yards have distinctive Islamic-style flour-ishes. Exhibits call up the era of Columbus and Spain's New World dominance. The lush, sprawling gardens invite exploration.

Cost and Hours: €12.50, €17.50 includes worthwhile audioguide, buy tick-ets in advance online; daily 9:30-19:00, Oct-March until 17:00; tel. 954-502-324, www.alcazarsevilla.org.

Rick's Tip: *Visiting the Royal Alcázar? Buy a* **timed-entry ticket in advance online,** *then pass the hundreds of visitors (being let in 20 at a time every 15 minutes) who didn't book ahead, and head to the short line for savvy travelers.*

Tours: The fast-moving audioguide gives you an hour of information as you wander. Or consider Concepción Delga-do's Alcázar tour (see "Tours," earlier).

Upper Royal Apartments Option: With a little planning, you could fit in a visit to the 15 lavish, chandeliered, Ver-sailles-like rooms used by today's mon-archs, including the official dining room, living rooms, and stunning Mudejar-style Audience Room. Your group (15 people max) will be escorted on a 30-minute tour while listening to the included audioguide. It's a delightful and less-crowded part of the palace, but you'll need to book well in advance (€4.50, must check bags in lock-ers, check in 15 minutes before reserved time, last tour departs at 13:30). With this ticket, you become an Alcázar VIP and can enter the complex any time you like that day (go to the front of the line and present this ticket).

❍ SELF-GUIDED TOUR

This royal palace is decorated with a mix of Islamic and Christian elements—a style called Mudejar. It offers a thought-pro-voking glimpse of a graceful Al-Andalus world that might have survived its Cas-tilian conquerors...but didn't. The floor plan is intentionally confusing, to make

experiencing the place more exciting and surprising. While Granada's Alhambra was built by Moors for Moorish rulers, what you see here is essentially a Christian rul-er's palace, built in the Moorish style by Moorish artisans (after the Reconquista).

• *Just past the entrance, you'll go through the garden-like Lion Patio (Patio del León), with the rough stone wall of the older Moorish for-tress on your left (c. 913), and through the 12th-century arch into a courtyard called the...*

❶ Courtyard of the Hunt (Patio de la Montería): For centuries, this has been the main gathering place in the Alcázar. The palace's main entrance is directly ahead, through the elaborately decorated facade.

History is all around you. The Alcázar was built over many centuries, with rooms and decorations from the various rulers who've lived here. Behind you, the court-yard you passed through has remnants of the original 10th-century Moorish palace. The towering entrance facade before you dates from after Sevilla was Christianized, when King Pedro I built the most famous part of the complex. To the right are rooms dedicated to Spain's Golden Age, when the Alcázar was home to Ferdinand and Isabel and, later, their grandson Charles V (the most powerful man in Europe...the Holy Roman Emperor). Today's king and queen still use the palace's upper floor as one of their royal residences.

• *Before entering the heart of the palace, let's get a sense of its history. Start in the wing to the right of the courtyard.*

❷ Admiral's Hall (Salón del Almi-rante): In the first room, find the **biggest painting**, showing the crucial turning point in the Alcázar's history. The king who defeated the Moors in 1248, and turned the palace from Moorish to Christian, is kneeling humbly before the bishop, sym-bolically giving his life to God.

Queen Isabel put her stamp on the Alcázar by building this series of rooms (1503) to administer Spain's New World ventures. In these halls, Columbus

Altarpiece painting in the Admiral's Hall

recounted his travels, Ferdinand Magellan planned his around-the-world cruise, and Amerigo Vespucci tried to come up with a catchy moniker for that newly discovered continent.

Continue into the pink-and-red Audience Chamber, once the Admiralty's chapel. The **altarpiece painting** is *St. Mary of the Navigators (Santa María de los Navegantes,* Alejo Fernández, 1530s). The Virgin—the patron saint of sailors and a favorite of Columbus—keeps watch over the puny ships beneath her. Her cape seems to protect everyone under it—even the Native Americans in the dark background (the first time "Indians" were painted in Europe). Kneeling beside the Virgin (on the right, dressed in gold, almost joining his hands together in prayer) is none other than Christopher Columbus. He's on a cloud and this is heaven (this was painted a few decades after his death). Notice that Columbus is blond. Columbus' son said of his dad: "In his youth his hair was blond, but when he

reached 30, it all turned white." The man kneeling on the left side of the painting, with the big gold cape, is King Ferdinand.

Left of the painting is a **model** of Columbus' *Santa María,* his flagship and the only of his three ships not to survive the 1492 voyage. Columbus complained that the *Santa María*—a big cargo ship, different from the sleek *Niña* and *Pinta* caravels—was too slow. On Christmas Day it ran aground off present-day Haiti and tore a hole in its hull. The ship was dismantled to build the first permanent structure in America, a fort for 39 colonists. (After Columbus left, the natives burned the fort and killed the colonists.) Opposite the altarpiece (in the center of the back wall) is the family **coat of arms** of Columbus' descendants, who now live in Spain and Puerto Rico.

As you return to the courtyard, don't miss the room (beyond the grand piano) with display cases of ornate **fans**. A long painting (designed to be gradually rolled across a screen and viewed like a primitive

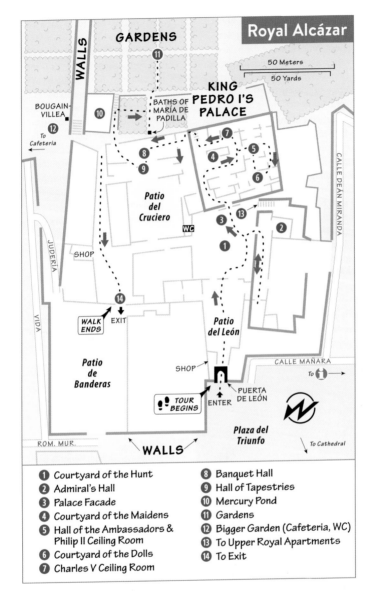

Royal Alcázar

GARDENS

WALLS

50 Meters
50 Yards

KING PEDRO I'S PALACE

BATHS OF MARÍA DE PADILLA

BOUGAIN-VILLEA

To Cafeteria

CALLE DEÁN MIRANDA

Patio del Cruciero

JUDERÍA

SHOP

WC

VIDA

WALK ENDS   EXIT

Patio de Banderas

Patio del León

SHOP

CALLE MAÑARA

To

TOUR BEGINS   ENTER   PUERTA DE LEÓN

Plaza del Triunfo

To Cathedral

ROM. MUR.   WALLS

1 Courtyard of the Hunt
2 Admiral's Hall
3 Palace Facade
4 Courtyard of the Maidens
5 Hall of the Ambassadors & Philip II Ceiling Room
6 Courtyard of the Dolls
7 Charles V Ceiling Room
8 Banquet Hall
9 Hall of Tapestries
10 Mercury Pond
11 Gardens
12 Bigger Garden (Cafeteria, WC)
13 To Upper Royal Apartments
14 To Exit

movie) shows 17th-century Sevilla during Holy Week.

• *Back in the Courtyard of the Hunt, face the impressive entrance to the...*

3 Palace Facade: This is the entrance to **King Pedro I's Palace** (Palacio del Rey Pedro I), the Alcázar's 14th-century nucleus. Though it looks Islamic, it's a classic example of Mudejar style. Looking closer you'll see Christian motifs mixed in—coats of arms of Spain's kings and heraldic animals. About two-thirds of the way up, find the inscription dedicated to the man who built the gate (center of the top row)—"Conquerador Don Pedro." The facade's elaborate blend of Islamic tracery and Gothic Christian elements introduces us to the unique style seen throughout Pedro's part of the palace.

• *Enter the palace. Go left through the vestibule (impressive, yes, but we'll see better), and emerge into the big courtyard with a long pool in the center. This is the...*

❹ Courtyard of the Maidens (Patio de las Doncellas): You've reached the center of King Pedro's palace. It's an open-air courtyard, surrounded by rooms. In the center is a long, rectangular reflecting pool. Like the Moors who preceded him, Pedro built his palace around water.

King Pedro cruelly abandoned his wife and moved into the Alcázar with his mistress, then hired Muslim workers from Granada to re-create the romance of that city's Alhambra in Sevilla's stark Alcázar. The designers created a microclimate engineered for coolness: water, sunken gardens, pottery, thick walls, and darkness. This palace is considered Spain's best example of the Mudejar style.

Courtyard of the Maiden

Pedro's original courtyard was a single story; the upper floors were added by Isabel's grandson, Charles V, in the 16th century. Today, those upper-story rooms are part of the Spanish monarch's living quarters. See the different styles: Mudejar below (lobed arches and elaborate tracery) and Renaissance above (round arches and less decoration).

• *Let's explore some rooms surrounding the courtyard. Start with the room at the far end of the long reflecting pool—beneath the big octagonal tower. This is the palace's most important room.*

❺ Hall of the Ambassadors (Salón de Embajadores): Here, in his throne room, Pedro received guests and caroused in luxury. The room is a cube topped with a half-dome, like many important Islamic buildings. In Islam, the cube represents the earth, and the dome is the starry heavens. In Pedro's world, the symbolism proclaimed that he controlled heaven and earth. As you marvel, remember that this is original, from the 1300s.

The stucco on the walls is molded with interlacing plants, geometrical shapes, and Arabic writing. Despite this being a Christian palace, the walls are inscribed with unapologetically Muslim sayings: "None but Allah conquers" and "Happiness and prosperity are benefits of Allah, who nourishes all creatures." The artisans added propaganda phrases, such as "Dedicated to the magnificent Sultan Pedro— thanks to God!"

The Mudejar style also includes Christian motifs. Find the row of kings, high up at the base of the dome, chronicling all of Castile's rulers from the 600s to the 1600s. Within the intricate patterns inside the dome, you can see a few coats of arms—including the castle of Castile and the lion of León. The Mudejar style also incorporates birds, seashells, and other natural objects you wouldn't normally find in Islamic decor, as it traditionally avoids realistic images of nature.

Hall of the Ambassadors ceiling

Notice how it gets cooler as you go deeper into the palace. Straight ahead from the Hall of the Ambassadors, in the **Philip II Ceiling Room** (Salón del Techo de Felipe II), look above the arches to find peacocks, falcons, and other birds amid interlacing vines.

• *Make your way to the second courtyard (with your back to the Hall of the Ambassadors, circle right). This smaller courtyard (with the skylight) is the...*

❻ **Courtyard of the Dolls** (Patio de las Muñecas): This delicate courtyard was reserved for the king's private family life. Originally, the center of the courtyard had a pool, cooling the residents and reflecting decorative patterns that were once brightly painted on the walls. The columns—recycled from ancient Roman and Visigothic buildings—are of alternating white, black, and pink marble. The courtyard's name comes from the tiny doll faces found at the base of one of the arches. Circle the room and try to find them. (Hint: While just a couple of inches tall, they're eight feet up—kitty-corner from where you entered.)

• *Wander around before returning to the big Courtyard of the Maidens. In the middle of the right side an arch leads to the...*

❼ **Charles V Ceiling Room** (Salón del Techo del Carlos V): Emperor Charles V ruled Spain at its peak and, flush with New World wealth, expanded the palace. His marriage to his beloved cousin Isabella—which took place in this room—joined vast realms of Spain and Portugal. Devoutly Christian, Charles celebrated his wedding night with a midnight Mass, and later ordered the Mudejar ceiling in this room to be replaced with the less Islamic (but no less impressive) Renaissance one you see today. At the base of the ceiling, find Charles' coat of arms—the black double eagle.

• *Return to the Courtyard of the Maidens, then turn right. In the corner, find the small staircase. Go up to rooms decorated with bright ceramic tiles and Gothic vaulting. Pass directly through the chapel (with its majestic mahogany altar on your right) and into a big, long room.*

❽ **Banquet Hall** (Salón Gótico): This airy banquet hall is where Charles and

A *Hall of Tapestries*
B *Courtyard of the Dolls*
C *Tilework detail*
D *Gardens*

Isabella held their wedding reception. Note the huge coats of arms: Charles' double eagle on one end and Isabella's shield of Portugal on the other. Imagine a formal occasion here, as elegant guests took in the views of the gardens. To this day, city officials and VIPs still host receptions here.

• Midhall, on the left, enter the...

❾ **Hall of Tapestries** (Salón Tapices): Next door, the walls are hung with 18th-century Spanish copies of 16th-century Belgian tapestries showing the power, conquests, and industriousness of Charles' prosperous reign. This series of scenes depicts the pivotal Conquest of Tunisia (1535), which stopped the Muslim Ottomans in North Africa at a time when they were threatening Europe on different fronts. The map tapestry of the Mediterranean world has south pointing up. Find Genova, Italy on the bottom; Africa on top; Lisbon (Lisboa) on the far right; the large city of Barcelona in between; and Tunisia (Tunis). The ships of the Holy Roman Empire gather in anticipation of a major battle. The artist included himself (far right) holding the legend—with a scale in both leagues and miles.

At the far end of the room is a big, dramatic portrayal of the Spanish Navy. Spain ruled the waves from 1492 until the defeat of the Spanish Armada in 1588; after that, Britannia's navy started to take over the helm, and it was her crown that controlled the next global empire.

• Return to the Banquet Hall, then head outside at the far end to the extensive landscaped gardens. First up is the...

❿ **Mercury Pond:** The Mercury Pond was a reservoir fed by a 16th-century aqueduct that irrigated the palace's entire garden. As only elites had running water, the fountain was an extravagant show of power. The long stucco-studded wall along one side of the garden was part of the original Moorish castle wall. In the early 1600s, when fortifications were no longer needed here, that end was redesigned to be a grotto-style gallery.

• From the Mercury Pond, steps lead into the formal gardens. Just past the bottom of the steps, a tunnel on the right leads under the palace to the coolest spot in the city—the Baths of María de Padilla. This long underground pool was a rainwater cistern, named for Pedro of Castile's mistress who frequented the place. Its mysterious medieval atmosphere is like something out of Game of Thrones—which actually did use this and other Alcázar settings in several episodes. Finally, explore the rest of the...

⓫ **Gardens:** The intimate geometric zone nearest the palace is the Moorish garden. The far-flung garden beyond that was the backyard of the Christian ruler. Both Christian and Islamic cultures used water and nature as essential parts of their architecture. The garden's pavilions and fountains only enhance this. Wander among palm trees, myrtle hedges, and fragrant roses. While tourists pay to be here, this is actually a public garden, and free to locals. It's been that way since 1931, when the king was exiled and Spanish citizens took ownership of royal holdings. In 1975, the Spanish people allowed the king back on the throne—but on their terms...which included keeping this garden.

• Your Alcázar tour is over. When you're ready to leave these gardens, return to the Mercury Pond and step back into the palace into a small courtyard with palm trees. From here, consider your options:

Just a few steps away, on the other side of the stucco wall, is a massive bougainvillea and a ⓬ **bigger garden with cafeteria and WCs.** Once a farm that provided for the royal community, the garden is now home to a cool and convenient cafeteria with a delightful terrace. If you've booked a spot to visit the ⓭ **Upper Royal Apartments,** return to the Courtyard of the Hunt, and head upstairs. Otherwise, follow ⓮ **exit** signs and head out through the **Patio de Banderas,** once the entrance for guests arriving by horse carriage.

Between the Cathedral and the River

▲ARCHIVO GENERAL DE INDIAS (GENERAL ARCHIVES OF THE INDIES)

To the right of the Alcázar's main entrance, the Archivo General de Indias houses historic papers related to Spain's overseas territories. Its four miles of shelving contain 80 million pages documenting a once-mighty empire. While little of interest is actually on show, a visit is free, easy, and gives you a look at the Lonja Palace, one of the finest Renaissance edifices in Spain. Designed by royal architect Juan de Herrera, the principal designer of El Escorial, the building evokes the greatness of the Spanish empire at its peak (c. 1600).

Cost and Hours: Free, Mon-Sat 9:30-17:00, Sun 10:00-14:00, Avenida de la Constitución 3, tel. 954-500-528.

▲▲HOSPITAL DE LA CARIDAD

This charity hospital, which functioned as a place of final refuge for Sevilla's poor and homeless, was founded in the 17th century by the nobleman Don Miguel Mañara. Your visit includes an evocative courtyard, a church filled with powerful art, and a good audioguide that explains it all. This is still a working charity, so when you pay your entrance fee, you're advancing the work Mañara started back in the 17th century.

Cost and Hours: €8, includes audioguide, daily 10:30-19:30, Calle Temprado 3, tel. 954-223-232, www.santa-caridad.es.

Visiting the Hospital: Entering the **courtyard** you're greeted by a statue of a woman and two ecstatic cherubs, filled with the love of mankind. It's Charity, the mission of this hospital. The statues come from Genoa, Italy, as Mañara's family were rich Genovese merchants who moved to Sevilla to get in on the wealth from New World discoveries. This charming red-and-white courtyard, surrounded by offices, was the administrative hub of the hospital's charitable work and its

Christopher Columbus (1451-1506)

This Italian wool weaver ran off to sea, was shipwrecked in Portugal, married a captain's daughter, learned Portuguese and Spanish, and persuaded Spain's monarchs to finance his bold scheme to trade with the East by sailing west. On August 3, 1492, Columbus set sail from Palos (near Huelva, 60 miles west of Sevilla) with three ships and 90 men, hoping to land in Asia, which Columbus estimated was 3,000 miles away. Ten weeks—and yes, 3,000 miles—later, with a superstitious crew ready to mutiny after they'd seen evil omens (including a falling meteor and a jittery compass), Columbus landed on an island in the Bahamas, convinced he'd reached Asia. He and his crew traded with the "Indians" and returned home to Palos harbor, where they were received as heroes.

Columbus made three more voyages to the New World and became rich with gold. But he gained a bad reputation among the colonists, was arrested, and returned to Spain in chains. Though pardoned, Columbus fell out of favor with the court. On May 20, 1506, he died in Valladolid. His son said he was felled by "gout and by grief at seeing himself fallen from his high estate," but historians speculate that diabetes or syphilis may have contributed. Columbus died thinking he'd visited Asia, unaware he'd opened up Europe to a New World.

ongoing assistance to the poor. You're likely to see seniors shuffling in and out, as this is still a home for the poor—Mañara's legacy in action.

The **Sala de Cabildos,** a small room at the end of the courtyard, is Mañara's former office. It has rotating exhibits from

Mañara's art collection. Stepping out of the Sala de Cabildos, the chapel is on your right. But first, head left into a small, evocative courtyard. These arches are part of the 13th-century **shipyards.** Wander around and imagine the huge halls where the ships were produced that enabled Columbus, Vasco da Gama, and Magellan to broaden Europe's horizons and make Portugal a power.

Next, cross the inner courtyard and head up a few steps into the **chapel.** It's an over-the-top masterpiece of Sevillian Baroque—a fusion of architecture, painting, and sculpture. Don Miguel hired Sevilla's three greatest artists (who were also his friends): the painters Bartolomé Murillo and Juan de Valdés Leal and the sculptor Pedro Roldán. Mañara himself worked with them to design the church and its themes.

Start with the painting at the back of the nave, on the left wall, Leal's *In the Blink of an Eye (In Ictu Oculi).* In it, the Grim Reaper extinguishes the candle of life. Filling the canvas are the ruins of worldly goods, knowledge, power, and position. It's all gone in the blink of an eye—true in the 1670s...and true today.

Directly opposite is Leal's *The End of the Glories of the World,* showing Mañara and a bishop decaying together in a crypt. Above, the hand of Christ—pierced by the nail—holds the scales of justice: sins on the left and good deeds on the right. The placement of both paintings gave worshippers plenty to think about during and after their visit.

Strolling up the nave, you'll see paintings and statues that show various good deeds and acts of self-sacrifice and charity performed by Jesus and the saints. Most of the paintings leading up to the altar are replicas of Murillo's pieces, lost during Napoleonic times. On the left wall, Moses strikes a rock to bring water to the needy Israelites. A trademark Murillo beggar-boy atop a horse points at Moses as if saying, "Do what he did." On the right wall, Jesus gives loaves and fishes to thousands of hungry people. Murillo, a devoted member of this charity, was hammering home one of the institution's functions—give food and drink to the poor.

The giant altar is carved wood with gold leaf, with a dozen hardworking cupids providing support. Christ's lifeless body has been taken from the cross and some workers are bringing in the dark-gray tombstone. This illustrated the mission of the monks here—to provide a proper Christian burial to society's outcasts, like executed criminals. The carved-and-painted statues by Roldán are realistic and emotional, in the style of his famed *La Macarena* statue. Atop the altar are three female figures representing faith (left), hope (right), and—the star of this place—charity.

As you leave the church, do Don Miguel Mañara a favor. Step on his **tombstone.** It's located in the back, tucked within the big wooden entranceway. He requested to be buried here so everyone would step on him as they entered. The

Hospital de la Caridad

tombstone reads, "Beneath this stone lies the worst man in the world." By focusing on the vanity of his own life and dedicating himself to charity, Don Miguel hoped to be saved from his sins. Outside, more big shots—many of Sevilla's top families to this day—are featured on tombstones paving the exit.

North of the Cathedral

▲▲CHURCH OF THE SAVIOR (IGLESIA DEL SALVADOR)

Sevilla's second-biggest church, built on the site of a ninth-century mosque, gleams with freshly scrubbed Baroque pride. While the larger cathedral is a jumble of styles, this church is uniformly Andalusian Baroque—the architecture, decor, and statues are all from the same period. The church is home to some of Sevilla's most beloved statues that parade through town during religious festivals. The statues depict events from the Passion (the week leading up to Easter), showing Jesus being tortured and crucified, and showing Mary mourning her son. (If you visit here just before Holy Week, you might see floats being assembled and bedecked in flowers in the nave.)

Nearby, the **Christ of the Passion chapel** is where the faithful have come for centuries to pray, marvel at the sadness that fills the chapel, then kiss Jesus' heel (free, daily 10:00-14:00 & 17:00-21:00). To reach the chapel, exit the church, go right, and then right again. Under the stubby tower, go through a small door into a courtyard and then through a small pilgrims' shop. To kiss the heel, head up the stairs behind the altar. Jesus is flanked by John the Evangelist and a grieving, red-eyed María Dolorosa, with convincing tears and a jeweled dagger in her heart. In the adjacent shop (above the cashier), a wall tile shows the Christ of the Passion statue in a circa-1620 procession.

Cost and Hours: €4, covered by cathedral combo-ticket, buy ticket in advance online; Mon-Sat 11:00-18:00 (July-Aug from 10:00), Sun 15:00-19:30; audio-guide-€2.50, Plaza del Salvador, tel. 954-211-679, www.catedraldesevilla.es.

▲FLAMENCO DANCE MUSEUM (MUSEO DEL BAILE FLAMENCO)

Though small and pricey, this museum is worthwhile for anyone looking to understand more about the dance that embodies the spirit of southern Spain.

The main exhibition, on floor 1, features well-produced videos, flamenco costumes, and other artifacts collected by the grande dame of flamenco, Christina Hoyos. The top floor and basement house temporary exhibits, mostly of photography and other artwork. On the ground floor and in the basement, you can watch flamenco lessons in progress—or even take one yourself (one hour, first person-€60, €20/person after that, shoes not provided but yours are OK).

Cost and Hours: €10, €26 combo-ticket includes evening flamenco performance, daily 10:00-19:00, pick up English info sheet at front desk; follow signs for *Museo del Baile Flamenco*, about 3 blocks east of Plaza Nueva at Calle Manuel Rojas Marcos 3; tel. 954-340-311, www.museoflamenco.com.

▲MUSEO DE BELLAS ARTES

Sevilla's passion for religious art is preserved and displayed in its Museum of Fine Arts. While most Americans go for El Greco, Goya, and Velázquez (not a forte of this collection), this museum opens horizons and gives a fine look at other, less-well-known Spanish masters: Zurbarán and Murillo. Rather than exhausting, the museum is pleasantly enjoyable.

Cost and Hours: €1.50; Tue-Sat 9:00-20:00, until 15:00 on Sun and in summer, closed Mon year-round; tel. 955-542-942, www.museosdeandalucia.es.

Getting There: The museum is at Plaza Museo 9, a 15-minute walk or cheap taxi ride from the cathedral. It's also on the #C5 bus route.

Background: As Spain's economic Golden Age (the 1500s) blossomed into its arts and literature Golden Age (the 1600s), wealthy Sevilla reigned as the sophisticated capital of culture (its New York City) while Madrid was still a newly built center of government (its Washington, DC). Several of Spain's top painters—Zurbarán, Murillo, and Velázquez—lived in Sevilla in the 1600s. They labored to make the spiritual world tangible, and forged the gritty realism that marks Spanish painting. You'll see balding saints and monks with wrinkled faces and sunburned hands, radiating an inner spirituality. This highly accessible style inspired the Catholic faithful in an age when Protestants were demanding a closer personal relationship with God.

Zubarán, Apotheosis of St. Thomas Aquinas

◑ SELF-GUIDED TOUR

The permanent collection features 20 rooms in neat chronological order. It's easy to breeze through once with my tour, then backtrack to what appeals to you. Pick up the English-language floor plan, which explains the theme of each room.

• *Enter and follow signs to the permanent collection, which begins in Sala I (Room 1).*

Rooms 1-4: Medieval altarpieces of gold-backed saints, Virgin-and-babes, and Crucifixion scenes attest to the religiosity that nurtured Spain's early art. Spain's penchant for unflinching realism culminates in Room 2 with Michelangelo friend/rival Pietro Torrigiano's 1525 statue of an emaciated San Jerónimo, whose gaze never falters from the cross, and in Room 3 with the painted clay head of St. John the Baptist—complete with severed neck muscles, throat, and windpipe. This kind of warts-and-all naturalism would influence the well-known Sevillian art teacher Francisco Pacheco (also Room 3) as well as his student and son-in-law, Velázquez (Room 4). Velázquez's *Head of an Apostle*—a sober portrait of a bearded, balding, wrinkled man—exemplifies how Sevillian painters could make once-inaccessible saints seem flesh and blood like you and me.

• *Continue through the pleasant outdoor courtyard (the convent's former cloister) to the grand, former church that is now Room 5.*

Room 5: Large-scale religious art now hangs in what was once a church nave. On the left wall is the *Apotheosis of St. Thomas Aquinas (Apoteosis de Santo Tomás de Aquino,* 1631) by **Francisco de Zurbarán** (thoor-bar-AHN, 1598-1664). In his most important work, Zurbarán presents the pivotal moment when the great saint-theologian experiences his spiritual awakening. What's unique about Zurbarán is the setting. He strips away any semblance of 3-D background to portray how these real people are having a surreal experience. Thomas has suddenly found himself in a heavenly cloud surrounded by long-dead saints, while his contemporaries below gaze upward, sharing the vision.

As you approach the former church's main altar, you find works of another hometown boy, **Bartolomé Murillo,** including several paintings of the Virgin Mary, his signature subject (for more on Murillo, see the sidebar earlier). He portrayed the Immaculate Conception of Mary, the doctrine that she was born

An Immaculate Conception *by Murillo*

without the taint of original sin. Typically, Mary is depicted as young, dressed in white and blue, standing atop the moon (crescent or full). She clutches her breast and gazes up rapturously, surrounded by tumbling winged babies. Murillo's tiny *Madonna and Child (Virgen de la Servilleta*, 1665), at the end of the room in the center, shows the warmth and appeal of his work. Murillo's sweet naturalism is quite different from the harsh realism of his fellow artists, so his work was understandably popular. For many Spaniards, Mary is their main connection to heaven. They pray directly to her, asking her to intercede on their behalf with God. Murillo's Marys are always receptive and ready to help.

• *Now head back outside to enjoy the coolness of the cloister and the beauty of its tiles, then go up the Imperial Staircase to the first floor.*

Rooms 6-9: In Rooms 6 and 7, you'll see more Murillos and Murillo imitators. Room 8 is dedicated to yet another native Sevillian (and friend of Murillo), Juan de Valdés Leal (1622-1690), whose work is also featured in the Hospital de la Caridad (see listing earlier). He adds Baroque motion and drama to religious subjects. His surreal colors and feverish, unfinished style create a mood of urgency. In Room 9, art students will recognize the work of José de Ribera—a Spaniard living in Italy—who merged Spanish realism with Caravaggio's strong dark-light contrast.

Room 10: Here you'll find more Zurbarán saints and monks, and the miraculous things they experienced, with an unblinking, crystal-clear, brightly lit, highly detailed realism. Enjoy the weathered faces, voluminous robes, and precisely etched details. These photorealistic people are shown against a neutral background, as though existing in the landscape of an otherworldly vision.

In Zurbarán's *St. Hugo Visiting the Refectory (San Hugo en el Refectorio),* white-robed Carthusian monks gather together for their simple meal in a communal dining hall. Above them hangs a painting of Mary, Baby Jesus, and John the Baptist. Zurbarán created paintings like this for monks' dining halls. His audience: celibate men and women who lived in isolation, as in this former convent, devoting their time to quiet meditation, prayer, and Bible study. Zurbarán's people often stand starkly isolated against a single-color background—a dark room or the gray-white of a cloudy sky. He was the ideal painter for the austere religion of 17th-century Spain as it led the Counter-Reformation, standing strong against the rising tide of Protestantism in Europe.

Adjacent to *St. Hugo,* find *The Virgin of the Caves (La Virgen de las Cuevas)* and study the piety and faith in the monks' weathered faces. Zurbarán's Mary is protective, with her hands placed on the heads of two monks. Note the loving detail on the cape embroidery, the brooch, and the flowers at her feet.

Rest of the Museum: Spain's subsequent art, from the 18th century on, generally followed the trends of the rest of Europe. Of particular interest is the large *Death of the Master* by José Villegas Cordero, in which bullfighters touchingly express their grief after their teacher, gored in the ring, dies in bed. Enjoy these painted slices of Sevilla, then exit to experience similar scenes today.

Far North of the Cathedral

▲▲▲BASÍLICA DE LA MACARENA

Sevilla's Holy Week celebrations are Spain's grandest. During the week leading up to Easter, the city is packed with pilgrims witnessing 60 processions carrying about 100 religious floats. If you miss the actual event, you can get a sense of it by visiting the Basílica de la Macarena and its accompanying museum to see the two most impressive floats and the darling of Semana Santa, the statue of the Virgen de la Macarena. Although far from the city center, it's located on Sevilla's ring road and easy to reach.

Cost and Hours: Church-free, treasury museum-€5, church daily 9:00-14:00 & 18:00-21:30, shorter evening hours mid-Sept-May, audioguide-€1; museum closed in days before Holy Week. Tel. 954-901-800, www.hermandaddelamacarena.es.

Getting There: Wave down a taxi and say "Basílica Macarena" (about €6 from the city center). Buses #C1 through #C5 go there, but the quickest ride is on circular routes #C3 and #C4 from Puerta de

Basílica de la Macarena

Jerez (near the Torre del Oro) or Avenida de Menéndez Pelayo (the ring road east of the cathedral).

Visiting the Church: Despite the long history of the Macarena statue, the Neo-Baroque church was only built in 1949 to give the oft-moved sculpture a permanent home. Grab a pew and study the statue.

La Macarena is known as the **"Weeping Virgin"** for the five crystal teardrops trickling down her cheeks. She's like a Baroque doll with human hair and articulated arms, and is even dressed in underclothes. Sculpted in the late 17th century (probably by Pedro Roldán), she's become Sevilla's most popular image of Mary.

Her beautiful expression—halfway between smiling and crying—is ambiguous, letting worshippers project their own emotions onto her. Her weeping can be contagious—look around you. She's also known as La Esperanza, the Virgin of Hope, and she promises better times after the sorrow.

Installed in the left side chapel is the **Christ of the Judgment** (from 1654),

showing Jesus on the day he was condemned. This statue and La Macarena stand atop the two most important floats of the Holy Week parades. The side chapel on the right has an equally remarkable image of the **Virgen del Rosario** that's paraded around the city on the last Sunday of October.

To see the floats and learn more, head to the **Tesoro** (Treasury Museum; to reach the entrance—on the church's left side—either exit the church or go through a connecting door at the rear). This small, three-floor museum tells the history of the Virgin statue and the Holy Week parades. Though rooted in medieval times, the current traditions developed around 1600, with the formation of various fraternities (*hermandades*). During Holy Week, they demonstrate their dedication to God by parading themed floats throughout Sevilla to retell the story of the Crucifixion and Resurrection of Christ. The museum displays ceremonial banners, scepters, and costumed mannequins; videos show the parades in action (some displays in English).

The three-ton **float** that carries the Christ of the Judgment is slathered in gold leaf and shows a commotion of figures acting out the sentencing of Jesus. Pontius Pilate is about to wash his hands. Pilate's wife cries as a man reads the death sentence. During the Holy Week procession, pious Sevillian women wail in the streets while relays of 48 men carry this float on the backs of their necks—only their feet showing under the drapes—as they shuffle through the streets from midnight until 14:00 in the afternoon every Good Friday. The men rehearse for months to get their choreographed footwork in sync.

La Macarena follows the Christ of the Judgment in the procession. Mary's smaller 1.5-ton float seems all silver and candles—"strong enough to support the roof, but tender enough to quiver in the soft night breeze." Mary has a wardrobe of three huge mantles, worn in successive years; these are about 100 years old, as is her six-pound gold crown/halo. This float

La Macarena

has a mesmerizing effect on the crowds. They line up for hours, then clap, weep, and throw roses as it slowly sways along the streets, working its way through town.

The museum collection also contains some **matador paraphernalia.** La Macarena is the patron saint of bullfighters, and they give thanks for her protection. Copies of her image are popular in bullring chapels. In 1912, bullfighter José Ortega, hoping for protection, gave La Macarena the five emerald brooches she wears. It worked for eight years...until he was gored to death in the ring. For a month, La Macarena was dressed in widow's black—the only time that has happened.

▲▲Triana Walk

In Sevilla—as is true in so many other European cities that grew up in the age of river traffic—what was long considered the "wrong side of the river" is now the most colorful part of town. Sevilla's Triana, west of the river, is a proud neighborhood that identifies with its working-class origins and is famed for its flamenco soul. Known for their independent spirit, locals describe crossing the bridge toward the city center as "going to Sevilla." To trace the route described next, see the "Sevilla" map.

⊙ *Self-Guided Walk*

• *To reach Triana from downtown Sevilla, head to the river and cross over…*

Puente de Isabel II: Note the bridge's distinctive design as you approach. It was inspired by an 1834 crossing over the Seine River in Paris—look for the circles under each span that lead the way into Triana. While crossing the Guadalquivir River, to the right you can see Sevilla's single skyscraper—designed by Argentine architect César Pelli of Malaysia's Twin Towers fame. Locals lament the Torre Sevilla because according to city law, no structure should be taller than the Giralda bell tower. But since this building doesn't sit within the city center, developers found a way to avoid that regulation. The **Capilla**

del **Carmen** sits at the end of the bridge. Designed by Expo '29 architect Aníbal González, the bell tower and chapel add glamour to the entrance to Triana.

• *At the end of the bridge, walk down the staircase on the right.*

Triana's Castle and Market: The **Castillo de San Jorge** is a 12th-century castle that in the 15th century was the headquarters for Sevilla's Inquisition (free small museum). Explore the castle briefly, then retrace your steps to visit the neighborhood's covered market. Built in 2005 in the Moorish Revival style, it sits within the ruins of the castle. The market bustles in the mornings and afternoons with traditional fruit and vegetable stalls as well as colorful tapas bars and cafés.

• *Exit the market downstairs, out the back door, and turn left.*

Ceramic Museum and Shops: Here you can discover the district's ceramic history, starting with the **Museo de la Cerámica de Triana,** which focuses on tile and pottery production. Located in the remains of a former riverside factory, the museum explains the entire process

(€2.10, free with Alcázar ticket, Tue-Sat 11:00-17:30, Sun 10:00-14:30, closed Mon, Calle Antillano Campos 14, tel. 954-342-737). Walk along Calle Antillano Campos, then turn left on Calle Alfarería. This area is lined with the old facades of ceramic workshops that once populated this quarter. Most have either closed up or moved to the outskirts of town, where rent is cheaper. But a few stalwarts remain, including the lavishly decorated Santa Ana and the large showroom Santa Isabel (at Calle Alfarería 12).

• *Continue down Calle Alfarería to...*

Calle San Jacinto: This is the main—and now pedestrian-only—street of the quarter. It's the hip center of the people scene—a festival of life each evening. Venturing down side lanes, you find classic 19th-century facades with fine ironwork and colorful tiles.

• *Walk down Calle San Jacinto in the direction of the bridge. The final cross-street (to the right) is...*

Calle Pureza: This street cuts through the historic center of Triana. As you wander, pop into bars and notice how the

Colorful Triana

decor mixes bullfighting lore with Virgin worship. It's easy enough to follow your nose into Dulcería Manu Jara, at Calle Pureza 5, where tempting artisan pastries are made on the spot. At #12 is La Antigua Abacería (an *abacería* is a traditional neighborhood grocer that also functions as a neighborhood bar), and at #28, sculptor José Gómez is busy with his restoration work and sculpting.

Chapel of the Mariners: Across from #54 is the Capilla de los Marineros, home of the beloved Virgin statue called **Nuestra Señora de la Esperanza de Triana** (Our Lady of Hope of Triana). She's a big deal here. Step inside to see her presiding like a queen from the high altar. In the pilgrims' shop adjacent, see the photo of this Mary in the streets being mobbed by what seems like the entire population of Triana. The brotherhood of this Virgin runs a delightful (if you're into Mary) museum where you can see her actual float, lots of regalia, and video clips (€4 entry fee).

• *Continue down Calle Pureza to explore the...*

Rest of Triana: The next church is the **Church of Santa Ana,** nicknamed the "Cathedral of Triana." The recommended **Bar Santa Ana** (on the corner before the church) is a classic Virgin Mary bar (with a little bullfighting tossed in). Walking around the little church, on the far side is a delightful square with two recommended eateries, **Bar Bistec** and **Taberna La Plazuela.** Circling farther around, return to Calle Pureza and the tiny Calle Duarte, which leads to the river. Gazing across the water, imagine the ships that kicked off the Age of Discovery sailing from here—then consider making the neighborhood you just explored your destination for a tapas crawl.

EXPERIENCES

Bullfighting

▲**BULLFIGHTS**

Some of Spain's most intense bullfighting happens in Sevilla's 14,000-seat bullring, Plaza de Toros. The arena hosts about 45 fights each year, which are held (generally at 18:30) on most Sundays in May and June; on Easter and Corpus Christi; daily

The matador sidesteps the bull.

during the April Fair; and for two weeks in late September (during the Feria de San Miguel). These serious fights, with adult matadors, are called *corrida de toros* and often sell out in advance. On many Thursday evenings in July, the *novillada* fights take place, with teenage novices doing the killing and smaller bulls doing the dying. *Corrida de toros* seats range from €25 for high seats looking into the sun to €150 for the first three rows in the shade under the royal box; *novillada* seats are half that—and easy to buy at the arena a few minutes before showtime (ignore scalpers outside; get information at a TI, your hotel, by phone, or online; tel. 954-501-382, www.plazadetorosdelamaestranza.com).

▲▲BULLRING (PLAZA DE TOROS) AND BULLFIGHT MUSEUM (MUSEO TAURINO)

This 40-minute tour (escorted with audioguide) takes you through the bullring's strangely quiet and empty arena, its museum, and the chapel where the matador prays before the fight. (Thanks to readily available blood transfusions, there have been no deaths here in three decades.) The two most revered figures of Sevilla, the Virgen de la Macarena and the Jesús del Gran Poder (Christ of All Power), are represented in the chapel. In the museum, you'll see great classic scenes and the heads of a few bulls—awarded the bovine equivalent of an Oscar for a particularly good fight. The city was so appalled when the famous matador Manolete was killed in 1947 that even the mother of the bull that gored him was destroyed. Matadors—dressed to kill—are heartthrobs in their "suits of light." Many girls have their bedrooms wallpapered with posters of cute bullfighters.

Cost and Hours: €8, includes audioguide, entrance with escorted tour only—no free time inside; 3/hour, daily 9:30-21:00—last tour at 20:30, Nov-March until 19:00; until 15:00 on fight days, when chapel and horse room are closed. While they take groups of up to 50, it's still wise to reserve a spot in the busy season (tel. 954-210-315, www.sevilletourexperience.com).

April Fair

Two weeks after Easter, much of Sevilla packs into its vast fairgrounds for a grand party that brings all that's Andalusian together. The passion for horses, flamenco, and sherry is clear—riders are ramrod straight, colorfully clad girls ride sidesaddle, and everyone's drinking sherry spritzers. Women sport outlandish dresses that would look clownish elsewhere, but are somehow brilliant here en masse. Every day for one crazy week, horses clog the streets in an endless parade until about 20:00, when they clear out and the streets fill with exuberant locals. The party goes on literally 24 hours a day.

Countless private party tents, called *casetas,* line the lanes. Each tent is the private party zone of a family, club, or association. You need to know someone in the group—or make friends quickly—to get in. Because of the exclusivity, it has a real family-affair feeling. In each *caseta,* everyone knows everyone. It seems like a thousand wedding parties being celebrated at the same time.

Any tourist can have a fun and memorable evening by simply crashing the party. The city's entire fleet of taxis (who can legally charge double) and buses seems dedicated to shuttling people from downtown to the fairgrounds. Given the traffic jams and inflated prices, you may be better off hiking: From the Torre del Oro, cross the San Telmo Bridge to Plaza de Cuba and hike down Calle Asunción. You'll see the towering gate to the fairgrounds in the distance. Just follow the crowds (there's no admission charge). Arrive before 20:00 to see the horses, but stay later, as the ambience improves after the *caballos* giddy-up on out. Some of the larger tents are sponsored by the city and open to the public, but the best action is in the streets, where party-goers from the livelier *casetas* spill out. Although private tents have bouncers, everyone is so happy that it's not tough to strike up an impromptu friendship, become a "special guest," and be invited in. The drink flows freely, and the food is fun, bountiful, and cheap.

Flamenco Classes

Eva Izquierdo shares her passion for flamenco culture with two classes at a studio in Triana (both 45 minutes and offered Mon, Wed, and Fri). **Rhythm and Palmas** (at 17:00) introduces you to the essentials of flamenco: its origins, rhythms, and different styles (*palos*). Learn to clap properly—technique is everything—in order to accompany flamenco music and song. **Flamenco Dance** (at 18:00) is geared toward beginners, men and women alike. After basic foot and leg work, Eva will guide you through a unique routine—*olé!* Reservations are required (€28, Calle Castilla 94, tel. 626-007-868, www.ishowusevilla.com).

Shopping

For the best local shopping experience in Sevilla, visit the popular pedestrian streets Tetuán, Velázquez, and Cuna near Plaza Nueva. They, and the surrounding lanes, are packed with people and shops.

Clothing and shoe stores stay open all day. Other shops generally take a siesta, closing between 13:30 and 16:00 or 17:00 on weekdays, as well as on Saturday afternoons and all day Sunday. Big department stores such as **El Corte Inglés** stay open (and air-conditioned) right through the siesta. Popular souvenir items include ladies' fans, shawls, mantillas (ornate head scarves), other items related to flamenco (castanets, guitars, costumes), ceramics, and bullfighting posters.

Collectors' markets hop on Sunday at Plaza del Cabildo (near the cathedral). You can browse art on Plaza del Museo (by the Museo de Bellas Artes). The El Postigo **arts and crafts market,** in an architecturally interesting old building behind the Hospital de la Caridad, features artisan wares of all types (Mon-Sat 11:00-14:00 & 16:00-20:00, Sun 16:00-20:00, at the corner of Calles de Arfe and Dos de Mayo).

▲▲SHOPPING PASEO

The lively pedestrianized shopping area north of the cathedral is well worth a wander. The best shopping streets—Calle Sierpes and Calle Cuna—also happen to be part of the oldest section of Sevilla. A walk here is a chance to join one of Spain's liveliest paseos—that bustling celebration of life that takes place before dinner each evening, when everyone is out strolling, showing off their fancy shoes and checking out everyone else's. This walk, if done between 18:00 and 20:00, gives you a chance to experience the paseo scene while getting a look at the town's most popular shops.

Start on the pedestrianized **Plaza Nueva**. From here wander the length of **Calle Tetuán,** where old-time standbys bump up against fashion-right boutiques. **Juan Foronda** (#28) has been selling flamenco attire and mantillas since 1926. A few doors down, you'll find the flagship store of **Camper** (#24), the proudly Spanish shoe brand that's become a worldwide favorite. Calle Tetuán (which changes names to Calle Velázquez) ends five blocks later at La Campana, a big intersection and popular meeting point, with the super department store, El Corte Inglés, just beyond, on Plaza del Duque de la Victoria.

Turn right at the end of the street. At the corner of Calle Sierpes awaits a venerable pastry shop, **Confitería La Campana,** with a fine 1885 interior...and Sevilla's most tempting sweets. In front of the pastry shop is a traditional newsstand, **Prensa Kiosk Sierpes.** It's been in Miquel's family for 100 years, and while times are tough as newspaper sales decrease, he still has his loyal customers. A few steps down Calle Sierpes at #5 is **Papelería Ferrer,** where the Ferrer family has been selling traditional stationery and pens since 1856. Such elegance survives and is appreciated by the people of Sevilla.

Next, at #19, is the clock-covered, wood-paneled **El Cronómetro** shop, where master watchmakers have been doing business since 1901. At #33 is another Juan Foronda shop, filled with traditional ladies' accessories for Sevilla's many festivals. For a fancy festival hat, stop at #40. **Sombrerería Maquedano** is a styling place—especially for men. They claim to be the oldest hat seller in Sevilla.

If it's tea time, #45 is a handy next stop. Since 1910 **Ochoa** *confitería* and *salón de té* has been tempting locals with a long display case of sweets. In back is a buffet line for tapas and a light lunch. At the corner of Sierpes and Jovellanos/Sagasta, you'll find several fine shops featuring more Andalusian accessories. Drop in to see how serious local women are about their fans, shawls, mantillas, and *peinetas* (combs designed to secure and prop up the *mantilla*). Andalusian women accessorize with

fans, matching them to different dresses. The *mantilla* comes in black (worn only on Holy Thursday and by the mother of the groom at weddings) and white (worn at bullfights during the April Fair).

From here turn left down **Calle Sagasta**. At #5, **Galán Camisería** is a traditional men's store that sells the "uniform" for the older gentlemen of Andalucía. While young men dress casually in T-shirts and jeans, older men still dress up to go out (especially for the Sunday paseo).

Just before you hit the charming Plaza del Salvador, stop at #6 for a peek into the windows at **BuBi**. This *boutique infantil* displays pricey but exquisitely made baby clothes. Now jump in to **Plaza del Salvador**—it's teeming with life at the foot of the Church of the Savior. Finish your shopping stroll by heading left up **Calle Cuna** for about 100 yards. This street is famous for its exuberant flamenco dresses and classic wedding dresses. Flamenco dresses custom-made for the April Fair are considered an important status symbol. At #46 a shop displays

Window shopping in Sevilla

A shopping street

this year's dress fashions (or last year's at clearance prices).

Nightlife

▲▲ EVENING PASEO

Sevilla is meant for strolling. The paseo thrives every evening (except in winter) in these areas: along either side of the river between the San Telmo and Isabel II bridges (Paseo de Cristóbal Colón and Triana district), up Avenida de la Constitución, around Plaza Nueva, at Plaza de España, and throughout the Barrio Santa Cruz. The best paseo scene is about 18:00 to 20:00, but on hot summer nights, even families with toddlers are out and about past midnight. Spend some time rafting through this river of humanity.

▲▲▲ FLAMENCO

This music-and-dance art form has its roots in the Roma (Gypsy) and Moorish cultures. Even at a packaged "flamenco evening," sparks fly. The men do most of the flamboyant machine-gun footwork. The women often concentrate on the graceful turns and smooth, shuffling step of the *soleá* version of the dance. Watch the musicians. Flamenco guitarists, with their lightning-fast finger-roll strums, are among the best in the world. The intricate rhythms are set by castanets or the hand-clapping (called *palmas*) of those who aren't dancing at the moment. In the raspy-voiced wails of the singers, you'll hear echoes of the Muslim call to prayer.

Sevilla's flamenco offerings tend to fall into one of three categories: serious concerts (about €20 and about an hour long), where the singing and dancing take center stage; touristy dinner-and-drinks shows with table service (generally around €40—not including food—and 90 minutes long); and—the least touristy option—casual bars with late-night performances, where for the cost of a drink you can catch impromptu (or semi-impromptu) musicians at play. Here's the rundown for each type of performance.

Serious Flamenco Concerts: While it's hard to choose among these concerts, I'd say enjoying one is a must during

Spirited flamenco erupts nightly in Sevilla.

your Sevilla visit. To the novice viewer, each company offers equal quality. They cost about the same, and each venue is small, intimate (congested seating in not-very-comfy chairs), and air-conditioned. **La Casa del Flamenco** is in a delightful arcaded courtyard right in the Barrio Santa Cruz (€18, €2 discount for Rick Steves readers with this book who book directly and pay cash; shows nightly at 19:00 and 20:30 in April-May and Sept-Oct, one show nightly the rest of year—check their website; no drinks, 60 relatively spacious seats, next to recommended Hotel Alcántara, Calle Ximénez de Enciso 28, tel. 955-029-999, www. lacasadelflamencosevilla.com). **Flamenco Dance Museum,** while the most congested venue (with 150 tightly packed seats), has a bar and allows drinks inside, and has a bigger production (six performers). It has festival seating—the doors open early so for earlier performances, you can grab the seat of your choice, then tour the museum before the show (€22, nightly at 17:00, 19:00, 20:45, and 22:15; €26 combo-ticket includes the museum—described earlier under "Sights"; reservations smart, tel. 954-340-311, www.museoflamenco.com). **Casa de la Guitarra Flamenco** is another venue in the tourist zone with cramped seating (75 seats) and a strong performance (€17, daily at 18:00, 19:30, and 21:00, no drinks, next to recommended Restaurante San Marco, Calle Mesón del Moro 12, tel. 954-224-093, www.flamencoensevilla.com).

Razzle-Dazzle Flamenco Shows: These packaged shows can be a bit sterile—and an audience of tourists doesn't help—but I find these entertaining and riveting. **Los Gallos** presents nightly 90-minute shows at 20:30 and 22:30 (€35 ticket includes drink, €3/person discount with this book—limited to 3 people, arrive 30 minutes early for best seats, bar, no food served, Plaza de Santa Cruz 11, tel. 954-216-981, www.tablaolosgallos.com, owners José and Blanca promise goose bumps). Their

box office is open at 11:00 (you'll pass it on my Barrio Santa Cruz Walk). **Tablao El Arenal** is more of an old-fashioned dinner show with arguably more professional performers and a classier setting (€40 ticket includes drink, €60 includes tapas, €72 includes dinner, 1.5-hour shows at 19:30 and 21:30, likely later in summer, near bullring at Calle Rodo 7, tel. 954-216-492, www. tablaoelarenal.com).

Impromptu Flamenco in Bars: Spirited flamenco singing still erupts spontaneously in bars throughout the old town after midnight—but you need to know where to look. Ask a local for the latest. **La Carbonería Bar,** the sangria equivalent of a beer garden, is a few blocks north of the Barrio Santa Cruz. It's a big, opentented area filled with young locals, casual guitar strummers, and nearly nightly flamenco music from about 22:30 to 24:00 (no cover, daily 20:00-very late; near Plaza Santa María—find Hotel Fernando III, along the side alley Céspedes at #21; tel. 954-214-460).

EATING

Eating in Sevilla is fun and affordable. Make a point to get out and eat well when in Sevilla.

A clear dining trend in Sevilla is the rise of gourmet tapas bars, with spiffed-up decor and creative menus, at the expense of traditional restaurants. Old-school places do survive, but they often lack energy, and it seems that their clientele is aging with them. My quandary: I like the classic *típico* places, but the lively atmosphere and the best food are in the new places. One thing's for certain: if you want a good "restaurant" experience, your best value these days is to find a trendy tapas bar that offers good table seating, and sit down to enjoy some *raciones*.

Triana

Colorful Triana, across the river from the city center, offers a nice range of eating options, especially around trendy Calle San Jacinto and the neighborhood scene behind the Church of Santa Ana. Also consider the covered market, home to a world of tempting lunchtime eateries (busiest Tue-Sat morning through afternoon). The riverside fish joints just beyond the Isabel II Bridge change names like hats and charge a little extra for their scenic setting, but if you want to eat reasonably on the river, they're worth considering.

On or near Calle San Jacinto

The area's pedestrianized main drag is lined with the tables of several easy-to-enjoy restaurants.

$$ Taberna Miami is a reliable bet for seafood. Grab a table with a good paseo-watching perch right on the street (daily 11:30-24:00, Calle San Jacinto 21, tel. 954-340-843).

$$ Blanca Paloma Bar is a classic wine bar offering a delightful bar (for tapas), plenty of small tables for a sit-down meal (no tapas), and a fine selection of good Spanish wines by the glass, listed on the blackboard (Mon-Sat long hours, closed Sun, at the corner of Calle Pagés del Corro, tel. 954-333-640).

$$ Las Golondrinas Bar ("The Sparrows") is famed in Triana for its wonderful list of tasty tapas. The dining area is limited to big and pricier *raciones* (ideal for groups). For one or two people, the tapas scene in the bar is best. Favorites here are the pork *punta de solomillo* (tenderloin) and *champiñones* (mushrooms). Cling to a corner of the bar and watch the amazingly productive little kitchen jam (daily 13:00-16:00 & 20:00-24:00, Calle Antillano Campos 26, tel. 954-331-626).

Behind the Church of Santa Ana

This is a more rustic and casual neighborhood scene, offering a charming setting where you can sit down under a big tree in the shade of the old church and dine with locals.

Eat afuera *(outside) in Sevilla.*

$$ Bar Bistec is enthusiastic about their cod fritters, fried zucchini *(calabacín)*, and calamari, and brags about their quail and snails in sauce. Before taking a seat out on the square, consider the indoor seating and the fun action at the bar (tapas only, daily 11:30-16:00 & 20:00-24:00, Plazuela de Santa Ana, tel. 954-274-759).

$ Taberna La Plazuela is simpler, doing fried fish, grilled sardines, and *caracoles* (snails) in spring. They serve from the tapas menu in the bar and at tables on the square (long hours daily, Plazuela de Santa Ana 1, tel. 686-976-293).

$ Bar Santa Ana is a rustic neighborhood bar—run by the same family for a century—with great seating on the street and a classic neighborhood-bar ambience inside. Peruse the interior, draped in Weeping Virgin and bullfighting memorabilia. It's always busy with the neighborhood gang, who enjoys fun tapas like *delicia de solomillo* (pork tenderloin). I like to be engulfed in the scene—sitting at the bar, where they keep track of your bill by chalking it directly on the counter (long hours daily, facing the side of the church at Calle Pureza 82, tel. 954-272-102).

Barrio Santa Cruz and Cathedral Area

For tapas, the Barrio Santa Cruz is *romántico* and *turístico*. Plenty of atmospheric joints fill the neighborhood near the cathedral. Walk up Calle Mateos Gago, where classic old bars—with the day's tapas scrawled on chalkboards—keep the tourists (and a few locals) well fed and watered.

$ Bodega Santa Cruz (a.k.a. **Las Columnas**) is a popular, user-friendly standby with cheap, forgettable tapas but an unforgettable scene. You can keep an eye on the busy kitchen from the bar, or hang out like a cowboy at the tiny stand-up tables out front (daily 11:30-24:00, Calle de Rodrigo Caro 1A, tel. 954-213-246).

$$$ La Azotea is a modern place that makes up for its lack of traditional character with gourmet tapas—made with local, seasonal ingredients, explained with a fun and accessible menu. It's run by Juan Antonio and his partner from San Diego, Jeanine. You can dine elegantly on tapas for reasonable prices (served only at the bar) or enjoy a sit-down meal—but you'll need to arrive early (daily 9:00-24:00, Calle Mateos Gago 8, tel. 954-215-878). Another branch is not far from Plaza Nueva (daily 13:30-24:00, Calle Zaragoza 5, tel. 954-564-316).

$$ Las Teresas is a characteristic little bar draped in festival posters and memorabilia—with ham hocks dripping from the ceiling. Prices at the bar and outside tables (for fun tourist-watching) are the same, but tapas are only available inside, at either the bar or tables (daily 10:00-24:00, Calle Santa Teresa 2, tel. 954-213-069).

$$ Restaurante San Marco Italian serves basic dishes under the arches of what was a Moorish bath (a thousand years ago) and then a disco (in the 1990s). The air-conditioned atmosphere feels upscale, but it's easygoing and family-friendly, with live Spanish guitar nightly after 20:30 (daily 13:00-16:15 & 19:30-24:00, Calle Mesón del Moro 6, tel. 954-214-390, welcoming Ángelo).

$ Freiduría Puerta de la Carne is a fried-fish-to-go place, with great outdoor seating. Study the photos of the options available; *un quarto* (250 grams, for €5-7) serves one person. Then head out front and grab a table (daily 13:00-17:00 & 20:00-24:30, usually no lunch service in summer; Calle Santa María la Blanca 34, tel. 954-426-820).

$$ Bar Restaurante El 3 de Oro is a venerable place with old-school waiters and a fun energy. The menu offers the full range of Andalusian classics (long hours daily, Calle Santa María la Blanca 34, tel. 954-422-759).

Ice Cream: The neighborhood favorite is **Bolas,** where *maestro heladero* Antonino has been making ice cream in Sevilla for the past 40 years, with a focus on fresh, natural, and inventive products (daily 12:00-24:00, Puerto de la Carne 3).

Between the Cathedral and the River

The area between the cathedral and the river, just across Avenida de la Constitución, is a wonderland of tapas, cheap eats, and fine dining. Calle García de Vinuesa leads past several colorful and cheap tapas places to a busy corner surrounded by an impressive selection of happy eateries (where Calle de Adriano meets Calle Antonia Díaz).

$$$ Bodeguita Casablanca is famously the choice of bullfighters—and even the king. Just steps from the touristy cathedral area, this feels like a neighborhood spot, with stylish locals and a great menu. I'm partial to the *solomillo* (tenderloin) and the artichokes. Tapas are available outside Monday through Thursday and inside anytime, while *raciones* are available inside or out (Mon-Fri 12:30-17:00 & 20:00-24:00, Sat 12:30-17:30, closed Sun and Aug, reservations smart, across the way from Archivo General de Indias at Calle Adolfo Rodríguez Jurado 12, tel. 954-224-114, www.bodeguitacasablanca.com).

$$$ La Casa del Tesorero Italian is a good, dressy alternative to the tapas commotion, with mellow lighting and music. It creates its own world, with a calm, spacious, elegant interior built upon 12th-century Moorish ruins (look through the glass floor) and under historic arches of what used to be the city's treasury (daily 12:30-16:00 & 19:30-23:30, Calle Santander 1, tel. 954-503-921).

$$ El Postiguillo has a fun ambience—sort of bullfighting-meets-*Bonanza*—where stuffed heads decorate the walls of a fanciful wooden stable. Locals come for the top-quality, traditional dishes, while tourists like the easy menu and snappy service (daily 12:00-24:00, Calle Dos de Mayo 2, tel. 954-565-162).

$$$ La Isla, tucked away in a narrow alley behind the Postigo craft market, is dressy, expensive, and sought out for its food—locals say it serves the best seafood and paella in town. Classy service is the norm whether dining outside, at the bar, or in the restaurant (daily 12:30-24:00, Calle Arfe 25, tel. 954-215-376).

$$ La Bulla, the brainchild of a gang of local foodies, mixes up traditional dishes, creating an inventive international menu that's a welcome break from the usual fare. It's bohemian-chic, with rickety tables gathered around a busy kitchen (no bar and no outdoor seating). While risotto is their signature dish, I prefer their other offerings, which are easily splittable (daily 12:00-16:30 & 20:00-24:00, midway between cathedral and Torre del Oro at Calle 2 de Mayo 26, tel. 954-219-262).

$ Bodega Morales oozes old-Sevilla atmosphere. The front area is more of a drinking bar; for food, go to the back section (use the separate entrance around the corner). Try the *salchicha al vino blanco*—tasty sausage braised in white wine—or the spinach with chickpeas (order at the bar, good wine selection, daily 13:00-16:00 & 20:00-24:00, Calle García de Vinuesa 11, tel. 954-221-242).

Near Plaza Nueva

$$$ Zelai Bar Restaurant is completely contemporary, with pricey gourmet tapas and *raciones* that are a hit with a smart local crowd. Study the English menu, which works in both the bar area and the dressy little restaurant out back, where reservations are generally required (daily 13:00-16:30 & 21:00-23:30, off Plaza

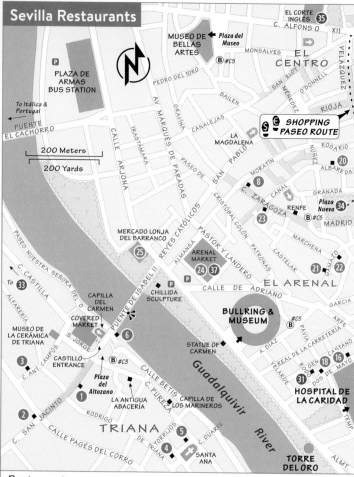

Restaurants

1 Taberna Miami
2 Blanca Paloma Bar
3 Las Golondrinas Bar
4 Bar Bistec & Taberna La Plazuela
5 Bar Santa Ana
6 Fish Joints
7 Bodega Santa Cruz
8 La Azotea (2)
9 Las Teresas
10 Restaurante San Marco Italian
11 Freiduría Puerta de la Carne
12 Bar Restaurante El 3 de Oro
13 Bolas Ice Cream

14 Bodeguita Casablanca
15 La Casa del Tesorero Italian
16 El Postiguillo
17 La Isla
18 La Bulla
19 Bodega Morales
20 Zelai Bar Restaurant
21 Bodeguita Antonio Romero
22 Abacería Casa Moreno
23 Taberna del Alabardero
24 Marisquería Arenal El Pesquero
25 Mercado Lonja del Barranco
26 El Torno Pastelería de Conventos

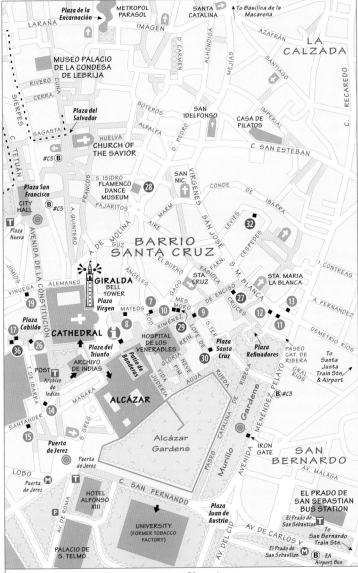

Flamenco

27 La Casa del Flamenco
28 Flamenco Dance Museum
29 Casa de la Guitarra Flamenco
30 Los Gallos
31 Tablao El Arenal
32 La Carbonería Bar
33 To Triana Flamenco Classes

Shopping

34 Shopping Paseo Starts
35 El Corte Inglés
36 El Postigo Arts & Crafts Market
37 Mercado del Arenal

Nueva at Calle Albareda 22, tel. 954-229-992, www.restaurantezelai.com).

$$ Bodeguita Antonio Romero has served millions of *montaditos* (little sandwiches) over the years. It's a tight, stools-or-stand kind of place. They're known for their tasty *pringá* (a meaty mix of beef, pork, sausage, and fat simmered for hours), but my favorite is the *piripí* (mini mouthful of pork tenderloin, bacon, cheese, tomato, and mayo). They also offer many good wines by the glass (Tue-Sun 12:00-24:00, closed Mon, Gamazo 16, tel. 954-210-585).

$$ Abacería Casa Moreno is a classic *abacería,* a neighborhood grocery store that doubles as a standing-room-only tapas bar. Squeeze into the back room and you're slipping back in time—and behind a tall language barrier. Rubbing elbows here with local eaters, under a bull's head, surrounded by jars of peaches and cans of sardines, you feel like you're in on a secret (Mon-Fri 9:45-15:30 & 18:30-22:30, Sat 10:30-16:00, closed Sun, 3 blocks off Plaza Nueva at Calle Gamazo 7, tel. 954-228-315).

$$$ Taberna del Alabardero, one of Sevilla's top restaurants, serves refined Spanish cuisine in chandeliered elegance. Consider their €20/person (no sharing) starter sampler, followed by an entrée. For €64 you can have an elaborate, seven-course fixed-price meal with lots of little surprises from the chef (be sure to understand your bill, daily 13:00-16:30 & 20:00-23:30, air-con, reservations smart, Zaragoza 20, tel. 954-502-721, www.tabernadelalabardero.es).

At or near the Arenal Market Hall

Mercado del Arenal, Sevilla's covered fish-and-produce market, is ideal for snapping photos and grabbing a cheap lunch. You'll find a world of picnic goodies—and a riverside promenade with benches just a block away (Mon-Sat 9:00-14:30, closed Sun, sleepy on Mon, on Calle Pastor y Landero at Calle Arenal, just beyond bullring).

$$$ Marisquería Arenal El Pesquero is a popular fish restaurant that thrives in the middle of the Arenal Market. It's a great family-friendly, finger-licking-good scene that's much appreciated by its enthusiastic local following (Tue-Sat 13:00-17:00 & 21:00-24:00, Sun open for dinner only, closed Mon, reservations smart for dinner, enter on Calle Pastor y Landero 9, tel. 954-220-881).

$$ Mercado Lonja del Barranco, an old fish market, is now a food hall with a wide variety of trendy, chain-like eateries filling a 19th-century building designed by Gustave Eiffel (of Parisian tower fame). It's just opposite Triana, facing the Isabel II Bridge (daily 10:00-24:00).

SLEEPING

All of my listings are centrally located, mostly within a five-minute walk of the cathedral. The first are near the charming but touristy Barrio Santa Cruz. The last group is just as central but closer to the river, across the boulevard in a more workaday, less touristy zone.

Room rates as much as double during the two Sevilla fiestas (Holy Week and the April Fair). In general, the busiest and most expensive months are April, May, September, and October. Hotels put rooms on the discounted push list in July and August—when people with good sense avoid this furnace—and from November through February.

If you do visit in July or August, you'll find the best deals in central, business-class places. They offer summer discounts and provide a (necessary) cool, air-conditioned refuge. But be warned that Spain's air-conditioning often isn't the icebox you're used to, especially in Sevilla.

Barrio Santa Cruz

These places are off Calle Santa María la Blanca and Plaza Santa María. The most convenient parking lot is the underground Cano y Cueto garage.

$$$$ Casa del Poeta offers peace, quiet, and a timeless elegance that seem contrary to its location in the heart of Santa Cruz. At the end of a side street, Trinidad and Ángelo have lovingly converted an old family mansion with 17 spacious rooms surrounding a large central patio into a home away from home (free breakfast if you reserve on their website, family room, air-con, elevator, Calle Don Carlos Alonso Chaparro 3, tel. 954-213-868, www.casadelpoeta.es, info@casadel-poeta.es).

$$$$ Hotel Las Casas de la Judería has 178 quiet, classy rooms and junior suites, most of them tastefully decorated with hardwood floors and a Spanish Old-World ambience. The rooms are a romantic splurge (RS% in low season, air-con, elevator, pool in summer, valet parking, Plaza Santa María 5, tel. 954-415-150, www.casasypalacios.com, juderia@casasypalacios.com).

$$$$ Hotel Casa 1800, well-priced for its elegance, is worth the extra euros. Located dead-center in the Barrio Santa Cruz (facing a boisterous tapas bar that quiets down after midnight), its 33 rooms are accessed via a lovely chandeliered patio lounge, where guests enjoy a daily free afternoon tea. With a rooftop terrace and swimming pool offering an impressive cathedral view, and tastefully appointed rooms with high, beamed ceilings, it's a winner (family rooms, air-con, elevator, Calle Rodrigo Caro 6, tel. 954-561-800, www.hotelcasa1800.com, info@hotelcasa1800.com).

$$$ Hotel Palacio Alcázar is the former home and studio of John Fulton, an American who moved here to become a bullfighter and painter. This charming boutique hotel has 12 crisp, modern rooms, and each soundproofed door is painted with a different dreamy scene of Sevilla (air-con, elevator, rooftop terrace with bar and cathedral views, Plaza de la Alianza 11, tel. 954-502-190, www.hotelpalacioalcazar.com, hotel@palacioalcazar.com).

$$$ Hotel Amadeus is a classy and comfortable gem, with welcoming public spaces and a very charming staff. The 30 rooms, lovingly decorated with a musical motif, are situated around small courtyards. Elevators take you to a two-tiered roof terrace with an under-the-stars hot tub (air-con, elevator, iPads in some rooms, laundry service, pay parking nearby, Calle Farnesio 6, tel. 954-501-443, www.hotelamadeussevilla.com, reservas@hotelamadeussevilla.com, wonderfully run by María Luisa and her daughters Zaida and Cristina).

$$$ Hotel Murillo enjoys one of the most appealing locations in Santa Cruz, along one of the very narrow "kissing lanes." Above its elegant, antiques-filled lobby are 64 nondescript rooms with marble bathrooms (air-con, elevator, Calle Lope de Rueda 7, tel. 954-216-095, www.hotelmurillo.com, reservas@hotelmurillo.com). They also rent apartments with kitchens (see website for details).

$$ El Rey Moro encircles its spacious, colorful patio with 18 rooms. Colorful, dripping with quirky Andalusian character, and thoughtful about including extras, it's a class act (free breakfast with this book, air-con, elevator, Reinoso 8, tel. 954-563-468, www.elreymoro.com, hotel@elreymoro.com).

$$ Hotel Alcántara offers clean and casual comfort in the heart of Santa Cruz. Well situated, it rents 23 slick rooms—most with patio views—at a good price (RS% if you pay cash, nice buffet breakfast available, air-con, elevator, outdoor patio, Calle Ximénez de Enciso 28, tel. 954-500-595, www.hotelalcantara.net, info@hotelalcantara.net).

$ Giralda Santa Cruz, once an 18th-century abbots' house, is now a homey 14-room hotel tucked away on a little street right off Calle Mateos Gago, just a couple of blocks from the cathedral. All rooms are basic but neatly appointed (air-con, Calle Abades 30, tel. 954-228-324, www.alojamientosconencantosevilla.

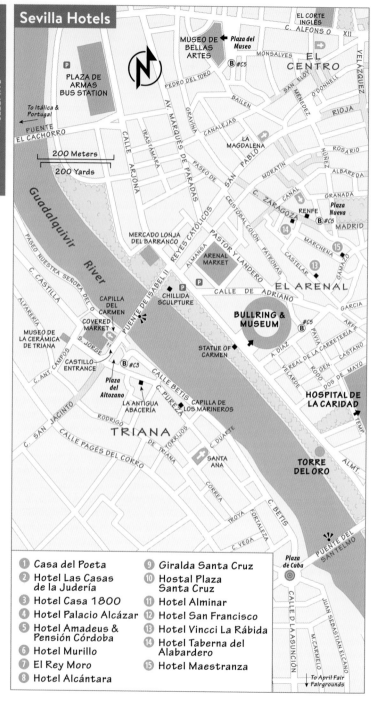

Sevilla Hotels

1. Casa del Poeta
2. Hotel Las Casas de la Judería
3. Hotel Casa 1800
4. Hotel Palacio Alcázar
5. Hotel Amadeus & Pensión Córdoba
6. Hotel Murillo
7. El Rey Moro
8. Hotel Alcántara
9. Giralda Santa Cruz
10. Hostal Plaza Santa Cruz
11. Hotel Alminar
12. Hotel San Francisco
13. Hotel Vincci La Rábida
14. Hotel Taberna del Alabardero
15. Hotel Maestranza

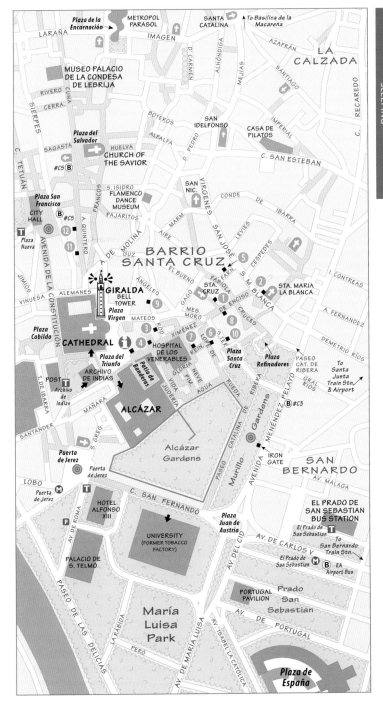

LARAÑA

Plaza de la
Encarnación

METROPOL
PARASOL

IMAGEN

SANTA
CATALINA

To Basílica de la
Macarena

AZAFRÁN

LA
CALZADA

C. RECAREDO

D. CARMEN

ALHÓNDIGA

MEJÍAS

SANTIAGO

RIVERO

CUNA

MUSEO PALACIO
DE LA CONDESA
DE LEBRIJA

SIERPES

CERRA.

SAGASTA

#C5 B

Plaza del
Salvador

HUELVA

CHURCH OF
THE SAVIOR

BOTEROS

ALFALFA

D. PEDRO

SAN
IDELFONSO

IMPERIAL

CASA DE
PILATOS

C. SAN ESTEBAN

C. TETUÁN

Plaza San
Francisco

CITY
HALL

B #C5

Plaza
Nueva

FRANCOS

A QUINTERO

12

11

S. ISIDRO
FLAMENCO
DANCE
MUSEUM

PAJARITOS

AIRE

A. DE MOLINA

GUZ.

SAN
NIC.

VIRGENES

MARM.

SAN JOSÉ

CONDE

LEVIES

DE IBARRA

BARRIO
SANTA CRUZ

EL BUENO

FABIOLA

STA.
CRUZ

S. M. BLANCA

CESPEDES

5

2

STA. MARIA
LA BLANCA

I. CONTRERAS

JIMIOS

VINUESA

ALEMANES

ÁNGELES

GIRALDA
BELL
TOWER

Plaza
Virgen

9

MATEOS

GAGO

MES
MORO

ROD.

DE ENCISO

CRUCES

1

8

A. FERNÁNDEZ

DEMETRIO RÍOS

AVENIDA DE LA CONSTITUCIÓN

Plaza
Cabildo

CATHEDRAL

3

4

i

XIMÉNEZ

FLIN. DE

LOPE DE

HOSPITAL
DE LOS
VENERABLES

7

6

GLORIA

PIM.

NEVE

AGUA

S. TER.

10

Plaza
Santa
Cruz

Plaza
Refinadores

PASEO
CAT. DE
RIBERA

GRAL
RÍOS

To
Santa
Justa
Train Stn
& Airport

POST

T. DE IBARRA

Plaza del
Triunfo

ARCHIVO
DE INDIAS

Patio de
Banderas

Archivo
de
Indias

MARAÑA

ALCÁZAR

JUDERÍA

VIDA

RUEDA

PASEO CATALINA DE RIBERA

MENÉNDEZ PELAYO

B #C3

SANTANDER

Puerta
de Jerez

S. GREG.

Alcázar
Gardens

Gardens

IRON
GATE

SAN
BERNARDO

AV. MALAGA

LOBO

Puerta
de Jerez

M

Puerta
de Jerez

T

HOTEL
ALFONSO
XIII

AV. DE ROMA

P

PALACIO DE
S. TELMO

PASEO DE LAS DELICIAS

LA RÁBIDA

C. SAN FERNANDO

UNIVERSITY
(FORMER TOBACCO
FACTORY)

Plaza
Juan de
Austria

AV. DEL CID

AV. DE CARLOS V

María
Luisa
Park

PERO

AV. DE MARÍA LUISA

AV. ISABEL LA CATÓLICA

EL PRADO DE
SAN SEBASTIÁN
BUS STATION

El Prado de
San Sebastián

T

To
San Sebastián
Train Stn.

El Prado de
San Sebastián

B

EA
Airport Bus

PORTUGAL
PAVILION

Prado
San
Sebastián

AV. DE PORTUGAL

Plaza de
España

com, giralda@alojamientosconencantos-
evilla.com).

$ **Pensión Córdoba** has 11 tidy, quiet rooms with cool-tone decor, and a show-piece tiled courtyard (air-con, on a tiny lane off Calle Santa María la Blanca at Calle Farnesio 12, tel. 954-227-498, www. pensioncordoba.com, reservas@pension-cordoba.com, twins Ana and María).

$ **Hostal Plaza Santa Cruz** is a charming little place, with thoughtful touches that you wouldn't expect in this price range. The 17 clean, basic rooms surround a bright little courtyard that's buried deep in the Barrio Santa Cruz (air-con, Calle Santa Teresa 15, tel. 954-228-808, www. alojamientosconencantosevilla.com, plaza@alojamientosconencantosevilla. com).

Near the Cathedral

$$$ **Hotel Alminar,** tidy and sophisticated, rents 11 fresh, slick, minimalist rooms. Double-pane windows keep it quiet at night (air-con, elevator, loaner laptop, just 100 yards from the cathedral at Calle Álvarez Quintero 52, tel. 954-293-913, www.hotelalminar.com, reservas@ hotelalminar.com, run by well-dressed, never-stressed Francisco).

$ **Hotel San Francisco** has 17 simple, dated rooms. It's centrally located, clean, and quiet, except for the noisy ground-floor room next to the TV and reception (air-con, elevator, small terrace with peek-a-boo cathedral view, located on pedestrian Calle Álvarez Quintero at #38, tel. 954-501-541, www.sanfranciscoh.com, info@sanfranciscoh.com, Carlos treats guests as part of the family).

West of Avenida de la Constitución

$$$$ **Hotel Vincci La Rábida,** part of a big, impersonal hotel chain, offers four-star comfort with its 84 rooms and huge, inviting courtyard lounge (elevator, Calle Castelar 24, tel. 954-501-280, www.vincci hoteles.com, larabida@vinccihoteles.com).

$$$$ **Hotel Taberna del Alabardero** has a special charm with seven spacious rooms occupying the top floor of a poet's mansion. It's nicely located, a great value, and the ambience is perfectly circa-1900 (air-con, elevator, pay parking, may close in Aug, Zaragoza 20, tel. 954-502-721, www.tabernadelalabardero.es, hotel.alab-ardero@esh.es).

$ **Hotel Maestranza,** sparkling with loving care and understated charm, has 17 simple, bright, clean rooms well-located on a street just off Plaza Nueva. It feels elegant for its price (family rooms available, 5 percent discount if you pay cash, air-con, elevator, Gamazo 12, tel. 954-561-070, www.hotelmaestranza.es, sevilla@ hotelmaestranza.es, Antonio).

TRANSPORTATION

Getting Around Sevilla

Most visitors have a full and fun experience in Sevilla without ever riding public transportation. The city center is compact, and most of the major sights are within easy walking distance.

By Taxi

Sevilla is a great taxi town; they're plentiful and cheap. Two or more people should go by taxi rather than public transit. You can hail one showing a green light anywhere, or find a cluster of them parked by major intersections and sights (€1.35 drop rate, €1/kilometer, €3.60 minimum; about 20 percent more on evenings and weekends; calling for a cab adds about €3). A quick daytime ride in town will generally fall within the €3.60 minimum. Although I'm quick to take advantage of taxis, note that because of one-way streets and traffic congestion it's often just as fast to hoof it between central points.

By Bus, Tram, and Metro

A single trip on any form of city transit costs €1.40. A Tarjeta Turistica card is good for one (€5) or three (€10) days of unlimited rides (€1.50 deposit, buy at TUSSAM kiosks, airport, El Prado de San Sebastián station, or Santa Justa station). For half-price trips, you can buy a Tarjeta Multiviaje card that's rechargeable and shareable (€7 for 10 trips, €1.50 deposit; buy at kiosks or at the TUSSAM transit office near the bus stop on Avenida de Carlos V, next to El Prado station, daily 8:00-20:00; scan it on the card reader as you board; for transit details, see www.tussam.es).

The various #C **buses,** which are handiest for tourists, make circular routes through town (note that all of them except the #C6 eventually wind up at Basílica de La Macarena). For all buses, buy your ticket from the driver or from machines at bus stops. The #C3 stops at Murillo Gardens, Triana, then La Macarena. The #C4 goes the opposite direction, but without entering Triana. And the spunky #C5 minibus winds through the old center of town, including Plaza del Salvador, Plaza de San Francisco, the bullring, Plaza Nueva, the Museo de Bellas Artes, La Campana, and La Macarena, providing a relaxing joyride that also connects some farther-flung sights (see route on "Sevilla" map).

A **tram** (tranvía) makes just a few stops in the heart of the city, but can save you a bit of walking. Buy your ticket at the machine on the platform before you board (runs about every 7 minutes Sun-Thu until 23:00, Fri-Sat until 1:45 in the morning). It makes five city-center stops (from south to north): San Bernardo (at the San Bernardo train station), Prado San Sebastián (next to El Prado de San Sebastián bus station), Puerta Jerez (south end of Avenida de la Constitución), Archivo General de Indias (next to the cathedral), and Plaza Nueva (beginning of shopping streets).

Sevilla also has an underground **metro,** but most tourists won't need to use it. It's designed to connect the suburbs with the center and only has one line. There are stops downtown at the San Bernardo train station, El Prado de San Sebastián bus station, and Puerta Jerez.

Arriving and Departing

Note that many destinations are well served by both trains and buses.

By Train

Most trains arriving and departing Sevilla, including all high-speed AVE trains, leave from the larger, more distant **Santa Justa** station, with banks, ATMs, and a TI. Baggage storage is below track 1 (follow signs to consigna, security checkpoint open 6:00-24:00). The easy-to-miss TI sits by the sliding doors at the main entrance, to the left before you exit. The plush little AVE Sala Club, designed for business travelers, welcomes those with a first-class AVE ticket and reservation (across the main hall from track 1).

Many cercanías and regional trains heading south to Granada, Jerez, Cádiz, and Málaga also stop at the smaller **San Bernardo** station a few minutes from Santa Justa, which is connected to downtown by tram. Hourly cercanías trains connect both stations (about a 4-minute trip).

Getting Downtown: From Santa Justa, it's a flat and boring 25-minute walk or about an €8 taxi ride. By city bus, it's a short ride on #C1 or #21 to the El Prado de San Sebastián bus station (find bus stop 100 yards in front of the train station, €1.40, pay driver), then a 10-minute walk or short tram ride.

TRAIN CONNECTIONS

For schedules and tickets, visit a Renfe Travel Center, either at the train station (daily 8:00-22:00, take a number and wait) or near Plaza Nueva in the city center (Mon-Fri 9:30-14:00 & 17:30-20:00, Sat 10:00-13:30, closed Sun, Calle Zaragoza 29). Many travel agencies sell train tickets; look for a train sticker in agency windows. Train info: tel. 912-320-320, www.renfe.com.

From Sevilla by AVE Train to Madrid: The AVE express train is expensive but fast (2.5 hours to Madrid; hourly departures 7:00-23:00). Departures between 16:00 and 19:00 can book up far in advance, but surprise holidays and long weekends can totally jam up trains as well—reserve as far ahead as possible.

From Sevilla by Train to Córdoba: There are four options for this journey: slow and cheap regional, *media distancia* trains (7/day, 1.5 hours), fast and cheap regional high-speed **Avant** trains (12/day, 45 minutes, requires reservation), and fast and expensive **AVE** trains (almost hourly, 45 minutes, requires reservation). Unless you must be on a particular departure, there's no reason to pay more for AVE; Avant or Alvia trains are just as quick and a third the price.

Other Trains from Sevilla to: Málaga (14/day, 45 minutes on AVE; 7/day, 2 hours on Avant; 5/day, 2.5 hours on slower regional trains), **Ronda** (4/day, 3 hours, transfer in Bobadilla or Córdoba), **Granada** (4/day, 3.5 hours, transfer in Córdoba and Antequera), **Jerez** (nearly hourly, 1.25 hours), **Barcelona** (2/day direct, more with transfer in Madrid, 5.5 hours).

By Bus

Sevilla's two major bus stations—El Prado de San Sebastián and Plaza de Armas—both have information offices, basic eateries, and baggage storage.

The **El Prado de San Sebastián bus station,** often called just "El Prado," covers most of Andalucía (information desk, daily 8:00-20:00, tel. 955-479-290, generally no English spoken; baggage lockers/ *consigna* at the far end of station, same hours). From the bus station to downtown (and Barrio Santa Cruz hotels), it's about a 15-minute **walk**. Sevilla's **tram** connects the station with the city center (and many of my recommended hotels): Turn left as you exit the bus station and walk to Avenida de Carlos V (€1.40, buy

ticket at machine before boarding; ride it two stops to Archivo General de Indias to reach the cathedral area, or three stops to Plaza Nueva).

The **Plaza de Armas bus station** (near the river, opposite the Expo '92 site) serves long-distance destinations such as Madrid, Barcelona, Lagos, and Lisbon. **Taxis** to downtown cost around €7. Or, to take the **bus**, exit onto the main road (Calle Arjona) to find bus #C4 into the center (stop is to the left, in front of the taxi stand; €1.40, pay driver, get off at Puerta de Jerez).

From El Prado de San Sebastián station to Andalucía and the South Coast: Regional buses are operated by Comes (www.tgcomes.es), Damas (www.damas-sa.es), and Autocares Valenzuela (www.grupovalenzuela.com). Connections to **Jerez** are frequent, as many southbound buses head there first (7/day, 1.5 hours, run by all three companies; note that train is also possible—see earlier). Damas runs buses to some of Andalucía's hill towns, including **Ronda** (7/day, 2.5 hours, fewer on weekends) and **Arcos** (2/day, 2 hours; more departures possible with transfer in Jerez). For Spain's South Coast, a Comes bus departs Sevilla four times a day and heads to **La Línea/Gibraltar** (4.5 hours). There is one bus a day from this station to **Granada** (3 hours); the rest depart from the Plaza de Armas station.

From Plaza de Armas station to: Madrid (9/day, 6 hours, www.socibus.es), **Córdoba** (7/day, 2 hours), **Granada** (7/day, 3 hours), **Málaga** (7/day direct, 3 hours), **Nerja** (1/day, 5 hours), and **Barcelona** (2/day, 16.5 hours, including one overnight bus).

By Car

To drive into Sevilla, follow *Centro Ciudad* (city center) signs. The city is no fun to drive in and parking can be frustrating. If your hotel lacks parking or a recommended plan, pay for a garage (€20-24 per day) and grab a taxi to your hotel from there. For hotels in the Barrio Santa Cruz area, the handiest parking is the Cano y Cueto garage near the corner of Calle Santa María la Blanca and Avenida de Menéndez Pelayo (open daily 24 hours, at edge of big park, underground).

By Plane

Sevilla's San Pablo Airport sits about six miles east of downtown and has several car rental agencies in the arrivals hall (airport code: SVQ, tel. 954-449-000, www. aena.es). The Especial Aeropuerto (EA) bus connects the airport with both train stations, both bus stations, and several stops in the town center (2-3/hour, runs 4:30-24:00, 40 minutes, €4, buy ticket from driver). The two most convenient stops downtown are south of the Murillo gardens on Avenida de Carlos V, near El Prado de San Sebastián bus station (close to my recommended Barrio Santa Cruz hotels); and on the Paseo de Cristóbal Colón, near the Torre del Oro. Look for the small *EA* sign at bus stops. If you're going from downtown Sevilla *to* the airport, the bus stop is on the side of the street closest to Plaza de España. To taxi into town, go to one of the airport's taxi stands to ensure a fixed rate (€25 by day, €28 at night and on weekends, extra for luggage, confirm price with the driver before your journey).

BEST OF THE REST

Córdoba

Straddling a sharp bend of the Guadalquivir River, Córdoba has a glorious Roman and Moorish past, once serving as a regional capital for both empires. It's home to the Mezquita, a splendid mosque-turned-cathedral that dates from AD 784. During the Dark Ages, when much of Europe was barbaric and illiterate, Córdoba was a haven of enlightened thought.

Day Plan

Don't rush the magnificent Mezquita. With extra time, wander the evocative Jewish Quarter and climb the tower of the Museum of Al-Andalus Life for a city overview. If overnighting, consider a flamenco show.

Orientation

Córdoba's big draw, the Mezquita (meth-KEE-tah), is buried in the characteristic medieval town. Around that stretches the Jewish Quarter, then the modern city.

Tourist Information: Córdoba has helpful TIs at the train station and Plaza de las Tendillas (daily, tel. 902-201-774, https://turismodecordoba.org) and another near the Mezquita (daily, Plaza del Triunfo).

Local Guides: Consider **Isabel Martínez Richter** (€137/3 hours, more on weekends, isabmr@gmail.com) or Ángel **Lucena** (€100/3 hours, lucenaangel@ hotmail.com).

Getting There

Córdoba is on the slick AVE train line (reservations required), making it an easy stopover between Madrid (almost hourly, 2 hours) and Sevilla (45 minutes). The Avant train connects Córdoba to Sevilla just as fast for nearly half the price (12/day, 45 minutes).

Córdoba's **train station** is located on Avenida de América; the **bus station** is across the street. There's no luggage storage at the train station, but the bus station has lockers (next to ticket booth #11, look for *Consigna/Locker* sign and buy token at machine, lockers are around corner). To get to the old town, hop a **taxi** (€8 to the Mezquita) or catch **bus** #3 (stop is west of the train and bus stations, buy €1.30 ticket on board, ask driver for *"mezquita,"* get off at Calle San Fernando, and take Calle del Portillo, following the twists and turns—and occasional signs—to the Mezquita). It's about a 25-minute **walk** from either station to the old town.

By **car,** the easiest way to enter the city center from Madrid or Sevilla on A-4/E-5 is to track signs for *Córdoba sur* and *Plaza de Andalucía,* following palm-tree-lined A-431 (Avenida del Corregidor). You'll find underground public parking off Paseo de la Victoria.

Sights

▲▲▲MEZQUITA

This massive former mosque—now with a 16th-century church rising up from the middle—was once the center of Western Islam and the heart of a cultural capital that rivaled Baghdad and Constantinople. A wonder of the medieval world, it's remarkably well-preserved, giving today's visitors a chance to soak up the ambience of Islamic Córdoba in its 10th-century prime.

Cost: €10, ticket kiosk and machines inside the Patio de los Naranjos, Mon-Sat

free entry 8:30-9:30 (during 9:30 Mass); detailed but dry audioguide-€3.50; bell tower climb-€2.

Hours: Mon-Sat 8:30-19:00, Sun 8:30-11:30 & 15:00-19:00; Nov-Feb closes daily at 18:00; Christian altar accessible only after 11:00 unless you attend Mass; usually less crowded after 15:00.

Information: Tel. 957-470-512, www.mezquita-catedraldecordoba.es

Visiting the Mezquita: The Mezquita's big, welcoming **courtyard** is free to enter. When this was a mosque, the Muslim faithful would gather in this courtyard to perform ablution—ritual washing before prayer, as directed by Muslim law. Gaze up through the trees for views of the **bell tower** (c. 1600), built over the remains of the original Muslim minaret. For four centuries, five times a day, a singing cleric (the *muezzin*) would ride a donkey up the ramp of the minaret, then call to all Muslims in earshot that it was time to face Mecca and pray.

Entering the former mosque, you pass into a forest of more than 800 red-and-blue columns topped with double arches.

The Mezquita's interior blends Islamic and Christian architecture.

The columns seem to recede to infinity, as if reflecting the immensity and complexity of Allah's creation.

The mosque's focal point is the **mihrab,** the mosque equivalent of a church's high altar. Picture the original mosque at prayer time, with more than 20,000 people kneeling in prayer. Built in the mid-10th century, the exquisite room reflects the wealth of Córdoba in its prime.

Rising up in the middle of the mosque is the bright, restored **cathedral.** In 1523 Córdoba's bishop proposed building this grand church in the Mezquita's center. If that seems like a travesty, consider what some locals will point out: Though it would have been quicker and less expensive for the Christian builders to destroy the mosque entirely, they respected its beauty and built their church into it instead.

*Rick's Tip: Climb the tower of the Museum of Al-Andalus Life for the **best panoramic view** of Córdoba and the cathedral rising from the Mezquita (€4.50, daily 10:00-14:00 & 16:30, Oct-April 10:00-18:00, Torre de la Calahorra). The view is better than the museum.*

JEWISH CÓRDOBA

Córdoba's Jewish Quarter dates from the late Middle Ages, after Muslim rule and during the Christian era. For a sense of the neighborhood in its thriving heyday, head to Calle de los Judíos and the **Casa de Sefarad.** This museum, set inside a restored 14th-century home, brings to life Córdoba's rich Jewish past (€4, daily 10:00-19:00, opens and closes one hour later in winter, 30-minute guided tours in English by request if guide is available, at corner of Calle de los Judíos and Calle Averroes, www.casadesefarad.es). Then, if it's open, visit the small yet beautifully preserved **synagogue** across from the museum. Built between 1314 and 1315, it

was in use right up until the final expulsion of the Jews from Spain in 1492 (free, may be closed for renovation when you visit—check locally; Tue-Sat 9:00-20:30, Sun and summers until 15:00, closed Mon year-round; Calle de los Judíos 20).

Finally, step into the **artisan market** (*zoco municipal*) set in a charming series of courtyards off Calle de los Judíos (free to enter, daily 10:00-20:00, www.artesaniadecordoba.com).

Nightlife

The Caballerizas Reales de Córdoba at the royal stables combines an artful equestrian show with flamenco dance (€15, one-hour shows Wed-Sat at 21:00, Caballerizas Reales 1, www.cordobaecuestre.com).

For flamenco only, try **Tablao Flamenco Cardenal** (€23, includes one drink, dinner for €11 extra, 1.5-hour shows Mon-Thu at 20:15, Fri-Sat at 21:00, no shows Sun, confirm schedule online, Buen Pastor 2, mobile 691-217-922, www.tablaocardenal.es).

Eating

Near the Mezquita, touristy **$$ Bodegas Mezquita** is easy and handy (daily, branches at Calle Céspedes 12 and Calle Corregidor Luis de la Cerda 73); **$ Bar Santos** supplies the giant *tortilla de patatas* (potato omelettes) that you see locals happily munching (daily, Calle Magistral González Francés 3). Just inside the evocative Puerta de Almodóvar gate is **$$ Taberna Restaurante Casa Rubio,** serving reliably good traditional dishes (daily, Puerta de Almodóvar 5).

Sleeping

Within a five-minute stroll of the Mezquita you'll find the elegant **$$$$ Balcón de Córdoba** (Calle Encarnación 8, www.balcondecordoba.com); the quiet and romantic **$$ La Llave de la Judería** (Calle Romero 38, www.lallavedelajuderia.es); and the humble but sleepable **$ Hotel González** (Calle de los Manríquez 3, www.hotelgonzalez.com).

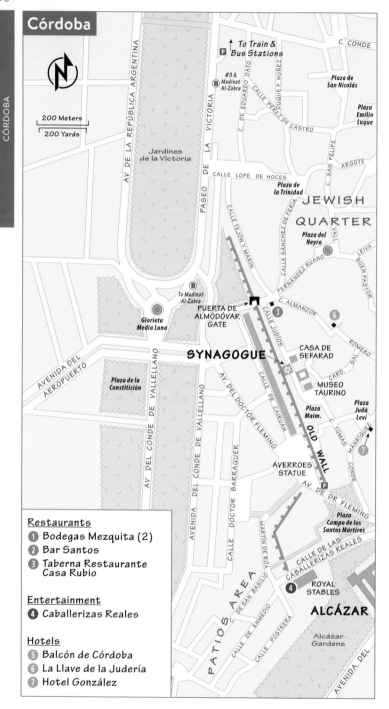

Córdoba

To Train &
Bus Stations

🅟

🅑 #3 &
Madinat
Al-Zahra

C. CONDE

Plaza de
San Nicolás

Plaza
Emilio
Luque

200 Meters

200 Yards

Jardines
de la Victoria

AV. DE LA REPÚBLICA ARGENTINA

C. DE EDUARDO DATO

CALLE PÉREZ DE CASTRO

CALLE DUQUE DE FERIA

CALLE F. NÚÑEZ

PASEO DE LA VICTORIA

C. SAN FELIPE

ARGOTE

CALLE LOPE DE HOCES

Plaza de
la Trinidad

JEWISH

QUARTER

CALLE TEJÓN Y MARÍN

CALLE SÁNCHEZ DE FERIA

FERNÁNDEZ RUANO

Plaza del
Neyra

LEIVA

BUEN PASTOR

🅑
To Madinat
Al-Zahra

Glorieta
Media Luna

PUERTA DE
ALMODÓVAR
GATE

C. ALMANZOR

❸

❻

ROMERO

AVENIDA DEL
AEROPUERTO

Plaza de la
Constitición

AV. DEL CONDE DE VALLELLANO

SYNAGOGUE

CALLE JUDÍOS

AV. DEL DOCTOR FLEMING

CALLE DE CAIRUAN

CASA DE
SEFARAD

CARD. SAL...

MUSEO
TAURINO

Plaza
Maim.

Plaza Judá
Levi

C. TOMÁS

MANRÍQUEZ

CONDE

❼

AVENIDA DEL CONDE DE VALLELLANO

CALLE DOCTOR BARRAQUER

AVERROES
STATUE

AV. DE DR. FLEMING

🅟

Plaza
Campo de los
Santos Mártires

Restaurants
❶ Bodegas Mezquita (2)
❷ Bar Santos
❸ Taberna Restaurante
Casa Rubio

Entertainment
❹ Caballerizas Reales

Hotels
❺ Balcón de Córdoba
❻ La Llave de la Judería
❼ Hotel González

PATIOS AREA

C. DE SAN BASILIO

CALLE DE ENMEDIO

CALLE POSTRERA

CALLE MARTÍN DE ROA

CALLE DE LAS
CABALLERIZAS REALES

❹ ROYAL
STABLES

ALCÁZAR

Alcázar
Gardens

AVENIDA DEL

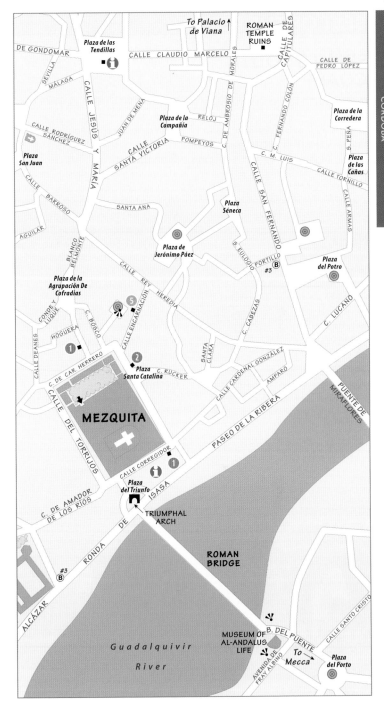

BEST OF THE REST

SPAIN'S SOUTH COAST

Much of Spain's south coast is so bad, it's interesting. Anything resembling a quaint fishing village has been bikini-strangled and Nivea-creamed. But the south coast holds a few gems. Unroll your beach towel at Nerja, the most appealing resort town on the coast. And jolly olde England beckons: the land of tea and scones, fish-and-chips, and pubs awaits you—in Gibraltar.

Nerja

While cashing in on the fun-in-the-sun culture, Nerja has kept much of its Old World charm. It has good beaches, a fun evening paseo, enough nightlife to keep you entertained, and locals who get more excited about their many festivals than the tourists do.

Day Plan

If you're coming from fast-paced Madrid or Barcelona, walking Nerja's streets, where everyone seems to have all the time in the world, is a psychological adjustment—but that's why you're here. The single best thing to do on a sunny day in Nerja is to hit the beach: swim, sunbathe, sip a drink, go for a hike along the rocky coves...or all of the above.

Orientation

The tourist center of Nerja is right along the water and crowds close to its famous bluff, the Balcony of Europe (Balcón de Europa). Fine beaches flank the bluff, stretching in either direction. The old town is just inland from the Balcony, while the more modern section slopes up and away from the water.

Tourist Information: The helpful TI is 100 yards from the Balcony of Europe (daily, tel. 952-521-531, www.nerja.es).

Local Guide: Carmen Fernández is excellent (€90/3 hours, mfeyus@gmail.com).

Getting There

Nerja, which doesn't have a train station, has direct **bus** connections with Granada

Nerja's Balcony of Europe

(6/day, 2.5 hours), Sevilla (1/day, 5 hours), and Málaga, the nearest major transit hub (1-2/hour, 1.5 hour *directo*). Málaga has train connections with all major cities in Spain, plus buses as well.

The Nerja **bus station** is just a bus stop with an info/ticket kiosk on Avenida de Pescia (www.alsa.es). **Drivers** can find the old-town center and the most central parking by following *Balcón de Europa, Centro Urbano,* or *Centro Ciudad* signs, and then pull into the big underground lot beneath the Plaza de España. The handiest free parking is about a 10-minute walk farther out (near the town bus stop, just off N-340).

Sights
▲▲BALCONY OF EUROPE (BALCÓN DE EUROPA)

The bluff, jutting happily into the sea, is completely pedestrianized. It's the center of Nerja's paseo and a magnet for street performers. The mimes, music, and puppets can draw bigger crowds than the Balcony itself, which overlooks the Mediterranean, miles of coastline, and little coves below.

BEACHES

Many of Nerja's beaches are well-equipped with bars and restaurants, free

Paella on the beach, Nerja style

showers, and rentable lounge chairs and umbrellas. Watch out for red flags on the beach, which indicate when the seas are too rough for safe swimming. Keep a careful eye on your valuables—or better yet leave them in the hotel.

Directly beneath the Balcony of Europe is pebbly **Playa Calahonda,** with fun pathways, crags, and crannies. To the east, a 20-minute walk (or €8 taxi) brings you to the bustling **Playa de Burriana.** West of the Balcony of Europe, choose from sandy but crowded **Playa del Salón, Playa la Torrecilla,** and local favorite **El Playazo.**

▲NERJA CAVES (CUEVA DE NERJA)

These caves (2.5 miles east of Nerja), with an impressive array of stalactites and stalagmites, are a classic roadside attraction. A visit involves a 45-minute audioguide tour, during which you'll climb deep into the mountain, up and down 400 dark stairs. At the end you reach the Hall of the Cataclysm, where you'll circle the world's largest stalactite column.

Cost and Hours: €10, daily 9:30-16:30, July-Aug until 19:00, timed entry on the hour and half-hour, smart to book online in July and August, last entry one hour before closing; easy pay parking, www.cuevadenerja.es.

Getting There: Catch a bus across the street from Nerja's main bus stop (€1.20, roughly hourly, 10-minute ride—get schedule from TI) or take a taxi (€10 one-way). Drivers take exit 295 on A-7 and follow the *Cueva de Nerja* signs.

Nightlife

Bar El Molino offers live Spanish folk singing nightly (starts at 22:00, Calle San José 4). **El Burro Blanco** is a touristy flamenco bar with shows nightly in the summer (corner of Calle Pintada and Calle de la Gloria). For more trendy and noisy nightlife, check out the **pub bars and dance clubs** on Antonio Millón and Plaza Tutti Frutti.

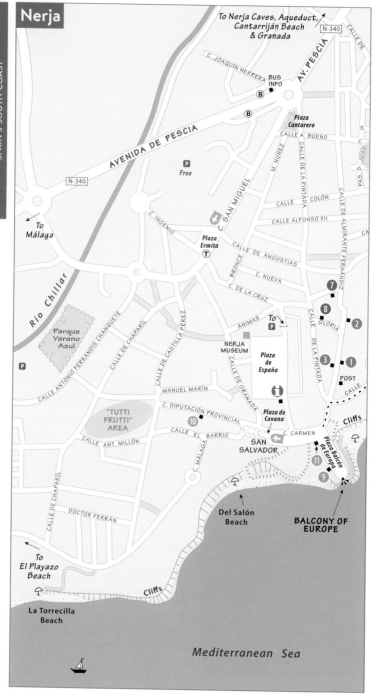

Nerja

To Nerja Caves, Aqueduct,
Cantarriján Beach
& Granada

N-340

CALLE DE

AV. PESCIA

C. JOAQUÍN HERRERA

BUS
INFO

Ⓑ

Ⓑ

Plaza
Cantarero

AVENIDA DE PESCIA

CALLE A. BUENO

M. NÚÑEZ

CALLE DE LA PINTADA

CALLE
COLÓN

CALLE DE ALMIRANTE FERNÁNDIZ

PAS. S.
JUAN

S.

C.

N-340

P
Free

C. SAN MIGUEL

CALLE

CALLE ALFONSO XII

CA

C. INGENIO

Plaza
Ermita
Ⓣ

CALLE DE ANGUSTIAS

BRONCE

C. NUEVA

C. DE LA CRUZ

7

8

CALLE
GLORIA

2

Río Chillar

Parque
Verano
Azul

CALLE ANTONIO FERRÁNDIS CHANQUETE

CALLE DE CHAPARIL

CALLE DE CASTILLA PÉREZ

ÁNIMAS

To
P

NERJA
MUSEUM

Plaza
de
España

CALLE DE LA PINTADA

3

1

POST

CALLE

P

MANUEL MARÍN

C. DIPUTACIÓN PROVINCIAL

CALLE EL BARRIO

CALLE DE GRANADA

10

"TUTTI
FRUTTI"
AREA

CALLE ANT. MILLÓN

C. MÁLAGA

i

Plaza de
Cavana

C. CARMEN

SAN
SALVADOR

Cliffs

Plaza Balcón
de Europa

11

9

CALLE DE CHAPARIL

DOCTOR FERRÁN

To
El Playazo
Beach

Del Salón
Beach

Cliffs

BALCONY OF
EUROPE

La Torrecilla
Beach

Mediterranean Sea

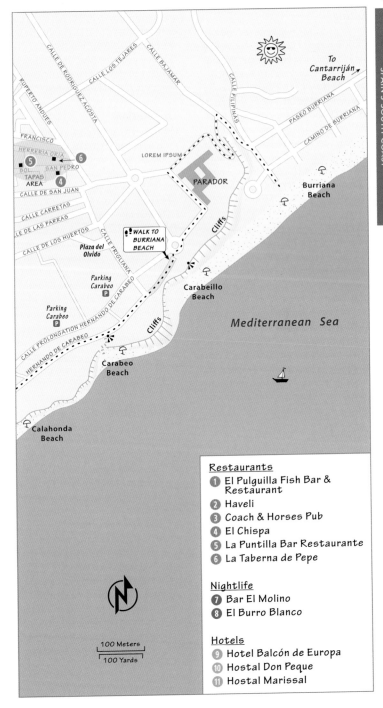

CALLE DE RODRÍGUEZ ACOSTA
CALLE LOS TEJARES
CALLE BAJAMAR
CALLE FILIPINAS
RUPERTO ANDIES
FRANCISCO
HERRERÍA OKIA
SAN PEDRO
BOL
TAPAS AREA
CALLE DE SAN JUAN
CALLE CARRETAS
LE DE LAS PARRAS
CALLE DE LOS HUERTOS
Plaza del Olvido
CALLE FRIGILIANA
Parking Carabeo
Parking Carabeo
CALLE PROLONGACIÓN HERNANDO DE CARABEO
HERNANDO DE CARABEO
LOREM IPSUM
PARADOR
Cliffs
WALK TO BURRIANA BEACH
Carabeillo Beach
Cliffs
Carabeo Beach
Calahonda Beach

To Cantarriján Beach
PASEO BURRIANA
CAMINO DE BURRIANA
Burriana Beach

Mediterranean Sea

100 Meters
100 Yards

Restaurants
1 El Pulguilla Fish Bar & Restaurant
2 Haveli
3 Coach & Horses Pub
4 El Chispa
5 La Puntilla Bar Restaurante
6 La Taberna de Pepe

Nightlife
7 Bar El Molino
8 El Burro Blanco

Hotels
9 Hotel Balcón de Europa
10 Hostal Don Peque
11 Hostal Marissal

Eating

Strolling up Calle Almirante Ferrándiz, you'll find a good variety of eateries, including **$$ El Pulguilla Fish Bar and Restaurant,** a high-energy place (closed Mon, #26); **$$ Haveli,** serving good Indian cuisine (closed Wed off-season, #44); and **$$ Coach and Horses Pub**, a little bit of old England (daily, #19). For a selection of tapas bars, continue uphill to find **$ El Chispa** (Calle San Pedro 12), **$ La Puntilla Bar Restaurante** (Calle Bolivia 1), and **$ La Taberna de Pepe** (closed Thu, Calle Herrera Oria 30).

Sleeping

The entire Costa del Sol is crowded during August and Easter Week, when prices are at their highest. **$$$$ Hotel Balcón de Europa** is the most central place in town, with the prestigious address Balcón de Europa 1 (www.hotelbalconeuropa.com). **$$ Hostal Don Peque** has cheery rooms, some with sea views (Calle Diputación 13, www.hostaldonpeque.com), and **$ Hostal Marissal** has an unbeatable location next door to the fancy Hotel Balcón de Europa (Balcón de Europa 3, www.hostalmarissal. com).

Gibraltar

One of the last bits of the empire upon which the sun never set, Gibraltar is famous for its dramatic Rock of Gibraltar, which rockets improbably into the air from an otherwise flat terrain. Britain has controlled this highly strategic spit of land since they took it by force in 1704. Virtually everyone speaks the Queen's English.

Day Plan

Head for the top of the Rock (by cable car or taxi), then walk down, seeing the sights along the way, and explore the town. Avoid visiting on a Sunday, when nearly everything is closed.

Before you walk across the border, decide whether you want to take the cable car to the top of the Rock or visit it via a private taxi tour. You can hire a taxi on the spot at a stand just inside the border. For the cable car, buy tickets at the Gibraltar info window on the left before passport control and take the free shuttle directly to the cable-car station.

Orientation

Gibraltar is a narrow peninsula (three miles by one mile) jutting into the Mediterranean and dominated by the steep-faced Rock itself. The locals live down below in the long, skinny town at the western base of the mountain.

Tourist Information: Gibraltar's main TI is at John Mackintosh Square (daily, tel. 200-45000, www.visitgibraltar.gi). At the border, there's a TI window in the customs building (closed Sat-Sun).

Money: Gibraltar uses the British pound sterling (£1 = about $1.40). Merchants in Gibraltar also accept euros, but at an unfavorable exchange rate. On a quick trip, don't bother drawing out cash; you can buy things with your credit card or use euros (though you may get pounds back in change).

Getting There

The nearest **bus station** is in Spain's La Línea de la Concepción, a five-minute walk from the Gibraltar border, with connections to Málaga (4/day, 3 hours), Sevilla (5/day, 4.5 hours), and Algeciras (2/hour, 45 minutes). The nearest **train station** is at Algeciras, the region's main transportation hub. You don't need a **car** in Gibraltar. It's simpler to park in La Línea and just walk across the border. The Santa Bárbara parking lot is closest to the border.

Crossing the Border: No matter how you arrive, you'll need your **passport** to cross the border. The "frontier" (as the border is called) is a chaotic hubbub of travel agencies, confused tourists, crafty pickpockets, and duty-free shops (pick up a map at the TI window in the customs building).

To get into Gibraltar town by **foot,** walk

Rock of Gibraltar

straight across the airport runway (look left, right, and up), then head down Winston Churchill Avenue. Angle right at the second roundabout, then walk along the fortified Line Wall Road to Casemates Square.

You can also ride **bus** #5 to Market Square, from where blue Gibraltar city buses head to various points on the peninsula (bus #2 goes to the cable-car station). The border bus and the city buses have different, nontransferable tickets at the same prices (€2.40/£1.80 one-way, €3.30/£2.50 all-day "Hoppa" ticket on buses; drivers accept either currency and give change).

A **taxi** from the border is €9/£6 to the cable-car station.

Rick's Tip: *The* **monkeys** *that congregate on the Rock have gotten more aggressive over the years. Keep your distance and don't feed them;* **it's best to have no food with you** *when you visit the Rock.*

Sights
ROCK OF GIBRALTAR
The actual Rock of Gibraltar is the colony's best sight. Its attractions include

the stupendous view from the very top, temperamental apes, a hokey cave (St. Michael's), and the impressive Great Siege Tunnels drilled through the rock face for military purposes. Hikers can ride the lift up and take a long, steep, scenic walk down, connecting the various sights by strolling along paved lanes (1.5 hours without stops).

Cost: £5 walkers ticket is required to enter the grounds. A £12 nature reserve ticket is required to visit any or all of these major sights within the reserve: St. Michael's Cave, Great Siege Tunnels, Moorish Castle, Military Heritage Centre, and City Under Siege exhibit.

Hours: Daily 9:30-19:15, until 18:15 late Oct-late March.

Visiting the Rock by Taxi Tour: Minivans driven by cabbies trained and licensed to lead these 1.5-hour trips are standing by at the border and at various points in town. They charge £27/person (likely 4-person minimum, includes nature reserve and sights ticket, www.gibraltartaxiassociation.com). The loop tour has four stops: a Mediterranean viewpoint, St. Michael's Cave, a viewpoint near the top of the Rock close to the monkeys, and the Great Siege Tunnels.

Visiting the Rock by Cable Car: A one-way cable-car ticket up is £13.50, plus either the £5 walkers ticket (total £18.50) or the £12 nature reserve ticket (total £25.50). A round-trip ticket for just the cable car is £15.50, but you won't be able to leave the upper cable-car area. The cable car runs continuously in busy times (daily from 9:30; April-Oct last ascent at 19:15, Nov-March last ascent at 17:15; http://gibraltarinfo.gi/en/tickets/).

Rick's Tip: *A prepaid* **Fast Track entry** *will save you time in line at the* **cable car** *up to the Rock. If you buy your ticket at the kiosk before the border, you can ride a* **free shuttle bus** *to the cable-car station.*

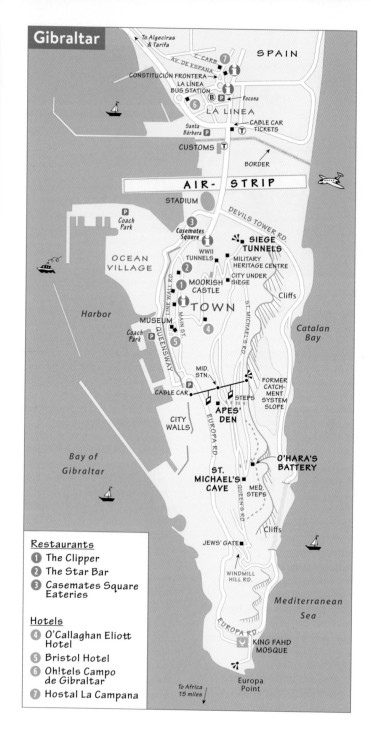

Gibraltar

To Algeciras & Tarifa

C. CARB.

SPAIN

AV. DE ESPANA

7

CONSTITUCIÓN FRONTERA
LA LÍNEA
BUS STATION

B
P
Focona

6

LA LÍNEA

Santa
Bárbara
P

CABLE CAR
TICKETS

CUSTOMS
T

BORDER

AIR-STRIP

STADIUM

DEVILS TOWER RD.

Coach
Park

3

Casemates
Square

SIEGE
TUNNELS

2

WWII
TUNNELS

MILITARY
HERITAGE CENTRE

OCEAN
VILLAGE

1

MOORISH
CASTLE

CITY UNDER
SIEGE

Cliffs

Harbor

TOWN

M. INTT RD.

MUSEUM

4

Catalan
Bay

Coach
Park

5

QUEENSWAY

MAIN ST.

ST. MICHAEL'S RD.

MID.
STN.

FORMER
CATCH-
MENT
SYSTEM
SLOPE

CABLE CAR

P

STEPS

Bay of
Gibraltar

CITY
WALLS

APES'
DEN

EUROPA RD.

O'HARA'S
BATTERY

ST.
MICHAEL'S
CAVE

QUEEN'S RD.

MED.
STEPS

Cliffs

JEWS' GATE

Restaurants
1 The Clipper
2 The Star Bar
3 Casemates Square
   Eateries

Hotels
4 O'Callaghan Eliott
   Hotel
5 Bristol Hotel
6 Oh!tels Campo
   de Gibraltar
7 Hostal La Campana

WINDMILL
HILL RD.

Mediterranean
Sea

EUROPA RD.

KING FAHD
MOSQUE

To Africa
15 miles

Europa
Point

▲▲▲**Summit of the Rock:** The cable car takes you to the real highlight of Gibraltar: the summit of the spectacular Rock itself (with a view terrace and a café). The limestone massif is nearly a mile long, rising 1,400 feet with very sheer faces. According to legend, this was one of the Pillars of Hercules (paired with Djebel Musa, a mountain across the strait in Morocco), marking the edge of the known world in ancient times. In AD 711, the Muslim chieftain Tarik ibn Ziyad crossed over from Africa and landed on the Rock, beginning the Moorish conquest of Spain and naming the Rock after himself—Djebel-Tarik ("Rock of Tarik"), which became "Gibraltar."

▲▲**Apes of Gibraltar:** The Rock is home to about 200 "apes" (actually, tailless Barbary macaques—a type of monkey). Legend has it that as long as the monkeys remain here, so will the Brits. And while guides may feed them, you shouldn't—it disrupts their diet and encourages aggressive behavior, not to mention there's a £500 fine.

▲**St. Michael's Cave:** Studded with stalagmites and stalactites, eerily lit, and echoing with classical music, this cave is dramatic, corny, and slippery when wet. Considered a one-star sight since Neolithic times, these caves were alluded to in ancient Greek legends—when the caves were believed to be the Gates of Hades (or the entrance of a tunnel to Africa).

▲**Great Siege Tunnels:** Also called the Upper Galleries, these chilly tunnels were blasted out of the rock by the Brits during the Great Siege by Spanish and French forces (1779-1783). The clever British used gunpowder to carve out a whole network of tunnels with shafts that would be ideal for aiming artillery. Eventually they excavated St. George's Hall, a huge cavern that housed seven guns. These were the first tunnels inside the Rock; more than a century and a half later, during World War II, 30 more miles of tunnels were blasted out. Hokey but fun dioramas help recapture a time when Brits were known more for conquests than for crumpets.

Eating

Take a break from *jamón* and sample some English pub grub. **$ The Clipper** pub offers filling meals and Murphy's stout on tap (daily, on Irish Town Lane). **$$ The Star Bar** claims to be Gibraltar's oldest (daily, 12 Parliament Lane). The big Casemates Square at the entrance of Gibraltar contains a variety of restaurants, ranging from fast food to inviting pubs.

Sleeping

In Gibraltar, try the plush **$$$$ O'Callaghan Eliott Hotel** (2 Governor's Parade, www.ocallaghanhotels.com) or the basic **$$ Bristol Hotel** (10 Cathedral Square, www.bristolhotel.gi), though you'll find cheaper accommodations across the border in La Línea de la Concepción: **$$$ Oh!tels Campo de Gibraltar** (at the intersection of Avenida Príncipe de Asturias and Avenida del Ejército, www.ohtelscampodegibraltar.es) or **$ Hostal La Campana** (Calle Carboneros 3, www.hostalcampana.es).

Spain: Past and Present

The distinctive Spanish culture has been shaped by the country's parade of rulers. Roman emperors, Muslim sultans, hard-core Christians, conquistadors, French dandies, and Fascist dictators have all left their mark on Spain's art, architecture, and customs. Start by understanding the country's long history of invasions and religious wars, and you'll better appreciate the churches, museums, and monuments you'll visit today.

The sunny weather, fertile soil, and Mediterranean ports of the Iberian Peninsula have long made it a popular place to call home. A mix from various migrations and invasions, the original "Iberians" crossed the Pyrenees around 800 BC. The Phoenicians established the city of Cádiz around 1100 BC, and Carthaginians settled around 250 BC.

Romans
(c. 200 BC-AD 400)

The future Roman Emperor Augustus finally quelled the last Iberian resistance in 19 BC, making the province of "Hispania" an agricultural breadbasket (olives, wine) to help feed the vast Roman Empire. The Romans brought the Latin language, a connection to the wider world, and (in the fourth century) Christianity. When the empire began crumbling around AD 400, Spain made a peaceful transition, ruled by Christian Visigoths from Germany who had strong Roman ties. Roman influence remained for centuries after, in the Latin-based Spanish language, irrigation methods, and building materials and techniques. The Romans' large farming estates would change hands over the years, passing from Roman senators to Visigoth kings to Islamic caliphs to Christian nobles.

Moors
(711-1492)

In AD 711, 12,000 zealous members of the world's newest religion—Islam—landed on the Rock of Gibraltar and, in three short years, conquered the Iberian Peninsula. These North African Muslims—generically called "Moors"—dominated Spain for the next 700 years. Though powerful, they were surprisingly tolerant of the people

Six Dates That Changed Spain

711 Arab Muslims ("Moors") from North Africa invade and occupy Iberia.

1492 Under the Catholic Monarchs Isabel and Ferdinand, Columbus sails Spain into a century of wealth and power. This same year, Spain conquers the last Moorish stronghold in Granada, expels its Jews, and ramps up the Inquisition to root out "heretics."

1588 Spain's Armada is routed by the English, and the country's slow decline begins.

1898 Thrashed by the US in the Spanish-American War, Spain reaches a low ebb.

1936 The Spanish Civil War begins, hundreds of thousands are killed during its three-year span, and nearly four decades of Franco's fascist rule follow.

1975 Juan Carlos I becomes king; he later leads the nation to democracy and the European Union.

they ruled, allowing native Jews and Christians to practice their faiths, so long as the infidels paid extra taxes.

The Moors themselves were an ethnically diverse culture, including both simple Berber tribesmen from Morocco and sophisticated rulers from old Arab families. From their capital in Córdoba, various rulers of the united Islamic state of "Al-Andalus" pledged allegiance to foreign caliphs in Syria, Baghdad, or Morocco.

With cultural ties that stretched from Spain to Africa to Arabia to Persia and beyond, the Moorish culture in Spain (especially around AD 800-1000) was perhaps Europe's most advanced, a beacon of learning in Europe's so-called "Dark

Ages. Mathematics, astronomy, literature, and architecture flourished. Even winemaking was encouraged, though for religious reasons the Muslims didn't drink alcohol. The Moorish legacy lives on in Spain mainly in architecture (horseshoe arches, ceramic tiles, fountains, and gardens), of which Granada's Alhambra is an exquisite example.

Reconquista
(711-1492)

For more than 700 years, the Moors were a minority ruling a largely Christian populace. Pockets of independent Christians remained, particularly in the mountains in the peninsula's north. Local Christian kings fought against the Moors whenever they could, whittling away at the Muslim empire, "reconquering" more and more land in what's known as the Reconquista. The last Moorish stronghold, Granada, fell to the Christians in 1492.

The slow, piecemeal process of the Reconquista split the peninsula into many independent kingdoms and dukedoms, some Christian, some Moorish. The Reconquista picked up steam after AD 1000, when Al-Andalus splintered into smaller regional states—Granada, Sevilla, Valencia—ruled by local caliphs. Toledo fell to the Christians in 1085. By 1249 the neighboring Christian state of Portugal had the borders it does today, making it the oldest unchanged state in Europe. The rest of the peninsula was a battleground, a loosely knit collection of small kingdoms, some Christian, some Muslim. Heavy stone castles dotted the interior region of Castile, as lords and barons duked it out. Along the Mediterranean coast (from the Pyrenees to Barcelona to Valencia), three Christian states united into a sea-trading power, the kingdom of Aragon.

In 1469, Isabel of Castile married Ferdinand II of Aragon. These so-called Catholic Monarchs (Reyes Católicos) united the peninsula's two largest kingdoms, instantly making Spain a European

Significant Spaniards

In Politics

Ferdinand (1452-1516) **and Isabel** (1451-1504): Their marriage united much of Spain, ushering in its Golden Age. The Catholic Monarchs (Reyes Católicos) drove out Moors and Jews, and financed Columbus' lucrative voyages to the New World.

Charles V (1500-1558): The Flanders-born grandson of Ferdinand and Isabel assumed the Spanish throne in 1516 (as King Charles I) and led the Holy Roman Empire from 1519 to 1555 (as Emperor Charles V), ruling over much of Western Europe, the Far East, and the Americas.

Francisco Franco (1892-1975): This general led the military uprising against the elected Republic, sparking Spain's Civil War (1936-1939). After victory, he ruled Spain for nearly four decades as an absolute dictator, maintaining its Catholic, aristocratic heritage while slowly modernizing the country.

King Juan Carlos I (b. 1938): Taking over Spain after the death of dictator Franco, Carlos turned Spain into a democracy in 1977. He abdicated in 2014 in favor of his son, now serving as King Felipe VI.

In Exploration

Juan Ponce de León (1460-1521): He's primarily known for being the first European to explore Florida. His quest for the Fountain of Youth is a myth popularized by American author Washington Irving three centuries later.

Francisco Pizarro (1476-1541): This conquistador vanquished the Incan Empire in the 1530s and founded Peru's capital city, Lima.

Hernán Cortés (1485-1547): A Spanish nobleman seeking his fortune, Cortés conquered Mexico in 1521, explored the New World, and exploited its indigenous peoples.

power. In 1492, while Columbus explored the seas under Ferdinand and Isabel's flag, the Catholic Monarchs drove the Moors out of Granada and expelled the country's Jews, creating a unified, Christian, militaristic nation-state, fueled by the religious zeal of the Reconquista.

The Golden Age
(1500-1600)

Spain's bold sea explorers changed the economics of Europe, opening up a New World of riches and colonies. The Spanish flag soon flew over most of South and Central America. Gold, silver, and agri-

cultural products (grown on large estates with cheap labor) poured into Spain. In return, the stoked Spaniards exported Christianity, converting the American natives with persistent Jesuit priests and cruel conquistadors.

Ferdinand and Isabel's daughter (Juana the Mad) wed a German prince (Philip the Fair), and their son Charles (1500-1558) inherited not only their crowns but that of his grandfather, the Holy Roman Emperor Maximilian I. Known as King Charles I of Spain, and as Emperor Charles V, he was the most powerful man in the world, ruling an empire that

In the Arts

El Greco (1541-1614): Born in Greece, but an honorary Spaniard for spending nearly 40 years in Toledo, this artist created ethereal, spiritual paintings of saints, using bold colors and dramatic poses and settings.

Miguel de Cervantes (1547-1616): Author of the classic satirical romance *Don Quixote,* Cervantes was also a poet and a playwright whose works shaped Spanish literature and the language itself.

Diego Velázquez (1599-1660): His masterful royal court portraits were studies in camera-eye realism and cool detachment from his subjects.

Bartolomé Murillo (1617-1682): He painted a dreamy, sentimental world of religious visions: pastel soft-focus works of cute Baby Jesuses and radiant Virgin Marys.

Francisco de Goya (1746-1828): This artist's liberal tendencies shone through in unflattering portraits of royalty and in emotional scenes of abuse of power.

Antoni Gaudí (1852-1926): A famous Catalan architect and a leader in the Modernista movement in Barcelona, he designed the astonishing Sagrada Família and other unusual buildings and public spaces (La Pedrera, Casa Batlló, Palau Güell, Park Güell, and more).

Pablo Picasso (1881-1973): The 20th-century's greatest artist explored Spanish themes, particularly in his inspirational antiwar *Guernica* mural, depicting the horrors of war.

Joan Miró (1893-1983): This modern artist was known for his playful artistic compositions with a Surrealist bent.

Salvador Dalí (1904-1989): The flamboyant, waxed-mustachioed painter created Surrealist, mind-bending art and installations.

stretched from Holland to Sicily, from Bohemia to Bolivia. The aristocracy and the clergy were swimming in money. Art and courtly life flourished during this Golden Age, with Spain hosting the painter El Greco and the writer Miguel de Cervantes.

But Charles V's Holy Roman Empire was torn by different languages and ethnic groups, and by protesting Protestants. He spent much of the empire's energies at war with Protestants, encroaching Muslim Turks, and Europe's rising powers. When an exhausted Charles announced his abdication (1555) and retired to a monastery, his sprawling empire was divvied up among family members, with Spain and its possessions going to his son, Philip II (1527-1598).

Philip II inherited Portugal in 1581, moved Spain's capital to Madrid, built the palace of El Escorial, and continued fighting losing battles across Europe (the Netherlands, France) that drained the treasury of its New World gold. In the summer of 1588, Spain's seemingly unbeatable royal fleet of 125 ships—the Invincible Armada—sailed off to conquer England, only to be unexpectedly routed in battle by bad weather and Sir Francis

Drake's cunning. Just like that, Britannia ruled the waves, and Spain spiraled downward, becoming a debt-ridden, overextended, flabby nation.

Slow Decline
(1600-1900)

Easy money from the colonies kept Spain from seeing the dangers at home. The country stopped growing its own wheat and neglected its fields. Great Britain and the Netherlands were the rising sea-trading powers in the new global economy. During the centuries when science and technology developed as never before in other European countries, Spain was preoccupied by its failed colonial politics.

By 1700, once-mighty Spain lay helpless while rising powers France, England, and Austria fought over the right to pick Spain's next king in the War of the Spanish Succession (1701-1714), which was fought partly on Spanish soil (Britain held out against the French in the Siege of Gibraltar). Spanish king Charles II didn't have an heir, so he willed his kingdom to Louis XIV's grandson, Philip of Anjou, who was set to inherit both France and Spain. But the rest of Europe didn't want powerful France to become even stronger. The war ended in compromise: Philip became king of Spain (Spain lost several possessions), but he had to renounce claims to any other thrones. The French-born, French-speaking Bourbon King Philip V (1683-1746) ruled Spain for 45 years. He and his heirs made themselves at home, building the Versailles-like Royal Palace in Madrid and La Granja near Segovia.

The French invaded Spain under Napoleon, who installed his brother as king in 1808. The Spaniards rose up (chronicled by Goya's paintings of the second and third of May 1808), sparking the Peninsular War—called the War of Independence by Spaniards—that decisively won Spain's independence from French rule in 1814.

Nineteenth-century Spain was a backward nation, with internal wars over which noble family should rule (the Carlist Wars), liberal revolutions put down brutally, and political assassinations. Spain gradually lost its global possessions to other European powers and to South American revolutionaries. Spain hit rock bottom in 1898, when the upstart United States picked a fight and thrashed them in the Spanish-American War, taking away Spain's last major possessions: Cuba, Puerto Rico, and the Philippines.

The 20th Century

A drained and disillusioned Spain was ill-prepared for modern technology and democratic government.

The old ruling class (the monarchy, church, and landowners) fought new economic powers (cities, businessmen, and labor unions) in a series of coups, strikes, and sham elections. In the 1920s, a military dictatorship under Miguel Primo de Rivera kept the old guard in power. In 1930 he was ousted and an open election brought a modern democratic Republic to power. But the right wing regrouped under the Falange (fascist) party, fomenting unrest and sparking a military coup against the Republic in 1936, supported by General Francisco Franco (1892-1975).

Thus began the bloody Spanish Civil War (1936-1939), fought between Franco's Nationalists (also called Falangists) and the Republic (called Loyalists). Adolf Hitler and Benito Mussolini sent troops and supplies to their fellow fascist Franco. It was Hitler's Luftwaffe that helped Franco bomb the town of Guernica (April 1937), an event famously captured on canvas by Pablo Picasso. On the Republican side, hundreds of Americans (including Ernest Hemingway) steamed over to Spain to fight for democracy.

The civil war resulted in Franco's victory and thousands of deaths (estimates range from 200,000 to 500,000—the exact total will never be known). For nearly the next four decades, Spain was ruled by Franco, an authoritarian, church-blessed dictator who tried to modernize the backward country while shielding it from corrupting modern influences. Spain was officially neutral in World War II, and the country spent much of the postwar era as a world apart.

Before Franco died, he handpicked his protégé, King Juan Carlos I, to succeed him. But to everyone's surprise, the young, conservative, mild-mannered king stepped aside, settled for a figurehead title, and guided the country quickly and peacefully toward democratic elections (1977).

Spain had a lot of catching up to do. Culturally, the once-conservative nation exploded and embraced new ideas, even plunging to wild extremes. In the 1980s Spain flowered under left-leaning Prime Minister Felipe González. Spain showed the world a modern face in 1992, hosting both a World Exhibition at Sevilla and the Summer Olympics at Barcelona.

Spain Today

Spain enjoyed a strong economy through the late 1990s and early 2000s, thanks in part to EU loans and subsidies, a thriving tourism industry, and a boom in housing construction. But the country was hit hard by the 2009 global economic downturn, and its economy entered a recession. Spain's banks stopped lending, many people lost homes to foreclosures, and by 2013 unemployment had soared to 27 percent. So many young Spaniards were out of work (one-fourth of those under 30, and nearly half of those under 25) that a new name was coined to describe them: *generación ni-ni* (the neither-nor generation).

Even the once-admired King Juan Carlos lost popular support due to some ill-timed, expensive hijinks while Spain's economic woes mounted. After almost 40 years on the throne, he abdicated in 2014, turning over the crown to his well-respected son, who now reigns as King Felipe VI.

Meanwhile, Catalunya, the Basque Country, and other regions of Spain have called for more autonomy or outright independence. It's clear that in Spain, history is unfolding in front of us.

Practicalities

TOURIST INFORMATION

Spain's national tourist office **in the US** will fill brochure requests and answer your general travel questions by email (newyork.information@tourspain.es). Scan their website (www.spain.info) for practical information and sightseeing ideas; you can download many brochures free of charge. If you're going to Barcelona, also see www.barcelonaturisme.cat.

In Spain, a good first stop is generally the *Oficina de Turismo,* the tourist information office (abbreviated **TI** in this book). Swing by to confirm sightseeing plans, pick up a city map, and get information on public transit, walking tours, special events, and nightlife.

HELP!

Emergency and Medical Help: For any emergency service—ambulance, police, or fire—call **112**. If you get sick, do as locals do and go to a pharmacist. Or ask at your hotel for help—they'll know the nearest medical and emergency services.

Theft or Loss: To replace a passport, you'll need to go in person to an embassy or consulate. If your credit and debit cards disappear, cancel and replace them (see "Damage Control for Lost Cards" on page 409). File a police report, either on the spot or within a day or two; you'll need it to submit an insurance claim for lost or stolen rail passes or travel gear, and it can help with replacing your passport or credit and debit cards. For more info, see www.ricksteves.com/help.

US Embassy in Madrid: Tel. 915-872-200, Calle Serrano 75, https://es.usembassy.gov

US Consulate in Barcelona: Tel. 932-802-227, after-hours emergency tel. 915-872-200, Passeig de la Reina Elisenda de Montcada 23

Canadian Embassy in Madrid: Tel. 913-828-400, in Torre Espacio skyscraper at Paseo de la Castellana 259D, www.espana.gc.ca

TRAVEL TIPS

Time Zones: Spain, like most of continental Europe, is generally six/nine hours ahead of the East/West coasts of the US. The exceptions are the beginning and end of Daylight Saving Time: Europe "springs forward" the last Sunday in March (two weeks after most of North America), and "falls back" the last Sunday in October (one week before North America).

Business Hours: Many businesses respect the afternoon siesta. When it's 100 degrees in the shade, you'll understand why. Shops are generally open from about 9:30 to 14:00 and from 17:00 to 21:00, longer for big chain shops or touristy places. Small shops are often open on Saturday only in the morning, and closed all day Sunday.

Watt's Up? Europe's electrical system is 220 volts, instead of North America's 110 volts. Most newer electronics convert automatically, so you won't need a converter plug, but you will need an adapter plug with two round prongs, sold inexpensively at travel stores in the US.

Discounts: Discounts for sights are generally not listed in this book. However, seniors (age 60 and over), youths under 18, and students and teachers with proper identification cards (www.isic.org) can get discounts at many sights—always ask. Some discounts are available only to European citizens.

Avoiding Theft and Scams

Like anywhere, thieves in Europe target tourists, especially in bigger cities and towns. Pickpockets often stage a commotion or a fight to enable them to work unnoticed. Someone in a small group pushing you as you enter or exit a crowded subway car may slip a hand in your pocket or daybag. Thieves snatch purses and break into cars.

Be on guard, and treat any disturbance around you as a smoke screen for theft. Remember to wear a money belt (tucked under your clothes) to keep your cash, credit cards, and passport secure; carry only the money you need for the day in your front pocket.

Don't believe any "police officers" looking for counterfeit bills—one of many creative scams that lowlifes dream up. When traveling by train, keep your luggage in sight and get a berth in an attendant-monitored sleeping car for safety on overnight trips.

MONEY

Here's my basic strategy for using money in Europe:

- Upon arrival, head for a cash machine (ATM) at the airport and withdraw some local currency, using a debit card with low international transaction fees.
- Save money by minimizing your credit and debit card exchange fees. The trend is to pay for bigger expenses by credit card, but cash is still the standby for small purchases and tips.
- Keep your cards and cash safe in a money belt.

What to Bring

I pack the following and keep it all securely tucked away in my money belt.

Debit Card: Use this at ATMs to withdraw cash.

Credit Card: Handy for bigger purchases (hotels, shops, restaurants, travel agencies, car-rental agencies), payment machines, and ordering online.

Backup Card: Some travelers carry a third debit or credit card, ideally from a different bank, in case one gets lost or simply doesn't work.

Stash of Cash: I always carry US $100-200 as a cash backup. A stash of cash comes in handy for emergencies, such as if your ATM card stops working.

What NOT to Bring: Resist the urge to buy **euros** before your trip or you'll pay the price in bad stateside exchange rates. I've yet to see a European airport that didn't have plenty of ATMs.

Before You Go

Know your PIN. Make sure you know the numeric, four-digit PIN for all of your cards, both debit and credit. Request it if you don't have one and allow time to receive the information by mail.

Report your travel dates. Let your bank know that you'll be using your debit and credit cards in Europe, and when and where you're headed.

Adjust your ATM withdrawal limit. Find out how much you can take out daily and ask for a higher daily withdrawal limit if you want to get more cash at once. Note that European ATMs will withdraw funds only from checking accounts; you're unlikely to have access to your savings account.

Ask about fees. For any purchase or withdrawal made with a card, you may be charged a currency conversion fee (1-3 percent) and/or a Visa or MasterCard international transaction fee (1 percent).

In Europe

Using Cash Machines: European cash machines have English-language instructions and work just like they do at home—except they spit out local currency instead of dollars, calculated at the day's standard bank-to-bank rate.

In most places, ATMs are easy to locate—in Spain ask for a *cajero automático*. When possible, withdraw cash from a bank-run ATM located just outside that bank.

If your debit card doesn't work, try a lower amount—your request may have exceeded your withdrawal limit or the ATM's limit.

Avoid "independent" ATMs, such as Travelex, Euronet, Moneybox, Cardpoint, and Cashzone. These have high fees, can be less secure, and may try to trick users with "dynamic currency conversion" (see below).

Exchanging Cash: Avoid exchanging money in Europe; it's a big rip-off. In a pinch you can always find exchange desks at major train stations or airports—convenient but with crummy rates. Banks generally do not exchange money unless you have an account with them.

Using Credit Cards: US cards no longer require a signature for verification, but don't be surprised if a European card reader generates a receipt for you to sign. Some card readers may prompt you to enter your PIN (so it's important to know it for each of your cards). If a cashier is present, you should have no problems.

ATMs work just like back home.

Exchange Rate

1 euro (€)=about $1.20

To convert prices in euros to dollars, add about 20 percent: €20 = about $24, €50 = about $60. (Check www. oanda.com for the latest exchange rates.) Just like the dollar, one euro (€) is broken down into 100 cents.

At self-service payment machines (transit-ticket kiosks, parking, etc.), results are mixed, as US cards may not work in unattended transactions. If your card won't work, look for a cashier who can process your card manually—or pay in cash.

Drivers Beware: Be aware of potential problems using a US credit card to fill up at an unattended gas station, enter a parking garage, or exit a toll road. Carry cash and be prepared to move on to the next gas station if necessary. When approaching a toll plaza, use the "cash" lane.

Dynamic Currency Conversion: If merchants offer to convert your purchase price into dollars (called dynamic currency conversion, or DCC), refuse this "service." You'll pay extra for the expensive convenience of seeing your charge in dollars.

Security Tips: Don't use a debit card for purchases. Because a debit card pulls funds directly from your bank account, potential charges incurred by a thief will stay on your account while the fraudulent use is investigated by your bank.

To access your accounts online while traveling, be sure to use a secure connection (see the "Tips on Internet Security" sidebar, later).

Damage Control for Lost Cards: If you lose your credit or debit card, report the loss immediately to the respective global customer-assistance centers. Call these 24-hour US numbers collect: Visa (tel. 303/967-1096), MasterCard (tel. 636/722-7111), and American Express (tel. 336/393-

7111). In Spain, to make a collect call to the US, dial 900-990-011. European toll-free numbers can be found at the websites for Visa and MasterCard. You can generally receive a temporary card within two or three business days in Europe (see www. ricksteves.com/help for more).

Tipping

Tipping in Spain isn't as automatic and generous as in the US. For special service, tips are appreciated, but not expected. As in the US, the proper amount depends on your resources, tipping philosophy, and the circumstances, but some general guidelines apply.

Restaurants: If eating at the counter of a tapas bar, there's no need to tip, although it's fine to round up the bill with a few small coins. At restaurants with table service, if a service charge is included in the bill, add about 5 percent; if it's not, leave 10 percent.

Taxis: For a typical ride, just round up your fare a bit (for instance, if the fare is €4.85, pay €5).

Services: In general, if someone in the tourism or service industry does a super job for you, a small tip of a euro or two is appropriate...but not required. If you're not sure whether (or how much) to tip, ask a local for advice.

Getting a VAT Refund

Wrapped into the purchase price of your Spanish souvenirs is a Value-Added Tax (VAT) of 21 percent (in Spain, it's called IVA—*Impuesto sobre el Valor Añadido*). You're entitled to get most of that tax back if you purchase more than €90 (about $110) worth of goods at a store that participates in the VAT-refund scheme.

Get the paperwork. Have the merchant completely fill out the necessary refund document. You'll have to present your passport. Get the paperwork done before you leave the store to ensure you'll have everything you need (including your original sales receipt).

Get your stamp at the border or airport. Process your VAT document at your last stop in the European Union (such as at the airport) with the customs agent who deals with VAT refunds. Arrive early to allow time to find the customs office—and wait.

Collect your refund. You can claim your VAT refund from refund companies, such as Global Blue or Planet, with offices at major airports, ports, or border crossings. These services (which extract a 4 percent fee) can refund your money in cash immediately or credit your card.

Customs for American Shoppers

You can take home $800 worth of items per person duty-free, once every 31 days. Many processed and packaged foods are allowed, including vacuum-packed cheeses, dried herbs, jams, baked goods, candy, chocolate, oil, vinegar, mustard, and honey. Fresh fruits and vegetables and most meats are not allowed, with exceptions for some canned items. As for alcohol, you can bring in one liter duty-free.

To bring alcohol (or liquid-packed foods) in your carry-on bag on your flight home, buy it at a duty-free shop at the airport. You'll increase your odds of getting it onto a connecting flight if it's packaged in a "STEB"—a secure, tamper-evident bag.

For details on allowable goods, customs rules, and duty rates, visit http://help.cbp.gov.

SIGHTSEEING

Sightseeing can be hard work. Use these tips to make your visits to sights meaningful, fun, efficient, and painless.

Plan Ahead

Set up an itinerary that allows you to fit in all your must-see sights. Given how precious your vacation time is, I recommend getting reservations for any must-see sight that offers them. Many museums are closed or have reduced hours at least a few days a year, especially on holidays such as Christmas, New Year's, and Labor Day (May 1). A list of holidays is in the appendix; check online for possible museum closures during your trip.

At Sights

Here's what you can typically expect:

Entering: Be warned that you may not be allowed to enter if you arrive less than 30 to 60 minutes before closing time. And guards start ushering people out well before the actual closing time, so don't save the best for last.

Many sights have a security check. Allow extra time for these lines. Some sights require you to check daypacks and coats. (If you'd rather not check your daypack, try carrying it tucked under your arm like a purse as you enter.)

At churches—which often offer interesting art (usually free) and a cool, welcome seat—a modest dress code (no bare shoulders or shorts) is encouraged though rarely enforced.

Photography: If the museum's photo policy isn't clearly posted, ask a guard. Generally, taking photos without a flash or tripod is allowed. Some sights ban selfie sticks; others ban photos altogether.

Expect Changes: Artwork can be on tour, on loan, out sick, or shifted at the whim of the curator. Pick up a floor plan as you enter, and ask the museum staff if you can't find a particular work.

Audioguides and Apps: Many sights rent audioguides, which generally offer dry-but-useful recorded descriptions in English (about €3-5). Increasingly, museums and sights offer apps—often free—that you can download to your mobile device (check their websites).

EATING

Spanish cuisine is hearty, and meals are served in big, inexpensive portions. You can eat well in restaurants for about €15-

20—or even more cheaply and more varied if you graze on appetizer-sized tapas in bars.

The Spanish eating schedule—lunch from 13:00 to 16:00, dinner after 21:00—frustrates many visitors. Most Spaniards eat one major meal of the day—lunch (comida)—around 14:00, when stores close, schools let out, and people gather with their friends and family for the siesta. Because most Spaniards work until 19:30, supper (cena) is usually served at about 21:00 or 22:00. And, since few people want a heavy meal that late, many Spaniards eat a light tapas dinner.

To bridge the gap between their coffee-and-roll breakfast and late lunch, many Spaniards eat a light meal at about 11:00 (merienda). This can be a light lunch at a bar or a bocadillo (baguette sandwich). For your main meal of the day, you can either eat a late lunch at a restaurant at around 15:00, then have a light tapas snack for dinner; or reverse it, having a tapas meal in the afternoon, followed by a late restaurant dinner. Either way, tapas bars are the key.

Breakfast

Hotel breakfasts are generally handy, optional, and pricey. Start your day instead at a corner bar or at a colorful café near a market hall. Ask for the *desayunos* (breakfast special, usually only available until noon), which can include coffee, a roll (or sandwich), and juice—much cheaper than ordering them separately. Sandwiches can either be on white bread (called "sandwich") or on a baguette (*bocadillo*).

A standard savory breakfast item is tostada *con aceite,* toasted bread with olive oil (and sometimes tomato). For something more substantial, look for a slice of tortilla *española* (potato omelet). Those with a sweet tooth will find various sweet rolls (*bollos* or *bollería*). If you like a doughnut and coffee in American greasy-spoon joints, try the Spanish equivalent: churros (or the thicker *porras*) that you dip in thick hot chocolate or your *café con leche.*

Sampling Jamón

The staple of Spanish cuisine, *jamón* (hah-MOHN), is prosciutto-like ham that's dry-cured and aged. It's generally sliced thin (right off the hock) and served at room temperature. *Jamón* can be eaten straight, served in a *bocadillo* sandwich, or mixed into a wide variety of dishes. Bars proudly hang ham hocks from the rafters as part of the decor.

Like connoisseurs of fine wine, Spaniards debate the merits of different breeds of pigs, the pig's diet, and the quality of the curing. The two major types are *jamón serrano*, from white pigs whose meat is cured in the mountains of Spain, and the higher-quality *jamón ibérico*, made with the back legs of black-hooved pigs.

To sample this delicacy without the high price tag you'll find in bars and restaurants, go to the local market. Ask for 100 grams of top-quality ham (*cien gramos de jamón ibérico*; about €80/kilo, so your *ración* will run about €8), and enjoy it as a picnic with red wine and a baguette.

Ordering

More casual eateries (and tapas bars) may feature dishes served in portions called *raciones* (*racions* in Catalan), or the smaller half-servings, *media-raciones* (*mitja racions* in Catalan). Smaller tapas plates are more commonly served at bars than at sit-down restaurants.

Typically, couples or small groups can share a few *raciones*, making this an economical way to eat and a great way to explore the regional cuisine. Two people can fill up on four *media-raciones*.

For a budget meal in a restaurant, try a *plato combinado* (combination plate), which usually includes portions of one or two main dishes, a vegetable, and bread for a reasonable price; or the *menú del día* (menu of the day), a substantial three- to four-course meal that comes with a drink.

Spanish cuisine has many regional specialties, but the most famous Spanish dish is probably paella. Featuring saffron-fla-

vored rice as a background for seafood, sausage, chicken, peppers, or whatever the chef wants to mix in, an authentic paella takes time to prepare—expect a wait.

Tapas Bars

I can't resist stopping in local tapas bars to munch on tasty small portions of seafood, meat-filled pastries, deep-fried morsels, and other delicious bites (typically costing €5-10 a plate). Best of all, I can eat well any time of day in a tapas bar.

The authentic tapas experience is not for shrinking violets. You'll elbow up to a bar crowded with pushy locals, squint at a hand-scrawled chalkboard menu, and try to order from a typically brusque bartender. In some locales, a small, free tapa may be included with your drink. Order your drink first to get the freebie; then order additional food as you like.

Basque-style bars have an array of tapas (called *pintxos* or *pinchos*) already

Spanish Regional Specialties

Galicia: The green, rainy northwest of Spain is known for its octopus (*pulpo*, specifically *pulpo a la gallega,* served in pieces and sprinkled with paprika) and its many pork dishes (such as *orejas,* fried pig's ears). Other specialties include *pimientos de Padrón* (deep-fried, small green peppers) and Ribeiro white wine, traditionally served in little ceramic bowls.

Andalucía: Gazpacho and *salmorejo*, Andalusian specialties, are chilled, garlicky, tomato-based soups, served with chunks of bread or *jamón* and chopped egg. Both are refreshing on a hot day and are commonly available as soon as the weather heats up. Many dishes in this region rely on *sofrito*—a base of onion, tomatoes, and peppers.

Castilla y León: This high, central plateau of Spain was the home of vast flocks of sheep in the Middle Ages. This influence—in the form of lamb and the famous *manchego* (from La Mancha) sheep's cheese—persists today. Other popular Castilian and Leonese meats are sausages, *cochinillo asado* (roast suckling pig), and *cecina* (beef that's cured like *jamón serrano*).

Catalunya: Like its culture and language, Catalan food is a fusion of Spanish and French. Every meal starts with *pan con tomate* (or *pa amb tomaquet* in Catalan): a baguette rubbed with crushed tomatoes, garlic, and olive oil. Favorite dishes include *fideuà,* a thin, flavor-infused noodle served with seafood, and *arròs negre,* black rice cooked in squid ink.

Basque Country: Most consider this region to be the culinary capital of Spain, with *pintxos* (tapas) bars that display a mouth-watering array of choices (just grab what you like from the platters at the bar, and pay on the honor system). Look for *txangurro* (spider crab), *antxoas* (tasty anchovies), *marmitako* (tuna stew), *ttoro* (seafood stew), and *txakolí* (fresh white wine, poured from high up). *Cazuelas* are stews meant for sharing.

laid out and can be less intimidating, as you simply point to or grab what you want. To find this type of bar, look for a place with *vasca* or *euskal* (both mean "Basque") in the name.

Where to Sit: Eating and drinking at a bar is usually cheapest if you sit or stand at the counter (*barra*). You may pay a little more to sit at a table (*mesa* or *salón*) and still more for an outdoor table (*terraza*). Traditionally, tapas are served at the bar, and *raciones* (and *media-raciones*) are served at tables, where food can be shared family style. If you're eating a free tapa with your drink, you can't occupy a table.

Ordering: To figure out what you

want, read the posted or printed menu. Use the "Tapas Menu Decoder," later, to sort through your options. You can also just point to items in the display case or at your neighbor's plate to get what you want. Handwritten signs that start out *"Hay"* mean "Today we have," as in *"Hay caracoles"* ("Today we have snails").

Hang back and observe before ordering. When you're ready, be assertive or you'll never be served. Your bartender isn't a "waiter"—he wants to take your order, period. To grab his attention, say *"por favor"* (please); you can also say *"perdona"* (excuse me). To ask for the price of a dish, say *"¿Cuánto cuesta?"*

If you don't know what to order, try an

Tapas Menu Decoder

You can often just point to what you want on the menu or in the display case, say *por favor*, and get your food, but these words will help.

a la parrilla; a la plancha	barbecued; grilled
aceitunas	olives
al ajillo	with garlic
albóndigas	spiced meatballs with sauce
almejas, a la marinera	clams, in paprika sauce
almendras	almonds (usually fried)
anchoas	cured anchovies (salted or in oil)
atún	tuna
bacalao	cod
banderilla	mini skewer
bocadillo	basic baguette sandwich
bombas	fried meat-and-potato ball
boquerones, en vinagre	fresh anchovies, marinated in olive oil, vinegar, and garlic
brocheta	shish kebab (on a stick)
cabrillas	big snails in a tomato sauce
calamares fritos	fried squid rings
canapé	tiny open-faced sandwich
caracoles	small tree snails (May–Sept)
champiñones	mushrooms
charcutería	cured meats
chorizo	spicy sausage
croquetas	croquettes—breaded, fried béchamel with fillings like ham
empanadillas	meat or seafood hand pies
ensaladilla rusa	potato salad with lots of mayo, peas, and carrots
espinacas, con garbanzos	spinach, with garbanzo beans
flauta	sandwich on flute-thin baguette
frito	fried
fuet	Catalan salami-like sausage
gambas, con cáscara	shrimp, with shell

jamón	cured ham (like prosciutto)
judías verdes	green beans
lomo	pork tenderloin
mejillones	mussels
merluza	hake (whitefish)
montadito	tapa on bread
morcilla	blood sausage
paella	saffron rice dish with seafood and meat
patatas bravas	fried potatoes with spicy tomato sauce
pescaditos fritos	assortment of little fried fish
picos	little breadsticks
pimiento, relleno	pepper, stuffed
pimientos de Padrón	fried small green peppers, a few of which are jalapeño-hot
pinchos morunos	skewer of spicy lamb or pork
pisto	mixed sautéed vegetables
pollo, alioli	chicken, with garlic sauce
pulga, pulguita, or pepito	small baguette sandwich
pulpo	octopus
queso	cheese
queso manchego	sheep-milk cheese
rabas	squid rings
rabo de toro	bull's-tail stew
revuelto, de setas	scrambled eggs, with wild mushrooms
salchichón	salami-like sausage
sardinas	sardines
tabla serrana	hearty plate of meat and cheese
tortilla española	potato omelet
tortilla de jamón / queso	potato omelet with ham / cheese
tortillitas de camarones	shrimp fritters (Andalucía)
variado de fritos	mix of various fried fish

inexpensive sampler plate. Ask for *una tabla de canapés variados* to get a plate of various little open-faced sandwiches. Or ask for a *surtido de* (an assortment of) *charcutería* (a mixed plate of meat) or *queso* (cheese). *Un surtido de jamón y queso* means a plate of different hams and cheeses. Order bread and two glasses of red wine on the right square, and you've got a romantic (and inexpensive) dinner for two.

Paying: Don't worry about paying until you're ready to leave; the bartender is keeping track of your tab (except in the Basque Country, where you often pay on the honor system). To get the bill, ask for *"¿La cuenta?"*

Spanish Drinks

Spain is one of the world's leading producers of grapes, and that means lots of excellent **wine**, both red (*tinto*) and white (*blanco*). For a basic glass of red wine, you can order *un tinto*. But for quality wine, ask for *un crianza* (old), *un reserva* (older), or *un gran reserva* (oldest). For good, economical wine, I always ask for *un crianza*—for little or no extra money than a basic

tinto, you'll get a quality, aged wine. **Cava** is Spain's answer to champagne.

Sherry, a fortified wine from the Jerez region, ranges from dry (*fino*) to sweet (*dulce*)—Spaniards drink the *fino* and export the *dulce*. You'll also see *amontillado* and *manzanilla* sherries; both are variants of *fino*.

When ordering **beer,** Spaniards rarely ask for a "cerveza." Instead, they usually specify a size or type when ordering, such as a *caña* (7-8 oz. draft beer) or a *tubo* (10 oz.). Most places just have the standard local beer on tap. Cruzcampo is big in the south, whereas San Miguel is big in the north, and Madrid's Mahou is the choice in central Spain. In Barcelona, local options include Estrella Damm, the trendier Moritz, and various craft beers.

If ordering **mineral water** in a restaurant, request a *botella de agua grande* (big bottle). For a glass of **tap water,** specify *un vaso de agua del grifo.* If you insist on *del grifo,* not *embotellada* (bottled), you'll usually get it.

Spain's bars often serve fresh-squeezed **orange juice** (*zumo de naranja*). For something completely different, try

the sweet and milky *horchata,* tradition-ally made from chufa (a.k.a. tigernuts or earth almonds).

Quick, Cheap Meals and Picnics

Located in most cities, sandwich shops such as the Pans & Company chain serve fresh, affordable sandwiches and sal-ads. Try pizza shops for slices-to-go and empanadas (pastry turnovers filled with seasoned meat and veggies). Bakeries often sell sandwiches. Bigger cities have at least one El Corte Inglés department store, with a cafeteria and supermarket.

Picnicking saves lots of euros. At a *supermercado* or an open-air market *(mercado),* you can pick up cold cuts, cheese, rolls, yogurt, and other picnic treats. Ordering 100 grams of cheese *(cien gramos)* is about a quarter-pound, enough for two sandwiches.

Shopkeepers will sell small quantities of produce (like a couple of apples or some carrots), but it's customary to let the mer-chant choose for you; watch locals and imitate. Either say or indicate by gesturing how much you want.

SLEEPING

Extensive and opinionated listings of good-value rooms are a major feature of this book's Sleeping sections. Rather than list accommodations scattered through-out a town, I choose hotels in my favor-ite neighborhoods that are convenient to your sightseeing.

In Spain, high season *(temporada alta)* is from July to September. Shoulder season *(temporada media)* is roughly April through June and October, and low season *(tem-porada baja)* runs from November through March. Book your accommodations as soon as your itinerary is set, especially if you'll be traveling during busy times (such as Semana Santa—Holy Week—particu-larly in the south). See page 433 for a list of major holidays and festivals.

Rates and Deals

I've categorized my recommended accommodations based on price, indi-cated with a dollar-sign rating (see sidebar). The price ranges suggest an estimated cost for a one-night stay in a standard double room with a private toilet and shower in high season, don't include breakfast, and assume you're booking directly with the hotel (not through a booking site, which extracts a commission).

Booking Direct: To get the best deal, contact family-run hotels directly by phone or email. When you go direct, the owner avoids the commission paid to booking sites, thereby leaving enough wiggle room to offer you a discount, a nicer room, or a free breakfast (if it's not already included). If you prefer to book online or are consid-ering a hotel chain, it's to your advantage to use the hotel's website.

Getting a Discount: Some hotels extend a discount to those who pay cash or stay longer than three nights. And some accommodations offer a special discount for Rick Steves readers, indi-cated in this guidebook by the abbre-viation **"RS%."** Discounts vary: Ask for details when you reserve.

Types of Accommodations
Hotels

Spain offers some of the best accommo-dations values in Western Europe. Most places are government-regulated, with posted prices. Hoteliers are encouraged to quote prices with the 10 percent IVA tax included. If you have any doubts, ask.

Spain has stringent restrictions on smoking in public places. Smoking is not permitted in common areas, but hotels can designate 10 percent of their rooms for smokers.

Some hotels don't use central heat before November 1 and after April 1 (unless it's unusually cold); prepare for cool evenings if you travel in spring and fall. Summer can be extremely hot. Consider air-conditioning, fans, and noise (since you'll want your window open). Many rooms come with mini refrigerators.

Street noise in Spain is high (even late at night), and walls and doors tend to be thin—earplugs are a necessity. Always ask to see your room first. If you suspect night noise will be a problem, request a quiet (*tranquilo*) room in the back or on an upper floor (*piso alto*). In most cases, view rooms (*con vista*) come with street noise. You'll often sleep better and for less money in a room without a view.

Even at the best places, mechanical breakdowns occur: Sinks leak, hot water turns cold, toilets may gurgle or smell, the Wi-Fi goes out, or the air-conditioning dies when you need it most. Report your concerns clearly and calmly at the front desk.

For more complicated problems, don't expect instant results. Any legitimate place is legally required to have a complaint book (*libro de reclamaciones*). A request for this book will generally prompt the hotelier to solve your problem to keep you from writing a complaint.

To guard against theft in your room, keep valuables out of sight. Some rooms come with a safe, and other hotels have safes at the front desk. I've never bothered using one and in a lifetime of travel, I've never had anything stolen from my room.

Hostales *and* Pensiones

Budget hotels—called *hostales* and *pensiones*—are easy to find, inexpensive, and, when chosen properly, a fun part of the Spanish cultural experience. These places are often family-owned, and may or may not have amenities such as private bathrooms and air-conditioning. Don't confuse a *hostal* with a hostel—a Spanish *hostal* is an inexpensive hotel, not a hostel with bunks in dorms.

Paradores

Spain has a system of luxurious, government-sponsored, historic inns called *paradores*. These are often renovate   castles,

Sleep Code

Hotels in this book are categorized according to the average price of a standard double room without breakfast in high season.

$$$$ **Splurge:** Most rooms over €170

$$$ **Pricier:** €130-170

$$ **Midrange:** €90-130

$ **Budget:** €50-90

¢ **Backpacker:** Under €50

RS% **Rick Steves discount**

Unless otherwise noted, credit cards are accepted, hotel staff speak basic English, and free Wi-Fi is available. Comparison-shop by checking prices at several hotels (on each hotel's own website, on a booking site, or by email). For the best deal, *book directly with the hotel.* Ask for a discount if paying in cash; if the listing includes **RS%**, request a Rick Steves discount.

palaces, or monasteries, many with great views and stately atmospheres. They are generally pricier than hotels but do offer discounts for travelers 30 and younger, and 55 and older (for details, bonus packages, and family deals, see www.parador.es).

Hotel Alternatives

Located mainly in rural areas throughout Spain, **casas rurales** can be furnished rooms, whole farmhouses, villas, or sprawling ranches. Some are simple, but others are luxurious, and they are mostly used by Spaniards, so you'll really be going local. Many are in the countryside, so you will need a car. For more information and reservations, try www.ecoturismorural.com or www.micasarural.com.

Short-Term Rentals

A short-term rental—whether an apart-

Using Online Services to Your Advantage

From booking services to user reviews, online businesses are playing a greater role in travelers' planning than ever before. Take advantage of their pluses—and be wise to their downsides.

Booking Sites

Booking websites, including Booking.com and Hotels.com, offer one-stop shopping for hotels. To be listed, a hotel must pay a sizeable commission...and promise that its own website won't undercut the price on the booking-service site.

Remember: When you use an online booking service, you're adding a middleman. To support small, family-run hotels whose world is more difficult than ever, book direct.

Short-Term Rental Sites

Rental juggernaut Airbnb and other short-term rental sites allow travelers to rent rooms and apartments directly from locals. Airbnb fans appreciate feeling part of a real neighborhood as "temporary Europeans."

Critics view Airbnb as creating unfair competition for established guesthouse owners. As a lover of Europe, I share the worry of those who see residents nudged aside by tourists. But as an advocate for travelers, I appreciate the value and cultural intimacy Airbnb provides.

User Reviews

User-generated review sites and apps such as Yelp and TripAdvisor can give you a consensus of opinions about everything from hotels and restaurants to sights and nightlife. But a user-generated review is based on the limited experience of one person, while a guidebook is the work of a trained researcher who visits many restaurants and hotels year after year.

Both types of information have their place, and in many ways, they're complementary. If something is well reviewed in a guidebook and it also gets good online reviews, it's likely a winner.

ment, house, or room in a local's home—is an increasingly popular alternative, especially if you plan to settle in one location for several nights. For stays longer than a few days, you can usually find a rental that's comparable to—and cheaper than—a hotel room with similar amenities. Plus, you'll get a behind-the-scenes peek into how locals live. Aggregator websites such as Airbnb, FlipKey, Booking.com, and the HomeAway family of sites (HomeAway, VRBO, and VacationRentals) let you browse properties and correspond directly with European property owners or managers.

Hostels

A hostel (albergue juvenil) provides cheap beds in dorms where you sleep alongside strangers for about €20-30 per night. Travelers of any age are welcome if they don't mind dorm-style accommodations and meeting other travelers. Most hostels offer kitchen facilities, guest computers, Wi-Fi, and a self-service laundry. Family and private rooms are often available.

Independent hostels tend to be easygoing, colorful, and informal (no membership required; www.hostelworld.com). You

Making Hotel Reservations

Requesting a Reservation: For family-run hotels, it's generally cheaper to book your room directly via email or a phone call. For business-class hotels, or if you'd rather book online, reserve directly through the hotel's official website (not a booking website). For complicated requests, send an email. Almost all of my recommended hotels take reservations in English.

Here's what the hotelier wants to know:
- Type(s) of rooms you want and size of your party
- Number of nights you'll stay
- Your arrival and departure dates, written European-style as day/month/year (18/06/20 or 18 June 2020)
- Special requests (en suite bathroom, cheapest room, twin beds vs. double bed, quiet room)
- Applicable discounts (such as a Rick Steves reader discount, cash discount, or promotional rate)

Confirming a Reservation: Most places will request a credit-card number to hold your room. If you're using an online reservation form, look for the *https* or a lock icon at the top of your browser. If you book direct, you can email, call, or fax this information.

Canceling a Reservation: If you must cancel, it's courteous—and smart—to do so with as much notice as possible, especially for smaller family-run places. Cancellation policies can be strict; read the fine print before you book. Many discount deals require prepayment, with cancellation refunds.

Reconfirming a Reservation: Always call or email to reconfirm your room reservation a few days in advance. For B&Bs or very small hotels, I call again on my day of arrival to tell my host what time to expect me (especially important if arriving late—after 17:00).

Phoning: For tips on how to call hotels overseas, see page 421.

may pay slightly less by booking directly with the hostel. **Official hostels** are part of Hostelling International (HI) and share an online booking site (www.hihostels.com). HI hostels typically require that you be a member or pay a bit more per night.

STAYING CONNECTED

One of the most common questions I hear from travelers is, "How can I stay connected in Europe?" The short answer is: more easily and cheaply than you might think.

The simplest solution is to bring your own device—mobile phone, tablet, or laptop—and use it just as you would at home (following the tips described below). For more details, see www.ricksteves.com/phoning. For a very practical one-hour talk covering tech issues for travelers, see www.ricksteves.com/mobile-travel-skills.

Using a Mobile Phone in Europe

Sign up for an international plan. To stay connected at a lower cost, sign up for an international service plan through

How to Dial

To make an international call, follow the dialing instructions below. Drop an initial zero, if present, when dialing a European phone number—except when calling Italy. I've used the telephone number of one of my recommended Madrid hotels as an example (tel. 915-212-900).

From a Mobile Phone
It's easy to dial with a mobile phone. Whether calling from the US to Europe, country to country within Europe, or from Europe to the US—it's all the same. Press zero until you get a + sign, enter the country code (34 for Spain), then dial the phone number.
▶ To call the Madrid hotel from any location, dial +34 915 212 900.

From a US Landline to Europe
Dial 011 (US/Canada access code), country code (34 for Spain), and phone number.
▶ To call the Madrid hotel from your home phone, dial 011 915 212 900.

From a European Landline to the US or Europe
Dial 00 (Europe access code), country code (1 for the US, 34 for Spain), and phone number.
▶ To call my US office from Spain, dial 00 1 425 771 8303.
▶ To call the Madrid hotel from Germany, dial 00 34 915 212 900.

For a complete list of European country codes and more phoning help, see www.howtocallabroad.com.

your carrier. Most providers offer a simple bundle that includes calling, messaging, and data. Your normal plan may already include international coverage (T-Mobile's does).

Use free Wi-Fi whenever possible. Unless you have an unlimited-data plan, save most of your online tasks for Wi-Fi (pronounced *wee-fee* in Spanish). You can access the internet, send texts, and even make voice calls over Wi-Fi.

Minimize the use of your cellular network. Even with an international data plan, wait until you're on Wi-Fi to Skype, download apps, stream videos, or do other

megabyte-greedy tasks. Using a navigation app such as Google Maps over a cellular network can take lots of data, so do this sparingly or use the app in offline mode. Disable automatic updates so your apps will only update when you're on Wi-Fi. Also change your device's email settings from "auto-retrieve" to "manual" (or from "push" to "fetch").

Use Wi-Fi calling and messaging apps. Skype, WhatsApp, FaceTime, and Google Hangouts are great for making free or low-cost calls or sending texts over Wi-Fi. With an app installed on your phone, tablet, or laptop, you can log on

Tips on Internet Security

Make sure that your device is running the latest versions of its operating system, security software, and apps. Next, ensure that your device and key programs (like email) are password-protected. On the road, use only secure Wi-Fi hotspots. Ask the hotel or café staff for the specific name of their Wi-Fi network, and make sure you log on to that exact one.

If you must access your financial info online, use a banking app rather than accessing your account via a browser. A cellular connection is more secure than Wi-Fi. Avoid logging onto personal finance sites on a public computer.

Never share your credit-card number (or any other sensitive information) online unless you know that the site is secure. A secure site displays a little padlock icon, and the URL begins with https (instead of the usual http).

toll-free access number, enter the card's PIN code, then dial the number.

You'll only see **public pay phones** in a few post offices and train stations. Most don't take coins but instead require insertable phone cards, which you can buy at a newsstand, convenience store, or post office. Except for emergencies, they're not worth the hassle.

Most hotels have **public computers** in their lobbies for guests to use; otherwise you can find them at public libraries (ask your hotelier or the TI for the nearest location). On a European keyboard, use the "Alt Gr" key to the right of the space bar to insert the extra symbol that appears on some keys. If you can't locate a special character (such as @), simply copy and paste it from a web page.

Mail

You can mail one package per day to yourself worth up to $200 duty-free from Europe to the US (mark it "personal purchases"). If you're sending a gift to someone, mark it "unsolicited gift." For details, visit www.cbp.gov, select "Travel," and search for "Know Before You Go." The Spanish postal service works fine, but for quick transatlantic delivery (in either direction), consider services such as DHL (www.dhl.com).

TRANSPORTATION

Choosing between public transit or driving? Spain's trains and buses take you efficiently from city to city. A car gives you more freedom to explore the countryside, though it's worthless in big cities (park it).

For information on transportation throughout Europe, see RickSteves.com/transportation.

Trains

Renfe is Spain's national train system. For information and reservations, visit Renfe.com or dial Renfe's number (tel. 912-320-320) from anywhere in Spain.

to a Wi-Fi network and contact friends or family who use the same service. If you buy credit in advance, with some of these services you can call or send a text anywhere for just pennies per minute.

Without a Mobile Phone

It's possible to travel in Europe without a mobile device. You can make calls from your hotel, and check email or browse websites using public computers.

Most **hotels** charge a fee for placing calls—ask for rates before you dial. You can use a prepaid international phone card (*tarjeta telefónica con código,* usually available at newsstands, tobacco shops, and train stations) to call out from your hotel. Dial the

Spain's trains are modern and efficient.

Types of Trains

Trains get more expensive as they pick up speed, but all are cheaper per mile than their northern European counterparts.

The high-speed train called the **AVE** (AH-vay, stands for *Alta Velocidad Española*) whisks travelers between Madrid and Toledo in 30 minutes, and between Madrid and Sevilla, Barcelona, or Málaga in less than three hours. AVE trains are priced according to their time of departure. Peak hours (*punta*) are most expensive, followed by *llano* and *valle* (quietest and cheapest times). Tickets for these trains typically go on sale two months in advance.

A related high-speed train, the **Alvia,** runs on AVE lines but can switch to Iberian tracks without stopping. On the Madrid-San Sebastián route, for example, it reaches the Basque Country in five hours. **Avant** trains are also high-speed—typically about as fast as AVE—but designed for shorter distances.

The **Talgo** is fast, air-conditioned, and expensive. **Intercity** and **Media Distancia** trains fall just behind Talgo in speed, comfort, and expense. **Cercanías** and **Rodalies** are commuter trains for big-city workers and small-town tourists.

Reading Schedules: *Salidas* means "departures," and *llegadas* is "arrivals." On train schedules, "LMXJVSD" stands for the days of the week in Spanish, starting with Monday. A train that runs "LMX-JV-D" doesn't run on Saturdays. *Laborables* can mean Monday through Friday or Monday through Saturday.

Overnight Trains: The main overnight train routes remaining in Spain are between Madrid, San Sebastián, or Salamanca and Lisbon (and the *only* train service on these international routes) and between Madrid or Barcelona and Galicia (A Coruña, Ferrol, or Vigo).

Most overnight trains have berths and beds (*litera*) that cost extra, with the price depending on the route and type of compartment. To get the space you want, it's smart to reserve in advance, even from home.

Rail Passes

The single-country Eurail Spain Pass can be a reasonable value if you'll be taking three or more long train rides in Spain. But otherwise, it's unlikely to save you money. A rail pass doesn't provide much hop-on convenience in Spain, since most trains require paid seat reservations. (Passholders can't reserve online through Renfe but can reserve at www.raileurope.com before leaving the US.)

Buying individual train tickets in advance or as you go in Spain can be less expensive, and gives you better access to seat reservations (which are limited for rail-pass holders). For most trains, point-to-point ticket prices already include seat reservations when required (for instance, for fast trains and longer distances).

Even if you have a rail pass, use buses when they're more convenient and direct than the trains. Remember to reserve ahead for the fast AVE trains and overnight journeys.

For more detailed advice on figuring out the smartest rail-pass options for your train trip, visit www.ricksteves.com/rail.

Buying Train Tickets

Trains can sell out, so it's smart to buy your tickets at least a day in advance, even for short rides, at the station or a Renfe office, at a travel agency, online, or by phone.

At the Station: You will likely have to wait in a line to buy your ticket (and pay

Rail Pass or Point-to-Point Tickets?

Will you be better off buying a rail pass or point-to-point tickets? It pays to know your options and choose what's best for your itinerary.

Rail Passes

A Eurail Spain Pass lets you travel by train in Spain for three to eight days (consecutively or not) within a one-month period. Spain is also covered (along with most of Europe) by the classic Eurail Global Pass.

Discounted rates are offered for seniors (age 60 and up) and youths (ages 12-27). Up to two kids (ages 4-11) can travel free with each adult-rate pass (but not with senior rates). All rail passes offer a choice of first or second class for all ages.

Rail passes are best purchased outside Europe (through travel agents or Rick Steves' Europe). For more on rail passes, including prices, visit RickSteves.com/rail.

Point-to-Point Tickets

If you're taking just a couple of train rides, look into buying individual point-to-point tickets. Use this map to add up approximate pay-as-you-go fares for your itinerary, and compare that to the price of a rail pass. Keep in mind that significant discounts on point-to-point tickets may be available with advance purchase.

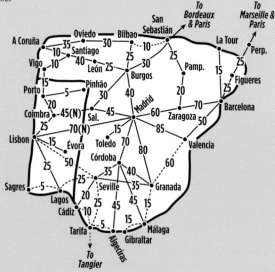

Fares in Spain (and Portugal): Map shows approximate costs, in US dollars, for one-way, second-class tickets on faster trains. Dashed lines show bus and ferry routes (not covered by passes). N indicates a night train.

a five percent service fee). First find the correct line—at bigger stations, there may be separate windows for short-distance, long-distance, advance, and "today" (para hoy) tickets. Renfe ticket machines usually take US credit cards but in some cases you may have to enter your PIN.

You can also buy tickets or reservations at the Renfe offices located in more than 100 city centers. These are more central and multilingual—also less crowded and confusing—than most train stations.

Travel Agency: The easiest choice for most travelers is to buy tickets at an English-speaking travel agency (look for a train sticker in agency windows). El Corte Inglés department stores (with locations in most Spanish cities) often have handy travel agencies inside.

Online: Although the Renfe website is useful for confirming schedules and prices, you may have trouble buying tickets online unless you use PayPal. (The website often rejects attempts to use a US card.) But with patience and enough Spanish language skill, you may nab an online discount of up to 60 percent (limited seats at these prices, available two weeks to two months ahead of travel). Online vendors based in the US include Raileurope.com and Petrabax.com (expect a small fee from either) or use the European vendor Trainline.eu.

By Phone: You can purchase your ticket by phone (tel. 912-240-202), then pick it up at the station by punching your confirmation code (localizador) into one of the machines. Discounts up to 40 percent off are offered a week or more ahead by phone (and at stations).

Buses

Bus travel in Spain gives you a glimpse at España profunda ("deep Spain"), where everyone seems to know each other and no one's in a hurry. The system can be confusing to the uninitiated, as a number of different companies operate throughout the country, sometimes running buses to the same destinations and using the same transfer points. The aggregator website Movelia.es is a good place to begin researching schedules and companies; local TIs also have bus information for their region.

Among the major companies are Alsa (www.alsa.es), Avanza (www.avanzabus.com), Comes (www.tgcomes.es), and Damas (www.damas-sa.es), but you will see many other regional carriers. Ticket desks are usually clustered within one bus station, and larger stations have a consolidated information desk with all schedules. In smaller stations, check the destinations and schedules posted on each office window. Whenever possible, choose a faster directo route over a slower ruta option (with more stops along the way).

On the Bus: You can (and most likely will be required to) stow your luggage under the bus. Your ticket comes with an assigned seat; if the bus is full, you should take that seat, but if it's uncrowded, most people just sit where they like. Buses are nonsmoking.

Drivers and station personnel may not speak English. Buses generally lack WCs, but they stop every two hours or so for a short break. Drivers announce how long the stop will be, but if in doubt, ask, "How many minutes here?" ("¿Cuántos minutos aquí?"). Listen for the bus horn as a final call before departure.

Renting a Car

Most of the major US rental agencies (including Avis, Budget, Enterprise, Hertz, and Thrifty) have offices throughout Europe. Also consider the two major Europe-based agencies, Europcar and Sixt. Consolidators such as Auto Europe/Kemwel (AutoEurope.com—or the sometimes cheaper AutoEurope.eu) compare rates at several companies to get you the best deal.

Wherever you book, always read the fine print. Ask about add-on charges—

Iberia's Public Transportation

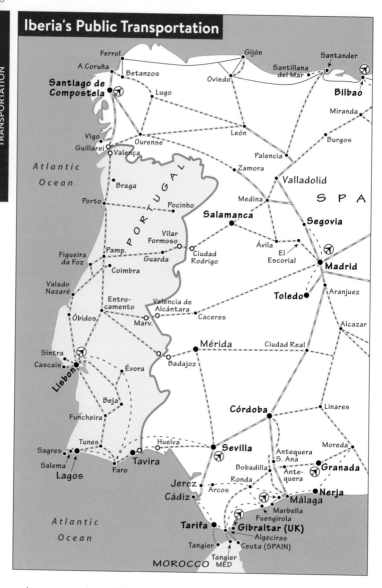

such as one-way drop-off fees, airport surcharges, or mandatory insurance policies—that aren't included in the "total price."

Rental Costs and Considerations

Figure on paying roughly $250 for a one-week rental for a basic compact car. Allow extra for supplemental insurance, fuel,

tolls, and parking. To save money on fuel, request a diesel car. Be warned that international trips—say, picking up in Madrid and dropping off in Lisbon—can be expensive if the rental company assesses a drop-off fee for crossing a border.

Manual vs. Automatic: Almost all rental cars in Europe are manual by

default—and cars with stick shift are generally cheaper. If you need an automatic, request one in advance. When selecting a car, don't be tempted by a larger model, as it won't be as maneuverable on narrow, winding roads (such as in Andalucía's hill towns) or when squeezing into tight parking lots.

Age Restrictions: Some rental companies impose minimum and maximum age limits. Young drivers (25 and under) and seniors (69 and up) should check the rental policies and rules section of car rental websites.

Choosing Pick-up/Drop-off Locations: Always check the hours of

Spain by Car

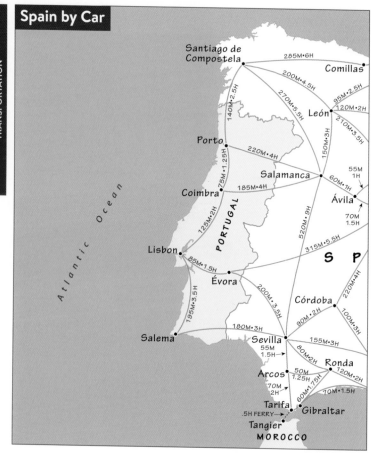

the location you choose: Many rental offices close from midday Saturday until Monday morning and, in smaller towns, at lunchtime. Wherever you select, get precise details on the location and allow ample time to find it.

Have the Right License: If you're renting a car in Spain, bring your driver's license. You're also technically required to have an International Driving Permit—an official translation of your license (sold at AAA offices for about $20 plus the cost of two passport-type photos; see www.aaa.com). While that's the letter of the law, I generally rent cars without having this permit. How this is enforced varies from

country to country: Get advice from your car rental company.

Picking Up Your Car: Before driving off in your rental car, check it thoroughly and make sure any damage is noted on your rental agreement. Rental agencies in Europe tend to charge for even minor damage, so be sure to mark everything. Find out how your car's gearshift, lights, turn signals, wipers, radio, and fuel cap function, and know what kind of fuel the car takes (diesel vs. unleaded). When you return the car, make sure the agent verifies its condition with you. Some drivers take pictures of the returned vehicle as proof of its condition.

NOTE: YOUR TIMES
MAY VARY BASED ON
TRAFFIC, CONSTRUCTION
& ROAD CONDITIONS.

m = miles
h = hours
···· = ferry

Car Insurance Options

When you rent a car in Europe, the price typically includes liability insurance, which covers harm to other cars or motorists—but not the rental car itself. To limit your financial risk in case of damage to the rental, choose one of these options: Buy a Collision Damage Waiver (CDW) with a low or zero deductible from the car-rental company (roughly 30-40 percent extra), get coverage through your credit card (free, but more complicated), or get collision insurance as part of a larger travel-insurance policy. For more on your car-rental insurance options, see www.ricksteves.com/cdw.

Navigation Options

If you'll be navigating using your phone or a GPS unit from home, remember to bring a car charger and device mount.

Your Mobile Phone: The mapping app on your phone works fine for navigation in Europe, but for real-time turn-by-turn directions and traffic updates, you'll need mobile data access. And driving all day can burn through a lot of very expensive data. The economical workaround is to use map apps that work offline. By downloading in advance from Google Maps, Apple Maps, Here WeGo, or Navmii, you can still have turn-by-turn voice directions and maps that recalibrate even though they're offline.

You must download your maps before you go offline—and it's smart to select large regions. Then turn off your data connection so you're not charged for roaming. Call up the map, enter your destination, and you're on your way. Even if you don't have to pay extra for data roaming, this option is great for navigating in areas with poor connectivity.

GPS Devices: If you want the convenience of a dedicated GPS unit, consider renting one with your car ($10-30/day). These units offer real-time turn-by-turn directions and traffic without the data requirements of an app. The unit may come loaded only with maps for its home country; if you need additional maps, ask. Also make sure your device's language is set to English before you drive off.

Maps and Atlases: Even when navigating primarily with a mobile app or GPS, I always make it a point to have a paper map. It's invaluable for getting the big picture, understanding alternate routes, and filling in when my phone runs out of juice. Buy a better map before you go, or pick one up at European gas stations, bookshops, newsstands, and tourist shops.

Driving

Freeways and Tolls: Spain's freeways come with tolls, but save huge amounts of time. Each toll road (*autopista de peaje*) has its own pricing structure, so tolls vary. Near some major cities, you must pre-pay for each stretch of road you drive; on other routes, you take a ticket where you enter the freeway, and pay when you exit. Payment can be made in cash or by credit or debit card (credit-card-only lanes are labeled *"vias automáticas"*; cash lanes are *"vias manuales"*).

Road Signs: Because road numbers can be puzzling and inconsistent, be ready to navigate by city and town names. Memorize some key road words: *salida* (exit), *de sentido único* (one way), *despacio* (slow), and *adelantamiento prohibido* (no passing). Mileage signs are in kilometers.

Road Rules: Be aware of typical European road rules; for example, many countries require headlights to be turned on at all times, and nearly all forbid handheld mobile-phone use. In Europe, you're not allowed to turn right on a red light unless a sign or signal specifically authorizes it, and on expressways it's illegal to pass drivers on the right. You should also stay in the right lane unless you are passing.

Seatbelts are required by law. Children under 12 must ride in the back seat, and children up to age 3 must have a child seat. You must put on a reflective safety vest any time you get out of your car on the side of a highway or unlit road (most rental-car companies provide one—check when you pick up the car). Those who use eyeglasses are required by law to have a spare pair in the car.

Ask your car-rental company about these rules, or check the "International Travel" section of the US State Department website (www.travel.state.gov.

Fuel: Gas and diesel prices are controlled and the same everywhere—about $6 a gallon for gas and $5.50 a gallon for diesel. Unleaded gas (*gasolina sin plomo*) is either *normal* or *super*. Note that diesel is called *diesel* or *gasóleo*—pay attention when filling your tank.

Theft: Thieves easily recognize rental cars and assume they are filled with a tourist's gear. Be sure all your valuables

Traveling by car

AND LEARN THESE ROAD SIGNS

Speed Limit (km/hr) — Yield — No Passing — End of No Passing Zone

One Way — Intersection — Main Road — Expressway

Danger — No Entry — Cars Prohibited — All Vehicles Prohibited

Through Road — Restrictions No Longer Apply — Yield to Oncoming Traffic — No Stopping

Parking — No Parking — Customs or Toll Road — Peace

are out of sight and locked in the trunk, or even better, with you or in your room. Parking attendants all over Spain holler, "Nada en el coche" ("Nothing in the car"). And they mean it. In cities you can park safely but expensively in guarded lots.

Flights

To compare flight costs and times, begin with a travel search engine: Kayak.com is the top site for flights to and within Europe, easy-to-use Google Flights has price alerts, and Skyscanner.com includes many inexpensive flights within Europe.

Flights to Europe: Start looking for international flights about four to six months before your trip, especially for peak-season travel. Depending on your itinerary, it can be efficient and no more expensive to fly into one city and out of another. If your flight requires a connection in Europe, see our hints on navigating Europe's top hub airports at www.ricksteves.com/hub-airports.

Flights Within Europe: Flying between European cities has become surprisingly affordable. Before buying a long-distance train or bus ticket, first check the cost of a flight on one of Europe's airlines, whether a major carrier or a no-frills outfit like Easy-Jet and Ryanair. Be aware of the potential drawbacks of flying with a discount airline: nonrefundable and nonchangeable tickets, minimal customer service, time-consuming treks to secondary airports, and stingy baggage allowances. To avoid unpleasant surprises, read the small print about the costs for "extras" such as reserving a seat, checking a bag, or checking in and printing a boarding pass.

Flying to the US and Canada: Because security is extra tight for flights to the US, be sure to give yourself plenty of time at the airport. It's also important to charge your electronic devices before you board because security checks may require you to turn them on (see www.tsa.gov for the latest rules).

Resources from Rick Steves

Begin Your Trip at RickSteves.com

My mobile-friendly **website** is *the* place to explore Europe in preparation for your trip. You'll find thousands of fun articles, videos, and radio interviews; a wealth of money-saving tips for planning your dream trip; travel news dispatches; a video library of my travel talks; my travel blog; and my latest guidebook updates (www.ricksteves.com/update).

Our **Travel Forum** is a well-groomed collection of message boards where our travel-savvy community answers questions and shares personal travel experiences—and our well-traveled staff chimes in when they can be helpful.

Our **online Travel Store** offers bags and accessories that I've designed to help you travel smarter and lighter. These include my popular carry-on bags (which I live out of four months a year), money belts, totes, toiletries kits, adapters, guidebooks, and planning maps.

Our website can also help you find the perfect **rail pass** for your itinerary and your budget.

Rick Steves' Tours, Guidebooks, TV Shows, and More

Small Group Tours: Want to travel with greater efficiency and less stress? We offer more than 40 itineraries reaching the best destinations in this book...and beyond. You'll enjoy great guides and a fun bunch of travel partners. For all the details, and to get our tour catalog, visit www.ricksteves.com/tours or call us at 425/608-4217.

Books: This book is just one of many in my series on European travel, which includes country and city guidebooks, Snapshots (excerpted chapters from bigger guides), Pocket guides (full-color little books on big cities), and my budget-travel skills handbook, *Rick Steves Europe Through the Back Door*. A more complete list of my titles appears near the end of this book.

TV Shows and Travel Talks: My public television series, *Rick Steves' Europe,* covers Europe from top to bottom with over 100 half-hour episodes (watch full episodes at my website). Or, to raise your travel I.Q., check out the video versions of our popular classes (covering most European countries as well as travel skills).

Radio: My weekly public radio show, *Travel with Rick Steves,* features interviews with travel experts from around the world. It airs on 400 public radio stations across the US, or you can hear it as a podcast. A complete archive of programs is available on my website.

Audio Tours on My Free App: I've produced dozens of free, self-guided audio tours of the top sights in Europe. For those tours and other audio content, get my free **Rick Steves Audio Europe app,** an extensive online library organized by destination. For more on the app, see page 29.

HOLIDAYS AND FESTIVALS

This list includes selected festivals in major cities, plus national holidays observed throughout Spain (when many sights and banks close). Before planning a trip around a festival, verify the dates with the festival website, the national tourist office (www. spain.info), or at RickSteves.com.

Jan 1	New Year's Day
Jan 6	Epiphany
Feb 2	La Candelaria (religious festival), Madrid
Feb 28	Andalucía Day (some closures, Andalucía only)
March/April	Holy Week (Semana Santa), Easter Sunday, and Easter Monday
Two weeks after Holy Week	April Fair (Feria de Abril), Sevilla
April 23	St. George's Day (flowers and books), Barcelona
May 1	Labor Day (closures)
May 2	Dos de Mayo, Madrid
May 3	Fiesta de las Cruces (religious festival), Granada and Córdoba
May 15	San Isidro (religious festival), Madrid and Nerja
40th Day after Easter	Ascension Day
May/June	Pentecost and Whit Monday
May/June	Corpus Christi
July 6-14	Running of the Bulls (Fiesta de San Fermín), Pamplona
July 25	Feast Day of St. James, Santiago de Compostela
Aug	Gràcia Festival, Barcelona
Aug 15	Assumption of Mary (religious festival)
Late Sept	Feria de San Miguel (bullfights), Sevilla; Little San Fermín (concerts, parades), Pamplona
Oct 12	Spanish National Day
Nov 1	All Saints' Day
Nov 9	Feast of the Almudena, Madrid (religious festival)
Dec 6	Constitution Day
Dec 8	Feast of the Immaculate Conception
Dec 25	Christmas
Dec 31	New Year's Eve

CONVERSIONS AND CLIMATE

Numbers and Stumblers

- Europeans write a few of their numbers differently than we do. 1 = 1, 4 = 4, 7 = 7.
- In Europe, dates appear as day/month/year, so Christmas is always 25/12.
- Commas are decimal points and decimals are commas. A dollar and a half is $1,50, and there are 5.280 feet in a mile.
- When counting with fingers, start with your thumb. If you hold up your first finger to request one item, you'll probably get two.
- What Americans call the second floor of a building is the first floor in Europe.

Metric Conversions

A **kilogram** equals 1,000 grams (about 2.2 pounds). One hundred **grams** (a common unit at markets) is about a quarter-pound. One **liter** is about a quart, or almost four to a gallon.

Clothing Sizes

When shopping for clothing, use these US-to-European comparisons as general guidelines.

Women: For pants and dresses, add 32 in Spain (US 10 = Spanish 42). For blouses and sweaters, add 8 for most of Europe (US 32 = European 40). For shoes, add 30-31 (US 7 = European 37/38).

Men: For shirts, multiply by 2 and add about 8 (US 15 = European 38). For jackets and suits, add 10. For shoes, add 32-34.

Children: Clothing is sized by height—in centimeters (2.5 cm = 1 inch), so a US size 8 roughly equates to 132-140. For shoes up to size 13, add 16-18, and for sizes 1 and up, add 30-32.

Spain's Climate

First line, average daily high; second line, average daily low; third line, average days without rain. For more detailed weather statistics for destinations in this book (as well as the rest of the world), check www.wunderground.com.

Madrid

J	F	M	A	M	J	J	A	S	O	N	D
47°	52°	59°	65°	70°	80°	87°	85°	77°	65°	55°	48°
35°	36°	41°	45°	50°	58°	63°	63°	57°	49°	42°	36°
23	21	21	21	21	25	29	28	24	23	21	21

Barcelona

J	F	M	A	M	J	J	A	S	O	N	D
55°	57°	60°	65°	71°	78°	82°	82°	77°	69°	62°	56°
43°	45°	48°	52°	57°	65°	69°	69°	66°	58°	51°	46°
26	23	23	21	23	24	27	25	23	22	24	25

Sevilla

J	F	M	A	M	J	J	A	S	O	N	D
61°	64°	69°	72°	79°	88°	96°	96°	91°	79°	68°	62°
43°	45°	48°	51°	55°	62°	66°	66°	64°	57°	50°	46°
25	23	26	25	28	29	31	31	28	26	25	25

Packing Checklist

Whether you're traveling for five days or five weeks, you won't need more than this. Pack light to enjoy the sweet freedom of true mobility.

Clothing

- ❏ 5 shirts: long- & short-sleeve
- ❏ 2 pairs pants (or skirts/capris)
- ❏ 1 pair shorts
- ❏ 5 pairs underwear & socks
- ❏ 1 pair walking shoes
- ❏ Sweater or warm layer
- ❏ Rainproof jacket with hood
- ❏ Tie, scarf, belt, and/or hat
- ❏ Swimsuit
- ❏ Sleepwear/loungewear

Money

- ❏ Debit card(s)
- ❏ Credit card(s)
- ❏ Hard cash (US $100-200)
- ❏ Money belt

Documents

- ❏ Passport
- ❏ Tickets & confirmations: flights, hotels, trains, rail pass, car rental, sight entries
- ❏ Driver's license
- ❏ Student ID, hostel card, etc.
- ❏ Photocopies of important documents
- ❏ Insurance details
- ❏ Guidebooks & maps

Toiletries Kit

- ❏ Basics: soap, shampoo, toothbrush, toothpaste, floss, deodorant, sunscreen, brush/comb, etc.
- ❏ Medicines & vitamins
- ❏ First-aid kit
- ❏ Glasses/contacts/sunglasses
- ❏ Sewing kit
- ❏ Packet of tissues (for WC)
- ❏ Earplugs

Electronics

- ❏ Mobile phone
- ❏ Camera & related gear
- ❏ Tablet/ebook reader/laptop
- ❏ Headphones/earbuds
- ❏ Chargers & batteries
- ❏ Phone car charger & mount (or GPS device)
- ❏ Plug adapters

Miscellaneous

- ❏ Daypack
- ❏ Sealable plastic baggies
- ❏ Laundry supplies: soap, laundry bag, clothesline, spot remover
- ❏ Small umbrella
- ❏ Travel alarm/watch
- ❏ Notepad & pen
- ❏ Journal

Optional Extras

- ❏ Second pair of shoes (flip-flops, sandals, tennis shoes, boots)
- ❏ Travel hairdryer
- ❏ Picnic supplies
- ❏ Water bottle
- ❏ Fold-up tote bag
- ❏ Small flashlight
- ❏ Mini binoculars
- ❏ Small towel or washcloth
- ❏ Inflatable pillow/neck rest
- ❏ Tiny lock
- ❏ Address list (to mail postcards)
- ❏ Extra passport photos

Spanish Survival Phrases

Spanish has a guttural sound similar to the J in Baja California. In the phonetics, the symbol for this clearing-your-throat sound is the italicized *h*.

English	Spanish	Pronunciation
Good day.	Buenos días.	**bway**-nohs **dee**-ahs
Do you speak English?	¿Habla Usted inglés?	**ah**-blah oo-**stehd** een-**glays**
Yes. / No.	Sí. / No.	see / noh
I (don't) understand.	(No) comprendo.	(noh) kohm-**prehn**-doh
Please.	Por favor.	por fah-**bor**
Thank you.	Gracias.	**grah**-thee-ahs
I'm sorry.	Lo siento.	loh see-**ehn**-toh
Excuse me.	Perdóneme.	pehr-**doh**-nay-may
(No) problem.	(No) problema.	(noh) proh-**blay**-mah
Good.	Bueno.	**bway**-noh
Goodbye.	Adiós.	ah-dee-**ohs**
one / two	uno / dos	**oo**-noh / dohs
three / four	tres / cuatro	trays / **kwah**-troh
five / six	cinco / seis	**theen**-koh / says
seven / eight	siete / ocho	see-**eh**-tay / **oh**-choh
nine / ten	nueve / diez	**nway**-bay / dee-**ayth**
How much is it?	¿Cuánto cuesta?	**kwahn**-toh **kway**-stah
Write it?	¿Me lo escribe?	may loh ay-**skree**-bay
Is it free?	¿Es gratis?	ays **grah**-tees
Is it included?	¿Está incluido?	ay-**stah** een-kloo-**ee**-doh
Where can I buy / find...?	¿Dónde puedo comprar / encontrar...?	**dohn**-day **pway**-doh kohm-**prar** / ayn-kohn-**trar**
I'd like / We'd like...	Quiero / Queremos...	kee-**ehr**-oh / kehr-**ay**-mohs
...a room.	...una habitación.	**oo**-nah ah-bee-tah-thee-**ohn**
...a ticket to ___.	...un billete para ___.	oon bee-**yeh**-tay **pah**-rah ___
Is it possible?	¿Es posible?	ays poh-**see**-blay
Where is...?	¿Dónde está...?	**dohn**-day ay-**stah**
...the train station	...la estación de trenes	lah ay-stah-thee-**ohn** day **tray**-nays
...the bus station	...la estación de autobuses	lah ay-stah-thee-**ohn** day ow-toh-**boo**-says
...the tourist information office	...la oficina de turismo	lah oh-fee-**thee**-nah day too-**rees**-moh
Where are the toilets?	¿Dónde están los servicios?	**dohn**-day ay-**stahn** lohs sehr-**bee**-thee-ohs
men	hombres, caballeros	**ohm**-brays, kah-bah-**yay**-rohs
women	mujeres, damas	moo-**heh**-rays, **dah**-mahs
left / right	izquierda / derecha	eeth-kee-**ehr**-dah / day-**ray**-chah
straight	derecho	day-**ray**-choh
When do you open / close?	¿A qué hora abren / cierran?	ah kay **oh**-rah **ah**-brehn / thee-**ay**-rahn
At what time?	¿A qué hora?	ah kay **oh**-rah
Just a moment.	Un momento.	oon moh-**mehn**-toh
now / soon / later	ahora / pronto / más tarde	ah-**oh**-rah / **prohn**-toh / mahs **tar**-day
today / tomorrow	hoy / mañana	oy / mahn-**yah**-nah

In a Spanish Restaurant

English	Spanish	Pronunciation
I'd like / We'd like...	Quiero / Queremos...	kee-**ehr**-oh / kehr-**ay**-mohs
...to reserve...	...reservar...	ray-sehr-**bar**
...a table for one / two.	...una mesa para uno / dos.	**oo**-nah **may**-sah **pah**-rah **oo**-noh / dohs
Non-smoking.	No fumador.	noh foo-mah-**dohr**
Is this table free?	¿Está esta mesa libre?	ay-**stah** ay-stah **may**-sah **lee**-bray
The menu (in English), please.	La carta (en inglés), por favor.	lah **kar**-tah (ayn een-**glays**) por fah-**bor**
service (not) included	servicio (no) incluido	sehr-**bee**-thee-oh (noh) een-kloo-**ee**-doh
cover charge	precio de entrada	**pray**-thee-oh day ayn-**trah**-dah
to go	para llevar	**pah**-rah yay-**bar**
with / without	con / sin	kohn / seen
and / or	y / o	ee / oh
menu (of the day)	menú (del día)	may-**noo** (dayl **dee**-ah)
specialty of the house	especialidad de la casa	ay-spay-thee-ah-lee-**dahd** day lah **kah**-sah
tourist menu	menú turístico	meh-**noo** too-**ree**-stee-koh
combination plate	plato combinado	**plah**-toh kohm-bee-**nah**-doh
appetizers	tapas	**tah**-pahs
bread	pan	pahn
cheese	queso	**kay**-soh
sandwich	bocadillo	boh-kah-**dee**-yoh
soup	sopa	**soh**-pah
salad	ensalada	ayn-sah-**lah**-dah
meat	carne	**kar**-nay
poultry	aves	**ah**-bays
fish	pescado	pay-**skah**-doh
seafood	marisco	mah-**ree**-skoh
fruit	fruta	**froo**-tah
vegetables	verduras	behr-**doo**-rahs
dessert	postres	**poh**-strays
tap water	agua del grifo	**ah**-gwah dayl **gree**-foh
mineral water	agua mineral	**ah**-gwah mee-nay-**rahl**
milk	leche	**lay**-chay
(orange) juice	zumo (de naranja)	**thoo**-moh (day nah-**rahn**-hah)
coffee	café	kah-**feh**
tea	té	tay
wine	vino	**bee**-noh
red / white	tinto / blanco	**teen**-toh / **blahn**-koh
glass / bottle	vaso / botella	**bah**-soh / boh-**tay**-yah
beer	cerveza	thehr-**bay**-thah
Cheers!	¡Salud!	sah-**lood**
More. / Another.	Más. / Otro.	mahs / **oh**-troh
The same.	El mismo.	ehl **mees**-moh
The bill, please.	La cuenta, por favor.	lah **kwayn**-tah por fah-**bor**
tip	propina	proh-**pee**-nah
Delicious!	¡Delicioso!	day-lee-thee-**oh**-soh

INDEX

442

INDEX

Damascene, shopping for: 15, 246

Debit cards: 29, 407–409

Domènech i Montaner, Lluís: 57, 70, 73

Drinks: 416–417. *See also* Sherry

Driving: *See* Car travel

Dürer, Albrecht: 179

E

Eating: 410–417; general tips, 30; budgeting, 28–29; restaurant phrases, 438; tipping, 409. See also *Jamón;* Markets; Roast suckling pig; Tapas; *and specific destinations*

Eixample (Barcelona): 35, 72–83; eating, 101–104; maps, 74–75, 102–103; shopping, 93; sleeping, 108–109

El Born (Barcelona): 35, 55; eating, 100–101; nightlife, 94–95; shopping, 93; sights, 64–72

El Café de las Monjas (Toledo): 233, 248

El Corte Inglés: 417; (Barcelona), 44, 54, 93–94, 95; (Madrid), 153, 191; (Sevilla), 371

Electricity: 407

El Escorial: 210–212; map, 211

El Greco: 15, 90, 123, 240–241, 403; biographical sketch, 243; Museum (Toledo), 226, 234, 243–244; Prado Museum (Madrid), 181, 183; Santa Cruz Museum (Toledo), 226, 234–235; Santo Tomé (Toledo), 226, 231, 233, 242–243

El Martes (Toledo): 246–247

El Playazo (Nerja): 393

El Prat de Llobregat Airport (Barcelona): 110–111

El Rastro Flea Market (Madrid): 13, 149, 191

Els Quatre Gats (Barcelona): 54, 97, 100

El Tajo (Ronda): 313, 316

El Torno Pastelería de Conventos (Sevilla): 352

Embassies: 407

Emergencies: 406

Escribà (Barcelona): 48

Espadrilles, shopping for: 92

Euro currency: 409

Euskal Museoa (Bilbao): 130

Events: 433; Sevilla, 338–339, 370–371

F

Fabrica Zamorano (Toledo): 233, 246

FC Barcelona: 46

Ferdinand: 60, 144, 164–165, 168, 244, 264, 274, 305, 353, 401, 402; Royal Chapel (Granada), 280–283

Feria de Abril (Sevilla): 20, 338, 370–371, 433

Ferpal (Madrid): 160–161

Festivals: 433; Sevilla, 338–339, 370–371

Fiesta de San Fermín (Pamplona): 130. *See also* Running of the Bulls

Figueres: 118–120

Flamenco: Arcos, 310; Barcelona, 94; Córdoba, 389; Granada, 17; Madrid, 148, 192–193; Nerja, 393; Sevilla, 20, 371, 373–374

Flamenco Dance Museum (Sevilla): 335, 362, 374

Font Màgica (Barcelona): 39, 91

Food: See *Bocadillos de calamares;* Cuisine; Eating; *Jamón;* Markets; *Mazapán;* Roast suckling pig; Tapas; *and specific destinations*

Food tours: Barcelona, 37; Granada, 259; San Sebastián, 121

Fortune tellers, in Sevilla: 338

Fountain of Canaletes (Barcelona): 44

Franco, Francisco: 42, 63, 152, 156, 165, 187, 213, 231, 235, 245, 322, 401, 402

Frederic Marès Museum (Barcelona): 39, 64

Fundació Joan Miró (Barcelona): 39, 86

Funiculars (cable cars): Barcelona, 85; Bilbao, 127, 130; Gibraltar, 397; Montserrat, 115–116, 118

G

Galería de Arte San Pedro (Arcos): 309

Garden of Earthly Delights (Bosch): 174–175

Gasparini Room (Madrid): 166, 168

Gaudí Antoni, in Barcelona: 10, 403; Casa Batlló, 39, 72–73; Casa Milà, 38, 73, 76; Exhibition Center, 39, 64; guided tours, 42; Palau Güell, 39, 50, 60; Park Güell, 10, 38, 83–85; Sagrada Família, 10, 38, 76–83; tomb, 81

Gehry, Frank: 126–127

General Archives of the Indies (Sevilla): 360

Generalife Gardens (Granada): 258, 278–280

Gibraltar: 396–399; map, 398

Gibraltar Museum: 399

Gimeno (Barcelona): 47

Giralda Bell Tower (Sevilla): 334, 342, 351–352

Girona-Costa Brava Airport: 111

Golden Age: overview, 402–404

Golondrinas, in Barcelona: 50

Gothic Quarter (Barcelona): *See* Barri Gòtic

Government of Spain: 405

Goya, Francisco de: 57, 90, 153, 166, 187, 240, 241, 317, 350, 362, 403; Prado Museum (Madrid), 183–184

MAP INDEX

Start your trip at

Our website enhances this book and turns

Explore Europe

At ricksteves.com you can browse through thousands of articles, videos, photos and radio interviews, plus find a wealth of money-saving travel tips for planning your dream trip. And with our mobile-friendly website, you can easily access all this great travel information anywhere you go.

TV Shows

Preview the places you'll visit by watching entire half-hour episodes of Rick Steves' Europe (choose from all 100 shows) on-demand, for free.

ricksteves.com

your travel dreams into affordable reality

Radio Interviews

Enjoy ready access to Rick's vast library of radio interviews covering travel tips and cultural insights that relate specifically to your Europe travel plans.

Travel Forums

Learn, ask, share! Our online community of savvy travelers is a great resource for first-time travelers to Europe, as well as seasoned pros. You'll find forums on each country, plus travel tips and restaurant/hotel reviews. You can even ask one of our well-traveled staff to chime in with an opinion.

Travel News

Subscribe to our free Travel News e-newsletter, and get monthly updates from Rick on what's happening in Europe.

Audio Europe™

Rick's Free Travel App

Get your FREE Rick Steves Audio Europe™ app to enjoy...

- Dozens of self-guided tours of Europe's top museums, sights and historic walks
- Hundreds of tracks filled with cultural insights and sightseeing tips from Rick's radio interviews
- All organized into handy geographic playlists
- For Apple and Android

With Rick whispering in your ear, Europe gets even better.

Pack Light and Right

Gear up for your next adventure at ricksteves.com

Light Luggage
Pack light and right with Rick Steves' affordable, custom-designed rolling carry-on bags, backpacks, day packs and shoulder bags.

Accessories
From packing cubes to moneybelts and beyond, Rick has personally selected the travel goodies that will help your trip go smoother.

Shop at ricksteves.com

Rick Steves has

Experience maximum Europe

Save time and energy

This guidebook is your independent-travel toolkit. But for all it delivers, it's still up to you to devote the time and energy it takes to manage the preparation and logistics that are essential for a happy trip. If that's a hassle, there's a solution.

Rick Steves Tours

A Rick Steves tour takes you to Europe's most

great tours, too!

with minimum stress

interesting places with great guides and small groups of 28 or less. We follow Rick's favorite itineraries, ride in comfy buses, stay in family-run hotels, and bring you intimately close to the Europe you've traveled so far to see. Most importantly, we take away the logistical headaches so you can focus on the fun.

travelers—nearly half of them repeat customers—along with us on four dozen different itineraries, from Ireland to Italy to Athens.

Is a Rick Steves tour the right fit for your travel dreams? Find out at ricksteves.com, where you can also request Rick's latest tour catalog.

Europe is best experienced with happy travel partners. We hope you can join us.

Join the fun

This year we'll take thousands of free-spirited

See our itineraries at ricksteves.com

A Guide for Every Trip

BEST OF GUIDES

Full color easy-to-scan format, focusing on Europe's most popular destinations and sights

Best of England
Best of Europe
Best of France
Best of Germany
Best of Ireland
Best of Italy
Best of Scotland
Best of Spain

COMPREHENSIVE GUIDES

City, country, and regional guides with detailed coverage for a multi-week trip exploring the most iconic sights and venturing off the beaten track

Amsterdam & the Netherlands
Barcelona
Belgium: Bruges, Brussels,
  Antwerp & Ghent
Berlin
Budapest
Croatia & Slovenia
Eastern Europe
England
Florence & Tuscany
France
Germany
Great Britain
Greece: Athens & the Peloponnese
Iceland
Ireland
Istanbul
Italy
London
Paris
Portugal
Prague & the Czech Republic
Provence & the French Riviera
Rome
Scandinavia
Scotland
Sicily
Spain
Switzerland
Venice
Vienna, Salzburg & Tirol

THE BEST OF ROME

ome, Italy's capital, is studded with
oman remnants and floodlit-fountain
uares. From the Vatican to the Colos-
um, with crazy traffic in between, Rome
onderful, huge, and exhausting. The
wds, the heat, and the weighty history

of the Eternal City where Caesars walked
can make tourists wilt. Recharge by taking siestas, gelato breaks, and after-dark
walks, strolling from one atmospheric
square to another in the refreshing evening air.

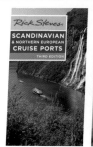

POCKET GUIDES

Compact, full color city guides with the essentials for shorter trips

Amsterdam	Munich & Salzburg
Athens	Paris
Barcelona	Prague
Florence	Rome
Italy's Cinque Terre	Venice
London	Vienna

SNAPSHOT GUIDES

Focused single-destination coverage

Basque Country: Spain & France
Copenhagen & the Best of Denmark
Dublin
Dubrovnik
Edinburgh
Hill Towns of Central Italy
Krakow, Warsaw & Gdansk
Lisbon
Loire Valley
Madrid & Toledo
Milan & the Italian Lakes District
Naples & the Amalfi Coast
Nice & the French Riviera
Normandy
Northern Ireland
Norway
Reykjavík
Rothenburg & the Rhine
Sevilla, Granada & Southern Spain
St. Petersburg, Helsinki & Tallinn
Stockholm

CRUISE PORTS GUIDES

Reference for cruise ports of call

Mediterranean Cruise Ports
Northern European Cruise Ports

Complete your library with...

TRAVEL SKILLS & CULTURE

Study up on travel skills before visiting "Europe through the back door" or gain insight on European history and culture

Europe 101
Europe Through the Back Door
European Christmas
European Easter
European Festivals
Postcards from Europe
Travel as a Political Act

PHRASE BOOKS & DICTIONARIES

French
French, Italian & German
German
Italian
Portuguese
Spanish

PLANNING MAPS

Britain, Ireland & London
Europe
France & Paris
Germany, Austria & Switzerland
Iceland
Ireland
Italy
Spain & Portugal

PHOTO CREDITS

Avalon Travel
Hachette Book Group
1700 Fourth Street
Berkeley, CA 94710

Printed in China

Third Edition. First printing October 2019.

ISBN 978-1-64171-115-9

For the latest on Rick's talks, guidebooks, Europe tours, public radio show, free audio tours, and public television series, contact Rick Steves' Europe, 130 Fourth Avenue North, Edmonds, WA 98020, 425/771-8303, www.ricksteves.com, rick@ricksteves.com.

RICK STEVES' EUROPE
Special Publications Manager: Risa Laib
Managing Editor: Jennifer Madison Davis
Assistant Managing Editor: Cathy Lu
Project Editor: Suzanne Kotz
Editors: Glenn Eriksen, Tom Griffin, Rosie Leutzinger, Jessica Shaw, Carrie Shepherd
Editorial & Production Assistant: Megan Simms
Graphic Content Director: Sandra Hundacker
Maps & Graphics: David C. Hoerlein, Lauren Mills, Mary Rostad
Digital Asset Coordinator: Orin Dubrow

AVALON TRAVEL
Editorial Director: Kevin McLain
Senior Editor and Series Manager: Madhu Prasher
Editors: Jamie Andrade, Sierra Machado
Copy Editor: Kelly Lydick
Proofreader: Patrick Collins
Indexer: Stephen Callahan
Interior Design & Layout: Tabitha Lahr
Cover Design: Kimberly Glyder Design
Maps & Graphics: Kat Bennett, Mike Morgenfeld

Let's Keep on Travelin'

Your trip doesn't need to end.

Follow Rick on social media!